THE ADMINISTRATION OF JUSTICE IN SOUTHERN INDIA

THE ADMINISTRATION OF JUSTICE IN SOUTHERN INDIA

JOHN BRUCE NORTON

GYAN

Published by

Gyan Publishing House
5, Ansari Road
Daryaganj, New Delhi-110002
Phone: 011-47034999, 9811692060
E-mail: books@gyanbooks.com

Distribution Network
gyanbooks.com
India, USA, Canada, UK, Australia

ISBN: 978-93-7133-136-4 (PB)

First Published, 1853

2nd Impression 2025

Printed at: Gyan Press, Delhi.

THE ADMINISTRATION OF JUSTICE IN SOUTHERN INDIA
Arthur JOHN BRUCE NORTON

THE

ADMINISTRATION OF JUSTICE

IN

SOUTHERN INDIA.

BY

JOHN BRUCE NORTON, Esq.
BARRISTER AT LAW.

1853.

THE ADMINISTRATION OF JUSTICE IN SOUTHERN INDIA.

WERE it not that my task is a self-imposed one, I should feel inclined at the very outset to complain of the sense of utter hopelessness under which I labour in undertaking it; for I believe that there are few attempts more hopeless than that of attracting public attention to Indian grievances in such a manner or to such an extent as to cause any practical remedy to be sought for or applied to them.

In India there is literally no public; and as far as our European population is concerned, any effort to arouse their sympathy is Quixotic—a highly cayenned article might possibly serve to pander for a moment to their listless, ephemeral and ever recurring appetite for novelty: while in England the most crass ignorance of all Indian wants and interests envelops the land in worse than Egyptian darkness. Nevertheless, though it is a 'far cry to Loch Awe', one voice, feeble an it be, shall be raised to give the people of England—that is the more influential portion of them—a knowledge of one of the most enormous evils of modern times; so that if they do not choose to apply a remedy, or institute farther inquiry, they shall not have at any rate to say that they have omitted to act through ignorance or for want of information.

The wrongs and the wants of many millions of men, unrepresented, and unable to explain their own requirements, possibly not even understanding them, are incentive enough to the labour; and the knowledge that now or never for the next five-and-twenty years, the British Parliament will have the opportunity of ameliorating the state of those unhappy multitudes is a sufficiently cheering solace, if the courage for a moment droops under an overwhelming sense of the magnitude and importance of the task, or of its all but utter hopelessness.

Therefore it is, that I an unknown man, without any personal object to serve, have taken upon myself at the cost of no mean labour to lay bare an evil of monstrous growth, of which the people of England have no idea; the very existence of which, no evidence will probably hint at before the Parliamentary Committees: and I will pledge myself to make out such a case, as, if it does not justify immediate interference, will at any rate call for the most serious attention and inquiry before a fresh Indian Charter is passed without the application of *some* remedy: and in doing this I purpose to confine myself exclusively to the Presidency of Madras, not that my facts and remarks will not be more or less applicable to the sister Presidencies, but because I wish to keep strictly within the limits of my own personal experience and observation.

The subject of which I am about to treat is the administration of justice—I had almost said *mal*-administration or non-administration—in the Mofussil Courts of the East India Company: and when I state that I am a Barrister practising now for some ten years in the Supreme Court, during the latter part of which I have given up a good deal of time and attention to the Procedure and practice of the Mofussil Courts, as well as to the Substantive Law which they administer, probably the results of my experience will be not altogether without value, if only as evidencing the opinions of one who observes the Courts of the Company from a different point of view to that whence others have

the present Head Assistant Registrar of the Court of Sudder and Foujdaree Adawlut.

All these volumes then are authoritative; and to these I earnestly entreat attention, as it is from their pages that I shall gather my facts: facts which speak for themselves, and upon which argument or inference is altogether unnecessary and thrown away. Now I might content myself with selecting some half dozen cases from each book, of such startling quality as would frighten not only English lawyers but the English public out of its propriety: but I know that if I were to restrict myself to that course, I should be accused, perhaps justly of a partial selection, and it would be boldly stated that the samples were not fair specimens of the rest of the staple. On the other hand it is impossible within the limits of such a production as this, nor indeed is it competent to its object, to enter into any minute discussions of the merits of all or even the majority of the cases. Such a course would weary if not disgust the general reader. I must therefore pursue a middle path, making extracts sufficiently copious, without any invidious distinction or preference between individuals or Courts, to ensure a conviction that I am merely giving a plain straightforward analysis of the general contents of the volumes, not picking out particular cases with a view to support a favourite proposition or theory.

Indeed one might be content to try a kind of 'Sortes Virgilianæ'; opening the books at haphazard; yet a little more method will be advisable; and as I must be necessarily somewhat long in this part of my undertaking, inasmuch as it is the principal proof and groundwork of my first proposition, I must ask the Reader to bear patiently with me; dipping into more or less of the selections as his inclination, incredulity or curiosity prompts him—giving me credit, if he feels inclined to skip any of these marvellous disclosures after reading one or more, for stating that the maxim "ex uno disce omnes" strictly applies to the matter in hand.

Present system.

But before I proceed to my selections I must, as shortly as is consistent with perspicuity draw attention to the circumstances which have given rise to the present anomalous state of things: because it is *in the system* that the vice resides.

The principal business of the Country is carried on by the Civil Service who fill all the chief Judicial and Revenue Departments and Offices. No line of demarcation is drawn between them, and a Revenue Officer is at any moment of his official career eligible for and liable to be removed to the Judicial Line. Inasmuch as the Collection of the Revenue is the main object of the Government, the Collector is in their eyes a more important Officer than the Judge, and it has ere now happened with a woful short-sightedness and ignorance of Political Economy on the part of the local Government, that a Collector or other Revenue Officer found incompetent for his office has been forthwith pitchforked on to the Judicial Bench; indeed I may add that it is now the well known practice to transfer such *Sub Collectors* as do not satisfy Government of their sharpness, from the Revenue to the Judicial branch, just when they are of sufficient standing to entitle them to be promoted to the office of Collector, rather than trust that important post to any but the most efficient hands. As a class therefore the Judges of this Presidency are on an average inferior in ability to their contemporaries in the Revenue department. Lest I should be accused of exaggeration in this statement, let me quote

Mr. Campbell.

the words of Mr. Campbell, a Civilian of Bengal, whose recent work has I understand obtained extensive circulation in England; he states as follows:

" When a Collector is old enough he is made a judge; and to this " step there is almost no exception if it is wished for. It seems to " be considered that if at this time of life a man is fit for any thing " at all he is fit to be a judge: and if he is fit for nothing at all " make him a judge and get rid of him, for once in that Office he "has no further claims to further promotions by seniority alone. The "judicial department being in a less satisfactory state than any other "is less sought after, and the ill effect of mis-management being less "immediately startling, the principle that (in a choice of evils) any "man will do for a judge seems to have become established. *Some "who mismanage their districts are said to be promoted to be judges "against their will.* Moreover all who can get any thing out of the "regular line have by this time got it. A crack Magistrate and Col- "lector probably prefers a Commissionership in the Punjaub, or "to wait for one in the Provinces: and men are now nearly entitled "to their Pensions before they get their judgeships. Altogether it "happens that comparatively few much above mediocrity remain to "be judges; and of those who do many are disappointed and ma- "ny hang on when they are old and worn out. A bad department "is then made worse."

He is speaking of Bengal. Hear his able commentator of Madras, a Civilian, whose Pamphlet on the "Judicial system of British India" gives a very clear outline of the constitution of the Madras Courts, stripped of the outlandish terms which offend an English ear.

"At Madras the principle adverted to by Mr. Campbell that *any "man will do for a judge*" has long been the established rule; "and notwithstanding the advantage afforded by the existence of "the Subordinate judgeships, *the higher appointments are not unfre- "quently bestowed upon revenue officers who have proved themselves "wanting in efficiency, and are considered unfit for a responsible reve- "nue charge. To such an extent has this mis-direction of patronage "been carried for many years past that the judicial line is commonly "talked of as 'the refuge for the destitute' at Madras.*"

Now the evil of this system is apparent: it has already drawn much of public attention to it in authoritative quarters, and has caused many remedies to be suggested; but all hitherto has been mere 'minuting' and 'reporting'; there it has stopped; nothing has been *done.*

But if the evil ceased here, it might be said that it was likely to be of such rare occurrence in practice, that it was almost beneath Legislative notice. Unfortunately however for the people of this country the evil does *not* cease here: for according to the present system *there is no school for training even those who are primarily destined for the judicial line;* and the only means they have of learning law, procedure, practice, evidence, is by trying their 'prentice hand' upon the cases which come before them when they first take their seat upon the Bench; which is as if a Surgeon should learn dissection upon the living body; but 'fiat experimentum in corpore vili;' the subjects are only 'niggers,' and provided a certain number of cases be decided monthly by the Mofussil Judge in accordance with a circular order of the Sudder Udawlut, it does not much matter *how* they are decided; especially as there is no Bar to watch the Bench; no Press to give voice to grievances; no Public to care for them, were they ever so declaimed against, and especially inasmuch as the mild Hindu is by nature long suffering, and not a little inclined to lick the hand that smites him.

At present we are only at the beginning of the end; for the Sudder Judges of the present day, and the senior Judges under them are the remnants of a system, wherein, although there was no regular judicial training, there was at least *one office* in which an active, observant, intelligent, laborious young man might learn *something* of the routine of judicial duties before he was himself elevated to the Bench: for there formerly existed attached to each principal Court *a Register*, who was not purely a Ministerial Officer, but who had cases of petty importance and trifling pecuniary amount handed over to him from time to time for trial when the hands of the Judge happened to be too full—and indeed his jurisdiction was ultimately extended to 3,000 Rupees. *But in* 1843 *the office of Registrar was abolished:* so that now there is literally not even the semblance of a school for judicial training. The results are even now apparent: but in the next generation all will be confusion worse confounded, outer darkness; and, on the part of the suitors at least, gnashing of teeth, however well the temple of justice may be paved with the very best intentions.

Effects as exhibited in the Reports.

Now in turning to the 'Reports,' the faults, errors, puerilities and mistakes which they exhibit are precisely those which we should expect to find emanating from men who have only 'common sense' and no well grounded acquaintance with the common principles of jurisprudence or the law of evidence to guide them. They exhibit an utter want of knowledge of those points to which judicial attention should be confined—a most lamentable ignorance of the Law of Evidence—an utter helplessness in the appreciation of testimony—a frequent oversight of material issues—perpetual digressions into purely irrelevant matter—wrong applications of the Law where they venture to apply it—an inability to control the proceedings before them—admissions of documents not legally proved, and of evidence the merest hearsay—decisions upon issues not raised or upon wrong or immaterial issues—strange and inconclusive lines of argument and reasoning foreign to the matter in hand—irregularities in proceedings—carelessness or inability in drawing up decrees—findings utterly contrary to evidence and so forth, of all of which copious instances shall be given: in short; it is one uniform dead level of incompetency.

The result of this is, as might naturally be expected, that the records are swollen and loaded to the most prodigious extent. A Judge who is so feeble that he does not know what *is* evidence, is too timid to trust himself to reject anything; and hence oral testimony is permitted to run to the most extravagant length, and to points the most irrelevant and in substance the most inadmissible; while almost every document that is presented by the ignorant Natives, Plaintiffs or Defendants, or their pleaders, is filed and received, till the record becomes a perfect labyrinth—another result, perhaps even more lamentable, is the frightful length and repetition of litigation which arises from the weakness of the Bench.

Litigious as the Natives naturally are, only too many loopholes are afforded for appeal : frequently upon the face of the proceedings is disclosed some complete bar which ought to have at once concluded the dispute, but which having been utterly overlooked, the case is tried, appealed, remanded, retried some four or five times, and at last ultimately disposed of on a point which ought to have settled it at the very outset.

Frequent instances of this will appear with respect to the Limitation of Suits; than which it is scarcely possible to conceive a more patent, palpable bar, especially as the Regulation of Limitations of Actions (2 of 1802, Sec. xviii.) is very express, plain and stringent in its terms; and from revenge or love of litigation the Natives are perpetually hawking up stale claims of many years standing, and instituting Suits concerning them.

With these remarks I proceed at once to the Reports: premising only that since their publication, their disclosures have frequently become the topic of conversation and wonder among reflecting men, who are scarcely to be put aside by the remark which usually greets any one who ventures to bring a more than ordinarily atrocious judgment to the notice of any of the 'Service'; 'Oh but that Judge is mad'— or 'he is an idiot,' or 'he drinks;' although politeness forbids one to put the question which naturally suggests itself—'why is such a man permitted to remain on the Bench'—for fear of reducing one's opponent to a perfectly Socratic stand-still.

No. 7 of 1848, vol. 3, p. 211.

The first case to which I shall draw attention is No. 7 of 1848, reported page 211 of Reports for 1851. It was an appeal from Mr. Anstruther, C. Judge of Rajahmundry.

Plaintiff sued for 55,270 rupees due on a bond. The defendant denied the claim in toto. The Judge nonsuited the Plaintiff *and fined him* 55,270 *rupees for bringing the suit !*

The Judge of the Sudder of course reversed this: and in paras. 41, 42, 43, 44 of his judgment he makes the following remarks.

41. "The Civil Judge has heavily fined the Appellant, as guilty "of urging a false claim. This sentence must of course now be can- "celled, the claim being considered a true one."

42. "The Civil Judge has furthermore grievously erred in the "standard adopted by him for determining the sum of the fine he "was prepared to exact. He has made the amount of the fine to "depend upon that of the claim, for the prosecution of which it was "adjudged, the one being fixed by him exactly at the sum of the "other, and thereby has quitted his position of administrator of the "law, which prescribed other considerations under which the amount "of the fine should have been regulated, to take up that of a maker "of law, and to propound a new standard for fining of his own."

43. "It has also to be deeply regretted that the Civil Judge "should have villified the character of the Appellant and his father, "as also that of the late Chinna Bungariah's manager Panungepully "Ramanah, in the manner he has done, upon grounds altogether "unwarrantable, imputing to them forgery, perjury, and subornation "of perjury, without other reason, it may be said, than that of his "own suppositions. This was the more reprehensible, as the position "of these parties should have served to prevent their being lightly "subjected to such imputations, while their circumstances made any "such stigma all the more grievously to affect them. I must add "that the characters of these individuals, so far as is to be judged of "by the matter of this Suit, stand in my mind wholly free of the "opprobrium cast upon them by the Civil Judge, and that I view the "transactions with the late Chinna Bungariah, which form the sub- "ject of this Suit, to have been conducted with all fairness and honor "and with every consideration for the party dealt with."

44. "I have to point out finally that the Decree of the Civil "Judge is defective, in not commencing with a clear statement of "the matter of the demand, and of the opposition raised to it, as also "in not containing lists of the witnesses examined, and of the docu- "ments filed."

61 of 1851, vol. 3, p. 161. I open the book again and we have No. 61 of 1851. Appeal from Mr. Baynes, C. Judge of Madura. He observes in his decree.

"The grand point for decision in this case as both parties admit is the authenticity or otherwise of the document No. 78," &c.

And he founds his judgment on it accordingly. Now it will be seen how pointedly the Judge has his eye fixed upon this document: yet it will perhaps be scarcely credited that this No. 78 turns out to be *the copy of a copy* of a deed: and the conduct of the Judge is thus set forth in the special appeal which was allowed by the Sudder Court.

11. "The Special Appellants urge that exhibit No. 78 is not the *copy of an original deed, but the copy of a copy*; that the witness (a Curnum) called to prove that the *original was deposited with him, declared he knew nothing about it,* and that the Civil Judge *refused to allow them to summon the alleged attesting witnesses to the deed, or to adduce documentary evidence to prove it to be a forgery!!!*"

47 of 1851, vol. 3, p. 135. Case No. 47 of 1851. An appeal from the decision of Mr. Boileau, C. Judge of Guntoor (formerly Judge of the Sudder.) This was a suit for the recovery of a piece of ground of the value of 40 rupees (£ 4.) It was tried over three times; and at the date of the Report was sent back by the Sudder for a fourth trial, from which it is to be remembered there might possibly be a further appeal. The Courts below had omitted to record points (in accordance with the Regulation) for the parties to prove: and both the District Moonsiff and the Civil Judge *had neglected to notice the plea urged by the Defendants that they had been in possession for* 40 *years.*

49 of 1851 reported p. 137, vol. 3. The case next in sequence is worthy of especial notice. It is from the decision of Mr. G. M. Swinton, Assistant Judge of Mangalore. (This Gentleman had been all his life in the Revenue branch; having acted in the Accountant General's Office, till he left for the Cape: and after his return he became at once a Judge.)

This suit was brought to enforce the Registry of certain land which plaintiff had purchased from 2nd Defendant, who pleaded that the land was not sold but mortgaged; and that Plaintiff had repaid himself by the usufruct.

Defendant also instituted a cross suit to recover the land. The Sudder Ameen who originally tried the suits discredited the evidence of the Defendant and gave the Plaintiff in the 1st suit a verdict in both suits.

On Appeal Mr. Swinton "affirmed *the Appeals*" (not reversed the decrees.)

On Appeal the Sudder observe that the mortgage deed was *not produced!*

The Sudder Ameen had commented on the absence of this deed: and also on sundry discrepancies in the Defendant's evidence.

The Assistant Judge remarks that the Appeal petition (i. e. the Appellant's own statement) "*sufficiently answers* the Sudder Ameen's objection as to the non-production of the document: and that he could not discover the discrepancies alluded to by that officer."

The Sudder remark "that it was the duty of the Judge to go "fully into the case as set forth in the judgment of the lower Court "and to record his opinion upon all material grounds of decision, "and to dispose of the reasons which have weighed with the lower "Judge for and against the claim in such a manner as the higher "Court may be able to judge of the validity of his own reasons."

And they then point out that oral testimony of the contents of a writing cannot be gone into when the writing is itself in existence; and that clear proof of its loss is necessary, &c.

Now here is a case tried over three times; remanded for a fourth, which surely should have been disposed of at once. Nor is it easy to conceive how any Judge could have placed credence in Defendant's story of a bond which he could not produce and did not account for: or how he failed to see that the whole story and the action upon it were trumped up to meet the Plaintiff's claim.

V. vol. 1, p. 80. *No.* 8 *of* 1848; appeal from the decision of Mr. F. M. Lewin, C. Judge of Combaconum.

The suit was brought to recover a Mosque and land. The Judge held that by Regulation VII. of 1817 he was precluded from interfering in the matter. However *he nevertheless proceeded to try the case on its merits:* disbelieved the Plaintiff's case: and then proceeded to declare the Defendant unfit to manage the property, and decreed it should *be made over to the Collector!* The Sudder Court on appeal consider that the removal of the Defendant was beyond the Judge's jurisdiction and they proceed "adverting to the opinion "of the C. Judge that the suit was barred by Reg. VII. of 1817 "the Court *are unable to comprehend* upon what grounds the Civil "Judge considered himself justified in passing a judgment upon the "merits of the case.

"It would however appear that the C. Judge has *overlooked* the "provisions of Sec. 14 of the Reg. in a question which *expressly per-* "*mits* the institution of suits of the nature of that under Review!"

This is a highly instructive case surely.

No. 56 of 1851, vol. 3, p. 155.

No. 56 of 1851 is amusing. It is an appeal from a decision of Mr. Bruere, C. Judge of Salem.

The Plaintiff sued for 125 rupees, money advanced to Defendant under a contract for the supply of oil. Defendant pleaded that he had been always ready and willing to fulfil his contract, but had been prevented by the Plaintiff.

The Moonsiff who originally tried the case disbelieved the Defendant's evidence, and gave the Plaintiff a verdict.

The Plaintiff appealed to the C. Judge who reversed the Moonsiff's decree.

The Defendant appealed to the Sudder who remanded the suit; making the following observations. "The Court of Sudder Adaw- "lut observe that the C. Judge has evidently mistaken the object for "which the suit was brought. It was instituted for the recovery of "125 rupees advanced by the Plaintiff to the Defendant, and not as "would seem to be the impression of the C. Judge *for a quantity of* "*oil!*"

A case this which may bring to mind the story of the Cambridge undergraduate who at his little go was required to find by Proportion if a lb. of butter cost 10*d.* how much a firkin and a half would cost. After a hard day's work he gave the matter up in despair, but handed in to the examiner a paper covered with figures to show he had not been idle, accompanied with a declaration that he had worked the problem over 13 times, but the answer always *would* come out in butter!

No. 67 of 1849, p. 6, vol. 1.

No. 67 of 1849 a short case from a decision of Mr. Murray, Acting C. Judge of Nellore, shows that he was totally ignorant of the law that a minor cannot bind himself—(the Hindu law is the same as the English in that respect.)

The Sudder Court remark "that there is nothing on the record "which tends to show that the 1st Defendant (minor) did at any "time after he came of age admit his responsibility on the Bond in "question," and they annul the decrees of both the Lower Courts.

No. 27 of 1847, p. 5, vol. 1.

No. 27 of 1849 is an appeal from the decision of Mr. Dowdeswell, C. Judge of Masulipatam.

The Defendants were charged in their *representative capacity;* and a verdict was given against them without any apparent enquiry as to whether they had possessed themselves of assets. The Sudder decided that they had not; and therefore released them from responsibility.

No. 80 of 1847, vol. 1, p. 9.

No. 80 of 1847 is a special appeal from the judgment of Mr. Harris, Assistant Judge of Mangalore.

The Judge on appeal reversed the Sudder Ameen's decision, and "*cancelled*" the deed of sale on which the Plaintiff relied. The Plaintiff appealed because the Judge's decree was "founded on inferences and surmises *not only not borne out* "*but contrary to the evidence as recited by himself*," (and the Judge certainly seems to have found directly in the teeth of his own argument, for the Sudder observe:

"The execution of the deed and payment of purchase money seem "to be established beyond all doubt: *a fact which the Assistant Judge* "*admits* while observing that the pleas urged by the Defendant in behalf of the sale being a nominal one are unsupported by the record."

No. 70 of 1849, p. 12, vol. 1.

Special Appeal No. 70 of 1849, is from the decision of the Chingleput Court.

Both the Lower Courts appear *entirely to have overlooked the* plea of the Plaintiff's that Document No. 13 purporting to have been executed in 1836 was a forgery, and that one of the parties alleged to have executed it died in 1835. The case was therefore remanded.

No. 32 of 1845, p. 16, vol. 1. This case (32 of 45) is a Special Appeal from the decision of Mr. Beauchamp, Sub Judge of Combaconum.

The defendant pleaded judgment recovered in a former suit about the same matter between the same parties, or those through whom they claimed. The Sudder pithily remark, "To sue again for the "same land which was disallowed by a decision in a former suit, and "that decree a final one is contrary to Sec. IX. Reg. 2 of 1802;" and they reverse the decisions of the lower Courts.

No. 4 of 1847, p. 36, vol. 1. Is a short but instructive case.

The suit was originally brought for a piece of ground of the value of 15 rupees (£1 10) and a house of the value of 40 rupees (£4) and for an "injunction to have a wall built." This case was tried *five* times; and the Sudder "as at present constituted" over-rule their predecessors.

No. 25 of 1847, p. 46, vol. 1. This was a Special Appeal from the decision of Mr. Morris, (afterwards a Judge of the Sudder Court.)

It was tried *six* times although the Court of Sudder are at last "*clearly of opinion that this suit is barred by the Statute of Limitations.*" ! ! !

And the case is further instructive because the lower Courts gave a verdict for plaintiff, who sued as heir against a personal representative, *without enquiring whether he was heir; or if defendant had possessed himself of assets ! ! !*

No. 43 of 1849, p. 66, vol. 1. This is a Special Appeal from the decision of Mr. Baynes, C. Judge of Madura, for the recovery of land of the value of Rs. 27-5-6, and Rs. 11-1-6 quit rent. It is tried over three times.

The Civil Judge finds directly contrary to the evidence.

The Sudder observe " the plaintiff's claim to the land in question " was founded on the plea, that the same had been bestowed upon " their ancestors as a gift, and although they *entirely failed* to prove " this averment, the C. Judge gave judgment in their favour because " they were *managers* of the land," and they reverse the decree, up- " holding that of the Sudder Ameen who originally tried the case.

No. 83 of 1844, p. 71, vol. 1. This is a Special Appeal from the Judgment of Mr. Glass, C. Judge, late Acting 2d Judge of the Northern Provincial Court. The Sudder admit the appeal on the ground that,

" The decree of the Provincial Court *was in direct opposition to the* "*facts admitted on both sides*;" and that it " *was equally clear that it* " *was erroneous* in other respects."

No. 42 of 1848, p. 75, vol. 1. This is a Special Appeal from the decision of Mr. Cook, Acting Sub Judge of Mangalore.

It was a case in which the Statute of Limitations had clearly run. It was tried over *five* times (being for the recovery of land of the annual value of Rs. 50-12.)

Once before it had been remanded because " the Appellate Court had reversed the original award *without receiving an answer from* the Respondent ;" and the present appeal shows how strange an idea the Judge must have had of what it was incumbent on the defendant to prove, in order to take advantage of the Statute of Limitations; for he held that the suit was *not* barred because " there " was no proof to show that the plaintiffs did not know of the sale, " but through negligence or indifference or doubt as to their rights, " they failed to institute the suit."

No. 35 of 1845, p. 96, vol. 1. This is a strange case.

Plaintiff sued for the recovery of 417 Rs. under the following circumstances. He delivered an order to the 2nd defendant at Trichinopoly, requesting him to send it to his (2nd defendant's) partner (1st defendant) at Madras, for the purpose of getting it cashed ; and sending the money by a Hoondie (order). A letter was put in evidence from 2nd defendant to 1st in which he specially directed his partner to transmit the proceeds by a Hoondie. Instead of this he chose to send the money by Bank Notes which never came to hand, and the plaintiff sued for its recovery.

It does not appear that the plaintiff ever gave any orders as to the mode in which the proceeds were to be remitted, and if not, quære his right to recover—this point never seems to have suggested itself throughout.

However the Sudder Ameen who originally tried the case found that

"The loss was occasioned by circumstances over which the par-"ties had no control; *and ought therefore to be borne equally by "the plaintiff and* 1st *and* 2nd *defendants;*" and he also apportioned the costs in the same ratio. Against this decree *all three parties separately appealed;* and the C. Judge (Mr. Greenway) dismissed the plaintiff's claim on the ground among others "that there *was no "proof that 2nd defendant directed* 1*st defendant* to remit the money "by an order," *although he had the 2nd defendant's letter before him;* for the Sudder in their decree expressly refer to it; and find "that the "decree passed in opposition to so important a document is con-"trary to the established practice of Courts." They find that the 1st defendant failed to carry out the orders of the 2nd; and they therefore absolve the 2nd defendant from all liability; decreeing the 1st defendant alone to make good the loss.

While I am on this case I may as well allude to it as one of a class to which I shall have hereafter to refer, when I come to look into the value of the *Sudder* Court's decisions; for *the* material point, namely, what were the Plaintiff's orders, seems to have entirely escaped their attention.

No. 53 of 1847, p. 102, vol. 1.

This is a Regular Appeal from a decision of Mr. Baynes, C. Judge of Madura. The case is too long to analyze, but the C. Judge misconceives the Substantive Law, the Decrees, and the proceedings of the Sudder Court, who declare that the C. Judge has

"Fallen into a singular error in applying that Section of the Law" (Section 12, Regulation 25 of 1801) "to the question at issue in this action;" and again: "the Civil Judge has likewise misunderstood

" the purport of the Court's decree No. 6 of 1841, as well as the " Court's proceedings of the 27th September 1841."

No. 2 of 1849, p. 105, vol. 1.

This is a shocking case. It is from the decision of Mr. Onslow, Actg. Asst. Judge of the Adawlut Court of Malabar. The amount in dispute was small. The amount of litigation frightful. It appears to have extended over a period from 1825 to 1849. It was tried over five times, besides a considerable amount of petitioning; and after all it turns out to be barred by the Statute of Limitations!

No. 20 of 1848, p. 119, vol. 1.

This is a Special Appeal from a decision of Mr. Anstruther, C. Judge of Rajahmundry.

Plaintiff's estate had been put up and sold by the Government for arrears of Kist; a proceeding, which according to the Law, satisfies the Government claim; and the Proprietor is expressly empowered by Sec. 18 of Reg. 28 of 1802 in such an event to sue his tenants for any arrears of rent due by them. The plaintiff brought his action to recover the sum of Rupees 45-12-10, the amount of rent due to him by the defendant his tenant. The Sub Judge gave him a verdict, which the Civil Judge reversed on appeal. The plaintiff thereupon appealed to the Sudder, who naturally reversed the decree of the Civil Judge.

The decision of the Chief Judge presents such a curious and indeed perversely ingenious obliquity of Judicial reasoning that I extract it entire from the Report.

6. " The Renter or Proprietor of an Estate," the Civil Judge remarked in his Decree, " rents from Government the difference " between the Peshkush the estate must pay to Government, and the " revenue the Cultivators or Sub-Renters pay to him. If these are " equal, the Renter gains nothing; if the revenue the Renter draws " from the Cultivators (or under-tenants, or Ryots or Sub-Farmers, " &c. &c.) be less than the Peshkush he has to pay to Government, " he loses; if it be more, so much more he gains. But it is evident " that not a Rupee, which he collects, can be really or justly his, until " he has collected and paid the Peshkush. Should he be unable to " collect the Peshkush in one Fusly, but pay it out of his own resour-

" ces, he has the right to recover from his Ryots what he paid in " advance for them. If he had collected those Rupees from the Ryots " during his rent, those identical Rupees belonged not to him but to " Government (the surplus only beyond the Peshkush belonging to " him,) and he would have paid them to Government. If the collec- " tion were delayed, the payment to Government must not be so, " wherefore if the Renter pays the Peshkush first out of his own " resources and then collects it from his Ryots, the money he paid " represents the same money as he collects from them ; it being on- " ly advanced by him. But, if he does not advance the money, he " cannot have the same rights as if he did. If it is the payment of " the Peshkush, which gives him the right to collect it, non-payment " takes away the right. If another person pays that Peshkush in ad- " vance, such payment confers the right to collect, and the person who " pays, not the person who does not pay, has the sole right to collect."

7. " If when he does not, and cannot pay, the Government were " to retain their demand against him, every Rupee, which he might " in any way recover, would to the extent of the Peshkush or his " arrear, be, not his, but the property of Government. If seeing " that he cannot and solely because he cannot, and on the ground, " condition, and agreement, and virtual declaration by him, that he " cannot collect even the Peshkush from the Ryots, the Government " have compassion on him, and waive their unquestionable right to " collect the full Peshkush from him, although he shall not have col- " lected and shall never be able to collect a Rupee of it, and shall " give him an acquittance, should he ever discover in the possession " of the Ryots the Rupees they unduly withheld from him, and which " he therefore only did not pay to Government, it is reasonable that " all so recovered, to the extent of the Peshkush, should go to Go- " vernment, and the contrary would be a palpable violation of reason " and justice. Should it ever appear that money, so discovered and " recovered, had been by fraud and collusion between the Renter and " Ryots withheld until the compassion of Government had been " moved, it is only what might be expected as the natural consequence " of ruling, that if a Renter collects punctually, he must pay what he " collects, but if he postpones collection he may enjoy what he col- " lects. Such however it is evident could not destroy the just and " reasonable right of Government to the whole so recovered, up to " the amount at least of the Peshkush or arrear." ! ! !

No. 21 of 1848, p. 122, vol. 1.

The next case, an Appeal from the decision of the same Judge, displays a sad state of things.

The Plaint disclosed a nonsuit on the face of it. The Plaintiff had exercised no right over the land in dispute since 1806. Yet the case was tried over *five times*, before the C. Judge's decree was ultimately reversed, and further litigation stayed by the declaration that the statute of Limitations barred it.

Nos. 41 of 1848, and 20 of 1849, p. 128, vol. 1.

No. 6 of 1846, p. 131, vol. 1.

These are Appeals from the decisions of Mr. Glass, C. Judge of Chicacole. They are too long and complicated to admit of abstracting. They are therefore transferred in full to the Appendix. A few remarks only will be necessary upon them. See Appendix No. 1.

The two first form one record: and afford a singular example of inability to appreciate the value of evidence.

It will be remarked that the Plaintiff was present when other lands, which, if his present claim were well founded, must have been also his, were publicly sold—that he *then* made no objection—but lay by for eleven years—and his whole case is a palpably false one. The Civil Judge ruled in his favour; though if his claim were established, upon what principle he was ordered to repay the sum of Rupees 2,863-12 (see para. 8 of the Report) is not easily conceivable.

Case No. 6 is also a very strong one. It shows an utter inability to weigh the value of testimony. The Plaintiff sued to annul a bond executed by him to Defendant for 1,600 Rupees, payable by yearly instalments of 200 Rupees; and for the recovery of 1,400 Rupees paid on the bond. His case was that it was executed under duress; see his absurd story; para. 4. The Defendant was an old woman. *Plaintiff admitted that he had paid seven instalments annually as they became due*, which it might be imagined would have been of itself conclusive. Nevertheless the case appears to have extended over eleven years, and to have been already *tried five times* with various fortune. Several Judges found in favour of the Plaintiff, as did the Judge from whom the present appeal was made. The Sudder of course reverse the decree ; though it is worthy of observation that with this all-important fact of *seven years' voluntary payment* before them, they had on a former occasion remanded the suit for further enquiry upon a point of tenure, a question which they at last see and admit (para. 20) is "of no importance to the issue in the suit."

Special Appeal Petition No. 56 of 1849, vol. 2, p. 10.

In this case the question was of one simple fact ; division or no division of family—yet it has been tried over four times already, and the Sudder has now remanded it for a fifth.

No. 18 of 1851, vol. 4, p. 53.

This is a case of singular hardship. It is an Appeal from a decision of Mr. Inglis, C. Judge of Chingleput.

It was brought to establish plaintiff's right of succession to the estate of one Soobaroya Moodelly, of the value of Rs. 4,414-2-3. He rested his case on one simple point, his adoption by the deceased : and in further support, he produced a will of the deceased recognizing him as his adopted son. The defendants denied the fact of adoption, and said the will was a forgery. The Principal Sudder Ameen who originally tried the case dismissed the plaintiff's claim. In a decree of considerable length and ability he went thoroughly into the evidence on both points, pointing out his reasons for disbelieving it, and found the adoption a lie and the will a forgery.

The plaintiff appealed to the Civil Judge (Mr. Boileau formerly in the Sudder) who reversed this decree, entering into a long disquisition upon the Hindu Law, as to whether any and what ceremonies were necessary to render an adoption valid ; and on other immaterial points, entirely losing sight of the *fact* found by the Sudder Ameen, that in this case there had been no adoption at all.

From this the defendants appealed to the Sudder, who remanded the suit in order that the opinion of the Pundits as to what was necessary in Law to constitute a valid adoption, (which had not been taken by Mr. Boileau and which they forwarded) might be considered.

In the meanwhile Mr. Inglis had succeeded Mr. Boileau. He pronounced his decree, reversing Mr. Boileau's, and agreeing on all points with the Sudder Ameen.

Against this decree the plaintiff again appealed to the Sudder Adawlut, who in the first instance refused to admit the appeal, but subsequently on a petition praying a review of their judgment, and containing a good deal of observation upon Hindu Law, the Sudder decided that it was a point of "general importance requiring further consideration," and accordingly determined to have the case orally argued. The defendants were thus forced to appear, and put in their answer, and ultimately Counsel were heard on both sides. The plaintiff's counsel went very fully into the Law of adoption; which the defendant's advocate declined to answer: and observed that so far as the decision of the case before the Court was concerned, any other thesis of Hindu Law might as well have been given out for disputation. He then pointed out that the original decree found that there was *no adoption in fact,* and of this opinion were the Court. So that here was a case depending upon a simple matter of fact tried over no less than five times; the amount being of the value of 4,000 and odd Rupees, the costs amounting to nearly 3,000; and all this entirely useless litigation about a point which had nothing whatever to do with the issue!

Special Appeal Petition No. 19 of 1850, p. 5, vol. 2.

This was a suit for the recovery of rent. Defendant *pleaded that he had not occupied the premises.* Both the lower Courts adjudged him to pay the rent *without deciding that issue, or taking any evidence upon it.* The Sudder remands it for a *third trial.*

Special Appeal Suit No. 33 of 1849, vol. 2, p. 16.

In this case a Special Appeal was admitted by the Sudder Court on the ground that the "decree contained much irrelevant matter, and was "in part recorded in a language not current in India, and un-"known to the parties concerned in the suit."

Special Appeal No. 58 of 1848, vol. 2, p. 19.

This is a pithy but important decree, as shewing the lax way in which judicial investigations are carried on. It is therefore given entire. It will be observed that here are three trials; a fourth ordered; and as yet nothing has been gained.

1. "The original Suit was instituted by the Plaintiff against the Defendants for the recovery of a tiled Bazar valued at Rupees 285-10, and which had been bequeathed to the Plaintiff by her deceased father in a will executed on the 24th March 1843.

2. The principal Sudder Ameen was of opinion that the validity of the will had not been clearly proved. He therefore rejected the Plaintiff's claim, but his decree was reversed in appeal by the Civil Judge, who considered the will in question to have been fully and satisfactorily established.

3. A special appeal was admitted on the application of the 3d Defendant on the 26th June 1847, as it appeared that the Civil Judge had omitted *to take an answer from him* previous to passing his decision. The Suit was accordingly ordered back that this omission might be supplied, and a fresh judgment passed.

4. The case then came before Mr. Story, the Acting Civil Judge, for disposal, and that officer reversed the former appeal decree and rejected the Plaintiff's claim, on the ground that "if the parties were divided, the will, whether false or true, was illegal."

5. A special appeal was admitted on the part of the Plaintiff, because the correct decision of the matter at issue depended in a great measure on the legality or otherwise of the will in question, and the opinion of the Law Officers on this point had not been taken.

6. And that this may now be done, the Court of Sudder Udalut remand the case back to the Civil Judge, with an injunction to replace the Suit on his file and, after following the above course, proceed to pass judgment de novo."

No. 1 of 1846, vol. 2, p. 23. This is a Special Appeal from a decision of Mr. Baynes, C. Judge of Salem.

The 1st para. of the decree discloses *four* trials :

"The Court of Sudder Adawlut gave judgment in this case on "30th December 1848 in favour of the Special Appellant; but an application having been made in behalf of the Special Respondent under date 2nd July 1849, the Court resolve to review the suit and "now proceed to pass judgment anew."

and they remand the suit for a fifth trial: the point being that a certain document (D) upon which the case hinged, had all along been dealt with as of a temporary character, whereas it was in fact of a permanent one, which the Sudder upon "again referring to the aforesaid document" find it actually is! There are some minor points in the case which it is not worth while to notice; they are however not without their import.

No. 14 of 1850, p. 25, vol. 2. This is a Special Appeal from a decision of Mr. Goodwyn, Sub. Judge of Calicut.

The matter in dispute was of the value of ten rupees, with one rupee damages for cutting plantains. The case has been tried over three times and is remanded for a fourth. "The District Moonsiff *went fully into the case* and gave his reasons "in detail for dismissing the Plaintiff's suit."

The Subordinate Judge set aside this decree without noticing the Moonsiff's reasons: because the Defendants would not abide by their first agreement to settle the dispute by oath! The Court observe:—

6. The Court of Sudder Udalut observe, firstly, that no final agreement was entered into by the parties to settle the dispute by oath, and that, if there had been, the non-observance of that agreement was not alone sufficient for reversing the decision of the District Moonsiff.

7. Secondly, that it was the duty of the Subordinate Judge to have recorded in detail, his reasons for setting aside the evidence on which the Moonsiff relied.

8. Thirdly, the Court of Sudder Udalut observe, from information furnished by the Civil Judge, that the notice issued to the 1st Respondent was not signed by him, and it does not appear that the course laid down by Law in such cases was observed.

9. The Court of Sudder Udalut therefore remand the case to the Subordinate Judge, who will be enjoined to issue a notice to the Respondent to make answer to the Appeal, and the record being completed, to pass judgment de novo.

No. 49 of 1848, vol. 2, p. 34. Appeal from the decision of Mr. Baynes, C. Judge of Madura. In this case the C. Judge decides upon an instrument in writing and a bond *neither of which were in evidence.*

No. 47 of 1849, vol. 2, p. 36. Special Appeal from a decision of Mr. Baynes, C. Judge of Salem. This is a very instructive suit. It will be found entire in the Appendix No. 1.

It will be observed that the suit was brought to recover a house alleged to have been forfeited under a mortgage bond. The bond was executed with an illegal object; to "save the "Defendant's property from liability to satisfy the claims of "other persons."

Yet the Sub. Judge gives the plaintiff (who was out of possession) relief, though wrongly in point of form, awarding him '*damages*,' not the house—instead of leaving the parties as he found them. His argument against the defendant is equally strong against the plaintiff, *both* are 'participes criminis.' Then the C. Judge in appeal having decided that the Plaintiff has no right, tells him he should sue in a regular suit; and though giving a right decision at last, basing it upon a wrong ground—that the sale was '*nominal*;' *(instead of* '*fraudulent*'.*)* Then one Judge of the Sudder admits an appeal which the other two overrule; laying down some bad law with respect to mortgages (para. 10) and after all it turns out that the suit is barred by limitation, and the amount is only for 124 Rupees!

What a jumblement.

No. 18 of 1850, vol. 2, p. 37. Special Appeal from Mr. Morris, C. Judge of Calicut (afterwards in the Sudder.)

"The C. Judge in Appeal decided against the Plaintiff, reversing the Sudder Ameen's decision in his favour. The plaintiff prayed for a review of judgment, and offered a document signed by the defendant's father which if true was conclusive as to his right;—*but this application was refused.* The Sudder remand the case on the ground "that written and material evidence for the plaintiff was not called "for and considered in the lower Courts.

No. 15 of 1850, vol. 2, p. 39. This is a Special Appeal from a decision of Mr. Baynes, C. J. of Madura. The suit was brought for damages in consequence of the defendants having blocked up a water channel which led to the inundation of the plaintiff's crops—he likewise sued for the removal of the bank in question, pleading that the land on which the bank was erected was in plaintiff's village.

The defendants generally denied the facts and their responsibility.

The case is a long one, but although the right to the land was plainly put in issue by the pleadings, the C. Judge says it was not, in the very teeth of them as well as of some pointed remarks of the Sudder Ameen. The decisions of both the lower Courts are entirely silent as to the plaintiff's right to keep the channel open. The C. Judge says the assessment of damages by the S. Ameen was correct, though he cannot tell on what principle it was decided: and shuffles out of it by saying the plaintiffs at any rate accepted these damages: which as the Sudder observe, of course they would, if they had in reality no right to the land in dispute.

The Sudder Court consider the C. Judge's decree to be "a loose "and unsatisfactory mode of disposing of the matter and one against "which the appellants very fairly complain:" they further observe that "from what is stated in the decrees of the lower Courts no "correct opinion can be formed as to whether the lands were flood-"ed or not at the time specified in the plaint, and if they were so "what was the amount of injury sustained:" and they remand the suit for further investigation.

No. 20 of 1850, vol. 2, p. 43.

The next case is a Special Appeal from the same Judge.

Plaintiffs claimed certain land as the widow and daughter of one Ramanooja Aucharry, who it was stated had acquired the land through adoption by its former owner. The defendants denied the adoption; but said the deceased had *inherited* the land and that they as his brother's sons were his heirs, the tenure of the land excluding females from succession.

If this tenure was proved there was an end of the case. It was *distinctly pleaded;* and Defendants were called upon to substantiate their plea; yet this point was entirely overlooked. The Sudder observe:

That the right of females to manage is "a very important point." They observe (para. 15) "this plea was *strongly urged by the defend-" ants as a decisive proof of the invalidity of the plaintiff's* claim, "and although the Court of first instance required the defendants "to substantiate their averment by proof, yet neither that Court nor "the Appellate tribunal made any references to it in their decrees!"

It is further to be observed that the plaintiffs being out of possession and only entitled to eject the defendants on the strength of their own title, and that title depending upon the disputed right of females to manage, the C. Court nevertheless passed a decree adverse to the defendants. The Sudder remand the case which has already been tried four times; so that there yet awaits it a fifth trial, besides the prospect of further appeals!

No. 21 of 1850, p. 45, vol. 2.

This is a Special Appeal from a decision of Mr. Story, Acting C. Judge of Salem. It will be found entire in the Appendix No. 1.

It will be observed that it is nothing but a continuance of errors from first to last. The 1st Judge decides upon a copy of an instrument. The next C. Judge decides that the defendants *have fraudulently made away with the very instrument which would prove their case!* and lastly the important point of law in it is overlooked altogether! The case has already been tried five times!

No. 29 of 1850, vol. 2, p. 65.

A Special Appeal from a decision of Mr. Lovell, C. Judge of Chittoor.

This is an extraordinary jumble of mistakes. 1st. The C. Judge nonsuits the Plaintiff (though on what the Sudder determine to be a total misapprehension of the Law) and then proceeds to decide on the merits; letting the Defendant file documentary evidence: no opportunity being given to the Plaintiff to rebut it.

No. 13 of 1849, vol. 2, p. 78.

This is a Special Appeal from a decision of Mr. Greenway, C. Judge of Trichinopoly.

It was brought for the recovery of a piece of ground of the value of 3 Rupees (6 Shillings). It has been tried three times, and remanded for a fourth trial. The defendants had been in "undisturbed pos-"session of the land for a lengthened period." The plaintiff proved his purchase from a *third* party: but the "title of that party to the "land not being satisfactorily established" the C. Judge reversed the decree of the Sudder Ameen in plaintiff's favour: but the investigation was carried on in such a way that the Sudder declare it "impossible from the evidence before them to arrive at any just or "satisfactory conclusion as to which party the land under litigation "rightfully belongs."

So here are four trials about a piece of land of the value of six Shillings.

No. 31 of 1850, p. 87 of vol. 2, and 256 of vol. 3.

This is a Special Appeal from a decision of Mr. Baynes. The Sub. Judge considered the title of the plaintiff to the land established, but as it would be "hard" upon the Defendants to call upon them to give it up, he decrees that they shall in lieu thereof *pay the Plaintiff the estimated value of the land*, Rupees 3,000.

The C. Judge reversed this decree considering it "clearly barred by the statute of Limitations."

The Sudder on appeal not agreeing with this, remanded the suit, and in page 256, vol. 3, we have it again as 97 of

No. 97 of 1851.

1851. The C. Judge stuck by his opinion, and the case comes up afresh. The Sudder stick by theirs, and send it back again—for a sixth trial!

But here I must take leave of this Judge. There are more decisions of his in the Reports: but I think the 'taste', as Coke would call it, already given of his judicial quality must be sufficient; and the necessity I am under of making as general selections as possible occupying more room than I can well spare, I shall say no more of the C. Judge of Madura. It would be unjust to that gentleman were I not to observe that he labours under the peculiar disadvantage, shared partly by the Judge of Salem, of having a clever European Vakeel practising before him, who does not let slips pass by unnoticed. The impression which these pages might otherwise convey would be to the prejudice of the Judges of Madura and Salem ; exhibiting their decrees as peculiarly deficient; whereas in truth and in fact if Vakeels of a similar quality to Mr. Fischer were practising before the other Mofussil Courts, it would no doubt be found that these gentlemen are not a whit behind their neighbours.

No. 38 of 1850, vol. 2, p. 89. A Special Appeal against the decision of Mr. Elliot, C. Judge of Cuddapah.

This is a case for the recovery of Rupees 12-10 damages in consequence of an interference of defendants with the exercise of certain privileges of plaintiff's deceased father. The case has occupied from 1845 to 1850. It has been already tried three times ; and is now to begin again.

No. 63 of 1848, vol. 2, p. 94. This is a Special Appeal from a decision of Mr. Story, Acting C. Judge of Trichinopoly. *When* this suit was instituted, does not appear, further than that it was *before* 1842. It was a simple question of fact ; it has been *tried eight times.*

No. 44 of 1848, vol. 2, p. 103. Special Appeal from a decision of Mr. Frere, Sub. Judge of Salem. This is a strange case.

Plaintiff sued on a bond dated 1838 for 125 Rupees, and interest at a rate stipulated in the bond.

The District Moonsiff gave a verdict for the plaintiff.

The Sub. Judge on appeal modified this decree—holding only one defendant liable, and giving only one year's interest.

This was appealed against to the Sudder who remanded the case on the ground that the Judge had failed "*to examine the witnesses whom the defendant was ready to produce.*" The Sub. Judge received the further evidence : and gave 50 Rupees interest instead of 40 on account of some supposed laches of the Plaintiff; and because a witness deposed that "an *attempt* at mediation was made about two "months before the filing of the suit, when *he* 'arranged' that "Defendant should pay 50 Rupees for interest—to which however "Plaintiff would not agree."

The Sudder of course declare the Plaintiff entitled to the full amount of his interest specified in the bond—but the case has been tried *five* times in order to arrive at this conclusion !

No. 48 of 1850, p. 109, vol. 2. Special Appeal from a decision of Mr. Davidson, late Sub. Judge of Combaconum.

This merely exhibits general carelessness and laxity in drawing up a decree. The appellant alleges that the decree was passed *behind his back without his being heard.* The Sudder remarking that the decree is silent upon this point, remit it for a fourth trial.

No. 52 of 1850, p. 126, vol. 2. A Special Appeal from Mr. Anstruther's decision. The whole case is worthy of the Appendix, wherein it will be found. See Appendix No. 1.

"The Sudder admit the Appeal because it was 'very faulty and "imperfect;' and they have read with much dissatisfaction the *very* "*objectionable epithets* made use of by the C. Judge *in speaking of* "*the Defendant and his witnesses;* and they expect Mr. Anstruther "will be more guarded and more circumspect in his language for the "future."

It will be observed that in this case the Judge relies on *mere rumours*, or *other* suits, instead of confining himself to the evidence before him.

No. 4 of 1851, vol. 3, p. 1. Special Appeal from a decision of Mr. G. Ellis, Acting Sub. Judge of Madura.

This is the continuation of a case sent back because the decree was irrelevant and in a language not current in India.* It now comes up again and is remanded again for a *sixth trial:* the case being a simple one which any competent Judge should have disposed of at the outset.

---

* See p. 16, vol. before quoted.

No. 5 of 1851, vol. 3, p. 3.

A Special Appeal from the decision of Mr. R. Cotton, Acting Sub. Judge of Salem. It is an amusing case, too long to be entered here in full, and therefore transferred to the Appendix. See Appendix No. 1.

It is tried seven times (besides the chance of future appeals.) The Defendant having executed a deed of gift, is perpetually allowed to shift his defence. 1st, his plea is that he executed it when about to go on a pilgrimage. In another trial, it is invalid because he has a son: 3d, he says it was never out of his possession. Then mark what an absurdity the Pundits lay down as law. A man cannot part with all his property so long as *he is able to beget children*, say these sages. Pray how is this precise time to be decided on? a pretty plea on which to defeat a purchaser without notice for valuable consideration!

No. 4 of 1850, p. 5, vol. 3.

This is a Special Appeal from Mr. Greenway, C. Judge of Trichinopoly. It is a case which ought to have been disposed of at once: it is tried over six times. The Sudder observe:

"In the record it is clearly shown that altho' the cause of action "arose in 1821 it was not until 1835 that the Plaintiffs took *any* steps "to establish their claims before a Court of competent jurisdiction. "They reverse the decrees of the lower Courts and declare the "suit barred by the statute of Limitations."

No. 11 of 1851, p. 1, vol. 3.

Special Appeal from a decision of Mr. Swinton, Assistant Judge of Mangalore.

This case exhibits an extraordinary jumble of suits, and deeds and just such confusion as might be anticipated in the decree of a Judge whose only training for the Bench has been in the Accountant General's Office.

No. 12 of 1851, p. 13, vol. 3.

Special Appeal from Mr. Bruere: an action this for 78 Rs. 4 As. tried over three times; sent back for a fourth; barred the whole time by the Law of Limitations.

No. 24 of 1848, vol. 3, p. 42. Appeal from the decision of Mr. Forsyth, C. Judge of Tellicherry. The case is so instructive that it is transferred to the Appendix: where it will repay perusal. See Appendix No. 1.

No. 61 of 1849, p. 48. Appeal from the decision of Mr. Scott, C. Judge of Combaconum. The case is so badly reported, that it is difficult to be sure one thoroughly gets at the facts.

It appears however that one subject of contest was a bill of sale: one party contending it was absolute, the other only conditional. The lower Courts held it the latter. The C. Judge in his decree observes as to the *non-execution* of the agreement for which a stamp cadjan had been purchased: "It is true that *mere intention* cannot as a *general* " *rule* be admitted as proof, more particularly when made in aid of a " fraudulent motive, and, were it not that the Court's rejection of the " conditional agreement on the part of the 2nd defendant, would lega- " lize the sale to the appellant, to their benefit, and to the serious injury " of the respondent, *the Court would be disposed to* require more full " and decided proof."

Strange reasoning, this, for admitting as evidence that which is not so.

A Special Appeal was admitted because the lower Courts " had rejected a document *admitted by all parties to the suit.*"

No. 24 of 1849, p. 12, No. 25. Special Appeal from Mr. Woodgate, Sub. Judge of Madura. The case is short; it is for 41 Rupees; tried four times; and full of a variety of errors. No. 25 is its fellow.

Nos. 16 and 17 of 1851, p. 60. Special Appeal from the decision of Mr. Beauchamp, Sub. Judge of Combaconum. The case is remanded; and it is only alluded to as a specimen of the enormous extent to which litigation runs in India, if unrestricted.

No. 55 [illegible]849, p. 78. Special Appeal from the decision of Mr. Goodwyn, Sub. Judge of Calicut. The decree is affirmed: but the action is for a piece of land valued Rs. 3-12 (about 7 shillings) and it is tried four times.

No. 32 of 1851, p. 80. Special Appeal from a decision of Mr. Anstruther.

Action on a bond. The Sudder Ameen found for the Plaintiff. The C. Judge reversed this decree, declaring the bond a forgery. He added " besides all this, *the probability always is that the suits* " *and bonds of Plaintiff are false*; he has long been *generally and* " *publicly considered* a forger and suborner of perjury."

A Special Appeal was admitted, and the suit remanded; the Court desiring the Civil Judge

" to abstain in his future decrees from stigmatizing, as he has done " in this case, the parties who may seek redress in Civil Courts."

They point out that if the case justified the Judge in his remarks, it was his duty to have committed the Plaintiff for criminal trial, but not having done so, the Court

" deem the remarks recorded by the C. Judge very unjustifiable and most improper."

No. 33 of 1851, p. 103. Special Appeal from the decision of Mr. Forsyth, C. Judge of Tellicherry. The case (on a bond) is tried over four times. The Sudder observe that

" *After the pleadings*, in which the Defendant totally denied the ex- " ecution of the instrument, were completed, and points recorded for " proof, he moved the Court to the effect that he had compromised the " matter with the plaintiff, and that the receipt then put in was an ac- " knowledgment of the plaintiff, and that he had fully satisfied all " demands. The lower Courts instead of confining their considera- " tion to the merits of the case as pleaded by the parties in their res- " pective pleadings, and to the evidence they might adduce in support " of the same, went into the question as to the genuineness of the re- " ceipt, and *without giving the plaintiff an opportunity of refuting the* " *same, decided that it was genuine, and that the plaintiff must abide* " *by it.*"

An easy way, this, for a defendant to meet a claim!

No. 34 of 1851, p. 112, vol. 3. Mr. Swinton in his decree fails to state his reasons for holding the claim barred by the Statute of Limitations.

No. 39 of 1851, p. 119, vol. 3. The decree of Mr. Davidson is careless and superficial, he stating no reasons for reversing the District Moonsiff's award.

No. 46 of 1851, p. 132. This is a case for recovery of a pair of gold ear-rings of the value of 47½ Rupees. It is tried four times.

No. 53 of 1851, p. 141. This is a Special Appeal from a decision of Mr. T. L. Strange, C. Judge of Bellary, (now in the Sudder). The Sudder observe that

"There are several points bearing on the matter in dispute which have not received consideration from lower Courts." They remark that is clear certain specified persons ought to have been parties to the suit, and that the Judge had adjudged the property to parties *not* before the Court.

No. 54 of 1851, p. 144. Special Appeal from the decision of Mr. Davidson, Acting Civil Judge of Trichinopoly. The Sudder observe :—

"The Civil Judge was of opinion that the only question to be de-"cided in the case is, &c. *No question has been raised as to the Plain-"tiff's right to redeem the land.* But this the Court would observe "is perfectly erroneous, for the Plaintiff pleaded all along that "the land in dispute never belonged to Peer Row, as stated in the "plaint"—

They further observe that the question as to whether the Statute of Limitations applies, has not been alluded to: and that the C. Judge has not recorded any opinion upon the facts found by the S. Ameen.

No. 13 of 1851, p. 147. Special Appeal from the decision of Mr. Lascelles, C. Judge of Honore. In this case the Judge quotes Law, and wrongly applies it.

No. 30 of 1851, p. 149. Special Appeal from Mr. Strange's decision. This case is only quoted on account of the curious notion which the Sub. Judge appears to have of a mortgage ; he observed,

" A mortgagee has no claim whatever to the property mortgaged : " his claim goes only as far as the amount of mortgage which he may " realize on the sale of the said property in case payment is refused :"

whereby a mortgagee's right are reduced to a bare right of Foreclosure.

No. 16 of 1850, p. 153. Special Appeal from the decision of Mr. White, C. Judge of Cuddalore. In this case the Judge relies upon a document which the Sudder pronounce utterly unworthy of credit.

No. 57 of 1851, p. 157. Special Appeal from the decision of Mr. Lovell, C. Judge of Chittoor ; the case will be found in the Appendix entire. See Appendix No. 1. I presume the accounts produced were the Plaintiff's own. The C. Judge seems to have arrived at a right decision, in fact, although erroneous in form. The accounts are not signed by Appavoo ; they are of course the Plaintiff's; and not evidence.

Then we have the Plaintiff dealing with defendant from 1825 to 1833 without any adjustment of accounts ; nor any such up to Appavoo's death in 1840, a period of 15 years. Then he says the accounts were settled, showing a balance in his favour of Rs. 288-14-3. The Settlement is not produced ; but the defendant immediately signs a bond for—not the balance, but 190 Rupees—yet no step is taken for 5 years after this. The Plaintiff is the Village Moonsiff ; and to adjudge him entitled under all these circumstances would be monstrous, and could only be awarded by one utterly incompetent to weigh probabilities.

No. 62 of 1851, p. 164. Special Appeal from the decision of Mr. Copleston, Sub. Judge of Mangalore. This si a case for property of the annual value of 38 Rupees : tried over three times, the C. Judge quite overlooking the Statute of Limitations, which stood staring him in the face.

No. 64 of 1851, p. 167. Special Appeal from a decision of Mr. Morris, Judge of Calicut. In this case the C. Judge disposed of the case on a compromise entered into by the plaintiff's brother, *without any authority from the Plaintiff.*

No. 65 of 1851, p. 169. Special Appeal from the decision of Mr. Story, Acting C. Judge of Cuddapah. In this case the Plaintiff's admission that he had received the money was not held evidence of that fact.

No. 66 of 1851, p. 172. Special Appeal from the decision of Mr. Lewin, C. Judge of Chittoor. Here the Judge goes out of his way to *disprove* defendant's admission.

No. 68 of 1851, p. 175. Special Appeal from a decision of Mr. Cook, Acting Sub. Judge of Calicut. The Sudder find his course very irregular.

No. 69 of 1851, p. 177. Special Appeal from a decision of Mr. Story, Acting C. Judge of Cuddapah. In this case law is applied, and, as usual, wrongly.

No. 2 of 1851, p. 154. Special Appeal from the decision of Mr. Walker, C. Judge of Nellore. This is an action for Rupees 147—Litigation dates from 1844. It has been tried over five times ; and quære whether Limitation does not apply ?

The Judge makes a funny ruling. He rejects a *settlement* of accounts : because the *accounts* themselves are not forthcoming.

No. 80 of 1851, p. 207. In this case the Sudder remark :

"The Civil Judge's decree contains no solutions of these questions, "but travels out of the real merits of the case as mooted by the par- "ties themselves, to decide thereupon on certain *foreign considera-* "*tions* which have *occurred to himself.*"

No. 81 of 1851, p. 209. Special Appeal from the decision of Mr. Anderson, C. Judge of Mangalore. The Sudder observe that no points were given out to the parties for proof; (this is required by the Regulations.)

No. 81 of 1851, p. 224. Special Appeal from the decision of Mr. J. Cotton, Sub. Judge of Combaconum. The Court notices

"That the Respondent having admitted the fact of the registry of "the land in question in the petitioner's family's name, the exception "taken to petitioner's case because of the non-production thereof is "a baseless one. They have to notice further that the Acting S. "Judge's decree is a very imperfect one, as it does not enter upon "the merits of the evidence adduced on each side."

The action is for lands of the value of 15 Rupees (£1-10) and it is remanded for a fourth trial.

No. 9 of 1850, p. 240. Appeal from the decision of Mr. Morris, C. Judge of Calicut. In this case the Judge finding that the plaintiff has no cause of action, nevertheless mulcts the defendant in costs!

No. 24 of 1851, p. 245. Special Appeal from the decree of Mr. Scott, C. Judge of Combaconum. In this case after three trials the S. Court discovers that the claim is barred by Limitations!

No. 96 of 1851, p. 255. Special Appeal from a decision of Mr. Swinton. Here is an action for 15 Rupees tried over four times. The C. Judge passed his appeal decree *without notice being served on the Respondent.*

No. 99 of 1851, p. 259. Special Appeal from the decision of Mr. Rhode, Acting C. Judge of Trichinopoly. This furnishes us with another curious dictum upon the law of English mortgage.

"That under the *English* practice, as the mortgagee *took the risk "of seasons,* he could not be called upon to account for usurious "interest."

The Sudder observe that the application of the Statute of Limitations to the case is quite "erroneous;" and observe that the C. Judge has not recorded his reasons for reversing the Sudder Ameen's decree. They consider the decree "defective and incomplete;" and remand it accordingly.

No 21 of 1851, vol. iv., p. 13. Special Appeal from the decision of Mr. Walker, C. Judge of Nellore. In this case, although the C. Judge dismissed Defendant's appeal, he "contrary to all practice of Courts of Law," directed certain property belonging to the Defendant, *(pronounced in the original decree not to be liable to the claim) to be "attached, until Plaintiff's claim is paid in full."*

No. 42 of 1851, p. 15. Special Appeal from the decision of Mr. Horsley, C. Judge of Cuddalore. Action brought on a bond for Rs. 10-8-7. The case tried three times; the Sudder reverse the decrees of the Courts below in favour of Plaintiff as there is

"no question," they consider, "as to the execution of the deed on "which Plaintiff's claim is founded with the full knowledge and con-"sent of Defendants."

No. 20 of 1852, p. 17. Special Appeal from the decision of Mr. Scott, C. Judge of Combaconum. Suit brought for land and house, value Rs. 154-15 (nearly £ 16.) The case is tried over eight *times* (besides the chance of further appeals.) The C. Judge records the following luminous decision.

"There is no particular reason for giving the preference to the "witnesses of either party, and as such a length of time has elapsed "since the marriage took place it is not very likely that any of them "can know much about the point at issue, since it is one in which they "had no actual concern, beyond that of guests, on the occasion, and "considering the great uncertainty that hangs over the matter, it "seems to the C. Judge that the fairest way to decide it will be to "*divide the property between the Claimants.*"

No. 22 of 1852, p. 22. Special Appeal from the decision of Mr. Lovell, C. Judge of Chittoor. The S. Court observe that it is contrary to practice " *to take fresh evidence* on a point which arose out of the suit, but which had been dismissed by the original Court without sufficient enquiry."

No. 23 of 1852, p. 23. This is an action for recovery of 25 Rupees. It has already been tried three times, and remanded for a fourth.

No. 24 of 1852, p. 25. This is a trumpery case for maintenance at 5 Rupees a month—4 Rupees per annum for cloths, the 'use of a cow' valued at 10 Rupees, a house of the value of 4 Rupees, 36 Rupees on account of expenses of marriage of Plaintiff's daughter, and 64 Rupees back maintenance. It has been tried over three times, and is returned to Mr. Rhode for a fourth.

No. 25 of 1852, p. 27. Special Appeal from the decision of Mr. Swinton. The suit is instituted for 69 Rupees principal and interest due on a bond for 35 executed by Defendant in 1835, Plaintiff admits payment of one Rupee in 1846. Defendant admitted execution, but pleaded payment in full in 1838, and said the bond had been left with Plaintiff to give him a better title to certain land, made over to him by Defendant in satisfaction of his claim. The Moonsiff found for the Plaintiff. The C. Judge reversed his decree. The Original Court did not consider whether the Statute of Limitations applied. The C. Judge disbelieved the payment of one Rupee, and applied the Statute. He observed that such a plea of payment

" was a clumsy ruse, often adopted by Native litigants, and happily seldom successful : a ruse which in this case bears the stamp of falsehood on the face of it."

The Sudder observe,

" This cannot be admitted. The Sub. Judge *has to deal with the evidence before him*, and *not with general practices:* and if he rejects Plaintiff's evidence on this point, he *must give his reasons* for doing so. The decrees are therefore manifestly incomplete." They are accordingly annulled, and the case stands for a fourth trial.

No. 26 of 1852, p. 29. Special Appeal from the decision of Mr. Glass, C. Judge of Chicacole. This was a suit for recovery of Rs. 136-12, due on a bond for Rs. 68-6. The case has been tried four times, and is remanded for a fifth. The proceedings however of the C. Judge are so extraordinary that I shall quote them in full.

12. "On a careful consideration of the matter of this petition, the Court of Sudder Udalut are of opinion that a Special Appeal must be admitted, in order to correct the error into which the Civil Judge has fallen. It appears on reference to the Decree in Appeal Suit No. 78 of 1849, and the order issued by the Civil Judge to the Moofty Sudder Ameen on 15th March 1850, copies of which have been received from the former officer, that although the award in Original Suit No. 41 of 1847 was not in Appeal before him, and had continued undisturbed since 30th November of that year, or nearly two years and a half, the Civil Judge took upon himself to "quash the whole of "the proceedings in Original Suit No. 89 of 1848, and Appeal Suit "No. 78 of 1849, *in toto*, and to direct that the Suit No. 41 of 1847 be "re-filed, and the Plaintiff in No. 89 made a supplemental Defendant "therein, and a fresh decree passed on its full merits." This course was clearly illegal, and a judgment so given cannot be allowed to retain the force of Law.

13. "In admitting a Special Appeal therefore the Court of Sudder Udalut resolve to set aside the Decrees now appealed from, and to annul the whole of the proceedings arising out of the illegal course adopted by the Civil Judge, thereby reviving the former Decree in original Suit No. 41 of 1847, and that in Original Suit No. 89 of 1848; and further to direct the Civil Judge to replace on his file Appeal Suit No. 78 of 1849, and to try and decide it according to the Regulations. Against the judgment given therein it will be competent to petitioner, if dissatisfied therewith, to prefer another Special Appeal, and in justice to the parties, the Court likewise resolve to return to them the value of the stamps used in carrying out the Civil Judge's aforesaid injunctions."

No. 60 of 1851, p. 59. In this case the C. Judge, Mr. Lovell, overthrows the original decree by a point not in issue.

No. 74 of 1851, p. 60.

Here the Judge, Mr. Scott, misapplies the Law.

I have thus gone through the whole of these Reports. I have not cited any cases of Appeal from decisions of Sudder Ameens, or Courts of Request : because they are foreign to my purpose, nor have I extracted by any means *all* the cases which present anomalous features. Many of less singularity are left untouched : nor have I cited any cases in which the decisions of the Courts below have been upheld.

Analysis of Reports.

It will be found that the Reports contain 249 cases: in 68 the decree of the Court below is confirmed : in 51 the decree is absolutely reversed ; in 17 modified; in 6 the application for appeal refused ; in 111 the cases are remanded; and it will be found in this last class of decisions that a remand is in point of fact generally equivalent to a reversal of the decree appealed from.

It is only fair to mention that these Reports do not contain in general the cases in which applications for permission to appeal have been refused: so that it is *possible* that there may be many very good decisions of the Courts below on which these Reports are altogether silent. An order has been lately passed under which all the decrees of the Lower Courts are published monthly : so that the curious in such matters will have now an opportunity of diving to the very bottom of the subject. For my own part I have not yet had courage to face one of these heavy blue books, though there can be little doubt this very desirable publicity will make some amusing disclosures. In the meanwhile I have, as I conceive, amply established my first proposition by the review of the volumes before me, so far as the Civil Law is concerned.

Turn we now to the Criminal Reports.

Foujdaree Criminal Reports, p. 1.

The volume opens with a startling case. A most cold-blooded murder is committed at Tellicherry. A man is stabbed in the belly, during the night, while sleeping on his cot, by the side of his son. The bowels protrude. He is taken to the Surgeon who appears to have acted with great laxity. He is ordered to the Hospital by the Surgeon: where *the Dresser* declares his inability to reduce the intestines. The *next morning* the Surgeon visits him, and states that *nothing can be done to save his life. He was then removed to the Hospital at Cannanore, a distance of many miles*, where the *Apothecary* replaced his intestines. The man however died before the operation was completed. The Judge, Mr. Forsyth, found the 2d prisoner guilty—but recommended that he should be transported for life, because *of the darkness of the night*, which rendered the testimony of those who said they saw the prisoner suspicious! as though this were not a reason for his acquittal, if anything—and because "the deceased might possibly have survived, had his wound been dressed without loss of time"! Thus letting the strange carelessness of the Surgeon—to call it by no stronger name—operate as an excuse in favour of as atrocious a murder as can be well conceived.

The train of reasoning is scarcely conceivable: but most assuredly such a mind is not fit to be trusted with adjudication in cases affecting life and death.

Page 9. A. B. and C. are committed on a charge of murder—the 1st prisoner charged *with having ordered the other two to kill the deceased*, which they accordingly did by blows and kicks. Mr. Anderson who tried the case convicted them all only of *culpable homicide*, because

"as water was thrown on the deceased in order to revive her, it does "not appear they *intended* to kill her!"

and the Foujdaree Adawlut confirm this decision!

Page 11. A man is charged with murder; he confesses:—and his confession is corroborated—that in a "fit of resentment" he stabbed the deceased, who interfered in a quarrel between prisoner and another. *Some hours elapsed between this event and the murderous attack.* The Judge, Mr. Elliot, finds the man guilty of *culpable homicide* and sentences him to transportation for life. The Foujdaree find him guilty of murder, " and wounding"—somewhat superfluous—and sentence him to be hung.

Page 48.

This was a case of murder. The prisoner stood charged with the murder of his concubine. The evidence was that on seeing her conversing with a barber in the yard, he *had gone into his house for a rice-beater** and struck her a single blow with it on the temple, which instantly proved fatal.

The Sessions Judge sentenced him to be hung. The Foujdaree Court mitigate the punishment to transportation for life. Mr. Morehead remarks, " *there is no proof* of premeditation or malice." The remarks of the Senior Judge are peculiarly naive, and were the subject less serious, might excite a smile.

" The blow, *only one, (!)* was I think inflicted in a sudden fit of vio-
" lent anger, on the spur of the moment, without any deliberate ma-
" lice before hand; and I scarcely think the fatal result *was intended*
" or expected by the prisoner: *although* the weight of the instru-
" ment, *had he considered for a moment,* would have shown the *dan-*
" *ger* of using it as he did."

Apparently quite forgetful that the prisoner *walked* into the house to procure this deadly weapon.

The 2d Judge is for the extreme penalty. He says

" The instrument with which the murder was committed, a heavy rice-
" beater shod with iron at both ends, must be taken into consideration.
" No one could deal a heavy blow on the temple with this instrument
" without intending to murder."

The 3d Judge points out a *slight* irregularity in the proceedings of the Sessions Judge; he says,

" *The examination by him of additional witnesses after the trial was*
" *closed* was *irregular* and *objectionable:* and the evidence so record-
" ed, *to which the prisoner was not called upon to plead,* could not be
" taken into consideration by the Court."

* Note—A " rice-beater" is a piece of very heavy wood, as thick as a man's arm, about 4 feet long, and shod with iron at either end.

Be it remembered this was a case of murder, involving a man's life.

Page 76. The Foujdaree observe on this case—one of murder—

" The prisoners should have been called upon *to plead to the evi-" dence*, which was taken *after* their defence was received."

Page 78. A case of murder—an awful case.

A woman was charged with the murder of her two children. She confessed that in consequence of gross abuse from her husband she drowned them. She says, *after the quarrel she went to sleep;* when she awoke it was dark; *she took up the youngest child and threw it into the well: she returned to the house; took up the eldest child, and threw it into the well.* She *says* she also threw herself in, but there not being water enough in the well to drown her, she went to the river—she was observed in the *morning, standing* in the river, and *calling* for help. She was brought to land in a boat. The Sessions Judge sentences her to death."

It will scarcely be credited that the Foujdaree changed this to transportation for life. The Sessions Judge remarks

" The Natives of this country, and particularly the females of the lower order, have no control whatever over their tempers."

Perhaps the example of one or two of them being hung, if the above is a specimen of their want of temper, might enforce a little restraint, at the same time that it saved the lives of children yet unborn.

Page 89. The case of Venkatachellem Pillay charged with child murder and robbery, appears to me to exhibit such a lamentable want of competency on the part of the Sessions Judge to weigh testimony, that I have transferred it entire to the Appendix. See Appendix No. 2. The remarks of the 3d Foujdaree Judge explain the whole matter so forcibly that I have no remarks to add.

Page 113. A case of murder.

The prisoners are convicted only of " culpable homicide under aggravating circumstances."

The reasoning on which the crime is reduced from murder is curious. It does not appear that there was any quarrel or affray, out of which the attack took place. On the contrary, though there seems to have been some ill-feeling between the parties, the Judge states:

"That it was the intention of the prisoners *at least to break* a leg "of the deceased; that they had tried to commit the offence on the "previous evening, and that they *deliberately arranged* to get the de-"ceased made drunk are highly aggravating circumstances."

The Judge says:

"I do not see any reason to suppose that they *intended* to kill "the deceased, but that they *intended* to do him some severe bodily "harm. I do not see any reason to think that the wounds were in-"flicted *with any other instruments but clubs!*"

Page 116. A murder case, in which two prisoners were convicted, and suffered death. The Foujdaree observe, casually as it were, as though it was not a matter of much importance:

"No evidence was recorded before the Session Court to prove the "identity of the corpse—an omission which should not have been "permitted to occur."

One would have imagined this alone would have been sufficient to have prevented the execution of the extreme penalty of the Law: strictly; the prisoners were entitled to their acquittal on account of this omission—at least further evidence should have been required on the point, if the Indian Courts are not very closely bound by forms.

Page 137. A case of murder.

The Foujdaree observe that the indictment "is defective, no men-"tion having been made therein of the *intent to kill*, which constitutes "the gist of murder"—and they say they could not have convicted upon this arraignment, "had not the crime charged been so described "in the question put to the prisoner by the agent, when calling upon "him for his defence, as to leave no doubt in the mind of the prisoner "as to the nature of the charge to which he was called upon to make "his defence."

Had the Court objected that the indictment did not make use of the terms "murder," and "feloniously," and "of his malice aforethought," I could have understood it—but it is singular that in almost the only instance in which they stickle for technicalities, they should insist upon the insertion of that which is never found even in our strict English forms.

Page 157.

This is one of the most singular cases perhaps to be met with in the annals of crime. It will be found in the Appendix. See Appendix No. 2. The circumstances were no doubt complicated; yet I cannot but think that any one, accustomed to weigh and judge of testimony, would have arrived at an opposite conclusion: at any rate, that such serious doubts must have arisen in his mind, that he would have felt himself bound to give the prisoner the benefit of them.

In the first place the circumstance of self-mutilation is so extraordinary, as to make it very questionable whether it *could* have been the prisoner's own act.

Then the testimony of the witnesses, who deposed that they heard deceased say prisoner was cutting her throat; who tried the door, and on finding they could not get in, and notwithstanding the gurgling sound they heard, did not arouse the police, is very suspicious. Their evidence is so full of contradictions as to render it altogether unworthy of belief. The fact that the bill-hook was the prisoner's property, even if proved, was not conclusive against him, as there was nothing singular in its being in the house, under the circumstances of intimacy with which he lived with the deceased. The prisoner's account that the whole was the act of the deceased's relations, is very consistent with native character. But the most astonishing point in the case is that all the Judges should have attached such weight to the supposition that the prisoner in his mutilated state *could* not have crawled to the door, although it never seems to have struck them that it would have required far greater physical exertion to have put the weapon in the loft. The evidence subsequently elicited shows in what a slovenly manner investigations, involving life and death, are carried on; and the report of the case scarcely gives a fair version of the minutes of the Foujdaree Judges. I have been informed by a gentleman practising in the Court, who has seen the whole record, that the 1st Judge *did* in his first minute express his doubts; indeed one may gather as much from the report itself. The 2nd *Judge expressed no doubts:* the 3rd Judge simply concurred generally with his colleagues. When the case came up again the 1st Judge again recorded that he all along had doubts—it is strange how a sentence of death could be awarded under such circumstances. The 2nd Judge took up the question as *though it had never come before him previously:* apparently forgetful that he had *formerly had no doubts*, and concurred in what the Report terminates by modestly calling the "amendment" of the sentence, which might better have been called by its right name, its unqualified reversal.

Page 162.

Murder. The prisoners, one a woman, were charged with the murder of a child six years old, and having thrown its body into a well, within the walls of a Hindu temple, after taking from its person ornaments of the value of Rs. 4-8-0. The crime was proved. It is scarcely possible to conceive a more cold blooded murder. The Sessions Judge however held out the 1st prisoner as an *object of mercy*, *because she was pregnant at the time of trial*—not that the execution of her sentence should be deferred, but that it should be commuted to transportation. Singular reasoning.

Page 184.

A case very unsatisfactorily disposed of.

An old man of 60 who had ploughed and sown a certain field, hearing that the prisoners were ploughing it up, proceeded to the spot: he stopped the prisoners' buffaloes: words arose; whereupon the 2nd prisoner stabbed him with a knife, and the others beat and kicked him after he fell. The Foujdaree Judge says; "*The attack* "*on the deceased was most unprovoked;* inasmuch as he simply en-"deavoured to prevent the prisoners ploughing up a field of seedlings "which he had avowedly reared:"—and again, he speaks of the 1st prisoner as "the man who *planned* and instigated the assault:" yet he concurs with the Session Judge in finding the crime to be "*culpable homicide without* aggravating circumstances!

One could scarcely anticipate such a finding except in a French Court.

Page 192. In this case the prisoner is convicted of the brutal murder of his wife, by letting a wooden mortar, 29lbs. weight, fall on her head, apparently because that night she refused to sleep with him. The Sessions Judge recommends him as an object of mercy because he is "of the Panion or slave "caste, a class *comparatively* deficient in capacity and intelligence."

Page 196. A man is convicted of a murder 19 years since. The Sessions Judge says, *he has behaved well ever since*—and suggests transportation—he gives other reasons for this. The Foujdaree 2nd Judge says:

"I cannot recognize the validity of *any* of the reasons advanced "by the Sessions Judge, many of which are only conjectures, for a "mitigation of the law; yet I am of opinion that considering *the* "*great lapse of time* which has elapsed since the murder was com-"mitted, *the execution of the prisoner is not required for public ex-*"*ample.*" The 1st Judge concurs.

I should have thought the argument was just the other way; that it was necessary to show the people that the successful concealment of crime for however long a period, would form no kind of screen from punishment.

It is only fair to the Sessions Judge to state that the merit of this decision entirely belongs to the Foujdaree; for he expressly repudiates the length of time as any ground for mitigation.

Page 210. Prisoner refusing to pay the toll (two pice, about a farthing) of the ferry boat after his passage, the ferryman ordered deceased to stop him. He accordingly did so; whereupon the prisoner stabbed him, and wounded several others. The

Mahomedan law officer declared him not liable to death, because his *intention to kill* was not clear. The Sessions Judge sentences him to imprisonment with hard labour for 14 years. The Foujdaree alter the sentence to transportation for life, the 2nd Judge observing: "The "2nd prosecutor, 3rd witness, and deceased were acting perfectly law- " fully in insisting on the payment of the regulated hire for ferrying the prisoner and his party over the river; and his attack upon them for doing so was *wilful and deliberate.*

Page 238. A prisoner is convicted of having received stolen goods. The Foujdaree revokes the sentence observing:

"That the property which the prisoner was charged with having "received has *not been proved to have been stolen;* and not only "has it not been claimed by the parties to whom it is supposed to "belong, but they have expressly declared before the Police that it "*did not belong to them.*"

The Court further remark that the conviction upon the evidence "reflects most seriously on the judgment of the Judge."

Page 251. *In this case the Judge convicts though the body of the deceased had not been found.*

He could never have read Lord Hale.

Page 260. In this case prosecutrix, a married woman, swore that the prisoner raped her "fully" The Sessions Judge, thinking there was not *sufficient proof of penetration,* but that the assault with intent was proved, referred the trial to the Foujdaree.

What better evidence on the point of penetration a case of this nature admits of than that of the prosecutrix, it is not easy to understand.

The Foujdaree convict him of the assault; and observe that "under *the English law,* upon an indictment for rape a prisoner may be convicted of an assault;" and refer to Russell on Crimes.

Apparently forgetful that in England, this is only under an express statute, made for that purpose.

Page 266. This is a case of one of the most deliberate cold blooded murders ever perpetrated.

It is merely referred to to show the absurdity of the Mahomedan law. The Futwah declares that the prisoner is not liable to death, because *he was the father of the murdered child !*

Page 277. The prisoner was arraigned on a charge of "culpable homicide." The facts clearly amounted to murder.

A quarrel had taken place between the parties—after the lapse of an Indian hour, (about 20 minutes) Prisoner goes up to the deceased, and gives the fatal blow with a bullock yoke, without saying a word. Deceased never spoke after. The judge who tries the case remarks on all these circumstances: states that the prisoner should *have been charged with murder*, of which he considers him guilty; and decides that he has subjected himself to death—(notwithstanding he is only indicted for culpable homicide).

He also states a strange matter for the consideration of the Foujdaree, with a view to their determining whether a lighter punishment than death might not be inflicted, namely:

"*That the parties were near relatives, and had been previously on friendly terms*" !

Page 281. In this case the Foujdaree object to the *reception* (not the credibility) of a witness, because his statement showed that he had himself been guilty of misprision of felony, and "there being strong grounds to suspect actual complicity "in the robbing upon his part."

Page 290. In this page I find a most extraordinary irregularity recorded. The case was one of murder, of which the prisoner was convicted, and for which *he actually suffered death*. The judge says:

"The trial of this case was conducted by *the late Agent, and the "principal witnesses had left* the Court previous to my arrival. It "devolved on me only to re-examine certain relatives of the 1st pri- "soner, who *happened* to be present, regarding the *ownership* of the "bandy, and to take the defence of the 1st prisoner."

Comment is needless.

Page 297. Here we have a very singular piece of reasoning of one of the Foujdaree Judges. He says,

"The prisoners are charged with fabricating a receipt (B), for the "payment of a moiety due on a bond (A), with the view of defraud- "ing the prosecutor of the residue claimable upon the bond, under "the representation that the prosecutor was liable for the same."

"There is no evidence of the *Bond* (A) *being a false one; and* "*without proof of this fact the charge of fraud cannot, it appears to* "*me, stand.*"

If the Bond (A) had been a *false* one, it might have been argued, probably unsuccessfully, that inasmuch as the Prosecutor could not then have been injured, the charge could not stand—but I am at a loss to comprehend the force of the reasoning above set forth.

Vol. 2, page 10. The 3rd Judge says, "I regret to observe that "the examinations held by the Judge are exceed- "ingly bald, evincing no effort on his part to draw out all the infor- "mation that the persons examined could give, and I concur with the "1st Judge in thinking his letter of reference extremely defective "and unsatisfactory."

The acting Foujdaree Judge adds:

"The examinations are certainly most defective, and his letter of "reference scarcely such as should have been submitted to the Court."

How slovenly that letter is we gather from the senior Judge's remarks.

"It is not clear from the letter whether the Judge intended to re- "commend that all the prisoners should be severally sentenced to (2) "two years' imprisonment with labour and irons, or only the '*other*' "prisoners referred to in para. 6. I can hardly imagine that he "could have intended under the aggravating circumstances of his "offence to have recommended so very inadequate a sentence for "the 1st prisoner, and therefore the only alternative is to suppose "*that he has inadvertently* omitted to recommend *any* punishment "for the 1st, 3rd, 4th and 5th prisoners"!

Page 11. This is one of the most revolting murders on record. It will be found in the

Appendix entire. See Appendix No. 2. It is not easy to conceive why the 2nd and 3rd prisoners, particularly the latter, did not undergo the extreme penalty of the Law.

Page 33. This case will be found entire in the Appendix. See Appendix No. 2. The Foujdaree observe (p. 40) that

"The proceedings before the Sessions Court evince throughout "either the most reprehensible negligence, or a great and deplorable "inaptness for judicial investigation on the part of the Acting Ses- "sion Judge."

It is worthy of remark that this gentleman has passed all his career in the Revenue Department, previously to his elevation to the Bench.

Such are the specimens of the *published* Criminal Reports. They are comparatively of little value, as testifying to the *general* conduct of Criminal Law in the Mofussil; as it is only in a particular, and comparatively small class of cases, that any reference to the Foujdaree is necessary from the Sessions Court. From a charge delivered to the Grand Jury by the Honorable Sir William Burton, Puisne Justice of Her Majesty's Supreme Court, in January 1845, I take the following figures.

The number of persons brought before all the criminal Courts of original jurisdiction during the decade 1832-41 was 103,247. Of these but 4,787 were referred to the Foujdaree. Hence it will be obvious how great a preponderance of cases passes unchallenged. How the odd 107,460 were disposed of: what errors, injustice, absurdities arose in these cases we cannot tell, although we may form a rough guess, if we bear in mind the principles, or rather want of principles exhibited in the comparatively few cases now before the Public.

But why should I fatigue my reader with figures? The last India Blue Book is full of them; and thither must be referred those who are fond of such statistics.

I have unfortunately no room left for specimens of Mr. Arbuthnot's Select Cases: nor for the numerous cases which have thronged in upon me since I commenced this undertaking. I select only one of three cases, which Sir William Burton, at my request, kindly placed at my disposal. It will be found in his own words in the Appendix. See Appendix No 3. I should premise that these cases were furnished to the learned Judge, some years back, by one of the then Sudder Judges, who forwarded them, not as anything extraordinary, but as testifying the ordinary run of business which came before the Court. It is known as the Cockspur case, and has been since reported by Mr. Arbuthnot in his 'Select Cases.'

I must also shortly advert before quitting this part of my subject to a case, not reported indeed, but in which I was professionally concerned, which exhibits such a distortion of reasoning, as makes it stand among the criminal selections pre-eminent for its monstrosity, as that of fining a man 55,000 Rupees for bringing an action does among the Civil Selections.

Achiah's case.

A wealthy Zemindar died leaving infant children, and, as is usual, a large amount of valuable jewels. A case was sent up to the Sessions Judge for trial, the depositions of which showed the following circumstances. It appeared that on the morning of the day on which the Zemindar died, he sent for Achiah, who had been his own guardian, and committed his children and property to his charge, with directions to take care of them till the Collector came. Achiah accepted the trust. On the morning after the Zemindar's death, Achiah removed 12 boxes, containing jewels and cloths, from the 'Treasury', in which they were kept, to his own house, and subsequently to his sister's.

The Collector's Sheristadar arrived to take charge of the property and accounts. The Zemindar had been a very careful man of business habits; keeping a large establishment of writers, to manage his public, and private accounts. The first thing that the Sheristadar found on opening the accounts was a very regular set of entries of all bribes paid to himself and other public servants. He consulted with Achiah, who consented to the removal of the distasteful items, for which purpose, the obnoxious sheets were abstracted, and others substituted in their places. The Collector arrived; he asked Achiah, as agent of the Court of Wards, for the Zemindar's property. Some 13,000 Rupees were given up, and a comparatively small quantity of jewels. The Collector, surprised at the smallness of the amount, asked Achiah for more. He distinctly denied that he knew of any more. He was asked to deliver up the records. He said he had not got them. They were however all traced to him by the evidence, and they were subsequently discovered mutilated and concealed, some in roofs of empty houses, others buried under trees and so forth. Achiah was committed to take his trial under the Breach of Trust Act. The Sessions Judge referred to the Foujdaree Court to know if he was at liberty to discharge a prisoner without trial, if there appeared no crime against him on the depositions. The reply was in the affirmative, although the Court added that they did not suppose he considered this as a case of that nature. Thereupon he discharged him without trial, and observed that the best way for the accused would be to admit all the facts. That it is clear he did not act with any guilty intention to defraud the minors; but to save the estate from the clutches of the Collector, whom he designates as "the Common Enemy;" and then he proceeds to argue that *if it is admitted that Achiah was justified in concealing the property, it follows that there was nothing criminal in his fabricating or destroying the accounts*: because this was *necessary*, to enable him to keep the property concealed! I do not give the language, but the general scope of the argument. It may seem incredible—but I will pledge my veracity for it. But this was not all. In the meanwhile Achiah had retained the services of Counsel; who filed a petition, applauding the justice of this decree, but stating that it was faulty only in one respect: inasmuch as it did not contain a declaration that Achiah was not liable to any future trial arising out of the same circumstances. The Judge accordingly made the order prayed for: thus extending the well known maxim, that no man shall be tried *twice* for the same cause, to this extent, that *non* trial shall operate as a bar to future accusation! The Magistrate sent the whole matter up to the Foujdaree who ordered the Sessions Judge to proceed to trial forthwith. At this period I was engaged on behalf of the Prosecution, and were it not that this Essay is already becoming too unwieldy, I could give one of the most laughable histories of irregularities, whims, and oddities, that ever came before the Public, from the first to the last moment when the other Counsel and I appeared before the Judge, presiding in his shirt sleeves: as Bon Gaultier sings of Judge Lynch:

> It was high noon, the month was June, and sultry was the air
> A cool gin-sling stood by his hand, his coat hung o'er his chair,
> All naked were his manly arms, and shaded by his hat
> Like an old Senator of Rome that simple Archon sat.

But I forbear.

"It is impossible," says the author of the Pamphlet before quoted, "to peruse the records of the most serious Criminal cases which are "referred for the final Judgment of the Sudder Court, without being "struck by the *utter absence* of a Judicial tone of mind on the part "of the Judge presiding at the trial, which these records very fre-"quently display. We find conclusions arrived at altogether unsup-"ported by the evidence upon which they are founded, and questions "omitted upon most important points—the result of the Judge "having arrived at a conclusion, without analysing in his own mind "whether that conclusion was justified by the premises upon which "it was based:"

A life-like portrait; which might be moreover transferred to represent the twin brother by the Civil Side.

Were I to travel out of the cases reported under authority, these pages might be multiplied almost infinitely; for scarcely a week elapses without some one or other of the Indian

Journals publishing details which almost tax belief; while every gentleman, practising in the Sudder, has a sheaf of curiosities of his own, calculated to confound the understanding of those who have not undergone the previous training of the Reports.

Indeed a learned friend of mine threatens to publish a few of the decisions in his possession, with annotations, to show how entirely Starkie, Phillips, and other writers, have misconceived the Law of Evidence, in all its fundamental points and principles.

Here let us pause awhile. What reflexions does the perusal of this monstrous melange of absurdity and iniquity excite in us? Can such things be? Do we feel more inclined to laugh, or to weep? to laugh, at the comicality of the mistakes into which the dispensers of justice have fallen, or to weep, at the miserable lot of the millions who live under such a dispensation? It is almost a question whether the slow torture, inflicted under the present system of administration, is not a worse evil than the despotic sway which it has superseded. *Life and liberty are not secure.* Property may be less subject to sudden irremediable usurpation; but a life time is now expended in defending it, under a system which professes to place it in safety, beyond the reach of uncontrolled liability. We may have blunted the axe-edge of the 'Insolence of Office;' but its substitute is the rack of the 'Law's Delay.'

Black Acts.

And yet it is to the tender mercies of Judges of such a calibre and quality, that the Government has long been striving to commit the lives and properties of British subjects, as well as Natives. Perhaps this exposure may satisfactorily account for the repugnance on the part of Englishmen to trust the safety, either of their persons, or fortunes, to the haphazard of such tribunals; and henceforth, the commotion and agitation roused whenever the hated Black Acts have been brought forward, may not appear either surprising or unnatural.

If it be, as no doubt it is, expedient, that in the present day, when the restrictions against British subjects holding property in the Mofussil have been withdrawn, the Englishman as well as the Native should alike be subject to one common tribunal; if injustice may arise from this not being the case; if great delay, expense, and inconvenience, may occasionally result from the necessity of sending offenders to the Queen's Supreme Courts for criminal trial, let the Company, or if the Company will not, let the English Legislature first provide us with decently competent Judges, before whose Judgment seats we shall not tremble for our safety, our property, our liberty, our lives; and then, but not till then, let agitation on this subject cease; or if it cease not, be unattended to.

Away with all such miserable expedients as have hitherto been tried, in order to reconcile British subjects to a submission to Mofussil Law. Twice have we seen drafts of these intended acts published within the last ten years; and rumour has it, that a third is about to be attempted. The last, which was in December 1849, embodied a recommendation of the Court of Directors, than which it is hard to conceive anything more monstrous, solely with a view to conciliate us to the introduction of the measure. It went a step further than the Draft Act of 1844, inasmuch as it made *all* offences cognizable by the Mofussil tribunals—but in capital cases, in accordance with a suggestion of the Court of Directors,* the sentence *was not to be death, but transportation;* and again a power was reserved to the Mofussil Judges to send the accused, if they thought proper, to Her Majesty's Courts at the Presidencies, for trial at Sessions—so that *this* was to have resulted. That if a Native was found guilty of murder, *he was to be hung;* if a European, *he was to be transported:* nay, the punishment of the European was to depend upon the caprice of the

* "You may try by taking away the capital punishment to make British subjects "amenable to the jurisdiction of these Courts in all matters whatsoever."—Despatch 10th December, 1834.

Judge; for if he was convicted *in the Mofussil*, he would be only *transported;* if at the Presidency, *hung!*

This may appear, perhaps, to some, a digression; but in truth it is not so; for if the expediency of subjecting Europeans and Natives to the same tribunal be conceded, it brings us, naturally enough, to a consideration of the fitness of that tribunal for such a responsibility.

Hitherto I have only spoken of the *ordinary* tribunals of the Country. There exists, however, occasionally, another class, to which I must necessarily call attention, notwithstanding their proceedings are not of such general concernment, as those of the regular Judicial Courts.

Special Commissions.

I allude to the Commissions, which are appointed, as occasion may require, for the investigation of cases against Government Servants, charged with peculation, malversation, fraud, or other mal-practices of a similar nature.

These Commissions sit under Regulation IX. of 1822, or Act XXXVII. of 1850; and they are usually composed of gentlemen selected from the Revenue Branch of the Civil Service.

It is indisputable that when these Commissions meet merely for the purpose of investigating and reporting to the Government, no very great *public* harm is likely to result from any irregularity or informality in their proceedings. The Government has a perfect right to dismiss any of its servants, if there exist reasonable grounds for suspecting their honesty, even although no strictly legal evidence may be procurable to bring the charge home to them. In such a case, nothing beyond the ordinary jurisdiction of a master over his servant is exercised: and possibly, even a formal enquiry is more than the party accused is in strictness entitled to.

A case in point is afforded by a Commission of this nature, which lately sat to enquire into a certain very clever but gross piece of roguery in the Accountant General's Office. I saw the whole of what was called *the evidence.** And certainly, such a mass of irrelevancies, hearsay, inadmissibilities, might perhaps be vainly sought for elsewhere, *out* of the Reports: although, at the same time, there was ample, in the shape of suspicion, to justify the dismissal of the parties, which shortly followed the Commissioner's Report.

But when a Commission is appointed, not simply to investigate, but *to adjudicate*, under the very extensive and highly penal clauses of Regulation IX. of 1822; or when a Collector acts summarily under that Regulation, or his Assistant under Regulation VII. of 1828, as it is not a question of simple dismissal, but the liberty and entire property of the accused are amenable to the judgment which may be passed, it is manifest that common justice requires that all such proceedings be carried on with at least as strict regard to the rules of evidence and law, as is supposed to obtain in the ordinary Civil and Criminal Tribunals of the Country. Regulation IX. of 1822: S. XV: in clauses 2, and 3, explicitly points this out. The late Act XXXVII. of 1850 was also expressly passed for this object. The Court of Directors, in their Despatch of the 1st of March 1843, (published page 339 of the Circular Orders of the Revenue Board) clearly draws the broad distinction between dismissing, and punishing a person, upon anything short of judicial evidence. In para. 6 they observe:

"Cases may indeed arise in which circumstances may be elicited, so "strong against an individual, as to produce a moral conviction of his "being unfit to continue in the Public Service, although it may be im-"possible to procure evidence of such a nature as would be received "in a judicial proceeding; *but in such cases of mere suspicion, unsup-"ported by judicial evidence, we cannot consent to the infliction of any dis-"qualification, disgrace, or pecuniary loss beyond deprivation of office.*"

Nothing can be more tender, fairer, more merciful than this. It might be imagined therefore, that if a case should

* I was not professionally engaged in this case, or the same feeling which has induced me to forbear in Achiah's case at the point where I was introduced into it, would have prevented my mentioning this.

arise, in which very many persons were accused of peculation and extortion, one single individual among them to the amount of 190,000 Rupees, for which he would be liable to be fined double, if found guilty, the greatest possible care and caution would be exercised in the selection of the very ablest member of the judicial line to preside over the trials: and that the investigation *would not* be committed to any of the Revenue Branch, whose "*unfitness in dealing with evidence,* "*or conducting any enquiry in the nature of a Judicial pro-* "*ceeding,*" the Court of Directors has "on several occasions "had reason to lament:" and that the accused would be allowed the amplest means and measure of Defence.

These observations will serve as an introduction to the history which follows.

Masulipatam affairs.

In 1849-50 the affairs of the district of Masulipatam were reported to be in great confusion. Very extensive charges of fraud, peculation, malversation, and bribery, were brought forward against many of the Native Revenue servants; and against the Sheristadar alone to the extent of 190,000 Rupees. A member of the Revenue Board, one of the ablest men in the Service, was appointed Commissioner in the Northern Circars, with all the powers of the Revenue Board. Now appeals lie from the decisions of the Collector under Reg. IX. of 1822 to the Revenue Board and not to the Sudder Court; so that the Commissioner, exercising all the functions of the Revenue Board, is in point of fact the Judge of Appeal. A gentleman of supposed capacity was appointed Collector: but inasmuch as it was imagined he would have quite enough to do in bringing the Revenue affairs into proper order, another gentleman of the Revenue Branch, also of supposed capacity, was appointed Special Assistant, who under Reg. VII. of 1828 was invested with all the summary powers of the Collector under Reg. IX. of 1822: and to him was committed the task of bringing the accused parties to justice.

The Commissioner opened the Ball—be it remembered he was also the Judge in Appeal—by himself investigating the charges. The Special Assistant then commenced upon their trials.

The Sheristadar, by far the most deeply implicated, bethought him of retaining the services of a Barrister; and a member of the Bar accordingly proceeded to Masulipatam. There he was informed, politely enough, by the authorities, that he could not be heard. He pointed out Act XXXVIII. of 1850, passed "to allow Counsel *to all persons* on the trial of offences." He was informed that the Act did not apply. He referred to Act XXXVII. of 1850, "For regulating enquiries into the behaviour of public servants," which in Sec. XI. expressly provides for the accused appearing, if he choose, by his "Counsel" or Agent. He was told that this was an enquiry under Reg. IX. of 1822. A reference was made to the Government, *who sent an exparte case to the Sudder Court*, for their construction of the Acts. The Barrister subsequently petitioned the Government against the Special Assistant's refusal to hear him. He was informed that the Sudder had already decided the point against him, and the Government could not interfere. He then applied to the Special Assistant to be allowed to confer with the Sheristadar, and assist him with advice out of Court, if he could not be heard in Court. *He was denied all access to his Client:* and finally, finding that he could be of no service, returned to Madras. The *details* of what followed I cannot profess to give, although it is far from improbable that they may yet see the light in a perfectly authoritative form; I can only give a general outline, the minute particulars of which *may* not be *quite* accurate; as a great deal of what passed between the officials, and the officials and the Government, has not been accessible by those who are my principal sources of information.

The trials proceeded; or rather the preparations for trial. Several cases, connected with Police matters, over which the

Special Assistant had no jurisdiction, were, when thought ripe, forwarded to the Sessions Judge for trial. They were one and all dismissed: the prisoners being respectively found not guilty. Thereupon the Special Assistant wrote to the Collector, complaining of the inutility of sending any more cases to be disposed of by the Sessions Judge, and intimating his intention of proceeding with the trials himself. He represented the influence of the people about the Court as altogether hostile to any conviction; the Collector indorsed his representation with the weight of his authority, in a long letter to Government: giving vent to some strange insinuations touching the judicial integrity of the officer who tried the cases: suggesting a change of venue for any future trials; and expressing his opinion that only some "thoroughly fearless and independent officer of Government" could carry the matter through, let the trials take place where they would.

The Government met, consulted, minuted; praised the Collector and the Special Assistant for their zeal; promised further acknowledgments for future services of the same nature; and, as usual, *referred the matter to the Foujdaree*, in order to obtain their opinion on the conduct of the Judge who had dismissed the cases, as to whether he had acted in a manner consistent with the impartial administration of justice. That Court expressed their opinion that the acquittals were the necessary result of the untrustworthiness, contradictions, and rottenness of the evidence; they amply vindicated the character of the Judge, and declared, that the way in which the Special Assistant had got up the cases, reflected very little credit upon himself.

Meanwhile fresh trials were proceeding before that Officer, and he has pronounced sentences against various offenders to the amount of about 70,000 Rupees. What has the Government done—has it superseded the Special Assistant as unqualified to decide in matters of such importance—and appointed another in his place—has it even stayed his hand—has it said to him

—"The result of the reference to the Foujdaree shows us that *you* at least do not know what *is*, and what *is not* evidence: that had you yourself decided upon the testimony which you sent forward to the Sessions Judge, and which you complained of that officer for not believing, you would have found innocent persons guilty; and you are therefore prohibited from taking any further proceedings."—So far from it, the Mail, only a few posts ago, brought down a letter from the Sheristadar, in which he complained that he had just been officially informed by the Special Assistant, that he had been found guilty on another charge, *which he had not even been called upon to answer.**

A year and ten months have now elapsed. All these decisions of the Assistant must be confirmed by the Collector, *before* the convicted have even a right of appeal. When they get it, they will go up to the Commissioner, who investigated their cases, in the first instance. Some have paid their fines; all have had their property confiscated to meet any demands which might be ultimately made against them on behalf of Government; some are confined; others are under surveillance; all are wretched; many, to use the language of indictments for murder, "languishing do live;" the most fortunate are dead. The Collector has from time to time put off considering the cases referred to him by the Assistant, for confirmation or reversal, on the plea of pressure of other business; but within the past week, and while these sheets were in the Press he has found time to confirm one decision against the Sheristadar, to the extent of 14,000 Rupees, the Sheristadar having a day or two previously given certain evidence before a Court Martial, arising out of these affairs, not likely to prove very agreeable to that "thoroughly fearless and independent officer" of Government.

I have this judgment of the Special Assistant, which has just been confirmed, now lying before me: and to show the

* The Sheristadar alone has been fined 64,000 Rupees. One other individual 4,500. I have therefore stated the gross amount of fines already inflicted at about 70,000; not knowing the amount of fines inflicted in other instances.

sort of way in which cases are tried and disposed of, let me as briefly as possible, advert to *some* of its more extraordinary features.*

No. XII. of 1851, Masulipatam.

The Sheristadar, it appears, was indicted on two counts; the 1st, for having, on the 17th of April 1844, received 2,000 Rupees, as a bribe from the *Nabob* of Masulipatam, for having obtained for him payment, through the Collector, of Rs. 14,494-14-6, due on a settlement of accounts between him and the Zemindar of Deevi.

The second count is for having received, on the 23rd October 1848, a bribe of 5,000 Rupees, from the same party, for having procured for him, in a similar way, a sum of Rs. 22,500, in part liquidation of a debt, due to him from the Zemindar of Devacottah.

It appears *from the Record*, that three witnesses were '*primarily*' examined by the *Commissioner*, and certain account books (A and B) filed on the 1st and 3rd September 1851.

This must have been behind the Sheristadar's back, because, 'a *portion* of the record of the investigation so held, was read to the Defendant, previous to the commencement of the trial.'

The Indictment was read to the Defendant on the 15th of September 1851: he pleaded not Guilty.

The first documents, (the account books) marked A and B, received in evidence against him, are thus described. They are the *private accounts of daily expenditure and receipt of the* WIFE *of the Nabob of Masulipatam.*

A witness is called, who deposes that he kept these accounts by order of the lady: that he entered therein the receipts of the two sums of Rs. 14,494-14-6 and 22,500; and that he also *made entries of the two bribes of* 2,000 *and* 5,000 *Rupees*, which he delivered to certain other witnesses to be given to the

* My strictures are confined to what appears upon the face of the judgment; the reception of testimony, contrary to the elementary principles of the Law of Evidence. I have not therefore at all alluded to the vivâ voce evidence; and not having that before me, I can form no opinion upon the effect which has been given to it.

Defendant, and which they *informed him the next day* had been accordingly given.

Now it will scarcely be credited that not only are these entries received as evidence against the Sheristadar, but through seven closely written pages of a laboured judgment, the Special Assistant gives his reasons in full, for believing and giving weight to the entries.

The following is the method by which he satisfies himself of the genuineness and authenticity of these two entries. He takes another independent entry at haphazard; one, be it remarked, in no way concerning the Sheristadar or his affairs; he finds that it purports to be the payment of a sum of 8,500 Rupees to a certain merchant of Masulipatam, who is accordingly sent for; he produces his accounts; he shows an entry therein of a sum of 8,500 Rupees paid to him by the Begum, corresponding with the entry in her books. An extract is accordingly taken from his books, and becomes evidence against the Prisoner, as document D. The same operation is twice more repeated; and we have the product, in two more 'extracts' from third parties' accounts, which become evidence, under the titles F and G.

Now setting aside, for the nonce, all consideration of the total illegality of this process—the permitting a party to make evidence for himself—the holding that the entries of X behind the back of Y, can be admissible as any proof against the latter, as exemplified by the documents A and B; and the extending of this ruling to their cousins once-removed, D, F, G, —the train of reasoning founded upon these illegal data is this; that *because* other entries with other individuals are correct, *therefore*, the two entries which the prisoner disputes, and says are part of a plot against him, must be, and are correct also!

The only other documents, C and E, are of minor importance, but both of them are inadmissible according to the fundamental principles of evidence.

The Assistant refers also to " the Collector's letter of the 16th May 1843 (not in evidence, and written behind the Sheristadar's back) to the Board of Revenue, as

"clearly showing that W Kristna Shastry the individual whose inter-" ests have been *proved in so many other instances*" (not in evidence) " to have been one with the defendant," was the principal party through " whose means the creditors were brought to agree to the terms pro-" posed by the Collector."

Again the 2d witness is allowed to give as evidence:

" that the sum in question, (the bribe of 2,000 Rupees) was given to " the Defendant in accordance with *an agreement entered into between* "*the said W Kristna Shastrooloo*" (dead) "*on the part of the Na-*" *waub and the Defendant, to the effect that the latter should receive* "2,000 *Rupees as his perquisite.*"

The document is not produced, called, or accounted, for.

Again, the Judge says:

" The person, Mahomed Ussan Khaji" (not a witness in the cause!) " who sold the garden at the sea side to the Begum for " Rs. 1,265-12-0, *informed me in person* that the money had been " duly received on the date alleged."

The Nabob of Masulipatam, who is supposed to have given the bribe, *is not even called as a witness;* nor are *his* accounts *allowed to be produced, although expressly demanded by the Defendant.*

It is not my purpose, nor is this the place, to go into any thorough discussion of the merits of this judgment. It is enough simply to point out what *stuff* is admitted against an accused, under what the judge is pleased to call " documentary evidence." The man has been convicted, and fined 14,000 Rupees on this charge by the Special Assistant, with imprisonment in the Zillah Gaol, until the fine is paid. The Collector has confirmed the decision: remarking that he sees no reasons to reject any of the evidence:—how should he—and the party has entered his appeal, which will in due course be disposed of by the Commissioner who 'primarily' tried the case, and who, be it remembered, himself filed the account books A and B.

These be strange doings. I have no interest in them; not having been in any way concerned for any of the parties; but I have given this narrative of what I believe to be a too true version of late events, only because in such a treatise as this, I could not pass over altogether in silence a subject so closely connected with the administration of justice; and because I shall have to suggest a check, if not a remedy, against the recurrence of such proceedings hereafter. Criminal cases conducted as this has been, are only calculated to bring Justice into disgrace. I do not profess to express any opinion as to the guilt or innocence of the accused;—all I say is, that he ought not to be condemned upon such illegal trash as the above:—but I will add this; that the form of trial, before these secret tribunals, where the accused is not allowed the benefit of counsel, or even advice, and where the Judge is of the quality and calibre above shown, had much better be dispensed with altogether. It is a delusion and a snare; a farce, a mockery and an insult.

The other decisions emanating from this gentleman, I have not seen: a pretty accurate guess may be formed of their quality by the one above partly examined. My learned friend who threatens to convict Starkie and Phillips by their publication, assures me that this is only a fair average specimen of the remainder.

Notwithstanding a nasty twisting against the prisoner of every point, capable of bearing two constructions, which pervades this document, and at first sight gives it rather the appearance of a Speech of Counsel, than a Judicial Decision, it revels and luxuriates so innocently in its supposed strength—it betrays such an honest unconsciousness that the data upon which it proceeds are peremptorily excluded from any consideration by the Law of Evidence; meandering, as it does, through seven pages of observation upon A, B, D, F, and G, until it arrives at the conclusion that "*the force of evidence can no farther go*"—it exhibits such a complacent well satisfied self-felicitation: such an 'I-am-Sir-Oracle-and-when-I-speak-let-no-dog-bark' air—as to carry conviction on the face of it, of the writer's perfect good faith and feebleness. We are constrained, even if Charity did not bid us, to attribute his lucubrations to their true cause, a pure, simple, virgin, blessed state of natural ignorance; for the mind rebels against any unworthy suspicion, that "thoroughly fearless independence" can have degenerated into an unscrupulous sycophant spirit of partisanship.

Sudder.

Having disposed of the Subordinate tribunals, I come now to the Court of Sudder and Foujdaree Udalut, the highest Court of Appeal in Civil and Criminal Cases in the Presidency: and inasmuch as the Judges of this Court come from the same ranks as those below them, and have been usually promoted more with reference to seniority than merit, (though latterly since the Marquis of Tweeddale took the very decided step of turning all three Judges out of their seats, this has not been quite so much the case) it is not to be expected that, further than more matured experience is a guarantee, they should perform their duties in a much more efficient or satisfactory manner than those whose errors they have to correct. If occasionally a man of some judicial power finds his way to the Sudder Bench, he is but what the Emperor Alexander described himself, 'a happy accident.' Accordingly we search in vain for any of those striking qualities which a Supreme Court ought to possess: their decisions do not display learning, or deep knowledge of the law; they are not employed in laying down luminous expositions of jurisprudence, or in building up a system commensurate to the wants of the people; all the more easy, because they exercise a regulating power over all the proceedings of all the Lower Courts. True they occasionally correct trumpery errors in practice, and procedure, into which the inferior Courts have fallen, by issuing Circular Orders, which are framed rather to meet the exigency of the moment, than to carry out any enlarged, well pondered, systematic scheme of general improvement. But their chief and ordinary jurisdiction over the Lower Courts, is exercised in reversing their absurdities, or remanding the cases for further investigation, on points either totally overlooked, not sufficiently considered, or raised before themselves for the first time; nor need we wonder, if when we find them attempting to expound the Law, especially when they go out of the Regulations, to rely upon what they suppose 'English' Law, be it of evidence, or otherwise, they are generally caught tripping. A few instances shall suffice.

No. 91 of 1849, Vol 1, S. Rep. p. 42. Special Appeal Petition.

The case is very badly reported.

The action was brought for recovery of 36 Rupees, for lace alleged to have been supplied to defendant's wife. The Sudder Ameen decreed in favor of Defendant; chiefly on the ground that the plaintiff had failed to produce evidence, *documentary* or oral, to prove that any articles were supplied. The C. Judge reversed the decree.

What actually was offered by the Plaintiff in evidence does not appear. I gather however that it was ***his own accounts***: if any thing.

The Sudder para. 7 observe that:

"a Merchant's accounts, if satisfactorily proved, constitute in themselves documentary evidence, sufficient to establish a claim to payment for goods sold and delivered."

An extraordinary decision, this, to emanate from the highest Court of Appeal in the land—no man would be safe if the plaintiff might thus make evidence for himself. I apprehend that the ruling proceeded from a confused, or mistaken idea of the law of evidence, as to a party's refreshing his memory from his accounts, or more possibly, the admissibility of entries in accounts made against interest, or by a deceased clerk, in the ordinary course of business.

No. 19 of 1851, Vol. 3, p. 191.

The case was remanded and we meet with it again, as a Special Appeal from the decision of Mr. Dowdeswell in 1851.

The C. Judge confirmed his original decree: he says no reliance can be placed on the account book.

" In fact, under no circumstances, could such a book be accepted as evi-" dence, unless signed by the parties, after examination," (wherein he is right) " or else the regular accounts, kept in proper order by a Merchant" (wherein he is wrong.)

The Sudder confirm this decree, because they agree with the C. Judge that the particular entries are

" such as may have been made at any time :" though (para. 8) they reiterate their former opinion, that " the account book kept by the " plaintiff was *clearly an admissible document.*"

The result of this is that we have a case for 36 Rupees tried over five times; and which a friendly reporter, such as Lord Campbell was to Lord Ellenborough, would label 'Bad Law' and put quietly away into his table drawer.

No. 16 of 1817, Vol. 1, p. 31.

In this case the Assistant Judge ruled, that as Defendant had not pleaded the Regulation of Limitation, she could not take advantage of it at the hearing. The Sudder hold that she can. The Rajah of Burdwan's case reported in 4 Moore's E. I. App. p. 403, is an express decision of the Privy Council to the contrary.

No. 35 of 1847, Vol. 1, p. 40.

In this case the Sudder observe

" It is proved that the land originally belonged to plaintiff's father, " and that by *his permission* the defendant and her ancestors have " held possession of it for a period of 40 years."

They therefore held the plaintiff's claim barred by limitation: —applying to *permissive* possession, a Law which only operates when the possession is adverse.

No. 68 of 1849, p. 41.

In this case after decree pronounced, the suit was remanded at request of appellant, to allow a certain document to be filed. The case presents no circumstances to show that the appellant was prevented from filing it earlier, or had since discovered it, and so forth; without which, I conceive, leave should not have been granted.

No. 15 of 1849, p. 111. This is a curious decision. Here a document, which was never produced before the C. Judge, and of which he was "in ignorance," is allowed to reverse his decree. The opposite party has no opportunity of meeting it. Under the English practice, such a document would of course have not been received on appeal. The most which the S. Court should have done, would, it appears to me, have been to remand the case, with directions for the C. Judge to receive and weigh this document, after the other side had had full opportunity of contesting it.

No. 5 of 1849, p. 115. This case contains some bad Hindu Law, for which however the Pundits seem more answerable than the Judges.

No. 10, of 1850, vol. 2, p 20., In this case the Court expresses a strange notion of Equity. They observe:

"The Courts of this country, *being quite as much Courts of Equity*, "as Courts of Law, have always recognized the right of a party to assign over a bond, for a valuable consideration, without requiring the "obligee (quære, obligor?) to be a party to the same."

In other words, the Judges seem to suppose that a creditor can, in Equity, more than he can in Law, assign over an instrument, not negotiable, to a third party, without the assent of his debtor to the transaction.

No. 44 of 1850, vol. 3, p. 25. In this case the decision is erroneous on the same ground as that of 16 of 1847, before quoted.

No. 13 of 1252, vol. 4, p. 9. In this case, the Sudder remand the suit for further investigation, upon a collateral point, when it is quite clear that the sale, being made during minority, cannot bind the infant.

No. 23 of 1852, vol. 4, p. 23. In this case, the action was brought against an agent contracting in his own name, but who had subsequently, and before action brought, disclosed his principal. The Sudder decide that the principal is a necessary party, whereas the Law says the Plaintiff, in such a state of circumstances, may sue either at his option.

This must suffice. I had marked other cases: but, as it is rather with the subordinate Courts that I have to deal, these few specimens are all that I shall offer under this head.

It is true these decisions are of no great importance ; but we should not look to find errors such as these, in the judgments of the highest Court of Appeal in the country. We look in vain through the Reports, for any general principles for our guidance. A student, seeking to digest the volumes, would reap a barren harvest: and his reward would be far from commensurate with his labour. From first to last the whole collection of cases exhibits, at the best, a general debility.

Lord Brougham's Speech.

Such are the judgments of the Sudder ; and this seems the proper place to notice a comparison which Lord Brougham instituted between the respective merits of the appeals to the Privy Council from the decisions of the Sudder, and Queen's Courts in India, very much to the disadvantage of the latter.

With all deference to such an authority, I cannot help thinking that the conclusion at which his Lordship arrived was not warranted by his premises ; for in truth, there is no analogy between the circumstances under which the two different classes of appeal reach the Privy Council.

Before the Supreme Courts, there is practising a Bar, not a numerous one it is true ; but still a Bar, composed of English Barristers, who watch the Bench carefully ; and it is only in those decisions which do not satisfy the Bar, that an appeal is ever advised or attempted : there is therefore the guarantee, or at least a primâ facie probability, that in these cases there is reason, more or less sound, for questioning the value of the judgment appealed from—in short, it is only the very bad law of the Supreme Courts which comes before the Privy Council. Not so with the Sudder. There, as it is wealth, or love of litigation, revenge, or other motive on the part of the Plaintiff or Defendant, or interest on that of the Pleader which prompts the appeal, there is no guarantee, no probability one way or the other; it is just as likely that the good decisions may be appealed against as the bad: and in forming any estimate of the quality and competency of these Courts, we must look to the *residue* of their decisions, not the sample exhibited before the Privy Council.

Subservient relation of the Sudder to Govt.

But there is another grave evil, which indeed applies forcibly to the lower tribunals, as well as the Sudder still remaining to be noticed. I mean its subservient to relation, the executive local Government. From highest to lowest, all stand in most holy dread of the censure of Government, or as it is here unclassically termed "a wigging."* All are alike dependent upon the local Government for promotion, or removal from the lower to the upper grades; and although it may be practically true, that the Government does not interfere to remove any man, except for grave misconduct, yet the independence of the judicial office, and the consequent security of property and liberty, especially in suits wherein Government is concerned, would, I conceive, be very much promoted by an express legislative declaration, that the Company's Judges hold their office on the same tenure as Her Majesty's—not 'durante bene placito' but 'dum bene se gesserint.'

* I was much amused, a few weeks since, with reading the Report of a recent case, in which a Mr. Fischer, the Mootadar of Salem, instituted a suit before the Subordinate Judge of that Zillah, for the establishment of what he conceived a right against the Government. He had however in the first instance, petitioned the Revenue Board and the Government without success. The Subordinate Judge decided against him—I do not undertake to say whether his Law was right or wrong—but he proceeds with inimitable gravity to express *his regret* that the Plaintiff should have *thought* of bringing an action after the Government had decided against him.

It is however, I believe, only in this Presidency, that the indecent spectacle is exhibited of a Government making a Standing Counsel of its own Highest Court. In the Sister Presidencies, law officers are appointed to the Sudder Courts, to whom the Government refers itself on matters requiring an opinion.

Two instances have been already given, in which the Government submitted exparte cases for the decision of the Court of Sudder Adawlut, in matters in which they required a construction of the Law for their guidance, or an opinion; it is their usual practice; and as this is generally with reference to some case which is pending before the lower Courts, and on which the Judge or Magistrate has required instructions, it follows that the Sudder Court is thus led to give an exparte opinion upon topics which may ultimately come before them upon Appeal—and there is even more behind: for the Government, not content with submitting *a mere* exparte case, first meet in consultation, minute their own views of the Law, and the course to be followed in the particular case, and then resolve that a copy of the proceedings, &c. be forwarded to the Sudder for their opinion. What wonder then if the Sudder adopts the already expressed views and wishes of their masters?

This may seem incredible: so I will support my assertion by an instance conclusive upon the fact.

Some two years since, a rich Zemindar died in the district of Rajahmundry, leaving several minor children. Under the Court of Wards Act (V. of 1804) a guardian was appointed; the Rajah's mother, however, one Bhaviah Row, claimed possession of the person of one of the children, a little girl; refused to give her up; declared her intention of using force, if necessary, to retain her; and there were reasons for supposing that it was intended to marry the girl to some of Bhaviah's friends.

The Magistrate represented the affair to Government: the Government consulted, minuted, and referred the whole matter to the Sudder for its opinion upon two points; first, what was the Law upon the subject: secondly, what course it was expedient to pursue. The Sudder adopt in terms the opinions of the Government; on the first point they say " the Court concur with the Government in its opinion," &c. and in para. 6 they add

" The argument set forth in paras. 12, 13, 14 of the extract of Mi-
" nutes of Consultation (Govt.) noted in the margin, &c. appear to the
" Court of S. U. to be *so conclusive* on that point, and are so *entirely*
" *expressive of their views on the subject, as to render the further enuncia-*
" *tion of them unnecessary,*"

and there, in the margin, in red ink, are paras. 12, 13, 14 of the Government minute. On the second point they say:

" Considering the course indicated in the 16th and 17th paras. of the
" Minutes of Consultation above referred to, to *be the most judicious*
" *which under the circumstances of the case can now be adopted,* the
" Court *deem it proper to suggest that they* be at once carried out,"

and here, red ink da capo—paras. 16 and 17!

I do not mean to question the soundness of the determination, either of the Government, or the Court, in this particular instance; but the shocking anomaly of an executive Government suggesting its own views to the highest Appellate Court in the land; and of that Court echoing them back, is something which makes English ears tingle.

The whole order will be found in the Appendix. See Appendix No. IV.

But one more fact is wanting, and that I now supply.

This very case has come up, and is now under Appeal before the Sudder Court.

Changes.

Another grievous evil in the constitution of the Sudder is the constant change of Judges. Independently of the vacancies which must necessarily occur from retirement or sickness, Government occasionally details the Judges for other duties. Thus in 1850

Mr. Morehead was sent as a Commissioner to Ceylon ; and, at the present moment, Mr. Strange is absent on a similar mission on the Coast of Malabar.

There have been no fewer than seven alterations within the last thirteen months; and as there is scarcely such a thing heard of as 'res Judicata,' each successor considering himself at liberty to review and differ from his predecessor, it constantly happens that after a matter has been solemnly argued before a full Court, and a decision pronounced, a review of Judgment is asked for, from no other reason that I can suggest, than because there *has been* a subsequent change in the constitution of the Court, and the Vakeels are willing to try one more last chance—so that literally no one is safe: when a cause is apparently laid and set finally at rest, the parties are never sure that its ghost may not arise to haunt and torment, though it may not be capable of inflicting much serious injury.

Pleadings.

The next point to which it is necessary to draw attention, is the extraordinary nature of what are called the pleadings. Instead of being mere records of the facts on which the respective parties rely, they run to the most enormous length ; being stuffed full of every argument which the ingenuity of the Native pleader can devise ; they travel into the most irrelevant matter, and I have seen a plaint, in which a man laid claim to a house, from which he wished to oust the defendant, conclude with a recapitulation of the eminent services, which his great grandfather had rendered the Honorable Company, upon the occasion of the invasion of Hyder Ali !

This is the more unaccountable, as the Regulation, (III. of 1802) which settles the *substance* of pleadings, is most express as to what shall, and what shall not be allowed. The pleadings are to be four in number —plaint—defence—reply, and rejoinder: certain cases are provided for in which a supplemental plaint and defence may be filed. It enacts as follows;

Plaint.

"Every complaint that may be presented to the Court of Adawlut of any Zillah, is *to state precisely the matter of complaint.*"

Defence.

"When the Defendant has delivered in his answer to the complaint, the Plaintiff is to reply to it on the next Court day. The Plaintiff *shall not introduce in his reply any matter not contained in his plaint.* He shall either acknowledge the answer of the Defendant to be true, or *simply and shortly* deny the truth of such of the facts in answer as he intends to dispute; or simply deny the truth of all the facts containted in it, or the competency of the answer.* The Defendant is to rejoin to the Reply on the same day. He "shall not introduce in his rejoinder any matter not contained in his answer. He is simply to deny," &c.

Reply.

Rejoinder.

and no further pleadings whatever are to be admitted in the cause. What was *intended* by the Legislature is clear enough: and I can only attribute the practice which has sprung up, to the absence of short forms by way of example in the enactment, in the first instance; and in the second, to the feebleness of Judges, totally unable to control the proceedings before them.

But the whole question of the state of Pleading in the Provinces requires to be taken up by the local Legislature. It is of the gravest importance, and surrounded with difficulty. It forms no part of the object of this treatise to enter upon it. At present it is certainly in a lamentable state. Our English system is probably not at all adapted for an agricultural semi-civilized population. Perhaps useful hints might be taken from the American Acts and Practice upon this topic. Oral pleadings, though suited to a rude state of society, would never serve to bind a people, so cunning, and truthless as the Hindoos; while the American system, even more than our own Common Law Procedure Act, seems to combine, in a remarkable degree, the great requisites of any

* By this term I presume is meant its sufficiency in law.

system of Pleading—speed—simplicity—cheapness—full notice to the opposite parties, and the Judge—and such a record of what really was decided, as suffices to prevent future disputes concerning it. But whatever changes may be effected, little practical benefit is to be looked for, till those who occupy the Bench are themselves so imbued with judicial principles, as to be able to watch the working of the pleadings, to check them where they are exuberant, and to foster and adapt them to the state and requirements of the society over whose welfare they preside.

This remark may however not be out of place; that the present state at which the pleadings have arrived, may probably be traced to a misunderstanding of the term itself. For, both the allegations of the parties, framed with a view to raise the issues, and the arguments of counsel, are, in common parlance, alike, termed 'pleadings.' Now in the Mofussil Courts the latter are unknown; and it appears to me, that it is by not paying attention to this distinction, that the 'pleadings', which the Regulation clearly intended to be confined to the object of raising issues, have, in process of time, been permitted to contain all the *arguments* as well as the facts of the case: and it was probably with a view to remedy the confusion introduced by this practice, that Reg. XV. of 1816, Sec. X, Clause 3, directs the Judge after a perusal of the pleadings, to record, somewhat after the fashion of the Prætor in the Civil Law, the points to be proved by the parties, a practice fraught with evil in this country; for informing a Native of a point which it is necessary for him to prove in order to substantiate his case, is almost tantamount to bidding him go into the Bazaar, where witnesses to any fact may be procured at an Anna a head, and setting in motion all the secret springs of a complicated machinery of forgery and subornation of perjury.

Fees.

Another monstrous evil is the absence of any scale or table of fees, and of a taxing officer, to take care that exorbitant charges are not made. This has been, to my knowledge, pressed upon the Sudder Court, but unsuccessfully: as they prefer allowing the suitors and the pleaders to make their own bargains.

Act 1 of 1846, Sec. 7.

By Act 1 of 1846, Sec. 7, it is provided

"That parties employing authorized pleaders in the said Courts, "shall be at liberty to settle with them, by private agreement, the re- "muneration to be paid for their professional services, and that it "shall not be necessary to specify such agreement in the Vakalutana- "mah."*

A pleader of the Sudder Court actually wished to argue with me, that under this section *any* agreement was valid! The remuneration is often made to depend upon the result of the suit—on the 'no cure no pay' system: and consequently the most iniquitous bargains are entered into, the needy suitor is glad to offer any amount, so that its payment is contingent upon his success: speculative suits are thus taken up: litigation, which would otherwise die out, kept alive, and champerty and maintenance are the order of the day.

There is one notorious case in this Presidency, where a pleader received 70,000 Rupees under one of these agreements. I have heard of an instance in which a bond for 100,000 Rs. has been taken; and those for petty sums of 10,000 and such small deer are, I fancy, common enough.

Whether the Courts would uphold these bonds in the event of their being sued upon I cannot say; in many cases it is obvious the parties may voluntarily pay; and in one instance where a bond of this nature, taken by one of its own pleaders, came before the Sudder Court, although they decided against him, it was upon the ground that he had not done the work contracted for: no objection seems to have been made, or suggested itself to the *legality* of the transaction, or the consideration of the bond.

* Power of Attorney, or Retainer from the client to the pleader which must be filed in Court.

No. 1 of 1851, S. A. Reports, vol. 3, p. 37. The case is as follows—One Mr. Varden Seth Sam (late a pleader in the Sudder Court) brought an action in the Madura Court, against the Minor Zemindar of Sheevagunga and his agent, to recover Rs. 34,850-5-4, principal and interest, due on an agreement, dated 10th March, 1844. The Civil Judge dismissed the case: and the plaintiff appealed to the Sudder. The case is No. 1 of 1851, reported in vol. 3, page 37 of the Sudder Reports, whence the following is taken:

" Mr. Sam stated that he was engaged by the 1st defendant, through the agency of the second, (a mere agent is made a party to the suit) to proceed to England as his private agent, in respect of a certain cause, then pending before Her Majesty in Council, in which the 1st defendant was appellant, for the purpose of explaining his case clearly to Mr. Clarke, his public agent, as also to the lawyers and barristers, and to await there, *and to obtain a favourable decision* in his favour, promising to give him 25,000 Rupees for doing so.

" That, agreeing to these terms, he went to England, at much inconvenience to himself, giving up his business at Madras, with a letter to Mr. Clarke, which he delivered, and remained in England till the case was heard, and a Decree passed in 1st Defendant's favour.

" That 1st Defendant executed to him a bond, engaging, on the conditions therein specified, to pay him the sum of 25,000 Rupees within 3 months after he should be put in possession of the Zemindary of Shevagunga, (the object in litigation) under such favourable decree. That a decree was passed by the Privy Council, under which 1st Defendant obtained possession of the Zemindary on 12th Sept. 1844, but had not paid his bond.

" The 1st Defendant stated in answer that it was suggested to him, that the plaintiff, being about to *proceed to England on his own business*, might be advantageously employed by him as a private agent in the matter, and on the plaintiff professing that he was *able and willling to render certain various important services in the cause*,

('unexpressed
and only from their wages to be guess'd')

ultimately executed the bond named in the Plaint. That he did so, trusting and believing, that the services of the Plaintiff would be useful and important, and *by his means he would obtain an absolute decree in his favour;* but that before the documents could be settled, Plaintiff, anxious on account of his *own business* to proceed to England, left India, desiring them to be transmitted to his elder brother. That *prior* to the bond being delivered, Defendant had obtained intimation of a decree having been passed by the Privy Council. That Plaintiff neither could, nor did, render any assistance to the cause: that he performed none of the acts or conditions requisite to entitle him to the reward: and, that, lastly, had he done so, the decree was not of the favourable nature contemplated; it being a mere direction to the Respondent to commence 'de novo,' and no adjudication of the rights of the Defendant."

" In a very long and laboured decree" observe the Sudder " which " might have been advantageously condensed, Mr. Baynes discussed " the plaintiff's claims, and directed both parties to bear their own " costs," and they proceed to dismiss the appeal with costs. They say the agreement is not denied: and the question for them is its construction: and they then observe upon the terms of the bond " we " bind ourselves after a *successful* decree is made in our favour, not to " object without paying the aforesaid sum. It is only when a suc- " cessful decree is made, and the zemindary is put in our possession, " that the aforesaid sum will be given on account of your labours. " Moreover in case of a decree *favourable to us not being made,* then " we have no reason to pay you even to the extent of a cash, on any " account whatever;" and conclude by deciding that the decision of the Privy Council was not a favourable one.

This is by no means an extreme case. There would have been some shadow of reason, or ground for so large a sum being demanded and given, if the whole were not based upon the merest false pretences—if the Vakeel had not been going to England on his own, but his client's affairs: had given up his business in Madras on that account, and had been really able to perform any services (even explaining to counsel the actual nature of the case): if a decree had not been already passed, before he could well have reached England, and if he had done anything more than, according to his own account, deliver his letter to Mr. Clarke, (who bowed him out) and—waited! But the Sudder do not seem to have doubted that the plaintiff would have been entitled to recover on this agreement, if the decree had been 'successful.' Not a word is said about the illegality of the transaction: and yet nothing can be conceived more detrimental to the character and dignity of justice, than permitting bonds of this nature to have any binding force or effect; especially in this country, where every Native has the most implicit credence in the all-sufficient value of money; fully believing with Sir Robert Walpole, that every one has his price; and that provided Judges, aye, even of H. M. Privy Council, can be only got quietly at, a douceur, liberally administered, will secure a successful termination to their suit. How completely this places them in the power of designing and unscrupulous persons need not be dwelt on. One case shall suffice. A Mr. Traveller, Editor of a small Newspaper, and "petition writer," came up before the Insolvent Court, to take the benefit of the Act. He was opposed by two wretched native country women who could not speak a word of English, and with scarcely a rag between them, who had walked up from one of the Provinces, to endeavour to get a brother released from Jail, to which he had been sentenced by one of the Mofussil Criminal Courts.

Traveller's Case Insolvent Court.

Mr. Traveller's 'Dubash'—a sort of Jackall—"happened" to be sitting under a tree, near the Sudder Court, when these poor women arrived. He took them to his 'gentleman,' who "had great influence;" and the result was that the Insolvent *undertook to procure the release of their relative for* 2,000 *Rupees*—which sum he actually extorted from his opposing creditors. In his defence he swore that this was not the nature of the agreement—no document was of course given: but that he had promised simply to write a petition to the Foujdaree Judges: and one also to Government. A good deal of very suspicious matter came out, showing how the poor women had been juggled, and imposed upon—for instance, an appointment was made with the women to meet Mr. Traveller at the gate of one of the Sudder Judge's premises:

whither Mr. Traveller drove, and telling them that he was about to have an interview with the Judge touching their matter, disappeared: though whether he ever got farther than behind the laurustinus bushes, was not clear. However the result was, that Sir W. Burton, the presiding Judge, committed him to Jail for six months, with some very pungent and appropriate remarks. From this sentence Mr. T. appealed to the Chief Justice, Sir C. Rawlinson, in the Supreme Court, who confirmed the Judgment, with the remark, that the only point in which he differed from the Puisne Judge, was that he thought the sentence was possibly too lenient.

These people are the pests of society. The mischief they do is incalculable: and every method ought to be resorted to to put a stop to their mal-practices. With regard to the Sudder Court, one remedy, which would of itself go a long way to cure the evil, would be to issue a table of liberal fees, and institute a taxing Officer, as I have before observed.

Appeal.

Another great evil is the facility of appeal. The people of India are by nature extremely litigious; and the reader of these pages can scarcely have failed to be struck with the number of times which suits of trumpery amount have been tried and appealed against.

Checks upon.

True it is, that so long as we have Judges of the present quality, it may be a hardship upon the people to limit their right of appeal in any way; but I cannot but conceive, that if we had a judicial bench of any strength, some limit might, and ought to be set upon the right of appeal; and indeed a greater boon could scarcely be conferred upon the people of India, than some legislative check imposed upon their unnatural inclination for litigation, and the designs of those who practice upon that inclination for their own interest.

Nature of checks.

What the nature or extent of that check should be, is a matter of detail and after consideration. Whether it should be made to depend upon amount, or upon the coincidence of the decision of two successive Judges upon the same subject matter—or both of these; or if any other checks may be successfully introduced, it is not my purpose here to discuss. I simply wish to draw attention to existing evils and abuses. Let others, who have the power, if they feel disposed, apply the remedy.

Stamps. Another great evil which I conceive ought no longer to be permitted to prevail, is the very high duty charged upon all Law proceedings. Jeremy Bentham has irrefragably established that the worst of all taxes is a Law tax: and all Political Economists agree with him. Now in India the tax is enormous. It is imposed in the shape of *stamps*; and they are of the most oppressive magnitude. By Reg. XIII. of 1816, Sec. XIII. it is enacted that,

1. In original regular suits institued in any court of judicature, and in appeals regular or special, preferred from the judgments of any such court to a superior court, if the amount or value of the property claimed shall not exceed sixteen Arcot rupees, the plaint or petition shall be written on paper of one rupee.

2. If above 16 rupees and not exceeding 32 rupees—two rupees.

3. If above 32 rupees and not exceeding 64 rupees—four rupees.

4. If above 64 rupees and not exceeding 150 rupees—eight rupees.

5. If above 150 rupees and not exceeding 300 rupees—sixteen rupees.

6. If above 300 rupees and not exceeding 800 rupees—thirty-two rupees.

7. If above 800 rupees and not exceeding 1,600 rupees—fifty rupees.

8. If above 1,600 rupees and not exceeding 3,000 rupees—one hundred rupees.

9. If above 3,000 rupees and not exceeding 5,000 rupees—one hundred and fifty rupees.

10. If above 5,000 rupees and not exceeding 10,000 rupees—two hundred and fifty rupees.

11. If above 10,000 rupees and not exceeding 15,000 rupees—three hundred and fifty rupees.

12. If above 15,000 rupees and not exceeding 25,000 rupees—five hundred rupees.

13. If above 25,000 rupees and not exceeding 50,000 rupees—seven hundred and fifty rupees.

14. If above 50,000 rupees and not exceeding 100,000 rupees—one thousand rupees.

15. If above 100,000 rupees—two thousand rupees.

By Section XVI. no exhibit is to be filed in any original or appeal suit, without an application praying its admission, written upon stamped paper, varying from 4 annas to 2 rupees, according to the rank of the Court.

By Section XVII. no summons shall be issued for attendance of any witness, without the like application, on stamped paper of like value.

By Section XVIII. it is not necessary to file a separate application for the admission of each exhibit or each witness—but any number of exhibits or witnesses may be included in one application—provided the same amount of stamp be paid as if there had been separate applications!

By Section XIX. every answer, reply, rejoinder, &c. in original or appeal suits is to be on stamped paper, varying from four annas to four rupees.

By Section XX. all proceedings in summary suits, miscellaneous petitions, are to be on stamped paper, varying from four annas to two rupees.

By Section XXIII. if the pleading cannot be contained on one sheet (only one side containing 30 lines 8 words to a line can be used by a Circular order of the S. Adaulut) further sheets are to be stamped as in Section XIX.

This will give some idea of the nature and amount of 'Law tax' levied upon suitors. Those upon the petitions for Appeal are positively preposterous; and the only argument that can be urged in their favour is that they *may* act as a check upon Litigation: but inasmuch as they act equally upon the just as well as the unjust Litigant, and operate very differently upon the rich and poor, such an argument is not of much worth. What adds considerably to this heavy burthen, is the constant remand of suits, which entails the necessity of fresh stamps innumerable.

It may be anticipated, that any proposition to alter this part of the system will meet with strong opposition at the hands of the Indian Government. They avowedly act upon the principle of making their Courts of Justice paying concerns. They like them to defray their own expenses, and would not even object to a surplus.* Any innovation which entails expense, or cuts down receipts, is sure to be looked upon with a jealous eye. Yet, if indeed a Law tax be the worst of all taxes, perhaps it is not beneath the British Legislature, now that it has the opportunity of interfering in Indian affairs, to take care that it be abolished. If *they* do not undertake this, we may rest perfectly assured that no measure of this tendency will spontaneously emanate from the Government of India, or the Court of Directors.

Inconvenient situations of Courts.

The next evil I would notice is the enormous distances at which the Courts are situated from the general body of the people. The districts are very large; and the Courts are very few, so that the suitors are put to great expense, both of time and trouble, in attending before the Courts. Indeed to such an extent is this felt in the case of witnesses, that the ends of justice are frequently frustrated by this very cause, joined as it is to the tardy pace at which cases proceed. I may mention two cases which have come lately within my own knowledge, instancing the snail's pace at which proceedings crawl. One was for forgery—the other was for an offence under the Breach of Trust Act. The two cases were connected together as arising out of the same subject matter, though the accused were different in them.

* See a late letter from the Government of Bengal to the Madras Judges on the subject of the new Small Cause Court.

In the former, in which five persons were joined, *the trial occupied 14 months*; during which the prisoners were in Jail. In the latter, the accused, who was on bail, was sent up for trial about January last: the trial commenced in July, and as counsel were employed on each side, whose time was valuable, irrelevant matter was by consent excluded, though not without some struggles on the part of the Judge. The actual examination of witnesses *only* occupied about three weeks; and the whole trial was got over and sentence pronounced by the beginning of November! Now it must be apparent that the hardship upon a man, especially a poor man, of dancing attendance during such prolonged periods, as a witness, must be very great; and with reference to this subject, an Officer of the 8th Regt. informed me that when he was on detachment at a place called Condapilly, three or four very serious assaults occurred, almost ending in murder. That no one interfered; and, that upon his asking the villagers how they could have kept out of the way upon such an occasion, the reply was that had they gone to render assistance, they would have had to go up to the Sessions Court as witnesses, and been kept away for months from their homes and harvests! It is not a week since I saw a poor old man who, a gentleman practising in the Sudder as a Pleader assured me, had walked up from Madura, a distance of 300 miles, four times about his appeal!

It would require but little arrangement to place the Courts in convenient localities. For this purpose the Subordinate Judge should hold his sittings, not as at present, in the principal Zillah town, in which the Zillah Judge also presides; but in some distant part of the district.

Different distribution of duties.

In order however to carry out this change, a different distribution of the duties of the respective Courts would probably become necessary.

The Subordinate Judge is a good deal occupied in work of a character from which he should be relieved, such as trying criminal cases in the first instance before sending them up to the Sessions Judge for final disposal.

The Zillah Judge, next in rank and standing to the Sudder, although his time is more than fully occupied in getting through his business, from his having to discharge duties which are properly the province of a Register, or ministerial officer, scarcely has such a class and character of cases for his investigation as his standing requires. He is in practice seldom other than a Judge of appeal: and although it is very expedient that more and more extended use should be made of Native agency, in carrying on the business of the Country, a more advantageous distribution of business might with ease be made among the different orders of Judges.

I barely glance at this, as it scarcely falls within the limits which I have proposed to myself.

Evidence.

Another source of great evil is the way in which evidence is too frequently taken. The Regulations of 1802 clearly contemplated all evidence being taken by the Judge who presided at the trial. But in 1809, two Regulations were passed, VII. Sec. 22, and XII. Sec. 8, by which the Judges are authorized to depute their Register, Assistants, or Native Officers, to discharge that all-important duty, when they themselves "may not have time."

True, the examination is to be in open Court, in the presence of the parties, and, I presume, in the presence of the Judge: but it might almost as well take place behind his back, so far as concerns his judging of the manner and bearing of the witnesses, the propriety of the questions, and the admissibility of the answers, if his time and attention are during the operation devoted to other business.

These pages afford an instance of a case wherein a man was hung, although the Judge who pronounced him guilty had himself examined only a few very unimportant witnesses.

Depositions before Magistrates.

So again, the way in which depositions are, as I have good reason to believe, ordinarily taken before the Magistrate, is a perfect farce. The Collector, who is also the Magistrate, has so much other business on his hands, that it is quite impossible for him to examine all the witnesses, who come before him in cases which he has to send up to the Sessions Judge for trial. I am not aware of any power given by the Regulations to the Magistrate, similar to that conferred upon the Judge, of discharging this duty by proxy. But I have myself seen witnesses under the process of examination before the Collector and Magistrate.

That officer is in his tent or his cutcherry, surrounded by a host of Natives, petitioners, complainants, peons, officers ; he is engaged in a rapid succession of trifling matters, or immersed in some subject of importance.

Meanwhile, seated on the floor in one corner may be seen a Native writer, jabbering to another Native squatted immediately beside him, and writing as fast as the two can talk. Should a stranger be tempted to enquire what is their occupation, he will learn that the Official is taking a deposition in a criminal case from a witness. The most abominable trash is taken down ; the whole is then read out aloud to the witness, who signs it ; it is attested by the Magistrate, and forwarded to the Session Court.

Such a system has only to be pointed out, in order most imperatively and peremptorily to demand, and it is to be hoped, obtain an immediate remedy.

It operates all the more injuriously, because by Regulation XV. of 1816, S. 4, Clause 1st, and by Act III. of 1843. S. 1., no Special Appeal is admissible *on the merits. The facts of the case are to be assumed to be as stated in the Decree ;* and an Appeal lies only where the decision appealed from " is " inconsistent with some law, or usage having the force of "law, or some practice of the Courts, or shall involve some "question of law, usage, or practice, upon which there may "be reasonable doubts."

Native Pleaders and Judges.

The ignorance of the Native pleaders in the Subordinate Courts is a subject of deep importance; as also is the character of the whole Native establishment of Principal Sudder Ameens, and Native judicial officers. If the European Judges have *no* training, neither have the Native; at least not any such as is worthy of the name: and some scheme ought to be devised for affording them also the means and opportunity of acquiring a knowledge of the law of evidence, procedure, and general jurisprudence, as well as of the Hindu and Mahomedan Law, and the Regulations, and Acts, under which justice is administered in the Mofussil.

Indeed there is a noble opportunity for him who shall undertake the task of rearing up a really useful body of Native Pleaders and Judges, and preparing Text-books of Mofussil Law. If he fitly perform his work, he may become the Story of India.

Law Officers.

The time seems to have arrived when the services of the Native Law Officers attached to the Courts may be beneficially dispensed with.

Futwahs.

Except in the Foujdaree Court, the Judge is obliged in every criminal case to receive the 'Futwah' or decision of his Mahomedan Law Officer, before he pronounces his own. Little weight is, I believe, attached to it in practice: and however politic it might have been at our first possession of this Country, somewhat to humour the vanity of the late rulers, no such motive any longer exists; it is a blemish in the administration of English justice, that even the *form* of bowing to the Mahomedan Law should be continued. The substance has long since gone; why does the shadow linger? The Mahomedan Law Officer sits as a sort of assistant with the Sessions Judge at all

Mahomedan Law of Evidence.

criminal trials—and inasmuch as the Mahomedan Law of Evidence prevailed when we first obtained dominion in India, the fiction of deciding by that law is still kept up, although it is notorious, as Mr. Arbuthnot remarks in the introduction to his work above quoted, that the English Law of Evidence is now, with some few exceptions of no great importance, the guide and rule of the Courts. Now inasmuch as that Law clashes with the Mahomedan Law in many points, and as we have not hitherto had sufficient resolution entirely to shake off the thrall of the latter, the Legislature has devised a compromise between the pretensions of the two Laws, by the following notable provision.*

Further question.

It consists in allowing the Judge to "put a further question"—Thus:—

The Mahomedan Law excludes, for instance, the evidence of women.

Suppose then that a woman is produced as a witness. The Mahomedan Law Officer objects that her evidence is not receivable, *because she is a woman*—whereupon the Judge is authorized to put the further question, "but suppose she were a man?" 'Oh! then her testimony would be good'—whereupon the Judge admits the evidence. Again, in almost all cases by the Law of England, one witness is sufficient to prove the fact. The Mahomedan Law requires three witnesses to prove adultery. Now as that crime is not usually perpetrated with such publicity, let us suppose one witness produced who swears point blank to the fact. The Mufti says the crime is not proved. The Judge 'puts the further question'—but suppose this witness were three witnesses? 'oh! then it would be proved'—whereupon the Judge decides that it *is* proved.†

* Reg. I. of 1825, Sec. 8 and Reg. VI. of 1829.

† I have given the substance, not the exact form of this Proceeding.

Now when we have arrived at such a state of things as this, I apprehend that few people will have much difficulty in coming to the conclusion that this 'fiction' should be abolished altogether. So with respect to the Hindu Pundits. They are literally worthless incumbrances. I believe there is no point—no contradiction—which a Pundit cannot produce authority for from one or other of the Hindu Law commentators. In case No. XI. of 1849, reported page 234 of the S. A. Reports for 1851, a question of Hindu Law was put to the two Pundits. They gave their respective answers, citing their respective authorities. In para. 17, the Sudder remark—

Pundits.

No. XI. of 1849.

Vol. 3, S. Rep. p. 234.

"The foregoing decisions being in *direct opposition to each other*, "and that of the senior Pundit *being contrary to one he had given* "*formerly in the same suit*, when pending before the Civil Judge, the "following question was put to that officer."

(Asking him to explain). A stronger instance can scarcely be conceived; and I believe the same result might be arrived at on any given point of Hindu Law. Again; they quote from all sorts of Authorities; citing the Dya Baga (which prevails in Bengal) to prove propositions diametrically opposed to the Metachsyra, which is the Code obtaining in Madras. I firmly believe that our English text writers, Colebrook, Strange, Macnaghten, together with such precedents as already exist, are amply sufficient authorities upon the Hindu Law, and that the Pundits may very advantageously make their exit with the Muftis.

Character of Native Officials.

Lastly, two other evils of the greatest magnitude, co-extensive with the whole surface of our dominions, are the fearful corruption in the Native Officers, and the degraded character of the people at large. True it is that no mere Legislative enactment can alter this state of things. It must be the result of patient years of education, and moral influence; yet it does not become me to pass over altogether in silence so crying an enormity, connected as it is with the subject before me.

Law Officers.

Pleaders.

Police.

I have no hesitation in stating my opinion, and I believe those who are most familiar with the Natives will bear me out, that the general rule of office is impurity.—Office is the badge of corruption, and the instrument of extortion, from him who sells his Futwah for thousands of Rupees, down to the village Peon who levies contributions in humble copper, as the price of his favour, or his silence.

The eagerness with which even the pettiest place is sought after—the price which is often paid for Office of the most trumpery nature, shows that the bait which attracts so many, is not the *mere* pay, which is trifling, but the opportunity which place offers for unlimited exaction.

I have myself seen as many as a hundred able-bodied men, drawn up in line, like a company of Soldiers, before a Collector's door, candidates for the vacant berth of a discharged Peon, whose pay is perhaps 5 Rupees a month; but whose place is in reality, worth a vast deal more, according to its owner's capacity of swallow.

The most commonplace order of every day life cannot be given without affording occasion for bribery and extortion. I must be pardoned if I give an anecdote in point, if it only serve somewhat to enliven these pages. During last Summer, when I was away some 400 miles from the Presidency, the gentleman with whom I was residing, sent a Peon (to whom an Officer on detachment added two Sepoys) to enquire at a village at some distance, if there were any hog in the neighbourhood, as we intended to try a little diversion with our spears. The envoys returned, reporting that there were none. Some few days after the villagers sent in a complaint which was still under investigation when I came away. They represented that the three worthies had arrived at their village early one morning: sent for the headmen, and representing that the "gentlemen" were coming there to hunt, told them that it would be their ruin; that their crops would be ridden down; that they would have to find provisions for a camp of several hundred followers; and that the only way to escape was to give the narrators a consideration—'buckshoesh' for which they would return, and tell the gentlemen there were no pig there, so that the devastation which threatened them, would be shifted to some other village. The elders consulted and consented; money was given: the officials then asked for food, and made themselves jolly until the evening; when they sent a further modest request to the headmen to furnish them with three women, not 'common women,' but 'respectable women of good caste.' This excited some commotion, and was ultimately refused, with a threat of reporting the whole circumstance to the Collector. Upon this the worthies drew in their horns, and having got their pockets and their bellies full, returned at their leisure to report to their employers that there were no pig in that village—a case this, as it was remarked at the time, going even beyond the old Border custom; for the good freebooters of former days confined themselves to black mail, whereas this was an attempt to levy 'black female.'

The People.

With respect to the people at large; they are utterly degraded; inconceivably so: to an extent of which those "gentlemen of England who live at home at ease" can form no idea. Lying is no disgrace to them, it is more than their habit; it has become their second nature: forgery, perjury and subornation of perjury are the common weapons on both sides in a contested suit. The Judge here starts from a diametrically opposite point to that from which he does in England. The probability here is that the witness is the witness, not of truth, but of falsehood; an oath, unless indeed it be on the cow's tail, is of no effect; the swearer comes to give his evidence according to his bribe. Whole scenes are got up and rehearsed before hand, when each witness takes his part; the dying man is placed upon his couch, the friends are gathered round; the will is prepared, read out, executed, attested; the closest attention is paid to form, with a truly awful mockery; and then the parties come into Court, where they act the farce with life-like veracity. Love of litigation, and love of revenge, are two of the strongest among Native passions: and when they have such means and tools ready at hand, and are utterly unscrupulous in their use, what wonder that our Courts are daily prostituted, and made against their will to pander to these abominable vices? Who can be surprized at hearing a judgment commence as it not unfrequently does:

> "This is one of those cases of conflicting testimony, unfortunately "only too common. There *must* be perjury on one side, probably on "both. The witnesses for the plaintiff and defendant are alike un- "worthy of credit. Several of the documents of both parties appear "to us evident forgeries, and we are unhappily left in a position in "which we are forced almost to guess at the truth. Our decision may "possibly be erroneous, but we can only, in such a state of things "be guided by what appear to us to be the probabilities of the case, "collecting them from our knowledge of what would be ordinarily the "conduct of parties placed in a similar possession to those before the "Court."

I have myself more than once heard a judgment commence in this way. Sir Henry Pottinger in a Minute on Education under date the 1st November 1852 makes the following remarks, para. 23:

> "He does not intend to deny but that there may be occasional "bright exceptions; but he is of opinion that whatever system of "Education may be enforced hereafter, its chief aim ought to be "directed to moral improvement, combined with extirpating the "foul vices of untruthfulness and dishonesty, *which are hardly now* "*held by the great masses to be a reflection, unless discovered.*"

A few days since a novel view of the *obligation* of a member of Hindu society was afforded in the Supreme Court by a worthy who conducted his case in person, and who ordinarily gained his livelihood as a 'Lawyer's Dubash,' a Trade whose quality has been previously explained. He cross-examined the Plaintiff, who claimed his house, with considerable ability; and elicited from him, that Defendant's ancestors, who had occupied the house for a long series of years, had some time since troubled him, by instituting an enquiry against him in the late Pauper Office, about this very property; that the case had been dismissed; that he nevertheless allowed the parties to continue in the occupation of the premises without paying any rent, as they were poor, and begged at his knees for this indulgence; and that he did not obtain from them at that time, or indeed at all, any written acknowledgment of his title. "What" burst out the Dubash, in a state of great excitement, "do you wish the Court to believe that after my "ancestors had brought you before the Pauper Office, you "acted in this way?—was it not your *duty* to have spent "15,000 Rupees in ruining them?" A piece of morality which I have no doubt the Dubash enunciated in the most perfect good faith, and without one touch of irony.

But this subject is far too serious to jest upon. It does not come within the scope of these pages to notice it further, or to suggest a remedy—though it may possibly be found that the only hope rests in a systematic and sound scheme of Education.

Supreme Court.

It remains for me to say a few words upon the Supreme Court; because its present state and future prospets are closely connected with the remedy which I am about to venture to suggest for the present mal-administration of Justice.

Macauley.

Many years have now elapsed since the Right Honorable Thomas Babington Macauley uttered his celebrated sneer that the Madras Supreme Court had already "fulfilled its mission," meaning thereby, that the population was ruined, beggared, prostrated by its operation. The saying was pithy and pointed; and, as often happens in such cases, has been frequently quoted; and has received, without hesitation, the readiest assent. The answer to it is, simply, that it is not true; or rather perhaps that there is a great deal of truth in it, though of a directly opposite character to that which its author intended it to convey. I am no apologist or defender of the Supreme Court; let there be no mistake upon that point. I am no stickler for class or exclusive interests, even when they happen to be my own. I conceive that every abolition of unnecessary forms, or obsolete fictions, is an improvement: that every measure which brings speedy and cheap justice home to the very doors of the people at large, ought to become Law; and be, as effectually as possible, carried into execution: though I must at the same time be permitted to entertain and express my doubts whether the means, now so much in vogue, are the wisest or best adapted for that end; whether the real remedy does not, after all, consist in sweeping away from the Supreme Courts all the abuses, fictions, technicalities, which, originating and growing up with a system now obsolete, have had their day, and are no longer adapted to the wants of a totally altered state of society; and in rendering the old Courts, as accessible, as speedy, and as cheap, as those of a lower quality: rather than in erecting new Courts, to be presided over by Judges of an inferior calibre, and handing over the practice in them to a lower grade and order of Advocates—and I will not refrain from expressing my fears, that there is in the present system the deep laid germ of an evil, which will only be witnessed in its full growth in the next generation, when it shall have destroyed that high, honourable Profession, to which I feel it a privilege to belong; and there shall no longer remain ranks, whence to recruit the breaches which Time must,

County Court System.

sooner or later, make in that phalanx of English Judges, whose long uninterrupted succession has given to the Administration of Justice all its purity, its dignity, and its authority. But,

λαμπάδια ἔχοντες διαδώσουσιν ἀλλήλοις

I believe yet in the destiny of the Bar: and that after the furor of satisfaction has passed over; when the present system shall have lost its first gloss of novelty; the strong common sense of the English People will revert somewhat to the old Courts of Judicature, provided that they are made accessible, cheap, and speedy: and that the anomaly of a practical distinction between Law and Equity being abolished, they are put much upon the footing of the Courts which now preside in America. The fashions of one Age become the fardels of the next: and although we are so tied and bound by the chain of habit, that *we* possibly may never shake off our prejudices, the time is probably not far distant, when Posterity will look, as an abuse, upon that division of Law and Equity, which our ancestors considered the very perfection of human wisdom; and the story, that formerly might be seen the spectacle of two sets of Courts sitting side by side in Westminster Hall, administering the Law upon totally different principles, will be pointed to with astonishment, even if it does not tax belief.*

Madras: its present state.

To return: it may be true that the great wealth of several important families has in early times been swallowed up by the Supreme Court: but so far from its having destroyed the well-being of the people at

* Such an opinion may probably startle the majority of the Profession in England, where not only are the Courts of Law and Equity distinct, but the division of labour is carried still farther by distinct branches in each Court; but practice before any of the Queen's polyedrous Courts in India or the Colonies, where every Barrister is Equity Draftsman, Special Pleader, Chamber Counsel, Advocate on all 'sides' of one and the same Court, the anomaly of the distinction between Law and Equity, and the comparative facility with which the two might be made to coalesce, do strike the mind very forcibly.

large, I believe that there never was so much wealth in Black Town as at this present time. Petty Native Shopkeepers have everywhere sprung up, in the closest imitation of the European retail, Auction, and Commission dealers; establishments are now conducted by Hindus, wherein the customer meets with as much intelligence, and civility, and articles of just as good a quality, as in those kept by Europeans: nay, Houses of Agency, carrying on large export and import traffic, have opened as competitors with the old established English Firms. Wealth may not be so concentrated as formerly in a few powerful families, but it is certainly far more widely and equally diffused. Altogether, such a state prevails in Madras, as can be pointed out in no other town throughout the whole Presidency; and it is the most conclusive and satisfactory proof, that the people *feel* that they are living under a Law, which, when properly administered, renders their property secure.

A similar state of prosperity *could not* have grown up under the present administration of Mofussil Law: not but that the Queen's Court has occasionally enforced the technicalities of English Practice in a manner totally unsuited to the state of Native Society—It has suffered in its credit accordingly. If the Supreme Court has now but little to do, assuredly it is not because it has left none to ruin. The true causes of its lack of business lie elsewhere.

It would be idle to attempt to conceal that at the present time the Supreme Court has little to occupy it on the Civil side, and that if the Small Cause Court jurisdiction is extended, as it is proposed, to 1,000 Rupees, it will have still less; probably nothing, or next to nothing.

Special Demurrers.

The causes of the present state of things appear to me to be principally three. In the first place, for the first seven years out of the ten which I have now practised in India, Judges unfortunately favoured

'Special Demurrers.' If these were an evil in England, it may be easily conceived how infinitely more so they were in India. Let any of my readers suppose Ramasawmy to sue Ram Doss, on his promissory note for 500 Rupees, to which the latter has no defence on the merits.

Both parties attend in Court when they understand their case is to come on: they sit listening 'from morn to dewy eve, a Summer day,' in silent admiration to their Counsels arguments, although they do not understand a single word of the language in which those arguments are uttered; and at the close, the Plaintiff betakes himself to his Attorney's Office, where some such speech as this is interpreted to him.

"Tell him" says the Attorney to his Interpreter, "that his case "has been heard upon special demurrer—I'm afraid I cannot exact- "ly make him understand what that is—but the case has been argu- "ed by two counsel on each side; very ably argued, the judge said: "but as the pleader had unluckily left out the word "said" in the "plaint, judgment has been given against him,—or liberty has been "given to amend on payment of costs, which will come to about 500 "Rupees!"

The result of this, often repeated, would naturally make Blacky shy of Law. A better state of things has succeeded, but too late: the mischief has been already done.

Insolvent Acts.

The next cause is the passing of the present Insolvent Act; which has nearly destroyed credit, and, for a time, almost paralyzed the operations of trade, of which credit is said to be the soul.

Before any Insolvent Act was passed for this Country, men who went to Jail, paid their debts. But as soon as it was found that by lying in Jail for 21 days, a man could claim to be freed from his liabilities, many took advantage of this, though the majority still paid. Passing through the Insolvent Court is not the slightest slur upon the generality of

Natives—indeed if an Insolvent succeed in entirely baffling all enquiry into his means, successfully masks his property, and unblushingly swears that he is not worth a doody in the world; he returns to the bosom of his family, and the circle of his friends, with a little increased eclat, as being a very clever fellow. Native families being 'undivided,' all members living together in one house, and having common rights, it becomes next to impossible to trace out individual property. Deeds are registered in other members' name: jewels belong to cousins' wives; houses are merely occupied in tenancy, and so forth; friends sit grinning by, while the investigation is going on, and the Insolvent and his relations are baffling Judge and Counsel, and however startling it may sound to English ears, it is notorious here, that whilst little is ever given up or discovered for the benefit of creditors, the debtor walks forth in just as comfortable circumstances as before his Insolvency; the only difference being, that his property is all in 'trust'; of which there have occasionally been brought to light some very laughable breaches.

But there was still a large class who call themselves 'respectable,' the wealthier and higher castes, to whom going to Jail even for 21 days was a discomfort, if not a disgrace; a benevolent Legislature has thought proper to provide for their wants; for by the last Insolvent Act, it is not necessary for a man to go to Jail at all, to entitle him to the benefit of the Act. The Jail is accordingly comparatively empty: but the number of Insolvents, and the work in the Chief Clerk's Office have wonderfully increased, and a practice has now sprung up, under which the candidate for irresponsibility puts up 'rails' in front of his door, prepares his schedule comfortably at home, files his Petition, and obtain his 'interim order' until the day appointed for hearing, when the solemn farce of an investigation is gone through; an adjudication is pronounced, and lo! the solution of what the fable in our younger days taught us to look upon as the ne plus ultra of impossibility: —a blackamoor white-washed.*

Import Trade. The import trade of Madras is carried on as follows. Firms in England consign their goods in large quantities to the English Houses of Agency here: who either send them to the Shops for sale on Commission, or by Auction, or dispose of them wholesale to large Native dealers for inland traffic. For transactions of the last nature each house employs a Dubash, who communicates between the vendor and purchaser, receiving a commission on the amount of sale effected through his agency. He is however himself personally responsible to his employer for the proceeds of the sale: he is always a man of considerable wealth, and gives heavy security to the firm that employs him.

How timid such a state of things, as is detailed under the working of the present Insolvent Court, must make these parties, mercantile men will easily understand: the same distrust operates everywhere, from the highest to the lowest dealer, and I believe the Act has very seriously shackled mercantile transactions. Certainly if the Legislature's object was to destroy credit, no better means could have been devised. The Insolvent Court also affords a compendious mode of discharging a Solicitor's bill: and the result upon the amount of Court practice has been disagreeably sensible.

* By returns furnished me from the Offices of the Sheriff, and Chief Clerk of the Insolvent Court, the following facts appear. From 1806 to 8th March 1829, (when the first Insolvent Act came into operation) there were confined on the Debtors side of H. M. Jail 1,828 prisoners.

There appear to have been no casualties, so that all these persons must have paid their debts, after a longer or shorter period of incarceration.

From 8th March 1829 to 22d August 1841, when the second Insolvent Act came out, were confined in all, 587 persons: of whom 152 took the benefit of the Act. The other 435 paid their debts.

From 22d August 1848 up to the present time, only about four and a half years, there have been confined in all, 120 persons. Of these only 24, *Natives*, have taken the benefit of the Act, but during this period there have been in all, 480 persons discharged under the Act so that 356 have never been in prison at all, a full proof this of the truth of the text above.

Small Cause Court.

Again the abolition of the old Court of Requests, whose jurisdiction went only to 200 Rupees in mere money demands, and the erection of a new Court of Small Causes, with a jurisdiction of 500 Rupees, over all classes of actions (except libel), upon the plan of the English County Courts, has taken away necessarily a large amount of business from the Supreme Court, and the measure

> 'Comes me cranking in
> And cuts into me from the best of all my land
> A huge half moon, a monstrous cantle out.'

True it is the Judges of the Supreme Court under a clause to that effect provided in the Statute, still keep their Court open for the trial of all such cases above 100 Rupees, as Suitors may choose to bring before them, rather than the Judges of the Small Cause Court: though it is inconceivable how they can fail to perceive the fact, that they have thereby done little more than give rise, as I heard an Attorney tell one of their Lordships in open Court a fortnight since, to a new trade in Madras—that of 'offering the head,' prize-fighter fashion, in the public streets, to be hit at; for nearly a third of the cases they try are for petty assaults, through which a decent livelihood may now be picked up in the shape of damages by an able bodied man, who does not care for 'punishment,' or regard his personal beauty.*

It is now proposed to increase the jurisdiction of the Small Cause Courts to 1,000 Rupees. In Calcutta, and possibly in Bombay, where there is plenty to do, such a measure would be a relief to the Supreme Courts: here, where mercantile affairs are of a comparatively limited nature, it must leave the Supreme Court with empty hands.

C. L. Procedure Act.

Whether the introduction of the Common Law Procedure Act, short as it falls of the changes proposed of Sir Lawrence Peel's previous

* From October 1851 when the Court determined to take cases above 100 Rupees up to 6th October 1852, the number of actions brought was 390, of which 112 were for Trespass and Assault.

draft, would not be a more prudent measure, it is not for me to decide. This I am certain of; that the whole Civil Service detests the Supreme Court, and would gladly see it abolished; and believing that the Government is jealous of it, as an 'imperium in imperio,' distasteful enough to an otherwise absolute rule, their policy is by all means to take away its business: and then the cry will appear natural enough: "Behold, "a Court kept up at an enormous expense: English Judges "with literally nothing to do; an Establishment utterly use- "less, and practically defunct. It has 'fulfilled its mission'— "away with it, away with it!"

I hope myself never to see that day arrive. I trust Her Majesty will always continue to have representatives in the highest judgment seats of British India, and be herself, through them, vicariously present, presiding over the due administration of justice; though I admit that large salaries and retiring pensions are not to be given without an equivalent in the shape of labour; and if the former employments of the Queen's Judges are taken away from them, it will be necessary to find something else for them to do; nor need we go far to search for that 'something,' which is indeed ready at hand, as I shall presently show.

It has been necessary for me to enter thus at length into the present position of the Supreme Court; but I must earnestly entreat, that the attention of my readers may not be thereby diverted from the main scope and object of this Essay: which is to show the present state of the administration of Justice in the *Company's*, not the Queen's Courts. That is the crying evil which it is my purpose to expose; and before proceeding further, I must ask my readers to pause: to carry back their recollection to my former observations upon that topic, and each for himself to reflect upon the facts which have been laid before him; and this being done; I would fearlessly ask, if I have not disclosed to them an enormous abuse, of the very existence of which they had previously no conception nor idea—or, if they think that I have not established a case calling for an immediate Legislative remedy, whether I have not laid open such a state of facts, as demands the serious consideration of all reflecting men, benevolently disposed towards the masses of India; and whether further investigation and inquiry are not absolutely necessary, before it is determined to allow things to remain in their present anomalous position?

Surely such an administration of Justice, as is shown by the Sudder and Foujdaree Reports, to exist throughout the length and breadth of this Presidency, must at least 'give us pause': and if further investigation is determined upon, I for one have no fear of the ultimate result.

Remedy.

I come now to a portion of my subject which I confess I approach with much less of confidence, and more of hesitation and embarrassment: I mean the suggestion of a remedy. Hitherto I have had to deal with facts; now I enter into the regions of speculation and opinion.

It is always far easier to find fault with an existing system, than to devise a better in its place; and in this particular instance, there are peculiar difficulties in the way of any such attempt. The very great differences which exist between the practice of the English Courts and those of the Mofussil; the caution which is necessary in trenching upon the customs and usages of the Natives; the want of experience in Mofussil practice and procedure, under which, one, not in the Civil Service, must necessarily labour; the knowledge that there exists great conflict of opinion among men very capable of judging upon the point; a feeling that it is almost presumption in an individual to point out what ought perhaps rather to be the result of mature Legislative deliberation; a sense of my own incapacity for so great and important a labour; all this oppresses and weighs me down at the very outset: nevertheless as the subject has been with me one of steady, continuous, protracted meditation and reflection; as I am on the spot, viewing the whole matter from a point whence others probably have not observed it; I will venture to make public the conclusions at which I have arrived; not enunciating them in any dogmatic spirit, as propositions which will not admit of dispute; nor putting them forth as novelties, the merit of whose discovery rests with me; but throwing them out as mere matter of suggestion, for the better consideration of those who are far more qualified than I can be to judge of them, with a view to court and cause further investigation; deprecating criticism; not affecting to pretend that the details are complete; or attempting anything more than a mere hasty outline; but at the same time, vindicating to myself a patient hearing, and professing my individual conviction in the expediency and practicability of my plan.

Conflict of opinion.

There has been great conflict of opinion as to the best or proper remedy among those who admit the inefficiency of the present system of administration of justice in India.

Barristers, Judges.

Some propose that Barristers should preside over the Mofussil Courts. I confess I think the remedy might prove worse than the disease.

There would be great danger of a constant clashing between such officers and a jealous Civil Service: the introduction of technicalities, which might possibly enough follow, would of itself be a great evil: the change would be very abrupt: and I believe that a thorough practical knowledge of the languages of the mixed people of this Presidency, and an intimate acquaintance with the habits, manners, and customs of the Natives, only to be acquired by long residence among them, and through their constant intercourse; together with a practical intimacy with the minute details and working of the whole Revenue system, are indispensably necessary in any one who is efficiently to discharge the duties of a Mofussil Judge. A mere knowledge of the substantive law, of the law of evidence; and a familiarity with the ordinary routine of business, is by no means sufficient—essential as such acquirements undoubtedly are; and certainly as we might expect to find them in Judges taken from the English Bar. But, for the reasons I have above stated, it appears to me that the propriety of such a measure is, to say the least, very doubtful: it would certainly be very distasteful to the Civil Service; nor above all do I think it is in any way necessary.

Wider base of the Civil Service.

Another suggestion has been to throw open, more widely, access to the Civil Service: to make the entrance to its ranks depend less upon patronage and connections; and more upon merit and talent—but for my own part, such a scheme strikes me as utterly powerless to effect any beneficial change in the present order of things. You might send all the young talents of England here; ship loads of mute inglorious Miltons, untried Bacons, embryo Shakespears: and still meditative Newtons, but unless something more were done; although we might have very good philosophical Essays, or extraordinary Epics and Plays by the bushel, yet so far as the administration of justice is concerned, things would proceed much as they do now.

Civil Service, quality of.

I have lived for many years in familiar intercourse with very many members of the Civil Service, old and young; and am acquainted with most of them; and I have ever found them in point of abilities and acquirements much the same as other men in average society, with here and there a really superior man. As a body, they are honorable, honest, benevolent, intelligent, laborious, high-spirited English gentlemen: and although throwing the entry into their ranks open to talent and merit, might offer a very convenient start to many young men in England, who can find no room for employment on that over crowded stage, where all the liberal professions are already overstocked, I do not think that such a measure could in any way enhance the respectability of the Service.

Real root of evil.

No—*the evil lies not in the men, but in the system.* Emphatically, there it is rooted; and thither we must descend, if we are to pluck it out.

This is probably the only civilized country in the world, or more properly speaking, country presided over by civilized men, where it is thought no special training is necessary to qualify a man for a due discharge of judicial duties.

I can by no means admit that the Subordinate Judgeship affords any such training—for although it is true that part of the duty of the Subordinate Judge consists in looking through the criminal cases which the Sessions Judge has to try, and, as it were, performing the functions of a grand jury; he is, nevertheless from the outset of his career, *a judge;* and one of very considerable importance; for although he has an original, in practice, he exercises little else than an *appellate jurisdiction:* and though he may perhaps gain a little experience during his incumbency of the Subordinate Judgeship, and before he is promoted to the superior grade, still it is gained at the expense of the unfortunate suitors; as Mr. Cameron has happily put it, he exhibits "the un-"seemly spectacle of a Judge learning to adjudicate *well* (?) "the rights of the great and opulent, by adjudicating *well or* "*ill* the rights of the vulgar." His career *commences* with an *appellate* jurisdiction of considerable magnitude, without his having any previous training whatsoever!

Magistrates.

It has been supposed by some, among the number Lord Auckland and Mr. Bird, that the Magisterial duties which every Civil Servant, even in the Revenue department, *must* perform, necessarily give him a certain degree of proficiency in the method of judicial investigation and decision. Nothing can be more fallacious. Upon this topic hear the Madras Civilian, whose recent pamphlet I have above quoted. It affords an answer, if not more complete, at any rate less open to suspicion, than any emanating from myself. He says—

" It might be supposed, and it is the general impression in India, that " in the Criminal department at all events, the duties of the Magistra- " cy afford a good preparation for the functions of a Criminal Judge. " It seems not unnatural to infer that a man who has passed several " years in adjudicating upon offences up to a certain limit, and, in his " capacity of committing officer, in investigating and preparing for trial " cases of a more serious kind should after a time become well qualifi- " ed for discharging the functions of the superior tribunal ; *and yet it* " *is in the criminal department, that, to judge from the printed reports,* " *the deficiencies of training and the want of habits of accurate inves-* " *tigation are most apparent.*"

But perhaps the Court of Directors' own testimony is the most conclusive which can be adduced on the point. They say in their letter of the 8th February 1837, para. 25, published page 242 of " the Circular Orders of the Madras Board of Revenue :"

" We have on several occasions had reason *to lament the unfitness so* " *frequently displayed by Revenue Officers in dealing with evidence, or* " *conducting any inquiry, in the nature of a judicial proceeding.*"

Certainly, if we may judge from the Masulipatam case herein before referred to, they have not improved since.

Haileybury.

Nor let the fatal error that Haileybury supplies the necessary education be any longer indulged in. Lord Brougham has drawn such a picture of that College, as might naturally enough result from a cursory visit to it on a show-day, and seem very plausible, addressed to an audience who had never been in India. He says :—

" The young men at Haileybury, who go out as writers, are quali- " fied to exercise these responsible functions, by being carefully edu- " cated at Haileybury by the most learned professors, among whom " I may mention Dr. Empson, the Professor of Law, and my excel- " lent friend Mr. Jones, the Professor of History and Political Eco- " nomy. Here these young gentlemen, to the number of eighty or

"ninety, are being instructed in law, in history, in the Oriental lan-
"guages, and every thing that can fit them for the discharge of their
"future duties. And this institution is a gratifying proof of the great
"improvement effected during the last twenty-five years in the
"Judges of the East India Company's possessions."

But the author of the pamphlet above referred to, himself a Haileybury man, and an Indian official, who has had ample means of testing the value of the legal education imparted at that College, after quoting the above passage, proceeds as follows:—

"To this position it is necessary to demur. It cannot be admitted that during the last quarter of a century any considerable improvement has taken place in the preparatory training of the Anglo Indian Judges. On the contrary, it has been proved by experience that in consequence of the changes which during that period have been effected in India in the constitution of the inferior tribunals, by the more extensive employment as Judges in them of Natives and other uncovenanted functionaries, the opportunities afforded to the members of the Civil Service, who under the present system alone are eligible to the higher judicial offices, of acquiring the necessary qualifications, have been very considerably decreased. The institution at Haileybury has been in existence for the last forty years, and for a very considerable portion of that period, the course of instruction has embraced all the subjects now taught there. It has of necessity followed from the number of subjects studied, that the students exercise a certain degree of selection as to the studies to which they shall more especially devote their attention; it having been found impracticable, or at all events inexpedient, that a high or even a fair standard of proficiency in *all* should be absolutely required. To the majority of youthful students the study of law is by no means an attractive one; and though perhaps of all others the one most calculated to tend to the efficiency of the future civilian, *it has been more generally neglected at Haileybury than any other, and few young civilians arrive in India with more than the merest smattering of legal knowledge.*"

I cannot profess myself to offer any opinion upon the working, the wants, or the efficiency of the College of Haileybury, as it is at present constituted and conducted.

It is a remarkable fact that not one of the witnesses examined before the Committees of the Houses of Lords and Commons, who have themselves been educated at Haileybury, and passed the better portion of their life in India—Mr. Bird, Sir George Clerk, Mr. Robertson, Sir Herbert Maddock, Mr. Millett—gives any information upon this subject.

Mr. Mills and Mr. Melville, neither of whom has been in India, nor, I believe, educated at Haileybury, are the only gentlemen examined on this head. The former appears not very well disposed towards the Institution: the latter supports it principally on account of the opportunity which it offers of acquiring a knowledge of the Oriental languages. Now it is curious that this is precisely the point upon which the supporters of the College in India seem least disposed to uphold it; and I believe that public opinion, could it be collected, would be almost unanimously in favour of devoting the time at present spent at Haileybury in studying the Oriental languages, to the acquisition of general substantive knowledge; and deferring the study of the languages of India until the arrival of the Civilian in this country; from a conviction, that generally speaking, very little really useful knowledge of the tongues is imparted at Haileybury: and that at any rate the facilities for such learning are infinitely greater here than at home.

Another ground, incidentally alluded to by Mr. Millett, is that Haileybury produces young men better qualified for Magisterial and Judicial duties than either of the Universities. This, though probably true in fact, amounts to nothing: for with the exception of lectures in Civil Law at Trinity Hall, neither Oxford nor Cambridge, so far as I am aware, even professes to train up Undergraduates in the study of the Law. What is the amount of the "smattering" of Law learnt at Haileybury, may be gathered from a perusal of the passage above quoted from the pamphlet on the Judicial System of India.

Common Sense. A vague rambling idea pervades the minds of the majority that a moderate acquaintance with the Vernacular, and such a knowledge of Native character, as a man picks up during his Revenue duties, are all that is requisite; and that 'Common Sense' (which might generally be more truly read 'uncommon nonsense',) will do the rest!

True it is that in the ordinary business of life we do not permit 'common sense' to cut off our leg, or even pull a tooth; nor do we expect a shoemaker to make a decent slipper without serving an apprenticeship—but for the purpose of adjudicating on points of life and death, and settling nice questions of title, and so forth, upon which depends the safe enjoyment of property—give a man a copy of the Regulations, and leave the rest to 'common sense'! Knowledge of the Law is perfectly unnecessary—indeed it is rather an incumbrance and a hindrance than otherwise. We don't want technicalities—English Law is full of quibbles—has he not the Regulations, together with a copious index, which renders reference easy, and almost mechanical, after a little habit? Procedure will be learnt with practice—and has he not the Circular Orders of the Court of Appeal, few and far between, it is true; but still all explanatory, as far as they go, of points of practice?—and then as to evidence; why let him *receive everything* that is offered, and give more or less weight to it, on perusal, according to the dictates of 'Common sense'; and if he is wrong—why there is an Appeal for the party imagining himself injured!

Such is literally the system, and the reasoning on which it is ordinarily sought to be supported—the results have been already sufficiently exhibited in these pages. If one ventures to hint that a practical and sound knowledge of the Law of Evidence would save a vast deal of time; shorten the record, prevent the frightful repetition of litigation; your antagonist does not see how that would be the case; if you proceed to point out that documents not receivable in evidence would be rejected, you are asked what is the use of that: the Judge *weighs* them—if you suggest that sheet after sheet of depositions are occcupied with Hearsay—The reply is "Hearsay! who does not know what hearsay is?" Though it would probably puzzle the gentleman to define it; or if you are cruel enough to venture to ask for such information, the answer is, as it has been to me, a ludicrous misapplication of Lord George Gordon's case; and if you should happen to produce one of the depositions in proof of your assertion, and proceed to point out a couple of consecutive pages or so of the merest hearsay, the answer is 'what a fool the Judge must be!'

Such are the arguments usually in vogue—though among the more reflecting portion of society the evil is admitted; the necessity of *some* remedy is obvious; and the controversy of opinions continues solely about the best nature of that remedy.

Law Com. Reports of 1838-42, laid before Parliament 1843.

It has formed the subject of anxious discussion before the Council of Bengal in 1838, and has been the subject of a special report of the Law Commission in 1842, the whole of which Papers have been presented to Parliament in 1843.

I shall refer copiously to these documents immediately. It will be observed that almost all who take up the question, however diverse their suggestions of amelioration, admit the defect of the system. The discussion arose out of a note, under date the 18th April 1836, by the late Mr. Shakespeare, calling for information from all the Presidencies, as to any rules which might exist for the training of Junior Civil Servants, from the time of their leaving College, until their employment as Joint Magistrate or Sub-Collector.

This arose, no doubt, from fears which suggested themselves to his mind, as to the effect which the abolition of the office of Register must sooner or later, have upon the fitness of the Civil Service for judicial office.

Abolition of Register's Office in Bengal.

It is to be observed, that in Bengal the Office of Register to the Provincial Courts was abolished in 1821, and that of Registrar to the Zillah Courts in 1831-32.

The effect of this measure was then beginning to be actually felt; or at any rate to suggest itself to those who took an interest in the subject.

In Madras.

The Office of Register was discontinued in the Madras Presidency in 1843.*

Plan.

Now before proceeding to these Reports, I may at once briefly state my own view of the most efficacious remedy, *in part*, for the present state of things.

Distinction of branches of service.

It is, first, to keep the Judicial Branch entirely distinct from that of the Revenue.

Preliminary Education.

Secondly, to have the young men *well* trained, *in the law of evidence;* not by mere lectures; but by absolute class-teaching, and frequent stringent examinations, until they are really thorough masters of the subject; let them also have a fair knowledge of the general principles of Jurisprudence, the Conflict of Laws, and an elementary acquaintance with the method of conducting civil and criminal trials; the examination and cross examination of witnesses; the usual grounds of objection to documentary evidence which arise during a trial; the way in which objections are taken, supported, disposed of, allowed, or overruled; the method of summing up, and the delivering of judgment.

Re-institution of Registerships.

Lastly, the immediate re-institution of the Office of Register to each of the Zillah Courts.

* By Act VII. of 1843, the Courts of Circuit were abolished, and the system put upon its recent footing. The office of Register was not abolished by the Act; but no Registers were appointed to the New Courts. No Act therefore would be necessary to re-institute them. The Government has only to nominate gentlemen to the office, if such a measure should be deemed expedient.

Mr. Shakespeare.

The Hon'ble Mr. Shakespeare in a Minute dated 3d May 1836, (page 486 of the Report) observes—

"I regret to find from the answer from the Secretary to the Bengal Government, in the judicial department, that no rules have been laid down for the employment of the junior civil servants on their first entering upon the public service. They are appointed assistants to the commissioners of revenue and circuit, to be employed, at the discretion of those officers, in any of the districts composing their respective divisions.

"2d. Is it possible that no better means can be devised for training men to the judicial administration of the country than this?

"3d. Is it possible that, under this course of tuition, they can acquire any knowledge whatever even of the forms of judicial proceeding, still less any acquaintance with the general principles of Hindoo and Mahomedan law, and the regulations under which they must, at no distant period, be called upon to administer justice to the people?

"4th. Defective as the system unquestionably was, under which young men, almost immediately on their quitting college, were intrusted with the decision of civil suits, though small in amount, the present system, under which the judge will take his seat on the bench, utterly ignorant of the forms of pleading, of the rules of appeal, and of the constitution and powers of the courts below, which he is expected to control, is a hundred times worse.

"5th. In the early stage of our administration, an assistant was directed to assist the register in procuring all acts of the courts to be executed, and in translating and transcribing papers, and in arranging and keeping the records of the courts.

"6th. When promoted to the office of register, he was empowered to try and decide suits to the amount of 200 rupees, which amount of jurisdiction was afterwards increased to 500 rupees. If of sufficient experience and tried ability, he might have been promoted to the office of assistant judge, or subsequently, when that office was abolished in 1814, he might have been specially empowered to decide suits equal in amount to those tried by the judge himself.

"7th. If from this grade he was appointed to the office of revenue collector, he obtained thereby an insight into the details of revenue management, of great assistance to him in adjudicating upon the relative tenures of the landed proprietors and their tenantry ; but he never could forget the instruction he had got during his judicial training, and he returned to that branch of the service (as was generally the case) better qualified than before for the high office of a judge.

"8th. But how is it now ? Literally in respect to the administration of civil justice, which I am particularly adverting to, he has no opportunity, as far as I can see, of acquiring the slightest information."

Mr. Pakenham.
Mr. McNaghten.

In the report of a Committee, held at Simlah, of which Mr. Pakenham and Mr. McNaghten were members, dated 24th May, and 23d June 1831, (page 487), we find as follows :—

Para. 3d. "In all countries considerable time is occupied in learning the principles of any liberal profession before an attempt is made at reducing them to practice, and this long after the ordinary period of education has passed. We see no reason why the office of judge in this country, more arduous perhaps than in any other, should alone be exempted from preliminary probation. The liberality of the pay granted during the probatory interval cannot alter the nature of the case. We should have thought that the preparation of cases, the collating or abstracting of papers, the taking of evidence, and reporting on accounts, were appropriate occupations for a young civil servant, and that if these duties can really be better performed by writers and mohurrers receiving one-tenth of their pay, the advantages of superior education cannot be very conspicuous; neither do we think that it by any means follows that the superior cannot derive relief from the employment of his subordinate without a transfer of responsibility.

Para. 5th. "We fully admit that the judge who has to pass a decision cannot be relieved from the duty of research and investigation ; but it is by no means evident to us that he might not derive most important aid from the employment of a junior civil servant in the conduct of ministerial duties. It does not follow that because this duty has been hitherto performed by the amlah, that it has been properly, impartially, and satisfactorily performed. Every thing is now done by ill-paid and irresponsible individuals, save only the actual decision or determination. We need not say how much the value of such decision or determination must depend on the fidelity of the preliminary proceedings.

Para. 6th. "We are of opinion that there is a great variety of duties in the Judicial Department in which the junior civil servants can be employed, independently of the decision of civil and criminal cases. We conceive that there are many ministerial duties, to aid in the performance of which their services would be most beneficial. The preparation of a case for decision is of itself a duty which would afford ample occupation to any junior servant attached to a civil court. It is a duty which, though of especial importance, requires only attention, integrity, and a competent knowledge of the native languages for its efficient performance. It is a duty, however, which is now of necessity left entirely to the amlah, and by the abuse of which there can be no doubt of their reaping a most abundant harvest, to the detriment of honest claimants and the general perversion of justice.

Para. 7th. "We see no objection to the junior servants being entrusted with the execution of decrees, or to their being employed in giving effect generally to all acts of the courts," &c.

It is true that Mr. Shakespeare says he has no wish to see the office of Register restored "which in fact has become in-"compatible with the extensive powers with which it was "necessary to invest the Native judges."

Mr. Ewer.

Mr. Ewer, Judge of the Sudder of the North West Provinces, on the 10th June 1836, minutes as follows:—(page 492).

"I would strongly recommend the re-establishment of the office of register, or something of the same description. At present I know not whence the supply of experienced judicial officers of the higher rank is to come from, while at the same time the administration of justice is hourly acquiring more importance, both in the eyes of the government and of the public."

"During the last year we have seen several instances of judges appearing in that character for the first time, without the slightest notion of the duties they were called on to perform in their own court, and altogether unable to control the proceedings of their inferiors. On one occasion, indeed, the Sudder have had the disagreeable duty of reporting an acting judge unfit for the office."

Sudder C. of N. W. Provinces.

And in a letter from Mr. Harrington, the Officiating Registrar of the Court, we find as follows:—

"The court concur generally in the sentiments expressed in Mr. Ewer's Minute: they apprehend that little doubt can be entertained that the abolition of the office in question, by doing away with the only school in which the junior servants of the Company had an opportunity of making themselves acquainted with the judicial regulations, and of acquiring an insight into the practical duties and powers of the civil courts before they were called upon to exercise the more extensive and responsible functions of a zillah or city judge, possessing under the system now in force original and appellate jurisdiction equal in extent to that which was vested in the late courts of appeal, must tend materially to impair the efficiency of the judicial establishment, while, as remarked by Mr. Ewer, on the occurrence of vacancies in that department, they must necessarily be filled up by men who have had little or no judicial experience, and who may then be called upon for the first time to preside in a court, whose decisions in a large proportion of the cases that come before it are final, and not open to appeal or revision by this court, or any other tribunal."

There is also a minute of Mr. Ross', dated 10th August 1836, (page 490) who disagrees with Mr. Shakespeare in certain suggestions of his for the better employment of young Civilians' time; and proposes that the whole matter be referred to the Law Commission: yet he acknowledges that "as "Mr. Shakespeare observes, they (the young Civilians) have "nothing to do with the administration of civil justice; and "consequently they cannot acquire that practical knowledge "of the business and proceedings of the Civil Courts, which "is requisite to qualify them for the office of a Civil Judge."

Sudder C. of Bombay.

The Sudder Court of Bombay in a letter dated 12th September 1837, express their opinions, thus—

Para. 17. "The defect under the existing system in the means of obtaining a judicial education for the junior members of the administration by that excellent school, the trying of original suits, adverted to in the 24th to 31st paras., has, I am directed to observe, more than once incidentally presented itself to the attention of the judges. The subject involves topics of the highest importance in the judicial system, and amongst these there appears to the judges a difficulty somewhat hard to be reconciled, which arises from the distinction of authority in the European and Native branches. If to the former are to be confined the high grades in judicature of appellate jurisdiction, it will, the judges conceive, be obvious that correspondent qualifications must be possessed by these functionaries; and amongst these the court would assign, at nearly the top of the list, a practical knowledge of the character, habits, and customs of the people, the attainment of which, however, appears to the judges to be hopeless, excepting by some such means as the schooling above adverted to. Upon the return of the absent judges, and when a full court can thereby be assembled, the subject will be brought on for consideration, with the able and judicious remarks Mr. Greenhill has offered, and the court will thereafter submit its sentiments to government."

Commissioners of S. Mahratta Country.

And the Judicial Commissioner of the Southern Mahratta Country writes on the 1st of August 1837, as follows:—

25. "The spirit of legislation has been of late to employ Natives as judges, either for the sake of economy merely, or for their supposed efficiency, reserving to the European civil servants the much more difficult and important office of judging on appeals, executing decrees, and of controlling the Native servants. These are delicate and difficult duties, requiring great practical knowledge of the detail of a court, and also an intimate acquaintance with the habits of the people, their usages, and rules of conduct. I shall not allude in this place to the knowledge of the rational rules of evidence, of practice, of procedure, and of jurisprudence generally requisite for a judge to possess; in short, I would say that something more is required of a judge of appeal and control than common sense, and a merely studied acquaintance with the Regulations, and that without it, a man of talent even, is not likely to fill the judgment seat, at first especially, with credit either to himself or the government."

26. "The operation, however, of our present Regulations is fast bringing the judicial branch of the service to a condition which I cannot contemplate without anxiety. The juniors have no opportunities of learning; they are partially employed in criminal cases only (and these necessarily of too serious a nature to be entrusted to a young

man on his first entrance on public employment), and probably have little or no opportunity of gaining an insight into the business of the civil courts, they are at once raised to the bench, where they have to sit in final judgment on the decrees of judges of far greater practical knowledge and experience than themselves; and that such a state of things would lead to a loss of public confidence, and to contempt of the judicial administration, I think there is too much ground for apprehension.

27. "The actual state of the judicial branch of the service seems to render an early and serious consideration of the subject of importance."

Lord Auckland.

On the other hand we have a long, washy Minute of Lord Auckland's—who objects generally to any early special training of young men—he doubts if a Judge in India can be pronounced as qualified,

"Who has not had considerable experience in revenue matters "and in the present business of the country; and who has not been "in that contact with the people and in that familiarity with their "prejudices, habits, attachments, merits, and faults, which a con-"nexion with their monied interest, an intimate knowledge of their "landed tenure, and the frequent view of their differences, apart "from the reserve and formality of a Court, seem best to promise."

To the truth of all of which a ready concurrence may be given. It is an argument which must cogently weigh against the introduction of English Barristers; but does not militate against teaching Judges a little Law.

He then goes on to observe that the Collector is a Magistrate and criminal Judge; that he must pick up a good deal of judicial knowledge in the course of his service; thinks the young men's leisure may be profitably employed in learning judicial business, but doubts if they have any leisure to spare; and refers the whole matter to the Law Commission.

Mr. Bird.

Mr. Wilberforce Bird follows on the same side, in a Minute of the 27th July 1838.

He thinks making a mere boy, just out of College, a Judge, was an anomaly—that the abolition of the Registrarship was therefore wise; and that it was proper to postpone the appointment of young men to the judgment seat, until they had obtained more experience. He thinks that a knowledge of judicial forms and proceedings is not the only requisite for a judge; (who ever supposed it was;) he should possess an intimate knowledge of the habits, &c. and then we have Lord Auckland repeated in other words.

He then quotes Lord Auckland, and continues:

" Moreover it is quite a mistake to suppose that a knowledge even " of judicial forms is not to be obtained in the offices of Magistrate and " Collector."

" Hence it appears that while the necessary qualifications of a Civil " Judge cannot be acquired without going through the office of a Col- " lector, *the offices of Collector and Magistrate afford an excellent pre- " paration for discharging the functions of a Civil Judge.*"

How excellent a preparation they really afford, let these pages testify! The records of cases which I have freely quoted are the decisions of the very men who have had this " excellent preparation." Observe especially the last criminal case cited in the Appendix, which is the decision of a gentleman who has had this " excellent preparation," and nothing else. And it is to be remembered that as the office of Register was only abolished in this Presidency in 1843, we are but at the beginning of the end; and if these judgments are the productions of gentlemen, some of whom had even the advantages which that school of training offered, what are we to expect when the present generation rises to the judicial bench?

Efficiency of Registers.

It has not escaped me, that this is an argument which may be turned against me. It may be fairly asked, if the office of Register produced no better fruits than those which are before us, what is the use of restoring it?

I would restore it *simply as an auxiliary;* the root of the evil lies deeper still. It is in the absence of any primary foundation in the principles of jurisprudence, and law of evidence, that it lies : formerly, even when a young man was a Register, he had to grope his way in partial darkness, according to the feeble light of his own reason—now, were he *primarily* instructed in the commonest rudiments of Law, the reinstitution of the Registrarship would afford him an admirable school for practice, and for the furtherance and perfection of his knowledge. Without this preparatory training, the reinstitution of the Office of Register would not, I am free to confess, be productive of much good.

Reasons against restoring Registrarships.

The main reason which appears to weigh with those who then considered the question, against the office of Register—I mean such of them as deemed *any* judicial training necessary—was, that as large jurisdiction had been given to the Native Officers, the Register would have nothing to do.

I confess I cannot think so. I should be averse to making the office one of even a partially judicial character—at any rate, if it were necessary partly so to employ the Registers, it should not be at the *commencement* of their career. They should be *purely ministerial* officers, such as are attached to the Court of Sudder and Foujdaree Adawlut, where there are no fewer than three, all of whose hands are fully occupied.

I have no apprehension but that there would be plenty of work of a purely ministerial kind for them to discharge ; from which the Judge might be advantageously relieved, and which in point of fact he ought not to be called upon to perform. Other duties might be attached to the office, were it necessary. I have asked the opinion of Civil and Session Judges well qualified to form an opinion upon the point ; and I have never heard but one reply, namely that there would be plenty for the Register to do.

Question of Expense.

It might probably entail an increase of expenditure, a serious stumbling block in the way, if the matter were left to the tender mercies of the Indian Government: but if the evil be apparent, and the remedy suggested appear likely to succeed, I apprehend that the English Legislature ought to step in, and take care, now that they have the opportunity for interference, to see that it is applied.

President of Council of Bengal.

On the 13th August 1838, the President in Council agrees with Governor General, but as no new arguments are offered, this Minute may be passed over without further notice.

Lord Ellenborough.

Here the matter appears to have slept, until Lord Ellenborough's arrival in India, who, on the 4th April 1842, addressed a letter to the Law Commission, the first topic of which was (p. 503.)

"The legal training in India of the Honorable Company's Civil "Servants, destined for the judicial branch of that service."

Law Commission.

This letter roused the Law Commission; from whom, on the 4th of November—verbosa et grandis epistola venit—we have a report of 163 paragraphs, of which, though it is difficult to understand why, those from 4 to 104 are taken up with a "concise "historical account of the several Judicial systems prevailing "at the three Presidencies of Bengal, Madras, and Bombay; "exhibiting their original character, and tracing them "through their various modifications to their present state." They then kindly add: "This narrative occupies paras. 4 to "104 of this address": as if with the express view of enabling his Lordship to turn at once to the matter on which he wanted information.

However, let us also get on to para. 105. They subscribe to the policy of giving Natives a greater share in the administration of justice; but they say, (page 522, para. 106.)

"In reducing it to practice an evil of a very serious nature has "been incurred, which already has been extensively felt, and which, "*if not remedied, will greatly impair the judicial administration.*"

This was written in 1842; yet here we are at the commencement of 1853, *and nothing* has been done.

They continue;

" We allude to that which has attracted your Lordship's atten-
" tion, the *absence of all previous training* in those, to whom as judges
" of first and local appeal, the Government must principally look for
" the guidance and control of the Courts of primary jurisdiction.
" *At present there is not a single situation in the civil branch of the*
" *judicial department of Bengal open to a covenanted servant before*
" *his elevation to the important office of Zillah Judge*; nor in Bom-
" bay do the Zillah or Assistant Judges exercise any original juris-
" diction before they are invested with appellate jurisdiction."

This was written in 1842, when the office of Register still existed in Madras; but in 1843 the present Madras judicial system was established: and thenceforth, the remarks of the Law Commission have been just as applicable to this as to the other Presidencies.

The Report then proceeds to suggest a remedy. It thinks that the field of selection for the Civil service should be as widely extended as possible; it points out the course of education which should be adopted in England, and immediately upon arrival in this country. The young Civilian, after acquiring a knowledge of two languages, should be attached to a Collector for three years, to the expiration of which the selection for the judicial department should be deferred, though it recognizes the necessity of an ultimate line of distinction and demarcation between the two branches of the services; and in order to secure this—

" The emoluments of the judicial branch (para. 141) should be so
" adjusted, as to render it on the whole the most lucrative branch of
" the service."

And I would add, honourable.

In paras. 124, 5, 6, the Commissioners make the following very important and judicious observations:

124. "It is chiefly at the beginning of his career, and whilst holding a subordinate situation, that the civil servant will find time for the prosecution of general inquiries, and the greatest readiness on the part of the natives to communicate their sentiments. The possession of superior office is at all times an obstacle to free communication with the people; nor would we advocate in the higher judicial functionary that familiarity of intercourse which would be useful and proper in the officers of revenue."

125. "To the acquisition of this description of knowledge the revenue systems of Madras and Bombay are peculiarly favourable; there, the annually recurring ryotwarry settlements require a constant and local intercourse between the revenue officers of government and the agricultural inhabitants, and the minute information respecting the interests of the different classes of the village communities, the various rights in land, and the instruments by which those rights are modified or transferred, necessarily acquired in the course of such detailed arrangements, cannot but prove valuable to the future judicial officer.

126. "We would therefore recommend for those presidencies that the civil servants, on being reported qualified to take a part in public business, should be attached as assistants to collectors and magistrates for the period of three years; that is, we would continue the initiatory system now in force there, which was introduced during the governments of Sir Thomas Monro and Mr. Elphinstone."

Balance of opinion.

On the whole, the balance of opinion seems vastly to preponderate in favour of an admission of a defective system; and the necessity for a remedy; and although the reinstitution of the Office of Register seems to have been thought generally not desirable, or indeed practicable, I confess that I have not seen reasons of any great weight adduced in support of that opinion; certainly none such as would counterbalance the good which might be expected to arise from such a measure. The reasons, so far as I can gather them, appear to be, a fear lest the Register should have nothing to do, and a natural unwillingness to incur outlay for the payment of a useless office. But if the first be not well founded, the second falls to the ground: if the institution of the office be a good, it should not be prevented, merely because it involves additional expenditure. The question may not be without its difficulties; its success may be problematical; but I can conceive no other scheme so likely to succeed.

And this brings me to the detail of the plan which has suggested itself to my mind as a practical remedy, if not the only one.

Law Commission—Results of.

One word, however, first, upon the substantive Law, and procedure, of the Civil and Criminal Law. I have, as I have before observed, purposely abstained from introducing this topic, as foreign to the immediate subject; and I only allude to it thus incidentally, in order that it may not be supposed, either, that I admit the perfection of the Law as it at present stands; or that its defects have escaped my notice. Very far from it. Much might be alleged upon this topic, were this the proper place for its discussion.

Paid Member of Legislative Council.

I will only remark in passing, that although from 1835 we have had a Legislative Council, one member of which has been nominally a Lawyer, and although the salary of that Officer has been enormous, amounting in 17 years to a total of £1,70,000, the amount of its practical labours has been by no means commensurate to the outlay, and public expectation has been year after year grievously disappointed, until, at last, hope deferred has made the heart sick of the whole concern.

Possibly a considerable amount of useful information has been collected; and certainly sundry very heavy blue books have been brought forth—a proposed Criminal Code proved an abortion, and was strangled at its birth; what few Acts have been produced, are drafted in the loosest and most unlawyerlike fashion, so that almost upon every oc-

Macauley's Code.

Legislative Acts.

casion when they have become the subject of discussion in the Supreme Court, a "coach and horses" have been easily driven through any given section: but, up to the present time no

Code for India.

Code, worthy of the name, has been prepared for all India; although it might have been imagined, that to any man wishing to illustrate his name, and hand it down immortal to Posterity, such an object would have been sufficient incentive to his ambition, even if he were not lured by the additional bait of £10,000 per annum, paid monthly, and with the strictest regard to punctuality. But the truth is, the office, from which so much has been expected, has been a mere job. From Mr. Macauley down to Mr. Bethune, we have never had a lawyer of any practice appointed. Theoretical men, having influence with the Ministry of the day, have been from time to time nominated. They have come out here at a comparatively advanced age, with the world before them where to choose, totally ignorant of the character and habits of the Natives, of their existing Laws and innumerable customs, and consequently unable to form any correct estimate of the wants and exigencies of the country.

Mr. Jackson.

During the few months which Mr. Jackson, the Advocate General of Calcutta, filled the office, he succeeded in pushing through a small but important body of Laws; and we have now unquestionably a ripe and able lawyer of large practice at the helm—but although

Mr. Peacock.

there can be little doubt that Mr. Peacock's drafts will be workman-like, it remains to be seen whether he will not be overwhelmed with the enormous amount of knowledge which he must necessarily acquire, before he can safely proceed to legislate for a country to which he is a stranger; and whether the habits of the Special Pleader will yield to the more enlarged requirements of the Legislator: but the appointment of a practical lawyer is an instalment of what is due to us; we must take the good the Gods provide us, and be thankful for it.*

But it is not after all, the state of the substantive Law, defective as that is, which is the main subject of just complaint; it is *the miserable system under which it is at present administered;* and the still more frightful prospect which awaits this unhappy country, if the British Legislature will still turn a deaf ear to our necessities. It is to the awful results of this feeble and insufficient system of judicial administration, the utter inability of the Judges to control the proceedings before them; the unnecessary swelling of the records, the prolongation of trials, and the increased repetition of litigation, which arise from the want of power in the Bench, and are permitted to rage unchecked, that we have all along pointed; for which we emphatically demand a speedy and effectual remedy; certain that if it be not extended to us *now*, we may look in vain for it for the next five and twenty years, unless indeed in the meantime, the evil should have become so intolerable, as to rouse even the unenergetic listless Hindoo to such an extent, as to endanger the continuance of our rule in India: and lastly it is to this state of things that I now address myself, with a view to submit for consideration, the plan, which, partly gathered from the conclusions and reports of others, partly the result of my own reflexions and experience, has suggested itself to my own mind.

Suggestions for a Remedy.

First then, the present confusion between the two branches of the service should forthwith absolutely cease and determine.

---

* Professor Wilson, in his history of India, suggests that the Chief Justice of Bengal should be a member of the Legislative Council. The proposition is not without its difficulties, and disadvantages; but it is not too much to say that if the present Chief Justice of Bengal, so learned a lawyer, so liberal a Reformer of the abuses of the Law, so accomplished a gentleman, and so experienced a man, could have had the task committed to him, years since we should have had Codes, Criminal and Civil, and of Procedure, well adapted to the wants of India at large.

Revenue and Judicial branches distinct.

The Judicial and Revenue Branches should be perfectly and permanently separate and distinct.

At what period selection for Bench to be made.

At what period those destined for the Judicial department should be selected; whether that selection should be deferred as long as possible, or made as early as possible, is a question which admits of much argument on both sides. I am disposed, however, to think that the sooner it is made the better, and that it should be made in England; although power should be reserved to draft into it such young Civilians, as, in the *earliest* part of their career in India, may display peculiar aptitude or inclination for the Judicial line.

Judicial Branch the more honorable.

The Judicial Branch should be made the object of ambition, as being the most honorable and distinguished, as well as being on the whole the more lucrative.*

Education at Home.

The Education of the young men at Home should include what is usually embraced, or rather what is not usually embraced in a liberal education, but by a fiction supposed to be so,

General.

History—Moral Philosophy—Natural Philosophy — Political Economy — Polite Letters.

Special.

Their Special education should comprise the general principles of Jurisprudence, conflict of Laws, procedure of Courts, and especially, the Law of Evidence, in which they could not be too thoroughly well ground-

* I wish to guard myself from the imputation of seeking to elevate the Judicial office at the expense of that of the Collector. The Collector is not, as his name would import, a *mere* Collector of Revenue. His office is one of a very high political character; the peace and well-being of the whole district rests mainly in his hands; and a union of no ordinary talents, firmness, kindness, accessibility, sound judgment, must centre in him who fitly fills this important post. Able men must always be selected as Collectors; but their duties will be all the lighter and easier of performance, if the Judges are made equal to a fit discharge of theirs.

ed. The greater part of the first Volume of Starkie, that most philosophical of Law writers, might possibly be the text book, well commented on, illustrated, and explained, by one fully master of his subject, practically, as well as theoretically.

This grounding in the elementary principles of Law *must take place at home, if at all.* Here, there is no one who can impart such knowledge; and without this foundation be laid, the reinstitution of the Registerships would be a mere farce.

In such an office, a young man, already tolerably acquainted with the principles of Law, might fairly enough be expected materially to improve, if not perfect himself; but to put him in such a position, without having previously enabled him to take advantage of it, would be, as though we should place a book before a man, and ask him to read it in the dark.

Neither could the present race of Judges impart to the tyro a learning which they themselves do not possess. True they might point out the Regulations and Acts as objects of study: and teach the practice and procedure of the Mofussil Courts; but of the philosophy of the Law, which is its life, they could teach nothing, because they know nothing.

There is a passage in Coke upon Littleton, which neither he who teaches, nor he who learns the Law, can too constantly bear in mind.

"The reason of the Law is the life of the Law: for though a man "can tell the Law, if he know not the reason thereof, he shall soon "forget his superficial knowledge. But when he findeth the right "reason of the Law, and so bringeth it to his natural reason, that he "comprehendeth it as his own, this will not only serve him for the "understanding of that particular case, but of many others: for "'cognitio legis est copulata et complicata:' and this knowledge "will long remain with him."

"Tunc unumquodque scire dicimur, cum primam causam scire "putamus. Scire autem est proprie rem ratione, et per causam "cognoscere."

The "*reason* of the Law which is the life of the Law" must be learnt in England: the particular laws, and their practice, by which this country is governed, may be taught here.

At the close of the first year, the examinations would, in the usual course, determine who were the most promising candidates for the Judicial Branch; although, as boys will be boys, there should be a locus penitentiœ, so that they should have an opportunity of recovering lost ground, say until the end of their second year.

Time of coming to India deferred.

The time at which the young Civilian comes out to India might be advantageously deferred, especially in the case of those of more studious habits, from among whom the future Judges would be selected. Little or no good results from learning the Oriental languages in England: the same time might be much more profitably employed: and the languages are more easily, as well as more thoroughly learnt in India, than at home. Finally, after the selection was made, the young Civilian for the last year of his English career should attend the English Courts of Justice, and watch their forms of proceeding, and methods of conducting trials.

Oriental languages.

Frequenting English Courts.

Education in India.

I would abolish the College here. But little good is attained by a prolonged residence at the Presidency. Debt is frequently incurred: and balls and parties are more attractive than work; though I am bound to say that as a body the conduct of the young Civilians of this Presidency is very exemplary. Still I think that all the advantages, without any of the disadvantages, of College, may be secured by the young men proceeding at once, on their arrival, to join some one of the Collectors in the Provinces.

Young Civilians to proceed to Collectors forthwith.

Necessity of acquaintance with the people.

It is impossible to feel more strongly than I do, the absolute necessity which exists for the future Judge intimately acquainting himself with the habits, manners, merits, and defects of the Natives; of a thorough knowledge of the working of the Revenue System: of his making himself a good practical Vernacular Scholar; not of the high-flown poetical language in which the Moonshee rejoiceth, but the every-day language of the ordinary body of the people. Too much stress cannot be laid upon the importance of a thorough mastery of the Native tongue. A want of complete familiarity with the language of witnesses, generally an ignorant, agricultural, half-savage population, speaking a mere patois, throws the Judge, it is to be feared, very much into the hands of the clever, unscrupulous, Native Officials of his Court; and I have myself seen an instance in which a Mofussil Judge, thoroughly master of the Telugu, repeatedly checked the Interpreter, in minute but important points, where, in expressions perfectly idiomatic, the spirit had evaporated in the process of translation; though an ordinary observer could find no fault with the sense of the sentence as rendered by the Officer. How different the spoken dialect of the people is from the College-taught language of the Moonshees, may be gathered from the following fact. A very active Member of the Civil Service, whom I met once, some two hundred miles in the interior, and whom I had not seen since he left College, told me that, although he had obtained the honorary reward for extra-proficiency at College, he found when he joined his Collector, he literally knew *nothing* that was practically of any service to him; and to use his own expression he had since picked up the language "at the plough-tail;" and that is where alone it can be picked up: by frequent, familiar, continual intercourse with the common people of the District.

Languages.

It is during his early years that this knowledge of character, language, Revenue System, is to be most readily and most surely acquired: and I think, therefore, that the young Ci-

Four years with Collector.

vil Servant should remain with the Collector for four years: at the expiration of which, upon his obtaining from his superior a certificate of a knowledge of the prevailing language of the district, and general qualification, he should be eligible for, and promoted to a Registership of a Zillah Court.

Registership.

This office I think should be purely ministerial; or at any rate no Jurisdiction should be attached to it until after some experience of its duties, and the general working of the Mofussil practice were attained.

General duties of.

The Register should prepare the cases for trial on both the Civil and Criminal sides of the Court; analyze pleadings; sit with the Judge in Court; be always accessible to the Suitor; issue all mesne process; file all papers: take minutes of all proceedings; and notes of evidence when so directed by the Judge; draw up all Decrees from the Judge's minutes; have the conduct of all Judicial correspondence; and issue and see to the carrying out of all process of execution. He might also be ex-officio Register of Deeds, if the Draft Act for Registration of Deeds becomes Law. I apprehend that if he effectually discharged these duties, he would have ample to occupy his time. Indeed the Judge's time is more than completely occupied. In page 22 of the Foujdaree Criminal Reports, Mr. Walker, Judge of Nellore, in answer to a query from the Foujdaree, as to how he came to omit to examine a witness to a point of particular importance replies: "By orders of 11th November 1847, I "am bound to set forth on the first page of the record of my "proceedings, that I have attentively perused and considered "the documents received with the criminal record, before pro-"ceeding to trial. *But the truth is, that if I were to attempt "such a task, the business of the Court would soon come to a "stand-still. I am obliged to trust to the eyes of one of my minis-"terial officers*:" and such, I believe, would be the candid avowal of the great majority, if not all, of the Judges of this Presidency.

In this office he should continue at least four years. His next step involves a further change in present arrangements, which requires a brief notice.

Separation of Magisterial functions from Collector's office.

Under the existing system, the Collector of the Revenue is also the chief Magistrate,* as well as head of Police,† of the entire District, often of enormous extent, and as large as several English Counties put together.

It is said, that if the Collector were to cease to be the head of Police, the collection of the revenue would be impossible. I know not how that may be; though if it be true, it does not speak very highly for the present method of collection : but if it be so, certainly the collection of revenue is not to be endangered; nor can there be any objection to the Collector continuing to be the head of the Police, if he has time to discharge such duties. Indeed, as it is desirable that there should not be frequent changes in the control of such an Establishment, perhaps his management is the best that could be devised; but I do think that ordinary Magisterial functions ought to be separated from the office of the Collector. If that officer does his duty, he has ample, more than ample, to employ him in the management of the District, and collection of the revenue: and although he should still be a Justice of the Peace, so as to enable him to act upon emergent occasions, I think the ordinary run of Magisterial business ought to be discharged by a distinct officer. I believe that such a change would be hailed by the heads of revenue departments, as a most opportune relief from their heavy and responsible duties. And this is the office to which the Judicial officer should be next promoted—he should however act under

Collector still to be Superintendent of Police.

Collector to be still Justice of the Peace.

* See Reg. IX. of 1816.

† See Reg. XI. of 1816.

the general orders and control of the Collector, who should have the power of ordering him to proceed anywhere in the district upon special duty. Steps ought also to be taken for rendering available the services of Zillah and Regimental Surgeons, for the purpose of instituting post-mortem examinations in cases of suspicious sudden deaths. A form of inquest is gone through by the Village and Police officers; but independently of their accessibility to bribes, it is apparent how very insufficient the inquest of ignorant Natives must necessarily be, especially in cases of poisoning, in a climate where corruption so speedily follows death, and where burning, not burying, is the ordinary mode of disposing of the body.

Inquests.

Duties of Magistrate.

The Magistrate, besides his summary powers, would take depositions, and prepare all Criminal cases for trial by the Sessions Judge. He would still be young enough to move rapidly about the District without personal inconvenience: and in this duty he should be employed for four years.

Bench.

Then, upon receiving a certificate of due discharge of his duties from the Collector, he should be eligible for the Bench; whither he would arrive after about twelve years training, of that miscellaneous character, which alone can duly qualify a man for the exigencies of Indian Judicial office.

Zillah Judge.

Then he would advance through the grades of Subordinate Judge, and Zillah Judge, to that of a Judge of the Sudder and Foujdaree Adawlut.

Thus, it appears to me, would be raised up a body of well trained Judicial officers. One great argument against the plan, is the lapse of time which must necessarily take place, before its effects come into sensible operation. I am not unaware of this; but I see no other course open.

Sudder Court.

With respect to the Sudder itself, I would entirely remodel it. At present the conflicting cries are 'abolish the Supreme Court,' 'smash the Sudder.' My views will either displease, or reconcile both parties. I would amalgamate the two. This is not an Age to be frightened at names, or to stand upon dignity or precedence. It matters not what the new Court should be called; College of Justice, Sudder, or Supreme Court; or whether the Judges, Queen's and Company's, should be placed upon a perfect equality, or whether the latter should sit as Assessors to the former. For my own part, I would have them all of equal rank. They should be four in all, two of each; and the Chief Justice should have the casting voice, when opinion was equally divided. They should retain the present original Supreme Court jurisdiction, and hold quarterly Sessions, as at present, for the delivery of the Presidency Jail; and they should be the Highest Court of Appeal for the whole of the Mofussil provinces.

Juncture of Supreme and Sudder Courts.

Jurisdiction.

By these means each class of Judges would be of much assistance to the other; and either would add considerable strength to the Judicial Bench. On the one hand the Company's Judges would bring intimate acquaintance with the language, character, customs of the people; on the other the Queen's Judges would add all the weight of their authority upon questions of substantive law; and with a Chief Justice of any calibre, we might look to see general principles laid down, and judgments adapting the Law to the wants of Society; while there is, perhaps, nothing which would so well serve to fill the gap, and ameliorate the present state of administration of justice, until the course which I have proposed, with a view to raise up a well trained body of Mofussil Judges, should have come into full and perfect operation.

Our own Mercantile Law, which owes its very existence to

the fostering hand of Lord Mansfield, is an instance of what may be done, in a Judicial way, in adapting the customs of a country to the extending wants of society. Never was there a kingdom offering better opportunities for a master-mind than India in its present transition state. The Supreme Court Judges have done somewhat. The Hindoo Law does not recognize a Will; yet I fancy that within the jurisdiction of the Supreme Court any decision seeking to uphold such a doctrine now, would be met with universal opposition. So, from the peculiar nature and frame-work of Native society, the members of a family, Fathers, Brothers, Uncles, Cousins living undivided, and having their property in common, it is obvious that opportunities must constantly arise for laying down fundamental principles for future precedent and guidance. Take for instance the rights of a party to insist upon division, the powers of the managing member, under what circumstances he may bind the other members; to what extent common property may be alienated, and a thousand others which might easily be suggested—on all of which authoritative law might be established by a Court understanding the principles of Jurisprudence: and we should no longer have the melancholy picture now exhibited, of the Sudder Court, as each individual case happens to arise, leaning on their Pundits, who put forth opinions contradictory to each other and to themselves, taking their authorities from works which do not apply in this Presidency; and then finding the highest Court in the land laying down, and publishing, at various times, diametrically opposite decisions upon the same point; looking only to the exigency of the case immediately before them, without reference to any general plan, or view of building up and constructing a system of Laws for the future governance of the millions over whom they preside.

Difficulties no doubt exist in the way of the execution of this project. The difference of forms of procedure between the two Courts is perhaps the principal: the right of preaudience of the Bar another; and others might be easily enumerated; but they are rather matters of detail, which difficult as they may be, could no doubt be made to yield to a little careful deliberation. I believe that so far as the Civil Service themselves are concerned, the change would not be distasteful. The Queen's Judges would thus have plenty of occupation found them; and there can be little doubt that the erection of such a Court, powerful as its hands would be, must prove of permanent and sterling benefit to the people at large.

Such a change might very much facilitate the introduction of the so-called Black Acts; and would, probably, ere long effectually check the present shameful abuse of pleading, as well as other anomalies of practice.

Another advantage would be the decrease in expense consequent upon keeping up one Establishment instead of two; a consideration which may probably go far in the eyes of those who can see no other advantages in it, to render this part of the scheme popular.

Tenure of Judicial Office.

All European Judges should hold their offices 'dum bene se gesserint.'

No exparte case for Sudder.

The Government should no longer consult the Sudder for opinions on exparte cases, but all references on such matters should be made to their own Law officers.*

Judges not to be employed on other duty.

The Sudder Judges, and indeed all Judges, should be exempt from liability to detachment on duties not specially judicial.

The Subordinate Judges should, however, cease to be, as now, partly ministerial officers, or rather grand jurymen, deciding in the first instance whether there is sufficient evidence on

---

* Since the earlier pages of this Essay were struck off, the Government has taken measures for putting a stop to the practice above complained of.

the depositions to secure the probability of a conviction. A great deal of valuable time is thus wasted, without any corresponding advantage gained; and I think, that if instead of

Situation of Courts.

holding the Civil Judge's Court and that of the Subordinate both at the Zillah or Principal station, the Court of the Subordinate Judge were removed to some such locality as might be found the best suited in each district, away from the Zillah Town, much of the evil at present resulting to the population at large from the enormous distances to which they have to travel in prosecution or defence of suits, and as witnesses, would be obviated.

Tables of Fees.

Tables of Fees should be prepared by the Sudder Court for all practitioners. Taxing officers should be attached to each Court. Taxation might

Taxing Officer.

form part of the duties of the Registers, and the most public notification of this innovation should be published in every Town and village in Madras.

Filing of Documents.

All documents should be filed with the pleadings, or at any rate be then marked by the Register, whenever practicable; this alone would put a stop to a considerable quantity of forgery and perjury.

Sentence to be passed by Sessions Judge.

The practice of the Sessions Judge not himself passing sentence, but merely recommending it, seems an anomaly. He who has observed the demeanour of witnesses, is the person who can best judge of their credibility. Constituted as the Courts are, it is true, one shudders at the idea of the power of life and death being entrusted to such hands; but if the Bench were once raised in quality, and the judgment-seat occupied by men capable of rejecting what is not evidence, and forming a correct estimate of the weight of what is, it would be probably found advantageous that sentence should be pronounced by the Court of original jurisdiction in the first instance, a power of reversal or mitigation being still vested in the Court of Foujdaree Adawlut.

Criminal Appeals.

Pleaders should be heard orally in criminal appeals, just as they are in civil appeals. It is not reasonable that while a man may be heard for hours on a question involving property of the amount of four Rupees; his mouth must be closed in a case which affects his life.

Arbitration.

Another point to which enquiry might probably be directed with advantage is the working of references to arbitration.* My own experience of the Punchayet in the Mofussil is too limited for me to offer any opinion—but if the practice there at all correspond with what takes place daily in the Presidency, the more restrictions that are placed upon it the better.

In Madras, a reference to arbitrators is generally the source of prolonged delay; and the office, as usual, is made the medium of extortion—each party appoints his arbitrators; customarily, far too many in number; and occasionally an umpire is named in the first instance.

The richer or more influential party bribes the arbitrators of the other side, and the result is that *years* often elapse before any decision is arrived at: or if the Punchayet be *virtuous*, each side proposes its own award in favour of the parties by whom it was appointed. If it comes to the umpire, he sides with the wealthiest or strongest.

Appeals checked.

Some measure should be introduced to check the excessive abuse of appeals. It may be a hardship, with the present quality of Judges, to

* See Reg. XXI. of 1802, V. and VII. and XII. of 1816.

make this act take immediate effect, but even as things are at present, I question if the general good and peace of society would not be advanced thereby, even though purchased at the cost of much individual hardship. 'Interest reipublicæ ut sit finis litium.'

Education for Native Judges and Pleaders.

As I have proposed a course of education for the European, so I would extend a similar system, although the instruction need not be either of so long duration, or so high a quality, to the Native Judges and Pleaders.

I fully coincide in the opinion that it was wise and just to give the Natives a larger share than heretofore in the administrations of public justice, and believe that, on the whole, the measure has worked well. It would be inexpedient to recede from that measure: indeed I hope to see the day when *educated* Natives shall be admitted to a far wider extent in all departments of the public service. My own conviction, arrived at by a careful perusal of the Sudder Reports is, that the Native Judges, as a body, are far more capable of weighing testimony, and far more often arrive at reasonable conclusions, than the English gentlemen who are placed immediately above them. Perhaps this is to be traced to the fact of their having generally either acted as Pleaders, or performed quasi Magisterial or Police duties for a considerable period, before they are appointed to the Bench; and still more probably to their more intimate acquaintance with the intricate mazes of Native character: still they would discharge their duties far more efficiently, if they were regularly trained. General education alone can guard against the chance of corruption.

Course of study.

If any Collegiate Class is ever to be established in connection with the High School, certainly a class in Law is that which is most needed, and which would be most easily carried out.* In this, all Native candidates for Judicial office, or the situation of Pleader, should receive plain, sensible instruction, unshackled by technicalities, in the Law of Evidence, the Regulations, and Legislative Acts, and the Mahomedan and Hindoo Law; they should pass examinations, and take degrees in Law; after which only should they be qualified for office; and indeed some such course as this would, in my opinion, go far to remove "the foul vices of untruthfulness and dishonesty," which the Native Pleaders and Judges at present have, in common with their fellow countrymen; because the pursuit and study of Law as a Science, and its application on scientific principles in practice, raise up, as it were, in most men's minds, a sort of artistic and technical love of justice. There does exist at present, an examination for Native Judges,† and Pleaders;‡ but it is scarcely necessary to observe that it can be of very little value, where the examiners themselves are nearly ignorant of the subject.

Degrees.

---

* A few days since, it was generally believed that Collegiate Classes, and among them, a Law Class, were on the point of being established, in conformity with the urgent recommendations of the University Board, and the Judges of the Sudder Adawlut.

However the whole has again been put off on the pretext of its prematurity—a jest so stale that it has ceased to be amusing.

But this last kick at Education will perhaps convince the Authorities at home, that if they really have the cause at heart, it is high time to take the whole matter into their own hands.

The following question would form a very pretty subject of inquiry; and elicit a curious mass of information.

"What has been the course pursued with reference to the Madras High School, "since its founder, Lord Elphinstone, left it, ten years ago; and how is it, that while "in Bengal and Bombay, Education, as a government measure, has spread far and "wide, it has been stationary or retrograding at Madras?"

Perhaps there are influential parties in England, who, being awake to this, will bring it forward.

† See Rules for the examination of Candidates for District Moonsiffships, and for granting Diplomas published in the Fort St. George Gazette 28th July 1843.

‡ See Reg. XIV. of 1816 and Act No. 27 of 1836, by which the Candidates for Pleaderships are to be examined—by the Mufti and Pundits of the Sudder Court!

Assessors.

Anything which gives the people an acquaintance with the method of administering the Laws is, so far, a good; and therefore I should retain the present Act (VII. of 1843, Sec. 32) under which two or more Natives can be chosen to sit as Assessors with the Judge in Criminal trials. It is true, that in practice, this plan is of little or no avail, for the Judge is empowered by the same Act to overrule the Assessors, if he does not agree with their opinion. Still it is an introduction of the people to a share in the administration of the Law under which they live, at any rate a semblance of it; if it answers no other purpose, it may help to spread among Native society a little more knowledge of the Law than they at present have; and at the worst, if it is productive of no good, I do not see how it can work any harm. Indeed I should pause long before proposing to invest the Natives, such as they are now, with any of the actual powers of Jurymen. They would probably use such powers very detrimentally to the ends of justice.

Jury, Petty.

It has been thought in some influential quarters, that the introduction of our Jury system into the Mofussil would be a wise measure, and productive of much good.

In such an opinion I cannot concur. In the present state of society and education among the Natives, it would not be safe to invest them with powers, which would, in their hands, be only fearful instruments of extortion or revenge. There exists in the Provinces no other body of men from whom Juries could be selected; and it is worthy of remark, that for the last five-and-twenty years all the machinery has been ready; but the Regulation "for the gradual introduction of trial "by Jury into the criminal judicature of the territories sub-"ject to the Presidency of Fort St. George"; (X. of 1827,) has ever been a mere dead letter, simply from the impossibility of applying it.

Grand Jury for Madras.

Whilst on this subject, it may not be out of place to notice the Grand Jury of Madras. Opinion at home seems to be somewhat divided as to the expediency of a longer continuance of this office in England; but in event of an amalgamation of the Supreme and Sudder Courts, the present criminal jurisdiction of the former being retained, I would most unquestionably keep the present Grand Jury system intact.

Seven years' service as Clerk of the Crown, has convinced me that it is a very useful and formidable barrier against Native vengeance and cupidity.

Private bills very seldom get safely through the Grand Jury room; and were it not for this safeguard, every Sessions would see the Court deluged with cases, preferred for the mere purpose of intimidating parties into the payment of money, or to avenge real or supposed injuries.

Mooftis and Pundits to be abolished.

I would abolish all Pundits and Mooftis as speedily as possible—perhaps the easiest way would be to let the present incumbents die silently out, appointing no fresh ones in their stead.

Pleadings reformed.

I would totally reform the present system of Pleading; but this is a point which appears to me to rest in a great measure within the power of the Judges;* the Regulation is plain enough in its terms and meaning: an enormous abuse has crept in, and the Sudder have merely to issue a Circular Order desiring Pleaders to state only facts, with a threat of fine if the order be disobeyed, at once to remedy this mal-practice.

* It is worthy of remark that although the Regulations of 1802 are silent on the point, Reg. VI. of 1816, (for District Moonsiffs) in Sections XVIII. and XXIV. expressly points out that it "shall be the duty of the District Moonsiffs to prevent, "restrain and discourage as much as possible the insertion of irrelevant matter" in the plaint and answer respectively. I presume that such a caution in the case of the superior Judges was deemed superfluous. Yet even the superior Judges are directed by Reg. XIV. of 1816, Sec. IX. cl. 3 to prevent the introduction of "irregular, irrelevant, and otherwise objectionable" pleadings.

Arguments.

At the same time, as the Pleaders would thus be cut out from offering any observations in support of their respective cases, some Legislative provision should be made for the allowance of arguments, either oral or in writing, as expediency might suggest, at some more convenient stages of the cause.

Stamps abolished.

All "Law-taxes" should be abolished: stamps on Appeals especially: and if this would seriously affect the Revenue, let some more equitable tax be levied in its stead.

Special Commissions.

In all investigations carried on by Special Commissions under Reg. IX. of 1822 or other Acts, not simply for the purpose of reporting, but of adjudication, Appeal should lie to the Foujdaree, and not, as now, to the Revenue Board.

Education of the people.

Lastly, but not least, I would move Heaven and Earth to educate the people.

Codes.

As before observed, I have purposely refrained from any observations upon the present state of the Substantive Law of the Land, as not falling within the province of this pamphlet. A Criminal Code, it is understood, there is some likelihood of our soon obtaining. This, if it finally throws off the shackles of the Mahomedan Law, will be one great step in advance. Another, not less important, would be to supervise and codify the Civil Regulations; for although, bating some vague generalities, such as ordering Judges to "act according to "justice and equity, and good conscience;"* and informing Collectors that they are to regulate their demands "on prin- "ciples of moderation, and with a just regard, to the rights "of Government, to the rights of the people, and the prospe- "rity of the country;"† it cannot be denied that the early

* Reg. 2 of 1802, Sec. XVII. † Reg. 2 of 1803, Sec. XXXIX.

Regulations of 1802-3, taken almost literally from the Bengal Regulations of 1793, present a bold, broad, admirable sketch of a judicial system, and,—'aut Porson aut Diabolus'—betray the hand of a right sound Lawyer, or his Personal Representative—yet the Acts of succeeding years become more and more feeble, and indefinite; they have been passed to meet particular exigencies, and not upon any general plan; and what with repealing Acts, or Sections of Acts, here and there, the whole body of Laws is in much the same state of confusion as the Statute Book of England.

Thus I think I have touched upon all the evils which have suggested themselves to me, and developed what I conceive a plan affording a specific remedy for each.

Necessity of Parliament taking the matter into their own hands.

I am aware that it may be said that a great many of these changes require no Legislative interference; that some are already within the power of the Judges of the Sudder Court; and others may be effected by the Indian Government—but this is not so with respect to all—especially with respect to the amalgamation of the Supreme and Sudder Court, one of the principal features, perhaps, the most important, in the whole scheme. But independently of this, the desirability of having the whole matter taken up at one time, and by one Power, instead of having fragmentary improvements carried out piecemeal by different authorities, and in different quarters of the Globe, is too obvious to require argument: but especially is it necessary in this instance; because if we may judge of the future by the past, looking to the fact that so far back as 1838 the highest authorities in India pointed out the evil, that in 1842 the Legislative Council proposed a remedy, and yet, with matters growing worse from day to day, nothing has been yet effected or even attempted, it requires no ghost to foresee, that if Parliament lets slip the present opportunity, the only one it may have for the next quarter of a century, nothing will be done; and the people of India will again be delivered over, bound hand and foot, to the apathy and neglect of the East India Company.

Conclusion.

And now my task is done. I could not come personally to England to give my testimony against the present system; nor indeed if I had, should I, an unknown man, in all probability have found either place or opportunity, for a hearing. It is perhaps better as it is. I have contributed my quota towards throwing light upon one of the many questions which must engage the attention of the Legislature at the present crisis. The fourth topic for Parliamentary Enquiry by the Committees of both Houses is "The judicial establishments of British, India, European, and Native: *the modes of administering justice*, civil and criminal, and the *working of the system*, "as exhibited by tables of *trials*, *appeals*, and *decisions*."

Noble and Honorable members shall at least, to use a legal phrase, be affected with such notice, as ought to put them upon further inquiry: and shall not have it hereafter to say, that it was for lack of information that they stood aloof, or neglected to investigate, report, or legislate upon the subject. Listening to vague generalities in the Palace at Westminster is of no avail. Let a Commission issue, to take evidence out here, upon the spot. Then only will the root of the matter be got at.

I have looked in vain through the late ponderous Blue Books on Indian Affairs to discover, if possible, any inkling of a disclosure of the present abuses; but in vain.

In the evidence taken before Committee of the House of Lords, I can only find one question (No. 2166) which immediately bears upon this subject. In that taken before the Committee of the Lower House, there are figures of formidable array, and statistical returns enough, in all conscience; and they may possibly afford a great deal of useful information, although there is no more magic in figures than there is in words.* I observe that the Governor of Madras, in his Minute, states that the work done in the course of the year is "on the whole satisfactory" in *quantity* perhaps; but the question of *quality* appears never to have been submitted to his consideration. Jeames's—"plentiful, but coarse—very" —would otherwise have more aptly characterized the formidable looking piece de resistance. So the work be done, no matter *how* it is done: and this is precisely the point on which it is to be feared that the Committees of both Houses would be kept totally in the dark, unless, as now, some one came forward to put them on the right scent—I have started and hallood the game—let better sportsmen run it down.

Full of my subject, I have written, "currente calamo," almost as I would have spoken, in haste to save the Post; careless about the graces of style, or even accuracy of diction: content to use such words as first suggest themselves to my pen's point; so my language does best serve, clearly and pointedly to convey my meaning. My opinions may be erroneous; my suggestions valueless; my plans impracticable; but my facts remain; they are above suspicion, and cannot be refuted. They require neither advocacy nor comment. They speak for themselves. I have called things by their right names, it is true. In my citations, I have still been mindful of Othello's caution—

> "In your letters,
> "*When you shall these unhappy deeds relate,*
> "Speak of them as they are: nothing extenuate,
> "Nor set down aught in malice."

I have attached my name to this Essay, not from a belief that that can add to its authority, but in order that it may not go forth anonymously, as though its author were either afraid or

* Truly does Carlyle observe of Statistics, "Tables are abstractions, and the object a most concrete one, so difficult to read the essence of. There are innumerable circumstances; *and one circumstance left out, may be the vital one* on which all turned."

Statistics, usually regarded as "the extracted elixir of the matter," are too often mere "wash and vapidity, good only for the gutters."

ashamed to own its parentage. I know what I have written; and am responsible for each word of it; able and willing to maintain the truth of every fact against all comers. I have done my ministering as gently as a strong sense of indignation would at times permit me. It may be, that in cutting somewhat rudely across the grain of the Civil Service's prejudices and habits of thinking, I may have raised against myself the hostility of a powerful and influential body of men, but I shall lay my head upon the pillow all the more easily this night, from a consciousness, that come what may of it, I have laid bare, and put my finger upon an ulcer, which must spread and fester, until it eats into and rots the very body of Society, so no remedy be applied.

The matter is now in the hands of the Parliament of England, either at once to interfere, or to institute fuller investigation; a course more imperatively imposed upon them by their national character for benevolence and generosity; because their assistance is asked on behalf of many millions who cannot represent their own grievances; nay possibly, as I have observed at the outset, scarcely comprehend the enormity of the evil under which they unfortunately, but at the same time, too surely suffer.

APPENDIX No. I.

Nos. 41 of 1848 and 20 of 1849.

1. This Suit was originally brought by the Respondent, as Plaintiff, for the recovery of a village called Goodam, with other lands, yielding annually Rupees 1,150. A further claim was also made for Rupees 12,650, the value of the produce of the above for a period of 11 years.

2. The Plaintiff alleged that the property in question had been transferred to his mother by his father the 5th Defendant, under a Deed of gift called a Hibbanamah, dated the 11th Rajaboo of Hejery A. D. $\frac{1236}{1823 \ \& \ 24}$, and that the Title Deeds, &c. were then made over to his mother; the management only of the property being left with his father.

That on the death of his mother his father having contracted a Nikah marriage, executed to him (Plaintiff) and his brothers an agreement dated 30th January 1830, conditioning to give up to them, whenever they might demand it, the whole of their late mother's estate to which under the Hibbanamah formerly executed by him to their mother, they were the legal heirs.

That his brother being dead he, Plaintiff, as the sole heir of his late mother, sued the Defendants for the property in question, they having obtained possession of it in 1836 and 1839 under bills of sale, which the 5th Defendant had fraudulently executed to them.

3. The 1st and 3d Defendants filed separate answers, alleging that the plea put forth by the Plaintiff was a false one; the Hibbanamah and the subsequent agreement alleged to have been executed by the 5th Defendant being forgeries got up by collusion between the 5th Defendant and the Plaintiff to defraud them of property, which they had legally acquired by open purchase, and at a price equal to its full value. That their bills of sale were duly registered in the Zillah Court, and immediate possession taken under them; and that moreover when the Deeds of Sale in 1836 were executed to the 1st Defendant, the Plaintiff and his brothers were present and stated nothing in objection to the transactions, in which their father the 5th Defendant was then engaged.

4. The 1st and 3d Defendants further observed that the whole of the property sold to them had been previously mortgaged to other parties by the 5th Defendant, and that it was to prevent the disadvantageous foreclosure of such mortgages that the lands, &c. were sold to them. That besides the above transactions Suits have been filed in the

Civil Courts against the 5th Defendant by different parties, and sales, have been effected under the decrees of the said Courts for lands, which are equally with the lands now sued for included in the Hibbanamah referred to; but that up to the institution of the present Suit no mention has ever been made of the existence of that document.

5. The other Defendants were proceeded against exparte.

6. The Civil Judge decided in favor of the Plaintiff.

7. In his decision the Civil Judge observed, that, "the case was a "simple one—the Plaintiff sued the 5th Defendant his father for "illegally selling and disposing of his mother's dowry, or Mahur, "which by rights he is the legal heir to, and the 1st and 3d Defen- "dants, &c. for purchasing it." The Hibbanamah and other documents the Civil Judge stated, to be "clearly proved by his (Plaintiff's) "witnesses and to be declared in Mahomedan Law legal, and legally "drawn up—and therefore that in the face of such any sale or trans- "fer in any way by the 5th Defendant was illegal, and that under "these circumstances the documents produced in defence although "clearly proved to have been duly executed by the 5th Defendant "were nevertheless of no value."

8. And in conclusion the Civil Judge observed "that as the Law "Officer of the Court had declared one-fourth of the said property "to be the 5th Defendant's share of his late wife's estate, the Court "allowed he had a right over that much, and directed that the pro- "perty should be restored to the Plaintiff by the 1st and 3d Defen- "dants on his paying them in the proportions to which they were en- "titled back, the sum of Rupees 2,863-12-0.

9. The Civil Judge disallowed the sum claimed by Plaintiff on account of produce, being of opinion "that it was his own fault that he had been so long kept out of the property." The Plaintiff was ordered to pay all costs on the sum disallowed, and the 1st and 3d Defendants were adjudged to pay the remainder of the costs incurred.

10. Of the 2d and 4th Defendants no notice was taken in the Decree.

11. From the above decision the 1st and 3d Defendants filed separate Appeal Petitions, which the Court of Sudder Udalut proceed to dispose of by one Decree; the nature of the question at issue in respect to both Appeals being one and the same.

12. The Appellants allege that the claim made by the Original Plaintiff is a fraudulent one; the Hibbanamah, and the agreement connected with it being forgeries. The Appellants also repeat that their purchases were openly made, and that from the date of the purchases they have been in undisturbed possession.

13. The Respondent filed no appeal answer.

14. The Court of Sudder Udalut having considered the points at issue, are of opinion that the decision of the Civil Judge should be reversed.

15. The Civil Judge in his Decree has stated that no suspicion attaches to the authenticity of the Deeds of Sale produced by the Ap-

pellants; but that he has felt compelled to reject them, as by the Mahomedan Law the 5th Defendant under the Hibbanamah given to him by his wife, had no power to grant them.

16. That such a document as the Hibbanamah in question would under ordinary circumstances have acted as a complete bar to any Sale, by the 5th Defendant to the 1st and 3d Defendants (Appellants), the Court of Sudder Udalut readily allow. But in this case, it appears to the Court that the Civil Judge has rejected on insufficient grounds the proof adduced to the fact of the Plaintiff being present and in no way objecting to the Sales in question, when his father executed the bills of Sale held by the Appellants.

17. That the Plaintiff was so present, and did so act, the Court consider to have been fully proved; and the Court are of opinion that by such conduct the Plaintiff virtually became a consenting party to the Deeds of Sale executed by his father.

18. The Court of Sudder Udalut feel that they would be countenancing a fraud were they to view the matter in any other light.

19. The Court of Sudder Udalut further remark, that strong grounds exist for doubting the truth of the Plaintiff's documents, inasmuch as the record of the case shows, that until the institution of this Suit no mention had at any time been made of this Hibbanamah, although for so doing many occasions had occurred. To reconcile therefore this previous silence with the execution of the Hibbanamah in 1824 is difficult, and does not in the opinion of the Court easily admit of satisfactory explanation.

20. The Respondent is adjudged to pay all costs in Original and Appeal.

No. 47 of 1849.

Exparte.

1. The Original Suit was instituted by the Special Appellant for the recovery from the Special Respondent of a tiled house alleged to have been forfeited under a mortgage Bond executed in 1828 by the Defendant in favor of the Plaintiff's deceased father.

2. The Defendant admitted the Bond upon which the Suit was founded but pleaded that it had been executed by him merely to save his property from liability to satisfy the claim of other persons; and that to this effect a counter agreement had been executed in his favor by the Plaintiff's father.

3. The Subordinate Judge recognized the validity of the Plaintiff's Bond, and rejected the counter agreement produced by the Defendant observing that if the latter were "a genuine document, the Defendant must be viewed as justly suffering the penalty of his own fraud and duplicity."

4. The Subordinate Judge accordingly adjudged to the Plaintiff the sum of Rupees 124—being the amount of principal and interest due on the aforesaid Bond, the house mortgaged being held liable for that amount.

5. The Defendant appealed to the Civil Court, and the Civil Judge reversed the Original Decree being of opinion that the Plaintiff's Bond was merely a nominal one, and conferred on Plaintiff, no title to the property claimed.

6. The Civil Judge was moreover of opinion that the Decree of the Subordinate Judge was irregular, inasmuch as it awarded to the Plaintiff a sum of money which was not sued for and which, if due, ought to be recovered by a regular Suit.

7. On the application of the Respondent (Plaintiff) a special appeal was admitted by the 3d Judge of Sudder Udalut on the ground that the Respondent was entitled to a definite decision on the merits of the case, and that therefore the award of the Civil Judge referring him to a fresh Suit for the recovery of any money that might be due to him on the mortgage Bond sued on was opposed to the general practice of the Courts.

8. The Special Respondent did not appear and the whole record of the case has been brought under the consideration of a full Bench.

9. The 1st and 2d Judges of the Court of Sudder Udalut concur in considering that the special appeal was admitted on insufficient grounds; they are of opinion that the Special Appellant did receive from the Appellate Court a decision upon the merits of the case, in- "asmuch as the Civil Judge expressly states "that the Plaintiff (Spe- "cial Appellant) has no title to the property claimed and accordingly "the Decree of the Subordinate Judge, which awards money not even "asked for, is reversed."

10. The 1st and 2d Judges observe that the Bond entered into by the parties conditioned for the forfeiture of a house, &c., in the event of a certain sum of money not being paid by the 7th May 1831; which sum not having been paid within that period, the 1st and 2d Judges are of opinion that the sale became absolute, and that therefore it was not competent to the Subordinate Judge to deal with the case as being one of money lent on security of a mortgage and to decree that the Defendant should pay the Plaintiff Rupees 100 with interest thereon for a period of two years.

11. The 1st and 2d Judges are moreover of opinion that the Suit was barred by the law of Limitations, the terms of the Bond extending only to the 7th May 1831, within twelve years from which date an action for the recovery of any property or money due under that Bond should have been brought; whereas the present action was not filed until the 17th August 1847, a period exceeding 16 years after the 7th May 1831.

12. For the foregoing reasons the 1st and 2d Judges of the Sudder Udalut resolve to dismiss the Special Appeal with costs.

No. 21 of 1850.

1. The Original Suit was instituted by the Special Respondent for the recovery from the Special Appellants and twenty-three other Defendants of Malgoozary Poonjah and Nunjah lands paying an annual revenue of Rupees 325-8-0, and yielding an annual profit of Rupees 79-8, and for the recovery of Rupees 636 the amount of profit for eight years, during which period the Plaintiff alleged that the lands in question had been usurped by the 1st and 2d Defendants, (Special Appellants,) aided by the other Defendants.

2. The Plaintiff stated in his plaint that the lands sued for had been made over to him by the 1st Defendant by a Pottah dated the 15th April 1834, but that they had subsequently been fraudulently usurped by the 1st and 2d Defendants.

3. The 2d Defendant denied the Plaintiff's claim, admitting the execution by the 1st Defendant of the Pottah upon which it was founded, but alleging that a counter agreement had been executed by the Plaintiff on the date of the execution of the Pottah re-transferring the lands, the execution of the Pottah having been merely a formal arrangement to enable the Plaintiff to manage the lands during a temporary absence of the 1st and 2d Defendants.

4. The 2d Defendant also denied that the 1st Defendant had any right to make over the whole of the lands to the Plaintiff, the lands in question having been inherited by the 1st and 2d Defendants as the undivided sons of their father, and the 2d Defendant contended that it was therefore competent to the 1st Defendant to transfer a moiety only of the same.

5. In regard to the 1st, 3d and 25th Defendants, the case was tried exparte.

6. The Plaintiff replied that the counter agreement was a fabricated document, and that his signature had been fraudulently obtained to it.

7. The Moofty Sudder Ameen passed a Decree in favor of the Plaintiff admitting the validity of the Pottah, upon which his claim was based, and rejecting the counter agreement, by which the Defendants sought to invalidate it; he accordingly awarded to the Plaintiff the lands sued for, adjudging the 1st Defendant to make good to him the sum claimed and to pay the Plaintiff's costs, and assessing the other Defendants with their respective costs.

8. From this Decree the 1st and 2d Defendants appealed to the Civil Judge, who considering the validity of both the documents above referred to to have been established, passed judgment in favor of the Appellants (Defendants) and reversed the original Decree, assessing the Plaintiff (Respondent) with the entire costs of Suit.

9. On the application of the Plaintiff (Respondent) a Special Appeal was admitted by the Court of Sudder Udalut on the ground tha

the counter agreement, upon which the Appeal Decree was founded, was a copy, and not the original counter agreement alleged to have been executed by the Plaintiff.

10. The Suit was accordingly remanded to the Civil Court, in order that the Original agreement in question might be examined and a fresh Decree passed.

11. The review of judgment devolved on the late acting Civil Judge Mr. Story, who found from a correspondence with the Revenue authorities that the original document in question was not forthcoming, but differing from the former Civil Judge in his estimation of the validity of that document, and considering that there were grounds for supposing that it had been fraudulently made away with by the Defendants (Appellants) confirmed the Decree of the Moofty Sudder Ameen.

12. From this decision the Appellants have presented an application for the admission of a Special Appeal, which application has been admitted by the Court of Sudder Udalut as it appeared to them that the investigation of the case by the Lower Courts had been deficient, in certain points material to the decision of the Suit.

13. It appears that the document No. 75 the alleged counter agreement, now stated to have been mislaid, wss delivered by the 1st Defendant to the Tahsildar of Kistnagherry and whilst in that Officer's custody was lost.

14. It is obvious that the production of this document was of the last importance to the Defendants (Special Appellants), and the Court of Sudder Udalut are therefore unable to concur in the opinion of the acting Civil Judge that they (the Defendants) were instrumental to its abstraction.

15. The Court observe that evidence to the execution of this document, that it was publicly recorded in the Tahsildar's Cutcherry and acted upon by that Officer, ought to have been received, and such weight given to the same as, in the opinion of the presiding Judge, it deserved.

16. The Court of Sudder Udalut are likewise of opinion that the extent of the land and the quantity and value of the produce claimed by the Plaintiff, and awarded to him by the Decrees passed in his favor, have not received the consideration they deserved from the Lower Courts.

17. And, finally, the Court remark that the land in dispute is acknowledged to have been the hereditary property of the 1st and 2d Defendants, and that it therefore becomes a matter for consideration how far the alienation of the same by the 1st Defendant alone is valid in itself, and binding on the 2d Defendant, and how far his interests are effected by that alienation.

18. The Court of Sudder Udalut accordingly resolve to remand the Suit to the Civil Judge who will refer it back to the Moofty Sudder Ameen for re-investigation and judgment de novo with reference to the foregoing remarks.

No. 52 of 1850.

1. From the Pleadings in this case it appears that the Plaintiffs had bound themselves by the Razeenamah, filed in No. 195 of 1839, on the file of the District Moonsiff of Seetanagarum, to pay Rupees 215 to the Defendants; that upon execution being sued out, Rupees 108-10-0 were realized by Court process and paid to the Defendant, between 1840 and 1843; that upon fresh process issuing, the Plaintiff averred that they had delivered over and above the sums collected by the Court; 15½ Pootties of grain in 1844 and 1845; but, as no formal notification of this payment had been made to the Court at the time they were referred to a fresh Suit for the purpose of establishing their right to credit the value thereof, Rupees 152-8-4, towards the Razeenamah in question.

2. The Defendant denied the receipt of the Paddy, and urged that on the date on which the delivery of 1843 is stated to have been made to him, he was in Rajahmundry, three cadums distant from the Plaintiff's village.

3. The District Moonsiff dismissed the claim—his decree was, in appeal, reversed by the Civil Judge, "from the plentiful marks of cheating in all Defendants' dealings, and the actual proof of the item of the 50 Rupees not being endorsed" on the Razeenamah, considered "that the Plaintiffs had established a strong presumptive proof, that they have long since cleared off their debt."

4. An application for the admission of a Special Appeal from the Decree of the Civil Judge, made by the Defendant, was admitted by the Court of Sudder Udalut, on the ground that the Decree was very faulty and imperfect.

5. The Special Appellant urges that the statement of the Civil Judge that "the Defendant got the District Moonsiff's Court to issue a warrant under that Razeenamah, and Plaintiff's declared Defendant had been paid," is contrary to fact, as the Plaintiffs, even then allowed that they still owed Rupees 48-6-8, as will be proved by the enclosed copy of their petition.

6. That the Civil Judge states "that throughout the transactions between these parties, the cheating and swindling appear all on the Defendant's side," but whilst thus aspersing the Defendant's character, he has failed to show in what the cheating and swindling consisted or the proofs that any cheating, or swindling at all occurred.

7. That no grounds are stated in the Decree for the assumption that the Defendant is "in the habit of lending monies to his friend "Taloo Vencana, who takes what he wants for himself, and tells the "lender to put down such sum as he likes to name to the account of "the Plaintiffs."

8. That the Civil Judge's observation "that the payment of 50 "Rupees admitted by Defendant not having been entered in the copy "of the Razeenamah, there is positive proof that the Defendant only "departed from the condition of the Razeenamah," will at least show that Defendant was ready to admit all payments actually made;

whilst, as the Razeenamah was filed in Court, he could not endorse the payment on it.

9. That the Civil Judge has vilified his witnesses, declaring "that some of them are the cleverest of the false Suit and false bond makers in this Zillah," without showing to which of the witnesses, this remark applies, or the grounds on which it is made.

10. That the Civil Judge's assertion that the Defendant did not disprove the deliveries of Paddy, is contrary to fact, for the Defendant and proved by oral and written evidence that he was in Rajahmundry on the date that 13 Pootties are said to have been delivered, whilst the delivery was not endorsed on the Razeenamah as stipulated.

11. The Court of Sudder Udalut remark that "the plentiful marks of cheating in all Defendant's dealings" which was one ground given by the Civil Judge for reversing the District Moonsiff's Decree are not matters of record in this case, which must be disposed of on its own merits, irrespective of what may have taken place in other Suits. Another ground given by him for the reversal of the Moonsiff's Decree, that the item of 50 Rupees paid by the Plaintiffs was not endorsed by the Defendant on the Razeenamah, filed in Suit No. 195 of 1839, ought not, in the opinion of the Court to be conclusive of fraud on the Defendant's conduct in this case, inasmuch as other previous payments, made under warrants from the Court, were also not endorsed, and this omission might have led the Defendant to suppose that he was justified in following the same course. The Sudder Udalut observe that the Civil Judge reported in his return of the 18th November, that the Defendant had publicly received the 50 Rupees, and on this point, therefore, there could have been no doubt.

12. The Court of Sudder Udalut further observe that the plea of the Defendant that when the alleged delivery of 13 khundys of Paddy took place at Jumbooputnum on the 2d March 1844, he was at Rajahmundry, and was a party to a bond executed at that place on the same date, has not been noticed at all by the Civil Judge. This was a very important point to be decided, and the Civil Judge was bound to have declared the plea proved or not.

13. The Civil Judge would seem to have been led into error in saying that when the District Moonsiff issued a warrant for the enforcement of the Razeenamah, in No. 195 of 1839, the Plaintiff declared Defendant had been paid, for the Court find on referring to the Petition presented by the present Plaintiffs, that they admitted that Rupess 48-6-8 were still due to the Defendant.

14. The Court of Sudder Udalut have read with much dissatisfaction the very objectionable epithets made use of by the Civil Judge in speaking of the Defendant and his witnesses, and they expect Mr. Anstruther will be more guarded and circumspect in his language for the future.

15. The Court of Sudder Udalut resolve to remand the Suit to the Civil Judge for judgment de novo, with reference to the above remarks, and if he reverses the decision of the District Moonsiff, Mr. Anstruther will record in detail his reasons for so doing, and discrediting the evidence upon which that Officer relied.

No. 5 of 1851.

1. This Suit was instituted to establish the right of the Plaintiff and his minor brothers to receive from the Mootahdar of Taudamputty Pottahs for 3 lots of land and a Tamarind Tree, all valued at 60 Rupees, and to account to the Mootahdar for the rent of the same for the year 1843-4 or Rupees 56-5-7.

2. The Plaintiff alleged that the Defendant, his paternal uncle by formal deed of gift on the 5th October 1840 gave the said land and other property to himself and his brothers. He urged that, as the Defendant had no male issue, and as possession was immediately given, the gift could not be revoked, and he explained that the Defendant, in whose name the Puttah continued to be issued, had induced the Mootahdar to refuse to receive the rent for the year in question from him (Plaintiff) and to file a Suit against the Defendant for the arrears.

3. The Defendant admitted the execution of the deed of gift, but alleged that he executed it when about to proceed on pilgrimage to Ramasserum, in order that his creditors might be paid, and his property duly preserved.

4. The District Moonsiff having passed judgment in the Plaintiff's favor, the Suit was remanded by the Civil Judge in order that further evidence might be received on the part of the Defendant, who then urged that a son had recently born to him, and that consequently the deed of gift could no longer be of any force or effect.

5. The District Moonsiff in his revised Decree awarded to the Plaintiff all that he had claimed, and this Decree was confirmed in Appeal by the Subordinate Judge.

6. Upon this the Defendant presented an application for the admission of a Special Appeal, urging that the property specified in the deed of gift had never been out of his own possession—that by the subsequent birth of 2 sons the gift had been nullified—that if the gift were held good his creditors would be defrauded, and that the property had been undervalued in the Plaint.

7. This application was rejected by the Court of Sudder Udalut.

8. On the presentation of a Petition for a review of the order rejecting the above application, the Court of Sudder Udalut submitted for the opinion of the Hindoo Law Officers the question "whether the birth of sons *after* the execution of the Bond (No. 10) giving the property of the Defendant to the Plaintiff rendered the gift invalid or not," and their reply was to the effect, that "the Defendant had not the power to dispose of *all* his property so long as he was able to beget children, but that he might alienate a small portion of the same, if by so doing he did not deprive his issue then born, or that might be born to him, of the means of support."

9. With reference to this exposition of the Law the Court of Sudder Udalut admitted a Special Appeal, on the ground that the Decrees of the lower Courts were defective, and that the opinion of the Law Officers as to the validity of the gift had not been obtained.

10. The Court of Sudder Udalut observe that the Decrees of the lower Courts are not sufficiently clear and specific as to the point, whether the whole or a portion only, of the property of the Defendant was included in the document No. 10, to enable the Court to dispose of the question involved in this Suit.

11. The Court of Sudder Udalut also remark that the course laid down by Section XVII. Regulation III. of 1802, which ought never to be omitted, was not followed either by the District Moonsiff or the Acting Subordinate Judge.

12. The Court of Sudder Udalut therefore resolve to remand the Suit back to the District Moonsiff for disposal, with reference to the above observations.

No. 24 of 1848.

1. This Suit was instituted by the Plaintiff (Respondent) for the recovery from the Defendant (Appellant) of Rupees 527-5-9 for a breach of contract.

2. The Plaint was to the effect that Defendant on 29th June 1844, signed a contract or agreement binding himself under a penalty of Rupees 300 to supply Plaintiff's predecessors with 227,846 laterite stones on account of Government at the rate of 14 Rupees per thousand, and that from 2d July 1844 to 5th March 1845, he (Defendant) received advances to the amount of Rupees 3,000, but only delivered 1,96,495 stones, the value of which Rupees 2,750-15-2 at the above rate, added to Rupees 63-2-0 cost of jungle wood received from him made an aggregate of Rupees 2,814-11-2 which, deducted from the said sum of Rupees 3,000, leaves a balance of Rupees 185-4-10, which sum with Interest thereon Rupees 42-0-11 and Rupees 300 the amount of the penalty, total Rupees 527-5-9, Plaintiff sued to recover.

3. The Defendant in his answer affirmed that he delivered 2,15,047 stones, and that he would, had he been permitted, have delivered the remainder according to the contract, the penalty could not legally be claimed.

4. The Civil Judge was of opinion that the Plaintiff's witnesses had proved the accounts filed by him, their testimony being clear and satisfactory as to the number of stones delivered and rejected, as well as to the admissions of Defendant and the frivolous excuses made by him for not settling his account; that it was shown that it had not been customary to grant receipts to contractors for stones delivered daily, but the number was duly entered in the Public Accounts of the Engineer's Department, the correctness of which there was no reason to question; that it was therefore manifest that the Memo. produced by Defendant, which does not bear the signature of any Public Officer, would have been of no use had it been filed, and that the time granted

by the Sub-Collector to Defendant, *at his own request*, to enable him to come to a settlement, was additional and conclusive evidence against him.

5. He therefore adjudged the Defendant to pay Rupees 185-4-10 Principal, with the amount of the penalty for breach of contract Rupees 300, Total Rupees 485-4-10 with Interest on that sum to the execution of the Decree. Costs of Suit to be paid by Defendant only on the amount adjudged against him, as the Interest sued for could not be legally claimed, the penalty for breach of contract having been clearly defined by the terms of the agreement.

6. The Defendant being dissatisfied with the above decision appealed therefrom, and in his detailed Petition of Appeal among other things affirms, that the Respondent's statement, that of the number of stones supplied by him (Appellant) 7,194 were returned to him as objectionable, that 400 belonging to Government had been erroneously inserted in the Memo. furnished to him, and that 11,000 had been entered therein in four items on four different dates over and above the actual supply, was not at all correct. That the Memo. furnished to him by Respondent's Subordinates (Respondent's 1st and 2d witnesses) in their own handwriting, exhibited a total of 2,15,047 stones supplied by him. That Peons were employed in the quarry to see that none but unobjectionable ones were sent to the work, they were examined again, and only those actually taken were entered in the said Account; that the 400 stones taken from the walls of the Fort might have been by an oversight erroneously entered in one account, but that the same error should have crept into all the accounts is improbable, and rests only on the unsupported statement of the 1st witness, who, as well as the 2d, is his enemy; and that the said witnesses may have purposely made false entries, i. e. less than the actual numbers, on the four dates above alluded to, with a view to cause loss to him (Appellant) and some advantage to themselves.

7. He then goes on to assert, that the Respondent had examined the said Memo. in presence of the said witnesses, and affixed his mark in pencil to each item which he found correct, and, after making the total also in pencil, returned it to him (Appellant): had it therefore contained an entry over and above the actual supply, the Respondent would have then detected it, but such was not the case—and that he (Appellant) made no admission to the Sub-Collector of their being a balance against him, nor obtained any time for the purpose of settling it, the time applied for and granted, being merely for the comparing of accounts.

8. He urges, moreover, that it is not shown in the evidence, nor stated in the Original Decree, how, or in what particular, he broke his contract; that the contract itself does not provide for the delivery of the whole number of stones *within any specified period*, in default of which the penalty should be paid; that other stone cutters were employed besides himself in order to expedite the work; that had his supply been deficient, he would, it is to be presumed, have been called upon through the Collector to furnish more, and that, as such was not the case, it is to be inferred that the stones supplied by himself and

others were found sufficient for all the purposes required; that, in fact, the whole of the stone work was completed before the departure of Captain Ditmas, Respondent's predecessor, with whom the contract was made, who then gave him (Appellant) a Testimonial (now in his possession) speaking highly of the services rendered by him; that he has undergone great trouble to supply stones for Government at 14 Rupees, when no one else would do it for less than 16, and that it is not just that he should be subjected to the payment of a heavy penalty on the ground of an alleged breach of contract, which is not shown to have occurred.

9. The concluding para. of the Appeal Petition contains matter which is highly objectionable and improper, consisting of imputations on the conduct and motives of the Civil Judge in the disposal of the Suit, which are obviously groundless, as well as absurd, and for which the Vakeel who filed the Appeal Petition deserves to be severely censured.

10. The Respondent answered, that it was not the custom to examine the stones on delivery, to find out whether any were objectionable, but after the stones were conveyed to the different places where they were wanted, and the building commenced, the Masons examined and selected those fit for use, and rejected such as were not so. That of those supplied by the Appellant 7,194 were rejected accordingly, and so entered in the public accounts.

11. That the said accounts show plainly that of the 500 stones entered in one item as supplied by Appellant, 400, which were taken from the walls of the Government Fort, were included by mistake, as recorded in a note after the mistake was discovered.

12. That the Appellant could have had no difficulty in altering the figures in the four items of the Memo. alluded to, so as to increase the total, after it had been examined by the Respondent, but not compared with the Office accounts, as alleged by the Appellant; that the Appellant had been given to understand that stones not of the dimensions or quality mentioned in the contract would not be accepted; that he should supply them regularly to prevent the Public work being stopped, and perform all the conditions of the contract punctually, but that he failed to do so, and showed great indifference as to the performance of the contract and caused delay, in consequence of which and the emergency of the work, other stone cutters had to be procured and the building was completed by means of the stones supplied by them. Therefore there is "hardly any doubt" that Appellant should pay the penalty stipulated in his contract, and that Appellant had himself admitted before the Sub-Collector, that he was indebted in the amount of balance sued for, as the orders of that Officer to the Police Ameen (exhibits B and D) and the Ameen's answer (exhibit C) will clearly show.

13. The Court of Sudder Udalut concur with the Civil Judge in considering the Plaintiff (Respondent's) claim to the balance of the amount advanced to Defendant (Appellant) viz. Rupees 185-4-10 to have been satisfactorily established by the evidence adduced, seeing

no reason whatever to doubt the correctness of the Public Accounts, or to discredit the testimony of the witnesses examined to prove them, whereas the Memo. produced by the Appellant in support of his assertions as to the number of stones delivered by him cannot be at all relied on.

14. It is obvious that nothing could be easier than for him to alter numbers entered therein on the dates referred to, by prefixing a numeral to represent *thousands*, and this is what appears to have been done, as the deposition given by the Appellant's Vakeel, who was examined regarding the said Memo. shows; the other figures in the place of units, tens, and hundreds, being found to correspond exactly with those entered in the Respondent's accounts, in which, it is evident, that no alteration has been made. No evidence has however, been adduced to prove the alleged breach of contract on the part of the Appellant.

15. The contract itself specifies no period, within which the whole number of stones was to be delivered, and there is nothing on the record beyond the Respondent's statements in the pleading to show that the Appellant neglected or refused to supply the whole quantity, or that the Public work was damaged or impeded in consequence.

16. The Court of Sudder Udalut are therefore of opinion that the penalty of Rupees (300) three hundred cannot legally be awarded against the Appellant, and modify the Lower Court's Decree to that extent, adjudging Appellant to pay the said sum of Rupees (185-4-10) one hundred and eighty five, Annas four and Pice ten only, with interest thereon, up to the execution of this Decree.

17. Costs to be defrayed by the Appellant in proportion to the amount he is adjudged to pay.

NOTE.—It will be observed that in this case (para. 4) the Plaintiff is allowed to use his own entries for himself: while an admission which he makes, may not be used against him. No evidence was given of any breach of contract: and the instrument on which the Defendant relies, turns out a forgery.

No. 57 OF 1851.

1. The Plaintiff alleged that the Defendants were the representatives of one Appavoo Pillay, with whom he had dealings from 1825 to 1833, and who died in 1840; that the accounts of these dealings were adjusted by the Defendants 1 to 4 on the 8th September 1841, when a balance was struck in his favor of Rupees 288-14-3, and the managing member, the 2d Defendant, executed a Bond in his favor for 170 Rupees, which however he declined to accept, not being willing to abate the remainder; that a charge was preferred by the 2d Defendant against him before the Head of Police, of having extorted the said Bond, but was dismissed on the 1st October 1841; and that the Suit was laid for the amount of settlement with interest, in the aggregate Rupees 451-10-9.

2. In their answer, the 1st to 4th Defendants denied that Appavoo Pillay had any dealings with the Plaintiff. They alleged that Appavoo Pillay had charged the Plaintiff with embezzlement, and commented on his never having signed any settlement during the 9 years in which the dealings are stated to have been carried on, or for 9 years after they had closed. They averred that Appavoo Pillay died in 1839. They admitted that the 2d Defendant had signed a Bond for 170 Rupees in 1841, but they alleged that he had done so upon compulsion, and immediately complained to the Police, upon which the Plaintiff surrendered the Bond.

3. In a supplemental answer, they further urged that the 2d, 3d and 4th Defendants were divided from, and had received no part of the estate of, Appavoo Pillay, who had been adopted by their divided grand uncle.

4. The 2d Defendant died, and his widow and sons, 5th, 6th and 7th Defendants, were made parties to the Suit.

5. The District Moonsiff found that the evidence of the Plaintiff's witnesses was confirmed by the depositions taken by the Tahsildar in 1841, and deeming that it had been proved that the settlement had been signed by the 2d Defendant, that the Bond above referred to had been voluntarily executed by him, and that the Defendants were undivided, he passed judgment for the balance shown in the settlement, viz. 249-8-9, with interest from the date of Plaint.

6. The Civil Judge reversed the Decree for the following reasons.

"There seems no doubt of the late Appavoo Pillay having been "adopted, as alleged by the Appellants. One of the witnesses for "the Respondent deposed to that effect, and this alters the nature of "the relationship to the Appellants, excepting the 1st Appellant who "is his son."

"The District Moonsiff has made all the Appellants answerable for "the debt, on the grounds that it has not been shown that any divi- "sion of property had taken place. But, on the other hand, it is not "proved that there was any property of which they could claim the "division, or that the deceased Appavoo Pillay lived with the Appel- "lants in a joint family; on the contrary it would appear from the evi- "dence that he did not, as he was living in a separate village from all, "except his son, the 1st Appellant."

"The accounts on which the Respondent founds his claim are most "unsatisfactory. There is nothing like a regular account current. "Thereare four separate accounts of transactions alleged to have taken "place, extending from the year Partheva to the year Vejeyah (1825 "to 1833), but no where is the balance struck, or the total amount "due to any particular date shown. One of them seems to relate to "a debt due by another person who has signed the document, but it "does not appear how it is connected with the present claim."

"It appears from the evidence that the Respondent was not on "good terms with the deceased Appavoo Pillay. It is very unlikely "that loose accounts of such long standing, and bearing no interest, "should have remained unsigned and unadjusted."

" Appavoo Pillay died in the year 1838 (not in 1840 as alleged by " the Respondent). He appears to have left some property, and if the " Respondent, who is the village Moonsiff, had any just claim thereon, " it might be expected that he would have then brought it forward. " In the year 1841 he seems to have made a demand against the late " 2d Defendant (who is represented in the Appeal by the three last " Appellants). His demand was resisted, and the Respondent has " since allowed about five years more to elapse before renewing it, by " the institution of the present Suit. Under these circumstances, the " Civil Judge is of opinion that the claim of the Respondent was in- " admissible. The Decree of the District Moonsiff is therefore set " aside, the Respondent paying all costs."

7. Upon the application of the Plaintiff, the Court of Sudder Udalut admitted a Special Appeal, on the ground that the Decree of the Appeal Court was imperfect.

8. The Court of Sudder Udalut observe that the Civil Judge has, in disposing of the Appeal, omitted all allusion to the Bond for 170 Rupees, admitted to have been granted to the Plaintiff by the 2d Defendant. The District Moonsiff found that the Bond in question had been executed voluntarily and not on compulsion, as alleged by the Defendants, and the Civil Judge ought also to have recorded his opinion on this point, which is a material one for the proper disposal of the Suit. Having done this, the Civil Judge ought then to have proceeded to determine in what way, and to what extent, the Deed in question affected the Plaintiff's claim, and disposed of the case accordingly.

9. In order that this course may now be followed, the Court of Sudder Udalut resolve to remand the Suit to the Civil Judge.

APPENDIX No. II.

VENKATACHALAM PILLE.

The Case of Vencatachalam Pille.

The prisoner in this case charged with child murder was acquitted by the majority of the Court of Foujdaree Udalut on the ground of contradictions and improbabilities in the evidence, and the omission of the Session Judge to cross examination certain

The prisoner was charged with having, on the 16th January 1851, taken to his house a female child named Marayummal, aged six years, and having given her intoxicating drugs, in a plantain fruit, murdered her by twisting her neck, robbed the body of jewels valued at Rupees 39-8-0, and thrown the corpse into a well.

The trial was held before the Session Judge of Salem.

It appears that the deceased was missed on the evening of the day specified in the indictment, and

of the witnesses with reference to the discrepancies observable in the evidence was noticed by the Foujdaree Udalut.

that suspicion having been attracted to the 1st witness Ramayi, who is stated to have been employed as a servant about the prosecutor's house, she was questioned by the prosecutor regarding the child, denied at first that she knew any thing about it, but in the course of the night, after having been pressed by the prosecutor, confessed that she had taken the child on the previous afternoon to the prisoner's house, where it was murdered by the prisoner, and was afterwards, in her presence thrown by him into a well in the neighbourhood of the village.

She stated that she had been requested by the prisoner to bring the child to him, in order that he might rob it of jewels, and that he had promised her a present of five Rupees for doing so; that on the previous afternoon having taken the child into the bazaar with her to see some dancing, she met the prisoner near a flat stone in the bazaar, and at his request followed him with the child to a neighbouring field, and then to the prisoner's house, into which he took the child, leaving her under a pandal at the entrance, and after remaining some time within, came out carrying a bundle tied up in a cumbly, and took her with him to the well already referred to, where he took out of the cumbly the dead body of the child, threw it into the well, and placed a stone upon it, and then returned with her to the village, told her that he would go back to the well on the following day for some jewels, which had been left by him on the body; and having strictly enjoined her not to divulge to any one what had occurred, left her at her house and proceeded to his own.

The purport of the witness' confession appear to have been reported to the village authorities at an early hour in the morning; and the well pointed out by her having been examined, the dead body of the missing child was found in it with a heavy stone placed upon it.

The prisoner was apprehended on the same morning when at work in his field. In a shed belonging to him a cumbly was found, which was identified by the 1st witness as that in which he had carried the dead body from his house to the well, and, on his house being searched, a gold "Cuppu" or earring was found in it, in a chatty, and was claimed by the prosecutor as having belonged to the deceased.

Jewels to the value of Rupees 32 were found on the corpse; others to the value of Rupees 36, which were alleged to have been worn by the deceased, being missing; and, with the exception of the "Cuppu" referred to, which is stated by the prosecutor to have been one of the jewels worn by her, none of them had been found when the trial took place."

After the apprehension of the prisoner a person belonging to the village came forward, and stated that on the previous evening, when passing near the well in question, on his return from his work, his attention was attracted by hearing the sound of a splash, and seeing a woman standing on the bank, he called out to know what was the matter, and was answered by the prisoner, who was in the well (and whom, although he did not see him, he recognized by his voice) to the effect that he, Venkatachalam Pille, (mentioning his name,) was washing himself in the well and had by accident kicked a large stone into it.

The fact of a person having passed near the well just at the time the prisoner threw the body of the child into it, having asked what was the matter, and having been answered by the prisoner in the manner above described, had, it is alleged, been mentioned by the 1st witness in her confession on the previous night.

Additional evidence, which was considered by the Session Judge to connect the prisoner with the fate of the deceased, was adduced by three other inhabitants of the village, who stated that they had seen the prisoner in company with the 1st witness and the deceased on the previous day, two of them adding that they had seen them proceed together to the house of the accused.

The prisoner and Ramayi having been committed for trial, and the latter having been subsequently admitted as an approver with the sanction of the Court of Foujdaree Udalut, the Session Judge in concurrence with the Mahomedan Law Officer convicted the prisoner of the murder laid to his charge, and referred the trial to the Court of Foujdaree Udalut recommending that he should be sentenced to suffer death.

By the Court of Foujdaree Udalut, E. P. Thompson. "I concur "with the Session Judge in convicting the prisoner of the murder "charged and would sentence him to suffer death."

W. A. Morehead. "The 1st witness' statements in regard to the "prisoner's conduct in the matter appear to me in the highest degree "improbable."

"It is alleged that the prisoner in broad daylight, through the pub-"lic street, conducted the deceased and the 1st witness to his house, "about which several of his relatives were employed at their various "avocations, and bidding the witness to remain close by, took the de-"ceased inside, murdered her, stripped her of some of her jewels, "and, although nothing occurred to hurry him or interrupt him in "his proceedings, left others on the corpse, exceeding in value those "which he appropriated to himself, brought it out in a cumbly, and "without any further attempt at concealment, carried it through the "village to a well, taking the 1st witness with him to witness in what "manner he disposed of it, without adopting any other precautions "for his own safety, then an injunction to the witness, a girl, who is "described by the Session Judge to be only 10 years of age, not to "divulge to any one what had occurred ; and having concealed, with "the exception of one article of trifling value, all the jewels which "were taken by him, so effectually, that after the most careful search, "they have not been found, placed that one article in a chatty in his "house, where he must have known that it could not fail to be dis-"covered, whenever a search was made."

"I cannot credit such a statement, when not supported by evidence, "the most cogent and irresistible ; and I consider the proof adduced "of the several circumstances upon which the Session Judge has con-"sidered the 1st witness' testimony to be corroborated, to be defective "and on some points contradictory."

"I do not consider it to be clearly established by the evidence for "the prosecution that the child had more ornaments on her person "on the day she met with her death, than were found on the corpse "when it was discovered."

"I cannot reconcile the fact of valuable jewels having been left on "the body of the deceased, with the motive which is alleged to have "impelled the prisoner to the commission of the murder; and, in the "absence of more conclusive evidence to the identity of the Cuppu "found in the prisoner's house, I see no sufficient ground for discre-"diting the prisoner's statement that it was his own property, which, "with reference to its value, is by no means improbable; while, if the "1st witness' statement be true, its discovery in the place in which "it was found, is altogether irreconcilable with the effectual precau-"tions, which must have been taken by him, for the concealment of "the remainder of the jewels, alleged to have been abstracted from the "body of the deceased."

"Adverting to the conclusions deduced from the discovery of the "Cuppu in question, I observe a most improper omission on the part "of the Session Judge in neglecting to notice the denial before the "Police of the witness who was named by the prosecutor, as the "maker of the ornament in question.

"This witness was not examined by the Session Judge, although "as it appears that he denied before the Police the "fact which he was called upon to establish, and "one which, if proved, must have had an impor-"tant effect upon the prisoner, it was clearly most important, in jus-"tice to the accused, that his evidence should have been taken.

See page 23.
Enclosure No. 3.

"The same remark is applicable in regard to the persons said to "have been about the prisoner's house, when the child was taken "into it, and the murder committed."

"It appears that these persons were examined by the Police, but "denied all knowledge of the facts alleged, and their examination "before the Session Court, although, considering their connection "with the accused, their evidence should have been received with "caution, was clearly most desirable to test the truth of the 1st wit-"ness' testimony."

"The evidence of the 3rd, 4th and 5th witnesses I consider in-"sufficient to prove the fact of the prisoner having been seen on the "day in question in the company of the 1st witness and the deceased. "It appears from the 3d witness' deposition, that when seen by him "in the bazaar on the day in question, the prisoner was at some dis-"tance from, and holding no communication with, either the 1st wit-"ness or the deceased; and, considering the publicity of the place in "which they were seen, the fact of their having been on the day in "question in the same street at a distance from each other appears to "me insufficient to justify any conclusion to the prejudice of the ac- "cused."

"The evidence of the 4th and 5th witnesses, who state that they "saw the prisoner, the 1st witness, and the deceased proceed from a "particular stone in the bazaar to the entrance of the prisoner's house, "contradicts the 1st witness' statement, from which it would appear "that they went in the first instance to a field in a different direction."

"It is possible that this discrepancy might have been reconciled by "a more careful examination of the witnesses in question; but on this "point many obvious questions have been omitted, and the Court are "left entirely to conjecture in regard to the fact to which the said wit- "nesses have deposed."

"On another important point, viz., the real age of the 1st witness "the information is far from satisfactory. By the Police she is repre- "sented to be sixteen years of age, while by the Session Judge her "age is fixed at ten; and for this difference upon a point of much im- "portance in the consideration of the case no reason whatever has been "assigned."

"The only remaining circumstance which has been adduced in "corroboration of the 1st witness' evidence, viz. the alleged recogni- "tion of his voice by the 2d witness near the well in which the body "was found, on the evening the murder must have been committed, "must be admitted to afford a strong link in the chain of presumptive "evidence against the accused; but in itself appears to me insufficient "to corroborate the truth of the 1st witness' statement, when the other "improbabilities by which it is characterized are taken into consider- "ation."

"Under these circumstances I feel it my duty to acquit the prisoner, "and would direct his unconditional release."

"I do not think that any thing would be gained by further evi- "dence being now taken."

G. S. Hooper. "This is a singular case, and one in which it is dif- "ficult to come to a satisfactory conclusion. Upon the whole how- "ever, I have been led, after much and anxious consideration, to take "the same view of it as the 3d Judge has done, and to join him in "acquitting the prisoner."

"The Session Judge ought to have put some further questions to "the 3d, 4th and 5th witnesses with a view to ascertain whether or "not the contradictions between their evidence and that of the 1st "witness (approver) on the important point alluded to by the 3d "Judge in his minute, could be explained away."

"The proceedings of the lower Courts are very often defective in "this respect."

CHINNATAMBI NADAN.

The Case of Chinnatambi Nadan.

The prisoner was convicted in the first instance by the Court of Foujdaree Udalut of the murder of a female and was sentenced to be hanged; but evidence having been subsequently brought forward which went to show that the crime charged must have been committed by other parties, the original sentence was recalled and the prisoner was acquitted and released.

The prisoner was tried before the Session Court of Tinnevelly for the wilful murder of a female named Meenatchee.

It appeared from the evidence adduced on the trial that the prisoner had for some years past carried on an illicit intercourse with the deceased Meenatchee who resided in a house by herself in the village of Murdaynuttam in the Talook of Suttoor, and that about 7 P. M. of the 12th April last the prisoner and the deceased were seen to enter the house, in which, on the following morning, the deceased was found murdered with a deep wound on her throat and the prisoner lying near her in a fainting state from a severe wound on his private parts, the organs of generation having been entirely severed from his body.

It was stated by three of the neighbours (1st, 2d and 4th witnesses) who were sleeping close by, that in the course of the night cries were heard by them, proceeding from Meenatchee's house, upon hearing which the 2d witness went to the door and on asking what was the matter heard Meenatchee call out that "Chinnatambi Nadan (the prisoner) was cutting her neck." This the witness stated was followed by a sound like "Koruttu Koruttu," after which all became silent and he being unable to open the door which was bolted inside, proceeded to the house of the Nattumgar (the 7th witness) and early in the morning reported to him what had taken place.

The latter, it appeared, proceeded to the house soon after sunrise in company with Number Curnum, (the 5th witness) and the Mettoo Peon (the 6th witness), and having broken open the door with a pestle found Meenatchee lying dead and the prisoner near her in the condition already described and in a loft which opens into the room, a bill-hook was discovered stained with blood, with which it was supposed that the murder of the deceased and the mutilation of the prisoner must have been effected.

The prisoner when first discovered, was unable to speak, but on the arrival of the Head of Police on the following day he stated that the murder of Meenatchee and the mutilation of himself had been committed by certain persons who were concealed in the loft in which the bill-hook was found, that the door was bolted by himself after the murderers had quitted the house for fear of their returning to dispatch him and that as they were walking outside after leaving the house he recognised the voices of seven persons, whom he named. He attributed the murder of the deceased, and the outrage which had been committed on himself, to an ill-feeling which existed on the part of Meenatchee's relatives who were of the Reddy caste, in consequence of her cohabiting with a man of an inferior caste; the prisoner being himself a Shanar.

This statement was discredited by the Head of Police, there being no access to the premises otherwise than through the door, which was stated by one of the witnesses to have been bolted by Meenatchee when she retired to rest, and it being in the opinion of the Head of Police impossible that any persons could have secreted themselves inside the house without Meenatchee's knowledge, as it was shown that she had been seated near the door spinning cotton for some time before she went to bed. These circumstances coupled with the evidence of a blacksmith in the village that the bill-hook with which the murder was supposed to have been committed, had been made by him for the prisoner a short time before and also by the evidence of certain of the relations of the deceased that a quarrel had recently taken place between her and the prisoner and that a few days before her death she had forbidden the prisoner to continue his visits to her, upon which occasion, according to the statement of one of the witnesses, he had declared his resolve, that rather than that she should attach herself to any other man, both he and she should die, led the Head of Police to the conclusion, which, it was stated, had been already arrived at by the inhabitants of the village, that the prisoner was the murderer, and that finding himself unable to leave the premises undiscovered in consequence of there being persons moving about outside, he had mutilated himself to make it appear that some one else was the perpetrator of the crime.

The prisoner was accordingly committed and having perfectly recovered from the effects of his wounds was tried for the murder of the deceased.

The evidence on the trial was generally to the same effect as that given before the Head of District Police. There were however variations in the statements of some of the witnesses. For instance the 2d and 4th witnesses who had deposed in the Talook that they entered the house in the morning with the Village Police and examined the premises retracted these assertions before the Sessions Court.

The 2d witness also alleged that he had communicated with no one but the 1st witness after hearing the cries of Meenatchee until he reported the matter to the Nattumgar, whereas the 4th witness stated that he went up to the door of the deceased's house when the 2d witness was standing there and was told by him the purport of the exclamation that had been made by Meenatchee from inside.

There was a variation in the 2d witness' statements regarding his own proceedings on going to the house of the Nattumgar. Before the Police he had stated that on going to the Nattumgar's house and finding that he was asleep inside, he lay down in the court yard until the Nattumgar came out, but before the Session Court he deposed, that on finding that the Nattumgar was asleep he returned to his own house to sleep and then went back to the Nattumgar's a little before daybreak and apprised him of what had occurred.

There was moreover a discrepancy in the evidence as to the place where the bill-hook was found; the 6th and 7th witnesses (the Mettoo

Peon and Nattumgar) deposing that it was found *on* the loft already referred to, whilst the 5th witness (the Curnum) stated that it was found at the door of a room inside the house.

The prisoner repeated in his defence the plea put forward by him in the Talook, having however retracted before the Principal Sudr Ameen, and omitting before the Session Court, the statement previously made by him, that he had recognized by their voices certain of the persons by whom the outrage was committed, and stating that he knew nothing of the bill-hook and had never seen it before, although before the Police he had asserted that it belonged to Meenatchee and that he had often seen it with her.

While the trial was proceeding the prisoner put questions to several of the witnesses for the prosecution with the view of eliciting from them an admission that he had been beaten by certain of the deceased's relatives on a former occasion; and some of them admitted having heard that some years ago something of the kind had occurred.

The Law Officer in his Futwah convicted the prisoner of the murder charged.

The Acting Session Judge (Mr. Frere) concurring in this Futwah referred the trial for the final judgment of the Foujdaree Udalut with a recommendation that in consideration of the evidence being entirely of a circumstantial nature, and adverting to the severe and irreparable injury which the prisoner appeared to have inflicted on himself, the prescribed penalty of the Law should be commuted to transportation for life.

In his letter of reference adverting to the variation above noticed as being observable in the statements of the 2d and 4th witnesses the Acting Session Judge observed that it did not appear to him to effect the general truth of these witnesses' statements. "The fact of an alarm "having been raised in the village, as they deposed before sunrise in "the morning, is," the Acting Session Judge remarked, "fully cor-"roborated by the testimony of the Head of the Village himself (the "7th witness) who was roused on the information given by the 2d "witness, and the state in which the deceased and the prisoner were "found is indisputably proved by that Officer as well as by the "Curnum and Peon (the 5th and 6th witnesses), who give a clear and "minute description of the premises in which the murder took place."

The Acting Session Judge pronounced the prisoner's plea to be wholly irreconcilable with the facts of the case and undeserving of credit. He considered it highly improbable that the prisoner, after having received injuries of so severe a nature, would have been physically able to fasten the door in so deliberate and complete a manner as it was shown to have been fastened, having, according to the evidence of the 5th and 6th witnesses, been found, when it was broken open, bolted above and below with a chain in the middle; and he observed that the manner in which the door was fastened was perfectly in accordance with the supposition that the murder was committed by the prisoner himself, after having first secured the door with a view to prevent interruption and that he then mutilated himself in a paroxysm of anger or despair.

The evidence of the 3d witness who identified the bill-hook found on the prisoner, as the property of the prisoner, and whose statement appeared liable to no suspicion, as he was of a different caste from the deceased and her relatives and a resident of the same village with the prisoner himself, the Acting Session Judge considered strongly corroborative of the prisoner's guilt. The handle of this weapon, the Acting Session Judge stated, was of horn, of more elaborate workmanship than usual, and capable therefore of easy identification.

On perusing the record of the 1st and 2d Judges of the Foujdaree Udalut were of opinion that the evidence (entirely circumstantial as it was) left no doubt that the prisoner was the perpetrator of the murder. They deemed it impossible that after receiving the injuries inflicted on him he could have barred the door in the manner stated, and this fact, coupled with the rest of the evidence adduced, they considered to be conclusive to his guilt. On the ground that the evidence was so entirely circumstantial and adverting to the discrepancies above noticed in the testimony of some of the witnesses for the prosecution, the 1st Judge suggested that the recommendation of the Acting Session Judge should be acted on and that a sentence of transportation should be adjudged in preference to the irrevocable sentence of death. The 2d Judge being satisfied of the prisoner's guilt and considering the murder to have been a most cruel and deliberate one did not consider that any grounds existed for a mitigation of the prescribed penalty, and the 3d Judge on a perusal of the minutes recorded by his colleagues and of the Session Judge's letter, having stated his opinion that no grounds existed for any commutation of the penalty to which the prisoner had rendered himself liable by the commission of the murder of which he was convicted by the 1st and 2d Judges, in concurrence with the Acting Session Judge and the Mahomedan Law Officer of the Session Court, the prisoner was ordered for execution.

Upon the warrant for the prisoner's execution being received at Tinnevelly, the Assistant Magistrate (J. Hunter Blair) addressed a letter to the Session Judge, (the Acting Session Judge, before whom the trial had been held, having in the meantime quitted the station) in which he stated that the Head of Police by whom the case had been committed, a man whose character had never stood high in his estimation, being then under suspension, he had taken the opportunity of a visit from the Head of Police who was sent to relieve him, to ask him if he knew any thing about the charge, and was then told by him that "he had strong reason for believing that the prisoner was not guilty "of the crime he was accused of, and that his statement that the mur-"der of the woman and the mutilation of himself was committed by "some person connected with or employed by the Reddy party was "correct."

The Assistant Magistrate accordingly suggested, that if a further enquiry conducted by the present Head of Police were permitted, important information might be obtained.

On receiving this letter the Session Judge suspended the execution of the sentence and reporting the same to the Court of Foujdaree Udalut recommended that the trial should be re-opened with the view of further evidence being adduced.

This proceeding having been sanctioned by the Court of Foujdaree Udalut a further enquiry was instituted by the present Head of Police and additional witnesses were forwarded to the Session Court, by whose evidence it was clearly established that on the day the prisoner was alleged to have made use of the threat deposed to by the 1st witness for the prosecution, as having been made by him in consequence of the deceased having forbid his continuing his visits to her, he and the deceased were absent at a feast in another village upon the best possible terms. The fact of their having gone together to the feast in question was partially admitted by the 1st and 2d witnesses on their re-examination by the Head of Police, and also before the Session Court.

It was also ascertained that the distance from the spot where the prisoner stated that he had been lying when the assault was made upon him to the door of the house was so little, that it was easier for him to have fastened the door in the manner stated after having undergone the injuries inflicted on him, than to climb into the loft for the purpose of deposing in it the bill-hook, which, according to the evidence for the prosecution, as originally recorded, it was to be inferred had been placed there by him after the mutilation had taken place: blood having been besmeared on the wall about the height of a man's middle, which the witnesses for the prosecution alleged to have resulted from the prisoner having climed into it in his wounded state.

Additional evidence was adduced to show that enmity against the prisoner existed on the part of several of the witnesses for the prosecution and the fact of his having been assaulted on a former occasion by the 7th witness (the Nattumgar of the village) and others, to which reference was made by the prisoner in the questions put by him to certain of the witnesses when they were originally examined, was clearly proved.

On consideration of the additional evidence adduced, the Court of Foujdaree Udalut (present G. S. Hooper and E. P. Thompson) arrived at the conclusion that the charge preferred against the prisoner was the result of a conspiracy on the part of the principal inhabitants of the village in which the murder was committed to rid themselves of an obnoxious relative, whom they considered to have disgraced them, and to revenge themselves on the author of their disgrace by acts the most savage and revolting to humanity that had ever come under the observation of the Court.

The Court of Foujdaree Udalut accordingly recalled the sentence passed by them under date the 21st July last and issued an amended sentence acquitting the prisoner Chinnatambi Nadan of the crime laid to his charge and directing his immediate release.

The Court of Foujdaree Udalut further directed that the Magistrate of Tinnevelly should use every exertion to bring to justice the real prepetrators of this atrocious crime either by the offer of a reward for any information that might lead to the apprehension of the principals, or by the adoption of such other measures as might seem best calculated to lead to their discovery.

PIRUGADU, CHUNTAVADU and B. ATCHI.

The Case of Pirugadu and two others.

Of three prisoners in this case convicted of murder, the 1st prisoner who was shown to have been the planner and proposer of the murder was sentenced to suffer death, and the 2d and 3d prisoners to transportation for life.

The facts of this case are fully stated in the following extracts from the Session Judge's (W. Elliot) letter of reference.

" The three prisoners were charged with having " about midnight on the 1st of September 1851 " murdered Rungadoo aged about 20 years, whilst " asleep in front of his house in Soogamunchipully, " appertaining to the Talook of Jummalamadugoo " the 3d prisoner holding the legs, and the 2d pri- " soner the hair of the deceased, whilst the 1st " prisoner sat upon him, held him fast and stab- " bed him at the top of the head, with a pointed " iron knife, such as is used by Natives for culinary purposes, and " thereby inflicting a wound, four inches deep, into the brain from " which stab Rungadoo then and there died."

" The prosecutor merely repeats what he heard from others ; but " from the whole record it appears that the 3d prisoner a married wo- " man left her husband about three years back and lived with her pa- " rents. For two years the 1st prisoner has had constant intercourse " with her. This coming to the knowledge of deceased, a washerman, " whether induced by considering such connection between a Mussul- " man and Hindoo incorrect, or from his own addresses being ne- " glected, he proclaimed the fact ; it seems moreover that 1st and 3d " prisoners had a dispute on which occasion they were placed in the " village watchhouse as disorderly persons."

" Some months afterwards the 3d prisoner takes a fancy to the " washerman, which the 1st prisoner detects, and resolving to put a " stop to it, threatens the deceased by saying he would see how he " could manage to live—a menace which deceased does not appear to " have thought much of. The 1st prisoner however found another " young man the 2d prisoner who was accustomed to visit Atchi, but " instead of feeling displeased or at least concealing his anger, deter- " mined with him to kill the washerman, their common enemy. They " also resolved to make Atchi a party to the deed and calling upon " her one night mentioned their intention, which from certain infor- " mation given by herself made it appear a favorable opportunity. " They called for the knife they knew her to possess, which she brought " and on the road settled the part they were each to act."

"It occurring to them that their victim might not be asleep, Atchi "willingly undertook the errand which was not a very hazardous one "for her, and soon brought back the welcome news of his sleeping "soundly, upon which they advanced and fell upon Rungadoo, the "3d prisoner holding his legs and the 2d his hair, whilst the 1st pri- "soner, the strongest of the party, sat upon the breast whilst he gave "him a severe stab on the top of the skull which appears to have pe- "netrated the brain and at once to have perfectly paralysed the de- "ceased who is said not to have moved, but who uttered for a short "time a groaning or gurgling sound and then died; a small wound "was also inflicted near the right eye."

"The 1st and 3d prisoners, being suspected, were apprehended; "the 1st prisoner affected ignorance, but on Atchi's confession being "known, he fully acknowledged the cruel deed and the motives which "incited him to commit the murder in concert with the 2d and 3d "prisoners. The 2d prisoner also confessed the crime in the Talook "and before the Subordinate Criminal Court."

"The witnesses to those confessions are the 2d, 4th, 5th, 6th, 7th, "9th, 10th and 16th as found at pages 22, 31 and 32, 38, 41, 42, 45, "48 and 59 of the Sessions Court proceedings."

"The cloths worn by the 1st and 2d prisoners bore marks of blood, "the 1st prisoner had tried to wash the stains out of the sella cloth; "he acknowledged having wrapped round his waist at the time of the "murder, and which the 3d witness states he had previously seen "him wear. Indeed the 1st prisoner acknowledges before the Ses- "sions Court (page 65) that there was blood on the same, and endea- "vours to account for it by saying he was at a cock fight which "caused it, and cited witnesses to support his statement but totally "fails; the witnesses to the delivery of the sella cloth are the 4th and "9th to 13th."

"The 2d prisoner was apprehended with the trousers on, which he "wore at the time of the murder, on which there were spots of blood; "to hide which, the trousers had been tucked up or folded in; the "4th, 5th and 10th witnesses depose to this point."

"The delivery and ownership of the knife are shown by the 4th, "5th and 18th witnesses. This instrument although stated to have "been wiped at the time, is nevertheless rusty and appears to pos- "sess still some faint appearance of blood. The mother of the 3d "prisoner was sent for, but being reported sick, her evidence was dis- "pensed with."

"Although the prisoners confessed the crime in the Talook and "acknowledged the truth of such statements when before the Subor- "dinate Criminal Court and had no questions to put to the witnesses, "it was considered advisable to ascertain the strength or otherwise of "the deceased in order to give perfect credit to the likelihood of the "3d prisoner undertaking the part assigned her, of holding his legs, "and the evidence was uniformly to the effect that the deceased was "less strong than the 2d prisoner who is comparatively slim and the "undertaking was therefore without any danger and perfectly easy, "witnesses were called for the defence, but their evidence, as above "shown, was of no avail to the prisoners."

"The participation of 3d prisoner in the murder would by her own "statements in the Talook appear at first to have been forced upon "her by the threats or otherwise of the 1st prisoner, but her readily "furnishing the knife and recommending to see the position, &c., of "the deceased, her giving the information which led immediately to "the carrying out of their express determination, when she had it in "her power to warn him of his danger and so prevent the murder, "show she was a willing participator in the deed and therefore they "are all equally guilty."

"The Session Judge perfectly concurs in the opinion recorded by "each of the assessors convicting all the prisoners of wilful murder "and feels it his duty to recommend that Pirugadu, Chintivadu and "Atchi be condemned to death."

The Court of Foujdaree Udalut, (present G. S. Hooper and H. Morris,) convicted the prisoners of the crime laid to their charge, but being of opinion that a capital sentence in the case of the 1st prisoner who as the planner and proposer of the murder was shown to have been the most guilty of the three, sentenced the 1st prisoner to suffer death, and the 2d and 3d respectively to transportation for life.

GANUGAPENTA SOMAYA and APPANA CHINNI.

The Case of Ganugapenta Somaya and another.

Two prisoners in this case charged with murder were by the Court of Foujdaree Udalut who considered that the evidence had been fabricated with the connivance of the Head of Police by whom the Prisoners were committed for trial.

The omission from the indictment of any statement of the part of the body in which the deceased was stabbed, was pointed out by the Court of Foujdaree Udalut.

The prisoners in this case were charged with having at 12 o'clock on the night of the 18th October 1851, in company with two other persons, not apprehended, stabbed the prosecutrix's husband Papaya with a chisel, as he was sleeping on a cot under a shed in front of his house in the village of Sakunapalli in the Division of Pamur and with having thereby caused his immediate death.

The trial was held before the Session Court of Nellore.

The fact of the murder was reported on the following day by the village authorities to the Head of District Police, but without any intimation of suspicion against any particular person or persons, the wording of the report being, that "some one "having stabbed him (the deceased) in the right "ear he is now lying dead."

A further report was addressed to the Head of Police by the village Officers two days afterwards in which they stated that they suspected one Ganugapenta Somaya (1st prisoner) a carpenter in a neighbouring village; that they had sent for him and examined his cloths, and having found stains of blood on his upper cloth concluded that he must have been the perpetrator of the crime.

In this report the grounds upon which the suspicions of the villagers had been attracted to the said Ganugapenta Somaya, were not stated, nor was any mention made of any other party being suspected of having been concerned in the murder.

On the same day that this second report was written, viz., the 21st October (the murder having been committed on the night of the 18th) the Head of Police proceeded to the village and held an inquest on the body, when a verdict of wilful murder was recorded against the 1st prisoner G. Somaya and the 2d prisoner Appana Chinni, (the sister of the deceased) the prisoners being, according to the Head of Police's report, in the custody of the village Officers when he arrived.

On the following day the Head of Police commenced his investigation, which, after being continued for five days, (the wife of the deceased who gave evidence as prosecutrix and fourteen other persons having been examined) resulted in the commitment of the 1st and 2d prisoners for trial upon the evidence of the 1st and 2d witnesses; the former of whom was the sister-in-law of the deceased; and had deposed before the Head of Police, that she was sleeping in his house on the night of the murder and was awakened by the noise of persons walking about it, when she saw three persons standing near the cot of the deceased, one of whom, on her attempting to get up, went over to her cot and threatened to kill her as they had done her brother-in-law, and that in consequence she lay trembling on her cot till daybreak, when a friend of her brother-in-law came and called him to go out and plough with him, and receiving no answer called to her, upon which she got up and found her brother-in-law lying dead with a wound in his right ear, and then told the villagers, who speedily collected on hearing her cries, what had happened in the night.

She stated that she had distinctly recognized the 1st prisoner and the other two persons who were with him in the house, and added that before the villagers entered the house, the 2d prisoner, the sister of the deceased, came to her and begged her not to implicate her; in reply to which she charged the 2d prisoner with having instigated the murder in consequence of the quarrels which were constantly occurring between her and the deceased on account of the intimacy she (the 2d prisoner) had contracted with the 1st prisoner.

She stated that the villagers had come up when she made the above charge against the 2d prisoner, and that in consequence of what she said, they took the two prisoners into custody.

She did not mention before the Head of Police having seen the 2d prisoner in the house at the time the murder was committed.

The 2d witness, a ryot of the same village as the deceased, deposed before the Head of Police, that on the night in question he had seen the 1st prisoner and the two other individuals named by the 1st witness in the neighbourhood of the house of the deceased; that in answer to a question put by him they all told him their names, and that he afterwards returned and saw the same three persons leaving the premises and on going in found the deceased lying dead.

He mentioned having met Chinni the 2d prisoner, but contradicted himself in regard to the time of his meeting her, stating in the first instance that he met her going in at the gate as he was coming out, and afterwards that he met her coming from the house as he was going in.

He added that when he met her he charged her with having been accessory to the murder with the other three persons he had seen, and that in reply she admitted that they had committed it "for want of sense" and prayed him not to divulge it.

This witness was not examined until seven days after the commission of the murder, and it does not appear what led to his examination; the fact of his having gone to the house of the deceased on the morning after the murder not having been mentioned by the 1st witness in her deposition before the Head of Police, nor by any of the other witnesses examined by that Officer.

The evidence of the other witnesses examined by the Head of Police had reference principally to the alleged causes of enmity on the part of the 1st and 2d prisoners towards the deceased.

In addition to the ill-feeling caused by the resentment of the deceased on account of the intimacy between the 1st and 2d prisoners, which was shown to have been of long standing, it was stated, that high words had very recently passed between the deceased and both the prisoners on account of the latter having been accessory to the removal of the deceased's wife from his house to that of her parents in consequence of a domestic quarrel.

The statements of the 1st witness in regard to her recognition of the 1st prisoner and two other persons on the night of the murder were contradicted by the evidence of the individual* named by her as having come in the morning to call the deceased, he having deposed that on the deceased not answering him the 1st witness called to him which she would hardly have done, if, as she asserted, she had already been made aware that he had been put to death.

* Coommara Vemavarapu Venkata.

Evidence equally contradictory to that given by the 1st witness on this point was furnished by two other persons examined by the Head of Police (Comarasetti Pullaya and Chitta Boyana Guruvappa) the tenor of whose testimony went to show that the fact of her having recognized the murderers had not been mentioned by the 1st witness on the morning after the murder; one of them (Comarasetti Pullaya) distinctly stating that the 1st witness, when questioned by him on the subject, had told him that she was prevented by the darkness from seeing who the murderers were, but that in the morning the 2d prisoner had informed her that the 1st prisoner and the other two persons named by her were the perpetrators of the crime.

Only the 1st and 2d witnesses however with the prosecutrix, the wife of the deceased, who had been absent from her house on the night in question, were forwarded to give evidence before the Subordinate Criminal Court.

The case was committed as it stood by the Principal Sudder Ameen for trial before the Session Court, and on the requisition of the Acting Session Judge, nine of the villagers, of whom only two had been examined by the Head of Police, were forwarded as additional witnesses to the Session Court.

In her evidence before the Session Court the 1st witness declared that the 2d prisoner was present with the other three persons in the house of the deceased when the murder was committed; a fact which she had stated before the Principal Sudder Ameen, but had omitted all mention of before the Head of Police.

In other points also her evidence before the Session Court differed materially from that given by her before the Head of Police. She stated that as soon as the murderers left the house she got up and looked at the deceased, her previous statement being that she had remained terrified on her cot and unable to rise till daybreak. She for the first time mentioned the 2d witness as having been one of those who came to the house in the morning, and in contradiction of her previous statement, asserted, that the moon was rising at the time of her recognition of the prisoners and their companions in the house of the deceased.

Contradictions equally important in regard to his own conduct on having become cognizant of the facts to which he deposed marked the evidence of the 2d witness before the Session Court.

Seven of the additional witnesses sent up at the requisition of the Acting Session Judge gave evidence in support of the general purport of the 1st witness' testimony, deposing that she had mentioned to them on the morning after the murder what she had witnessed during the night.

On several important points, however, the evidence of these persons contradicted that of the 1st witness; while of the only two who had previously been examined by the Head of Police, one (Comarasetti Chinnappa) entirely contradicted his own previous statements, deposing before the Session Court that on going in the morning to the house of the deceased he found several persons there, and was then informed by the 1st witness of what she had witnessed in the night; whereas before the Head of Police he had stated that the 1st witness having been awakened by Coommara Vemavarapu Venkata (as stated by that individual in his deposition before the Police), had got up and called the deceased, obviously implying that up to that moment she was ignorant of what had occurred.

The 1st prisoner pleaded an alibi, and named two witnesses in support of his plea, to prove that he was absent at a feast in another village on the night the murder was committed; but both these persons denied having seen him on the night in question, which denial was attributed by the prisoner, when asked whether he had any questions to put to them, to the influence of the village Officers by whom he had been taken into custody.

The 2d prisoner confined her defence to a simple denial of the charge.

The Mahomedan Law Officer of the Session Court pronounced the evidence sufficient to convict both prisoners upon strong presumptive proof of having been concerned in the murder of the deceased, and the Acting Session Judge (M. Murray) concurring in this Futwah referred the trial to the Court of Foujdaree Udalut with a recommendation that the prisoners should be sentenced respectively to transportation for life.

The Acting Session Judge observed in his letter of reference that "the evidence rested chiefly on the statements advanced by the 1st "and 2d witnesses for the prosecution," which, he stated that he "saw "no ground to doubt, as they were in a great measure corroborated "by the depositions of other witnesses called by the Court."

These persons the Acting Session Judge remarked "had no time "to concoct a story against the prisoners; they state what they saw "and their statements form very presumptive proof that the 1st and "2d prisoners were actually present at the murder, if the 1st prisoner "is not the person who struck the fatal blow."

The Court of Foujdaree Udalut (present G. S. Hooper, H. Morris and T. L. Strange) on the perusal of the record of the trial considered the evidence altogether undeserving of credit, and acquitting the prisoners, directed their unconditional release.

The view taken by the Court of Foujdaree Udalut of the evidence for the prosecution is to be gathered to a certain extent from the foregoing statement of that evidence, and the remarks already made in regard to the discrepancies it contained. The further grounds assigned by the Court for the judgment passed by them are contained in the following extract from their proceedings.

"The perusal of the record of this case has led the Court of Foujdaree Udalut to entertain a very different appreciation of the evidence from that arrived at by the Acting Session Judge, and they are at a loss to understand how any Judicial Officer could have founded a conviction upon testimony, abounding in such glaring discrepancies and improbabilities, and bearing on the face of it such obvious marks of having been falsely concocted with a view to the conviction of the accused."

"The murder is described as having occurred on the night of the 18th October last. On the following morning the village authorities attended at the spot, and it is deposed that they were then informed of the prisoner and the two other persons charged having been seen by the 1st witness in the house where the murder was committed, and of three of the same persons having been seen near it about the same time by the 2d witness, and a fourth, viz., the 2d prisoner, leaving it."

"One of the village Officers, the Curnum, was examined on this point by the Acting Session Judge, and was one of those who deposed to the above effect.

"That this evidence is altogether false, and that no such information was given at the time alluded to, appears plain from the reports of the village authorities of the 19th and 21st October, the 1st of which documents gives the information that the deceased had been stabbed by "some one" making it evident that it was not then known *by whom*: while the other intimates that the 1st prisoner having been suspected, his cloths had been examined and stains of blood appearing thereon, it had been "concluded that the crime must have been committed by him;" no others furthermore being then implicated, from which it is manifest that the evidence relied upon by the Session Judge had up to that period not been furnished. The Punchayetnamah, dated also on the 21st October sets forth the case in the same way, detailing grounds of suspicion against the 2d prisoner, as well as the 1st arising out of enmity existing on their parts towards the deceased, and speaks of the stains found on the 1st prisoner's garments, the narrative being wound up in these words, "this is what we have understood from examining the corpse, and other persons, both when we first saw the corpse, and when we looked at it again this day at 2 o'clock in the presence of the Head of Police."

"Such was the position of the case when the latter functionary appeared on the scene. After this it underwent a marvellous transformation, and on the following date, that is on the fourth day after the murder, the testimony above recited, as given by the 1st witness, at length appears; the evidence of the 2d witness, whose name in the meantime is not mentioned by any of the deponents, not being produced until the 25th or seven days after the murder took place."

"In the face of these facts the Acting Session Judge observes in his letter of reference that these witnesses had no time to concoct a story against the prisoners, and he repeats the observation when commending to the Court the evidence of the 2d witness, on the ground that he "had very little time to fabricate such a story."

"In the sketch of the evidence given at the commencement of these proceedings the Court have noted the various discrepancies and contradictions which mark the evidence for the prosecution throughout; but they would especially refer to the testimony given before the Head of Police by the 3d additional witness for the prosecution (Comarasetti Chinnappa) and by Coommara Vemavarapu Venkata (who was examined only before the Head of Police), both of whom deposed befor that Officer that the 1st witness, so far from having been cognizant of the murder during the night, as has been since asserted by her, called to the deceased in the morning to waken him up and then for the first time learnt what had occurred."

"The Court have already noticed the contradictory statement made on this point by Comarasetti Chinnappa when examined before the Session Court."

"That the statements of the 1st and 2d witnesses were fabricated, appears further from the testimony given before the Head of Police by Comarasetti Pullaya Carampudi Narappa, and Chittaboyana Guruvappa, who were among the earliest who went to the house of the deceased on the morning in question, and whose statements show that neither the 1st witness nor any other person had then any information to give as to the murderers of the deceased.

"None of those persons were examined by the Session Court, and the omission to call for their evidence, as well as that of Coommara Vemavarapu Venkata, which was obviously calculated to expose the falsity of the accusing witnesses, appears to the Court of Foujdaree Udalut to argue the most culpable neglect of duty on the part of the Acting Session Judge."

"There are furthermore internal marks of falsehood in the evidence of the 1st and 2d witnesses, which of themselves appear to the Court to render their testimony altogether undeserving of belief."

"The 1st witness represents that the murderers were observed by her when standing round the cot of their victim, after the deed had been accomplished, and that she was threatened by one of them and told of what they had done; a course of conduct which it is difficult to suppose that persons having just committed a murder would be betrayed into, as being so obviously calculated to lead to their detection and conviction of the crime. The 2d witness in like manner deposes, that when seen by him outside, these murderers stopped and revealed their names to him, thus again gratuitously exposing themselves when the way was clear for them to have decamped."

"The Court have already adverted to the contradictions and discrepancies in the evidence of these witnesses as given by them before the Police and before the Session Court."

"The additional witnesses relied on by the Acting Session Judge, as having afforded corroboration to the 1st and 2d witnesses, from having, as they say, been early recipients of their information, were with the exception of the 3d and 5th not examined till the case came before him, and there is thus no security that their declarations have not been concocted, while there is much to falsify them."

"The contradictory nature of that given by the 3d witness (Comarasetti Chinnappa) has been already pointed out. The 1st additional witness, a Curnum, is one of those who sent in the village reports, the 7th was present when one of these reports was written, and the 4th and 5th signed the Punchayetnamah, and these documents pointedly falsify their testimony. Such of these witnesses, moreover, as depose in reference to the 1st witness' information, have fallen in with her amended declaration that the 2d prisoner was present at the murder which is of itself a most suspicious feature."

"Not one of the contradictions above noticed appears to have attracted the attention of the Acting Session Judge; not a single question has been put by him with reference to them, and from the course of examination it would appear that that Officer could have paid no attention whatever to the record of the preliminary investigation; thus losing sight of the best criterion by which to test the value of the evidence adduced."

"The Court of Foujdaree Udalut are constrained to remark that the proceedings before the Session Court evince throughout either the most reprehensible negligence or a great and deplorable inaptness for judicial investigation on the part of the Acting Session Judge, and they deem it necessary to direct that that Officer will submit any explanation he may have to offer of the negligence displayed by him in the trial and reference of the case."

"The Court of Foujdaree Udalut further resolve to direct that the Magistrate will institute an enquiry in regard to the circumstances under which the evidence of the 1st and 2d witnesses was produced; the evidence in question appearing so manifestly to have been fabricated after the arrival of the Head of Police at the scene of the murder."

"The Court desire that the Magistrate will require the Head of Police to account for having accepted this evidence as true, and so sent on the case to the Criminal Court in the face of the village reports of the 19th and 21st October; the Punchayetnamah, and the testimony of Vemavarapu Venkata, and the three other individuals above referred to, as given before him, as also of the 3d additional witness, all of which were so calculated to convince him of the utter falsehood of the statements of the said 1st and 2d witnesses; and in communicating the result the Magistrate will be pleased to report generally upon the conduct of the Head of Police as a Police Officer."

"The Court observe that in the record of the trial the additional witnesses who are entered as Court witnesses from 1st to 9th should have been numbered consecutively to the 1st and 2d witnesses, as witnesses from 3d to 11th."

"The indictment upon which the prisoners were arraigned does not state in what part of the body the deceased was stabbed; an important omission which should not have been permitted to occur."

"The Court of Foujdaree Udalut have directed the unconditional release of both the prisoners charged, and they consider the commitment of the case by no means creditable to the Principal Sudder Ameen."

In reply to the requisition made to him for an explanation of the negligence displayed by him in the trial of the case, the Acting Session Judge submitted a lengthened statement in justification of his proceedings, in which he endeavoured to refute the reasons assigned by the Court of Foujdaree Udalut for rejecting the evidence upon which he had relied.

The gist of the arguments advanced by the Acting Session Judge in his return (the length of which precludes its being published in this report) is given in the accompanying extract from the proceedings of the Court of Foujdaree Udalut dated the 13th April 1852.

"The Court of Foujdaree Udalut proceed to review the explanation offered by the Acting Session Judge in the foregoing return on the several points noticed in their proceedings of the 5th ultimo with reference to the trial of the case above referred to; and in recording their remarks thereon the Court will advert seriatim to those paragraphs of the return, in which the Acting Session Judge has endeavoured to combat the grounds assigned by the Court for rejecting the evidence for the prosecution."

"With reference to the remark in para. 2 that "there seems little "doubt that a murder has been committed, and that the deceased was "killed by a chisel, and that this is acknowledged by all the parties "examined," the Court of Foujdaree Udalut observe that as to the fact of a murder having been committed no doubt whatever can exist, but that for the reasons which have led them to discredit generally the evidence of the witnesses for the prosecution, they consider their testimony as to the nature of the instrument with which it was perpetrated to be deserving of no weight whatever."

"The absence of all mention in the primary reports of the murder addressed to the Head of Police by the village Officers of the nature of the stab which had caused the death of the deceased, or of the instrument with which it was supposed to have been committed, appears to the Foujdaree Udalut to render the evidence subsequently given on this point open to much suspicion; the more especially when it is considered how materially the addition of such evidence would be calculated to strengthen the accusation against the 1st prisoner, who, being a carpenter, would naturally be possessed of such an instrument for the purposes of his trade."

"The Acting Session Judge in a subsequent para. of his return (29) lays some stress on the circumstance of no such instrument having been found in the 1st prisoner's possession, but the Court of Foujdaree Udalut would observe that the only direct evidence on this point consists in the statement made by the Court's 1st witness Nakaraz Subbaya, the Curnum of the village, in his answer to the 36th question put to him by the Session Court;—an answer, which, it appears to the Foujdaree Udalut, should have suggested the necessity of a further examination in regard to the nature of the search made, both of this witness himself and of the other persons who were present when it took place."

"No evidence was taken to show that the prisoner did possess such an instrument or when it was last seen in his possession, nor was any opportunity afforded him of explaining, if he did possess one, what had become of it."

"The next point to which the Acting Session Judge adverts is the inference drawn by the Court of Foujdaree Udalut from the omission from the reports made regarding the murder by the village Officers, of all mention of the circumstances which they subsequently stated had been made known to them by the 1st witness previous to the dispatch of either of those reports."

"The inference of the Court of Foujdaree Udalut was, that if the information in question had been in the possession of the village Police when their reports were written, some mention of it would then have been made and that, as it was not even alluded to, their subsequent statements to the effect that they were at that time in possession of it, were false."

"The Acting Session Judge impugns the correctness of this conclusion, and contends that the fact of the prisoners having been apprehended and kept in custody from the morning after the murder, makes it manifest that the village Officers had been informed of the circumstances subsequently stated by them, when they wrote their original reports."

"This, the Court of Foujdaree Udalut observe, is begging the whole question, for it assumes the correctness of the report of the Head of Police and the truth of the evidence for the prosecution, both of which the Court of Foujdaree Udalut, for the reasons already stated by them, have considered to be undeserving of credit."

"The Acting Session Judge throughout his return proceeds upon this assumption, attaching apparently no importance to the circumstances which have led the Court of Foujdaree Udalut to discredit the evidence subsequently adduced, and then urging that evidence as proof, that the omissions in the reports proceeded from another cause than ignorance of the facts to which the subsequent evidence referred."

"The Court of Foujdaree Udalut on the other hand do not consider the fact of the prisoner's apprehension before the arrival of the Head of Police, to have been at all satisfactorily established. It is clear from the second report of the village Officers that suspicion had been attracted to the 1st prisoner; but, as observed by the Foujdaree Udalut in their proceedings of the 5th February last, it is not stated therein from what cause such suspicion originated; nor does it follow that the real cause was that which was subsequently assigned, viz., the information given by the 1st witness; and that it arose upon other grounds than those afterwards stated, the omission from the report of all mention of the 1st witness' statements, or of the other persons named by her, affords, in the opinion of the Court of Foujdaree Udalut, proof the most convincing that from presumptive evidence can be derived."

"The Court attach no importance to the informal manner in which the reports in question were drawn up, and from the mention which the 2d report contains, of the grounds upon which the village Officers concluded that the 1st prisoner must have been the murderer, the Court of Foujdaree Udalut consider it may fairly be inferred, that some allusion to circumstances so specific as those afterwards stated by the 1st witness, would not have been omitted, if they had been known at the time."

"The inference therefore derived by the Court of Foujdaree Udalut from the reports above alluded to, is not, in their opinion, obnoxious to the epithets which the Acting Session Judge has thought fit to apply to it."

"In regard to the Punchayetnamah referred to in paras. 10 and 11 of the Acting Session Judge's return, the Court of Foujdaree Udalut observe an error in their proceedings wherein it is stated that mention was made in that document of the two persons who are said to have absconded ; but this does not in any way affect the conclusions to be arrived at from the Punchayetnamah, unless it be that the omission from it of the names of two of the persons mentioned by the 1st witness would lead to the inference that that individual's subsequent statements were not then known to the members of the inquest, or to the Head of Police in whose presence the Punchayetnamah was drawn up."

"The Court of Foujdaree Udalut are of opinion that the Acting Session Judge has failed entirely in reconciling the discrepancies noticed by them as being observable between the statements of the 1st witness and the accounts given by the persons to whom those statements are said to have been made. The Court still consider the 1st witness' assertions in regard to what she had witnessed during the night of the murder altogether irreconcilable with the fact deposed to by the witness Coomaravarapu Venkata, of her having got up to call the deceased, and making no mention to the former of what had occurred ; and her alleged denial to Comarasetti Pullaya of having recognized any of the prisoners appears to the Court to be equally contradictory to her own evidence, whether it was made on the morning after the murder or at a later period. The Court do not give the evidence of this witness Pullaya any more credit than that of any of the other witnesses for the prosecution, but they see no reason for supposing it to be less credible, and they have merely referred to it as one, among many instances, of the contradictory nature of the evidence upon which the Acting Session Judge founded the conviction of the accused."

"In the 15th para. of his return the Acting Session Judge has applied a most extraordinary construction to the answer given by the 1st witness, when asked by the Head of Police whether on the morning after the murder she had informed the Capoos and Curnum of the three persons previously named by her, having murdered the deceased. The witness had previously made no mention of the 2d prisoner, but in answer to this question she stated that as the villagers were coming up to the house, on hearing of the murder having taken place, the 2d prisoner came up to her and begged her not to implicate her, in reply to which she charged her with having been accessory to the murder, and that the accusation was overheard by the villagers who had in the meantime come up. The terms of the accusation were, "are you and Camsala Somaya not the persons who caused the murder?" "This expression," the Acting Session Judge observes, "among the "Telcogoos amounts to a direct affirmation that they were the very "persons;" and the gist of the argument based on it by that Officer appears to be, that the 1st witness thereby intended to accuse the 2d prisoner as having been one of the persons present, and that therefore the express mention subsequently made by her before the Principal Sudder Ameen and Session Court of the 2d prisoner's presence at the murder, was in no way contradictory to her evidence on this point before the Police."

"Such a construction of the answer above referred to appears to the Court of Foujdaree Udalut to be altogether untenable, and to afford additional proof of the deplorable want of judgment evinced by the Acting Session Judge in weighing the evidence in this case, and in arriving at conclusions altogether unsupported by the facts upon which they are based."

"Admitting for the sake of argument that the answer given by the 1st witness to the question above alluded to was perfectly true, and that the interrogation alleged to have been put by her to the 2d prisoner on the morning in question virtually amounted to an assertion of that prisoner's guilt, the utmost that can be inferred from it would seem to be, that at that time she saw reason to suspect the 2d prisoner of complicity in the murder, and that she charged her with the same; —not surely that she had *seen* her present at it, as she afterwards alleged."

"In the 16th para. of his return the Acting Session Judge points out that the words used by the 1st witness in her deposition before the Session Court, in narrating her conduct after the departure of the murderers, were, "*after* they went out I got up and having looked, &c." not, "*as soon as* they went out" which term was made use of by the Court in commenting on the difference between this statement and her previous one before the Police, to the effect that after they left the house she had remained terrified on her cot."

"The difference appears to the Court to be very immaterial, and assuming the word actually used by the witness to have no more definite meaning than that ascribed to it by the Acting Session Judge, it is sufficient (if it be true) to prove that when the witness was roused by Coommara Vemavarapu Venkata in the morning and when according to the statement of the latter individual she proceeded to call the deceased, she was already aware that he was dead."

"The discrepancy between this witness' statement in regard to the rising of the moon appears to the Court of Foujdaree Udalut to be irreconcilable. The witness stated before the Police that the moon had not risen, leaving it clearly to be inferred that it was dark when the murder was committed. Before the Session Court she stated that it was just rising, this statement being made in reply to a question put by the Court to ascertain by what light she had been enabled to recognize the accused."

"The Court of Foujdaree Udalut adhere to their opinion as to the improbability of the line of conduct attributed by the 1st and 2d witnesses to the prisoners and their accomplices, immediately after the commission of the murder; but, though they still consider it most improbable that persons having just committed a murder should in such a gratuitous manner have exposed themselves to detection, the records of criminal jurisprudence afford such numerous instances of equally unaccountable conduct on the part of persons after just perpetrating a crime, that the Court would not have deemed themselves justified in rejecting the statements of the witnesses on this point, had the rest of their evidence and of the other witnesses for the prosecution been less open to exception than it is."

"In the opinion of the Court of Foujdaree Udalut the Acting Session Judge has entirely failed to explain away the circumstances which have appeared to them to render the evidence of the 2d witness undeserving of credit. This witness was not examined for some days after the murder, having, according to his own statement, been absent from his village from the morning of the murder till the evening of the day before his examination. The Court consider the cause which led to his being examined to be involved in much doubt and suspicion, for no mention was made of him by any of the persons who gave evidence before the Head of Police; and his own statement before the Session Court that he mentioned in the morning after the murder what he had seen in the house of the deceased, to three of the villagers, is contradictory to his Police deposition, wherein he averred that previous to his examination by the Head of Police he had not mentioned to any one the facts then stated by him."

"The statement made by him before the Session Court on this point is also contradicted in its details by the persons who were then alleged by him to have been the recipients of his information on the morning after the murder, and who are supposed by the Acting Session Judge by their communications to the Head of Police to have caused his examination on his return to his village."

"As an instance of the contradictory nature of this portion of the evidence, the Court of Foujdaree Udalut would advert to the deposition of the village Curnum, Nakeraz Subbaya, before the Session Court, wherein it is stated that the 2d witness came to his (the Curnum's) house and informed him of the murder of the deceased, whereas the 2d witness himself states in his evidence before the same tribunal, that the only information he gave, was given in a field outside the village, and that he did not return to the village after leaving the house of the deceased."

"The explanation given by the Acting Session Judge of the contradictory statements made by this witness in regard to the time of his meeting the 2d prisoner on the morning after the murder, appears to the Court of Foujdaree Udalut extremely unsatisfactory."

"The Acting Session Judge infers from the evidence that the witness met the 2d prisoner twice, once when she was coming out and he was going in, and again when he was coming out of the house of the deceased, and that on the second occasion she being conscious that he had discovered the murder, went to him for the purpose of requesting him not to divulge it."

"This view of the evidence is supported by the witness' Session Court deposition, but it does not explain the discrepancy in his evidence before the Police, where he distinctly stated, first that his conversation with the 2d prisoner was as he was leaving the house, and afterwards that it took place as he was entering it."

"To this discrepancy in itself the Court do not attach any material importance, but coupled as it is with others, for which it is impossible to account, except on the supposition that the witness' evidence was concocted, and especially considering the suspicious circumstances under which it was given, the Court consider that the opinion recorded by them regarding the evidence of this witness cannot be deemed an "arbitrary rejection of evidence," as it is designated by the Acting Session Judge."

"The Acting Session Judge would seem to have misunderstood the meaning of the expression made use of by the Court, to the effect that "the seven additional witnesses sent up at the requisition of the Acting Session Judge gave evidence in support of the general purport of the 1st witness' testimony," and to construe it as an admission on the part of the Court that the evidence of the seven witnesses in question went to prove the truth of the 1st witness' statement."

"It is hardly necessary to observe that such was not the meaning of the Court, and how such a construction could be applied to the words made use of, it seems difficult to understand."

"The meaning of the Court was, that these witnesses gave their evidence in conformity with the general outline of the 1st witness' story, but exposed the falsity of their statements by differing, and contradicting each other, in regard to important details."

"The evidence of C. Narappa, to which the Acting Session Judge adverts as proving that the 1st witness early in the morning denounced the murderers of the deceased, has not been taken before the Session Court, and could not therefore be taken into consideration in weighing the evidence against the accused."

"The evidence of this witness is somewhat vague in regard to the most important fact related in it, the time of the communication alleged to have been made to him by the 1st witness not having been stated; and it is therefore impossible to ascertain whether this communication was said to have been made in the presence of the other witnesses who were named by C. Narappa as having been present when he inspected the corpse of the deceased ; a point of much importance in comparing his evidence with that of the other witnesses and forming a judgment as to its truth."

"That the Acting Session Judge should have deemed the examination of these witnesses unnecessary, the Court of Foujdaree Udalut consider to reflect most seriously on his judgment and aptness for judicial enquiry."

"The only other point, requiring notice from the Court, is the alleged fact of the persons accused with the prisoner having absconded from their village. The evidence to the fact consists of bare statements made by several of the witnesses for the prosecution, but *when* the individuals referred to left their houses ; *when* they were last seen; whether they may not have quitted the village for some other reason than that assigned, is all left to conjecture, no question having been put regarding any of these points by the Police or by the Acting Session Judge."

"After the above review of the arguments advanced in the Acting Session Judge's return, it is hardly necessary to observe, that the Court of Foujdaree Udalut see no reason to modify the censure pronounced by them upon that Officer's proceedings in the conduct of the trial under notice. Many of the arguments now put forward in reference to those proceedings afford additional evidence of the Acting Session Judge's great want of judgment, and the general tone of his comments on the observations of the Foujdaree Udalut, while they prove his inability to understand the errors committed by him in mistaking contradictory assertions for proof and drawing inferences from insufficient premises, even after those errors have been pointed out to him in the clearest terms, evinces at the same time a total forgetfulness of the deference due by him to the Higher Court."

"The Judges of the Court of Foujdaree Udalut have no wish to restrict the Officers presiding over the Lower Courts from a free expression of opinion on all points on which their proceedings may have been commented on by the Higher Court, but it is obvious that all such communications should be couched in respectful language, and although the Court of Foujdaree Udalut are willing on this occasion to attribute many of the objectionable expressions made use of in the Acting Session Judge's return to an anxiety to relieve himself from the censure which had been recorded on his proceedings, they deem it proper to inform the Acting Session Judge that any similar instance of disrespect in the communications addressed by him to the Court will be brought to the notice of Government."

The Head of Police, by whom the case was committed for trial, and with whose connivance the Court of Foujdaree Udalut stated, that they saw every reason to believe, that the whole of the evidence had been concocted, was dismissed from his office by order of the Court of Foujdaree Udalut.

APPENDIX No. III.

"THE COCKSPUR CASE."

FROM A NOTE BY THE HON'BLE SIR WILLIAM W. BURTON, PUISNE JUDGE OF THE SUPREME COURT.

"The next case I am obliged to quote from memory, having lost my note of it; but it is impressed so strongly on my mind, that I have no doubt of the accuracy of my recollection as far as my statement of it will go, although minor points may have been lost from it.

"Five men were tried in one of the country district Courts in 1844 held before Mr. Bird (the same gentleman who tried the case) for the murder of a young boy 7 or 9 years old.

"The accepted witnesses of the fact were two boys, one 12, the other 16 years of age.

"The child who was murdered was missed from the neighbourhood of his parent's house on the evening of the day on which it was murdered. It had on its person at the time the little ornaments worn by children on festival occasions, and which were of some little value. In the afternoon of that day it had been seen by some of the neighbours, a little way from the house, in the company of one of the boys: and in consequence of that circumstance coming to the knowledge of the father in the course of the search for the child, he went to the house of the two boys at about 9 in the evening, (they were then in bed) and questioned them, if they had been with or seen the child. They both said "they had not seen him;" and persisted in that account.

"Next morning the body of the child was found in a well, just outside the village; dead; and there were wounds on its throat inflicted by some sharp instrument, which it appeared were the cause of death.

"The boys were arrested by the Native Police authority of the village, and charged with the murder.

"They persisted in their first statement, and made no other.

"The Police official forwarded them to the next authority, I believe a Magistrate, and after they had been in custody for some time, I believe two or three days, they joined in telling a story which was incredible in all its facts; but nevertheless obtained implicit credence by the Magistrate, the Judge, and the inferior Court, and Judges of the Foujdaree Udalut.

"It was this—that they had witnessed the murder. That it was committed by four men of the village, whom they named: that they, the boys, were employed by the men, one to fetch a rope to bind the child, the other to watch if any one should approach; and that they thus witnessed what followed.

"They described, particularly, without either deviating from the other, the part which each of these four men took in the murder. It was this. They laid the child on his back. They described particularly to what point of the compass the head lay, and each arm, and the legs, one held one arm of the child, and covered his mouth; two others held, each, a leg; and the fourth held the other arm, and cut the throat of the child with a steel cockspur, such as is used by Natives for fighting cocks: an instrument about 2½ inches long: he then took the ornaments off the child's person, and threw the body into the well. They then proceeded towards the house where the two boys lived, and then under a hedge, only 1½ yard from the house, in the presence of the two boys buried the ornaments, and the cockspur with which the murder had been perpetrated, together with a small purse, containing other cockspurs, which the boys alleged belonged to one of the prisoners, and had been left by him with their father who was a blacksmith, and a maker of such instruments, for the purpose of being sharpened, and had been returned to the prisoner.

"To confirm this story they took the Police to the spot where the articles were buried, and there they were found.

"This was their first story: they afterwards amended it, both concurring in all the particulars of the amendments, that a fifth man was party to the murder, whom they accused, and being asked what part he took, they answered that he held the child's head, and gave orders 'cut here.'

"There was one other witness, a woman, who might be said to give some probability to the story of the boys, as she proved that the five men had been seen by her at the spot where the boys said it had been committed that evening, about the time the boys spoke of. It was a place where seeds or shrubs grew: and so thickly, as not to be seen through; but there was a path that way to the village; the five prisoners and the woman had to go that way home from their work in the fields.

"So there was really nothing in this evidence. The boys might have been there unseen of either man or woman, and yet have heard, whilst in confinement, that those men had been seen that evening about the spot, where the well was, in which the body was found.

"After the body had been found there, it was likely enough that any one who had been seen there would be remembered. But the gross improbabilities in the story consisted in the fact that these two boys in no way concerned in the murder, or to derive any benefit from it, should one of them be sent for a rope, and bring it, and the other be put to watch, and that they should not be struck with fear and horror, and run away and give the alarm on the first appearance of what was going to take place—that the men should allow two such witnesses to be present and they should conceal the property near the boys' residence, rather than anywhere else, and in a spot known to them. All this was so monstrous that one is lost in astonishment at its finding credit from any one. It did however obtain it from Magistrate and Judge. All concerned in the case in the Country (except the old Police Peon who charged the boys themselves with the murder), believed it, and the Law Officers and the Judge convicted the five prisoners.

"The case being capital, it went up to the Foujdaree Udalut.

"That Court consists of three Puisne Judges and a Chief Judge, the latter, however, is a Member of Council, and is only called in when the others differ.

"Messrs. Waters and Boileau minuted their opinion; found the prisoners all guilty, and awarded their sentence accordingly, four to be hanged, one to be transported.

"Mr. Lewin was one of the Judges. When the case came to be considered by him, he at once stated his opinion that the prisoners were innocent, and the boys were the murderers, and begged the case might be referred to Mr. Dickenson, Chief Judge. He concurred with Mr. Lewin. Thus the Court was divided in opinion. Government appointed a fifth, Mr. Thomas, who concurred with Mr. Lewin and Mr. Dickenson, and the men were saved."

APPENDIX No. IV.

(No. 89.)

Extract from the Proceedings of the Sudr Udalut Court under date the 9th July 1852.

Read again Extract from the Minutes of Consultation of Government in the Revenue Department under date the 29th April 1852.

(Here enter F. U. No. $\frac{1059}{1852}$)

Read also Extract from the Minutes of Consultation of Government in the Revenue Department under date the 6th May 1852.

(Here enter S. U. No. $\frac{921}{1852}$)

Read also letter dated the 21st May 1852 from the Magistrate of Rajahmundry soliciting the instructions of the Court of Foujdaree

Udalut regarding the matters contained in the Petition presented by the Guardian of the minor Zemindar of Pittapoor.

(Here enter F. U. No. $\frac{1296}{1852}$)

Read also Miscellaneous Petitions presented on the 25th May and 7th June 1852 by R. Teroomala Row Vakeel on behalf of Kolaghen Venkatarow the aforesaid Guardian of the minor Zemindar of Pittapoor.

(Here enter F. U. P. No. 65 and $\frac{73}{1852}$)

Read also Return dated the 26th May 1852 made by the Civil Judge of Rajahmundry to the requisition contained in the proceedings of the F. U. under date the 13th May 1852 calling upon that Officer to explain the circumstances under which he deemed himself justified in interfering with the orders issued by the Collector and Magistrate of Rajahmundry relative to one Bhaviummah sister of the minor Zemindar of Pittapoor, and requiring him to suspend all orders issued by him in the matter pending the final instructions of Sudr Udalut.

(Here enter S. U. No. $\frac{1083}{1852}$)

Read also letter dated the 9th June 1852 from the Civil Judge of Rajahmundry submitting copies of the correspondence connected with the above matter.

(Here enter S. U. No. $\frac{1196}{1852}$)

1. In the foregoing Return, the Civil Judge adverting to the requisition contained in the proceedings of the S. U. above recorded, states that the orders of the Court are obeyed, and all orders issued by him on the matter in question are placed in abeyance.

2. These orders Mr. Anstruther observes were necessarily issued by him in his joint capacity of Civil and Session Judge in consequence of the orders appealed from having been placed by Mr. Prendergast, some in his capacity of Collector and others in that of Magistrate. Mr. Anstruther denies that he exercised any undue interference in the Officers of the Zemindary beyond that which was called for by the importunity of the parties; and he maintains that the course of procedure ultimately adapted by him will be found on reference to certain cases on the records of the S. U. to be borne out by practice and precedent as well as sanctioned by the Regulations.

3. The two principal points arising out of the foregoing correspondence which now demand the consideration of the Court of Sudr Udalut are—

1. The power of the Court of Wards to provide for the Guardianship of all the minor children of the deceased Zemindar and

3. The right of the Magistrate to interdict the marriage of the female minor " Bhaviummah" at the instance of the Guardian of the minor Zemindar.

4. In regard to the first point, the Court of S. U. *concurs with the Government in its opinion that the power* to provide for the Guardianship of all minor children (male or female) of a Zemindar deceased, whose estate as in the present instance, has been taken under the Administration of the Court of Wards, must be held to be vested likewise in that authority.

5. Regulation V. of 1804, it is true in providing for the Guardianship of the immediate heir or heirs to an Estate (being minors or otherwise incapacitated) contains no direct or explicit provisions authorizing the Court of Wards to appoint a Guardian to the other minor member of the family nor on the other hand it must be observed does it contain any provision sanctioning that appointment by the Zillah Judge and the effect of the omission is consequently equally applicable to the latter as to the former authority.

6. The question of jurisdiction therefore in each case must necessarily be determined in accordance with what may appear on a fair and liberal construction of the legislative in enactment, *and the argumentsset forthin paras.* 12, 13, *and* 14 *of Extract from the Minutes of Consultation noted in the margin in support of the opinion* that such authority is vested in the Court of Wards and not in the Zillah Judge, *appear to the Court of S. U. to be so conclusive on that point and are so entirely expressive of their views on the subject as to render the further enumeration of them unnecessary.*

7. The Court remark that the cases cited by the Civil Judge as analagous to the one now under consideration are altogether irrelevant and his application to it of the provisions of Section II and VII Regulation V of 1804 is clearly erroneous, those Sections being obviously applicable only to cases in which females or persons incapacitated from any of the cause therein specified may succeed to the property as heirs to the former proprietors deceased. In the case now under notice it is to be observed no property was inherited by the female Ward,

REVENUE DEPARTMENT.

No. 390.

Extract from the Minutes of Consultation under date the 29th April 1852.

12. The power of the Court of Wards to provide for the guardianship of all the minor children of a Zemindar deceased, whose property has been taken under their administration (which it is observed is now challenged by the agent of the grandmother and C. Atchiah the uncle) is a power which it is believed has never before been questioned. It has been the invariable practice of the Court to make provision as seemed meet for the tutilage, maintenance and education of female minors as well as males. The Regulation is certainly not very explicit, but the usage of nearly half a century ought to be taken as settling the construction. The property may be regarded as having devolved on the eldest son as head of the family, but all the sons and daughters have a certain heirship in it: a certain interest has devolved on them by inheritance, they are entitled to maintenance out of the estate, and indeed from what other source could they be supported; they are therefore so much concerned in it that the administration of it by Court of Wards may be taken to be for their behalf partly, they are also reversionary heirs. Upon some such view as

this the younger children have always been considered as falling within the scope of the Regulation and entitled personally to the protection of the Court of Wards as well as the elder, and no distinction has been made in this respect either between the elder and younger male children or between male and female children. They have been cared for equally as an undivided family. The construction now contended for would cause a division in every family.

13. Mr. Salmon the Vakeel for those who oppose the appointment made by the Court of Wards contends that the authority of the Court, to appoint a guardian is confined to the minor to whom the estate or property descends and that the Zillah Judge as representing the Supreme authority "is the person on whom the law vests the duty of seeing that a fit person is guardian of a minor girl under such circumstances." He does not however point out the law. The Supreme authority in the land is undoubtedly competent to vest this duty in the Zillah Judge and it has done so in some cases, but not where the property concerned is subject to the Jurisdiction of the Court of Wards. In one set of cases the duty is vested in the Court of Wards, in another it is vested in the Zillah Courts. The same latitude of construction as to the term "heirs" as has been observed prescriptively by the Court of Wards would be necessary to admit of the Zillah Court appointing a guardian to this female minor, if the case were one within its Jurisdiction as it is not.

See Sec. XX. to XXII. of Reg. V. of 1804, extended by Sec. III, Reg. X. of 1813.

14. The argument that the girl is of an age to choose where she will reside does not seem valid. It is clear she could not make such a choice against her father's will if he were alive, a guardian stands in locoparentis—a guardian appointed by the Court of Wards has the same powers as a guardian appointed by the father. If therefore the Court of Wards has the power to appoint a guardian to the girl, no party can interfere between the girl and the guardian so appointed without committing a misdemeanour of which the Magistrate might take cognizance. Or if the girl be in the charge of other persons, the guardian so duly appointed is entitled either directly or through the medium of the Collector as agent to the Court of Wards to demand

Reg. V. of 1804, Sec. XXI. C. 8.

who so far as the Court can learn is wholly dependant for her maintenance on the proceeds of the Estate which is confessedly under the Collectors management on behalf of her brother the minor Zemindar.

8. Having arrived at the foregoing conclusion as regards the first point the Court of S. U. have no hesitation in regarding this opinion in respect to the second, that the Collector, as Agent to the Court of Wards had full authority to interdict the proposed marriage of Bhaviummah, and that the Civil Judges interference with that order whether issued by the Collector ostensibly in the capacity of Magistrate, or as it ought to have been in his capacity of Collector and his ex-Officio Agent to the Court of Wards was most irregular and uncalled for, and the Court cannot but consider that Mr. Anstruther has both incurred a very serious responsibility, and rendered himself obnoxious to grave censure by the ill-judged pertinacity with which he insisted upon acting upon his own view of so important and doubtful a question resolutely refusing to refer the queries submitted by the Magistrate for the consideration and orders of the Court of S. U.

9. The two points in question having been thus disposed of, it now only remains for the Court of S. U. to express their opinion as to the measures which should be adopted by the Court of Wards preliminary to the removal of the minor Bhaviummah from the custody of her paternal Grandmother and Aunt the absolute prohibitions of the proposed marriage and disposal of her in marriage to some other person and

from them the person of his Ward and if not delivered to him, he may call upon the Magistrate to support him in the exercise of his just and legal authority over her, and to put down all forcible opposition to it. The Government resolve to call upon the Board of Revenue to report whether there are upon their records any precedents bearing upon this point.

considering the course indicated in the 16*th* and 17*th paras. of the Minutes of Consultation above referred to, to be the most judicious which under all the circumstances of the case, can now be adopted,* the *Court deem it proper to suggest that the same be at once carried out.*

Here paras. 16 and 17 are entered in the margin.*

Ordered that Extract from these proceedings be forwarded to the Civil Judge of Rajahmundry for his information and for communication to the Magistrate.

---

* **The copy of the order furnished the Vakeel of Row Bhaviah, unfortunately does not contain Sections 16 and 17 of the Government Minute. Sections 12, 13, and 14 however suffice to show how thoroughly the Government argues its own exparte case before submitting it to the Sudder for its decision.**

THE AFFRAY BILL

AND THE

CRIMINAL ADMINISTRATION

OF BENGAL.

BY

A MEMBER OF THE BRITISH INDIAN ASSOCIATION.

1854.

THE AFFRAY BILL

AND THE

CRIMINAL ADMINISTRATION

OF

BENGAL.

THE natives of Bengal are known to be industrious, peaceful and mild in their disposition. They are patient under wrongs, and possess a power of endurance under a complicated system of oppressions and exactions hardly to be equalled by any other nation. Why then do we witness such frequent and bloody affrays attended with loss of life and limbs as well as property, and harassing criminal prosecutions which often result in imprisonment and fine? These affrays are not, as Mr. Welby Jackson states in his report to Government, chiefly conducted by Upcountrymen, but by Bengally Rajpoots, Mussulmans, Bagdeēs, Harries, and Goalas. The employment of Upcountrymen, on such occasions, is an exception, not the rule. But it will be asked, what are the causes that lead to such anti-national and suicidal conduct, and convert such a peaceful people into something approaching to an armed populace? Simply and emphatically, self-defence. No one class in the community, from the Zemindar down to the sweeper, feels itself safe from the aggressions of others—including Magistrates and their subordinate Police. Not that we are without excellent and stringent laws for putting down affrays and punishing other crimes, but people have no trust in their administration. To the defects in the administrative agency and the total inadequacy of the Police force, much of these evils may be traced. Our Magisterial Courts have become the focus of perjury, forgery and false complaints, arising chiefly from the incompetency of the presiding officers to discriminate truth from falsehood, and to protect the honest from the arts of the wicked. They are chiefly the resort of the latter class of persons. The peaceful portion of the community would rather put up with many evils than come into contact with one of these courts. In fact, in the language of one who now occupies a high position, our Police "is as bad as can be." An impression has gone abroad that might is right. Every one who can afford it acts upon this principle. If a Planter does not avail himself of clubmen, his indigo will be cut and carried away by either the neighbouring Planter or the Zemindars. Even, sometimes, the Ryots would turn round and deprive him of it. If the Ryots be not impressed with a belief that their Zemindar is all powerful, they will not pay him their rents but at once drive his Gomastah out from the village. The *Huptums, Punjums and Bistoms* (summary laws for the realization of rent) will avail him naught unless accompanied by the one thing essential. If he wishes to measure the lands or to make a new settlement of rent in his estate, or to inquire into the validity of rent-free tenures and institute legal proceedings, woe be to him if he depends for the success of his measures or his lawsuits upon his own exertions and the potency of the laws. If a Ryot complains to the Court of the loss of his crops, he must either be a favorite of the Zemindar or belong to a knot of influential men in the village, with clubmen at their disposal; else he will not get a witness to depose in his favor. By turns, the Zemindar, the Planter and the village clique—the latter, consisting of disreputable but shrewd and clever persons, get the upper hand in the village, according to accidental circumstances, such as the smiles, obstinacy, prejudice, freaks and caprices of a Magistrate, a Collector, or even the corrupt support of a Police Darogah. While such favor lasts, the possessor of it has everything his own way, but, by another change, his opponent gets the upper hand, and retaliates upon the fallen enemy and his party. It is during such crises that recourse is had to clubmen and clubs. When a man finds that ruin is staring him in the face, though by the illegal acts of his opponent, indirectly countenanced by Magistrates, he becomes desperate, and in self defence he takes himself to unlawful measures. If he succeeds in the use of force, he, in his turn, becomes the aggressor, and goes on from one step to another, encroaching and trampling upon the rights of others. The other party in time retaliates and repays old grudges tenfold while his sunny days last. Such is and will be the conduct of poor human nature in this as well as in every other country, when in possession of unlimited or irresponsible power. A peaceful or honest man, be he Zemindar, Planter or Ryot, finds it very often impossible to preserve his rights by lawful means, and therefore from sheer necessity either becomes himself an aggressor or joins with one dominant party or other. In Bengal, village society is thus divided into two opposing, irreconcileable factions. Morality, good sense, peace and happiness are thus alternately sacrificed at the altar of strife, and a settled conviction takes place that right is might. A person of property who commences life with good and peaceful intentions is gradually hardened by this lawless state of the country into an habitual peacebreaker. Not unfrequently a Magistrate, sometimes from prejudice and sometimes from excess of zeal, takes a liking to a Planter, a Zemindar, or the village clique, and gradually settles down into a partisan, and supports him or them through thick and thin as long as he remains in the zillah. We can point out many instances in which a number of Planters, Zemindars, or Ryots, as the case may be, have uniformly secured decrees from a Magistrate. His successor adopts perhaps an opposite course, and gives a lift to one of the parties to the ruin of the others. Thus this system of alternate predominance interminably goes on, to the disorganisation and corruption of society. The present limited system of appeals mends the matter very little. In a numerous class of cases, there is no appeal from the decision of a Magistrate. A large number of cases decided by Assistant and Deputy Magistrates, Sudder Ameens, Cazees, and Pundits with limited powers, are only appealable to the Magistrate, whose orders are final. A person need but be known to be obnoxious to the Magistrate, or an indirect hint thrown out by him in conversation—it is enough to seal the doom of the accused, however falsely he may have been arraigned. After all these deductions, there remain indeed a very limited number of cases that are appealable to the Sessions Judge, and the privilege of appeal after all is of very little avail, as a Magistrate has so many ways of annoying people, and possesses such an amount of irresponsible and undefined power, in his double capacity of Superintendent of Police and Criminal Judge, that few dare to provoke his hostility, and therefore most try to avoid it by bribing the Sudder and Mofussil Amlah, and put up with a large amount of unnecessary annoyance and trouble which the Magistrates and their subordinates inflict on all classes of the community who do not submit to their caprices and humours. It is very unfortunate, but nevertheless true, that a very erroneous impression exists in the minds of the higher classes of our public officers, whose opinions more or les regulate the making and unmaking of laws, that all serious and important cases are adjudicated by the Sessions Judges, men of mature understanding and judgment; but the fact is quite the reverse. The cases generally made over to their tribunals are Dacoities, murders, culpable homicides, in which a man of property or respectability is very seldom a defendant, but those concerned are chiefly persons of abandoned character, outcasts from society, to whom imprisonment and irons are no disgrace. All other cases, which constitute the vast majority, and in which the innocent, the virtuous and the respectable portion of the community are concerned, are disposed of, as I have described above, by men of little or no experience, temper and judgment. From the peculiar nature of our society, the trial and decision of this class of cases exercise the greatest influence on the condition of the community. A few decisions, entailing the imprisonment or disgrace of a few innocent persons, create a great sensation in the community, and for a time the honor, property and liberty of the rest of that community may be said to be at the disposal of the victorious party. Under the influence of such circumstances, Talookdars, Lakerajdars, and Planters are known to have been ousted from their estates, and Ryots despoiled and plundered of their all. To prevent such disasters, large bribes are offered, recourse is had to perjury and forgery, and not unfrequently a person jeopardizes his all by flying from our so called Justices of the Peace.

Until the trial of this class of cases, the largest and most important, is placed on an improved footing, and people are sure to meet with a fair hearing, an unbiassed and deliberate judgment, pronounced by properly qualified judges, and not according to the present fashion, dragged into jail with little or no evidence and hardly any hearing, to be spit upon and abused by other prisoners, Burkundazes and Darogahs, unless a large sum of let-alone-money (if I may be allowed to use the term) is given, the well-being and security of the community will always be precarious, and recourse had to affrays and other unlawful means. I have known and am ready to adduce hundreds of cases in which respectable persons thus huddled into jail had to pay let-alone-money from five to 500 Rs. in each case, according to their wealth and respectability. But there is not the slightest hope of a change for the better as long as the head of the executive police is permitted to engross in his person, with little or no check, the largest and most important portion of judicial functions, unaided by jury, experience, age or legal training. For the corroboration of this statement, I appeal unhesitatingly to the intelligent portion of the Mofussil residents, both European and native, as well as to those members of the Civil Service who are known for their impartiality and justice. I will here quote the opinions of two of this class of civilians. Mr. Hawkins, the late Sudder Judge, said, when called upon to state his opinion as to the propriety of doing away with appeals from the decisions of Magistrates,

"17. But let it be admitted, that the Magistrate or other court "of first instance does examine all the witnesses. The question "must be asked whether all the officers, vested with power to sen- "tence offenders to punishment, can be safely entrusted to deal "finally with matters of evidence and facts. An inexperienced "youth, just out of College, who has never been trained to weigh "evidence, probably ignorant of the first principles of the law of "evidence, cannot surely be safely entrusted with a power so "great. It appears to me, that the means and materials with "which we are compelled to work in this country do not admit of "an entire abrogation of appeals upon matters of evidence and "fact, with running the risk of doing incalculable mischief such as "cannot be compensated for by any additional celerity in the "despatch of business, and consequent diminution of vexation and "annoyance to parties attending our Criminal Courts.

"18. Again, as to the abrogation of appeals on matters of evi- "dence and fact, in cases decided by the Magistrates themselves. "I give every credit to the Magistrates as a body of zealous and "intelligent men, but it must be borne in mind that they exercise "an authority far exceeding that of the Magistracy of our own "land, or indeed I believe of any civilized people. This authority "too is exercised by men discharging the functions of the twofold "capacity of the Criminal Judge and the Executive Police. The "Magistrate cannot but feel that the conviction and punishment of "offenders is, in its own place and in no small measure, essential to "the maintenance of that efficiency of Police for which he is respon- "sible; he has a bias (possibly imperceptible to himself) towards "the conviction of offenders, and has the power, on conviction, of "sentencing a man to a long term of imprisonment, according to "the nature of the offence, to the extent of three years Would "it be safe to leave this power in the hands of Judges, the execu- "tive duties of whose office, as officers of Police, are calculated to "induce a bias on their mind against the accused, and to lead "them, however unintentionally and imperceptibly, to place the "accused in that position in which the vast powers of punishment "with which they are armed may be called into action, without "giving a higher court an appellate jurisdiction in matters of evi- "dence and facts? I cannot think so."

Mr. Trevor, on the same occasion, says,

"3. It may perhaps be asserted generally that in all systems,

" denying the privilege of appeal, there should be on the part of " the Judges, first, considerable legal attainments conjoined with " great knowledge of human nature in general, and especially of " the character of the people amongst whom they have to admi- " nister justice, and secondly, the absence of every official influence " likely to cause disturbance or fluctuation in the mind of the ju- " dicial authority.

" 4. It is further submitted, that both the conditions above " mentioned should be realised together, before the finality of the " orders of a court of first instance can work out other results than " injustice; the absence of influencing circumstances, if unattended " with legal knowledge, will not save a Judge from committing " errors of law; whereas the highest legal acquirements, if accom- " panied by influences disturbing the judgment, will be no safe- " guard against the commission of errors in matters of fact.

" 5. I do not presume to say whether the first condition is " realised in the present state of things or not. I may venture to " assert that the second is not; the union in the same person of " the offices of thief-catcher and thief-trier (offices requiring very " different habits of mind) gives a bias to the judgment of the Ma- " gistrate unfavorable to persons apprehended through the instru- " mentality of his own Police, when on their trial; it is not ne- " cessary that Magistrates should be aware of the bias; it is not, " however, the less real or less prejudicial to justice by reason of " this unconsciousness."

It does not require much argument to convince us that the evils depicted by Mr. Trevor would be augmented tenfold when coupled with the ordinary frailties of human nature, from which our Magistrates cannot be said to be exempt, such as prejudice, passion, self-interest, obstinacy, indolence, &c. It is well known that Darogahs, partly from overzeal, but mostly from interested and corrupt motives, continue to keep alive in the imaginations of Magistrates intended or actual scenes of affrays, plunder and other crimes, the intended flight of individuals, and the opposition of wealthy and powerful Landholders, Planters and others, both by written and oral communication, in as exaggerated a manner as official forms and the character and gullibility of the superior officer will permit them to do with impunity, when in reality the greater part of these representations, if not the whole, are only the creations of their own brains. Is it possible for a juvenile Magistrate to remain unprejudiced against individuals and communities, to prevent or curb whose supposed evil disposition and opposition to his authority he has so frequently and seriously been called upon to exercise his ingenuity and wisdom? Is it human nature that the Head of the Police should bring discredit on his own management and control by frequently passing adverse decisions as a judicial officer, condemning the preliminary steps taken by himself and his subordinates for preserving peace and checking crime? Are all these or any of these circumstances favorable to the forming of habits of viewing clearly and dispassionately the merits of a case, so necessary to arrive at a just conclusion? It will, however, be urged that notwithstanding theoretical argument, a large number of acquittals are in practice to be found in the proceedings of our Magistrates. I am aware of the fact, and ascribe it to the necessity imposed upon them to send up such cases only as will stand the scrutiny of another tribunal, and in those case which are appealable to the Sessions Judge, I think I shall not be far from the truth when I affirm that, were a person judicially trained and unprejudiced, or even a Merchant, a Planter or a respectable native of mature judgment and age, and who is in the habit of mixing with all classes of the people, to go over the decisions (both dismissals and decrees) recorded by our Magistrates, he would quash on an average at least half of them, if not more. This is one of the peculiar results of the union of executive and judicial powers in the same person. This doubling system is also admirably adapted for gagging the throats of the people, for, if a person opposes the wrong-doing of a Magistrate in the Police department, the latter turns round and shelters himself as a judicial functionary under the impunity *law*, Act 18 of 1850, or has his revenge indirectly in a judicial proceeding. A Magistrate is very seldom without an opportunity of gratifying his personal dislike, as the mere circumstance of a person falling foul of that functionary will bring in a number of false complaints supported by false testimony against that individual. What a temptation these occasions offer to those Magistrates who are vindictively inclined. Magistrates, generally, may not be chargeable with this weakness, but nevertheless, as long as they are endowed with this double capacity it is very difficult to eradicate such a conviction from the minds of the people. And after all a great deal of the efficiency of a public functionary depends upon the popular belief of the impartiality of his proceedings. The present system is injurious both ways; a man of honour and delicacy feels himself constrained from giving full force to the convictions of his mind, while it is worse than injustice to invest an officer of an opposite disposition with such tremendous powers.

The superintendence and control exercised over this class of officers is very slight. On a recent occasion one of them sentenced a respectable man to ten days' imprisonment on the pretext of his having cut down a tree. The Sessions Judge very properly recommended to the Nizamut Court to take a serious notice of such improper conduct, which he ascribed to an unjudicial state of mind, but the controlling Court simply reversed the order, without expressing a single word of disapprobation. On a private ferry being taken possession of by a Magistrate, the Sudder Court held in 1848 that the official acts of Magistrates are not cognizable by the Civil Courts of the country. An Indigo Planter, some years ago, with the direct cognizance of a Magistrate, who was living with him at the time, wantonly attacked and robbed the houses of a number of respectable Mussulman Talookdars, in revenge for his being denied the farm of their estate. This, as well as other improper acts of that officer, was officially brought to the notice of government, without bringing down any other punishment on the offender than simple removal from one district to another. I can fill up a volume with such recitals; but my object is to attack and criticise the system, and not individuals.

The following observations of Mr. W. Jackson, a late Sudder Judge, on the qualifications necessary for a Police Magistrate, are very appropriate, and add not a little to the reasons already adduced for separating the Police from the judicial functions of Magistrates. The two posts require distinct and not unfrequently opposite qualifications very rare to be met with in the same individual.

" 131. POLICE OFFICERS SHOULD BE CHOSEN FOR QUALIFICATIONS, NOT BY GRADATION.—The examinations of Civil Servants which they must pass before they can exercise the full powers of Collector and Magistrate, are such as to ensure their being sufficiently acquainted with the law and language of the country; but this will not alone render any one an efficient Police officer; indeed there are many men who from want of natural energy, and of the habit of acting readily and effectually, can never be made fit to be trusted with the control of a district Police; in their hands there would be a want of regular discipline in the administration, which is fatal to efficiency in the subordinate Police force; it appears to me that such men ought not to be entrusted with Police: it is quite certain that in their hands the improvement of a Police cannot be effected.

" 132. The regular steps by gradation in the Civil Service cannot, in every instance, be occupied, each in succession, by every member of the service; some of them are not fit to be Magistrates, some well adapted for that purpose, but not possessing the qualities required to fill the office of Judge; it seems to me that this kind of personal fitness should receive more at-

"tention: I would not pass over a fit man in filling up an appoint-"ment, but would not appoint him to a charge to which he was "known to be unequal."

An ex-Zemindar or Talookdar out of possession for many years finds that his opponent is not in favour with the Collector or his Deputy, institutes a false *huptum* or a *punjum canoon* suit, supported by some old and worthless document, or, may be, by forged ones, and secures the aid of the village clique. In many instances such a claimant would obtain a decree in his favor, either through the carelessness, inattention, or the influence of the Omlah. Notwithstanding the remonstrance of the opposite party against such a decree, the successful party would proceed to dispossess the present proprietor from a large estate containing many hundreds of Ryots, while the decree is perhaps only against a single tenant, and not against the proprietor. Cases of such shameful dispossession of large estates by the means of Act 4 of 1840, do not unfrequently occur. Such acts of flagrant injustice seldom, if ever, happen in any other well regulated country, but in this, people are habituated to such scenes from their frequency. Every body in the community knows and talks over the real merits of the cases, while our public officers are alone ignorant of such outrages, because many of them possess so small a share of legal talent and training, and are so little acquainted with the habits, feelings and customs of the people. It is thus that designing persons not unfrequently obtain possession of other people's property, to the disgust and alarm of the community. Not more than seven or eight years ago, a wealthy Planter and Zemindar of one of the Presidency districts, with the help of a fabricated deed of sale and of clubmen, took forcible possession of a large estate containing twenty villages, and notwithstanding decisions under Act 4 of 1840 and several revisions, modifications and retrials in favour of the party wronged, the aggressor managed, with the help of clubmen and in consequence of the incapacity and indifference of our public functionaries, to retain possession of the property for nearly two years, and would have perhaps kept it for ever had not the weaker party consented to pay 200 or 300 Rs. in the shape of expenses that his aggressor had been put to by this daring act of robbery. Another outrage of this kind occurred in the same vicinity soon after. Such acts of misrule (it is nothing less than that) can be quoted and proved by hundreds in every district.

The system of training civil servants, when scarcely of an age to get out of College, by investing them with judicial powers in criminal and revenue cases, though of small value, has not a little tended to foster a feeling of self-sufficiency and carelessness in the assistants, which materially mar their usefulness and future improvement. They imbibe in early life the habit of hearing and looking at so much only as the Amlahs choose to point out and interpret to them, and pass judicial decisions more by dictation than from any deliberation of their own. The Amlahs take care to draw up the decisions in a manner that implies the possession of a large amount of erudition and investigation in the assistant; they are generally accepted as such by the appellate authorities; and to his delight, as well as that of his amlahs, the greater portion of these decisions are upheld. Who is there among the people and such of the civilians as mix with the people and care for their welfare that does not know that while the novitiate lasts the favourite amlah of the Assistant Collector or Magistrate makes from 200 to 500 Rs. a month? What a wholesome example such scenes hold out to our Moonsiffs and Sudder Ameens, who after labouring honestly and zealously for a series of years find their income unequal to that of the Mohorir or clerk assistant of a covenanted assistant. The cases made over to our assistants for trial may be and are considered by their seniors as trivial, but we know to our cost that a large portion of such decisions inflict an amount of injustice and legal oppression that can hardly be imagined by any one not initiated into the mysteries of Mofussil life, and tends not a little to disturb the peace and harmony of society. Our Magistrates, Collectors and Judges are not selected for their aptitude and habits of business, nor for their enlarged views and knowledge of jurisprudence, but because they require promotion and large salaries and cannot conveniently be employed in the political or commercial departments. A few years ago a sensible Magistrate used frequently to remark to the writer of this paper what an awkward position he would be in when pushed up to the bench of a Civil and Sessions Judge. With little or no knowledge of law and practice, and hardly any acquaintance with the different systems of accounts, professions, trades and a vast variety of customs and usages as regards the land tenures and their produce, he would be called upon to scrutinise in appeal the decisions of such experienced native judges as Lokenauth Bose and Hurro Chunder Ghose, and to extricate truth and justice from the cobwebs of sophistry and ignorance with which cases are sometimes enveloped by incompetent subordinate judges or from the heap of perjury and forgery in which they are buried—to superintend and give tone to the whole of the judicial establishments of a large district, perhaps as large as Yorkshire. It must be remembered that this is the language of a sensible and modest young gentleman who feels the deficiency, but how few there are who ever think about such stupid things! Is it not notorious that many covenanted Judges are compelled from necessity at first to adopt, and in time are reconciled to the plan of upholding the decisions of their subordinate judges generally in toto, or sometimes with slight alterations to keep up appearances, such as sending back cases for retrial on slight and technical grounds, or non-suiting them. I have known several of this class of Judges who uniformly decree bond and rent cases whenever two or three witnesses depose to a transaction, Magistrates who hardly know the difference between a crime and a civil wrong, and Collectors who are not fit to be included among the 10 European Assistants of Mr. Forlong. Is it a wonder then that forgery, perjury, affrays and false complaints should abound in the Mofussil? The case would have been still worse, if we had not occasional relief by the advent of a good Judge, Collector or Magistrate, much more the work of accident, than the result of the system in which he is brought up. As long as he remains in the zillah he manages to give an improved tone to the whole local administration and tries to give a shape to the discordant materials at his disposal; perjury, forgery, false complaints and affrays are checked for a time, to be revived with perhaps double fury on his departure. It is a very true statement of the Decca Planters and zemindars that our present laws are sufficiently stringent to enable a good Magistrate to manage a district properly, and to give greater powers to incapables is worse than folly. Lord William Bentinck, a shrewd observer of mankind, by a single stroke of his pen, removed a load of oppression from the heads of the people of this Presidency. That measure was no less or more than to abandon one of the legitimate functions of Government, *i.e.*, to refrain from enquiring into thefts and burglaries. He had heard and was convinced that the people of Bengal suffered more from the interference of our Police officers than from thieves and burglars, and he put a stop to one of the fruitful sources of legalized oppression by enacting Regulation VI. of 1832. After an experience of 22 years very few persons will deny that the result has not fallen short of his expectations; people have got rid of the vexatious interference of Police officers, and strange to say, thefts and burglaries, either in character or number, have not increased since then.

The tendency of the legislature in those days of unlearned but practical legislation was to grant relief to the people by curbing the powers of the executive. But it seems that our present rulers, more learned in the art, have turned over a new leaf, as the current of legislation for the last ten years tends more towards heaping unnecessary and ill defined powers upon our youthful Magistracy without taking any measures for increasing adequately the quality or the numerical strength of the Police officers. It may be very pleasant to a young gentleman to summon without much reason a Zemindar, Planter or a knot of their working and useful servants, and demand large securities from him to keep the peace under Act 5 of 1848, or to compel his attendance under the general regulations, and then keep him dancing attendance for months on one plea or other, but the question is, is it equally pleasant and convenient to the community to be subjected to all these annoyances, loss of time, and unnecessary expense? The bribes given to Nazirs and other amlahs for the single item of security or Bailbonds amount in the 35 zillahs in the Lower Provinces to some lacks of rupees per annum. This is no exaggeration. Government or any one inclined to question this assertion has only to reckon from the books of the Nazir or Court Sheriff of a single zillah the number and extent of securities demanded and taken, let him then take 10 per cent as the *average* charge, and he will find the sum total swell to many thousands in a year. The account books of the community and the universal testimony of all classes of pleaders, Mooktears, suitors and witnesses will corroborate the percentage. In the case of a high Civilian in Delhi, Sir Charles Trevelyan seized the account Books of Mohajuns and substantiated the charge of corruption. If Government be desirous of arriving at the truth, let them follow a similar course in a single zillah, and their exertions will be amply rewarded by relieving the people from an evil of far greater magnitude. It is the custom for nazirs to take from influential parties, under a good Magistrate, 5 per cent upon the amount of bail tendered, his Deputy or Buxy 1 per cent, chuprassees &ca 1 per cent, and the Mooktear who becomes security 2 per cent. From uninfluential and ignorant parties the Nazir alone exacts 7 or 8 per cent, but under an incapable, indolent absentee or *too Pucca* Magistrate, the Nazir's fee varies from 5 to 15 per cent according to circumstances. This is not authorized by law, but is generally submitted to under a feeling of helplessness, as the alternative of not paying is to go to jail. The Nazir has merely to say that he is not satisfied with the security tendered and the offending party will immediately be lodged in jail. A large number of Magistrates and their Assistants seldom remain in office more than 2 or 3 hours a day; during that short interval a Magistrate has to decide 10 or 12 cases judicially, pass orders on the reports of a dozen Police officers, order securities and muchlokhas to be taken from a score or two of individuals, and for the rest of the day he is inaccessible for business. A too Pucca Magistrate, on the other hand, cannot be approached either in court or out of court by suitors and others who are not sent for. Under these circumstances it is not difficult for the Nazir, an officer receiving 20 or 30 Rs. salary from Government, to manage things in his own way or to dictate his own terms. This state of things is not unknown to some of our Magistrates and other officers. The good deprecate the necessity and try to lessen the hardship as much as possible. The rest are quite indifferent to the suffering and loss of the community.

It has become quite a fashion with our Magistrates, their Deputies and Assistants, to demand large bail securities for misdemeanour or slight affray cases, for no purpose but just to ensure the attendance of parties in Court during the pendency of the cases. It is not uncommon with Magistrates in such trivial cases to demand from persons in the receipt of 3 or 4 Rs. monthly salary bail securities from 50 or 100 Rs. In fact, the vexatious annoyances and expense to which the community is subjected under this head have become quite intolerable. The subject is not unworthy the attention of our Lieutenant Governor, whose great Mofussil experience will enable him to check the evil to a great extent. Both European and native suitors are much censured for giving bribes to the amlah; they do it from necessity, because Government will not give them good and qualified officers to administer justice and an efficient police to protect them. Who would give money and become a criminal by the act without necessity? If it be said that this is one of the vices inherent in the Asiatic character, why do the European Planters and Zemindars have recourse to the same when they know that they have a covenanted and highly-educated European Magistrate or Judge to deal with. It is urged also that the covenanted Civilians being selected from the middle and educated classes in England cannot but act as gentlemen in whatever position they may be placed. I do not pretend to say anything against their gentility, but on the contrary greatly admire the high integrity, independence and good intentions of a large majority of them. What the country deplore is the unfitness of a great number to fill the important places to which they are indiscriminately appointed, the serious defects in the system under which they are trained, the very early age at which they are invested with judicial powers, the slight control exercised over their proceedings, the certainty of promotion and increase of emoluments apart from official qualifications, the investing them almost with unlimited power by law and practice, the indulgence with which their faults and misdeeds are viewed, the doubling and tripling several incongruous functions in the same individual, and lastly, the removing them frequently from one appointment to another more to suit their convenience and interest than with a view to the happiness and comfort of the people, such as promoting a salt agent to a Collectorship, or an opium agent or a Post Master General to a judgeship &ca. It is not necessary that the whole of these depressing causes should exist in the case of every individual; a number of them are quite enough to make a man unfit for the efficient discharge of his duties, whether they be those of a Judge, a Collector or a Magistrate.

There are serious defects also in the mode of selecting uncovenanted officers in the Judicial, Revenue and Police departments. A person who is successful in a parrot-like examination, or gives satisfaction to his Covenanted Master in his capacity of head clerk, or writes a good English Essay, gets one of these appointments. No inquiry is made as to his acquaintance with the different systems of accounts in use among different professions and trades, intricate revenue accounts, the process necessary to arrive at a sound conclusion as to the credibility or otherwise of witnesses, the experience and knowledge necessary to trace out forgery and perjury. Native functionaries are not, however, independent enough to lay much of good or evil to their own account. There is undoubtedly a large class of sensible, talented and upright men in their ranks, and they in their way achieve a great deal of good to the country, but their power and numbers are much too small, and their dependence upon their European superiors much too great, to lead us to expect that they can exercise any great influence over the complicated affairs of a whole country. It is generally known and admitted that many of them pass judicial decisions and in other respects act according to the known views and predilections of their superiors. This defect, however much to be regretted, cannot be denied as a fact. It is owing partly to a desire to gain the good opinion of the judges, upon which so much of their present and future prospects depends, and partly to save themselves from the ruinous consequences of too many reversals of their decisions in appeal. Considering the great power and influence of Covenanted officers and the reliance which Government [illegible] the necessity of placing in their reports and opinions, the [illegible]viency of the native agency is not a matter of surprise. In [illegible] revenue department the evils of this dependency were so much [illegible] that not long ago the Bengal Government was compelled to [illegible] a circular to the Zillah Collectors to give a greater share of freedom to the Deputy Collectors. This trait in the character of our subordinate Judges and revenue officers ought to be a warning, if a warning is necessary, to Government how it commits the des[illegible] of whole districts, containing in each of them more than a million of persons, into the hands of an incompetent head. But it is urged that the local Government is merely an instrument to carry out a system established by the authorities in England. It must select its officers according to rules laid down for its guidance, and the sphere of its selection is limited. The limitation is certainly an evil, and ought not to be continued. But even with the present limitation the system is susceptible of great improvement. Instead of considering a Civil Servant fit for every branch of the administration, train him up according to the bent of his mind and the amount of his acquirements in particular branches; such as Police, Criminal and Civil Justice and Revenue, retain him there as long as he conducts himself properly, let him rise in that line from grade to grade, and let his wishes, hopes and prospects be mixed up in the organisation and improvement of that particular department, impose sufficient checks on his proceedings, curtail a portion of the salary paid in the higher grades at present, and increase the number of hands by means of that saving, instead of doubling and tripling appointments in the hands of one individual. This is no new plan, nor is the principle an unrecognised one. Before the late reconstruction of the civil establishments of this country in Lord William Bentinck's time, there was some provision for the species of training alluded to in the judicial department. Young civilians, as Registrars to the Zillah Courts, were initiated into the practice of dispensing justice, and though owing to the number of civil servants in employment being much too small for the demands of the country, incongruous appointments were doubled up in the same person, the good effects of the training were always distinctly observable in the after life of the Registrars. Sir Charles Wood, also, in his memorable speech of the 3rd June, 1853, promised to separate the judicial service from the rest of the Civil List, and we claim a redemption of that promise. Reform must begin with this indispensable modification in the judicial branch of the administration. The uncovenanted judicial, revenue and ministerial officers must also be selected under a better system, and adequately paid and made more secure and independent in their position than they feel at present, to induce men of talents and property to enter the service. If from the Revenue and Judicial, we turn to our Police, the prospect is not much improved. It is miserably bad both in point of number and quality, and totally inadequate to afford protection to the people. The mixing up the two incongruous functions of Superintendent of Police and Criminal Judge in the same individual, and that individual an inexperienced youth, is an unmixed evil, and quite sufficient to account for the disorders and irregularities in those two important departments. The contemplated change of making these officers subordinate to Collectors of Revenue will, if possible, increase the evils so generally and loudly complained of at present. Instead of having Officers, however incompetent, with direct responsibility, at the head of affairs, we shall have Subordinate Officers, practically with similar powers, but without the same incentive to exertion and activity and the fear of exposure. These departments will be considered by Collectors as subordinate to their revenue duties, and the multiplicity of his tasks will always furnish him with a good plea, when charged with neglect or mismanagement.

Numerous and repeated suggestions and recommendations both from its own Officers and the public have failed to induce Government to take any decisive step for improving the department of Police and Criminal Justice, the two most important functions of state, and upon which, more than upon anything else, depends the woe or weal of millions. The utter inefficiency of the present system is too well known to require any proof; I will, however, adduce one in every respect unquestionable. Whatever may be said of Mr. Piddington's opinions as a man of science, nobody can deny his extensive acquaintance with the state of the Mofussil. He says, in the preface to the second edition of his work on agriculture—" We are told, and I believe truly, not only that we " cannot afford roads and bridges and canals and schools, but more, " that we cannot afford the adequate means of protecting pro- " perty, and of administering justice between man and man. " Every volume of evidence and reports on the subject of India, " from the days of Warren Hastings till now, teems with proof of " this startling assertion, and the experience of every individual " who has resided in the country, and seen the working effects of " our Government, confirms it." The plea of want of funds is not tenable, as I shall show in the sequel. A radical change is required, involving a large amount of expenditure, and Government tries to avoid it, if possible, by patchwork, such as the appointment of a few Deputy Magistrates, and by despotic legislation, *vide* Act 5 of 1848, and the Bill on which we are commenting. But an organic disease is never cured but by the most efficacious remedies. The proposed law is calculated to increase rather than diminish the difficulties of the Bengal Government. The unprecedented and extraordinary amount of discretion and latitude of action, or rather the power of coercion, allowed to our youthful Magistrates, and other palpable defects in the systems of criminal justice and Police, pointed out above, induce in the minds of the people a corresponding degree of exasperation and uncertainty.

No man, however peaceful and honest, feels himself safe from the clutches of the Police. A few instances of injustice and unmerited disgrace and unjust dispossession of property soon turns this feeling of uncertainty and terror into one of hatred and hopelessness, the precursor of despair. Persons or a community in despair are capable of committing any enormity. Those persons who, from a sense of wrong or from a dread of disgrace, refrain from joining or assisting in affrays or false suits, often find themselves entangled in the meshes of a criminal prosecution, or are suddenly deprived of their property by the machinations of the wicked, without any fault of their own. It is this general want of security and safety that has induced the present state of disorganisation, by turning the law-ridden Englishman and the peaceful citizen of Bengal into clubmen, and employers and retainers of clubmen; the Bagdees and Domes into organised bands of robbers. The proposed bill, if passed into law, will tend greatly to augment the evils, by rendering our moveables and immoveables, peace and liberty, at the disposal of a knot of informers and corrupt policemen, under no control, save that of an inexperienced and young Magistrate.

It is a matter of great surprise and no little concern that while the people of Bengal are, under one head or other, taxed for Police purposes more than four times the amount now expended in that department, and the surplus is applied for the benefit of the Punjab, Burmah and Bombay, we are left for want of a few lacs of Rupees, without a Police and criminal justice deserving the name. Nor is this all. The present disorganisation is ascribed to our cowardice, falsehood and lawless conduct, and at last we are threatened with a law under which no man of property and respectability can feel secure, as if Government Officers take pleasure in adding insult to injustice. We are condemned before we are tried. We never had a good and efficient Police and criminal administration. It is the duty of the Government to supply the deficiency in the first instance, and to allow a sufficient time to inspire confidence and a feeling of security from the encroachments of the ill-disposed who have been encouraged by the inefficiency of our Magistrates and their corrupt subordinates, as well as to eradicate the vices and habits engendered by the mal-administration of a century. If, after such a probation, the people be found disinclined to assist the Police, to refrain from entertaining clubmen and to preserve the peace, the Government will be perfectly justified in using coercive and harsh measures, but not till then. The country is under a deep debt of gratitude to the British Government for protecting it from foreign aggressions, and those internal political commotions that so often disgraced the administrations of our former rulers; but that is no reason why an enlightened Government should neglect to reform the civil administration of the country, particularly when that object is attainable at a moderate expense and exertion.

The table of expense of the present establishment and the one I shall venture to suggest at the close of this paper will show that an increase of 50,000 Rupees for each district, or about 17 lacs of Rupees per annum for the 35 districts of the Lower Provinces, is absolutely necessary to place the departments of Police and criminal administration on an efficient footing. No patchwork will do. I am certain that if the enormity of the evils to which the people of this country have been long subject, and which is the principal cause of undermining the good qualities and exciting the evil passions of the population, both European and Native, be fully laid before the Noble Lord at the head of the administration, we shall not be long without a remedy. His reforming zeal and perseverance in other departments is a guarantee that no amount of money or exertion will be a bar to a successful issue. If his Lordship requires further information, let him invite deputations of intelligent Landholders, Planters, Merchants and Bankers, and consult such Civilians as have established a reputation for promoting the interests and welfare of the people. Among other things it must be impressed on his Lordship's mind, if he is not already aware of the fact, that the present Mofussil Jury law (Act) is simply a nullity. All the honor and power is on the side of the sessions Judges, the trouble, annoyance and disgrace on the side of the jurors. The verdict of a jury on facts goes for nothing if the Sessions Judge disagrees with it. What respectable people will undergo trouble, expense and loss of time for such unenviable work? The decisions of Mofussil juries must be treated as they are in other countries where the institution exists, to give dignity to the institution, as well as to induce respectable people to become juries. To say that very few persons can be met with who are fit to be jurors, and that the people would rather be tried by Public Officers than by juries, is simply a mis-statement. The latter objection, or more properly deception, will soon be dispelled by the mode of proceeding I have suggested below. As soon as a defendant is required to answer a charge, give him the option of being tried by the Court or jury, and in a few years the result will clearly show that people have more sense than they are supposed to possess. The other objection is soon answered. The intelligent portion of a community must necessarily know more of the habits, customs, vices and virtues of that community, and consequently is better able to distinguish truth from falsehood, than a stranger can ever be. On the introduction of the system there will, no doubt, be some irregularities, and perhaps injustice in some instances, but as the people become gradually accustomed to this change, the defects will one by one disappear. And if the plan permanently succeeds, as there is every reason to hope it will, what a saving of expense to Government and of trouble to public Officers; what a check to injustice and corruption, which are now reigning triumphantly; what an elevation of the national character, the forerunner of every social good. The Punchayet or Jury system was in vogue in this country long before the illustrious Alfred introduced it into Britain, and a great majority of cases are still actually decided partly by village Punchayets and partly by Zemindars, Planters and their Omlahs, according to the circumstances of each locality, but as such powers are exercised against the existing law of the land, it is liable to great abuse. The people of this country therefore are not altogether strangers to the Jury system, they only require to be accustomed to the forms and checks introduced by modern Jurists.

I am aware that many officers of Government will object from conscientious motives to the introduction of Juries in the trial of petty cases, chiefly on the ground that even in boasted England, the great nursery of the system, petty cases are disposed of by Justices of the Peace without the aid of Juries, and that while it will take away the sense of responsibility from the public Officers, it will be merely to substitute an unpaid, irresponsible and generally speaking ignorant agency. I would at once admit that these reasons are very plausible, and would carry great weight if the actual circumstances of this country were otherwise than what they are. In the first place, it must be admitted that the sense-of-responsibility system, introduced in this country from the very dawn of British supremacy, has failed in securing the object we mutually have in view, the peace and comfort of the great mass of the people. The introduction of the obnoxious Bill by Government is a positive proof of the fact, if a proof be deemed necessary at this time of day. In the second place, the circumstances of England and this country are quite different. In the former, Justices of the Peace are men of mature understanding and selected from the mass of the people, they are controlled by an independent and intelligent public opinion and an all-powerful press; they administer justice among a people the most jealous of any of personal liberty, and their proceedings can at any time be arrested by a writ of *certiorari*, or that of *habeas corpus*, and generally their powers are quite insignificant when compared with that of one of our youthful Magistrates, or even of his more juvenile Assistant. We look in vain for any of these safeguards in this country. On the other hand we have an hereditary reverence and confidence in the decision of a plurality of judges over that of a single individual. With this national partiality in our favor, the removal of other obstructions to the complete establishment of the Jury system will be a work of a short time.

It will not perhaps be out of place to advert here to a prevailing rumour that Government intends shortly to appoint a number of Honorary Magistrates from among the intelligent portions of the Indigo Planters and Zemindars. If it really be the case, I warn my countrymen, as well as the *Blues*, to pause before they accept such appointments, until a thorough change in the appointment and selection of Zillah Magistrates takes place; any one that accepts such an appointment must necessarily be subject not only to the orders of the Zillah Magistrates, but also to their caprices and whims. As these honorary functionaries must decide in favor of one of the litigating parties, the party cast will leave no stone unturned to misrepresent their motives and doings, directly and indirectly. Insinuations against them, in one shape or other, will not only be indulged in, but in many instances readily believed and acted upon by public Officers, as many of them now swallow any charges, however unfounded, that are preferred against men of property and respectability. Our motives will be misconstrued in the cases of our Ryots and Asamees, and ultimately the system pronounced to be a failure from the misconduct of Planters and Zemindars.

The village watch is a remnant of the ancient municipal institution that flourished under the Hindu and Mahomedan Kings. Lord Cornwallis's Government, in attempting to derive the greatest possible aid from them, placed their services at the disposal of Police Darogahs by Section VIII., Regulation XXII. of 1793, while their appointment and dismissal, under ordinary circumstances, remained in the hands of Landholders in some places, and in others with the village communities; no provision was made for paying them, but on the contrary the chackran lands they were previously enjoying in lieu of wages were unconditionally made over to Zemindars by Section XLI., Regulation VIII. of 1793. Thus they were placed between the two horns of a dilemma, and the result has been what is very lucidly stated in the following extract of a petition presented by some Landholders and others to the Government of Bengal a few years ago:—

"In certain entire districts, and again in mere portions of 'others, Chowkeedars are maintained by a money tax, called

" *dowar massreh*, originally fixed by the inhabitants among themselves, while in others and even in parts of the same district they are paid by chackran lands. The rates of such wages differ considerably, varying from Rupees 4 to 2 per month for each Chowkeedar, and the quantity of chackran land assigned is equally diverse, *viz.*, from ·6 to 20 biggahs, which yield from Rupees 15 to 36 per annum, and from this ostensible out-turn of the land the Chowkeedar in reality receives on an average about one-half, owing to the influential villagers not paying, and the poorer classes being unable to pay, and also for the fact of the chackran land being either dry or inundated every second year at an average.

"There is no law to enforce the village Chowkeedaree Tax (*vide* C. O., Superintendent of Police, Lower Provinces, No. 14 of 1839, and No. 8 of 1841, Government Order on Police Report for the first six months of 1838). Some of the Magistrates enforce the payment through the agency of the Darogahs, others consider the issue of a purwanah to the Zemindar a sufficient remedy for ensuring payment, while many others do not interfere at all. In fact a Chowkeedar, after fagging and running here and there, ultimately finds that there is very little chance of his receiving an honest and adequate salary. The Zemindars, on the other hand, deeming themselves entitled to the rents of the chackran lands under Section XLI., Regulation VIII. of 1793, and Government order, dated 1st October, 1790, feel themselves ill-used and illegally deprived of their just dues, when opposed by any Magistrate, and spare no fair and foul means to gain their ends. They have generally succeeded in their attempts all over Bengal, excepting in Burdwan and a portion of the Hooghly district, and may be in one or two more, but even in these districts, vigorous measures are in progress on the part of the Landholders for the purpose of resuming these lands.

"The uncertainty and evils of the present system do not end here. The village Gomastah, the Darogah and every other grade of inferior Thanna Officers employ Chowkeedars to carry their loads from place to place, and perform other drudgeries for them. Even when Magistrates are out in the District these poor fellows are made to carry loads and provisions for those functionaries and their Omlahs, though it may be not always with their knowledge. The Zemindars and Talookdars expect them to collect their rents. They are also expected to give something annually *purbunee* to the Darogahs and other principal Omlahs of the Thanna. The Chowkeedar is moreover "made to pay something occasionally to Ghattee Burkundauzes, "or Jemadars, as the case may be, in which he is employed, or "else these worthies frequently report him as absent from the "watch, not to say the sound thrashing that he gets frequently "from every grade of Police Officers for slight inattention, real or "fancied; hence it is no wonder why better classes cannot be in- "duced to accept the post of Chowkeedars."

To make the matter still more confused, our present Lieutenant Governor (Mr. Halliday), when a member of a Police Committee that sat in Calcutta about 16 years ago, recorded a Minute to the effect that the whole of the village Chowkeedars be dismissed, and the amount of their pay thrown into the general Police Fund of the country for augmenting the Police force, while a large majority of the Committee recommended the continuance of the institution upon an improved system. The Court of Directors approved of the latter plan, and at the same time authorised the local Government to take proper measures for restoring them to efficiency, as will appear from the following paragraphs of the Court's letter:—

"To deprive the community of the services and protection af- "forded them by 170,000 persons answering this description, "would be an act which nothing could justify, unless a complete "substitute were provided, and to deprive such a body of men of "their subsistence and lawful occupation and to let them loose to "prey upon society would create such a degree of disorder and "outrage as the best constituted system of Police must be quite "unequal to repress."

"Not less objectionable than the dismissal of the village watch- "men would have been the imposition of a commutation tax of "sixty lacs of Rupees, instead of the precarious and in a great "measure voluntary allowances which they now receive from the "people. In its amount the tax has greatly exceeded that at "which those allowances have been estimated; in its distribution, "it would in many cases have fallen upon parties hitherto ex- "empted from payment; and in its effects it would have been felt "as a new exaction, and it would have excited general discontent. "We should have deemed it matter of deep regret and serious "concern if a project fraught with so much mischief had met with "any degree of support or encouragement."

"In our Despatch, bearing date the 9th of November, 1814 "(from paras. 91 to 135), we took full view of the importance of "maintaining, and when necessary restoring, the village institu- "tion as the only effectual groundwork of any system of Civil "Government, and we referred particularly to the testimony in "their favor by many of your ablest and most experienced public "officers. As the principles and details therein discussed retain "all their force and applicability, it is sufficient that on the pre- "sent occasion we should recall your attention to that Despatch. "We were then aware, as has been strongly recommended by the "Police Committee, that these institutions have been much ne- "glected and have fallen into great decay, but we entirely co- "incide in the opinion of the Committee as explained in paras. 53 "and 59, that the object should be not to abolish them, but to as- "certain their actual condition and to apply such remedies as may "be necessary for restoring them to efficiency."

As Zemindars and village communities are more interested and far more trustworthy than Police Darogahs and Burkundauzes, the municipal feature of the institution ought to be restored, and the Chowkeedars placed under the control of Zemindars and village communities, under certain restrictions as regards their number, pay and liability, to aid the Police Officers on emergent occasions. This will be giving back to John what really belongs to John. As the people pay the Chowkeedars, it is but just that they should command their services without the interference of Police Officers. They (the people) surely know much better what persons are qualified to look after their crops and other little things. The idea of the Zemindar running away with all the advantages of such a change is absurd, and should find no place in the minds of statesmen. A simple law enacting that for every 50 houses there shall be a Chowkeedar on a salary of 3 Rupees in remoter districts, and Rupees 3-8 or Rupees 4 in districts close to the Presidency, to be paid by the village communities, whose property and crops they are required to guard, will answer the purpose. The management and control may rest in a village Punchayet including the Zemindar. The village occurrences may be reported to the Thanna by Zemindars, as at present; a double report of the same by the Chowkeedars is unnecessary, and should be dispensed with. The suspicions lurking in the minds of some of the Public Officers that by such a straightforward measure the burden of maintaining the Chowkeedars will be shifted from the Zemindars to the people, are deserving of very little consideration. From after the Permanent Settlement to the present time, a period of more than 60 years, every ingenious argument has been exhausted for saddling the Landholders with this charge, but without success. I should very much like to see the supporters of this opinion come forward openly and establish their position or abandon it for ever, instead of impeding a fair settlement of the question by guesses, insinuations and conjectures.

I will now proceed to point out both the defects and the dangerous tendency of particular sections of the proposed law.

Section II. gives jurisdiction to Magistrates, both as regards moveable and immoveable property of whatever description; and Section III. authorizes a Magistrate, pending inquiry, to attach and take possession, &c. The present law (Act IV. of 1840,) as well as those which preceded it, confined the summary jurisdiction to "lands, premises, water-fisheries, crops and other products of land." This is perhaps the best limitation that can be imposed on the operation of such a summary mode of procedure. To extend it to all descriptions of moveable property, which necessarily include title deeds, cash, bank notes and public securities, jewels, household furniture, clothing and other domestic utensils, will give rise to an amount of litigation that our Courts are numerically incapable of adjudicating upon, and open a wide door to petty and malicious contention, which it is undesirable to bring before such tribunals. Under the pretence of taking possession of disputed articles, domestic sanctity will be invaded by Police Officers and other strangers. Title-deeds, Government securities, jewels, cash, &c., &c., often amounting to large sums, will be suddenly removed from responsible and proper custody to the hands of irresponsible and corrupt officers, who may waste, change, alter or damage them with very little chance of detection. The people of this country mostly live in co-partnery. Any slight disagreement or momentary irritation among the members of a joint family, will produce a number of such vexatious and petty suits. The power already possessed by Magistrates under the general regulations is quite sufficient to put down any affray or breach of peace arising from such disputes.

Section III. of the Bill authorises Magistrates to take possession *pending inquiry*. The existing law is also silent, and judiciously so, as regards the custody of disputed property *pending inquiry*. No doubt in some cases the existence of such a power is very desirable and necessary to secure property from waste, and no less for removing the object of contention from the litigating parties. But, on the other hand, the danger of waste, spoliation, change and abstraction by unprincipled and corrupt Police Officers and others, is palpably so great, that the advantages of the proposed alteration will sink to insignificance. Besides, the knowledge of such power will give a great stimulus to subordinate Police Officers to frame their reports, inquiries and proceedings in such a manner as to induce Magistrates, who generally live at a distance, in ignorance of real facts, to order an attachment in almost every case. Besides, inquiries will be interminably postponed and lengthened, to retain, when once in possession. Under all the circumstances, then, the present mode of procedure appears to be preferable. To meet extreme and urgent cases, however, a discretion may be given to attach disputed property *pending inquiry* through the Collector, as prescribed in Section IV., Act IV., of 1840.

Section IV. chiefly provides for the realization of the expenses of the custody and care of the subject in dispute, pending inquiry, but it will be rendered unnecessary if the suggestion made in the preceding para. be attended to. At any rate any expense which the Government incurs either for the protection of disputed property or for enquiry into the same, is a part of the legitimate charges of the Police department, and should be borne by the State.

Section IX. is extremely objectionable. The legislature in proposing this Section, has doubtless been influenced by the consideration that parties, if injured, can have redress from the Civil Courts. But we would submit that cases coming under this head are often of great importance, not unfrequently involving nearly all a man has in this world, and to invest with final powers to adjudicate such cases young Officers who, from prejudice, inexperience, or caprice, have been often found to pass unjust and discordant orders, will be to increase, if possible, the insecurity and dissatisfaction which the community already feels and which are mainly the cause of affrays at present. The intended virtual abrogation of appeals will augment tenfold the affrays so much deprecated. For the people of this, or of any country, will never suffer their all to be taken possession of by others, or ousted and plundered by unprincipled and subordinate public Officers, and abstain from violent means, in the hope of a tardy and uncertain civil suit, the final adjudication of which generally occupies from 2 to 10 years. Men will do anything when in a state of exasperation or desperation. It behoves the legislature to diminish rather than alarmingly increase such causes of discontent and dissatisfaction by enacting such a Section. It will remove the only check existing at present on the conduct of our youthful Magistracy, otherwise it will verify the saying of a well-known Indigo Planter, that the "Government in "proposing this measure wish to establish that youth and rashness "are to be preferred to age and experience."

The decisions of Collectors passed under this law, should be made appealable to the Sessions Judges, for most of the reasons stated in this para.

The penal provisions in Section XI. are very vague, and should be defined as to persons, time, place and extent.

It is not unfrequently the case that in the absence of the elder brother the younger complains in the Court, and obtains, through the Magistrate, the possession of a property from a third person, though the same belongs equally to both the brothers; on the return of the elder he takes possession of his share of the property. Will it be construed into "knowingly contravening, &c.?" Two parties connive together, as is sometimes the case, one becomes plaintiff, the other a defendant; after a sham fight one of the parties is decreed possession by the Magistrate, a false execution and delivery takes place; none of these acts are done with the knowledge of the rightful owner, who all this time retains possession as before; all of a sudden the latter individual, to his utter surprise, may be summoned for "knowingly contravening," or at the time of the execution he may be handed up for obstructing or impeding. A person obtains a decree for possession of a certain malgoozaree Estate only, within the limits of which many persons may hold lakhiraj tenures, ayemahs, mucrorees, &c., will these be punished for resisting any invasion of their rights? Any person after obtaining possession may sell or let the property in putnee six months thence, and put the purchaser in possession, but chooses to deny the transaction and complains within a week to the Magistrate for "knowingly contravening." A multiplicity of other instances may be quoted, but those already stated ought to induce our Legislators to place sufficient safeguards to prevent abuse of the powers herein vested.

Section XII. belongs to a new species of legislation. To quarter a small army of hired Policemen on private individuals, "whenever "it shall appear to the Magistrate that a breach of the peace is "likely to be committed," is giving a dangerous and unlimited power to Magistrates very little subject to official control and still less to public opinion; a Magistrate himself unconsciously will very often inflict and prolong the infliction of such punishment upon unoffending and innocent parties for supposed criminal intention, which perhaps exists only in the fancy of the Magistrate, arising from corrupt and interested reports of venal subordinates, the truth or falsehood of which he has very little means of knowing, living, as most of our Magistrates do, at a great distance from the scenes of action. The preservation of peace and order is one of the principal functions of Government, and the legitimate instrument to be used for the purpose is the regular Police force of the country. If it be insufficient for the object, the most obvious remedy is to improve it and make it efficient. The course proposed in this Section, besides being objectionable on the ground of making private individuals pay for the general protection of property when the community is once taxed for the same purpose, places in the hands of Magistrates a power which will be liable to the greatest abuse, as shown above.

Section XIII. which requires that the Magistrates shall be furnished with a list of guards, &c., will be quite unobjectionable, if certain periods be fixed and wilful omissions only made punishable.

Section XIV. arms the Magistrate with the power of compelling Landholders, Farmers, and others, who own and possess land, to discharge any servant or retainer whenever he (the Magistrate) has reason to believe that such a servant is likely to be employed to commit a breach of the peace. This is monstrous and uncalled for. Why is a man, be he Landholder, Planter, or Farmer, to be restricted in the choice of his own servants? The Section is not confined to clubmen, but extends to all descriptions of servants, Dewans, Naibs, Cashiers, Tehsildars, Gomastahs, &c. If this law be passed, will any Dewan, Naib, Gomastah presume to remonstrate or appeal against the proceeding of a Magistrate? If he does, he is a marked man, he must be discharged for the peace of the country. In the collection of rents, in guarding persons' property, houses, corn-fields, gardens, in travelling, as well as marriage and other ceremonies, and in thousands of other things, a person exercises his own judgment and employs any person in whom he has confidence and trust. This natural state of things will be changed, and the Magistrate of a district will be made the Director General in the selection, retention and dismissal of private servants. It is questionable if the Legislature ever pictured to itself the extent and variety of the task they were imposing upon Magistrates by this Section. If the law is meant to be effective, it is no stretch of imagination to say that the Magistrate of a district, sometimes as large as Yorkshire, must have the extraordinary faculty of knowing not only the qualifications, motives, and actions of all classes (saving the domestic servants) of servants entertained by every individual in the community, but also the extent and variety of the circumstances, the time, place, and number of servants required on each and every occasion. Until it can be shown that our Magistrates are capable of possessing a thorough knowledge on all these points, and of performing satisfactorily the novel and extraordinary functions that will devolve on them, it will be a grievous injustice to place in their hands such despotic powers.

Besides entrenching upon private right, and disturbing the economical arrangement of individuals, it will be depriving people of, or at least putting great obstacles in the way of their employing, the only means they have at present of preserving their lives and property, while the present miserable Police of the country is admitted on all sides to be quite inadequate for the purpose.

It is also violating one of the sound principles of political economy to require the dismissal of suspicious characters (presuming that means exist of arriving at a correct conclusion, though every body knows that such does not exist in fact), from the service of private individuals, and casting them upon society, branded as such, without the means of support. One would suppose that it is a great safeguard for the peace and comfort of society, that such characters should have some honest employment, and be under the control of their masters, and, through them, of the public authorities. The provisions in Section XIX. are strong enough for the purposes of a good Police. The existing law prohibiting the assemblage of large bodies for unlawful purposes may be rendered, with a slight amendment, quite sufficient as a check. Where then is the necessity for enacting Sections XV. and XVI.? If it had been the object of the Legislature to exasperate the feelings of the country, and take away the little security they at present enjoy from the aggressions and interferences of Police Officers and others, these Sections could not have been better suited to the purpose. After the passing of the law no man, of property or no-property, will feel himself safe, as any private servant might be construed into a hired clubman, and the intention of committing affrays inferred or imagined, with the aid of perjured or interested witnesses. The awful disclosures made by the proceedings of the Dacoity Commissioner of many scores of innocent men being prosecuted, tried, convicted, and lodged in the jail for crimes never committed by them, should have made Government pause before proposing such an extraordinary law, the vague and despotic provisions of which may, by misapplication and through the instrumentality of marked persons, at any time be made the means of destroying the prospects, and taking away the personal liberty of any individual, however honest.

If the word "arrest" be expunged from Section XVII. it will be rendered unobjectionable. Section XVIII. crowns and completes a series of clauses unparalleled even in Indian legislation. If this Clause be maintained, how any honest person or man of property can feel secure, will be a matter of grave consideration. The vast and unlimited field that will be thrown open for the exercise of villany and perjury, will not be left unemployed by the numerous class of persons indicated in this Clause. The men of property and wealth will have enemies, and what a field for the gratification of enmity and revenge! The country has had some little taste of the extent to which approvers are capable of harassing and oppressing innocent families, but, their field being very limited and contracted by previous records, their depredations will dwindle down into insignificance compared with those to be realized by this piece of legislation.

I will now briefly sum up here the causes that have chiefly contributed to lower our Police and the administration of criminal justice in the public estimation.

1st. The coupling in the same individual of the conflicting duties of the Police Magistrate and Criminal Judge.

2nd. The incompetency and inadequacy of the agency employed in the administration of criminal justice.

3rd. The total inadequacy of the material and quality of the subordinate Police force.

4th. The want of a plain and intelligible criminal code for all classes of the people, including British-born subjects.

5th. The want of a regular system of village watch, of the absence of plain and tangible rules for the guidance of Police Officers, and defects in the present laws for Indigo contracts, defalcations and several other matters.

6th. The want of Trial by Jury.

It is not without a feeling of diffidence, as the subject is beset with difficulties, that I venture to offer the following suggestions, under each of the foregoing heads, for remedying the defects pointed out above, as much as possible.

I. A complete and entire separation of these two functions. A police Magistrate should never be allowed to exercise judicial powers over persons and property subject to his control in his executive capacity. People will then have confidence in and respect for the criminal administration of the country, feelings which do not exist at present. Mr. W. W. Bird, a Civilian of high standing and eminent talents, energetically advocated this separation as long as he remained in this country. Other eminent persons in favor of the change, such as Mr. Dick, of the Sudder Court, may be named, but there is very little need of argument or authority to bring home the injustice and impolicy of such an incongruous junction of functions.

1st. The powers of the Sessions Judge to remain as at present, with this restriction, that he will be bound to summon Jurors in every case, and the decision of Juries regarding facts to be final, unless the judge has reason to believe the failure of substantial justice; in which case he will have power to summon another set of Jurors, whose verdict shall be final. Appeals to the Sudder to be limited to law points only.

2nd. There should be a Judicial Magistrate above 30 years of age, who has served before at least two years as a Police Magistrate or Deputy, and two years as an Assistant Judicial Magistrate, with the powers at present possessed by a Magistrate.

When a defendant is called upon to answer a charge, he is to be questioned by the Magistrate whether he is willing to be tried by the Court or by a Jury. If he prefers the latter, the Magistrate to be bound to summon and try him by Jurors, whose verdict as to the fact shall be final, with the proviso mentioned in the preceding paragraph when failure of justice may be apparent. He is also to exercise a control over his subordinate criminal Judges, such as the civil Judge exercises over the Sudder Ameens, &c., &c. Appeals from his decision on law points only to the Nizamut in cases decided by the assistance of Jurors and upon both fact and law in other cases.

3rd. Assistant Judicial Magistrates above the age of 25 with the powers at present excercised under Regulation 5 of 1821, under the proviso for Jurors as above. Appeals to the Sessions Judge under the above restrictions.

4th. Moonsiffs at present employed, or those among them who may be deemed fit to be called Sudder Ameens, with a salary of rupees 250, to try both civil and criminal cases within certain limitations. Proviso for Jurors and appeals to the Judicial Magistrate with the above restriction.

II. *1st.* Jury lists to be prepared and forwarded to the Sessions Judge by division Sudder Ameens, and also by the Collector and Judicial Magistrate. These lists to be finally settled by the Judge, Collector, Magistrate, and two Principal or Sudder Ameens.

2nd. The Jury to consist of at least five persons, chosen from the Jury list, and to give their verdicts according to the majority. The parties to be furnished with a list of Jurors to be summoned, and to have a right of challenging, within reasonable bounds.

III. One Police Magistrate for each district above 25 years of age, with as many Deputies as will admit of one for every 200 square miles; Darogahs to be done away with. Two Jemadars in every division at Rupees 20 each, and an adequate number of Burkundauzes, say one for every 4 square miles, at Rupees 6 per month; each Magistrate to have a guard of 12, each Deputy 4, and each Jemadar 2 Burkundauzes.

IV. A Criminal Code for all classes of the people, including British-born subjects, in which, among other things, a legal definition of the right of self-defence, as well as of the offence of conspiracy, should be embodied. Our British fellow-subjects are not unwilling, as far as I am aware, to share with the natives the same laws, provided the Police and Criminal Courts be placed on a proper footing, and a plain, intelligible Code of Laws published.

V. The village watch to be restored to the village communities under certain restrictions, as detailed in page 25 of this paper.

VI. The suggestions made on the second head also include my plan for the employment of Juries.

VII. Plain and intelligible rules for the guidance of Police Officers, and especially for the prevention of disputes about indigo, the apprehension and punishment of defaulting servants, and a few other laws to define the rights of parties and the remedies open to them.

There are some other minor changes and details necessary to complete the proposed system, but the above outline will suffice to demonstrate the principle. The change proposed involves a large increase of expenditure, which must be incurred, as without it no improvement can take place. I believe the Court of Directors profess to be not unwilling to incur some expense, if a tangible and well-digested plan be submitted to them. This is the time then for all classes of the community to be up and doing. The whole question lies in a nutshell; Government must expend more money, or nothing can be done; no great ingenuity or wisdom is required to devise an improved plan, when we find that in the districts nearest to the Presidency (the most populous ones), there is only one Policeman in the shape of a Burkundauz on a salary of Rupees 4 per month for every 10 square miles on an average, and one for 15 or 20 miles in remoter districts. The executive and judicial functions jumbled together, and lower grade Darogahs and Mohurirs, Jemadars and Burkundauzes so ill-paid that no honest man can accept any of those appointments, and as for prospects for the future, " nil." It is necessary to see what is the difference in point of expense between the proposed and present system. I will take a Zillah, 48 miles in length by 48 in width, which is about the extent of the Hooghly district.

Present Establishment per Month.

1	Covenanted Magistrate both as Police Superintendent and Criminal Judge... ...	Rs.	1,000	0	0
	Travelling allowance at an average	,,	50	0	0
2	Deputy Magistrates, each 350	,,	700	0	0
1	Covenanted Assistant	,,	600	0	0
2	1st Grade Darogahs	,,	200	0	0
2	2nd ditto ditto	,,	150	0	0
8	3rd ditto ditto	,,	400	0	0
12	Mohurirs, each 7	,,	84	0	0
24	Jemadars, each 8	,,	192	0	0
240	Burkundazes, or 20 per each Thanna, at an average each 4	,,	960	0	0
		Rs.	4,336	0	0

The Proposed Establishment.

1 Judicial Magistrate	Rs.	1,200	0	0
1 Assistant ditto ditto	,,	700	0	0
1 Police Magistrate	,,	800	0	0
Travelling allowance for ditto	,,	100	0	0
2 Deputy Magistrates each 300	,,	600	0	0
4 Ditto ditto, each 250	,,	1,000	0	0
5 Ditto ditto, each 150	,,	750	0	0
24 Jemadars, each 20	,,	480	0	0
625 Burkundazes, each 6	,,	3,750	0	0
	Rs.	9,380	0	0

N.B.—The pay of Sudder Ameens is not included in either, as they more properly belong to the Dewanny or Civil branch of the administration.

The writer of this paper, in submitting the above scheme of a reform in the Police and the criminal administration of the country, is willing to admit that it is in many respects a crude one, and having no ready access to authentic sources of information on every point, may possibly be somewhat out in his calculations. The principles of the reform, however, are such as may be judged of independently of these contingencies. The description given in the preceding pages of the actual condition of the Police, and of the mode of administering Criminal Justice in the Courts of the Magistrates will, he hopes, not be found substantially incorrect, and the opinions advanced on that part of the subject are the result of twenty-five years' experience in a sphere of life in which the opportunities of observation are more abundant than in any other that can be conceived. The writer has been during that period in the management of extensive estates in two of the Metropolitan districts, and has had to deal extensively with other Landholders, Indigo Planters, Ryots, and Officers of Government of every grade. Some of those opinions, he fears, are likely to give offence, but as they are honestly entertained, and have exclusive reference to a subject of general interest, he has not hesitated to state them at a time when they will at least not be deemed uncalled for.

A LETTER

TO THE

RT. HON. ROBERT VERNON SMITH, M.P.,

PRESIDENT OF THE BOARD OF CONTROL,

UPON THE

PROPOSED JUDICIAL REFORMS IN INDIA

BY

THEODORE HENRY DICKENS,

Of Lincoln's Inn, Barrister-at-Law,
and late an Officer of the Supreme Court of Calcutta.

1857.

PREFACE.

The Author desires to record his grateful sense of the valuable information placed at his disposal by Mr. Dickinson, Honorary Secretary of the India Reform Society. Want of space has alone prevented his making more extensive use of these materials.

A LETTER

TO THE

RIGHT HON. ROBERT VERNON SMITH.

Sir,—After the lapse of many years, the Penal Code of the Indian Law Commission, commonly called "Macaulay's Code," has been fitted with a code of procedure for the Presidency of Bengal, and published with an announcement of the intention of the Indian Government to make it the universal law of that country. This announcement at once raised the alarm of the whole non-official European population of Bengal, and drew forth an immediate expression of their hostility to the proposed legislation. The native population have not as yet, I believe, made any similar demonstration, for an obvious reason, which will be hereafter pointed out; but I know from private sources that some of the most intelligent of them disapprove of the measure as much as their European fellow subjects. Nevertheless, if we may trust the assertions of the semi-official organ of the Indian Government, the *Friend of India*, and of the Calcutta correspondent of the *Times*, the code, as published in England, is now being patched and altered by the local legislative council, and is to be hurried into actual law as precipitately as the necessary forms will permit. I trust, however, that it is not too late to ask you to interfere, and pause before you make that code the law of India, or, at least, of Bengal, upon some of whose many important provisions its own propounders are disagreed among themselves; upon others of which provisions the local legislative council differ with the propounders; and to the leading principles of which those Europeans who will have to live under the administration of the law which it proposes to introduce offer an unanimous opposition. Surely it becomes the minister of a free country to pause before he plunges into a legislation which excites so much alarm among those for whose supposed benefit it is intended.

It is not my intention—indeed, I do not possess the requisite knowledge, if I had the wish—to discuss the minor provisions of the code. But there are in its leading principles objections which would be fatal, were all the minor provisions absolutely perfect in themselves. To these objections I respectfully beg your attention.

The principle upon which the proposed legislation rests is, in the abstract, perhaps wise and sound, namely, the introduction of one universal system of law, and of law courts, for every dweller in India, whether Hindoo, Mahomedan, European, half-caste, Armenian, or Jew. The idea of such a code is grand; and if judiciously framed, and administered by competent tribunals, it might be productive of unmixed benefit. But I think it will not be hard to show that this code is wanting in these essentials of excellence.

It is necessary to state here very shortly the present state of law in India. There are two descriptions of courts,—the Queen's Courts, called Supreme, presided over by judges appointed by the Crown, administering English law, and whose proceedings are conducted in

English. These courts have a local jurisdiction in each of the Presidency capitals, and a criminal jurisdiction over British subjects through all India. Secondly, there are the Company's Courts, which are the only tribunals in the Mofussil, and which administer the civil and criminal law of the respective Presidencies, as modified by the regulations and the circular orders of the Sudder Courts, which are courts of appeal from the other Company's courts, to Hindoos and Mahomedans, with a deference to their own laws and religion. When Europeans settle in the Mofussil, they are subject to these courts, to a certain degree, in civil matters; and the half-caste and Armenian are subject to the criminal and civil courts; that is, though Christians, they are subject to Mahomedan criminal law; and as an illustration, I may mention one instance in which a Christian clerk was, for adultery with a Christian woman, sentenced by a civilian, not, indeed, to the hideous mutilation prescribed by the Mahomedan law for that offence, but to imprisonment for three years. There is, therefore, a large Christian population in the interior of India who are the descendants of Europeans, and yet are subject to laws which are repugnant to civilized men. For this state of things the judicial commission propose a remedy. Let us see what that remedy is.

They propose to abolish the Supreme and Sudder Courts, and to form a High Court, which is an amalgamation of these two courts, and is separately and collectively to discharge all the functions these two courts at present discharge; the criminal jurisdiction to be confined within the limits of the present Supreme Court, as a Court of Oyer and Terminer, together with its criminal Admiralty jurisdiction. In all Mofussil cases,

Europeans are to be subject to the Company's criminal courts, presided over by the servants of the Company, administering the laws of Macaulay's Penal Code, as regulated by the procedure of the code now under consideration.

This measure, therefore, sweeps away the special privileges of the British subjects. By the process of amalgamation, it, as they allege, swamps and destroys their peculiar court, a tribunal which they have always held in reverence, and whose administration of the law is the only administration which has given satisfaction and security to the litigants. It introduces a law to which they have grave objections in itself, which is in many respects contrary to the spirit of the constitution, and to whose proposed administrators they have still graver objections.

The judges of the Supreme Court are men of mature age and legal education, unconnected with, and not appointed by, the Executive Government of India. And though it has been asserted by some well qualified to express an opinion on the subject, that even these judges are not sufficiently independent, yet they have, in that respect, an immense superiority over the civil servants of the Company, who are all under a covenant to the Government, are all part and parcel of the executive power, and who, if their decisions run counter to the wishes of Government, are liable to fall, and often have fallen, under its severe displeasure. The proposed amalgamation will constitute a court of eight judges, three to be men appointed, as the present judges of the Supreme Court are, by the Crown, and the remainder by the Governor-General in Council, from among members of the Civil Service, barristers and advocates, uncovenanted servants of the Company, and vakeels, or native lawyers. Upon this most important provision there was strange disunion among the judicial commissioners. It was carried by the Master of the Rolls, Sir Edward Ryan, Mr. Cameron, and Mr. Robert Lowe, against the late Lord Chief Justice, Mr. Macleod, and Mr. Ellis. The minute of Mr. Macleod shows what some of his objections were; and as they are those entertained in general by civil servants, I shall proceed to examine them as briefly as possible, premising here that while the non-official population view the proposed alterations with the same dread as Mr. Macleod, the cause of their apprehension is exactly the opposite to his, —they fear that those results will *not* accrue of which he is so apprehensive. They know that as long as the government of India remains in its present hands, persons other than the covenanted servants of the Company will *not* be appointed to the majority of the seats on the bench of the proposed High Court. Mr. Macleod fears that barristers, natives, and "other persons" will ultimately "elbow out" the favoured service.

Mr. Macleod's minute contains so many assertions which are untrue (though I doubt not his belief of their truth), and so many strangely illogical conclusions and apprehensions, which are inconsistent with other conclusions and apprehensions expressed in the same paper, that it is not easy to ascertain exactly what his fears are, beyond the general one that the judicial power will ultimately be taken out of the hands of the Civil Service, and vested in judges who will not be completely under the control of the Government. This he regards as an unspeakable evil, political and judicial. Sir John Jervis and Mr. Ellis, in their remarks upon Mr. Macleod's minute, regard it as a purely political question, and therefore out of their province to determine. It may be doubted whether they were right in this conclusion, and whether it is possible, in the consideration of this point, completely to separate these elements: but, at any rate, the whole question, in all its bearings, is one for *your* consideration. Although Mr. Macleod's minute has not met with the concurrence of his fellow commissioners, it is important to comment upon it as an exposition of the views of the civilians upon the judicial system of India, and the principles which should guide any contemplated reform; and as indicative of the point of view from which Indian politics are regarded by that official class, from which alone Parliament received evidence to any extent as to the state and requirements of that country, during the late Charter discussion. I will now proceed to state and comment on what appear to me the salient points of Mr. Macleod's minute.

His first expression of alarm is at the fact that by the new code "it is not provided that even a single seat on the bench [of the High Court] shall be filled by a member of the Indian Civil Service. This is a great, and, in my opinion, an impolitic innovation. The interests of India, I think, require that at least half the seats on the bench of the new court shall be secured by law to the Civil Service." The proposed law does not indeed *compel* the Governor-General in Council to appoint civil servants in such a proportion; but it *permits* him to appoint them in a larger proportion, namely, of 5 to 3. Mr. Macleod is in dread of a fewer number being appointed than the law permits. We, who know how these things are managed in India, well know the fear to be unfounded. We are only in dread lest the action of the independent judges of the Crown should be swamped by the numerical force of the subservient and dependent servants of the Company. We feel perfectly certain that four of these five judges will always be civilians, and the fifth occasionally a favourite native, whenever it may suit the purposes of the East India Company to make a flourish at home about their liberal and paternal government, and secure the votes of the British Indophilist. The grounds upon which we base our apprehensions of the constitution and servility of the proposed court will be stated hereafter, and you can judge of their validity.

In short, from the first page of Mr. Macleod's minute, it is clear that his objection to the proposed amalgamated court arises from his apprehension of the infusion of too large a portion of independence, legal training, and knowledge into the Supreme Court of the country, and from the door which it opens to the admission of barristers, natives, and uncovenanted lawyers to the seats of the High Court. He rightly regards it as a move tending to the breach of the barriers so long and carefully erected for the preservation of the close Civil Service. The non-official European population of India, the natives, and uncovenanted servants, would rejoice beyond expression if they thought it would have that effect. *Their* fear is, that many of the framers of the code have been led away by the belief that the permission granted to the Governor-General in Council will be wisely and liberally used by the appointment of the best man, irrespective of class, station, or colour: while they know that as long as the Governor-General is so much under the control of the Court of Directors, and has, moreover, the possibility of a pension as a reward for his subserviency dangling always before his eyes, he will never run counter to their wishes by a bold infringement on the places of their pet Service; and that thus, under the pretence of a liberal reform, the Supreme Court will be swamped and rendered ineffective, which was wisely erected as a protection for British subjects against the servants and laws of the East India Company—a corporation whose policy has been always despotic and anti-national in spirit, and hostile to the immigration and settlement of Europeans in India.

Mr. Macleod proceeds to assert that under the present system:—

"India is governed wisely, strongly, mildly, and *justly*, to a degree far beyond what would otherwise be possible; *and to the mass of the people of any country it matters little who are its rulers, or what is the form of the government, except in as far as whether it is governed with wisdom, justice, power, and mildness, may depend on those circumstances.*"

How far India is governed in this magnificent way, —what manner of thing that is which is there called "Justice," will be shown hereafter. But whether the writer means that it matters little to a country who are its rulers, or what its form of government; or whether he means to assert that the results of that rule are not dependent upon the two circumstances which he regards as of such small importance, I cannot pretend to say. But he clearly must mean to assert one of these two things. And whichever it be, it is quite enough to terrify one to think that an important legislative task has been entrusted in any degree to the holder of such an opinion.

He then proceeds to say that this scheme "holds out judgeships in the gift of Indian Governors to the ambitious hopes, not only of barristers, but of other and far more extensive classes of men." Having asserted this, he goes on, in the same breath, to show that the class will not be a very extensive one:—

"I am convinced that Europeans not in the Civil Service, and descendants of Europeans, are the only classes on which the advantage of an extended field for their employment by the Government will really be conferred. It is by them that the civil servants will be elbowed out. The notion that the native population will be benefited is a delusion. The natives will not even be able to keep hold of what they now have in possession."

Why the natives will not be benefited, it is impossible to conceive, as they form the majority of that class—viz., vakeels and uncovenanted servants in judicial employ—which the clause, upon which Mr. Macleod is commenting, admits to these honours. Still stranger is it, that with this conviction he should devote the greater remaining portion of his minute to a vivid description of the fearful danger of their admission. Still more incomprehensible is the assertion which he reiterates at page 241, that the removal of the barriers, "which fence off men not of the close Civil Service from the offices appropriated to that body," would not only give the natives no chance of admission into the coveted precincts, but would deprive them of the petty offices they now hold by favour of the Civil Service; "that protection removed, the energy of the Anglo-Saxon race would triumph over them, and trample them under foot." In short, Mr. Macleod is afraid, first, that the admission of natives to seats of the High Court will upset the whole basis of the British power in India;

then, he is sure that giving them the chance of admission will not only not result in their admission, but will result in their exclusion from all other offices. A man entertaining two such conflicting opinions would only be fit for an asylum. But, as Mr. Macleod is not a fool, we may be sure that he blunders in this fashion in a desperate attempt to conceal the real cause of his evident panic. That cause is easy of discovery. He does not, I am sure, in his inmost soul, fear,—or, if he does, I am sure his fear is groundless,—that the energy of the Anglo-Saxon will trample the native *only* under foot in the contest for judicial honours. His real terror is that the Anglo-Saxon, *and* the native, will "elbow out" the civil servants. He trembles for the slothful security of his fellow civilians, and acutely masks his defence of their overwhelming and improper advantages over all other classes, by an appeal *ad misericordiam* for the "mild Hindoo." Under pretence of a cry for charity, he cloaks a defence of monopoly. He well knows, that if ever the Governor-General used his power of selection with an eye to merit alone, the civilians would stand, as a body, no chance whatever with their non-official competitors, native or European. As to the assertion that the natives would have no chance against the European in a struggle for judicial honours, on account of their want of energy and industry,—it is simply untrue*. As a nation, they are

* It is but fair to Mr. Macleod to state that he apparently forms his opinion on a mistaken assertion of Mr. Halliday's (page 241):—"English barristers from the Calcutta Supreme Court are now largely practising in the Sudder Court, and bid fair to monopolize the practice there." When I left India, in September, 1855, there was not, and had not been for some time, a single barrister practising in the Sudder

very inferior to the Anglo-Saxon in bodily energy; but they are marvellously industrious in many respects. They will not walk or run an unnecessary yard, but they will work sitting for hours. Law may be learnt even in a recumbent posture, and they often learn it remarkably well. It is a notorious fact that a very large number of the uncovenanted service, European, native, and half caste, are far superior to the great majority of civilians as lawyers. How many civilians would Mr. Macleod dare to bring into competition in a fair examination with such men as Ramapersaud Roy, Lokenath Bose, or Prosonocoomar Tagore, or Mr. Waller,* and many others that might be mentioned? I much doubt if there is one single individual in the whole Civil Service who would approach anywhere near these men: the difficulty would be to find examiners sufficiently learned and able to form an estimate of their learning. Do you doubt my assertion, that the uncovenanted judges are often abler than their covenanted superiors? I refer you, in reply, to an answer of Mr. Marshman before the late Charter Committee (p. 343), a witness undoubtedly well-affected towards the Company, and the intimate friend of some of its most distinguished members:—"The business of the Judges' Court is to

---

Court. There is now one; and I believe this gentleman is the only barrister who has *ever* practised regularly in the Sudder, and he gets little business. It is true, that in very important cases the leaders of the bar are sometimes taken into the Sudder; but they demand such heavy fees for going, that the occurrence is not more common than the 500 guinea special retainers to our leaders in England in circuit cases.

* The first, third, and fourth are or have been practising vakeels in the Sudder Court. The second is a member of the uncovenanted service, in judicial employ, and distinguished for his knowledge of revenue law.

hear appeals from the subordinate courts, which are for the most part filled by natives, thoroughly versed in the law and procedure of the courts, and men who have obtained long and admirable judicial experience,—*to hear appeals from men who are far better acquainted with the law and practice of the courts than himself.*"

Such is the evidence of Mr. Marshman (whose testimony, by one of the soundest of all rules of evidence, must be taken as strongest when against civilians, from his bias in their favour) as to natives and those "other persons" whose admission to the chance of a seat on the bench of the High Court is so feared by Mr. Macleod. Why should men, who for a small salary, and under every disadvantage, can thus surpass their more favoured brethren, be beaten in the race for higher places on equal terms? If they *are* beaten, let them not win the prize; but let them at any rate have the option of a start, and a fair trial. If they then fail, no blame can attach to the Government for their failure. Does any man, who has the slightest knowledge of human nature, suppose that the mere remote chance of success will not be a stimulant delight, and consolation to these men, even if they never attain the prize? Does not every young donkey who goes to the bar in England delude himself with the belief that he may be Attorney-General or Lord Chancellor some day? The chances are a thousand to one against him, to be sure, but he trusts to the unit and ignores the long figure. How many would go through the law's wearing work and sickening delays without this infinitesimal hope—this shade of a shadow? Yet Mr. Macleod, quoting Mr. Halliday, does not think the admission of a native —of one of those men declared by Mr. Marshman to be so well versed in their business—can be of the slightest use to the High Court, and fears the mere chance of their admission will upset the whole political system of India; to which, what is it possible to reply, but that if your political system rests on no sounder basis than the exclusion from judicial offices of judicial merit, if possessed by a certain class, the sooner it is destroyed the better for the nation who live under it?

As to there being no advantage in the admission of a native judge to the bench, it is self-evident that it depends on the question of his comparative superiority. If a barrister, a civilian, a person of mixed blood, and a native, are all candidates for the seat, and the latter is superior in learning and ability to his competitors, the bench must be benefited by his admission in the exact ratio of his superiority. The benefit of the admission to the bench of a particular individual must always be a question of comparison at the moment when a vacancy occurs. But the general possibility of admission—the right of eligibility—will have a wide and permanent beneficial effect. It will induce a superior class of men to enter into the judicial service, when they know the highest prizes are within their grasp. I am not contending for any advantage for the natives over their European fellow subjects; but I would impose no disadvantage upon them. If they cannot, by reason of indolence or want of intellect, beat their white competitors, by all means let them not be placed above them: if they do beat them, let them win the reward they deserve. Mr. Macleod states his belief that the natives themselves would not desire this boon. It is unnecessary for me to refute this assertion, as he refutes it himself, by subsequently asserting their value of the inferior dignities now open to them; and why men who love small rewards and places should dislike greater, is a riddle which an Œdipus could not solve.

It would take up too much of my space were I to attempt an exposition of all the incongruities of this minute. I must merely notice a few more instances. It is not worth while to point out the fallacy of the case put, of Sir L. Peel being over-ruled by a native judge. As Mr. Macleod rightly says, "it requires no comment;" its absurdity being self-evident.* So, also, is that of the argument that if natives are to be admitted into the higher judicial seats, they must also be admitted to the higher posts of the army. I may, however, again call attention to the inconsistency in the last paragraph of page 242, where he urges against the admission of natives to eligibility for these high judicial posts, that the bestowal of that privilege upon them now will prevent Government from granting it to them hereafter—"a grace which is not a valueless thing;" and "the consciousness of having got which gratifies generous impulses, and affords pleasure in other ways;" and yet, *eodem flatu*, he declares that it "would in his opinion be detrimental and unacceptable, instead of being a thankfully accepted boon." Neither need I refute the strange relative value which he deems money to possess for the native and European. But I may say, that I fully concur with him in believing, that when once the principle is established of admitting natives and "other people" to the higher seats of the Indian Bench, "consistency will forbid that the existing privileges of the regular Civil Service should be upheld with respect to the appointment to any inferior judge-

* See *post*, page 99.

ship or magistracy." This he regards as a result pregnant with evil,—I, as the only possible basis on which a remedy can be found for the present fearful judicial state of India; and the same remark applies to what he truly calls his "bold opinion" as to the inadvisability of forming a separate judicial service.

I should not have deemed it necessary to enter at such length into this minute, but for the fact that Sir John Jervis and Mr. Ellis subsequently voted in the minority with Mr. Macleod, in the division on the question of the constitution of the High Court,—a vote which I certainly was not prepared for, after reading the minute of those two gentlemen in answer to Mr. Macleod's.

To conclude this portion of my remarks, then, I venture to observe, that if an amalgamated court is to be formed at all, sound policy and justice require the admission of natives, and uncovenanted servants, to a chance of a seat on its bench; not to a *right* of a seat, but to a *chance* of a seat; because amongst these men are to be found some of the ablest servants in the judicial employ of the Company: men profoundly versed in the peculiar law of the Company's courts; possessed of great knowledge of the intricacies of the revenue system, and a much deeper acquaintance with the feelings, customs, and springs of action of the native population than Europeans can hope to attain.

Whether such an amalgamated court as that now proposed is possible, is a matter of opinion upon which there may be some doubt. I confess mine is, that it is wholly impossible, without at least raising the number of the Crown judges to six. The judges of the Supreme Court of Calcutta are already as severely worked as the human frame will permit in that country. They do not, like the judges of the Sudder, avail themselves of the constantly recurring native holydays,—with one exception.

If both his colleagues are in health, one judge gets three months' holiday every other year. They sit all the rest of the year till five o'clock, and often later; with the exception of about a week at Christmas, a fortnight in October during the great native festival of the Doorgah Poojah, and a few days at the end of May, when the heat becomes nearly insupportable, and the frame, weakened by its long continuance, can no longer stand exertion in the foul atmosphere of the Court. How can men, so worked, add to their labours Circuit and appeal duties? You must clearly increase their number from their own class, appointed after their own fashion, and not by the Governor-General in Council. Five judges are not too many for the Sudder work alone; and the result would be, that if the Crown judges are to lend their assistance to the judges of the Sudder, the business of the Supreme Court would fall into hopeless arrears; for the Supreme Court would derive no counter assistance from the ludicrous lawyers of the Civil Service, most of whom certainly do not possess the knowledge of English law possessed by an average attorney's clerk, and who would lead a life of misery and ridicule if they attempted to adjudicate under the eyes of such an able bar as that of Calcutta. If they dared to meddle with English law, a few weeks would suffice to display their ignorance in so glaring a light, that the force of public opinion would drive them with contumely and disgrace from their seats.

I do not mean for one moment to deny that there are among the civilians men of great talent and industry, who are well acquainted with the leading principles of law, and who are as good lawyers as it is possible, perhaps, for men to be, who do not make the profession their sole study. But the Sudder judges do not very often consist of the best men in the service; and there is not, even among the best—it is quite impossible that there should be—any man possessed of a knowledge of technicalities and practice and case law, sufficient to fit him for a seat in the Supreme Court. I can conceive no spectacle more amusing than would be the hopeless bewilderment depicted in the faces of the Sudder Bench, while listening to the subtle arguments and distinctions of such a man as the present learned Advocate-General upon a point of pleading.

I am perfectly certain, therefore, that none of the judges of the Sudder could undertake the work of the Supreme Court; and the judges of the latter court have not time to attend to their present duties, with the addition of the Sudder appeal business. If, therefore, the proposed High Court is established, it will be an amalgamation only in name. The avowed object, I take it, of this measure, is to infuse the element of legal training and knowledge into the Sudder Court, by the admission of properly educated judges. That can only be done by an increase in the number of Crown judges; and they must be appointed by the Crown. We cannot trust the Governor-General in Council with the bare permission to select the judges of the High Court from among any others than the civilians; he is too much under the influence of the Court of Directors to set what we know will be their wishes in this matter at defiance. The admission of barristers to a majority of these seats must be guarded by direct legislative enactment. The ministers of the Crown must not part with a patronage, the exercise of which cannot be more agreeable to them than beneficial to the people of India. Upon these terms alone will the High Court be a really Amalgamated Court; that is, a court in which the English legal knowledge and judicial experience of the Crown judges will be amalgamated in proper proportions with the knowledge of regulation law, and experience of the revenue system, possessed, or supposed to be possessed, by the civil servants of the Company.

Since the foregoing pages were written, the Calcutta correspondent of the *Times* has informed us that the Local Legislative Council objects to the proposed amalgamation. "The civilians," says this writer, very naively, "have no desire to submit their decrees to revision by barristers." How very singular! Ignorance is too conscious of her deformity to venture on an exhibition by the side of knowledge; knowledge dislikes subjection to the caprices of ignorance. This point, which affects the comfort and dignity of the official classes of India,—the only classes, I pray you to remember, who are represented either in the Local Legislature or in Parliament,—is to be "referred" back to England. The officials of India no sooner get hold of the proposed code, than they set about the removal of the only feature in it which affects them personally, turning, however, a deaf ear to the universal remonstrance of the non-official population against the points to which it objects. They will blot out at once the provision which affects them, though they thereby destroy the leading feature of the measure itself, and cut away the main argument upon which the necessity of the code has been defended; but they declare their immediate intention of passing the penal code into law, and thereby subjecting all Europeans in the Mofussil to the criminal courts of the East India Company, a measure which those men declare is an unconstitutional deprivation of their birthright as British subjects—a measure which they have hitherto successfully opposed, and which, in their universal opinion, will surely, though gradually, destroy the value of their property, and drive them out of the country. The Legislative Council dare to do this, with ample evidence before them of the frightful state of those courts, and the utter incompetence of the judges to which they are proposing to subject the lives and liberties and property of their fellow countrymen; and it is well worth your while, Sir, to note with what cavalier indifference this representation of the governing classes treats the complaints of the governed, not merely with a view to the present judicial question, but with regard to the often-urged request of the non-official population for a proper representation of themselves in their Local Legislature. This question must sooner or later come before Parliament, and I beg you to observe this one instance of the *animus* of the Legislative Council, as at present constituted, and to store it up in your memory. The non-official population of India, native and European, are the only subjects of Her Majesty who have no sort of representation of their own, either local or parliamentary, and no hand in making their own laws.

Let us see how this rejection of the scheme of amalgamation affects the proposed code. In their second report, the majority of the Commissioners observe that the present anomalous state of the law in India would become more insufferably apparent when one High Court presided over the whole country. That objection is quashed by the refusal of the Local Council to amalgamate the existing courts, and the argument as to the necessity of a code, upon that ground, falls to pieces. But a very grave consideration arises out of the destruction of the scheme of a High Court, coupled with the determination to subject all classes to the criminal courts of the East India Company. To what court is the appeal to lie from these tribunals, and who are to be the arbiters of life and death? The Sudder Judges? I do not think that such a proposal would be ventured upon in the case of British subjects. Then is it to be the Sudder in cases other than those of British subjects, and in their case the Supreme Court? Why, the anomalous state of law in India will be quite as apparent as it is now, and the business of the Supreme Court increased. You will remember that there is no attempt in the proposal of the Commissioners to supply one of the great wants of India,—a *lex loci*,—and that Mr. Robert Lowe and the late Chief Justice Jervis differed from their colleagues as to the best mode of supplying this want. The effect, therefore, as I understand it, of passing the penal code into law, without forming the amalgamated court, will be, first, to subject all Europeans to the criminal courts of the Company, with an appeal, in cases where death and some of the higher punishments are the award, to either the Supreme Court or the Sudder; and, secondly, it will provide a more rational criminal law, instead of the Mahomedan law, for those classes who are not British subjects, and are also not Mahomedans. It will introduce, as far as regards courts of first instance, an uniform criminal law into the country, by the objectionable process of depriving the British subjects of their indefeasible right of being tried by competent judges and a jury of their peers, according to the meaning of that institution within the laws of England. But as it appears to me that it cannot be seriously proposed to give British subjects a right of appeal to the Sudder only, the uniformity of the criminal law will be confined only to the courts of first instance, and to the perpetrators of minor offences. The appeal will be to the Sudder or the Supreme Court, as the offender is a British subject or not. If, again, it be proposed to give an appeal in *all* criminal cases to the Supreme Court, you will have the anomaly of one court of appeal from the lower tribunals in criminal cases, of another in civil cases; and I have already observed that you cannot increase the business of the Supreme Court without increasing the number of its judges.

Then, in the present state of proposed reform,—namely, the enactment of new laws without the amalgamated court,—what is to be done with the civil code as proposed by the Commissioners? It clearly cannot be passed in its integrity. Is the jurisdiction of the Supreme Court to be limited, as at present, to British subjects, and those who choose artificially to subject themselves to its jurisdiction? If so, many of the provisions of that code will have to be altered, and the anomalous difference of the law between the Presidencies and the Mofussil will remain *in statu quo*.

To sum up, therefore, the results of the proposed reforms of the law in India,—as far as I have means of ascertaining what they will be when the scheme of the Commissioners has been altered by the Local Legislative Council,—they amount to these:—

The British subjects will be subjected to criminal

courts to which they object, and which they undertake to prove incompetent to administer any law whatever.

The native population will gain no great advantage, unless it be deemed that they will prefer the laws of the penal code to their own criminal law; but they will not (like the British subjects) be subjected to any loss of existing privileges, as they have always been (to their great misery) subject to these courts of the Company.

The Armenian, the Christian who is not a British subject, and the Jew, will be subject to a defined law, and to these same courts; whereas heretofore they have been subject to these courts, either administering the Mahomedan criminal law, or endeavouring to discover what law they ought to administer to the particular delinquent before them.

The first of these three classes vigorously object, not so much to the proposed law, as to subjection to the courts which are to administer it, as a scheme ruinous to their welfare.

It may be doubted whether the second class care much about the matter, one way or the other. Feeling that their condition is already as bad as it can be, they may hope for some amelioration by any reform; but I know, as before stated, that the more thoughtful among them are sincerely grieved that so infinitesimal a portion should be awarded, since their condition is to be made the subject of discussion.

The third class is to a certain degree benefited. They will have *some* law, with the pleasure of knowing that it will be administered by a class of officers and courts which would not give satisfaction if administering a revealed law; and they will have the undoubted gratification of knowing that everybody is in the same predicament as themselves.

That is the amount of the proposed reform, after a lavish expenditure of money and of the time of many able men—a scheme which terrifies and abuses one class; hardly, if at all, benefits another; and presents a third with a homœopathic improvement of its condition. Is it worth while to take any trouble at all for such a result?

It appears to me that a consideration of the whole question will show you, Sir, that, however desirable the proposed measure of reform may be in some points of view, it is yet a remedy applied only to very small parts of the diseased judicial system of India, and cannot be expected to effect a valuable cure even of those parts: while it will have the effect of spreading the existing disease to a portion of the body politic (and the most intelligent and energetic portion) not hitherto affected by it. There is really no necessity for this. I am so convinced in my own mind that the scheme of amalgamation in its present form will not be carried through the Legislative Council of India, that I think we may assume its rejection. In that case, as before remarked, the main feature of the whole scheme, namely, the introduction of one uniform law, presided over by one High Court, for the whole population of India, is destroyed. But if Government is still desirous of trying a partial reform, if it thinks some use should be made of the penal code, why not confine the trial to those classes who cannot suffer by it to any great degree, and that class who must benefit by it to some degree? This may be done by enacting the penal code as the law to be administered by the East India Company's Courts to all save British subjects, and leaving the latter subject, as at present, to the Supreme Court and their own laws. I have said, as far as I have means of ascertaining, that I believe the natives would not object to the exchange of this law for the Mahomedan criminal law; and its introduction would undoubtedly be a benefit to those classes who may be said to possess no laws of their own. I see no objection to this as an experiment, a compromise, and temporary measure, though it is to be ardently hoped that the day is not far distant when a nobler and ampler reform will be granted to the judicial evils of India.

But any such reform, deserving of the name, must begin in another direction—with the courts of the East India Company, and the men who preside over them. The best tools in the hands of bad workmen can never produce anything but indifferent results; and in this case you have judges and magistrates wanting in legal knowledge; without administrative experience; without the check of a bar; hardly able to speak, and certainly not to read, the language in which their proceedings are recorded, and very often not understanding the dialect of the witnesses; at the mercy, in an extraordinary degree, of ill-paid native underlings; men of extreme youth, discharging other functions incompatible with judicial duties; totally without independence; each man *ex officio* a judge, whether fit for the office or not; with more work than he can do, however honestly disposed, and yet without any incentive to work at all:—what in the world can you expect from an *average* man under such circumstances? and what manner of thing, think you, is that which they dispense, and which Mr. Macleod, with grim facetiousness, calls Justice? A law made by the angels of heaven, and administered by such judges sitting in such courts, could scarcely be anything short of a curse.

The British settler has always been exempt from these courts in criminal matters. Had he not been so, he would not now be found in the country. His subjection to them in civil matters has operated in a most deleterious manner upon his enterprise, and consequently upon the commerce of England. A true statement of the sums spent by Zemindars and Planters in the maintenance of men for the defence of their property, and in the necessary bribes to judicial officers, would astound the House of Commons, and show what an enormous tax the shameful neglect of the Indian Government to provide for the peace and law of the country entails upon all classes out of the jurisdiction of the Supreme Court; and yet the Government do nevertheless tax the population enormously and directly for the maintenance of their courts and police, and spend a large portion of the money so obtained on other purposes. The British settler, knowing how his property has suffered from subjection to these courts, struggles against an extension of their jurisdiction to his life and liberty as against his absolute ruin. *That* he knows will be the result, whether the law under which he is harassed be Macaulay's Code or the Mahomedan Law.

An opinion, I am informed, is prevalent in England, that the British subjects object to be placed on an equality with natives, and I can easily guess the reason why such an impression has been fostered by the East

India Company's partisans. It is utterly false. The British subjects would be delighted to see the natives *raised* to an equality with them, and enjoying the benefit of laws and courts as good as their own. Such an amelioration would be of incalculable mutual benefit. But they undoubtedly object to reach that equality with the natives by *degradation* to the unhappy condition of the latter. That cannot and will not benefit either party. To that measure they have quite as great an objection as Her Majesty's ministers would show to a reduction to the condition and salaries of Her Majesty's footmen. And, as I have before stated, the intelligent and thoughtful among the natives do not desire it themselves. Perhaps, among the mass, some slight feeling of selfish gratification might be felt for a moment at the thought that all others were as badly off as themselves; but the better sort hope to have their condition raised to ours, and derive no pleasure—as indeed no rational man can—at the prospect of a measure which will simply have the effect of involving others in their own misfortunes. I have seen it so stated in so many words by more than one distinguished native; and if you will make inquiry among the members of your own Government, you will easily learn that I am justified in making that assertion, if you do not already know it.

If Parliament yield, as I think they are bound in justice to do, to the remonstrances of their fellow countrymen, and refuse to subject them to the courts of the Company in criminal matters, there is no necessity to pass the Penal Code for them. The judges of the Supreme Court are as well acquainted with the criminal law of England as the judges of England,

and can continue to administer it with the same facility as their British brethren. There is no need to impose upon them the necessity of learning a new set of definitions and laws. I am bold enough to think there are very grave objections to Macaulay's Penal Code, and that much difficulty will arise in administering it. But it is certainly easier to learn, and superior to the law now administered by the Criminal Courts of the Company. Pass it, therefore, if you please, at once for these courts, and for the people who are now subject to them; and hereafter, when you have rendered these courts unobjectionable to British subjects, the code will have been tested, and amended in all probability; and it may then be made the criminal law of India, if it has been found to be productive of a benefit sufficient to warrant the change.

I may make a few observations upon this code. It certainly is not my intention to enter upon the subject at any great length, or to take all the objections which might be taken to its language, provisions, and definitions, but to confine myself to a few leading remarks. In the first place, it was drawn up by men, not one of whom was a practical or learned lawyer. I do not know in what degree it is the handiwork of the distinguished man whose name it bears; but he brought to his task neither a practical knowledge of law, nor an acquaintance with India. He is a barrister only in name; and yet he is the only one of the framers who is a barrister even in name. The others were civilians of the Company's Service—men of ability, no doubt, and who brought to their task a knowledge of India, but marred by their ignorance of English law, and by the peculiar prejudices which attach, as I shall hereafter endeavour to show, to their whole service, as a body. Of this there is abundant evidence in the code itself.

The Act which appointed this Commission, of which Mr. Macaulay was the President, pointed out the preliminary steps to be taken by them. (3 and 4 William IV., c. 85, sec. 53 and 54.) They began by flatly disobeying the provisions of the Act, and neglecting the necessary steps for informing themselves of the state of things for which they were to legislate. Upon this point, see the evidence of Sir Edward Ryan before the late Parliamentary Committee for Indian Affairs,—one of the richest pieces of satire I ever read, and infinitely more amusing from the apparent unconsciousness, on the part of the witness, of the tremendous revelation he was making :—

"Q. 2,114. Have the provisions of the Act of 1834 effected the objects which were contemplated in 1829? Certainly not. It was the intention of the Legislature, under that Act of Parliament, as is to be gathered from the words of the Act itself, that the Commission should make inquiry into the existing system of the courts, and examine the state of judicature generally in both the Queen's and the Company's Courts: *that after a full examination into the subject it should report the results of their inquiries;* that the Governor-General should direct what inquiries it should make, and what places it should visit for the purpose of making those inquiries. No searching inquiry has been made by that Commission into the state of the existing courts; NOR into the state of the Queen's Courts; NOR have any reports of that nature been made; NOR has the Commission personally visited or inspected the state and condition of ANY of the courts in the interior; BUT IT

DID PROCEED IN 1835, WHEN IT WAS ESTABLISHED, TO THE CONSIDERATION OF A CODE OF CRIMINAL LAW."

I do not know any parallel to this statement. It may be a question whether this disobedience of the Act does not nullify the proceedings of the Commission. Without any information upon the subject, these gentlemen proceed headlong to make laws for a hundred millions of people; the civilians taking the English law, I suppose, from the mouth of Mr. Macaulay, who is no lawyer,—whose very devotion to other pursuits shows that he can have had but a superficial knowledge of the maxims and principles of that "Ladye Law," of whom Coke quaintly says, that she "loveth to lie alone," —and who certainly never had the slightest experience of their practical working; and Mr. Macaulay receiving his information as to the state of the courts from the civilians, who, for the honour of the Government they served, and for their own exoneration from blame, were directly interested in keeping him in the dark as to the true state of things. Is it wonderful that under these circumstances the code should be objectionable? Was not this disobedience of the Act an insult to the Legislature of these realms? Is it unreasonable to expect that the remonstrances of the people so legislated for will receive courteous hearing from Parliament, and a compliance with their just demands?

I have discussed this code with lawyers of long standing and practical experience, and never knew one of them who approved of it in any degree, except in so far as it was *a* code of some sort. We all feel what a boon a good code would be. But when we reflect that after the English Criminal Law Commissioners had made themselves acquainted with the state of things for which they were to legislate—had taken all those necessary preliminary steps which the Indian Commission neglected to take—the result of their labours was a complete failure, in the opinion of the judges of England, it is not marvellous that the code of the unlearned Indian Commission should be a bad one. When you have got a code in England, it will be time enough to alter it in the slight degree required for India, and to pass it for British subjects, when it can be administered by competent courts. The definitions and principles of the criminal law by which British subjects in India are to be ruled, they as such subjects have, I contend, an indefeasible right to demand should be co-equal and con-similar with those of the law enacted for their countrymen in England. They do not denaturalize themselves by voluntary exile, and do not lose the right of being tried by the laws and courts, for the establishment and integrity of which their forefathers fought and conquered.

Independent of the fact that the enactment of this code is sought to be made the pretence of subjecting British subjects to corrupt courts and incompetent and dependent judges, it is itself unconstitutional in some of its leading principles. It is a code in which the principle of despotic dictation by the Supreme Executive Government to the judicial officers is recognized as a fit principle to be made the supreme law. It is a code in which laws for the suppression of European immigration into India are recognized, re-affirmed, and re-enacted, when they ought to be repealed. It is a code containing a provision which makes the bare possession of a printing press punishable with fine and imprisonment, even though it be not used,—with fine to the amount of £500, and imprisonment for two years! It is a code which entrusts enormous powers to very young, dependent, and incompetent men, and makes no attempt to improve the courts of India. It is, moreover, full of strange definitions and loose language, to which a thousand objections might be taken. The grand merit of the English criminal law is, and has ever been, that as far as trial is concerned, its code of procedure has been popular and republican. It has been the Legislature, by endless statutes of no small absurdity, and judges, by decisions of marvellous narrowness, that have caused its encumbrance with a heap of rubbish which is not yet half swept away. But this code presents the Indian public with a mockery of trial by jury; with a law despotic in its leaning and principles, and with judges and magistrates who habitually refer to, and act under the actual and immediate control of, the Executive Government,—the magistrates, more especially, on whom the whole preliminary investigation is thrown, and who have the power, of course, of holding to bail, or refusing it, and committing for trial. Moreover, it is a *sine qua non* that the Local Legislature, as at present constituted, out of purely official elements, should not have unlimited power of altering any code which may be presented to them. Such a code as the one now under consideration, altered by such a local legislature, will put the residents in India bound hand and foot into the power of any judges and magistrates who may choose to exercise the almost unlimited powers of oppression which they will possess. And that there are many such I will proceed to show.

I now come to the point to which I most specially

desire to direct your attention,—the class of men who exercise judicial and magisterial functions in India, the civil servants of the East India Company. It is not unusual to say that one intends to speak of them with great respect, and to profess a high respect for them, as a body. I shall make no such avowal, but shall endeavour to show exactly in what points they are deserving of respect and of blame, in my opinion. They are selected from the middle class of English gentry, and are, as a body, just what the average Jones and Thompson of English society would be, under the same circumstances of climate, position, and education. I willingly allow the great excellence of some individuals; but with these we have nothing to do. They are happy accidents. In speaking of a body of men, and considering their fitness for being entrusted with large powers, we must not proceed upon the hypothesis that some may be Pitts or Mansfields; but upon the fact that the great majority must be the sort of average being against whom you brush in the drawing-rooms of the society whence he comes.

If this proposed reform takes place, the vast majority of the men by whom the British subjects in India will be tried will, for many years, be men who entered the service under the old system of appointment by the Court of Directors, and my remarks will chiefly apply to them, though their force will not be materially affected by the alteration to the examination system now introduced.

Let us, for the purpose of illustration, take the case of two brothers, average boys, rather clever than the reverse, and, judging by general rules, consider the probable effect upon their character of their different positions, the one entering upon the career of a barrister in England, the other of a civilian in India. Mr. Jones, we will say, is blessed with two sons, Jack and Tom, who have both gone fairly through the ordeal of a public school, got one or two prizes, reached the sixth form, written some sweet things in their sister's album, and are considered geniuses by their own family and their own selves, and not particularly stupid by other people. While Jones, *père*, is debating to which University he will send them, an East Indian Director takes a fancy to Tom, and offers him a writership, and he is sent to Haileybury, where we will leave him for the present, to follow Master Jack. He is sent to Oxford, and of course such a very clever fellow is sure (in his own opinion) of a first class, with moderate work. The lists come out, and lo! Jack has only "got a third." For a moment his self-esteem receives a little shock; but he soon recovers. The examiners notoriously had a prejudice against —— College men; and if they had not, by the cruellest luck, set him a paper in the only passage of Aristotle which he had not read carefully, he would have been certain, &c., &c., &c. Mrs. Jones and his sisters believe every word of the excuses, and by the time he has muttoned and beefed himself into the degree of utter barrister, his self-complacency is completely restored; besides, though he did not get a first class, he cannot forget how he distinguished himself at the debating society. Nature meant him for an orator, he feels: only let him get the chance, and the effect he will produce in Queen's Bench will be something astonishing. He does get it at last, through a benevolent attorney, who fancies he sees a resemblance in Jones to his dead son, and determines to give him a chance of showing his mettle. With what pride Jones eyes his brief! How he will show cause against that rule! How he will pound, triturate, and utterly demolish the other side! His leader seems to entertain no great hopes, but his leader clearly has never got a right hold of the point. *He*, the great Jones, will have to do it all himself. So much the better; in about five years a silk gown; in ten, if the right ministry are in power, Mr. Attorney! Down he goes on the eventful morning, with a most carefully prepared speech; points duly marshalled, like steps on a ladder, a tremendous peroration, and a secret hope that the judges will snub him, in order that he may "come out strong." Need I say that he will arrange his facts and arguments with the lucid force of Lyndhurst, and descant upon them with the nervous eloquence of Erskine?

At last the moment arrives. He gets up, and says very glibly, "My Lords, I also have the honour to appear in this case with my learned friend," when a sudden doubt suggests itself as to whether he had not better begin with his third point. He hardly attempts it, before he finds himself in an inextricable confusion. The oddest sensation ensues. Sparks seem to flash from his eyes; something rises up and bobs against his uvula, choking his voice; the judges seem all running into one; Lord Campbell has suddenly laid aside the grave decorum of his manner, and is winking at him with indecent hilarity; and clear amid all the confusion he sees, rife with malicious fun, the detested face of his stupid cousin Robinson—that Robinson whose waltzing and hideous boots he has so often ridiculed, in his neat way, to Miss Charming—that Robinson who never wrote album verses in his life, and yet has, in this very case, acquitted himself fairly on the other side, as he,

Jones, cannot but allow. Now at this juncture, instead of snubbing him, one of the judges kindly tries to give him a help; he cannot understand or catch the suggestion; it is the last feather on his burden; he sits down abruptly, with burning cheeks and a heavy heart. He sneaks home with suicidal intentions; but his spirits improve gradually after dinner with each glass of port. He begins to reflect and take a new measure of himself. He perceives that he made a little mistake in thinking he was a huge piece of ordnance, whose weighty metal and loud bang would astonish the world the moment it was discharged, and that it will take long time and labour to make even a pocket pistol of him. He takes a more favourable and respectful view of Robinson; he dare not, cannot, quiz him any more. However, if he has pluck, luck, and (ah! most necessary of all) a friendly attorney, he will try again, and may in time get his silk gown. Such is the rude lesson through which a professional man learns modesty and charity. Many a fine intellect and sensitive nature have shrunk from the horrors of a second attempt; many more have never got the chance after the first dismal defeat. But the lesson, stern and cruel though it often is, has an all-pervading and beneficial effect. Jack Jones, after that miserable day, is a wiser and better man, and fitter to judge of his fellow men.

Now turn to the other picture, and follow the civilian's career. He is "highly distinguished" at Haileybury, and after hearing a few eloquent and touching remarks upon duty from the good Sir James Hogg, he sails, amid sororial lamentations and maternal blessings, for Calcutta. He gets an inkling into his good fate upon the voyage. He hears congratulations on his luck from the old military men who are returning from furlough, and notes the semi-divine assumption of the old civilians; and probably one or two of the more knowing girls make a dead set at him. Once at Calcutta, his progress in conceit is exceedingly rapid. He goes to stay with a married relation, who is high in the service. The house is a palace; the splendour of the living, the number of the servants, the style of furniture, present a rather striking contrast to the paternal mansion in Bloomsbury Square. This, then, will be his lot too. Every morning as soon as his eyes open, in answer to the gentle call of his bearer, that polished individual makes the most graceful and lowly prostrations, and salutes him by the loftiest appellations. Two of them wipe and dress him. Whenever he eats, a servant attends to his sole wants. The tradesman is only too happy to give him unlimited credit. Does he want money? Who so happy as the money-lender to oblige him with any amount? The lessons taught by the adulation of the native and the shopkeeper are enforced by the demeanour of his own pretty countrywomen. Beauty bows before him; the brightest eyes light up at his approach. Emily and Ann seem to have made a bet as to who shall produce him the greatest number of sweet smiles in a given time. For, alive, his value ranges, as soon as he is employed, from about £500 to £10,000 per annum; and when he is bricked up in his grave (to give the worms a fair start against the jackals, the wealthy are bricked up in India), his miraculous carcase is still pecuniarily productive to his widow. "Three hundred a year, my dears, dead or alive, and pensions to the children!" is the remark of the sagacious matron to her daughters, when enforcing the necessity of catching a civilian; "to say nothing of the position." He stays about a year in Calcutta, snatching just time enough from dissipation to enable him to pass through a very easy examination in the native languages, and he is then sent up into one of the interior districts, to officiate as assistant to the magistrate—a gentleman who presides sole arbiter over from one to three millions of men. The young civilian, who from the date of his appointment has been drawing from £300 to £360, now begins to draw from £480 to £600 a year, according to the number of examinations which he has passed, and proceeds to deal out "justice" to an enormous population, without any sort of judicial training, but with no small opinion of himself and his powers. His age, it will be remembered, is twenty-two. I shall copy a short description of his *modus operandi* from the pen of the late Mr. Wilson, for upwards of twenty-five years a resident in Tirhoot, a man profoundly versed in Oriental character and languages, and of the highest character:—

"The embryo magistrate instals himself in a dwelling-house, the property of the principal landholder in the vicinity; a nominal rent is, for appearance sake, negotiated, while double the amount is usually spent in repairs and improvements. The landlord impresses upon his tenantry the obligations the authorities are under to him, and he is enabled to give them an extra squeeze. A room in the building is set aside as a court; all the procedure is in writing; a nephew of the magistrate's confidential native functionary presides as confidant and mentor to the youthful Englishman; several other writers, a few attendants, porters, and policemen arrayed in blue turbans and badges, describe this official retinue ; and with all the lighter charges and petitions of the magistrate's file handed to him for adjudication, the young man commences his career, taking lessons on the wrongs of indigent men, much in the same way as Majendie experimented upon living animals.

"The language of the court is not the dialect of the people. The evidence, therefore, of the witnesses, the accuser, and the accused, must be taken in writing by a native examiner ; and the whole proofs of the most trivial assault, or the foulest murder, are carefully arranged by a man who receives ten shillings a month! A *douceur* modifies the evidence materially. When all is ready, the papers are read aloud by the head native functionary, while the young magistrate is drawing a horse or a ship on some blotting paper, or hacking the table with his penknife. At the conclusion, the bench intimates to his sable mentor to give a 'suitable order.'

"But the decisions here pronounced do not rest upon the affidavit of witnesses present, so much as upon the report and details of an investigating officer, who possesses the most anomalous power in the interior of the province. At the distance of some twenty or thirty miles from each other, small police stations are distributed ; these are occupied by a few paid and unpaid policemen, the latter being rewarded for their zeal by a levy upon the inhabitants, in which the former share. This posse is commanded by a sergeant called a darogah, a corporal called a jamadar, and a clerk ; for it very often happens that, although engaged in the most extensive paper correspondence, the two former cannot write. Under these officers, again, are placed a body of village watchmen, said to amount in Bengal, in round numbers, to no less than 200,000 men, and supported by a local tax upon all huts. These guardians of the night are thieves by profession, and thieves by hereditary descent.

"The duty of the sergeant is to inquire into all unlawful causes of offence, take down evidence, and report his own convictions on the case to his superior, the magistrate, who in most cases decides accordingly, as he cannot help relying on the accuracy of a man writing from the spot; and thus the lives and fortunes of the people depend upon the good will of a set of the most unmitigated scoundrels on earth."*

Under this advantageous training, the young civilian speedily becomes a magistrate, and a good deal more than a magistrate, as we understand it in England. He is not simply a judicial officer, but a thief-catcher, police superintendent, accuser and magistrate in one. A conviction by him, in his judicial capacity, is a compliment to himself as thief-catcher and policeman. Is it strange that he should have, therefore, a strong leaning to severity? In fact, as there is no sort of division of labour in the service, the education above described is supposed to fit a civilian to be thief-catcher, police superintendent, accuser, magistrate, judge, an intricate tax collector, a commissioner of revenue (with nearly indescribable powers), a postmaster, an opium agent, a salt salesman, an exciseman, a secretary to Government, a diplomatist, a finance minister, a professor of English law, a director of public instruction, and an ædile, or commissioner of sewers and public works, all in turn; but if he is remarkably idle, or remarkably foolish, his elevation to

* "A Letter to John Bright, Esq., M.P., on the India Question." By James Wilson, Esq., Twenty-five Years Resident in Bengal. London: Edward Stanford, 6, Charing Cross.

the bench becomes a certainty, as he is considered unfit to be employed in what are deemed the more important branches of the public service. You will think I exaggerate; but I am stating a truth as notorious in India as that the earth goes round the sun. I know an instance in which an exhibition of remarkable folly on the part of his senior gained a friend and connection of my own an unexpected promotion. That senior, for his folly, was immediately made a judge, because he could not, in the opinion of the authorities, be intrusted with revenue matters, and my friend got the post his senior would have had, if no doubt had been entertained of his sanity. Every man, as he attains sufficient standing, can be made a judge; in fact, he is only *not* made a judge if he has shown too much ability to be spared from the other branches of the service, or if he pushes his interest with a view to other employment. This fact is broadly stated by Mr. George Campbell, who is, nevertheless, a thorough-going partisan and admirer of his own service:—

"It seems to be considered, that if at this time of life a man is fit for anything at all, he is fit for a judge: *and if he is fit for nothing, make him a judge, and get rid of him:* for once in that office, he has no *claim* to farther promotion by mere seniority alone." This being the case, the judicial is naturally the despised branch of the service, and nearly all the more able and ambitious servants of the Company seek employment either in the revenue or secretarial or financial departments, as through these paths only are the highest dignities, such as lieutenant-governorships and memberships of Council, likely to be attained. I am well aware that the present Lieutenant-Governor of the North-Western Provinces was raised to that dignity from the Sudder Bench; but he was not so promoted from any abilities displayed as a judge, but from those shown in other employments, and from strong interest; in fact, he was a very bad judge in some respects, as the *Friend of India* has lately confessed, though, of course, a man of his ability and industry was vastly superior to the majority of his service. And after this confession on the part of the civilians' own organ, of the judicial unfitness of the Sudder Bench generally, and especially of this undoubtedly able man, and after Mr. G. Campbell's statement, it may well be conceived that the average judge is a very queer animal indeed.

I think I might almost leave my case as to the judicial unfitness of the civil servants where it now stands, and ask any man of common sense whether he wonders much at the dislike shown by his countrymen to the prospect of entire subjection to such courts, and such officers, and such a police? But their greatest disqualifications for the judicial office have not yet been hinted at.

It cannot be denied that the judicial training of the civilian is totally deficient in every requisite for the improvement of his natural capacity. Let any kind of fault be proved against him, no notice is taken of it, or if any is taken, it is generally in the nature of a kick up-stairs. Mr. Wilson, just quoted, cites an instance: "A judge, condemned by the Court of Directors for open fraud in the performance of his judicial duty, is deprived of an appointment yielding £2,300, and is installed in another worth £6,000 per annum," and adds:—"This one instance is given, where twenty more might be added." This is true when the delinquency is not of a nature to offend the Government; but if the judge decides against the Government, he is nearly sure to feel its displeasure sooner or later. He has entered into a covenant with them, of the precise nature of which we are not aware; but that, and the fact of his promotion depending not on his own merits, but on the goodwill of the Executive Government, render him totally subservient. The Government do not hesitate to tell the judges how they are to decide in cases of which the decision affects its own interests, as I shall presently show. This evil spreads through all the subordinate judicial officers. The latter obey the slightest hint of the magistrate, whom they regard as the exponent of the wishes of those in power. Let him be known to have a prejudice against a given zemindar, or planter, and the obnoxious individual is ruined. The slightest expression of his bias—an indirect hint even—and the man indicated never gains his case. Assistant magistrates, deputy magistrates, cazees, pundits, amlah, nazir, sudder ameens, moonsiffs, darogahs, police, all are banded against him. Not only does he suffer defeat in every case which he himself brings into Court, but endless accusations are trumped up against him, and supported by perjury and forgery. The darogah, or serjeant, is only too happy to gain credit for zeal by bringing accusations forward; the magistrate begins to think him a very excellent officer, and himself a very energetic and successful detector of abuses. The darogah sees the pleasure his charges give, and continues producing new ones. The magistrate can hardly help believing some of them, even if the majority are found to be false; and the man, against whom charges are weekly or monthly preferred, is at last believed to be an accomplished villain; though perhaps all these accusations had their origin in some hasty word, or heedlessly displayed dislike of the magistrate himself. If he leaves the district, he probably tells his successor, "You had better keep your eye on So-and-So;" and thus the successor too imbibes a prejudice against a man who is very likely to be entirely innocent. The result is invariably that the man is either ruined, or driven to hold his own by the worst means: by the strong hand, by extensive bribery of the magistrates' underlings, or fraud, perjury, and forgery. If the latter be the case, the chances are that by the time he has become a thoroughly accomplished villain, and has got all the understrappers in his pay, and a well organized band of perjurers, he becomes a great favourite with the next magistrate, who now finds him always to be in the right, looks upon him as an injured individual, who was shamefully oppressed by his predecessor, finds every case in his favour, and the man in his turn rides rough shod over all his neighbours, and indemnifies himself for his previous unjust losses by present unjust gains. Conceive the effect on the planter when the magistrate has a spite against him!

I have said that the best intentioned magistrates cannot do their work, and that they have no incentive to work. The first assertion does not admit of argument; a glance at the extent of their jurisdiction, and a consideration of the badness of their police (of which I am informed a late Report by Mr. Halliday, which I have not seen, is as demonstrative as the most ardent Indian reformer could wish), will convince you of its truth. As to the second, it is to be remembered that, except in very rare instances, energy is not rewarded. The civilian is sure of his promotion, whether capable or incapable, whether idle or industrious. In those rare cases where an extraordinary promotion takes place, it will be found that the more important element of interest, either in India or at home, was not wanting in the candidate; at least, I cannot call to mind an instance to the contrary. All that the Government require is, that a certain number of cases should be decided in the month. When, therefore, the officer finds his tale growing short, he rattles through his remanets in a helter-skelter fashion, till he gets his decisions up to the required number. This is, I believe, absolutely necessary under the present system; and it is easy to conceive that an indulgence in this rapid mode of decision becomes habitual, the more readily as it generally brings the magistrate into favour with his superiors, and gains him credit for vigour and diligence; while, on the other hand, a conscientious representation of abuses, and schemes for their reform, as frequently bring the official into disgrace; he is ordered not to be troublesome and meddling, but to do as others do. Moreover, the climate must not be left out of consideration; that of Bengal is relaxing to an astonishing degree; the most vigorous are not free from its irritating and weakening effect; the majority alternate between a savage irritation and effete listlessness. And yet to discharge the duties of a magistrate properly, a man must be a good horseman, and able "to stand the sun," in addition to his other qualifications.

Besides the obvious tendency to severity, which the possession of judicial and executive functions by one and the same individual must superinduce in him, this double capacity has another most injurious effect. It precludes the possibility of obtaining redress against his wrong doing; for if convicted of evil practices in his executive department, he turns round and shelters himself as a judicial officer under Act 18 of 1850, commonly called "The Impunity Act." This was one of the three "Black Acts," which the European residents unanimously opposed in 1849, and the only one of them which was passed. It was expressly passed to give the civil servants more impunity than Lord Wensleydale had decided they were entitled to under the statute 23 Geo. III., c. 70, in the well known case of *Calder* v. *Halkett.* It was an Act contrary to the intention of the Legislature when it passed the statute of George III. It was an Act contrary to the principles of the Privy Council's judgment, and it was laughable for the absurdity of its phraseology; but nevertheless it was passed, and seems to have the effect of preserving the magistrates from the consequences of punishment in case of mis-behaviour. I will, as a specimen of the manner in which some of these gentry behave, quote the case of a Mr. Thomas, the collector and magistrate of Coimbatore, in Madras. The last few mails have brought us news of the final decision of this case.

Bhawanny Lallah is a wealthy merchant, trading between Coimbatore and Madras. Mr. Thomas is collector and magistrate of the former place, but in September, 1854, was residing at Ootacamund, distant seventy to eighty miles from Coimbatore. On the 20th September, he sent a note—not a summons—to Bhawanny Lallah, ordering him to appear before him at Ootacamund, the object of the requisition not being stated. Bhawanny Lallah very naturally did not go. On the 23d December Mr. Thomas had him taken into custody, dragged backwards from prison to his cutcherry day after day, until he was pleased to sentence him—Heaven knows what for (for there was no charge)—upon the 6th January, to find two sureties in 100 rupees each. Then Mr. Thomas pretended that this wealthy trader could not find such sureties, or at any rate he refused to accept them, and the man was further imprisoned for another week. Subsequently, Bhawanny Lallah brought his action in the Supreme Court at Madras, and Sir C. Rawlinson delivered judgment in his favour, from which judgment I extract the following sentences:—

Sir C. Rawlinson, C. J. "*I cannot find in my notes that any charge whatever was made against this plaintiff; nor does all alleged against him in the highly-coloured statement called 'a sentence,' amount to any charge. In fact, I cannot make anything at all out of this piece of paper; for I cannot look upon it as a record at all—merely a sort of memorandum.*"

This "sentence," or "record," or "piece of paper," is the official record of what passed with regard to Bhawanny Lallah. It described the charge against him, and the sentence upon him, in the language of an advocate, and not of a judge; but one very remarkable fact is worth noting. When Bhawanny Lallah brought his action in the Supreme Court, he applied for a copy of his "sentence" to Mr. Thomas: one was furnished to him. At the trial this was produced, and what purported to be a copy of the same sentence, was put in upon behalf of the defendant Thomas: *there was great discrepancy between the copies, and one was much longer than the other!* Upon which the Chief Justice thus commented:—

"*I have here two papers, both signed by the defendant, and both (singular to say) purporting to be the record of the case—both dated on the same day; but their contents are very dissimilar. No explanation is given of this, though there has been ample time for such explanation, for the case has been the reverse of hurried on. Yet the two papers widely differ. True, I can make little of either—both are so confused and irregular.* * * * * * * What are the facts, the *undisputed facts* of the case? On the 23rd December the plaintiff was taken into custody, and subsequently was taken before the defendant, by whose orders he was day after day dragged backwards and forwards from the prison to the cutcherry, and from the cutcherry to the prison, *being confined in the prison* each night. *Nothing would have been easier than to disprove this, had it been untrue.* At length, *after many days of this dragging about in custody, the defendant proposes to hold an inquiry into something which took place in his absence, more than two months previously. There had been other magistrates there during these two months, but there had been no inquiry, no charge, nothing done till the defendant returns as described.* On the 6th of January the plaintiff was sentenced to find two sureties in 100 rupees each, or to go to jail: *and on that day he was thrown into jail. The question then comes, what took place before he was thrown into jail?* The plaintiff swears he had friends, respectable and wealthy men, there, whom he tendered as his securities, *and there is also other evidence of the fact.* Coimbatore is a large place, and has many respectable and wealthy inhabitants; *and can the Court then be expected to believe the suggestion for the defence, that the plaintiff, who is a very rich and influential man, could not get two securities for* 100 *rupees each?* It is also suggested that the plaintiff flatly refused to give security. It does not become necessary to inquire into this, *because the magistrate had no jurisdiction to make him do so.*"

This is an abbreviated account of a case tried in Madras within the last few months. The report is taken from the Madras papers, and the very words of Sir C. Rawlinson's judgment are given; the parts omitted do not in any way affect these passages. The Chief Justice upon this occasion found a verdict for the plaintiff, with 1,000 rupees damages. This was subsequently upset by the same judge and his colleague, upon a point of law; both judges, however, in their judgment, intimating their opinion that Mr. Thomas had been guilty of "*mala praxis.*" It is not for me to question the legality of this decision; but it certainly seems greatly to exceed the principles laid down in *Calder* v. *Halkett*, and must therefore, I presume, rest upon the Act 18 of 1850, before noticed, and if so, proves the impropriety of that Act. For it must be remembered, that both the judges find a verdict for the plaintiff on the merits; and we may deduce from the first judgment of Sir C. Rawlinson the following facts:—

1. That Mr. Thomas ordered Bhawanny Lallah to appear before him, seventy miles off, without any reason or proper forms.

2. That he kept him in prison without any charge a fortnight.

3. That he then, for no offence and upon no charge, ordered him to find bail.

4. That he refused his bail, and imprisoned him for a further term.

Sir, this is *torture!* It would be bad enough in England, but you have no conception of what it is in

India. A respectable native would abandon a very large amount of money rather than be obliged to appear in person in a civil court—nearly his whole fortune, I verily believe, rather than go into jail, or even appear in a criminal court. He loses caste, and honour, and feels it much as you would feel being kicked out of a gentleman's drawing-room. To regain the position he has lost costs him an immense sum of money, if he be a man of position and wealth, in religious ceremonies, feasts, and fees to the priests of his caste. The police subject him to every indignity, spitting on him, flinging dirt on him, sending him food which he cannot eat, or threatening only to send him his food by the hands of men whose touch is pollution, and thus starving him; and force from him large sums of money to purchase exemption from their cruelty; even if they do not proceed to actual torture by any given instrument named in the late Report. I know nothing of Madras personally, but unless the police there are very different from what they are in Bengal, I have no hesitation in saying that this iniquitous proceeding of the magistrate probably cost Bhawanny Lallah £1,000, at least, from beginning to end. Yet his oppressor goes unpunished.

Now, observe the difference between this case and that of an English magistrate acting in a similar way. It may be that this magistrate is exonerated from punishment upon principles similar to those which wisely hold our judicial officers free from the consequences of their judicial acts, though I confess I doubt it. *But*, if an English magistrate acted thus, the force of public opinion would drive him at once from the bench. Mr. Thomas, on the contrary, will be considered a martyr by the Local Government, and will perhaps be specially favoured, but most certainly will suffer no loss of station or one step of promotion. This gentleman, by the way, was one of those whose veracity appeared in a somewhat unfavourable light in the Torture Report. He denied the existence of torture, and yet it appeared in the tables attached to the Report that he had convicted two men for the practice himself. To judge from Sir C. Rawlinson's judgment, he does not seem to have improved in his conceptions of truth.

Think what the effect upon the poor natives must be of letting such instances of misconduct go unpunished; they never dare complain of any oppression: and let me ask again, if it is surprising that Englishmen object to being tried for their lives by such men, and desire that the natives should have the benefits of their courts, instead of themselves being subjected to the Company's Courts? And yet Mr. Thomas's sins are mere peccadilloes in comparison with those of some of his brethren. I cannot refrain here from quoting a paragraph from the *Madras Athenæum* on this subject:—

"It is not the bare acting without jurisdiction from which the natives so much require protection, as all those irregularities, eccentricities, oppressions, illegalities, which may, and often do, occur during a trial and investigation, and which are simply '*pessima praxis*'!"

Surely the British subjects require this too!

Are you acquainted with the case of Mr. Solano, and the charges he has brought against a magistrate named Swinton? The case has been before Parliament, before the Government of India, before the Court of Directors, and has been noticed by one, at least, of the English papers. But (supposing that Mr. Solano was right in his allegations) his wrongs have received no redress, and the last news from India reports that he has been all but murdered. It is impossible to deny that the attack on him is directly traceable to the ill-will of the magistrate. The case is one of such importance, that I shall make no apology for quoting an article upon the subject from the leading journal of Calcutta, and extracts from the case which Mr. Solano laid before the Government of India. Mr. Solano is a foreigner of substance, who has been for many years a planter and landholder in the district of Shahabad. Mr. Swinton chose to believe that Mr. Solano was in the habit of oppressing his tenantry, and consequently commenced what, if Mr. Solano's statements be true, was a system of persecution and denial of justice against him. It is impossible to doubt the truth of a large portion of Mr. Solano's statements, because he states facts which were matters of judicial record, and the falsity of which must have been so easy of proof, that no sane man would have ventured on such assertions if false. He describes a long and most vexatious proceeding, the adverse decisions of the magistrates, and the reversal by the judge of those decisions. We know well in India that civil servants have frequently been guilty of such conduct, and the proceedings of the Government in this case lead almost irresistibly to the belief, that Mr. Swinton is not able to exculpate himself from the charges made against him; for when Mr. Solano applied to Government to let him see Mr. Swinton's reply, *the Government refused the request.* And yet, Sir, since you have been at the Board of Control the Home Government promised to furnish a copy of Mr. Swinton's reply, but has never fulfilled the promise. Is it because they dare not? A gross wrong has thus been done to one of these two gentlemen.

Either Mr. Swinton is guilty, or he is not guilty. If the former be the case, those in power, who kept him in office after they had proof of his wrong doing, are directly chargeable with the moral guilt of the murderous attack upon his victim; if the latter, they have behaved most cruelly to Mr. Swinton, in permitting him to lie for years under the stigma of being a shameful and reckless oppressor. The evil results of such a policy are not confined to this particular case; they spread through the whole country, and every honourable and upright member of the service suffers from the suppression of inquiry into such charges. Suppose a parallel case in England. Suppose that a charge of corruption or oppression was brought in this circumstantial manner against a magistrate or a judge of England. Would the public be satisfied—would his learned brethren be satisfied—if Sir George Grey rose in the House, and said that he had received an explanation from the accused personage which he deemed satisfactory, and that therefore the Ministry intended to take no further steps in the matter, but that he certainly did not intend to publish that explanation? Would not the public be still more suspicious if the accused man happened to be the Home Secretary's own nephew? Yet this is an exactly parallel case. I defy anybody to say that it is not a fair analogy. Mr. Swinton is a very near connexion of Sir J. W. Hogg's, and has, I believe, other interest to back him. I know nothing of this case, save from the published documents. It may very likely be true that Mr. Solano has at some period resorted to illegal proceedings. There is hardly a Mofussil man in the oldest settlements of India, who is not driven, by the inefficiency of the courts and the police, to hold his own at times by illegal means.

But Mr. Solano is not only a planter, but a zemindar and landowner. In such cases oppression on any large scale is very rare, for the best of all reasons; it militates against his own pecuniary interest. It is very possible that Mr. Solano, as soon as he had discovered the uselessness of appealing to the judicial authorities, determined to protect his property by the strong hand, and enforced his legal claims by illegal means. But the blame of such not uncommon proceedings attaches to the Government, who provide no effectual means of preserving order, or enforcing just claims in legal ways. And surely a man is not likely to be cured of evil practices by finding the law courts shut against him, and the police, who obey every hint of their official superior, turned into so many enemies against him, from that superior's personal ill-will and prejudice. It requires no reflection to suppose that a man, who has invested his whole fortune in the country, will prefer holding his own by bribery, fraud, and violence, to certain and imminent ruin. I subjoin the article, and extracts from Mr. Solano's petition to the Bengal Government, taken from the *Calcutta Englishman*, under date the 12th and 24th May, 1855.

"The *Press* has noticed the case of Mr. Solano, and the ***Friend*** insinuates, as if it was a fault, that the *Press* must have been moved by the legal adviser of that gentleman. It indeed does not name him, but it points at him. Now, let us observe that Mr. Solano printed his case many months ago, with the view to give it a more or less extended circulation; and the notice which it has attracted in England is owing, we believe, entirely to its importance. This so-called Case is a miscellany of cases, furnishing individually and collectively a striking illustration of the extent to which the abuse of office and maladministration of justice may be carried with impunity by an East India Company's civilian. In this point of view it illustrates the spirit of the authorities here, in dealing with the best grounded complaints against any of that class of persons. The case has also been before the Court of Directors, which has supported the nephew of Sir J. W. Hogg and the local Government. The part taken by these authorities gives the case a public, we may say a political, importance.

"We shall have occasion hereafter to advert more particularly to the conduct of the Government; at present we shall deal only with that of Mr. Swinton. One of Mr. Solano's complaints against him was, that practically he shut him and his servants out from redress, by the manner in which he dealt with their complaints when brought before him. We will give an illustration. One of his servants, who was in charge of some of his cultivated lands, had to drive off a herd of cattle which was trespassing upon them, and was beaten and threatened by the owners of the cattle. The man complained to Mr. Swinton, who referred the case to the Joint Magistrate, and in the order of reference, cast on Mr. Solano the following imputation:—'As on the part of Mr. Solano great oppression is practised, you will inquire into the matter and pass proper orders.' To appreciate the malignity of this remark, it must be observed that it does not stand alone; it was not a momentary aberration from proper judicial decorum, but the invariable treatment which Mr. Solano and his servants received from Mr. Swinton, and conduct of this kind in another case formed the matter of an express charge against Mr. Swinton. Any magistrate not belonging to the privileged service, acting in such a manner, would, we will venture to say, be visited with the highest displeasure of this Government, if not instant dismissal. What would be said of a magistrate in Calcutta if he took the occasion of a complaint on the part of a banian to vilify the firm that employed him, and that, apparently, with no object but to prejudice the banian's complaint when it should come under investigation? Such would be a parallel to the conduct of Mr. Swinton in this instance. And what probably would be the conduct of the banian in the case supposed, appears also to have been that of Mr. Solano's servant. He declined to prosecute his complaint before such a prejudiced tribunal, and who could blame him? But, therefore, what shall we say of Mr. Swinton?

"Our readers will see that the case described grew out of cattle trespass. It is not surprising that cattle trespass should prevail in any district under such a man. The manner in which Mr. Swinton dealt with this subject forms one of many very strong grounds of complaint against him. Pitching his tent, in one of his cold weather tours, near Mr. Solano's residence, he invited, according to Mr. Solano's pamphlet, complaints against him. As might be expected on such an invitation, twenty or thirty complaints were brought to him. Even Mr. Swinton could entertain only two of them, and they were complaints that Mr. Solano had distrained cattle trespassing, and in one of the cases taken a fine of five rupees. A Punchayet of respectable zemindars had investigated the case, and fixed that fine. Giving no weight to their decision, Mr. Swinton fined Mr. Solano a hundred rupees in each case, and required from him a security bond in two thousand rupees not to oppress any ryots in future. Here, then, we plainly see what is Mr. Swinton's idea of oppression. Mr. Solano's servant complains of cattle trespass, and of being beaten in driving cattle off his master's cultivated fields; Mr. Swinton takes occasion of that complaint to brand Mr. Solano as an oppressor of the people. Mr. Solano is called before him in consequence of his servants having distrained cattle trespassing, and Mr. Swinton fines him heavily, and binds him over not to oppress the people. Obviously the distraining of the cattle is here the oppression in Mr. Swinton's opinion, and his decision in these cases, practically and logically, amounted to a license for all the owners of all the cattle in the country to feed their cattle on Mr. Solano's crops.

"Outrageous as was the imposition of fines on Mr. Solano himself, and the extortion of a security bond from him, it was but a small part of Mr. Swinton's misrule on that one occasion. On the same day (we quote Mr. Solano's petition to Government) on which the security bond was taken from Mr. Solano, Mr. Swinton summoned Mr. Solano's dewan, a man upwards of seventy years of age, and two others of his principal native servants, the naib and jemadar, and required them to give similar security bonds not to oppress the ryots. And besides taking security from servants, Mr. Swinton summoned from Arrah, the civil station thirty miles off, Mr. Solano's law mooktear, and extorted a security bond from him. We cannot better express our opinion of these proceedings than in the words with which Mr. Solano concludes his representation of this conduct to Lord Dalhousie, as Governor of Bengal:—

"'Your petitioner submits that this conduct of Mr. Swinton, in relation to these several security bonds, was as outrageously arbitrary and unreasonable as it was illegal. Though the bonds were cancelled on appeal, to your petitioner the proceeding has produced consequences almost beyond the reach of legal redress. It occasioned alarm and terror throughout your petitioner's establishment; in consequence of it some of your petitioner's most valuable servants immediately abandoned your petitioner's service and their native villages, leaving their accounts unadjusted, and causing no small amount of confusion and disorder in the affairs of your petitioner; and your petitioner has not been able to supply their places. The collection of rents has consequently fallen into arrears, and cattle trespass on your petitioner's indigo cultivation has been committed to a ruinous extent, unchecked and unpunished.' "

Extracts from Mr. Solano's Statement.

" In May, 1853, the magistrate, Mr. Swinton, without a written complaint before him, which is generally considered necessary under Reg. 9, 1807, §§ 3, 6, to initiate his jurisdiction in such a case, recorded a charge in which three persons (Jowahir Ram, Tanto, a police burkundaz, and Keolapate and Rizun Sing) were complainants, of rescue of cattle by Bhowani Rai and others, and in the same record or proceeding Mr. Swinton ordered that depositions should be taken. Depositions were taken, and they exhibited the usual amount of exaggerations, such as cutting and wounding, and at the bottom of the whole lay another more serious charge, viz., that the cattle rescued had been stolen seven months before from the two prosecutors who claimed the cattle, and also stated that they had at the time reported and complained of the theft at the thannah of Arwell. This proved to be false, for the magistrate of Behar, in which Zillah Arwell is situated, reported to the magistrate of Shahabad that no charge of theft of cattle had been made by the complainants at the thannah mentioned : the case was thus reduced again simply to a complaint of assaulting the burkundaz and rescuing cattle from him.

" The case disclosed on the depositions was, that as the two prosecutors were passing by the village of Dunwar, they saw their cattle (six head) depasturing among others, which they learned from the herdsman belonged to Bhowani Rai, and they went and informed Jowahir, the police burkundaz, who, with three police chowkidars, accompanied them back, and they were taking away their own cattle, when the rescue complained of took place. Upwards of a hundred villagers, it was said, assisted in the rescue, and some of the witnesses alleged that Mr. Solano encouraged and directed the rescue from the verandah of his factory bungalow of Dunwar ; but they did not know Mr. Solano personally. They did not agree in their statements; and the three police chowkidars, who may be considered as the principal witnesses, said that no sahib was present. The depositions of seven persons, including the prosecutors, having been taken, and the case for the prosecution closed, Mr. Swinton made it over to his assistant Mr. Richardson.

" It should here be noted, that three or four days before this case came on, Mr. Swinton had received a copy of the charges which Mr. Solano had preferred to the Government of Bengal against him : and, as can be distinctly proved, displayed in his conduct animosity when Mr. Solano's name was mentioned. Mr. Solano heard of the case going on, and the information he received alarmed him and led to Mr. Norris's letter to Government of the 2nd June being written.

"Before noticing the next step in these proceedings, it will be proper to premise for information, that there is a practice in the Mofussil, warranted no doubt by the regulations, of employing darogahs (native superintendents of police) to inquire into facts alleged to have happened within their local districts, and report the result to the magistrate. The darogah of Dhungaeen was directed to investigate and report on the alleged transaction of rescue of cattle: he did report, and his report, which was based on the evidence of thirty witnesses of respectability, in no way involved Mr. Solano as a party concerned. This report did not satisfy the assistant magistrate, Mr. Richardson; he ordered another darogah, him of Ekwaree, to make a fresh investigation, which was made, and a report upon it, according to which Mr. Solano was *not* present or concerned at the said rescue of cattle; and this report was founded on the evidence of twenty-four witnesses, whose depositions were forwarded with it; but on the evening of the same day this worthy sent a letter varying, on no intelligible grounds, his report of the same morning; the letter was sent express and reached first, and on hearing it read and without waiting for the formal report, viz., on the 14th June, Mr. Richardson issued a summons against Mr. Solano, which gives a new phase to the case, and now we have the case of *Jowahir* v. *Solano.* The summons purported to be on the complaint of the police burkundaz Jowahir, and required Mr. Solano to appear on the 30th June, to answer a charge of having 'caused him' (Jowahir) 'to be forcibly resisted when in discharge of his duty, whereby he was wounded and beaten,' he, 'Solano, being personally present aiding and abetting.'

"The tenor of this summons naturally under the circumstances struck terror in Mr. Solano's mind and suspicion of Mr. Swinton; it was false to his knowledge, and his friends could plainly see in it the marks of concoction: it is hardly necessary to refer to them, but this may be mentioned, viz., that Jowahir, the complainant, had been but lately stationed by Mr. Swinton in a police chowkey between two of Mr. Solano's factories, and this trumped up case took place at a time when Mr. Swinton was most inimical to Mr. Solano, having been called upon by Government to answer the charges preferred by the latter against him.

"On the day appointed, viz., 30th June, Mr. Solano sent one of his assistants (the one in charge of the Dunwar factory, near which place the rescue was said to have happened) to represent him, and he subsequently made various endeavours to be excused from a personal appearance, on the *bona fide* ground of ill-health occasioning an inability at that time to travel; and on legal grounds, also, he appealed for this purpose to the Sessions Judge and Nizamut Adawlut, without success, however, on the ground that he was *personally* charged with the offence in question; and at last, on the 1st of October, he appeared before the magistrate. His answer to the charge was a total denial: it was true he has a factory at Dunwar, near where the rescue was alleged to have happened, but it is in charge of an assistant; his own sudder factory at Bullea, where he resides, is several miles off, and he was not at the Dunwar factory on the day of the rescue, and had not been there for a considerable time. He stated then, and it was repeatedly stated afterwards, and is unquestionably the fact, that neither can the factory bungalow be seen from the road, nor the road from it; that the distance between them is upwards of 1,400 feet, and the vats and all the factory buildings also are between; it was therefore impossible that Mr. Solano or any one else should have directed and halloed on the rescue, standing, as alleged, in the verandah of the bungalow. Mr. Solano also urged the extreme improbability that he would compromise himself personally in a matter so petty, and in which his factory interests were in no way concerned; and he also appealed in refutation of the charge to the two regular reports of the two darogahs.

"Having put in his answer to the charge, the trial was adjourned to the 17th of October, on which day Mr. Solano attended, and his witnesses, sixteen in number, were also present: of these sixteen, two were Europeans, and the rest respectable landholders, and two police chowkidars, and Mr. Solano was accompanied by Mr. Norris the pleader. The following points were established in evidence by these witnesses:—(1) that on the day when the rescue happened, Mr. Solano was all the day at Bullea, where some of the witnesses were transacting business with him; (2) that he was not at the Dunwar factory at all on that day; (3) that no sahib (gentleman) was present at the rescue; (4) that hedged round as the Dunwar bungalow is by walls, trees, &c., and the side nearest the road intercepted by vats and factory buildings, it was utterly impossible that any person in the verandah of the bungalow should be seen from the road; (5) that the top only of the bungalow is visible from the road; (6) that it was impossible for orders given at the bungalow to be heard on the road; (7) that while the nearest part of the road is 1,400 feet from the bungalow, the part where the rescue is alleged to have taken place was upwards of 2,500 feet from the bungalow; and lastly, witnesses present at the quarrel proved that no weapons were used—that it was a case of a common kind, in which there was more noise than violence of any sort.

"This evidence having been given for the defence, Mr. Norris requested on behalf of Mr. Solano that the witnesses for the prosecution should attend in order to be examined in Mr. Solano's presence; to this request a very determined refusal was given, but it was at last granted, on Mr. Norris's finding a decision of the Sudder Court in support of the application, and the case was adjourned for some days for the prosecutor's witnesses to attend: all, excepting two, did attend. It has already been stated that they did not agree in their original depositions; that the three chowkidars had all deposed that no sahib was present; the others, whose evidence went to implicate Mr. Solano, did not know him, though they mentioned his name; and now, on the occasion of their cross examination, when for the first time confronted with him, they one and all said he was not the person, and they described the person as tall and dark, which Mr. Solano is not; on the contrary, he is short and stout, of a florid and thoroughly European complexion, and of the kind of hue usually regarded as Saxon.

"Observe now, the situation. There was Mr. Solano, in the magistrate's presence; there were the prosecutor's witnesses, asserting that he was not the person, and describing the man whom they meant to charge as altogether a different kind of person, and there was the evidence for the defence in direct exculpation. One would expect, in any court of justice that is guided by evidence, the instant dismissal of the case; instead of which, when one of the witnesses for the prosecution was examined, the magistrate, with manners and features distorted by passion, addressed Mr. Norris,—'Well, Mr. Norris, what did you give for the perjury of those witnesses?' (be it recollected, they were the witnesses for the prosecution),—or words to that effect; and at the end of the hearing adjourned the case to the 25th October, when Mr. Richardson recorded a sentence of conviction, fining Mr. Solano 500 rupees,—simply stating as his reasons, that he disbelieved the evidence for the defence, and only credited the original depositions of the very witnesses for the prosecution who, in cross examination, in Mr. Solano's presence, declared he was not the person whom they charged!

"The above result did not astonish those who knew Mr. Solano's position and Mr. Swinton's influence, only because the monstrous injustice is of common occurrence; Mr. Solano himself, also, could not be surprised at any sentence against him, passed under the eyes and nose, as it were, of Mr. Swinton; his anticipation of this result had been shown by the application of Messrs. Theobald and Norris, that cases against him should be transferred to another jurisdiction, so long as Mr. Swinton remained at Arrah. Mr. Solano paid the fine, and appealed, not on the ground (which was open to him) that a fine of 500 rupees was, as is the fact, beyond Mr. Richardson's jurisdiction to impose, and therefore illegal, but on the merits of the case with reference to the evidence; and the judge has set aside the conviction: but for what, in the name of justice, if not on the ground of the impossibility of convicting legally on such evidence,* and, finally, to save Mr. Solano from this cruel persecution? No: two witnesses for the prosecution, as already stated, did not attend on the day appointed for cross-examination, and the case is remanded for them to attend, and is again on the same magistrate's file for investigation: and the magistrate, Mr. Richardson, was ordered to go to Dunwar and see if a person could be identified, and his voice heard from the bungalow, at the spot pointed out by the complainant as the place of the rescue.

"But the whole of this flagrant case of wrong has not yet been told. To complete it, we must revert to the time appointed for Mr. Solano's appearance. Mr. Solano's application to be allowed to appear to the charge by his vakeel being, as above stated, refused, in seven days after a warrant was issued to apprehend him, and was given to the nazir of the Fouzdary Court for execution; a proceeding, precipitate in point of time, the excuse of illness existing; equally unusual in point of form, the Nazir of the Fouzdary Court not being the officer to employ in such a trifling case, according to custom; and it was violent to order an arrest in so short a time without further communication in such a case. But the sequel is that to which attention is more especially invited.

"Mr. Solano was at Tarar, another of his factories five miles off, on the opposite side of the Soane river, but in Behar, when the nazir arrived at Bullea; the nazir was informed where he was, and the magistrate was informed by the nazir; there was neither flight nor

"* This is not intended as a reflection on the judge, but on the regulation under which he has given the decision referred to; so far as the judge has been free from the trammels of a bad system, he has exercised his appellate jurisdiction with fairness and a just discrimination."

concealment, and if the warrant was legal there still remained means of getting it executed; yet, on the fact of his absence from Bullea the magistrate sent a precept to the collector to attach all his factories and other properties in Shahabad. This precept was unprecedented; it was flagrantly illegal; the collector refused to execute it, alleging that it was illegal, and that its execution at a time when the manufacturing of the indigo was going on would ruin Mr. Solano, and throw great responbility on those executing it. Thus warned, a pause or halt might have been expected; instead of which, this young magistrate issued orders to the several darogahs, within whose district Mr. Solano had factories, to report to him the particulars of Mr. Solano's property, including the number of bigahs which he had under indigo cultivation, as if he intended still to enforce the attachment which the collector had refused to execute. The tendency of this proceeding, to injure Mr. Solano's mercantile credit and terrify him, is obvious.

"The nazir's conduct also must be stated. In reporting to the magistrate the absence of Mr. Solano from Bullea, and his consequent inability to execute the warrant, he did his duty. But he did more. Mr. Solano having factories on both sides of the Soane River, he summoned the farmers of lessees of the Government ferry, and gave orders to them to carry nothing across belonging to Mr. Solano's factories, and took mochulkas or security bonds from them, to secure their compliance with these orders. The orders and bonds did not remain a dead letter. Mr. Solano's indigo seed was accordingly refused at the ferry; the favourable time for sowing was lost to some of his factories; a stinted crop was the consequence, and from this resulted a pecuniary injury to Mr. Solano, estimated at nearly rupees 20,000=£2,000. Whether these orders were authorized by Mr. Swinton, or his successor, is unknown to Mr. Solano; but there is no doubt the nazir acted according to his view of their wishes.

"The reader may now be curious to know whether any persons have been made responsible for the illegalities just related. It may therefore be stated, that Mr. Solano represented the whole case to the deputy magistrate of Sasseram, an uncovenanted judicial officer; he summoned the farmers of the ferry; found them guilty, of course, as they were, and sentenced them to two months' imprisonment in the criminal gaol; he also sent a letter to the magistrate requesting an explanation of the nazir's conduct: the nazir explained—justify he could not; impeach his superiors in office he dared not;—he prudently confessed to having acted *proprio motu*, or on his own assumed authority; he remains to this day unpunished, and is doubtless looking forward to similar promotion or reward to that which has been reaped by the other prosecutors of Mr. Solano. Mr. Swinton's position has been advanced from that of magistrate to that of acting collector, in the same zillah, with increased power of injuring Mr. Solano, and increased salary. In like manner Mr. Richardson, his assistant and pupil, is officiating as a full magistrate with increased salary. And Mr. Swinton, following the example of Government, has promoted the prosecutor Jowahir to the Sudder station, where he may daily worship the presence, and, like a faithful omedwar, watch and learn the passions and interests of his superiors. It will be hard if the nazir alone goes unrewarded.

"It might now be left to the reader to say whether Mr. Solano, or any other person having anything to lose, may not justly feel the greatest alarm at the state of the authorities in this district. But it remains to be observed that the case is still pending. The hearing, appeal, annulment of the conviction, and remand of the case to the magistrate for further investigation,—all took place in the space of a few days; months have elapsed since, and still the case remains not decided. The subsequent and recent incidents, therefore, have to be mentioned.

"On receipt of the judge's order remanding the case to him, the magistrate proceeded to the spot to ascertain personally whether Mr. Solano and his witnesses had given a true account of the relative situation of the road or place of rescue, and the bungalow, and had justly represented that it was impossible for orders given in the verandah of the latter to be heard, or the person giving them seen, by persons at the former, as he and they stated. The magistrate sent the prosecutor to the spot before him, and met him there. It would have been only fair to have secured the attendance on the spot of Mr. Solano also, and he and Mr. Norris did of course wish to attend: but, in fact, they were prevented by means which probably were contrived by the amlah, but cannot here be explained or commented on. Suffice it to say that no palankeen bearers were procurable for love or money, though there were hundreds at the station at the time. Mr. Norris, however, by great efforts, reached on horseback so far as to meet the magistrate on his return journey, and in a brief conversation on the road the latter stated, that the burkundaz, prosecutor, had pointed out a spot considerably nearer to the bungalow than he had named before; but that he, the magistrate, was of opinion that no one could be heard, at the spot even now pointed out, giving orders from the bungalow, and that no one could be identified from such a distance. It is six months since this happened, and still the case is undecided.

"It is obvious, now, that the charge is deprived of every tittle of proof ever brought in support of it; its real character is now apparent, and justice requires not only that it be dismissed, but that the tables should be turned on the prosecutor and his co-conspirators. That there was a rescue of cattle, it is true, but the cattle belonged to Bhowani Rai, as was notorious to the villagers, and therefore they turned out in support of their fellow villager, and helped him to recover his property, as they had a right to do; to this, the real character of the transaction, Mr. Swinton and the assistant magistrate seem to have been blind, through their zeal to find or make a case against Mr. Solano. When all the strange circumstances of this case are summed up, from the appointment of the prosecutor burkundaz, little doubt can be entertained that the whole affair was a preconcerted one, got up and contrived by the police to gratify the animosity of Mr. Swinton towards Mr. Solano: and it may be added that it is a type of a numerous class, which in their gradual and eventful effect have uprooted justice, and corrupted and enslaved the people; but they remain comparatively unknown to the world, through the well grounded fears the sufferers have of the ruinous consequences of disclosure, especially against a civilian of Mr. Swinton's connections and influence. This is the real cause why many persons of capital and respectability feel so averse to settle in and develop the resources of the Mofussil, where the whim or malice of a man in power may cause his disgrace and ruin.—*April*, 1854.

"THE REMAINDER OF THE CASE IS SOON TOLD.

"We have seen above that the judge, in reversing the orders of Mr. Swinton's assistant, directed him to go to Dunwar and see whether a person at the bungalow could be heard and identified from the spot where the rescue is said to have taken place, and to summons the two remaining witnesses to be examined again. In the same Roobukaree the judge directed that, after the case was finally disposed of, Keolapate, one of the plaintiffs, should be transferred to the Sessions to take his trial for perjury, which crime was apparent in the proceedings. The order was given the 1st November, 1853, and it was not till the middle of September, 1854, that Mr. Richardson disposed of the case,—which, contrary to all law and custom, was kept pending for eleven months, for no other imaginable purpose than to prolong Mr. Solano's anxiety and vexation. The two witnesses were duly summoned, but never made their appearance, and as their former depositions were given in private, and they were never confronted with Mr. Solano, it is generally believed they were tools of the police burkundaz, who falsely personified the witnesses. At all events, the law requires, that, when the witnesses do not come forward, the case must be dismissed and the accused acquitted; this is also the universal practice; but as no law is observed in Mr. Solano's case, the magistrate, to the astonishment of the whole district, confirmed his former fine of 500 rupees, and refused to transfer to the Sessions the perjurer Keolapate, stating he did not consider him guilty! This order, which stands as a monument of how justice can be administered in the Mofussil, was again appealed to the Sessions Judge, who reversed it on the 29th October last, directed the fine to be returned to Mr. Solano, and declared in his record that there was no evidence whatever. Thus ended this extraordinary case, which, though so trivial in its nature, without a particle of evidence, and which every one knew to be perfectly false and trumped up, has been used for eighteen long months as an instrument of torture to satisfy private vexation. What redress can be obtained for the harassment and losses Mr. Solano has experienced? None; from the highest personage who had a share in this *conscientious and honourable transaction*, to the lowest police spy, all and every one is protected by the laws, or rather by the system—the system which presses down India, and which will keep it down till it is removed."

Whatever justification Mr. Swinton may have been able to offer for his proceedings, it is impossible to deny that a prejudice existed in his mind against Mr. Solano. It was matter of notoriety throughout the country; and all who have the slightest knowledge of India know that the result of such a feeling on the part of a vindictive official is ruin, more or less rapid, to the individual who has raised his ire. In Mr. Solano's case the result has been very nearly ruin, and perhaps will be death. The circumstances, the locality of the outrage upon him, are such as must convince every dispassionate reader that it could not have been attempted, had the assailant not been sure of no interference on the part of the police authorities. I have been favoured with the sight of a private letter from an assistant of Mr. Solano's, who describes the attack and its motives. I will give the substance of his statement. Mr. Solano was not attacked by oppressed ryots or tenants, but by a servant whom he had dismissed for oppressing them, the man having been employed in collecting his rents. This man, a bold and vindictive villain, assembled a band of about 300 men, chiefly his own tenants, commanded by himself, and about seven others on horseback, and attacked Mr. Solano, who was on a tour of inspection round his estate, in an outlying cottage, at midnight, and left him for dead. *This cottage was within sight of the police station, and the police made their appearance upon the spot half an hour after the ruffians had decamped*, leaving Mr. Solano in a pool of blood, his arm broken, covered with sword and spear wounds. How he escaped with life is marvellous. Let me ask if it is credible that the police should have no information of the assembly of such a band, which, according to Mr. Solano's assistant, took a whole day to gather? and also how it was that they took no steps to interfere till the outrage was completed, when the attack was within 300 yards of their station? It is impossible to doubt that it is directly traceable to the well known ill-feeling of the magistrate against Solano, whether that feeling was founded in reason or not. The question is one of vital importance; it directly affects the settlement of Europeans in India. Are we still to be told that Mr. Swinton's reply to Mr. Solano's charges is satisfactory, without having the opportunity of judging for ourselves?*

In 1849 nearly the whole non-official European popu-

* Three weeks before this attack, Solano wrote to his legal adviser in Calcutta, that if the magistrate were not removed from his district, he should be obliged to leave the country.

lation of Calcutta attended a Meeting in the Town Hall, to protest against the Black Acts; the main principle to which the Meeting objected being the one which is now sought to be introduced, namely, their subjection to the courts of the Company. At that Meeting a Mr. Cruise, a settler in the Mofussil, gave a description of the treatment he had received at the hands of a judge named Pringle, and a magistrate named Pearson. I give the substance of his statement abbreviated, though it will lose by condensation, for it is too lengthy for me to extract it in its entirety.

Mr. CRUISE.—"I hold in my hand a copy of a summons, addressed to me by one of those boy magistrates, of whom we have all heard so much, which in itself would be nothing singular, were it not that you will presently find a judge of twenty years' standing approving of its tenor and substance.

"'*Summons.*

"'TO RICHARD CRUISE, ESQ.

"'*Inhabitant of Purnea.*

"'WHEREAS I have been directed by the sessions judge of this district to take *your defence in the matter of a letter written by Mr. J. C. Johnson*, dated the 5th ultimo, to my address, *you being his legal adviser*, and *the said letter containing some improper remarks*, you are hereby required to appear before me *in person* (even the words, by mookteyar [attorney] are scratched out), on Monday, the 7th instant, at nine o'clock in the forenoon, *to answer to the said charge.* Herein fail not. Dated the 5th day of May, 1849.

(Signed) "'E. S. PEARSON,

"'*Magistrate.*'

"I considered this summons a curiosity, and determined to retain it for my future justification in refusing to obey it—acknowledged its receipt thus:—'Whereas the above summons is irregular, illegal, and in all respects extremely improper, I refuse to obey it.' The magistrate tried to get back the original summons, and refused the acknowledgment, which his burkundauze (police officer) finally threw in my compound (enclosure round the house), and ran away. I walked to the magistrate's house, and threw the acknowledgment into his verandah. As I returned, I was assaulted, by his order, by his peons (constables), sepoys, and others. In the scuffle which ensued, I wrested a musket and bayonet out of the hand of one of the sepoys, who had presented it to my breast, and made good my way home. I immediately applied for protection to the judge, but that gentleman replied, '*There is nothing whatever in the summons issued by the magistrate, a copy of which you submit for my inspection, to call for my interference.*' Accordingly I waited upon him, and in the presence of two other gentlemen gave him a letter, in which was this notice:—'That I was at all times ready to obey any and every legal order, but that I would not submit to illegal violence or outrage, or place myself in the power of the magistrate to insult or injure me (as he had already done in his court on a previous occasion); and that as the judge refused to protect me, I should avail myself of my right as a British subject to carry arms for my self-defence; and that I would not obey any warrant which, like this summons, was in its form and substance illegal.' After having given this notice, I carried arms for self-defence, and every one knew it. On the 10th I was obliged formally to withdraw an appeal pending in the Judges' Court, in which I was agent of the appellant, to protest against the judge's misconduct, and to give notice that I would make a representation on the subject to Government. On the 11th I again attended to advise and protect a poor man, who was about to prefer a complaint of maltreatment against both the magistrates. It was well known that this petition would be presented, but the man dare not present it without the aid and protection of some one whose presence would ensure respect. He applied to me, and I freely rendered my assistance. I went to court, attended by two other Christian gentlemen as witnesses of what might occur, and by four orderly peons,* who, as usual in the Mofussil, carry swords, which, on reaching the court-house, they put into my buggy. The man presented his petition. The judge asked what it was about. I advised him not to tell, but to request that it might be read. The judge ordered it to be given back to have an abstract made of it, *as he pretended, according to custom.* The man put out his hand to take it back, when I quietly put my hand on his arm, and told him to follow my advice in everything. 'Let Mr. Cruise be fined 25 rupees,' said the judge. 'For what, sir,' said I, 'have you fined me?' Whereupon, without answering my question, he coolly declared to his amlah the following falsehood:—

'Whereas, a certain man presented a petition, and it was ordered that it be given back to him to have an abstract made of it, according to custom; and it was given back. *Whereupon, Mr. Cruise, snatching the petition out of the hand of the man, threw it down in the face of the Presence*—'

* Every private gentleman in the Mofussil keeps a few of these in his service.

'I observed that I did not do that. But he persisted in dictating the lie,—which every one in court knew to be a lie. I then said, 'Let not the Presence write that which is false.' *Whereupon, dashing back his chair, rising up and striking the table with his fist,* he said, '*Let Mr. Cruise be fined* 50 *rupees, and if he does not pay, let him be sent to jail for twenty days.*" (Mr. Cruise then states the law upon the subject, and the illegality of these proceedings.) "I said quietly, I would not pay, and turned to leave the court. The judge roared out to his myrmidons to seize me; in an instant a dozen or more seized and dragged me back to his presence. *He instantly ordered me to be tied up, and as no ropes were at hand, ordered the punkah ropes to be cut, and with these I was bound.* An officious retainer asked him what was to be done with the two gentlemen who had accompanied me, when he ordered them to be seized too; and accordingly, they, and one of my peons, were all tied up in a bundle together. I was honoured with a separate rope to myself. I then said that in my pockets were two small pistols, and requested they might be taken care of. The judge does not deny this. But it was pretended that I went to court to shoot him with them. It now became necessary to justify this outrage. My buggy and palankin were searched, and the arms in them found. The judge caused all the doors to be shut, a great uproar to be made, sent off for a company of sepoys to quell the pretended affray, and despatched a letter to the magistrate to come forthwith. When he arrived, the judge and he seated themselves in the *iljas,* or tribunal of justice, and the official document, in which had been recorded that I threw the petition down in the face of the Presence was read aloud. I declared that this was false. The judge ordered me to be silent. I replied, I would not be silent; when he said, with vehement anger, '*If you will not be silent, I will order you to be gagged.*' To which I replied, '*You would order me to be crucified if you dared.*' '*Gag him,*' said he to his burkundauzes, gnashing his teeth; and immediately a cloth was thrust in my mouth, and tightened round my throat till I was nearly strangled. I was kept nearly two hours in this manner, my face twisted up to the ceiling, not permitted to open my lips, a Mahomedan burkundauze holding the ends of the cloth and giving it every now and then an additional wrench."

He then asserts that some native officers of the court were brought forward as witnesses against him, but "I will do them the justice to say that these swore nothing against me, but against the judge, how I had been fined, seized, tied up, &c. *They did not accuse me of any offence whatever*, but it was all the same, they were supposed to have sworn against me; *and I was directed to give bail to the amount of* 5,000 *rupees, that I would attend and answer any charge which might be preferred against me thereafter, and to find security in a similar amount that I would keep the peace towards all Her Majesty's subjects.* I put in a protest against the jurisdiction of these gentlemen, declaring myself a British subject, and claiming the protection of the Supreme Court. They would neither receive nor record it. I tendered bail on the spot. They refused it, and declaring it was now late (noon), drove home to breakfast, leaving us in custody of the sheriff. I soon procured other good and sufficient bail,—Company's paper,—and tendered it to the sheriff, but he could do nothing without leave of his master. About sunset I was marched down to the magistrate's house, where I waited outside the compound while my mookteyars (attorneys) waited on him for the execution of the necessary bonds. *The two gentlemen who had accompanied me to the court being, unfortunately, East Indians, and amenable to the jurisdiction of the court, were unceremoniously sent to jail.* As the sun was setting, the mookteyar brought the bonds to me, which I instantly endorsed, and the deeds and money were taken back to the magistrate, who *observed the sun had set; that it was after hours; that he would not now receive the bonds, the earlier execution of which had been prevented by his own impudent delay; and to jail I was sent. And there we remained that night.*

"On the following day we were released, but our bail bond requiring us to appear and answer any charge that might be preferred against us, we so appeared on the 14th. The first thing the magistrate did was to compel us to stand in the felons' dock, among the murderers and dacoits. I remonstrated, reminding him that *we were neither prisoners, nor as yet charged with anything.* 'You shall stand, Sir,' he said, 'where the Court orders you.' After a while, I and another gentleman were allowed to leave the dock; the other two, not being sufficiently respectable, were obliged to remain in it. The depositions of the 11th were read, and I was asked what I had to say to the charge? I asked what the charge was? The magistrate said he had not time to argue with me. I had heard the depositions read. I answered, Yes; it was stated that I had been maltreated and bound; but what was the charge against me? He said, if I would not plead, *he would take down that I had nothing to say to the charge.* 'Sir,' said I, 'you can record that falsehood if you choose; but you ought rather to record that I asked to know what the charge against me was, and the magistrate refused to tell me.' *He recorded that I had nothing to say to the charge, and declined to answer.* I read aloud a protest against his jurisdiction. He refused to receive or record it. He then turned to Mr. Babonau, another of the pretended defendants, and asked him what he had to say to the charge? I advised him to ask what it was, when the magistrate ordered me to be silent; and Mr. Babonau, thus ensnared, admitted there was a charge, by pleading not guilty to it. A bundle of depositions by some fifteen or twenty Mahomedan burkundauzes, *taken when, where, and by whom, none of us knew,* were then read, and the deposers sworn *with so little decency, that I pointed out to the magistrate a Hindoo swearing on the text of the Koran.* Not one of the respectable persons present in the Judges' Court on the 11th was produced, but burkundauzes and convicts—creatures entirely dependent on the judge—were brought forward to swear that Mr. Cruise had a large body of armed men at the Judges' Court on the 11th May, *ready to make an affray; for as there had been no breach of the peace, 'ready to make' was held to be synonymous with 'to make.'* When these depositions had been read, the magistrate read from a paper, *which he had prepared before he came into court,* that the case had now assumed a much more serious aspect, and that we must give heavier bail for our attendance, and heavier security to keep the peace. He accordingly extorted from me bail to the amount of 8,000 rupees, and security in 10,000 rupees; the alternative being, to go to jail. If I had not been able to give this security on the instant, to jail I must have gone; and the magistrate did all in his power to make it difficult. I gave it, and was released. We were summoned again on this bail two days afterwards, viz., on the 16th; and a charge was preferred, that on the day on which the magistrate had caused me to be assaulted, I had a large body of West Country peons at my house. So impudent and desperate a perjury was this, and so easy of disproof, that *it was not considered safe to retain these depositions along with the other proceedings, and they have been made away with*, so that I have been unable to obtain copies of them. *Copies of all these atrocious proceedings have been denied to me invariably on repeated applications*, preventing my taking the necessary steps for redress."

Mr. Cruise proceeded to state a similar altercation which ensued between him and the magistrate as to the bayonet and musket which he had wrested from the hands of the sepoy who attacked him on the 5th of May; that this resulted in his house being searched, and the imposition of a fine of 500 rupees; that the magistrate levied this fine by what he calls "the plunder of his property;" that he was again summoned on his bail; that he then set the magistrate at defiance, and challenged him to levy his bail; that the magistrate then finding that he could not deal with the case as a justice of the peace, transferred the case to "his fellow-conspirator," the judge, as a civil case; and that the latter functionary, "after having kept me in attendance on bail to the amount of 8,000 rupees for two months, termed the charge a case of resistance to process; held an *ex parte* proceeding *on the infamous proceedings of the magistrate; and, during my absence in Calcutta, fined me 500 rupees for resistance to a process which was never issued."*

Now here was a case in which the gravest charges were publicly brought forward in the largest meeting ever assembled in Calcutta. Mr. Cruise may have been in the wrong, his law may have been bad, his conduct unbecoming. But if so, why was not the matter inquired into, and a public justification of the proceedings published? I believe there was never any denial of Mr. Cruise's statement put forth, and I know it is generally believed to have been true in India to this day.* Yet he got no redress, and his persecutors, if such they were, remained in the service. Here, again, I say, a gross wrong was done. If the officials were innocent, why leave all men in the belief that they were guilty? If Mr. Cruise's statement was true, did not justice and policy demand the removal of such men from the bench? Does not such a system of burking charges, upon the rare occasions when men are bold enough to come forward and make them, lead irresistibly to the inference, that a hundred cases of oppression may occur, and must occur, of which nothing is ever heard—that every poor victim of an official's wrong-doing will submit in silence and fear, when he sees that men of wealth and station cannot gain redress?

These three cases are known, through the whole length and breadth of India, to every one who ever reads the papers. There are hundreds of similar and worse cases which are well known and talked of privately, but which the sufferers have never dared to publish, because they know that such a proceeding would only result in their own ruin and persecution, and in perfect impunity,

* The judge ever after went by the nickname of "Gagging Pringle."

perhaps in increased favour and preferment, to the official accused. I could mention many such from my own knowledge, which have been communicated to me under promise of not revealing my informant's name. But I have no wish to encumber my pages with many such cases. I must leave it to the reader, after having shown the shield which Government throws over its officers, to conclude that it is impossible but that such evils as I have mentioned must have a wide existence. I will, however, quote a few instances, upon the authority of Mr. Wilson, which were communicated by him to Mr. Dickinson, the Secretary of the India Reform Society, and have been kindly placed at my disposal. Wilson is in his grave, and therefore the publication can do him no harm :—

"If the civilians are convicted of the gravest faults, they are generally promoted and rewarded by the Government, as if to defy public opinion in India, and to show that proof of a civilian's malpractices is all that is required to assure him of the favour of Government. For example, the judge mentioned in my letter to Bright was convicted of the most disgraceful frauds; it was impossible that he should remain a judge: they gave him a better berth, with an increased income, and increased opportunities of fraud, though they reprimanded him; and he is now (1853) employed in the opium department.

"Another, named ——, imprisoned two English proprietors, and exposed them to all sorts of indignities. He was completely mad. That was proved. The Government released his victims, of course, without any indemnification of loss, or making them any amends, and gave —— leave of absence to England for two years. On his return, as mad as ever, he was again made magistrate, and again commenced persecuting an Englishman in the same fashion. The Government again released his victim, *and sent him to a district where there were no English, knowing that he might do what he liked among the natives, without exciting much public uproar.*" This was, I believe, the same judge who, as lately stated by the *Englishman*, tried, convicted, and *hung* a man within two hours! A not unnatural consequence of keeping maniacal pets in power; but, perhaps, as the last mentioned victim was "only a nigger," and there are a hundred millions of them, one more or less does not much matter.

Mr. Wilson continues:—"With regard to criminal justice, I will give an instance of a petty theft. I lost 10lbs. of Indigo, value, perhaps, £2. I was obliged to send for the police. They came to my house, and took away the prisoners and witnesses, all bound, to dance attendance for five weeks, until it pleased the magistrate to hear the case. During this time (and in similar instances it is always some weeks before the case is decided) the witnesses remained prisoners; and although such detention is their ruin, they were put in the stocks, to prevent their escape. During this interval, the prosecutor must pay each witness two rupees a month for diet, even though he may be a poor man, not gaining as much himself. In this case, the police cavalcade extended over half a mile of ground, marching in Indian file. I was obliged to pay all the functionaries of the police and of the magistrate's court. The affair cost me above £8 in expenses, and some months of time."

Mr. Wilson then recounts a case of bribery, in which "another planter, a Mr. M——, tried to bring the parties to justice." This account was afterwards corroborated by Mr. M—— in person. "Mr. M—— having learnt that a certain native had been obliged to pay a sum of £400 to the mother-in-law of a certain collector, who had married a native woman, under threat of losing an estate about which proceedings were then pending in the collector's court, went to a young magistrate, and called upon him to report the proceedings. He would do nothing. M—— then went to a sub-collector, and threatened to publish the facts in the newspapers, if a report were not made. Thereupon the sub-collector made an official report of this corruption. The collector summoned the accuser to prove the facts before him. The native's account-books were examined, and proved the payment of the sum, but not the person to whom it was paid. Upon that the accused were declared innocent by the collector, and the accuser dismissed. Soon afterwards, M—— learnt that persecution, instigated by the authorities, had driven the accuser out of the country. He immediately made a fresh complaint, and demanded a judicial inquiry. This time the collector was frightened; *he demanded and obtained his removal from that district, and employment elsewhere.*"

I will also quote the statement of a very common mode of persecution on the part of the magistrates, the guilt of which it is obviously almost impossible to bring home to them:—

"It is easy to involve a man in some accusation, and for the magistrate to summon him, not to the nearest court, but to some place fifty or sixty miles off," (as in the case of Thomas and Bhawanny Lallah.) "When the victim gets there, he finds no lodging; he waits his turn in the magistrate's court; but from day to day his case is not called on, so that he is obliged to follow the magistrate all round his district for many weeks, without having an audience. At last, if there is the least ground for legal proceedings, the magistrate can refuse his bail, and there he is detained and imprisoned for some time longer. All this is done with impunity to natives, and often to planters also."

I have myself heard a civil servant declare that he so punished a man of whose rascality he was convinced, but against whom no legal proof could be obtained.

I will conclude with one more quotation from Mr. Wilson :—

"A very common cause of the armed affrays between planters and zemindars arises in this way. A ryot, the tenant of a zemindar, offers himself, when short of money, to the planter as a cultivator of indigo, points out his lands, and receives advances for the purpose of cultivating indigo. Afterwards, he declares that the lands so indicated did not, or do not now, belong to him; that he raises some other crop; and the planter, finding himself robbed, enforces his rights by the strong hand, if he can. On such occasions we never think of appealing to the Courts of the Company, for we well know what a difference there is between 'justice' and the proceedings of these Courts. But in consequence of this want of law in the country, the planters suffer immense losses. In short, so far from the Company having aided the planters by its government, it has done nothing but increase the facility of their ruin; and they would have created a hundred times more commerce in India, had they not been hampered by the existing system. They now run enormous risks; and make, in twenty to thirty years, fortunes which they would make in five years with perfect ease, if there were any law or order in the country, such as are to be found in every other civilized country. From want of it, their loss of capital each year is at a rate which would not be credited in England. I myself have lost, during the past year, £2,500 in debts, which have been accumulating for three years, from the impossibility of obtaining redress in the Company's Courts. Every planter is pillaged in the same fashion every year, and they are obliged to calculate on these losses, as part of their working charges. I never dreamt for a moment of seeking my remedy in the law courts; that could only have increased my loss."

Mr. M—— confirmed this statement, and said that he had, in his own case, abandoned bonds and debts to the amount of a lac of rupees—£10,000. He added, that he had now depending, in the Moonsiff's Courts, suits of two years' standing, although these officers are obliged, by law, to decide their cases within six months.

You can easily conceive, after reading these statements, that a real *bonâ fide* case is hardly ever brought into an Indian law court. In fact, no man who has had any experience of them, would dream of stating the plainest and truest case in its bare simplicity and truth. He would not, indeed, meddle in the matter himself; but his law agent, or mookteyar, would cook it up to the requisite degree. I have the permission of Mr. Forlong, one of the few men who have had the boldness to come forward openly and state their grievances, to mention an instance or two of his experience. I extract the following notes, taken of his conversation immediately after the last interview I had with him:—

"While I was at Mulnath, the head factory of the

Bengal Indigo Company, within fifty miles of Calcutta, and at a time when I was general manager of the whole of the factories belonging to that Company, I had occasion to go and settle the rents of a certain village, and receive the rents due from the people round about. My servants went the day previous to pitch my tent. The tent, I found on my arrival, had been destroyed, the ropes cut, &c. The magistrate, to whom I at once went and stated the case, said, 'Now, do bring that case into Court just as you have stated it to me; don't employ any mookteyar, but let us have the plain statement, and your servants as witnesses.' After some weeks the case came on; another magistrate, or the deputy magistrate, had to decide upon it, and my fine truthful case was most unceremoniously kicked out of Court.

"I remember another instance at the same factory. I expected an attack on one side of the factory; a neighbouring zemindar, I was informed, intended to carry off a portion of my crop. I therefore set a number of men to watch it. Suddenly, one day, a false alarm was raised that the police were coming. The men rushed headlong over the river, and in the scurry one was drowned. Some time after a darogah was sent to inquire into the death of this man. It was the height of the manufacturing season; if my servants had been dragged off to the Court, the loss would have been immense. I therefore begged the darogah to make a true report. He demanded a *douceur*; and after some discussion I agreed to give the man 250 rupees, to make a true report of what had occurred. A week after, the magistrate sent another: I had to make him a similar bribe. Shortly after, two were sent, and demanded the same sum each; I paid it, and represented the case to Government. The magistrate was reprimanded, and shortly afterwards removed to another district."

But I need scarcely say, the Bengal Indigo Company were not indemnified. English people would perhaps think this payment a folly in the first instance. But if it had not been made, the indigo manufacture would have been stopped, the servants on whose superintendence it depended carried off prisoners, as in the case recited by Mr. Wilson, and the loss would have been thousands of pounds instead of a hundred; that Mr. Forlong was forced so to act, in order to protect his employers' interests, is owing to the abominable want of all law and order and efficient police in the country, and the blame attaches to the Government for neglecting their primary duty of providing means of proper protection, a duty, upon the fulfilment of which their right of taxation rests. In fact, as stated by Mr. Wilson, in his letter to Mr. Bright, an accidental death is a "calamity under which the whole village suffers;" to conceal it is bad, to reveal it, worse: the darogah marches down, and extorts money from everyone able to pay, under threat of accusation of murder. Finally, if the magistrate is suspicious of foul play, or anxious for a conviction, the darogah seizes on some poor and friendless individual, tortures him into a confession, suborns witnesses, gets him convicted, and everybody (but one insignificant unit) is perfectly satisfied.

I shall now quote one more witness in corroboration of my statements, Mr. Francis Horsley Robinson, now dead, but formerly a member of Council in the Agra Presidency. From many of the assertions in the able little pamphlet from which I quote, I dissent; but these only show that this liberal and amiable man was not quite free from the prejudice which a civilian's position infallibly produces. The whole pamphlet is well worth the perusal of all who take an interest in India.* It abounds in sentences which point out the abominable state of the law; the favouritism shown to civilians, and their great arrogance; the hatred of the natives to our Government; the evils resulting from that rampant proselytism now prevalent in India, through the influence of the fanatical "Saints," who have long been the dominant party in the Indian Government; the dictation of Government to their judicial officers; the despotic demeanour of these officials, and their subserviency; the means which their duplicate functions give them, at once of oppression and escape from its consequences; the extraordinary consanguinity of the Civil Service; the necessity of independence in judges; and the necessity of an easy mode of recovering damages against an officer for exceeding his authority or acting illegally. I shall extract a few things apposite to my argument:—

"A civil servant takes a dislike to two highly respectable native revenue officers; knowing that they would be protected by the Board of Revenue, he does not attack them in that department; but he institutes proceedings against them as magistrate, imprisoning them, and, under pretence of enforcing jail discipline, shaves their beards off—an intolerable insult, according to the notions of the people. The sentence of imprisonment is reversed by a higher court, but the sufferers receive no

* "What Good may Come out of the India Bill, or Notes of what has been, is, and may be, the Government of India." By F. H. Robinson. Hurst & Blackett, 13, Great Marlborough Street, 1853.

compensation, and the civil servant is suspended barely for six weeks."

"There is no mode of prosecuting a magistrate, whatever wrong he may commit. . . . . So strongly is the irresponsibility of the magistrates felt, that the highest court in the country, when I was in it, objected unanimously to the subjection of British subjects to the magistrates of the country, and they did so on the specific ground that the power of the magistrate was too absolute, and that there was no redress, by an action, for damages or otherwise, against the abuse of authority by a magistrate—no means of enforcing compensation for injury done."

[There are, undoubtedly, clauses in the proposed Penal Code for the punishment of public servants; but they are so worded, especially when taken in conjunction with the before-mentioned Impunity Act, that I do not hesitate to say it would be all but impossible to obtain a conviction under them. And if obtained, the result would be this: a man, ruined by an official's spite, would have the satisfaction of seeing him slightly punished, and probably restored to the service in a higher and better post immediately afterwards, but would never get the least indemnification of his own losses from Government.]

"In the next place, the Courts are inefficient. A judge can be removed by Government for any order they do not like. This power has not, of late years, been used;* but there it is, and unless a judge be prepared to risk his place, he dare not act in opposition to Government. *I have known a judge refuse to join me*

* This is not strictly correct, though I believe no absolute removal from the service has taken place.—T. H. D.

in issuing an order which he thought right, because it would draw down upon him a reprimand from Government. There are, besides, other ways of influencing a Court; THUS, I HAVE BEEN AWARE OF A GOVERNOR COMMUNICATING PRIVATELY WITH THE JUDGES OF THE HIGHEST COURT IN THE COUNTRY, AND GIVING THEM HIS VIEWS AND ARGUMENTS IN A CASE OF IMPORTANCE, IN WHICH HE WAS ANXIOUS TO SECURE A DECISION FOR GOVERNMENT, AND HE GOT THE DECISION. It is impossible to read men's hearts, and the decision must be taken to have been given on conviction; but the fact of the communication between the Governor and the Judges was known, and where such things happen, the distrust of independence of the Court must be great. I HAVE KNOWN AN INSTANCE OF A GOVERNOR-GENERAL CALLING FOR AN EXPLANATION OF ONE OF THE SAME COURT'S DECISIONS. I HAVE KNOWN A MAGISTRATE HOLD SECRET AUTHORITY FROM GOVERNMENT TO DISOBEY THE ORDER OF THIS COURT ON A PARTICULAR POINT. In the third place, the Courts are inefficient. I was myself appointed to the Chief Court, though I had been a revenue officer all my life, because it had got into such confusion, that it was thought necessary to appoint some one unconnected with the squabbles existing in it, to make the machine work at all. I have seen many men sitting in that Court as incompetent as myself."

I most specially beg your attention to this passage:—

"This state of the country, this uncertainty of rights, and the great power lodged in the hands of the collectors and magistrates—although Englishmen are personally exempt from their jurisdiction—form powerful preventives to Europeans undertaking extensive works and speculations in India. Hence, one sees them becoming scarcer as they get farther from the Supreme Court, although it would be natural for them to cluster more thickly in the more congenial climate of the north of India.

"Everywhere, out of Calcutta, the position of the European settler is this,—either he possesses the favour of the authorities, in which case he has unfair advantages; or he is under their displeasure, in which case he is at an unfair disadvantage. But neither position suits an independent, prudent man. I HAVE KNOWN A HIGHLY RESPECTABLE ENGLISH MERCHANT TOLD IN OPEN COURT BY A MAGISTRATE THAT 'THE GOVERNMENT HAD THEIR EYE ON HIM, AND THAT HE WAS A MARKED MAN,' BECAUSE HE HAD TAKEN A PART IN A CASE WHICH THE MAGISTRATE DID NOT LIKE."

Mr. Robinson proceeds to state, that if he were to settle in India, he would not trust his property out of the Supreme Court's jurisdiction. He complains, I am bound to say, of its expensive procedure; but I do not think he can be well informed on this point. But, supposing his averment true, there is the fact that he would prefer its jurisdiction to any other now constituted in India.

Mr. Robinson mentions one more case, which I think worth quoting, to show the English public how subscriptions are got up in India. It is needless to state that subscriptions to testimonials to high officials are not seldom raised in the same way. I condense Mr. Robinson's statement:—

"A man of respectability complained to the Board of Revenue that he had been induced, through hope of gaining the collector's favour, to subscribe to a dispensary; was disappointed in this hope, and withheld his subscription, and was consequently subjected to a series of petty persecutions, *and especially had been summoned to a distance, to be asked why he had not paid his subscription.** We called on the collector to answer. He did not deny the facts. We reported the matter to Government. *We were told in answer that the collector was right, and the man eventually paid his subscription.*" He then says that he has asked natives, "'Why do you subscribe' (to purposes of charity or utility) 'against your will?' And I have been silenced by the reply, 'What would become of me if I were to displease the magistrate and collector?'

"Some years further back,—I think about 1835 or 1836,—a magistrate, with a view to put a stop to burglaries and thefts, ordered that in every village a party of the inhabitants should perambulate the village and its purlieus all night. He had no more authority to do this than to order the Governor-General to keep watch and ward. He reported to Government at the end of the year what he had done, and actually, instead of a reprimand and removal from his situation, he was highly commended, and all other magistrates were urged to follow his example. And they did so, almost without an exception, so that the whole country was nocturnally worried and disturbed in this way for a year or two, till the madness of the project became too evident, and the whole thing died away."

I shall now quote a few passages from "A Letter to the Court of Directors of the East India Company, regarding Judicial and Revenue Administration in Bengal, by a Member of the Bengal Civil Service, lately

* Another confirmation of Wilson's statement, and of the frequency of such cases as that of Bhawanny Lallah.

retired" (London: Parker, Furnivall, and Parker, Military Library, Whitehall, 1853). I condense again:—

"In 1800, the Government of Bengal dispossessed the proprietor, Gokul Chunder Gosaul, of certain villages, 906 in number, yielding an annual rent of about 8,200*l.*, situated in Chittagong. These villages were all subject to the terms of the Marquis Cornwallis's solemn pledge in the perpetual settlement. The Government appropriated these villages. This act was committed without the intervention of any legal process, done under 'the good old rule, the simple plan,' by the Government, the wielders of a powerful arm, and the possessors of a full purse.

"In the year 1804, however, the heiresses and successors of Gokul Chunder Gosaul brought an action against the Government for the recovery of these lands; and in August, 1815, it was finally decided by the Sudder Court, that the suitors should hold of the lands which formed the cause of action, such portion as might have been ascertained to have been, in the year 1764, the undoubted property of their family. The Court visited the illegal act of the Government by saddling them with the entire costs of the action; for the Court held that the course pursued was illegal, as their own Regulations expressly provided that all questions connected with the financial rights of the Government should be decided by the established courts of judicature.

"By the terms of the decision, it appears, moreover, that the Government, even if so disposed, could not have instituted any action for the lands they seized on, because the date of the cause of action was previous to 1764. Notwithstanding this clear definition of the law by the highest Company's Court of Bengal, it will be distinctly shown, in the following pages, that the Government in Bengal have persevered in dispossessing hundreds of individuals of land under pretexts similar to and equally illegal as in the case of Gokul Chunder Gosaul, and in an equally summary manner, without the intervention of any suit in any court, and of course without any decree in justification of their exercise of power. Also, that they have proceeded thus irregularly to increase their own revenue in Chittagong by separately assessing those lands, and settling for the payment of revenue with individuals other than those from whom they, the Government, took them.

"This course was persevered in, notwithstanding that it was stated, in language so strong as to all but overstep the boundaries of respect, by their own subordinate officer, that they, by their proceedings, had gone beyond the law. The Government acted thus in prosecution of claims founded on alleged rights originating before 1765. Four commissioners of revenue in Chittagong successively endeavoured to enforce the claims of Government to lands in that district, 'by the exertion of executive power,' notwithstanding 'the Government had lost its right to sue.'"

And the author proceeds to prove his assertions irrefutably. But the Judge at Chittagong was disposed to act in accordance with the law, and consequently to thwart the intentions of Government: whereupon the Secretary to Government, who was the prime mover and director of the bewildered Governor in the matter, addressed to that official a letter.

The "Retired Member" thus proceeds :—"I will here quote a letter. No. 13, dated the 5th of January, 1837, written by the Secretary to the Bengal Government to the Judge of Chittagong. I do so to show the support that the officer, who, in this paper is described as having been removed, must have received from the highest authority years previous to his removal; and also to show what are the ideas of the independence of our Judges held by the Bengal Government, when such a letter is addressed to a Judge, whose duty it was to hear and decide all cases impugning the acts of the Government Collector, brought by parties aggrieved by him. Here is the letter:—'Sir,—The Right Honorable the Governor of Bengal, having had before him a copy of a letter addressed, under date the 12th ultimo, by the Collector of Chittagong to the Commissioner of the division, a transcript of which, as appears from the last paragraph, has been forwarded to you by Mr. Harvey, the Collector, I am directed, with reference to the great importance of the subject, as regards both the due maintenance of the authority of the Government, and preservation of the peace of an extensive district, to address you direct, for the purpose of impressing on you the mischievous consequences which must be expected to ensue, if those classes of the agricultural population of Chittagong, who appear to be opposed to the survey now in progress, and to be in a state of considerable excitement in consequence of that measure, should be deluded by designing persons into a belief that you, the highest judicial functionary, are disposed to support them in opposition to the views of Government, and to become a partisan in their cause.

"'With reference to your established character as a public officer, the Governor feels confident that you have not, in any manner, willingly afforded grounds for erroneous impressions of the nature above alluded to;

and this communication is not made with the slightest intention of imputing blame to you, but merely in order to remove at once, at a time when a considerable degree of excitement appears to prevail, and on a point of much importance, all room of misunderstanding, and to place you fully in possession of the views and determination of the Government. You must, doubtless, be well aware with what avidity, in moments of excitement, the support of the local authorities, whose views are assumed to be opposed to those of the Government, is caught at by the disaffected; and that, therefore, special caution is necessary to prevent misconception, which must embarrass the public service, and not improbably lead those who labour under it to commit overt acts of resistance to constituted authorities, seriously affecting the peace of the community, and compromising themselves. As these overt acts have been committed, you will no doubt feel it to be your duty to take every suitable and proper measure to correct any false impression in regard to your sentiments that may have gone abroad. . . . . . Operations having been already carried on, with the best result, to a considerable extent, his Lordship is of course determined to push the measure to completion. In itself, it must be productive of good to all honest persons; and those who may think themselves aggrieved by any ulterior proceedings, founded on the data which it furnishes, will have, of course, full opportunity to appeal either to the Court (I may remark that this Court was presided over by the Judge to whom this letter was addressed) to which the Revenue authorities in such cases are amenable, or to lay their complaints before the Government, where they will have due attention. It will be your duty, as a high public officer of the Government, thus made acquainted with its views and objects, to forward them by the zealous exercise of your influence, and the employment, on all fitting occasions, of the authority which is vested in you.'

"The last paragraph need not be quoted, as it refers to the conduct of some native judicial functionaries. It may again be observed, that the Judge, addressed in the dictatorial tone of the Government Secretary, was the functionary presiding in the Court to which the Revenue authorities are liable; and it may be inquired whether the tenor of the letter cited was such as to encourage the self-possession of the presiding functionary, and tend to his arriving at a prompt and judicious decision in any case between the Revenue authorities and the aggrieved agriculturists? Would the Secretary to Government in any of our Colonies, or the Home Secretary of State, be tolerated in addressing any of the Judges in such a tone? Is it only in remote India that such a tone is to be adopted?"

I submit that I have proved, as completely as can be expected within such limits, that the judicial officers of the Civil Service deserve the epithets I have applied to them as a class, and are unfit for the proper discharge of judicial duties. If they were in all other respects fit for their dnties, their want of dependence alone would render them objectionable. The power which the Executive Government possesses over them has never been suffered to lie dormant: it has occasionally been exercised, in cases where the Government was not concerned as a party, to promote the ends of justice, and to compel them to act legally and rightly; but the delinquent official, if a covenanted civilian, has never been visited with condign punishment. The last mail has brought news of a case in which the effect of a young magistrate's unjust proceedings was remedied by the interference of the Executive Government. This man's oppression nearly stopped the working of a large indigo factory within twenty miles of Calcutta. He crowned his misdeeds by striking one of his head native officers in open court: his punishment was the usual one,—leave of absence until the affair has blown over, and then, no doubt, he will get a better place. The honourable member for Guildford will be able to give you every information about this case.

But if this controlling power of Government is occasionally exercised in the interest of right and justice, how much oftener has it been exercised in its own interest, with the sole motive of its own gain. The resumption robberies have not been confined to Chittagong. In spite of the Privy Council's decision in the Rajah of Burdwan's case, numbers of estates in Bengal have been resumed on precisely the same grounds as were there held to be invalid; and it is hardly too much to say, that in the item "gain by resumptions," mentioned in one of the Blue Books of 1852, you might with propriety erase the word "resumptions," and substitute "larcenies."

I may also remind you that your own relative, Mr. Courtenay Smith, was turned out of office for a decision, which, if the facts have been correctly stated to me, was undoubtedly right in law, and which, whether right in law or not, was one which, in the exercise of his discretion, he had a perfect right to give, and which he would have given in any other country without the least risk of his office. You will also remember, that Sir J. P. Grant, a Crown Judge, was suspended and removed by the Local Government, until public opinion forced his restoration to a higher and better seat upon the bench. Mr. Lewin, too, one of the witnesses examined before the Charter Committee, was turned out of office for doing his duty as a judge; and I beg you to refer to his evidence, and read the account given by him of the improper conduct and ignorance of his fellow civilians, and the difficulty with which he stopped a series of judicial murders of innocent men: how, in one case, it was proved that a Session Judge, who had recommended a man to be hung, had not even seen the document on which he made that recommendation; and how the Government, upon a representation of the matter, treated it lightly, and simply reprimanded the man; and how, in another case, two judges, who had for years been passed over for incompetence, were with great difficulty prevented by Mr. Lewin himself from hanging four innocent men on the evidence of the real murderers.

Indeed, what can be expected from uneducated men, who are sure of incurring the displeasure of Government if they disobey its hints and decide against its interests, and on the other hand are certain of promotion and support from the Government, whatever may be the impropriety of their conduct, if only they will unscrupulously serve it, when its own interests are concerned? The support of Government is extended in the same fashion to native and uncovenanted officers on whose subservience they can depend. It took eighteen months of ceaseless remonstrance on the part of the residents in Serajgunge to persuade Mr. Halliday to remove a native deputy magistrate, whose incompetence was asserted by the whole district, and the assertion confirmed by the reports of every official in it. Mr. Halliday has never paid the slightest attention to the public remonstrances which have been made against the inefficiency of the present junior magistrate of Calcutta, a native; though such remonstrances have been continually made for the last two years; and though scarcely a session passes without strong observations by the Judges of the Supreme Court upon the state of the depositions drawn by him. The case is one so flagrant that I shall again quote from the *Englishman* a specimen of the proceedings:—

"On the 19th of May, the junior magistrate committed Kadernath Bonnerjea on a charge of forgery, and held him to bail: on the 28th of May, he committed him again on a charge of embezzling the monies which he received as the proceeds of his successful forgeries, refusing in this instance to admit the prisoner to bail, who, in consequence, appealed to the Supreme Court for his discharge from custody. Mr. Justice Colvile, in granting his prayer, observed, that 'Kadernath Bonnerjea was committed for two inconsistent offences. If the bills, by virtue of which the prisoner obtained the money, were forged, then he could not have received it on account of his master, and consequently the offence of embezzlement could not have been committed.' And it does appear to us that the learning of a judge is not indispensable for the discernment of so obvious a fact.

"Again, he committed a man named Hurrynarain Day for embezzlement: according to Sir James Colvile's charge to the grand jury, this prisoner had been guilty of no criminal offence whatever, 'as far as from the very confused manner in which the depositions had been taken he was enabled to judge.' And now we come to a case which the Judge described as the most preposterous of the kind he had ever met with. It was a case of rape. One Jaranimo goes to his friend's house, and takes him and a girl, who lives under his guardianship, out for a drive in a buggy; and they finally go to his (Jaranimo's) house. When there, Jaranimo persuades the girl to go into his bedroom, where they remain some time. The friend becomes impatient, and calls to the ravisher that he wants to go home. Jaranimo responds that he had better go, 'as the *missee baba* (little miss) will sleep there that night.' He does go, and the young lady remains a *whole fortnight*, after which she brings a charge of rape against her admirer, whom the native magistrate actually committed to the sessions! The case, however, was so absurd, that, as we are informed, the learned Judge ordered the clerk of the crown not to prepare an indictment."

This article appeared in 1855, and one of the last mails brings papers which contain fresh instances of this officer's ignorance, and animadversions upon it by another judge of the Supreme Court; in fact, the misconduct and the complaints have been continuous ever since the magistrate was promoted from the Mofussil to Calcutta, and his actions came under the eye of the public. To what conclusion can officers, so upheld, come, but that their conduct is of no moment, provided they can secure the favour of the Executive Government?

It was also proved, as stated in the same paper, against the Chief Magistrate of Calcutta, a civilian, about the same time, that he was in the habit of hearing and deciding charges without putting the accusers upon their oath, or proceeding with the proper formalities; that he was ignorant of his own powers, and, in one case, of the capacity in which he was acting; that he actually dismissed a charge against one man, not because he was convinced of his innocence, but for fear the individual should deem he was an object of persecution by the police; and that the magistrate drew upon himself a severe rebuke from the Chief Justice for the way in which he permitted the police books to be kept. It is true, that the benevolent disposition of this most kindhearted Judge led him in his written judgment to soften down his expressions; but those who were in Court at the time (and I was one), and heard the oral judgment, did not soon forget the dignified and calm severity of its language.

Such are the Indian officials; and, be it remembered, that I have, with one exception, confined myself to proof of the incompetence of the English officials,—gentlemen of the middle classes of our own country; I leave you to guess how much worse the lower native classes of deputy magistrates, &c., are as a body. Yet many of these exercise the enormous powers of the Indian magistrate; and it is to such men that European settlers are to be subjected in matters affecting life and liberty. That immigration into India has not been stopped before, from the partial subjection already existing to these courts, is matter of great wonderment; that they have operated as a grievous check upon commerce and enterprise, and given rise to fraud and violence, there cannot be a shadow of doubt; but that, in spite of all these evil inducements, there are to be found many admirable civilians, men who strive earnestly to do their best, manfully contending against a system which cramps their energies, nullifies their efforts, and holds out no reward for their exertions; that there are still to be found planters, who, despite all the temptation to crime, would rather suffer ruin, and lose the reward of their long toil, than resort to illegal violence, or uphold their legal rights by chicane and fraud, is proof of nothing but the high morality and dauntless courage of our race. It shows only that Englishmen have not yet degenerated from the lofty spirit of their fathers; that their energy will triumph over obstacles in the fields of peaceful enterprise with the same stubborn resolution and unfailing heart, which they have so often proved in the ranks of war; that the country-women of Lucy Hutchinson are still upon occasion the mothers of men who may challenge comparison with him whom she so truly loved, and of whom she has left us a memorial so noble.

But if laws are to be made, not to order what men may do, but to prohibit things they may not do,—which I have always understood to be the right principle of legislation,—conceive the effect of trusting the average men of the Indian Civil Service with such powers as they now have, and will have generally extended by such chapters as those in the proposed code on Abetment; on Offences relating to the Press; on Defamation; on Offences against Public Servants; on Illegal Entrance; on Mischief, the first clause of which is—"Mischief: *having taken precaution not to be detected.* Bailable. Punishment, imprisonment of either description for six months, or fine, or both." But if I were once to begin on the *minutiæ* of the code, I should write a book, and not a pamphlet.*

Then, such being the officers and the courts, what is to be the jury by which men are to be tried? According to the last accounts, it is to be a jury of five. I presume this number is fixed from the common and erroneous notion that it is one for which the natives

* See Appendix.

have an especial affection; that the Punchayet is an old Hindoo institution, an error which was fully exposed by Sir John Malcolm, and especially by Major Munro, Resident at Travancore, in a report, dated 7th March, 1818.

How are the jury to be appointed? In such manner as the Governor-General in Council may direct, with the consent of the High Court. I suspect that will result in an appointment by the judge or magistrate who tries the cause, with, perhaps, a very limited power of challenge; for in the Mofussil there can only be a limited number of jurymen fit to try a cause of any sort. It is admitted on all sides that Indian juries will be severe, and under the influence of the presiding judge. Unanimity, or a majority of two-thirds, with the concurrence of the judge, is necessary for conviction; but if any number short of the whole are for conviction, the decision will rest with the judge. This is meant, I suppose, as a humane provision; but observe the door which it opens to the exercise of the judge's will. From the acknowledged subserviency and severity of Indian juries, it is probable he will always be able to secure a conviction if he wants it; but if he is anxious, from any reason, to get an acquittal, he has only to bias one man, and he gains his object. Suppose that a man in Mr. Solano's position prosecuted another before such a judge as Mr. Swinton; what would be his chance of getting a conviction?

The provisions as to appeal are also bad. The High Court will be swamped with them. It appears to me that every conviction by a magistrate will be appealed against. It is most important that the right of appeal from such functionaries should be retained, but there ought to be a provision restricting it to cases where reasonable grounds can be shown for the proceeding.

It seems to me, on re-consideration, that what I have said at page 14, about Mr. Macleod's assertion as to the possibility of the Chief Justice being over-ruled by a native, may be liable to misconstruction. The case, indeed, as put by Mr. Macleod, is sufficiently absurd, and there is less danger that a native judge would overrule the decision of the Chief Justice, than that he might be overruled by a civilian.

But there is a defect, or rather an omission, and a very important one, in the provisions of the code, of which this observation reminds me. There is nothing to show what majority of the High Court is to be competent, in cases of difference of opinion, to give a final decision; and, consequently, it is easy to conceive a case in which one uneducated judge of the High Court might overrule the whole three judges of the Crown.

For instance, suppose that three of the judges of the High Court sat as a Court of first instance, consisting of two Crown judges and one civilian. The civilian differs in opinion from his colleagues, and the case is appealed to the High Court, which I will suppose to consist of the Chief Justice and two more civilians. The Chief Justice is for upholding the decision of his learned brethren below, the civilians for supporting their unlearned brother; the verdict, therefore, of the third civilian in such a case will overrule the three Crown judges. If, again, one civilian only should dissent, what is to be the result, for it is not stated whether unanimity is necessary in the High Court or not? If unanimity be considered necessary in the Appellate Court, as I conceive it ought and must be, the dissension of one ignorant man will nullify, in the case put, the decision of four men. And it is obvious that this may happen when the point for decision is a case of pure English law, of which the best civilians must be, in a great measure, ignorant; as, for instance, an intricate question of commercial contract or wagers, such as the well known Opium cases; and thus, by the obstinacy of one uneducated man, a wrong decision, affecting millions of money, may be pronounced, notwithstanding the numerical and intellectual superiority of his brethren. If, again, a majority, in a court of eight judges, is to determine, it is obvious that they may be equally divided, supposing the whole of them sit, and in that case no decision can be come to; or if the number be raised to nine, or consist of a lower uneven number, you may again have one unlearned man overruling all the learned ones, or else the anomaly will arise that the decisions of the Court of Appeal will not be final.

Such are some of the difficulties attendant on an attempt to amalgamate ignorance and learning. I think, however, that the settlement of all such minor objections may be left safely to the local Legislative Council, and to such men as Mr. Peacock and the Judges of the Supreme Court. I wish I thought the leading principles could also be entrusted with safety to their discrimination; but I do not think so, and I will state why I entertain that opinion.

The Judges of the Supreme Court, during the time that I held office in it, were three as learned lawyers and upright gentlemen as ever sat upon a Colonial Bench; and I shall ever speak of them, not only with the respect due to their high station, and with professional reverence for their learning, but with personal gratitude for the kindness invariably shown to me during the years that I had the honour to be their servant. I do not hesitate to say that, all things considered, they were fully the equals in learning of their brethren in England. But I am perfectly certain that they have no conception of the state of the country without their jurisdiction. Their high station prevents their mingling, to any degree, with non-official classes; and even if they could do so, those classes would not speak without reserve before such high officials. The very conscientious diligence with which they discharge their laborious duties prevents their acquirement of any personal knowledge of the country. Their knowledge of it is drawn almost solely from their conversation with high officials of the Civil Service. Moreover, two of the judges now are, and have been for many years, ex-Advocate-Generals of the East India Company. I cannot believe that men who have once canvassed the Court of Directors for their appointments, who feel that they owe their fortune and station to that body, and who mingle chiefly with men similarly circumstanced, can be entirely free from a bias in favour of the Government. I know that such a bias could never affect their decisions as a Court of Justice, but I am convinced that, however unconscious they may be of it themselves, it must and will affect their political views. Many of the most illustrious judges of England have given instances of a political bias, and so have the predecessors of the present judges of India. I cannot forget that two judges and Mr. Peacock were in Council when the Affray Bill was discussed—an enactment of which the atrocity was only equalled by the grammatical blunders and legal ignorance with which it was drawn—that they all appeared to approve of the principle of that measure—and that Sir James Colvile made a sort of soothing speech in Council upon it, in which he showed that he entirely misapprehended the grounds upon which the public founded their objections to it. It is true that Mr. Justice Buller is now in Council, who was never an Advocate-General of the East India Company; and a long personal intercourse with him has given me so deep a respect for his wisdom and liberality, that upon him I should most confidently rely, had I any belief in his possession of a tithe of the knowledge of Mofussil matters which I myself possess. But I know the contrary to be the fact, and that he is not in this respect superior to his colleagues. I fear, therefore, that they will not offer a sufficiently stern opposition to some of the politically objectionable parts of the code, which the other Members of Council will, I am sure, approve, and strive to enact.

The real rulers of India, as far as concerns internal administration, at least, are the Government Secretaries. The Governor-General, when first appointed, must rely upon them, from his ignorance of the country; the reliance upon, and reference to, them generally become habitual; and just as the Governor-General acquires sufficient knowledge to act independently of them, his term of office expires; and during its continuance his attention is generally directed solely to what are called, by a singular perversion of terms, "Imperial matters." Lord Dalhousie, I am sure, had never inquired much into the state of law or of police; his attention was so much occupied with making war, and putting kingdoms into his pocket—operations which did not bring him within the power of these charming establishments—that he forgot others were subject to them. I am confident that if he had known their state and effect, he would have found a remedy for the misery they produce. But as to the internal state of the country, the Governor-General is always kept as much as possible in the dark. We have Lord Ellenborough's own statement that he knew nothing of the existence of torture; and yet almost every other man in India was as conscious of the fact as of his own existence. The last Governor-General who devoted his time to the examination of the judicial evils was the great and good Lord William Bentinck—the man to whom is due the fact that there is now a single Englishman to be found in India. It is high time we had another Governor-General of his temper and calibre. Most of his important measures were carried in the teeth of the Court of Directors: he thwarted them whenever opposition would tend to the benefit of India, or the interests of the Crown; and they took very good care not to give *him* a pension. His opinion of the police and courts was such, that he deliberately "abandoned one of the legitimate functions of Government—inquiry into thefts and burglaries. He had heard and was convinced, that the people of Bengal suffered more from the police officers than from thefts and burglaries, and he put a stop to one of the fruitful sources of legalized oppression by enacting Regulation VI. of 1832."

I beg you, Sir, to remember also that Lord Campbell, in 1853, expressed his opinion of the Courts of the Company in language which he would not have employed had he not been sure of its truth. It was upon the occasion of Lord Ellenborough's presenting a petition from Madras:—

"The noble Duke who had spoken in the course of the debate (the Duke of Argyll) had, he thought, been somewhat prudish in his criticism on the phrases which had been used by the natives of India in describing their grievances; it was not reasonable to expect them to be very mealy-mouthed: and, for himself, as far as regarded the administration of justice in the interior courts, he thought no language could be too extravagant in describing its enormities."

It is easy for the Postmaster-General, sitting serene on the cozy benches of the House of Lords, to cast a classically critical eye on the productions of half-ruined men. But if he were in a situation similar to that of a man like Solano—if the revenues of the house of Argyll depended on the cultivation of clover and corn; if those domains were surrounded by large breeders of horses and cattle, and each morning saw numbers of these quadrupeds in the Argyll crops; if the neighbouring justice of the peace would not listen to his Grace's complaints, or gagged and fined him for making them, instead of impounding the voracious animals: then, when he saw poverty staring him in the face, and the heritage of the future little Macallum More vanishing partly into equine and bovine bellies, partly into the pockets of the police and of the clerk to the justice of the peace; then, I must say, I think his Grace of Argyll would be seen rushing about, *passis capillis*, invoking the gods, and denouncing his enemies in the strongest terms with which his vocabulary could furnish him. I even deem it possible that he might occasionally be heard to swear.

Or, again, if he attempted to right himself by the strong hand—if he assembled his clan, buckled on his claymore, bid his pipers strike up "The Campbells are coming," and made a swoop down upon the intruding cattle—then, if he had to deal with an Indian magistrate, administering the late Affray Bill, he might find himself summarily fined five million pounds, and sentenced to imprisonment for 200 years. Nay, he would very likely find himself in the same predicament, though he had never stirred out of his house, if any of his neighbours thought it worth while to bribe the police, and to suborn testimony against him. And, under the bill quoted, he would have no power of appeal.

This specimen of Indian legislation was introduced into Council while Mr. Peacock and two judges were members of it.

The cry of the Indian public for redress, accompanied by complaints against the officers, the police, and the courts, and proof of their incompetence and abuse of power, has always been answered by nothing but a proposal to increase the powers of these courts and police: and it has then taken a long and expensive agitation to convince the Government that this curious *sequitur* was objectionable.

To these courts, in their desire for uniformity, the Commissioners now propose to subject Europeans. I have been asked, with an air which showed my interrogator's belief that his question was unanswerable, "If a native were to say to you, 'What right have you to be exempt from the jurisdiction of courts to which I am subject—what answer could you make?" I answer, "Considered politically, my sable friend, our right to be well governed does not rest on the same basis: you are one of a conquered race, who have therefore no original and strictly political right to be well governed: you are at the mercy of your conquerors. But I am one of a nation who have their rights guaranteed by such things as Magna Charta, the Bill of Rights, the Act of Settlement, and a few other conditions, upon whose due and faithful observance by the Crown my allegiance to it depends. I cannot, therefore, admit that you are politically my equal. But your right to be well governed, I nevertheless admit: it rests upon a higher basis—upon moral and religious grounds, upon which a Christian nation is more especially bound to build its government—upon principles which should lead it to follow the golden rule of doing unto others as it would be done by, and to seek the peace and well-being of all its subjects. But you admit that the courts to which you are subject only add to your misery and disturbance; how will my subjection to them improve your condition, or conduce to peace and order? I will do all I can to raise you to my advantages, and that is a better way of giving us the desired equality in the eye of the law: what you desire, or rather, what the civilians pretend you desire, would simply reduce us to an equality in lawlessness and misery; and against these evils it is the duty of our Government to guard."

The truth is, that this argument of my interrogator contains a fallacy which is not inapt to charm the unthinking, but which conceals the very essence of Socialism. What would become of us if any wretched creature could claim a right to reduce every one to his own level? A healthy, wealthy, tall, and handsome man might start for a morning walk eastwards from Hyde Park, and if the levelling wishes of those he met could be at once carried into action, he would find himself maimed, ruined, and afflicted with every disease in the world, before he got to Temple Bar. "He is six feet high," one would shout; "I am only five; compress him a foot." "His face is smooth," another would cry; "mine is pitted; pit his too." "He has a handsome nose; mine has a polypus; let his be similarly afflicted." "I have a 'shocking bad leg;' he must have one too." "The rascal has £10,000 a-year; I have nothing—'Halves!'" One hour's walk in the streets of London, and not homœopathy, nor hydropathy, nor mesmerism, nor even Holloway's pills and ointment, would effect his cure. Nothing but a motion for a writ of *habeas corpus* (supported by proper affidavits) would have a chance of restoring him to his former self.

Is this sound policy, or sound morality, or good religion? There was once a Reformer upon earth whose will ever found immediate fulfilment, and whose maxims Christian England professes to follow; and when blind Bartimeus sat by the wayside and cried his woes to Him, He answered the prayer, not by the deprivation of others' happiness, not by the infliction of darkness upon the rest of the multitude; but by widening the scope of human enjoyment, and bestowing the ineffable blessings of vision upon the clouded eyes of the Hebrew beggar. I would earnestly pray our statesmen to go and do likewise.

If you do not believe my assertions, you can apply to Mr. Theobald, who, though a private gentleman, comes as the representative of the whole non-official European population of Bengal. There he is, overflowing with evidence, and ready to answer any amount of questions. It is a notable fact, that that population were so alarmed by the proposed measures of judicial reform, that a few—I think about twenty—subscribed at once upwards of £2,000 to pay the expenses of their delegate to England. If, after hearing him and reading me, you are still unconvinced, let us have what we have so often demanded—what the missionaries now, too, with the best motives, but most mistaken impressions, join us in demanding—a Royal Commission to India. Nobody dreads it but the East India Company. If it is issued, and discharges its duties faithfully, and men are assured that they can give their evidence without the certainty of ruin from the vindictiveness of the civil officials, I will pledge my honour —I would pledge my life and fortune—that you will get a mass of evidence that will absolutely appall you.

All this will very likely be denied by the men who represent the East India Company at home; but they will deny anything that tells against them. It should never be forgotten, in weighing their testimony, that (to put their evident interest out of the question) they come before the public doubly and trebly convicted, either of the grossest ignorance, or of wilful falsehood. When it was proposed to destroy their commercial monopoly, they raised such a cry that one would have thought the world was coming to an end upon its destruction. The government of India could never be carried on without that monopoly; the territorial revenue showed a sad deficit; and the Government only continued solvent through the commercial gains: nay, the commerce with India would die away with the monopoly. The accounts were investigated by Mr. Wilkinson, and it was found—proved beyond the possibility of refutation—that these assertions were not only not true, but the direct opposite of truth; that their commerce was a loss; their territorial revenue the one which showed a surplus, and supported their commerce. The monopoly was destroyed, and the commerce has so increased, that the Hooghly can hardly hold the shipping.

They made the most terrible uproar about the immigration of Europeans into India, and vilified their conduct most outrageously. It would, to quote Mr. Macleod's words, "upset the whole basis of the British power in India." Lord William Bentinck inquired into the matter, and told them in reply, "That the whole of their objections rest on a train of argument, in meeting which the chief difficulty is that of so stating it, as to bear the semblance of sound reason."

They denied the existence of torture,—Mr. Mangles and others flatly, Sir James Hogg impliedly. The first mentioned gentleman had indeed "heard of it in certain matters of police, but he could solemnly declare he had never heard of anything of the kind in connection with the collection of the revenue." As if it is possible to believe that a man capable of reason, who knew the police were in the habit of torturing for confession of crime, and who knew that the same police were the collectors of revenue; and who knew the difficulty of collecting that revenue; could help knowing, whether he had "heard" it, or not, that they would resort to torture on the first difficulty! But Sir J. W. Hogg—that far-seeing man—was much too cunning to make any denial of the practice; he probably saw that public attention was roused to the pitch of action, that an inquiry would be made, and knew what the result would be. He, therefore, did not deny it: he simply contented himself with abusing Mr. Danby Seymour for asserting its existence. Let no one deprive him of the honour of the distinction, whose value he had the astuteness to perceive.

Indeed, that Torture Report, and the curious contradiction between the official assertions and the evidence in the appendices, would lead one to believe that there is something in employment by the East India Company which destroys the perception of truth. I may mention a little story which rather tends to confirm this view. There was, a couple of years ago, a squabble about an appointment in Calcutta between the Lieutenant-Governor of Bengal and the Governor-General's Private Secretary. It led to a rupture between these quondam friends. Of course, such an occurrence was greatly discussed in that Eastern little Pedlington; various reports got about; and the Private Secretary printed and circulated his version of the cause. Somehow it got into the papers; and the *Friend of India* took up the defence of Mr. Halliday, of course, as he was a civilian. Unfortunately, that paper could not deny that Mr. Halliday had told a fib; so it excused the little slip, and on these grounds, and in these words:—

"It was an act of official equivocation, which we can only account for by a reference to the circumstance of Mr. Halliday's having breathed too much of the parliamentary and official atmosphere of England during his residence there."

It really did,—it accused you all, my Lords and Gentlemen, of being such infectious liars, that a few days passed in your company served to upset Mr. Halliday's notions of truth. I cannot help thinking, if this be true, that the attack must have seized him very early in the delivery of his evidence before the Charter Committee.

But, deny it who may, the further you push your inquiries, the more firmly you will be convinced that the Europeans will not trust their capital willingly out of the jurisdiction of the Supreme Courts; that the badness of the Company's Courts has hindered, to an enormous degree, the immigration and enterprise of Europeans; and that an entire subjection to these tribunals will drive them out of the country. The amount of inconvenience arising from their exemption is very small. In the Memorial against the Black Acts it is stated, par. 17,—"When an inconvenience is alleged, from which such grave consequences as the disfranchisement of the whole body of Englishmen in India, their disherison of their own laws, and the denial to them of trial by jury and by competent courts, are to follow, it should at least have been stated in what it consisted, and what was its extent, for fraud lurks in generalities. We seek in vain for proof of its magnitude and reality. We find that the reality is that such alleged inconvenience has hitherto been exceedingly trifling and insignificant. We undertake fully to prove this by evidence. In the space of the last nineteen years, out of the total number of thirty-five British subjects committed for trial for offences of all kinds, within this Presidency (Bengal) beyond Calcutta, only seven can be shown to have been sent from a greater distance than a hundred miles, and the expense to Government must, therefore, have been utterly insignificant. The establishment of railways, the improvement of the navigation of the Ganges, and of internal communication generally, will greatly diminish this inconvenience, small as it is."

I am delighted to see that the attention of the cotton manufacturers is being turned again to India as a cotton field. In the debates which have already arisen this session in the House, you, Sir, have attributed the non-cultivation of cotton in India to the want of railroads and roads. Undoubtedly these are grave objections; but the main causes are the impediments thrown in the way of European enterprise by the East India Company, by the conditions they impose upon the tenure of land by Europeans, and by their revenue system, and the state of their laws and courts. Depend upon it, if Europeans had been encouraged to cultivate cotton, they would have got it to the sea-ports somehow or other. I extract and refer you to a portion of the letter of the Bombay Chamber of Commerce, published in the Cotton Committee's Report :—

Extract of a letter addressed to the Government of Bombay, by the Chamber of Commerce at that Presidency, on the subject of extending and improving cotton cultivation in India, 1841.

"Notwithstanding the last Company's Charter rules that British subjects may hold lands in any of the old British Indian territories, the terms which in your letter of the 30th May, 1840, you communicated to the Chamber, as those on which alone the Court of Directors permit land to be granted to persons desiring to engage in the culture of coffee, cotton, and other products, wholly exclude a real *bonâ fide* tenure. The Court, in the despatch therein quoted, expressly forbid Europeans from being allowed to purchase the land out and out ; all that is permitted is a lease of years, and the utmost extent of lease, under any circumstances, is fixed at twenty-one years. The land is, moreover, rendered liable to seizure, and the lease to forfeiture, at the discretion of the collector, and no judicial appeal is allowed ; the only appeal is to the Board of Revenue (whose functions in the Presidency the Committee suppose are exercised by the Revenue Commissioner), and the decision of that Board is to be final. On such a tenure the Committee think few British subjects will be found to risk their capital. Independently of the provisions regarding the Collector and the Board of Revenue, the shortness of the tenure is in itself an insuperable objection; for it takes away from the settler the fruits of his labour—his time and money, possibly just when they are beginning to ripen, and leaves another to reap where he has sown. Nothing short of the absolute and perpetual property in the land (subject, of course, to a fixed rate of taxation) will give that confidence which is necessary to cause capital, time, health, and labour to be freely expended upon it, and, when that possession is given, these will probably not long be wanting. The present flow of capital to Ceylon, and the great progress already made there, in converting the forests of Candy into flourishing coffee plantations, is a proof of this."

(The Cotton Committee's Report. Appendix No. 5, p. 513. Printed by order of the House of Commons, 17th July, 1848.)

Are you well acquainted with the result of Mr. Shaw's energetic promotion of cotton cultivation in Dharwar?

Do you know that he produced, in spite of the opposition of the money-lenders, excellent cotton, equal to the second quality of the American cotton, and at a price with which America could not compete?

But the moment Mr. Shaw left, the Government allowed the thing to lapse, the money-lenders resumed their power over the ryots, and there was an end of the matter. The *Times* lately, in a striking article, foreshadowed the effects of a possible failure of the cotton crop in America. If that evil day for England should come soon, it will be a happy day for India: then all these things will be inquired into, and their causes discovered; then they will build statues and get up testimonials to Colonel Arthur Cotton, and others who have laboured zealously and thanklessly for the true interests of India; then the British Lion (commercial) will wag his tail, and roar; then ruined Manchester will arise in its wrath, and (I hope) hang Messrs. Hogg, Mangles, and Melvill in cotton twist. Let us fervently pray that the then President of the Board of Control may not share the same fate.

It should also be remembered, that by the promotion of cotton cultivation in India, you will strike a deadlier blow than has yet been given to negro slavery.

The power of the East India Company over European settlers as to the right of deporting them from the country, and refusing them entrance into it, is involved in some doubt. Professor Wilson, in his history, denies the existence of any such power. But I think that learned historian is mistaken. The statutes are not very clear. My own opinion is, that the law upon this point is rightly stated by Mr. Dickinson, in his pamphlet on "Indian Government." There can be no doubt that the intention of the Legislature, in its more recent statutes, was to destroy the power of deportation; but I do not think those statutes have accomplished that object. The question is now awaiting the legal decision of the Supreme Court of Calcutta, and the time it has taken to consider its decision shows the difficulty in which the matter is involved. I hope when the judgment is delivered it will be broad and clear, beyond the possibility of doubt or cavil; and if, as I am inclined to think, it will rule in favour of the Company's right of deportation, the Legislature should step in and destroy it by a special enactment; and if the

Penal Code be unhappily passed, the chapter on Illegal Entrance should be struck out.

It may, perhaps, be asked what remedial measures I would myself propose for the evils I have described? Yet it may be deemed presumptuous in me to offer any suggestions, and I should hardly venture to do so, were my views not supported by the opinions of men whose right to attention is beyond question.

The main reform which I would propose is the employment at once to the largest extent practicable, throughout the country, of properly educated judges, chosen from barristers and advocates. This has been recommended by two judges, Sir Erskine Perry, who knows more of the internal state of India than any other Crown judge, and by Sir E. Gambier. Sir Edward Ryan, too, did not dissent from the advisability of the plan, but doubted its feasibility; he thought you could not get barristers to take the places. I am quite sure that if he were as well acquainted with the state of the profession, both in England and India, as I am, he would alter that opinion. Perhaps he founded it on the extraordinary assertion of Mr. Halliday, that barristers in Calcutta are making, on an average, £3,000 a year. This is the most preposterous mis-statement I ever read, even in Mr. Halliday's evidence. Three men at the Calcutta bar make from £5,000 to £8,000 per annum, one of whom occasionally makes as much as £10,000. About four more make a comfortable competence, and the rest manage as well as they can until they get places. There are some who make nothing at all by their profession. In fact, it is just as much a lottery as it is in England. It is a bar which requires peculiar and diverse qualifications; and there has been more than one instance of a man leaving an excellent rising practice in England to go to the Calcutta bar, in the vain assurance that he must make his fortune there, and finding, to his great astonishment, that he could not make enough to pay house-rent. In fact, six years ago it was probably the ablest bar, for its numbers, that was ever seen. The leaders were not inferior, as the judges declared, to the leaders of England. Wherever there are three or four such men, you may be sure there is a large proportion of briefless waiters on Providence.

I am perfectly certain, that if you offered to pay their passage out, and give them £600 a year until they passed the civilian's examination in native languages, and £1,500 upon their passing, with the chance of elevation by merit to the Sudder bench, you would get as many English barristers between twenty-five and thirty-five years of age as you wanted. An ordinarily clever and industrious man would, I am sure, pass the first examinations of the civilians in three months; indeed, I believe some of the first civilians who entered the service under the new competition system passed it in one or two weeks! And yet this is the marvellous knowledge of native languages, the want of which in English barristers has so often been declared by the East India Company's officials to be an insuperable bar to the employment of English lawyers. But you must, of course, take care to assure English lawyers that they will have fair play in the race for the higher seats of the Sudder bench.

The object of the East India Company has always been to keep lawyers out of the country, because their learning and fitness for their duties afford a too painful contrast to the ignorance of the civilians; and because, in Calcutta at least, the bar has always exposed, and stopped by public agitation, the grosser absurdities of their legislation. They have shown the greatest hostility to the profession, ever since they were defeated in their attempt to keep the bar also a closed nest for their own patronage. Their cry against lawyers has been always the same as that of Dick the butcher, in his little request to Jack Cade—"The first thing we do, let's kill all the lawyers." "Any law you please," say the civilians, "Mahomedan or Macauleian; but, for God's sake, no lawyers!" Their coyness, like Kate's, in the song of drunken Stephano, is confined to a class:—

> "The master, the swabber, the boatswain, and I,
> The gunner, and his mate,
> Loved Moll, Meg, and Marian, and Margery,
> But none of us cared for Kate;
> For she had a tongue with a tang,
> Would cry to a sailor, Go hang!
> She loved not the savour of tar nor of pitch,
> Yet a *tailor* might scratch her where'er she did itch;
> Then to sea, boys, and let her go hang."

So, according to the East India Company, every sort of person—I think a railway engineer was Mr. Halliday's last elevation to a judicial office—is fit for judicial employ except a lawyer.

I am no bigoted admirer of my own profession, but I confess my difficulty in meeting these objections is identical with that of Lord W. Bentinck in refuting the arguments against immigration—so to state the case of my opponents as to bear the semblance of reason. Do you go to your hatter for boots, and to your butcher for hats? Do you ask Kelly to take the stone from your bladder, and Brodie for his opinion upon the title of the property you want to purchase?

Every occasion has been seized on to circumscribe the jurisdiction of the Supreme Court, and now an attempt is made by the proposed code to take away, in a great measure, the independence of its judges. Mr. Halliday made the modest proposition to abolish the Supreme Court, and substitute for it the Sudder, with one presiding English lawyer. This proposition, to my mind, is conclusive as to the value of Mr. Halliday's evidence on all judicial matters. A counter proposition has been made, I am informed, by others, to retain that court in its integrity, and to appoint an English lawyer to preside over it. It is said to have the approval of the Crown judges. But there are, in truth, now *three* Sudder Courts. It consists of nine judges, who sit in batches as different Courts, and show their fitness for their office, according to the *Friend of India*, by diametrically opposite decisions:—while Messrs. Brown, Jones, and Robinson are laying down the law in one room as black, Messrs. Green, Stokes, and Nokes are laying it down as white in another room. Yet these decisions are of equal weight, and you can imagine the confusion they cause through all the courts of the country. It is evident that one man cannot keep three courts in order; it is clear there must be at least three fit men appointed. But why is even one wanted? To keep the ignorance of his colleagues in check by his learning. When we catch a wild elephant in the jungles, we secure him between two tame ones to keep him quiet; but here is a proposal to tie one sober and deliberative lawyer to eight wild and hasty civilians. If his learning could have any valuable effect upon their legal decisions, could he check them in their subserviency to the Executive Government, if, as stated by Mr. Robinson, they were to hold secret instructions as to their decisions, and be threatened with suspension and removal from office in case of contumacy? Is it certain that he would offer much opposition, when he himself might be turned out of office by a stroke of the Governor-General's pen? Let it not be said that the Government would never make such suggestions. They made a most improper request to the Judges of the Supreme Court, during my tenure of office; and I myself as the confidential clerk of Mr. Justice Buller, drafted the reply which conveyed to the Government the firm refusal of the Judges to comply with that request. I hope and believe most men would do their duty, even at the risk of office: but why subject them to such a trial? Why place such a power in the hands of a nearly irresponsible Government? "The eternal governing principle of the British Constitution," said Lord Lyndhurst in the most memorable debate of last year, "is jealousy and not confidence, and the principle upon which I proceed—the old constitutional principle—is, that I will give the Crown no power which is capable of being abused, unless some great and over-ruling necessity can be shown to exist. I look with all constitutional jealousy, and not with confidence, to those who are the depositories of power." Surely this applies with tenfold force to the servant of the East India Company, as the Governor-General undoubtedly is, who has a pension to gain by obedience to their wishes.

Eighty years ago, Lord Erskine, when counsel in a case against the Government, said to the Court of King's Bench, "I know that your Lordships will decide according to law, for the torrent of corruption which has overwhelmed every other part of the constitution is, by the blessing of Providence, stopped here by the sacred independence of the judges." That independence is as sacred now as it ever was: you must be aware that an attempt to destroy it here would raise a rebellion, if persisted in. It would be a grievous shame if it should be attempted in India. The Judges of the Supreme Court and the Sudder, at any rate, should hold their offices on the same tenure as the Judges of England. And on the very same ground upon which the introduction of one competent man into the latter court is proposed, I contend that ultimately all, and half at once, of its judges, should be selected from professional lawyers of some standing.

Every darogah should be an European, or half caste of the highest respectability. Every native of that class and station *will* torture upon the slightest difficulty.

Establish a Supreme Court at Agra. Pass the *Lex loci* as proposed by Mr. Lowe and Sir John Jervis. This measure does not rest on their recommendation alone.

I have advocated the bestowal upon natives of the right of eligibility to a seat in the highest court, chiefly because I think it will induce a much higher class of men to enter the judicial service. But the greatest care must be taken in their elevation. It must not be forgotten, that though many of those now in the service are well qualified in point of knowledge of regulation law, few of them are of very high character. I have taken the greatest pains to collect evidence on this point; and I find the evidence nearly unanimous in favour of the opinion expressed in the following extract of a letter from a planter of great experience:—

"I have known numbers—the great majority—of

native officers on the bench, who would not take money bribes: but I never knew one who would not obey the least hint of the Government officials, or of any very high caste man of their own nation, whom they very often respect more than the Governor-General. I have, I confess, myself used my influence with a man of the latter class successfully to induce a former native deputy magistrate of this district to give me fair play, when the civilian magistrate was doing everything he could to ruin me."

Let them have the chance of a seat, I say, on the highest bench; but let them clearly understand that they will have no favour in the struggle for that seat; that they will only gain the elevation if they are really superior to their white competitors. Let us have no more such specimens of incompetent men kept in office in spite of public opinion, as those previously quoted. Such a system tends to exasperate everybody, keeps the best men from seeking judicial employment, and makes all in it subservient and desirous only of securing the favour of the executive Governors.

Separate at once the judicial and executive functions. I know the opinions of Messrs. Halliday and Macleod are against this suggestion. But they are contradicted by men of much greater authority, and they advance but two arguments in support of their views—that it will weaken the Executive Government; which cannot be if the Government mean only to enforce their just claims—and that the civilians will be treated with less respect: they are now approached and treated with more adulation than our Protestant forms of worship permit to the Deity. It would do them no harm to learn that they are ordinary and fallible mortals.

Amid the mass of testimony by very distinguished men against the union of judicial and executive functions now existing, I shall quote two men, Lord Wellesley and Mr. Fullerton, probably the ablest civilian who ever went to Madras, and who was Member of Council there: he says;—

"The situation of judicial servants must be considered in another point of view. Judges are called upon to decide between Government itself and its subjects; to secure impartiality they must be free from bias, from the fear of losing their office thereby. No confidence can be placed by the public in the decisions of a judge holding an office only *durante bene placito*; the principle of *quamdiu se bene gesserint* must be scrupulously observed. The dismissal of a judge for a judicial opinion subverts the whole constitution of the Government. It is essential that distinct charges, judicial inquiry, and full hearing, should precede the dismissal of a judicial officer." And I would add that the inquiry and verdict should be public.

Here is the Marquis Wellesley upon the same subject.

Letter from the Marquis Wellesley, from Bengal, 31st December, 1799, to the Madras Government:—

Para. 115. "It is of essential importance to the security of private rights and property that a clear line should be drawn between the executive and legislative authority of the Government in India. The Governors in Council of the several Presidencies must necessarily act in both these capacities; the regulations in Bengal subject certain acts of Government in the executive capacity, as well as those of its officers, to the cognizance of the courts of justice, the judges of which are bound by solemn oaths to administer the laws impartially between Government and its subjects.

116. "By promulgating in print all our Legislative Regulations, and by subjecting Government itself, in its executive capacity, to the operation of those regulations, we afford to the inhabitants of these provinces the best security compatible with our situation in the country for the enactment of salutary laws for the protection of the person, rights, and property of the subject, and for the due administration of the laws. In addition to the check imposed on the legislative power by the publicity of the proceedings, those proceedings (as observed by your Board of Revenue) come regularly under the inspection of the public authorities at home, who thereby possess the means of an efficient control."

Letter from Marquis Wellesley to the Madras Government, 19th July, 1804.

18. "The most solemn and sacred obligations of the Government towards its subjects demand that just laws should be enacted and established for the general protection of the persons, rights, and property of individuals, and that judicial establishments should be provided, adequate to secure the prompt and impartial administration of the established laws. The new form of the internal Government provides for those salutary objects.* Experience of the happy effects of this system in other parts of our empire in India warrants a reliance that its introduction into the possessions in question

* Note by Mr. Fullerton. "Unfortunately, these establishments have not been adequate. Want of means had cramped their operation, produced imperfection, and imperfection has been urged in condemnation of the system."

(This is even truer now.—T. H. D.)

will promote the extension of agriculture and commerce, the increase of private wealth, and the permanent establishment of private security and public tranquillity, according to the degree in which those salutary effects may be produced; the sources from which the public revenue is derived will be augmented, and the means of obtaining a just proportion of the wealth of the country for the use of the State will be facilitated and improved.

19. "Instead of delaying the institution of courts of judicature; instead of suspending the authority of those already constituted; *instead of confounding all the powers of Government in the person of a Collector of Revenue*, the judicial authority should be strengthened by equitable regulations; justice and mercy should temper the severity of power; and the control of fixed law should manifest the certainty of protection to the lives and properties of our obedient subjects, while regular authority, sustained by sufficient force, should display an equal certainty of punishment to lawless violence and rebellious resistance. Were it possible for the Collectors of the Revenue to appropriate a sufficient portion of their time to the administration of justice, and to the maintenance of the peace of the country, the nature of their duties as officers of the Revenue disqualifies them for the discharge of judicial functions. The people cannot repose a firm confidence in the protection of the laws, while the administration of the laws shall be entrusted to the Collectors of the Revenue, because the conduct of those officers, and of the native agents and servants acting under their authority, necessarily forms a principal object of legal control." After stating that unless these principles were acted upon the system of administration would be no better than that of the

Native Governments, the Marquis Wellesley proceeds :—

25. "Under the most favourable exertions of individual talents and integrity, such a system must produce public and private oppression and abuse. It provides no restraint upon the exercise of power sufficient to ensure the uniform, impartial, and general operation of the laws, and to inspire the people with a sense of confidence and security in the ordinary conduct of private transactions, and in the undisturbed exercise of private rights. Exempt from those salutary restraints, the public officers may pursue a course of evil administration in many of the subordinate departments of the State without the knowledge of Government; and the Government may continue ignorant of the abuse of its name and power, until private distress and personal suffering shall compel the people to combine against the authority whose name and power have been perverted for the purposes of vexation and oppression. In this condition, open resistance affords to the people the sole mode of appeal to the justice of Government. To that dreadful appeal the most peaceable, industrious, and dutiful people must resort, whenever the laws shall afford no regular organ to convey the complaints of the subject to the ear of the Sovereign. Under such circumstances, it is to be apprehended that the resistance produced by the oppression of the State, or of its officers, may be ascribed to disaffection in the people, and the Government may be reduced to the necessity of vindicating its authority at the expense of its character for justice."

And in consequence of the systematic disregard of these nobly worded principles, we had the Santhal Insurrection, which has already cost the State at least a million sterling; for these savages—cheery, laughing fellows, as easily ruled as children—were driven to rebellion by the exactions of the subordinate revenue and judicial officers; they did enormous damage to all the European settlers in their districts; the Government refused the slightest compensation even to men who aided them in every way, and though their own troops did nearly as much damage as the Santhals; and the *Friend of India* had the impudence to assert that the insurrection arose from the erotic regards cast by railway servants and planters on the Santhal women; creatures one degree less hideous and ten times filthier than chimpanzees; with any one of whom her lawful lord would be delighted to part for a consideration of two rupees a month; and the very thought of amorous relations with whom makes the flesh creep.

I am half afraid, Sir, that my statements will not be believed, and yet I have carefully restricted myself to a very mild revelation of the judicial evils of India. I have always said that if those evils had been a tithe of what they are, a remedy would have been found for them long ago. But they are so atrocious, so incredible, that their description generally gains for the author the character of a Munchausen. It has often amused me to see the terror my many informants have one and all expressed, when I have begged to be allowed to publish their facts with their names. They knew that they would be an object of persecution by the great majority of officials in their district—in short, would be ruined.

However, I can only repeat, that I have but lifted a corner of the curtain; and you will find that assertion correct, if you will only inquire into the matter. No doubt it will be denied; but really there are two members of the House of Commons, who are called the members for Honiton and Guildford, but who ought to be called the members for the bewilderment of the House upon Indian topics. Whenever an enthusiastic member, who has never been in India, and has not the archives of the India House at hand, gets hold of a little bit of Indian grievance, then I know I shall soon see the comely presence of the member for Honiton rise in his place, and with fluent elocution, exquisite tact, great sophistical skill, some perversion, and no small suppression of truth, he will puzzle the honourable House; he will also lay a trap for Mr. Murrough, who will fall plump into it. Then the not so comely presence of the member for Guildford will rise in *his* place, and talk against time, with less tact and less skill, and will drive the honourable House frantic with boredom; and I shall read in the *Times* next morning that "the subject then dropped." But it is really high time that some one was listened to on the other side.

In the haste with which, among other avocations and many distractions, this letter has been written, it cannot be expected that I should have done more than hint at the objections to the scheme I oppose, or the remedies I suggest. I hope, however, that I have said enough to set other more powerful and abler men thinking, and to indicate the dangers of the scheme proposed.

I think, in all humility, that if the main principles I have advocated are followed, you would improve the internal state of India, increase European immigration, and consequently, extend your commerce and augment your revenues; and that you would advance far in the way of obtaining some law and order in the country, and some justice, very different from that Indian justice whereof Mr. Macleod is enamoured. Seventy years ago the eloquent fancy of Sheridan painted Justice as one "whose countenance was ever placid and benign; whose favourite attitude is to stoop to the unfortunate—to hear their cry and to help them—to rescue and relieve, to succour and to save: majestic from its mercy, venerable for its utility, uplifted without pride, firm without obduracy, beneficent in each preference, lovely though in her frown."

But the thing which went by her name in India he denounced "as a disgusting caricature—a halt and miserable object; the ineffective bauble of an Indian pagod; the portentous phantom of despair; like any fabled monster, formed in the eclipse of reason, and found in some unhallowed grove of superstitious darkness and political dismay."

This is as true at the present moment as it was when the old men of to-day were at their mothers' breasts. Indian justice might now be pictured as a hideous harpy, scouring the land, while the terror-stricken population fly before her; her right hand wielding the instruments of torture, her left hand grasping the pice wrung by their agency from the agonized ryot. Her favourite attitude is to stoop to the unfortunate to clutch him by the hair of his head; to hear his cry and laugh at it with horrid glee; to pluck out his beard by the roots; to force his feet into the stocks; to crush his fingers in the kittie; to place the many-legged beetle in his navel, and the burning chillie beneath his nostril.

You may alter all this if you have the will, for you have the power. You can destroy the Court of Directors, the ridiculous anomalies and irresponsibilities of, I will not say the double, but the treble Government of

India; and if you do this, you will give happiness to a hundred millions of human beings, increase the wealth and prosperity of your own countrymen, and gain for yourself an imperishable name. Then, to quote lines which you know exceedingly well,—

> "Qui motus animorum, et quanta pericula nostra
> Accipient facilem sine cæde et sanguine finem!"

Perhaps, as I have presumed to address you, I ought to say a few words about myself. I am no place-hunter, reviling official abuses from motives of disappointment; the office which I had the honour to hold was offered to me without any solicitation on my part, and resigned at my own wish. It is just as likely that any office in India which I would accept will be offered to me again, as that I should be asked to take a seat in the Cabinet. Had I ever hoped or wished for such an office, the chance of obtaining it would be destroyed by this publication. Lastly, I have no cause of dislike against the East India Company's Service. A very large number of my connections are in it—I might have been in it myself; and I have found amongst its members some of my most valued friends. I have therefore a right to demand that my evidence should be received as that of a man whose personal interests not only do not prompt its delivery, but urge powerfully to its concealment.

I have the honour to be, &c.,

T. H. DICKENS.

APPENDIX.

I THINK it worth while to extract the chapter on Mischief as a specimen of Macaulay's Code. It is taken at random from a mass of similar absurdities:—"Whoever causes the destruction of any property, or any such change in any property, or in the situation of any property, as destroys or diminishes the value of such property, intending thereby to cause wrongful loss to any person, is said, except in the case hereinafter mentioned, to commit mischief.

"*Explanation.*—A person may commit mischief on his own property.

"*Exception.*—Nothing is mischief which a person does openly, and with the intention in good faith of thereby saving any person from death or hurt, or of thereby preventing a greater loss of property than that which he occasions."

Of the illustrations, I take two again at random; here they are:—

"A, having joint property with Z in a horse, shoots the horse, intending thereby to cause wrongful loss to Z. A has committed mischief.

"A voluntarily throws into the river a ring belonging to Z, with the intention of thereby causing wrongful loss to Z. A has committed mischief."

It will be observed that it is not necessary that anybody else should have a reversion in the property destroyed by its owner. A man therefore wilfully breaking his own teacup is a felon under this law. Mischief is to be punishable by the magistrate: now think of the consequences of such a law to a man against whom that official had a spite. I will give a few illustrations, taking, on the supposition that Mr. Solano's charges against Mr. Swinton are correct, these two men as my *dramatis personæ.*

Case I.—Mr. Solano is joint proprietor with a friend, more remarkable for acuteness than morality, of a racing Arab which has cost 5,000 rupees, and which the acute friend has backed to win the Calcutta Derby. The horse gets a painful and incurable disease. "I really think," says Solano to his friend, "it would be a mercy to shoot him." "Perhaps it would," says the acute friend; and he is shot by Solano's orders. "Now, Solano," says the other, "if you don't pay me 10,000 rupees to hold my tongue, I'll have you up, you mischievous villain, for shooting our horse, before Mr. Swinton! You will think the sum I demand large; but read the clauses 400, 402, 403, 404, 406, of the chapter on Mischief in Mr. Macaulay's excellent code; and you will see that you are liable to conviction under them all. I leave you to guess whether Mr. Swinton will let you off with less than the highest punishment. I know that it is very inconvenient to you; but be wise, pay me 10,000 rupees, and I won't prosecute."

Solano, if wise, does pay it; if he does not, I can fancy Mr. Swinton thus delivering judgment:—

"It is not denied that the accused shot the horse, but it is said that he shot it with the prosecutor's assent. The latter denies this, and it would be too much to hold that the words, 'Perhaps it would,' in answer to the remark of the accused, 'That it would be a mercy to shoot the horse,' conferred any authority or assent. The prisoner is clearly liable to conviction under all the clauses mentioned by the prosecutor. It is also clear that he is liable to be fined ten times the value of the horse. It has been urged that half the property in the horse was the accused's own, and that he ought therefore only to be fined five times the whole value of the horse. But that objection is ridiculous, as the explanation of this chapter clearly says, that a man may commit mischief on his own property, and therefore must, of course, be liable to punishment for that offence. I therefore sentence the accused Solano to imprisonment with hard labour in irons for three years, and I fine him 50,000 rupees; in default of payment he will be imprisoned for a further term of nine months."

Case II.—Mr. Solano has lately bought one of Smith's best rifles, price £100. He goes out tiger shooting with a friend, misses every shot, and at last, in a pet, flings his rifle down from the howdah, and it is broken. The friend innocently relates the circumstance in Mr. Swinton's hearing. He summons Solano; convicts him under clauses 400 and 403, of mischief to his own property; and sentences him to imprisonment for two years with hard labour in irons, and fines him 10,000 rupees.

CASE III.—Mr. Solano breaks a teacup, value four annas, and picks up and throws the fragments into a rubbish heap. "Had you contented yourself with breaking your cup," says Mr. Swinton, "the highest punishment I could have inflicted for your crime would have been a fine of three shillings; but as you chose further to commit the crime of taking precaution not to be detected, as is clearly proved by your hiding the fragments of your cup, the sentence will be under clause 401. You are fined 2 rupees 8 annas, and will also be imprisoned for six months with hard labour in irons."

Well may the late Commissioners say, "We have not made [this code], collectively, a particular subject of our examination and consideration, further than was necessary, in order that we might be able to frame, in such a manner as to suit it, the Code of Criminal Procedure." But were they not bound to do this before they ventured to recommend its adoption?

T. H. D.

THIRD

PETITION TO PARLIAMENT

FROM THE MEMBERS OF THE

BOMBAY ASSOCIATION,

RELATIVE TO THE

REPORTS OF THE COMMISSIONERS APPOINTED BY
HER MAJESTY FOR THE REFORM OF THE
JUDICIAL ESTABLISHMENTS, CODES
OF PROCEDURE AND LAWS OF
INDIA.

1857.

To

The Honorable the COMMONS OF THE UNITED KINGDOM OF GREAT BRITAIN AND IRELAND, in Parliament assembled.

The Humble Petition of the Members of the Bombay Association.

SHEWETH,

That your Petitioners, whose Association comprises almost the whole of the Native Inhabitants of Bombay whose position and education enable them to form an opinion on the Legislative measures proposed for the benefit of their country, and who faithfully represent the views and wishes as well as the true interests of the whole population of the Presidency, have watched with the utmost interest the enquiries which have been conducted, and the proposals which have been made, with a view to the improvement of the Judicial Establishments of India; and while they highly approve of many of the recommendations made by the Commissioners appointed to consider this subject in their Reports presented to your Hon'ble House, they regard with serious concern some of the most important of those suggestions; and they have heard with great alarm that it is proposed to introduce a Bill founded on those Reports, which would give effect to the objectionable portions of the system devised by the Commissioners.

2. Your Petitioners have not been blind to, as they are not now unmindful of, serious defects in the forms and procedure of the Supreme Court. Into these much improvement has recently been introduced, and they believe that liberal and judicious persistance in this course would, before long, leave them nothing to desire. The needless technicalities, which yet remain, the arbitrary

differences in procedure in administering law and equity, the distinction of the functions of barrister and attorney, with some other anomalies, which still throw unnecessary expense and delay upon suitors, would, by the course of reform which has been entered upon, be gradually removed, and a Court, of which the reputation has never been tarnished by even the imputation of want of either capacity or integrity, would remain with its great and substantial advantages, freed from its defects of detail, and capable of extending to the whole Presidency those benefits which it has already conferred on the Town and Island of Bombay.

3. The Commissioners recommend the abolition of the present Supreme Courts and Sudder Adawluts, and the substitution of a High Court in each Presidency to exercise the functions of the two Courts which it supersedes, and to consist at Madras and Bombay of not less than five judges, two of them to be appointed by the Crown, and three by the Governor in Council of the respective Presidencies.

4. There are many other recommendations in the Commissioners' Reports which, though in themselves of very serious importance and open to grave objection, your Petitioners do not propose to make the subject of comment at the present time, as they consider them to be of little moment when compared with the proposed abolition or supercession of the Supreme Court, which if sanctioned by your Hon'ble House, will, your Petitioners apprehend, have the effect of withdrawing the only guarantee on which they can rely for the regular, systematic, and trustworthy administration of law and justice, under the protection of which they have hitherto lived, and to which they look with grateful confidence for the security of their persons and property.

5. In this Court, so justly respected by all classes, which is presided over by judges selected from the experienced members of the English bar—men who have been educated, as it were, in a legal and judicial atmosphere, and have imbibed not only the legal knowledge

but the tone and habit of thought which characterize the English lawyer, and constitute his fitness for the judicial office,—it is proposed to substitute a tribunal in which the majority, and therefore the preponderating influence, being appointed by the Governor in Council, probably will, as they certainly may, be taken from amongst the Civil Servants of the Hon'ble Company. Your Petitioners would not speak otherwise than most respectfully of these gentlemen, of whom many are not only distinguished by high abilities and a zealous desire to promote the welfare of the people whose affairs they administer, but who also possess habits of business and a knowledge of India to which barristers from England could lay no claim. But, great as these advantages are, and ready as your Petitioners are to appreciate them in their proper sphere, they cannot admit that they constitute the necessary qualifications for the judicial office. Even supposing that an improved system of training and appointment should be introduced, and the Civil Servants of the Company no longer be transferred from political and fiscal employments to the highest judicial appointments, of which so many instances have been seen, still the objections to the appointment of Civilians to the Bench of the Highest Court are not removed, hardly lessened. These gentlemen have not that one advantage, for which no other can be substituted, an education in the legal axioms and methods, in the habits of thinking and reasoning which prevail in and about the superior Courts of England, and of which your Petitioners see the excellence in every Judge who takes his seat on the Bench of the Supreme Court, whose demeanour and decisions command respect, notwithstanding his ignorance of the habits and language of the people; while the judgments of even the most experienced and intelligent servants of the Company fail to carry the weight which should attach to the decisions of the higher Courts of Justice.

6. Your Petitioners think it highly desirable, that all the important judicial offices in the country should, so soon as circumstances permit, be filled by professional lawyers, whether English or

Native, whether trained in England or in India, need not be now discussed; but that every superior judge in this country should be a lawyer by profession and a judge by right of superior abilities and character, your Petitioners humbly claim at the hands of your Hon'ble House; and they think this consummation will be well commenced and greatly facilitated by the immediate establishment of an ultimate High Court of Appeal (on the model of, and comprising the functions of the present Supreme Court,) to superintend and correct the defects of all the provincial tribunals. Such High Court to be composed entirely of trained and experienced lawyers, whose reputation and character, and the responsibility of those who appoint them, should afford sufficient security for their fitness for their important office. That such lawyers, fitted both by knowledge, integrity and experience suitably to fill even the highest judicial offices of the country may, before long, be found amongst the Natives of India, is the earnest hope and confident expectation of your Petitioners, who trust that no provisions may be admitted into any Acts of Parliament which would have the effect of excluding them.

7. Your Petitioners therefore trust, that the proposed High Court may be established by the addition of a general appellate jurisdiction, and the appointment of a sufficient number of additional judges to the present Supreme Court, and at the same time they think that the forms and modes of procedure of that Court might undergo a thorough revision with a view to their simplification, and in order to render them more suitable to the extended jurisdiction to which they would become applicable. But your Petitioners most earnestly deprecate the proposed virtual supercession of the Supreme Court by the Sudder, the merging of the better tribunal in the worse, and the subjection of the Queen's Judges to the preponderating voice of a majority of the Civil Servants of the Company. Your Petitioners attach little weight to the argument, that for appellate jurisdiction from the provincial Courts a knowledge of the language and habits of the people and of the Hon'ble

Company's Regulations is essential. At present the ultimate appeal is to English lawyers, who constitute the Judicial Committee of the Privy Council, most of whom have never been in India, and of whom none have ever been connected with the Judicial Establishments of this country, save as Judges of Her Majesty's Supreme Courts at the Presidencies, and who have consequently none of those advantages which are said to be so necessary, but whose judgments have ever been thought most sound and satisfactory.

8. Your Petitioners, however, have more especial reasons for objecting to the proposed alterations. Your Hon'ble House is aware, that Bombay is a place of very extensive European and general trade, the entrepot for all surrounding countries, the outlet for the productions of the interior, as it is the inlet for the British and foreign manufactures and productions which are consumed in Western India. Its extensive mercantile transactions now are, and for the future must be, founded on the refined but happily settled and well-known rules of English mercantile law,—rules which ages of judicious and well-considered enactments and decisions have prescribed to govern the various and complicated dealings of merchants, bankers, brokers, and shopkeepers, transactions in notes and bills of exchange, as well as questions on freight and salvage, and the innumerable other subjects that are constantly giving rise to litigation in the midst of so large a trading population as that of Bombay. It is obvious that the most serious injury to the trade not only of the port, but of the whole country, would be done by any irregularity in the decisions of the Courts or any departure from settled rules of law. No one would be disposed to send his goods or his capital to a place in which the law was either ignorantly or capriciously administered, and yet on all these subjects the Hon'ble Company's Judges are not only uninstructed, but are incapable, from want of legal education and practice, of appreciating the distinctions and principles upon which the mercantile law depends. It would thus happen that the High

Court, being the Court of first and last resort in the country for the large European and Native trading community, would be presided over by Judges of whom the majority would be entirely unacquainted with the Law of England, especially the Law Mercantile, and the course of decisions by which, and the principles on which, that Law has become settled. It is unquestionable that endless confusion would thus be introduced into this most important branch of the business of the Court, upon the skill, knowledge, and regularity displayed in dealing with which, the trade of the port and the prosperity of Western India, and of your petitioners, so mainly depend.

9. There is another point in the recommendations of the Commissioners to which your Petitioners must advert with equal earnestness. They believe that, as the introduction of Civil Servants into the new Court would detract from or destroy its efficiency, so the proposed subjection of its members to the authority of the local Government would subvert its independence, freedom of action, and integrity, or if these should stand the trial, would at least subject it to constant imputations of subserviency and time-serving timidity. It is proposed to give the Governor in Council the power of suspending any judge at his discretion, pending a reference to the Crown. Considering the high and dignified position which the Judges of the Supreme Court now hold, and which those of the proposed High Court ought always to maintain, it is certain that the indignity of suspension would practically be equivalent to deprivation and dismissal. No judge having proper respect for himself and his office, who should have the misfortune to incur the displeasure of the local Government and be suspended, would condescend to remain in India in a private station, awaiting the decision of the advisers of the Crown in England, and, if that should prove favorable, to re-take his place on the Bench. If he should do so, the spectacle would be as unseemly as it would be subversive of that respect which is now paid to the Court and detrimental to the administration of justice. Suspension would

therefore amount to dismissal and degradation; and your Petitioners humbly submit, that this power should not be given to the Governor in Council. That high functionary represents the East India Company, and they are owners of the greater part of the land of India. They are not only a Government, but a Company having proprietary interests and business dealings, which frequently involve judicial investigations. They may now sue and be sued directly in the Supreme Courts, and they not unfrequently appear as suitors there, while their officers are still more frequently parties to litigation arising out of their official proceedings and in which Government often takes a warm interest; and with what freedom can the Judges act, and what confidence can be placed in their decisions if they hold their offices at the discretion of the local Government? That power, which is not even held by the Crown in England, it is proposed to confer on the vicarious Governors in India.

10. Strongly therefore as your Petitioners object to these leading proposals of the Commissioners, there is one recommendation they have made, conceived in the wisest spirit, and in which your petitioners so entirely concur that they have heard with great regret that, on the objection of the Governor General, it is not proposed to carry out their suggestions in this respect. Your Petitioners refer to the abolition of Stamps on Judicial proceedings,—a species of tax which the reasoning of every political economist combines with the experience of every Court and every community to condemn. It is said that the finances of the country cannot dispense with the produce of these Stamp duties; but this argument must be but a comparative one; it is but a question between this and some other form of taxation, or some reduction of expenditure, which would render the taxation needless. Your petitioners are so strongly impressed with the conviction that the due administration of justice is utterly impracticable under the pressure of this species of taxation, that they earnestly recommend that at any cost the means should be found for dispensing with and abolishing it.

11. With the exception therefore of the important points to which your Petitioners have thus taken exception, and some minor points of detail, which they trust will be re-considered before any Act on this subject is passed, your Petitioners earnestly hope, that the proposals of the Commissioners for the establishment of an uniform procedure, and of a single Court of original jurisdiction for the Town and Island of Bombay and of appeal from the provinces, may speedily receive the sanction of Parliament and be introduced into this country ; for they look to this as one great means of remedying the very serious and lamentable evils and the constant failure of justice that the present judicial system is productive of, and which loudly calls for early and complete reform.

12. Your Petitioners therefore pray, that the present Supreme Court in all its essential and characteristic attributes may be retained, while its procedure is revised and improved ; that a general Court of Appeal from provincial tribunals composed entirely of English trained lawyers may be established, to be combined with the Supreme Court if the union should be found practicable ; that the entire independance of the Judges of any Indian authority should be preserved intact, and that all Stamp Duties should be at once abolished.

And your Petitioners, as in duty bound, will ever pray.

Bombay, 19*th*
March 1857.

PREFACE.

PREFACE.

On the motion of Sir T. E. Perry, a return was ordered by the House of Commons of Extracts from the following Minute. The Minute, not being at the India Board, had to be applied for at the India House, and the return made was—that it is not at the India House. I dare say this was a true return at the time when it was made; but it is no less true that two copies were sent from the Bengal Office to the Court, one to Colonel Sykes, and one to Mr. Mangles (the Chairman and Deputy Chairman). The return, therefore, though true, is not a *just* one; and there can be no doubt that the Directors are much afraid of the Minute, or they would have given it up.

Recently, to a subsequent order of the House, a return has been made, entitled, "Copy of the Minute recorded by the Lieutenant-Governor of Bengal," &c., and, to my knowledge, from similarity of description, this is supposed by some members to be the above-mentioned Minute. But it is no such thing. There are two Minutes; and they are very different. The Minute withheld runs on all fours with the representations which the British and Christian inhabitants have made respecting the Police and Administration of Justice in the Lower Provinces; the other Minute, without adverting to the former one, amplifies the assertion that the Government is doing all it can in the way of improvement. This may be true, and yet what is being done may be of very superficial action;

and it affords no reason why Parliament should not see what the Lieutenant-Governor has said respecting the local authorities under him: the Minute reflects credibility on all that we have represented. I therefore now publish it with the concurrence of gentlemen with whom I consult on all important matters connected with my mission.

W. THEOBALD,
On deputation from Bengal.

36 *Jermyn Street, S.W., June* 6, 1857.

Note. I am furnished by a friend with the following:—

"The Minute in question was written by the Governor of Bengal on the 20th April, 1856, and was in possession of the public at Calcutta within a few weeks from that time.

"It was noticed in the 'Friend of India' (semi-official paper), in the following month of June, 1856, as containing a stronger denunciation and more severe exposure of the corrupt and rotten state of the administration of justice in Bengal, than the fiercest radical had ever ventured to utter before;—and this article of the 'Friend of India' was immediately reprinted in the Indian journals, and reprinted in the English press as soon as it reached this country in August, 1856. About this period the Minute itself arrived in England, as it was shown to a friend of the writer's at the India House in the beginning of the month of September, 1856, by the then Chairman of the East India Company, Colonel Sykes.

"At the same period in India a Memorial was presented to the Government by the Bengal missionaries, dated September 2, 1856, quoting many of the startling admissions contained in the Minute; which Memorial was reprinted by the English press on its arrival in this country, on October 31, 1856. At the same period in India, on the 25th of August, 1856, an analysis of the Minute, with a long series of extracts from it, was published in the Transactions of the Indigo Planters' Association of Bengal. Shortly after this, on the 5th of February, 1857, Sir Erskine Perry moved for extracts from the above Minute, and the return was, that the paper in question could not be furnished, as it had not been received at the East India House."

INDIGO PLANTERS' ASSOCIATION.

MINUTE BY THE HON'BLE THE LIEUTENANT-GOVERNOR OF BENGAL.

POLICE AND CRIMINAL JUSTICE IN BENGAL.

Police.—For a long series of years complaints have been handed down from administration to administration regarding the badness of the Mofussil Police under the Government of Bengal, and as yet very little has been done to improve it. Such efforts as have occasionally been made for this purpose, have been usually insufficient to meet the greatness of the evil; partial remedies have failed to produce any extensive benefit; and, during long intervals, the Government has appeared to fold its hands in despair, and to attempt nothing new, because the last tried inadequate measure had ended in inevitable disappointment.

2. Meantime the ill success of our administration in this particular has been an endless theme of reproach to the Government, accompanied often by the grossest exaggerations, and very rarely by any sound and practical suggestions for improvement.* And the weight and moral authority of the Government have undoubtedly been affected by continual invective on a subject regarding which, while little or no defence was attempted, the Government yet appeared indisposed to make any real effort towards reform.

3. *Former Measures.*—For what, after all, has been done to improve the Police during the last thirty years? We have ceased, it is true, to expect integrity from Darogahs with inadequate salaries and large powers, surrounded by temptations, and placed beyond the reach of practical control; and we have somewhat curtailed the excessive and unmanageable extent of our Magistrate's Jurisdictions by the gradual establishment of thirty-three† Sub-division Magistrates. But beyond this, and not speaking at present of the special and peculiar machinery lately set up in a few Districts for the suppression of Dacoity, I know not what else has been attempted; and, even with regard to these two instalments of improvement, the halting, hesitating way in which they have been effected has prevented the full benefit which might otherwise have been expected from them. Before the first of these improvements, our stipendiary Police in the Regulation Provinces consisted of some four hundred and eighty-four Darogahs or Thannadars scattered at distant intervals over a territory of 150,000 square miles, and a population of

* Several very valuable suggestions have been submitted to Government from time to time by the late Superintendent of Police for the improvement of the system, and I shall have occasion to avail myself of them, more or less, in the measures I am about to propose.

† This is now the number of Sub-Divisions in the Regulation Provinces.

35,000,000 souls—being, say, one Darogah or superior Police Officer to 309 square miles and 72,314 souls. Each of these potent functionaries was paid Rupees 25 a month—avowedly less than he could live and move about upon—and each had under him, generally, a Mohurir or Clerk, and a Jemadar or head Constable, on salaries ranging from Rupees 4 to 8 a month each, but with powers equal on most occasions to the Darogah himself. Subordinate to these at each Thannah was an establishment of from ten to twenty Burkundauzes or Constables, often deputed with large powers into the interior, and paid, each man, from Rupees 3-8 to 4 a month—a salary notoriously inadequate. It was a step in the right direction, doubtless, when the Government of Lord Auckland determined thenceforth to pay no Darogah less than Rupees 50 per mensem, and to allow to one hundred of the number Rupees 75, and to fifty of them Rupees 100 per mensem. But the good of all this was tarnished by the omission to do anything for the lower grades of Police Officers. For it was impossible to become a good Darogah without an apprenticeship; and when the apprenticeship was to be served in the midst of great power, great temptation, and the traditions of unavoidable corruption in the station of a Thannah Mohurir on Rupees 7 a month, what was to be expected from such a training?—or how, train the Darogah as you might, could you expect purity and integrity until you had cleansed away from about him the foul atmosphere of corruption necessarily engendered by the aggregation of ill-paid and unscrupulous underlings with whom bribery and extortion were almost a necessity, and had long been the habit of their lives?

4. *Recent Recommendation.*—This great evil has been more than once commented upon by Mr. Dampier, the late Superintendent of Police, and a remedy proposed. I trust that it may now shortly undergo reform, as I last year submitted to the Government of India an earnest recommendation founded on Mr. Dampier's propositions for an increase to the salaries of Mohurirs, Jemadars, and Burkundauzes, by a system of gradation.* And, unless financial difficulties interpose, I cannot doubt that this measure must ultimately be honoured by the approval of the Governor-General in Council. But if this be not granted, all thought for the improvement of the Police will, I fear, be but thought thrown away.

5. *Sub-division Magistracies.*—The establishment of Sub-division Magistracies had in it, doubtless, the elements of a very important reform; and, as far as it has been yet carried, has certainly effected much good. But as yet it has been carried to a very small and inadequate extent, and it has, therefore, seemed to the public eye almost to have operated as a failure. Beyond all doubt, we shall ever fail to establish a good and trustworthy system of Police, unless—together with other improvements—we establish a close, constant, and vigorous control over our Police Agents, and a ready access to justice for all persons, so that the appeal of the weak against the strong may be at all times possible and effectual.

6. Throughout the length and breadth of this country, the strong prey almost universally upon the weak, and power is but too commonly valued only as it can be turned into money. The Native Police, therefore, unless it be closely and vigorously superintended by trustworthy Officers, is sure to be a scourge to the country in exact proportion to its strength and power. For this indispensable superintendence, no adequate provision has ever yet been made; nor can any provision be considered adequate which does not supply, at least, one capable and trustworthy Magistrate for every two, or, at most, every three Thannahs. At present, however, our establishments do not com-

* Full details of the proposed measure, and cogent arguments for its adoption, will be found in Mr. Grey's letter to the Government of India, No. 774, of 30th April, 1855. It was proposed to divide Mohurirs into three grades on Rupees 30, 35, and 40 per mensem; Jemmadars into three grades on Rupees 10, 15, and 20; and of the Burkundauzes, one-fourth at Rupees 6 per mensem, one-fourth at Rupees 5, and the rest on Rupees 4. The whole increased cost to be incurred would be Rupees 3,38,609 per annum.

prise more than seventy Executive Magistrates, covenanted and uncovenanted, over four hundred and eighty-four* Thannahs, being at the average rate of about seven-and-a-quarter Thannahs to each Magistrate—a proportion much below what is requisite, and the distribution of even this number of Magistrates is extremely irregular.

7. *Village Chowkeydars.*—Of the vast importance of the rural Police, the village Chowkeydars, and the strong necessity for fortifying and improving their character and position, there has never been but one opinion; and from as far back as 1784 down to the date of Lord Hastings' celebrated "Police Minute," and again from that time till the Police Committee of 1837, down to Mr. Dampier's frequent comments on the subject in his Annual Reports, all who have written or spoken on the subject have invariably urged the necessity of directing constant and vigilant attention to the preservation and improvement of this ancient institution of the country. Yet, though more than one expedient for this purpose has been devised and discussed, nothing has ever been carried into execution, and it is a lamentable, but unquestionable fact, that the rural Police, its position, character, and stability as a public institution, have, in the Lower Provinces, deteriorated during the last twenty years. It is now diminished in number and impaired in efficiency, while its rights have been seriously and successfully attacked and undermined; so that, unless some speedy measures be taken to save it, it is in danger of perishing altogether from the face of the land and passing out of use, if not out of remembrance.

8. Thirty years ago the old opinion was still prevalent among the Magistrates, an opinion handed down from the Dowdeswells, Elliots, Bayleys, and other Magistrates of renown, that it was the highest duty of a Magistrate to uphold the Village Police, to cause all vacancies to be properly filled, and to see to the fair payment of all members of the body. There is no doubt that these exertions were in those days effectual towards the object in view, and that the Village Police were kept from falling into decay by the determined and persevering interest shown by the Magistrates in their behalf.

9. The manner in which Mr. W. B. Bayley, when Magistrate of Burdwan in 1811, exerted himself to keep up the efficiency of the Village Police, which has often been held up as an example to succeeding Magistrates, has been explained by him in the following words, quoted from his report to Government of 1812—"I explained," he says, "to the Talookdars, Munduls, &c., the necessity of giving a sufficient provision to their respective Chowkeydars, and urged to them, as strongly as I could, the advantage which would result to the prosperity of the country and its inhabitants, by furnishing to every Chowkeydar such means of subsistence as might prevent them from committing thefts and robberies, in order to support themselves and their families. Upon this principle, I have to the utmost of my power prevented all attempts on the part of the Landholders, &c., to resume any portion of the Chakeran lands, or to remove or appoint any Chowkeydars without a previous inquiry into their conduct and character by the Magistrate."†

10. The great difficulty indeed regarding the Village Police, which has been commented upon by all who have directed their attention to the subject since the beginning of the century, is that they are inadequately and uncertainly paid. They are kept in a permanent state of starvation, and though in former days Magistrates battled for them with unwilling Zemindars and Villagers, and were encouraged by Government to do so, it has been discovered in later times that this is all against the law; and Magistrates, contrary to the doctrine of earlier times, have been actually prohibited from

* I find this the number of Thannahs in the Regulation Provinces in the Appendix to the Circular Orders of the Superintendent of Police printed in 1854.

† Mr. Bayley's Report to Government of 1812.

interfering in favour of village watchmen, it being ruled that this is altogether an affair of the people themselves, who may pay watchmen or not just as they think fit. Village watchmen are now declared to have no legal right to remuneration for service, and (the help of the Magistrate being withdrawn) they have no power to enforce their rights even if they had any rights to enforce. Hence they are all thieves or robbers, or leagued with thieves and robbers, insomuch that when any one is robbed in a village, it is most probable that the first person suspected will be the village watchman.

11. Mr. Millett made a careful inquiry into the law on this subject in 1842, and came to the conclusion that it was optional with the Zemindars and Villagers to maintain the Village Police or not. I quote in the margin* a part of his Report to the Bengal Government on this subject.

12. Since that date, although very great advantage has been taken by the Zemindars and others of the law as thus declared, to get rid of Chowkeydars, and often to appropriate their old established service lands, a slight check has been given to the progress of this deterioration by a decision of the Sudder Court in April, 1854, whereby it was decided that an obligation lay upon a Zemindar to appoint to a vacant Chowkeydarship. It was however not decided, and on the contrary, the Judges were divided on the point, whether a Magistrate could enforce this obligation by fine, without which the obligation may be little more than nominal, and if so, the condition of the Chowkeydar is likely to remain as starved and helpless as ever. Yet, miserably impaired as the institution of the Village Police has become, it is still true that no Police can be effective without their help, and that, as stated in the Minute of Lord Hastings, dated 2nd October, 1815, "It is from the Chowkeydars that all information of the character of individuals, of the haunts and intentions of robbers, and of everything necessary to forward the objects of Police, must ordinarily be obtained; they are the watch and patrol to which the community looks for its immediate protection, and on the occurrence of a crime the Darogah's only mode of proceeding is to collect the watchmen of all neighbouring villages, and to question them as to all the circumstances, with a view to get from them that information which they only can afford."

13. The village Chowkeydars are in short the foundation of all possible Police in this country, and upon their renovation, improvement, and stability depends the ultimate success of all our measures for the benefit of the country in the prevention, detection, and punishment of crime. To what a state of corruption, however, this most important branch of the Police system

* It appears from the 12th Article of the Regulations of the 7th December, 1792, and parts of the correspondence above extracted, that it was not the intention of the Government to interfere with the establishments of the common Village Police, further than by registration, and by placing them under the control of the Darogahs, to make them more efficient auxiliaries to the Government Police.

"That Article was embodied in the Code as Section XIII., Regulation XXII. of 1793, and the registration of the Village Police, and in addition to them, of all watchmen or guards employed by individuals, was enforced by the penal provisions of Section XXI., Regulation XII. of 1807

"Section XIII., Regulation XXII. of 1793, was rescinded by Section II., Regulation XX. of 1847, but re-enacted in substance and extended in Section XXI. of the same Regulation. Although the Landholders and other persons to whom the right of nomination to vacancies in the village watch belong, are required to transmit the names of the persons they may appoint to the Police Darogahs, the law does not empower the Magistrates to compel such nomination, or interfere respecting the allowances whether in land or money of the village Chowkeydars actually employed, and the Magistrates have been directed" (by order of the Nizamut Adawlut, 26th August, 1831) "to confine their interference with the Chowkeydars paid by the people, to those cases in which they are authorised to interfere by the existing Regulation." And Mr. Millett, in another part of the same report, intimates his opinion, "that it is at the option of the Zemindars and the cultivators to maintain or discharge the village Chowkeydars."

had fallen, was strongly illustrated by the late Mr. Bethune, in his Minute of the 27th May, 1851, of which the following is an extract:—

"The evidence I have seen of this is now thirteen years old, but the complaints recently made of outrageous dacoities and acts of violence point rather to a deterioration than to an improvement of the practical working of the system since that time. I took the following striking comparison from Speede's Criminal Statistics of Bengal, in which some of the results obtained by the Police Commissioners in 1837, have been digested and arranged in a Tabular Form. The returns made to Government for the years 1833-4-5-6, show the average number of persons annually convicted for crimes and offences* *of all kinds* in those years to be 31,843, and taking the population of the districts to which these returns apply to have been 38,717,874, as estimated in the Magistrates' returns, the proportion is about 1 convict to 1,219 persons.

"The Commissioners of 1837 obtained also a Return of Chowkeydars dismissed from the Police force during the years 1835-6-7, with the causes of dismissal.† From this Return, it appears that the whole number of Chowkeydars (with the exception of six Districts from which accounts had not been received when the Table was compiled) was 1,30,365, and therefore, *were they no worse than the rest of the population*, the number of persons among them guilty of *every kind of offence known to the calendar*, at the rate of 1 in 1,219, would be under 107 annually, or 321 in the three years included in the Return. What were the facts? The whole number of Cowkeydars dismissed for misbehaviour in those three years, instead of 321, is 1,130.

Of whom for Murder and Thuggee	19
Burglary	39
Robbery and Theft	357
	415

that is to say:—

"Nearly one-fourth more, in proportion to their number, *for these heinous crimes*, than were convicted in all the Lower Provinces of Bengal *for all offences of every kind.*

"The full complement of 1,130 is made up as follows:—

Class 1st.		
Murder and Thuggee	19	
Burglary	29	
Robbery and Theft	357	
		415
Class 2nd		
Embezzlement or Forgery	42	
Perjury, False Evidence, or False Complaint	55	
Bribery, Extortion, or Oppression	28	
Affrays, Assaults, or Wounding	96	
Accessories to Crime	70	
Concealing Crimes or Aiding Escapes	178	
		469
Class 3rd.		
Bad character or suspected of Crime		246
		1,130

* Speede's Criminal Statistics, page 149; do., page 174.
† Speede's Appendix, page 7.

"I have not included in this list—

31 dismissed for contumacy.
33 . . . intoxication.
7 . . . being asleep on duty.
—
71

meaning only to select those offences, which it is the direct object of a Police force to prevent and discover."

It seems to me that this statement renders it superfluous to enumerate in detail the expressions of dissatisfaction, however strongly worded, of those who understand the working of the system. The whole is summed up by the Commissioners in the following terms:

"49. The most urgent necessity exists for a thorough revision throughout the country. The establishment (of village watchmen) is described not only as utterly useless for Police purposes, but as a curse instead of a blessing to the community. *It is even a question whether an order issued throughout the country to apprehend and confine them would not do more to put a stop to theft and robbery than any other measure that could be adopted.*"

14. Various plans have been proposed for amending this state of things, and a good deal of paper has been covered with written discussions regarding them, but nothing has ever been done; so that many persons have come to think it a thing impossible to do any good in that direction, and have ceased from all effort accordingly.

15. Not to disinter any more ancient projects of this kind, I will now go no further back than the last, which was a plan submitted to the old Legislative Council of India by the Marquis of Dalhousie, as Governor of Bengal, on the 11th July, 1853, and which was intended to give to the Government of Bengal the power of extending the system of Regulation XXII. 1816, now applicable only to towns in which a covenanted Magistrate is stationed, to all parts of the country at discretion. This, however, was objected to by the Hon'ble Mr. Peacock, on very valid grounds, as set forth in his Minute of the 6th March, 1854, in which it was shown conclusively that the length to which the proposed law would go would involve a violation of the engagement entered into by Government at the time of the Permanent Settlement. Accordingly the Bill of Lord Dalhousie was modified, so as to exclude the rural Police, and made to apply only to populous Towns, Stations, and Bazaars, and in that shape is at this moment pending before the Legislative Council.* Regarding rural Police, Mr. Peacock, while showing very strong

* As the establishment of this Town Police is a matter of great importance, and the method of taxing the inhabitants of towns for the purpose requires the most careful consideration, I desire to quote in this place the remarks I have addressed to the Legislative Council on the subject:—

"If the existing system be preserved, the Lieutenant-Governor would advise that the maximum limit of Rupees 2 be abolished. He has found this very generally complained of as unjustly favouring the rich, and causing obvious and invidious inequality of taxation.

"The plan, however, which, in the Lieutenant-Governor's deliberate judgment, is the most suited to the people, and would nowhere be unpopular, would be a system of town duties, levied and managed by a head Punchayet and a local collector under the control and direction of the Magistrate. This is a mode of taxation which the natives are quite accustomed to in their hauts and markets, which they accordingly prefer to any direct taxation, and under which they might gradually be induced to contribute more largely than would be required for mere watching, so as, without incurring unpopularity, to allow of the introduction of other municipal improvements into the principal towns.

"The present town Chowkeydaree system, with its always ill-chosen, reluctant, and jobbing Punchayets, its favouritism and inequality, its inquisitorialness, its direct monthly calls for cash, its summonses, its notices, and its harassing concomitants of distress and sale, is, the Lieutenant-Governor is thoroughly persuaded, one of the most unpopular institutions we ever forced upon the people, and of this, which is well known to the

reasons why it would be in his judgment impolitic to levy, as proposed by Lord Dalhousie's Bill, a Rent Tax of 5 per cent. for the support of that establishment, added—"I would not exempt the owners or occupiers of land from any liability to contribute to the support of village watchmen which may attach to them according to the custom and usage which has prevailed in each village. The custom to maintain watchmen seems to have existed from the earliest times in every village. I cannot think that it could ever have been intended that the maintenance of that class of officers should fall into disuse, or be considered as merely optional with those who have always contributed to their support. Where lands have been appropriated to their support, they should continue to be so. Where the watchmen have been paid by the contributions from the village community, either in money or grain, such contributions should be considered obligatory. I find that the continuance of the village watchmen is contemplated by the Regulations passed at the time of the Permanent Settlement."

16. Convinced by the reasoning of Mr. Peacock, Lord Dalhousie assented to the proposed modification of his Bill, by which the rural Police was excluded from its operation. But he suggested that the principle involved in the observation of Mr. Peacock regarding the reasonable liability of owners and occupiers of land to contribute to the rural Police according to established usage, might, if fully worked out, be rendered effectual to the end he had in view, the supplying gradually of the great and crying want of these Lower Provinces, to wit, an effective rural Police.* With this view he suggested that a local investigation should be made, in every village, throughout every zillah, of the liabilities to which the village is subject in respect of the maintenance of Village Police, in order to found thereon a legislative measure for the improvement of that institution.

17. That investigation has now been completed.

18. *Administration of Criminal Justice.*—I am satisfied, however, that it will be vain to improve the agency for the detection and apprehension of criminals, unless we improve also the agency for trying them.

Police reform, in India at least, is a word of large signification, and extends to our criminal judicatories as well as to the Magistracy and the Constabulary organisation. At present our criminal judicatories stand in need of much amendment, and unfortunately the method of amending them is a question which admits of much diversity of opinion.

19. They certainly do not command the confidence of the people.

20. That this is the case may, I think, be inferred from many parts of Mr. Dampier's elaborate reports. I have myself made much personal inquiry into this matter during my tours, which have carried me over nearly the whole of the Regulation Districts, and have brought me into communication with all sorts and conditions of men, official and non-official. Whether right or wrong, the general native opinion is certainly that the administration of criminal justice is little better than a lottery, in which, however, the best chances are with the criminals; and I think this also is very much the opinion of the European Mofussil community.

21. No complaint is more common among Magistrates and Police Officers of every grade than that of the disinclination of the people to assist in the apprehension and conviction of criminals. From one end of Bengal to the

Lieutenant-Governor from extensive personal inquiry and observation, the papers now submitted afford good proof. To extend this very unpopular system will be very distasteful to the people, but since there ought to be a Police in our large Towns, and this must be paid by means of a taxation of some kind, the Lieutenant-Governor would desire to record his conviction that the safest and best way of doing this (at all events in the Lower Provinces of Bengal), and the way most acceptable, or at any rate least unacceptable, to the people, will be by re-introducing a system of town duties in a form modified to suit the occasion."

* Lord Dalhousie's Minute, 14th April, 1854.

other the earnest desire and aim of those who have suffered from Thieves or Dacoits, is to keep the matter secret from the Police, or, failing that, so to manage as to make the trial a nullity before the courts. Something of this is due perhaps to the natural apathy of the people, though it cannot fail to be observed on the other hand that where they have any object to gain, the same people show no apathy or unreadiness, but remarkable energy and perseverance, in civil and criminal prosecutions. More no doubt is due to the corruption and extortion of the Police, which causes it to be popularly said that Dacoity is bad enough, but the subsequent Police inquiry very much worse. But after allowing for both these causes, no one, conversant with the people, can have failed to remark how much of their strong unwillingness to prosecute is owing to the deep sense which pervades the public mind of the utter uncertainty of the proceedings of our courts, and the exceeding chances of escape which our system allows to criminals; often have I heard natives express, on this point, their inability to understand the principles on which the courts are so constituted or so conducted, as to make it appear in their eyes as if the object were rather to favour the acquittal then to insure the conviction and punishment of offenders, and often have I been assured by them that their anxious desire to avoid appearing as prosecutors arose in a great measure from their belief that prosecution was very likely to end in acquittal, even, as they imagined, in the teeth of the best evidence, while the acquittal of a revengeful and unscrupulous ruffian was known by experience to have repeatedly ended in the most unhappy consequences to his ill-advised and imprudent prosecutor.

22. That this very general opinion is not ill-founded may, I think, be proved from our own records.

23. Appended to this minute, is a note and certain statistical returns prepared by Mr. Secretary Buckland, from which it may be gathered that for fourteen burglaries committed, only one burglar is punished, and that even in thefts, which are matters of easier detection and punishment, the average proportion of convictions is only of three persons to eight offences.

24. These two descriptions of offences are offences punishable by Magistrates. In the more heinous cases tried by the Sessions Judges, it will be seen from one of the Statements annexed to Mr. Buckland's note, that an average of 1,237 persons were annually acquitted to 1,935 convicted, being a ratio of 2 to 3. This is the more remarkable, because, in the practice of our courts, every case sent by a Magistrate before a Sessions Judge is carefully heard by the Magistrate, on both sides, as if the Magistrate had himself to pass sentence, every Magistrate being empowered by Law, and almost bound by practice, to send for and examine witnesses to the defence as well as for the prosecution, and strictly enjoined to send no case to the Sessions regarding which he does not see reason to believe that a conviction will follow. And the Magistrates are unfailingly censured if they commit on what the Sessions Judge and the Sudder Court may think insufficient, *i.e.*, not perfectly sufficient, grounds for committal, *i.e.*, for conviction. That under such a system a proportion of 2 to 3 committed prisoners should be acquitted at the Sessions, nearly every one of whom must have been considered by the Magistrate guilty on the evidence, is of itself a very startling fact, and one which cannot but leave a painful impression of the working of our institutions.

25. A Sessions Judge is obliged to refer for the orders of the Sudder Court the cases of all criminals regarding whose guilt he may differ in opinion with his Mahomedan Assessor or Law Officer, and also many classes of cases requiring in his opinion a higher punishment than imprisonment for 7 years. It appears from Mr. Buckland's Statements that the average annual result of such references is that no less than 148 persons are acquitted to 332 convicted, and this, it will be remembered, is in cases in which two

Judicial Officers* *must*, by the nature of the case, have found the prisoner guilty on the evidence. So that the solemn judicial conclusions of tribunals in various parts of the country, in each of which two minds have deliberately concurred, are found, or supposed to be, absolutely erroneous by the higher Court, in the proportion of 148 to 332.

26. From any sentence passed by a Magistrate beyond a fine of Rupees 50 or one month's imprisonment, there may be an appeal to the Sessions Judge, and from every sentence passed by a Sessions Judge there may be an appeal to the Sudder Court. This license is largely taken advantage of, so that a great number of cases undergo two complete trials. And indeed, in order to encourage appeal, and give appellants every possible advantage, and no chance of disadvantage, it is provided† that Appeal Courts may remit or mitigate to any extent, but must on no account enhance punishment. I have not at present any statement of the consequences of this system as regards sentences by Magistrates, though I am well aware that it leads to a considerable abatement of the Magistrates' convictions. As regards appeals from Sessions Judges to the Sudder, the case is thus stated by Mr. Buckland. From 1843 to 1852 inclusive, the number of petitions of appeal averaged (annually) 248, the sentences being modified or reversed in 85 cases and upheld in 152 cases As the average number of prisoners in each case appears to be about 2½, the annual average of prisoners convicted at the Sessions (amounting to 1,935,) suffers a reduction of 200 by the result of the appeal to the Sudder. Of the total 4,000 persons annually committed to the Sessions for heinous crimes, it thus appears that the conviction of 1,735 takes place in the Sessions effectually, and of 332 in the referred trials to the Sudder; so that of the whole number committed, very nearly one-half is eventually acquitted.

27. That a very small proportion of heinous offenders are ever brought to trial, is matter of notoriety. It now appears that half of those brought to trial are sure to be acquitted. Is it to be expected, then, that the people should have confidence in our system, or that they should show any desire to assist the Police, knowing as they do from experience the miserable results to be obtained?

28. I must say that this appears to me the weakest point of our whole system, and that which most loudly calls for an effectual remedy. No doubt the badness of the Police and the inefficiency of the tribunals act and re-act on each other, and both are concerned in bringing about the deplorable existing consequences. But until the tribunals are reformed, I can see no use in reforming the Police, and I think it will be money thrown away to attempt the latter unless we are determined vigorously to insist on the former. We have been hitherto debating about both for many years without much practical effect, and in the meantime, to take only one crime, and only the seven Districts round about Government House, we have seen dacoities increase from 82 in 1841, to 524 in 1851! It is true that under a special agency this has since been reduced to 111 in 1855. But the operations of this agency have shown more than anything else the utter inability of our ordinary institutions to cope with the enormous social evil that is ever rising up in defiance before it.

29. *Inexperience of Magistrates.*—Even if our tribunals were all we could wish, and if our Police were fully reformed, what would it avail us so long as our Superintending Magistracy was for the most part in the hands of inexperienced and therefore unqualified young men. Yet this has not only been long the notorious fact, but peculiar and accidental circumstances, partly temporary and partly arising out of the constitution of the Civil Service, have

* *i. e.* The Magistrate and the Sessions Judge, or the Magistrate and the Mahomedan Law Officer.

† Act XXXI. of 1841.

at this moment made the inexperienced condition of the Magistracy more observable than it has ever been before, while it seems certain that the evil during several succeeding years is likely very seriously to increase. I have appended to this paper a note by Mr. Grey on this very subject, together with a Tabular Statement, from which it will appear that whereas in 1850 the average standing of Magistrates was 9 years and 8 months, it had sunk in 1854 to 8 years and 5 months, and is now, in 1856, so low as 6 years and 10 months. "In 1850," says Mr. Grey, "there were only two Magistrates below the standing of 7 years. Now there are 15 such. The youngest Officer officiating as a Magistrate, in 1850, was of 5 years' standing. The youngest Officer now officiating as Magistrate *is of less than three years' standing.*" Those who are conversant with the working of our system are aware that this is (under present rules) an evil that cannot be resisted; while it exists, although certain of our young Magistrates often display efficiency and ability beyond their years, yet on the whole our Magistracy is losing credit and character, and our administration is growing perceptibly weaker, and yet I grieve to be obliged to affirm that the evil will infallibly increase within the next three years unless an early remedy be applied. Does anybody imagine that while this lasts our Bengal Police can be reformed?

30. *Five Measures Proposed.*—It appears to me then that in order to an effectual improvement of the Police in the Lower Provinces, the following principal measures are indispensably necessary :—

(1.) The improvement of the character and position of the village Chowkeydars or watchmen.

(2.) Adequate salaries, and, I may add, fair prospects of advancement to the Stipendiary Police.

(3.) The appointment of more experienced Officers as Covenanted Zillah Magistrates.

(4.) A considerable increase in the number of the Uncovenanted or Deputy Magistrates.

(5.) An improvement in our Criminal Courts of Justice.

31. *Improvement of Chowkeydars.*—Regarding the first of these measures, I have said that the inquiry suggested by Lord Dalhousie into the actual condition of the Village Police has been completed. By a Circular, dated 13th November, 1854, the several Zillah Magistrates were directed to adopt immediate measures for the collection of full and accurate information regarding the position of the village Chowkeydars, showing the number that are regularly kept up, by whom they are appointed, by whom paid, and the amount and nature of their receipts The Magistrates were told to call for this information in the first instance through the Thannah Police, and subsequently to test the accuracy of the information furnished to them by making inquiries in person in different parts of each District, as well as by one or two trustworthy Officers specially deputed for that purpose. The results were to be submitted to Government in a prescribed Tabular Form, and in the native language, as originally prepared.

32. The Tabular Statement so supplied, have been translated into English in the Secretary's Office. They appear for the most part to have been prepared with great care and accuracy, and they furnish an important body of information.

33. The following is an abstract of the results of this inquiry :—

PATNA DIVISION. *Chumparun District.*—Villages, 3,578; houses, 1,81,881; chowkeydars, 3,809, or 1 to 48 houses. Appointed by gomashtahs or head villagers, and paid annually by grain. Some had from 5 cottahs to 20 bigahs of land each.

Sarun District.—Villages, 4,347; houses, 2,10,425; chowkeydars, 5,926, or 1 to 36 houses. Appointed by zemindars; paid, by cash, from 4 annas to 36 rupees, a few having clothes given them;

by grain, from 2 to 24 maunds; by land, from 4 cottahs to 12 bigahs.

Patna District.—Villages, 3,908; houses, 1,32,122; chowkeydars, 4,380, or 1 to 30 houses. Appointed by zemindars and villagers, confirmed by magistrate; paid, by cash, from 8 annas to 36 rupees each; by grain, from 2 to 21 maunds each; by land, from 4 cottahs to 12 bigahs.

Shahabad District.—Villages, 4,948; houses, 2,19,949; chowkeydars, 6,283, or 1 to 35 houses. Appointed by zemindars or head villagers, or both; paid, by cash, 4 annas to 36; grain, 20 sun to 30 maunds; land, 10 cottahs to 24 bigahs each.

Behar District.—Villages, 4,343; houses, 1,42,229; chowkeydars, 4,582, or 1 to 31 houses. Appointed by the landholders, omlah, and the villagers; paid, by cash, 12 annas to 36 rupees; grain, 2 to 25 maunds; land, 1 bigah to 5 bigahs each.

Total in Patna Division.—Villages, 21,124; houses, 8,86,606; chowkeydars, 24,980.

BHAUGULPORE DIVISION. *Tirhoot District.*—Villages, 5,473; houses, 3,33,485; chowkeydars, 7,895, or 1 to 42 houses. Appointed by zemindars, and some by villagers; paid annually, by cash, 1 rupee 4 annas to 45 rupees; or land, 1 cottah to 2 bigahs each, and a few receive a little grain.

Purneah District.—Villages, 5,267; houses, 2,45,181; chowkeydars, 7,481, or 1 to 31 houses. Appointed by landholders or villagers; paid, cash, 12 annas to 36 rupees each, some receive a little grain.

Monghyr District.—Villages, 2,642; houses, 1,32,514; chowkeydars, 3,086, or 1 to 43 houses. Appointed by the zemindars; paid, cash, 1 rupee 2 annas to 36 rupees; land, 8 cottahs to 15 bigahs each.

Bhaugulpore District.—Villages, 3,740; houses, 1,71,482; chowkeydars, 3,687, or 1 to 47 houses. Appointed by zemindars; paid, cash, from 8 annas to 57 rupees; land, from 1 bigah to 20 bigahs each.

Total in Bhaugulpore Division.—Villages, 17,122; houses, 8,82,662; chowkeydars, 22,509.

RAJSHAHYE DIVISION. *Maldah District.*—Villages, 1,950; houses, 91,817; chowkeydars, 1,568, or 1 to 58. Appointed by the head villagers; paid annually, cash, 1 to 48 rupees each, some have grain.

Dinapore District.—Villages, 8,517; houses, 2,05,051; chowkeydars, 5,592, or 1 to 37 houses. Appointed by zemindars or head villagers; paid, cash, from 4 annas to 42 rupees each.

Rungpore District.—Villages, 3,383; houses, 2,17,471; chowkeydars, 5,077, or 1 to 43 houses. Appointed some by headmen, generally by zemindar's omlah; confirmed by the magistrate.

Bograh District.—Villages, 4,964; houses, 1,23,982; chowkeydars, 3,100, or 1 to 40 houses. Appointed by head villagers, a few by the zemindars; paid, cash, from 1 to 36 rupees each.

Pubnah District.—Villages, 3,526; houses, 1,81,811; chowkeydars, 3,611, or 1 to 50 houses. Appointed by headmen; paid, cash, from 3 to 52 rupees each, a little grain given to some.

Rajshahye District.—Villages, 3,416; houses, 1,41,918; chowkeydars, 3,839, or 1 to 37 houses. Appointed by headmen; paid, cash, 6 to 48 rupees each, one man has 15 bigahs of chakran.

Total in Rajshahye Division.—Villages, 25,756; houses, 9,62,045; chowkeydars, 22,787.

DACCA DIVISION. *Mymensing District.*—Villages, 13,162; houses, 3,06,133; chowkeydars, 4,080, or 1 to 75 houses. Appointed by head villagers or police; paid annually, cash, from 3 to 54 rupees each.

Sylhet District.—Villages, 6,937; houses, 2,24,336; chowkeydars, 3,259, or 1 to 69 houses. Appointed by landholders and villagers; paid, cash, 1 to 30 rupees.

Dacca District.—Villagers, 3,163; houses, 2,32,023; chowkeydars, 4,026, or 1 to 58 houses. Appointed by head villagers; paid 6 to 36 rupees each, and a few are said to be paid *monthly* from 1 to 3 rupees each.

Backergunge District.—Villages, 2,357; houses, 1,78,104; chowkeydars, 3,051, or 1 to 58 houses. Appointed by landholders; paid, cash, from 7 to 42 rupees each.

Furreedpore District.—Villages, 1,987; houses, 1,25,972; chowkeydars, 1,773, or 1 to 72 houses. Appointed by headmen; paid, cash, 1 to 52 rupees each; some have grain.

Total in Dacca Division.—Villages, 27,606; houses, 10,68,618; chowkeydars, 16,189.

CHITTAGONG DIVISION. *Tipperah District.*—Villages, 5,884; houses, 2,37,733; chowkeydars, 2,768, or 1 to 86 houses. Appointed by headmen; paid annually, cash, from 2 rupees 8 annas 9 pie, to 57 rupees 8 annas each.

Noacolly District.—Villages, 977; houses, 90,833; chowkeydars, 1,867, or 1 to 49 houses. Appointed by headmen and police; paid, cash; each receives 12 annas per house, monthly.

Chittagong District.—Villages, 944; houses, 1,79,763; chowkeydars, 2,431, or 1 to 74 houses. Appointed by head villagers; paid annually, cash, from 6 to 30 rupees (some get grain too), and a few monthly, at 2 rupees 8 annas each.

Total in Chittagong Division.—Villages, 7,805, houses, 5,08,329; chowkeydars, 7,066.

CUTTACK DIVISION. *Pooree District.*—Villages, 4,584; houses, 1,10,814; chowkeydars; 2,822, or 1 to 39. Appointed by gomastahs and headmen; paid annually, by cash, from 1 to 48 rupees; land, 1 bigah to 65 bigahs each.

Cuttack District.—Villages, 6,630; houses, 2,13,207, chowkeydars, 5,072, or 1 to 42 houses. Appointed by zemindars, confirmed by the magistrate; paid, cash, 1 to 55 rupees; land, from 1 bigah to 40 bigahs each.

Balasore District.—Villages, 4,317; houses, 96,457; chowkeydars, 1,978, or 1 to 49 houses. Appointed by the zemindars; paid, cash, 4 annas to 25 rupees; land, 1 bigah to 25 bigahs each.

Total in Cuttack Division.—Villages, 15,531; houses, 4,20,478.

BURDWAN DIVISION. *Midnapore District.*—Villages, 11,198; houses, 2,95,145; chowkeydars, 9,123, or 1 to 32 houses. Appointed by headmen or the magistrate; paid annually, cash, 2 to 61 rupees; land, from 4 bigahs to 143 each.

Howrah District.—Villages, 1,412; houses, 98,756; chowkeydars, 1,465, or 1 to 67. Appointed by the zemindars; paid, cash, from

19 rupees 4 annas to 39 rupees 12 annas, with some grain each.

Hooghly District.—Villages, 3,168; houses, 2,80,493; chowkeydars, 5,194, or 1 to 54 houses. Appointed by the zemindar and magistrate; paid, cash, 3 to 60 rupees; land, 1 bigah to 36 bigahs.

Burdwan District.—Villages, 2,873; houses, 2,13,036; chowkeydars, 8,848, or 1 to 24 houses. Appointed by zemindar and magistrate; paid, cash, from 12 annas to 72 rupees; some had land.

Beerbhoom District.—Villages, 6,928; houses, 1,88,182; chowkeydars, 10,850, or 1 to 17 houses. Appointed by zemindar and magistrate, and some by sirdar ghâtwâls; paid, cash, from 12 annas to 136 rupees each; or, land, from 3 cottahs to 228 bigahs each, or land and grain, producing an estimated income from 25 to 42 rupees each. The chowkeydars and ghâtwâls, who in Beerbhoom hold of the zemindar, but in Bancoorah of the government, should have been distinguished.

Bancoorah District.—Villages, 2,879; houses, 1,25,618; chowkeydars, 3,934, or 1 to 32 houses. Appointed by zemindars or villagers; confirmed by the magistrate; paid from 8 annas to 71 rupees, and also in kind.

Same District.—Ghats, 1,127; houses, 28,389; ghâtwâls, 4,325, or 1 to 7 ghats. Appointed by the magistrate; paid by land held of government, under engagements with the old Rajah of Bishenpore, at from 2½ bigahs to 4,152 bigahs per man.

Total in Burdwan Division.—Villages, 29,585; houses, 12,29,619; chowkeydars, 43,739.

NUDDEA DIVISION. 24-*Pergunnahs District.*—Villages, 2,605; houses, 1,53,905; chowkeydars, 2,788, or 1 to 55 houses. Appointed by headmen; paid annually, cash, from 3 to 220 rupees 11 annas, also in kind.

Nuddea District.—Villages, 3,054; houses, 2,13,576; chowkeydars, 4,134, or 1 to 52 houses. Appointed by headmen; paid, cash, from 1 rupee 8 annas to 60 rupees, grain added in some parts.

Jessore District.—Villages, 4,126; houses, 2,16,256; chowkeydars, 4,189, or 1 to 52 houses. Appointed by headmen; paid, cash, 1 rupee 8 annas to 48 rupees, grain added in some parts.

Moorshedabad District.—Villages, 3,014; houses, 1,89,871; chowkeydars, 4,467, or 1 to 43 houses. Appointed by zemindars or villagers, or both; paid, cash, from 1 to 48 rupees each, and must have some land or grain added.

Baraset District.—Villages, 1,981; houses, 96,901; chowkeydars, 2,157, or 1 to 45 houses. Appointed by headmen; paid, cash, from 11 rupees to 60 rupees each.

Total in Nuddea Division.—Villages, 14,780; houses, 8,70,509; chowkeydars, 17,735.

Grand Total.—Villages, 1,59,309; houses, 68,28,866; chowkeydars, 1,64,877.

34. It may be observed, as a general result of the inquiry, that, with few exceptions, the Zemindar or Zemindar's Agents are found to nominate the Chowkeydars, and this most commonly in the Bengal Zillahs. In these latter Zillahs though the Zemindars who nominate the Chowkeydars seem to be primarily answerable for the payment of their wages, yet the ultimate payment falls upon the village Ryots. In the Behar Zillahs this seems to be not so generally the case, the "Malik" or Zemindar more usually in those Zillahs having to incur the expense of paying the Chowkeydars, who, however, in Behar, as elsewhere, often receive a part of their income in the shape of pre-

sents from the villagers in kind. I am aware also that in some instances in the Behar Zillahs the liability to pay Chowkeydar's wages is disputed between the Zemindars and the Ryots. Where these disputes have been carried before the Magistrate, I have found the liability of the Zemindar usually enforced, though, as I have thought, with doubtful justice.

35. The number of houses to each Chowkeydar's beat is seen to vary considerably—from 86, the largest number, which occurs in Tipperah, to 24 in Burdwan.*

36. The general average for the whole of the Regulation Districts of the Lower Provinces is shown to be one Chowkeydar to 41 houses. This average is however affected by the introduction of Ghâtwâls into the lists. The traditionally proper proportion is believed to be one Chowkeydar to 50 houses.

37. The total number of villages by this return is 1,59,306 and of Chowkeydars 1,64,877, being 1,034 Chowkeydars to each village.

38. The average receipts of each Chowkeydar in land and wages, will be probably under-stated at Rupees 2 a month. Assuming, however, Rupees 2 a month as wages, whether in money, land, or kind, and Rupee 1 a month as customary presents, a very high estimate, we have a total for the annual receipts of Rupees 59,35,572; and calculating at 5 for each house in these returns, the population would be 3,41,44,330,† upon whom the above amount of taxation would fall at the rate of 2½ pie per head per annum, which is certainly a very light taxation, even at the high rate of receipts above assumed.

39. *A Law Suggested.*—What is, however, necessary to secure the old institution of a village watch from falling into utter desuetude, and for keeping it in a state of vigour sufficient for our present purposes, but doubtless to be further improved and reformed hereafter, is a law which shall enable a Magistrate, on finding a village without a Chowkeydar, or a Chowkeydar without wages, to make a summary inquiry, and, according to the nature of the case, either to cause the nominàtion of a fit Chowkeydar by the person or persons to whom the nomination may be proved by custom and usage to belong, or to cause payment of his wages at the rate found customary by the person or persons on whom the customary liability to pay such wages may be found to fall. Any very precise provisions would, I humbly think, be out of place at present. The people will not, I venture to say, feel it as any hardship that the Magistrate should be empowered to make such inquiries, and to exercise such powers as I propose; on the contrary, they will assent to them as in accordance with old customs, and as enforcing an acknowledged obligation, for the inquisition and the powers are such as were formerly very generally in use, and are even now employed by zealous Magistrates in districts where the people are not yet fully aware of the actual law on the subject. It will only be if any minute system of tax gathering on account of the village watch should be attempted that the law will be found to create any disaffection or dissatisfaction. At all events, I would desire to try the effect of the simpler method before resorting to any more complicated process. It may be safely, I think, reckoned upon, that, as soon as the law shall declare that the Magistrate has the power which in former years he always used, and which has only lately been brought into question, the necessity for putting the law into force will very rarely arise.

40. It has been objected by some very competent advisers on such subjects, that even when all this shall have been done, we shall be as far as ever from our object; that the village Chowkeydars at the best are an untrustworthy, unorganised rabble, and that no real improvement will be effected unless we

* There are lower numbers in Beerbhoom and Bancoorah. But this arises from the Ghâtâwls having been admitted into the lists, who are not Village Chowkeydars, but guards of jungle passes.

† The usual loose estimate of the population of the Regulation Districts subject to the Government of Bengal, has been 36 millions.

get rid of them altogether, and organise a rural Police according to the newest forms of occidental civilisation. And it is common with those who advocate this method of reform, to point to the 34 or 36 millions of the population, and to urge how easily a sum might be raised from them, not greater than they now pay for their imperfect village watchmen, which, in the hands of a skilful organiser, might be made to provide for the establishment in each Zillah of a well-paid, dressed, and disciplined force, inferior in numbers to the present rural Police, but far superior in trustworthiness and efficiency. To some such plan as this, I have myself leaned in earlier days; nor do I doubt either that, if it were practicable, it would provide a vastly improved rural Police, or that we may fairly look forwards to such an improvement hereafter, though as yet at a great distance. I am satisfied, however, that to press for such a measure now would be impolitic and unwise, and that we might lose all in our anxiety to attain a desirable end sooner than can be reasonably expected. We must do our utmost to carry the people with us in our Police reforms; at present they will readily admit old established obligations to maintain village watchmen in a certain customary proportion to the size of each village, and to pay them after a certain usage, which differs somewhat in different villages, but has long been accommodated to old habits and customs in all. They will not, however, regard with favour a distinct and precise taxation for a new Police, the application of which they will doubt, and the object of which they will be very likely to misunderstand; and, unfortunately, our knowledge of the people and our intercourse with them, through distantly placed, often inexperienced, and but too frequently changed, Mofussil Magistrates, is not sufficiently intimate and cordial to allow as yet of our acquiring their confidence, and thereby their co-operation, in plans for the improvement of their old institution. Hereafter, when we shall have placed trustworthy Magistrates in adequate numbers, and in the centre of manageable jurisdictions, I do not doubt that we shall be able gradually to influence the people more effectually than we can now pretend to do, and so to carry them with us as to obtain their intelligent assent, and with it their hearty assistance to all our measures. We must, in short, obtain their confidence in our Magistracy and Police system before we can hope for their co-operation, and this cannot be expected under our present imperfect organisation.

41. *Better paid Police.*—With regard to the second of the measures above enumerated, *viz.*, the adequate payment of the stipendiary Police, I have already submitted a proposition to the Government of India, by which, at an expense of Rupees 3,38,609, a reasonable increase may be made to the salaries and expectations of the Mohurirs, Jemadars, and Burkundauzes, as to render their situations more valuable than at present, and leave them at all events without the plausible excuse for corruption which they may now plead.* In order, however, to complete this part of the subject, I would very strongly recommend that a few considerable prizes be held out to Darogahs, in the shape of increased salaries for particularly distinguished service. It is not always, and not in fact often the case, that a good Police Darogah is fitted to make a good Deputy Magistrate. Occasionally this method of rewarding distinguished service by a Police Darogah may be resorted to with success. But I have seen several very remarkable instances of failure, and on the whole I am much disposed to think that this method of promotion cannot be relied upon, as generally practicable. It will be better, therefore, to grant a few enhanced salaries of Rupees 150 and 200 to meritorious Darogahs; and this may be done without any great increase of expense. There are now 50 Darogahs on Rupees 100 per mensem, one hundred on Rupees 75, the remainder on

* It has been my object in all my propositions to study a fair economy. I am sensible that the amount of increase I have proposed for the Burkundauzes may by some be thought below the mark, and that a larger amount might have been suggested. I think that what I have proposed will be a great improvement, and I should wish it tried before the amount is increased.

Rupees 50. I would propose that, for special services rendered, it should be competent to the Government to reward as many as fifteen or twenty distinguished Darogahs by promotion to salaries of Rupees 150 each, and ten more for a like cause to 200 Rupees each per mensem. These special promotions might be accompanied by other marks of distinction, so as to render the example in each case more striking and effective. The additional cost of this would not be more than Rupees 42,000 per annum

42. I may mention, while on this part of the subject, that I have found in some parts of the country some of the Thannah jurisdictions of a very disproportionate size. This I believe to be more particularly the case in some of the Behar Zillahs. It will be necessary in such cases to make an increase in the number of Thannahs. But this I think will involve no expense worth mentioning in discussing a matter of this magnitude.

43. *More experienced Magistrates.*—The third measure on my list relates to the youth and inexperience of the Covenanted Magistrates. This is a very serious evil, and it is absolutely necessary to remedy it. It arises out of the numerical inadequacy of the covenanted service to supply the number of offices required by the existing system. It has been a matter of reproach to the service for many years, but it has very much increased of late, owing to the growing disproportion of men to offices It has, in a manner painfully perceptible to me in my visits to the different Districts, impaired the force, dignity, and efficiency of our administration in the interior, and in all cases in which the youth and inexperience of the officer is not, as it sometimes is, counterbalanced by unusual ability and force of character, it has brought the all-important authority of the Zillah Magistracy into marked slight and disregard, and sometimes into actual contempt. It is certain still more to increase under the present system, and no addition to the number of the service can remedy it for many years to come. The method in which each Zillah was manned from 1793 down to 1830, was thus. There was in each an Officer styled Judge and Magistrate, who was Zillah Judge in Civil causes and also Magistrate of Police. He was usually an Officer of upwards of 12 years' standing. There was a Collector, who, under the old system, had very little to do, and was usually upwards of 10 years' standing. There was a Register, who had generally arrived at from two or three to five or six years' standing, and there might be an Assistant of any standing below that of the Register. Under this system the Magistrate was the Officer most experienced and highest in rank in the District; and he was therefore looked up to with a degree of respect, the recollection of which, to those who, like myself, have known "the Mofussil" in those old days, suggests a painful contrast with the uninfluential and comparatively insignificant and unregarded position of the juvenile functionaries, many of whom I have found ineffectually presiding over the Zillah Magistracies in my recent tours. But the Magistrate of those days was encumbered by the weight of duty imposed upon him as the (to use the native phrase) "incarnation of justice," civil and criminal, over an unmanageable extent of country; and partly with a view to remedy this, Lord William Bentinck's Government took the office of Zillah Magistrate from the Judge, and gave it to the Collector, turning the Register, who had been a subordinate to the Civil Judge, into a subordinate to the Collector-Magistrate. Thus the Zillah Magistrate, though no longer the Officer of highest standing in the Zillah, was yet of sufficient standing, position, and experience to command respect; especially as at the same time the Government began to exercise a much greater degree of care than formerly in the selection of Officers for Collectorships. It happened, however, that about the same period an extraordinary activity was infused into the revenue administration in the Lower Provinces, which had been previously much neglected; and for some years after the Offices of Collector and Magistrate had been united, the chief attention of the Government was given to remedying the grave neglects and

deficiencies which had pervaded the revenue management of former times; so that the business of a Collector became for a considerable time very engrossing and onerous, and the duties of the Magistracy were comparatively disregarded. This, which experience has since shown to have been merely a temporary difficulty, was treated, subsequently to 1838, and in consequence of the Report of the Police Committee of that year, as if it had been permanent, and the Offices of Collector and Magistrate were separated and put into different hands. But the number of the Civil Service employed in the Lower Provinces not being increased, but rather, I think, diminished, the inevitable consequence was, that the lower paid of these two offices, that of the Magistrate, fell into the hands of functionaries who had previously been the subordinates of the Collector Magistrate; and young officers became thenceforth Magistrates at about the same standing at which they had formerly become Registers, or (subsequently) Deputy Collectors and Joint Magistrates. At present the reasons which caused this change no longer exist. The nature of the duties and responsibilities of Collectors' Offices requires that they should be held by Officers of a certain standing and experience; but the actual work of those offices has become, with a few exceptions, so notoriously light, that full leisure is left for the efficient performance of a Magistrate's business; and there is undoubtedly nothing in the nature of the two duties in these Provinces, where the collection of the Government Revenue is almost mechanical, and the interference of the Collector in the realisation of the Zemindar's rent from his tenants is purely judicial, to make them in the smallest degree incompatible To re-unite them, therefore, is now the mere dictate of prudence. It will at once place the Superintending Magistracy of each district in experienced hands, will economsie labour, will remove a standing reproach against the Government, and will restore to the Mofussil administration that strength and weight which the present youth and inexperience of our "boy Magistrates" have very sensibly and seriously impaired. This measure was proposed by Lord Dalhousie in 1854, and the reasons in its favour which then existed have been greatly enhanced by the occurrences of the past two years. I earnestly trust that the advantages which it offers, and which are enjoyed by all other parts of India, including all our recent acquisitions, will no longer be denied to Bengal, where, in fact, they are most urgently needed, and where the theoretical objections to the system, weak as I believe them to be everywhere else, have literally no kind of practical application.

By those who object to this, in my judgment, most useful and necessary measure, two methods have been proposed of remedying the great present evil, which nobody denies, of the youth and inexperience of the Magistrates. One is to make the Magistrates and Collectors, as it were, change places, to let the young and inexperienced Officers become, after their present brief training, Collectors on the present salaries of Magistrates, and to let them thence rise to the office of Magistrate, receiving in that office the salary now given to Collectors.

This would merely transfer a disease from one part of the administration to another part, and cure the defect in the Magistracy at the expense of the efficiency of the Revenue Department. The Revenue Department, not less than the Magistracy, requires maturity of standing and experience, and the Government, as well as the people, would suffer if the office of Collector were placed generally in young, inexpert, and unpractised hands.

44. Another plan is to keep the two offices separate, and to divide the aggregate salary of a Magistrate and a Collector equally between each office, so as to make the standing of a Magistrate equal to that of a Collector. Bearing in mind that this is to be done with a limited service which, for many years to come, cannot possibly receive an increase of experienced Officers, it will be obvious that this would not prevent as large a proportion as at present of Officers in independent charge (whether Magistrates or Collectors) from

being too young for the duties of their position. At present a young Assistant becomes first a dependent and subordinate "Joint Magistrate and Deputy Collector," and next a Magistrate of a Zillah. And if there are a certain number of Magistracies vacant, the junior Officers *must* be taken to fill them whether they be experienced or inexperienced, two years out of College, or five or ten. This evil will not be cured by taking from the salary of a Collector and adding to the salary of a Magistrate; on the contrary, it will be in some degree increased. What is required is, that the office of Magistrate shall be moved up higher in the scale, so as to be, as it were, out of the reach of the inexperienced junior until he shall have passed through further stages of probation.—And this can *only* be done (the numbers of the service being inadequate as well as limited) by joining the Magistracy to some existing higher office, such as the Collectorship, and letting the young Officer continue in the subordinate, though gradually improved and improving position, until time and experience shall have fitted him for an independent charge. Nor can it ever be too strongly insisted upon, that the nature of a Collector's duties in this part of India is such as to offer no reasonable objection to the junction, but rather in many important respects to render it politic and advantageous.

45. If this were done, the step to which the junior now rises from his first and insufficient training, instead of being as now that of a Magistrate in full charge of a District as large as three counties, would be, with perhaps the same or nearly the same pecuniary advantages, the more suitable position of a Deputy or subordinate to the experienced Collector Magistrate, and the Zillah Magistracies, instead of being in the hands of youngsters of three, and perhaps even less than three, years' standing, would not be attained to under a standing of at least ten years, and probably much more.*

46. *Increase of Deputy Magistrates.*—The next necessary measure is an increase to the Magistracy, and this can only be by an increase to the number of Uncovenanted Deputy Magistrates.

47. It is vain to talk of Police reform so long as the Police are under no closer superintendence than that of a Magistrate from 30 to 60 miles off (or even more), in a country where, owing to the nature of the climate and the want of means of communication, a distance of 10 miles is often more than equivalent to 50 miles in England. I will not here parade any statistical facts. Every one acquainted with the country knows how few and far between are our Magistrates in the interior, as compared with even the worst organised country in Europe, and every one admits that one of the first steps towards improvement must be to have Magistrates at such tolerably convenient distances, that each functionary shall not be at all events more than a few hours' journey from the most distant village in his jurisdiction. I think that the proper size of a Deputy Magistrate's jurisdiction was not unreasonably stated by an intelligent and experienced Native friend, whom I consulted on the subject, as "so much as the Magistrate could go to one end of in his morning ride, and the other end in his evening ride." This would probably comprise two or at most three Thannahs. The total number of Thannahs is 484. But of these some belong to Sonthal Pergunnahs, and a good many are city Thannahs, such as the 15 Thannahs of the City of Moorshedabad. These may be for our present purpose deducted, as well as the Sudder or Station Thannah of each District, which should be under the immediate direction of the Zillah or District Magistrate. After these deductions there will be left about 400 Thannahs. If a Deputy Magistrate were appointed to every three of these Thannahs, we should require 133 Deputy or Assistant Magistrates. But we have already, between Covenanted Assistants and Uncovenanted Deputy Magistrates, 33 out-Stations or Sub-divisions esta-

* Our present Junior Collector is of eleven years' standing, and this is at a time of unusually rapid promotion.

blished, so that the new appointments actually required would be 100, a number which would hereafter be liable to some diminution as the lower ranks of the Covenanted service were increased. Taking the number at 100, and placing this number on salaries of from Rupees 200 to 700 in the proportion now assigned to the Uncovenanted executive service, the expense of this additional establishment would be Rupees 4,21,200 in salaries.—For a reason, however, to be hereafter stated, I am clearly of opinion that the maximum at present assigned to the Uncovenanted executive service is too low. Instead of the highest class embracing only one Officer on Rupees 700, the highest class should embrace two Officers on Rupees 1,000 each; below that should be a class of four on Rupees 800 each, and then (omitting the present class of Rupees 700) the classes should proceed downwards in the same proportions as at present This would raise the additional charge above quoted to Rupees 4,60,801. The additional establishments, allowing for some reduction in the present Zillah Magistrates' establishment, would certainly bring the expense up to five lacs and a half per annum, or say, with some additional Thannahs, six lacs. For this amount, however, I think this very desirable, not to say necessary reform, might be made. And even then, and after adding the amount of Rupees 3,38,609 required to render adequate the pay of Mohurirs, Jemadars and Burkundauzes,* which would raise the total additional annual expense to Rupees 8,88,609, or say, after allowing for all defects of the estimate, ten lacs of Rupees, the Police charges of Bengal would still be only a little more than the Police charges of the North-Western Provinces.† And it must be by no means left out of sight, that the diminution of expenditure at present, in consequence of the diminished numbers of Junior Civil Servants, as compared with the year 1850, is more than a lac and a half of Rupees;‡ and as it is in a great measure owing to this diminution, that an addition is required to the Uncovenanted Magistrates, it is reasonable to set off a large part of this lac and a half, say at least a lac, against the additional charge now asked for, thus reducing the total to a maximum of nine lacs per annum.

48. My reason for thinking it necessary to have a class on Rupees 800, and a class on Rupees 1,000 per mensem, is that, although I should contemplate filling the new Offices chiefly with Natives, it would be indispensably necessary to have a certain number of well-educated and respectable Englishmen among them; and experience as well as theory has shown that these cannot be had for the same pecuniary inducements as Natives of the country, but must be in general paid more highly. In Districts where there are many Indigo Planters, it is absolutely indispensable to have English Magistrates, and to attempt to administer the Magistracy with Natives in such Districts will always be productive of dissatisfaction and disappointment.

49. *Junction of Judicial and Executive Powers.*—There is, however, an opinion which has found favour with some persons of just weight and authority in matters of this kind, and which has indeed a certain plausibility which tends to recommend it to many, and especially to those whose experience or whose mode of thinking has been derived from European rather than from Oriental habits, against which I am especially desirous of raising my testimony in this place, the rather, perhaps, that in the days of my smaller experience, I myself have held and advocated the opinion which I now very heartily condemn. The opinion to which I allude is this, that Magistrates of every degree should be debarred from all judicial powers, and should have nothing but the executive duty of preventing and detecting offences, and that separate

* See para. 4 of this Minute.

† Provincial Police Charges, 1851-52, Bengal, Rupees 10,31,386. N. W. P, Rupees 16,97,607. See para. 15 of Mr. Secretary Grey's letter to the Government of India, No. 2137, of 30th September, 1855.

‡ The actual difference is Rupees 1,54,440.

judicial functionaries should always receive and try cases of every kind committed to them by the Magistrates of various degrees. Thus it is, I believe, contemplated by some advocates of this system, that at or near every place at which a Deputy Magistrate is stationed, there should be a Moonsiff, or a Sudder Ameen, or a Judicial Officer of some corresponding class to try all cases sent to him by the Deputy Magistrate, and that in the same way all cases coming before the Zillah Magistrate, whatever their nature and importance, should be sent for trial to a Judicial Officer at the Zillah Station, Native or European.

50. It is one very serious objection to this scheme that it will be very expensive; not unlikely, as I believe, to double the proposed additional charge. But I think this the smallest objection to which it is liable. It is a scheme foreign and unintelligible to Asiatic notions, and altogether founded on European ideas and habits, going indeed, in its excessive provisions, to a degree even beyond any general European practice.

51. I am very sure that our Mofussil administration will, "*cæteris paribus*," be generally efficient, while it is certain to be also acceptable to the people according to the degree in which it conforms to the simple or Oriental, in preference to the complex or European model. The European idea of Provincial Government is by a minute division of functions and offices, and this is the system which we have introduced into our older territories. The Oriental idea is to unite all powers into one centre. The European may be able to comprehend and appreciate how and why he should go to one functionary for justice of another kind. The Asiatic is confused and aggrieved by hearing that this tribunal can only redress a particular sort of injury, but that, if his complaint be of another nature, he must go to another authority, and to a third, or a fourth kind of judicature, if his case be in a manner incomprehensible to himself, distinguishable into some other kinds of wrong or injury. He is unable to understand why there should be more than one "*Hakim*," and why the "*Hakim*" to whom he goes, according to his own expression, as to a *father* for justice, should be incapable of rendering him justice, whatever be the nature of his grievance, or whatever be the position of his adversary.

52. Accordingly, not only in all our recent acquisitions, such as Scinde, the Punjaub, Burmah, Nagpore, Oude, but in most of those which date thirty and forty years further back, such as the Nerbuddah Territories, Assam, or Arracan, we have carefully framed our administration upon the Oriental plan, modifying it only where absolutely necessary to insure real benefit to the people. And while the Europeanised methods of our oldest territories have been notoriously unsuccessful, the result has, on the whole, been so decidedly favourable in the newer Districts, that no sound Indian statesman would now dream of proposing for any new acquisition any other plan of administration. Now, nothing can be more opposed to the Oriental plan of administration than the entire separation of judicial from executive duties, which is advocated by the over-much occidentalists to whom I have alluded, at the same time that it is going backwards from the course which experience has been gradually forcing upon our older territories ever since 1793. In that year the "Regulation system" began by denuding Zillah Magistrates of almost all judicial powers. But this was soon found to be practically intolerable; and first in 1807, and afterwards at different intervals, the judicial powers of Zillah Magistrates were increased from the infliction of one month's imprisonment to that of six months, one year, two years, and ultimately three years, which is the limit of judicial power now exercised by Zillah Magistrates. I know that the general opinion of the most trustworthy Officers is that if the Magistrates were not so young—that is, if by union of the office with that of the Collector, or in any other way, the age and experience of the Magistrates were raised to its former standard—it would be wise to increase (instead of diminishing) their judicial powers, and to give them, as is given to Magis-

trates in several of the "Non-Regulation" Provinces, a power of sentencing to imprisonment for as many as seven years, subject only to the revision of a higher authority. This was recommended by Mr. Dampier in his Police Report for 1848, for all cases of simple Dacoity.

53. Before 1830, the trial of heinous cases in each Zillah was by a Circuit Judge, who came at stated intervals, tried such cases as he found ready, and departed, to be succeeded on the next circuit by a different, and again at another interval by a third, and sometimes even a fourth Circuit Judge. Among some evils peculiar to the system as it then existed, there was undoubtedly much that operated with advantage in these successive Circuits by successive Judges. That system has been succeeded by one in which each Zillah Station has its permanent Sessions Judge. And though this change effected an undoubted remedy for some of the more obvious evils of the previous system, it has been found in practice to be open to certain special objections, such as have been thought by many almost to counterbalance its admitted benefits. For instead of the little known, and therefore the more honoured Circuit Judge, we have now a Judge who, in a small Station and a confined society, must of necessity be in such a degree of close and incessant intercourse with the Magistrate as usually breeds the familiarity which is proverbially destructive of respect. Small societies, too, are liable to jealousies, scandal, quarrels, over-friendships, over-enmities; and in all these, to the detriment of his official usefulness and his judicial dignity, the Judge is not seldom found to bear a part. Sometimes the Judge and the Magistrate are in open enmity; and then every counter-decision is apt to be attributed, by their keen-sighted Native observers, to the existence of ill-feeling between the two functionaries. As often, perhaps, the Judge and the Magistrate are in close intimacy; they dine together, they ride together, they shoot or hunt together, their tastes and feelings are obviously in unison; and then every judicial affirmation of commitments and appeals is liable by narrowminded and interested by-standers to be put to the account of friendship and influence. In one Zillah the Judge perhaps is weak, and exercises feebly and ineffectually the control over the Magistrate which the system expects of him. In another Zillah the Judge may be vigorous, encroaching, overbearing, and then the Magistrate is made a cipher, and his power, without his responsibility, passes into hands for which it was never intended. No one who is familiar with the state of the interior will deny that, amidst much that is good, our present system is often marred by one or other or all of the evils I have above depicted; and these evils, wherever they occur, arise undoubtedly from the antagonism of a locally opposed judicial and executive authority. But conceive this local antagonism, not merely at each Zillah Station, but all over every District; and the antagonism in each case, not of two liberally-educated Englishmen, but of two half-educated and Orientally-civilised Natives, and let those who know the country and people declare what would be the practical result. Conceive every Darogah opposed perhaps to an antagonist local Moonsiff, and every Native Deputy Magistrate to a Native Sudder Ameen at an out-station: imagine the bickerings, the criminations, and recriminations that would ensue. For though, under the greatest provocation, corruption is the last thing which a Native ever imputes to an English Judge or Magistrate, it is the first imputation which a Native casts on a Native, on great provocation, slight provocation, or no provocation at all. Thus, in but too many instances, would executive Officers account for every failure by insinuations against the judicial department; and thus as often would the judicial functionaries retort by insinuations against the purity of the executive. At the best, all the difficulties and embarrassments which even now not unfrequently impede the administration, owing to divided authority at the chief Zillah Stations, would be multiplied a hundred-fold. If it were asked why crime had increased in a given district, the executive Officers would reply—"Because of the pertinaciously unreasonable acquittal of all our criminals by

the judicial functionaries." If the judicial functionaries were in any way questioned for this result, they would answer—"It is because of the negligence and inefficiency of the executive." Nobody would be responsible. Power would be everywhere divided, and everywhere contending against power. The administration of the interior would be torn in sunder, and the result would be good made bad, bad made worse, and confusion everywhere worse confounded No one who has the personal acquaintance with the interior, which my present position no less than my past experience has given me, can say that this anticipation is exaggerated. All must agree that the mischiefs I have anticipated would, under such a system, be very likely to break out.

54. I believe, too, that to deprive our Magistrates of judicial power, while it would degrade them in the eyes of the Native community, who can never understand why, when the "*Hakim*" has caught a thief, he should not forthwith try and punish him, would take away a great cause of self-respect from the executive functionary and a great means of self-improvement. I have no doubt that the sense of judicial responsibility has a very large and important effect in raising the character and improving the conscientiousness of our executive Magistrates, while it certainly adds greatly to their useful influence among the people; and I am satisfied that justice is not likely to be less truly or satisfactorily administered under the present system, which intrusts large judicial powers to Magistrates and Deputy Magistrates, than under a system which, taking away from them all judicial power, should make them in their own view, and in the apprehension of the people among whom they act, nothing but a higher kind of Police Darogahs.

55. In recommending, therefore, a considerable addition to the number of Deputy Magistrates, I would be understood to advocate very strongly that they should, as at present, be permitted to exercise judicial powers varying with their known qualifications and experience, and subject to revision by a higher authority. This is in perfect accordance with recommendations of the recent Report of the Law Commissioners.*

56. *Improved Administration of Justice.*—The fifth and last general measure which I have enumerated is an improvement in our Criminal Courts of Justice.

57. This part of the subject has repeatedly been brought to notice in Mr. Dampier's Annual Reports, and there is undoubtedly a general consent of opinion as to the urgent necessity for an improvement.

58 But, as might be expected on a subject so difficult, there is much variety of opinion as to the manner in which improvement can best be effected.

59. On the whole, and after much careful consideration, I give in my entire adhesion to the recommendations of the London Law Commissioners, as stated in their recent Report, but with certain modifications, the most material of which I shall now proceed to describe.

60. *Jury Trial.*—The plan of the London Law Commissioners provides† for trial of heinous cases by the Sessions Judge in each Zillah, assisted by a jury in cases where certain privileged persons are defendants, or among the defendants.

61. The privileged persons are thus stated in the report.—"A British subject, or an European, or an American, or an East Indian, or Armenian, or a person of any other class to which the Governor General in Council may see fit to extend this rule, registered according to such rules as the Governor-General in Council shall prescribe." Unanimity, or a majority of not less than two-thirds, with the concurrence of the Judge, being necessary for a verdict of guilty. Of all other defendants the trial is to be before the

* See pages 98 and 99 of the Report.

† Chap. XIX., page 149.

Sessions Judge and two or more Assessors; the decision being vested exclusively in the Judge. I will enter in this place into no argument, but simply state that I disapprove of these provisions; and instead of confining trial by Jury to certain privileged classes, I would have all trials of heinous cases in the Mofussil before the Sessions Judge and a Jury.

62. *System of Appeal to High Court.*—The plan of the London Law Commissioners leaves the system of appeal very much as it is now, encouraging appeal by insuring every appellant against any disadvantage, and giving him every possible chance of advantage by appeal.* But in cases of trial by Jury, the High Court is not permitted to reverse a verdict as to facts; though it may try any point of law in appeal from such trials, and alter, in the way of mitigation, but not in the way of enhancement, any sentence passed by a Sessions Court in such trials.

63. If, then, Jury trial were made the rule, instead of the exception, there would be, even according to the scheme of the Law Commissioners, no appeal whatever from the Sessions Court on the facts, but only on the law. To this I have no objection. There would remain an appeal in mitigation of sentence, and this I should not object to leave, not, however, binding the High Court to take up any such appeal unless on strong *primâ facie* ground, shown to their satisfaction, for questioning the justice of the sentence appealed against. But I would restore the wholesome power of enhancing within certain limits as well as reducing sentences, which was formerly exercised by the Sudder Court. I can see no reason for withholding it, and a great many for giving it. Our Zillah Judges err at least as often by over-leniency as over-severity, and over-severity has never been imputed to the Sudder Court, but the contrary.

64. *Powers of Sessions Judges.*—The plan of the Law Commissioners gives to the Sessions Courts the power of sentencing to any legal punishment short of death. Capital cases are to be referred to the High Courts.†

65. This entirely accords with my view of what is required. But the large powers of revision given to the High Court by Chapter XXV. are, in my judgment, for the most part unnecessary, and I would either abrogate or greatly reduce them. In this country it is quite sufficient to give a power of revision on appeal, without encouraging the High Court to take up cases regarding which no one has appealed or complained. This is one of those excesses of cautious investigation which so frequently disfigure our system, and, by occupying time which might be better employed, as well as by adding to the uncertainty of sentences, do in the long run a great deal more harm than good.

66. *Moonsiff Magistrates.*—The plan of the Law Commissioners gives to subordinate Magistrates much the same powers as at present, but it makes every Moonsiff a subordinate Magistrate. The present system leaves the Government the option of making a Moonsiff a subordinate Magistrate or not; and I think the present system in this respect very much the most prudent and proper.

67. *Appeals to Sessions Judges.*—The plan of the Law Commissioners gives an appeal of right against every sentence or order, light or heavy, of every Magistrate and subordinate Magistrate, high or low, to the Sessions Judge. This is simply impossible, if the subordinate Magistrates are increased as I propose to increase them. Even now, the appeals from Magistrates and subordinates with the higher powers, go far to swamp the Sessions (who are also Civil) Judges. And if, as I propose, the Magistrates are doubled, it is vain to think that the present number of Sessions Judges can hear their appeals. And besides this, there is good reason for leaving all the subordinate Magistrates subject in all things to their chief Zillah Magistrate.

* Chap XXVI., page 163.
† Page 96, and see note at page 98, also Chap. XXII., Rule 304, page 157.

It has always been a mistake to transfer them in any way to any other authority; every purpose for which the new arrangement is proposed will be far better subserved if the Deputy or subordinate Magistrates were, as to their judicial, not less than their executive functions, made liable to the complete authority of the Zillah Magistrate by whom they are to be posted, and guided and controlled: by whom they are to be checked in their errors and encouraged in their successes; to whom they are to look for praise or blame, for repression or advancement; and to whom the Government must look for advice and opinions as to the conduct and qualifications of every member of the new organisation.

68. *Effect of Act* XXXI. *of* 1841.—But, both in regard to the revision of sentences of his subordinates by the Zillah Magistrate, and the revision of the sentences of the Magistrate by the Zillah or Circuit Judge, I would most earnestly counsel a return to the system in force before 1841, which gave no criminal appeal of *right* in any case, but allowed certain higher authorities a power of discretion, and on sufficient cause shown, of revising and amending sentences of certain subordinate Courts.

69. The old system was by the Honourable Court* well and wisely contrasted and compared with the newer system of 1841, and the practical superiority of the former strongly and convincingly insisted on. "We apprehend," says the Honourable Court, commenting on Act XXXI. of 1841, "that in this enactment the analogy of civil has been erroneously applied to criminal judicature. In the exercise of the right of appeal given to a party in a civil suit, he has to take into consideration the increased costs with which he will be chargeable in the probable event of the original decree being affirmed. But the convict will have no such motive to discourage him from exercising his right to appeal. The execution of the sentence must be suspended, which will itself be a positive benefit, and the superior tribunal, when it confirms the sentence, cannot enhance its severity as a punishment for the exercise of a legal right. The Act in question indeed expressly prohibits such enhancement, so that a committed prisoner has no inducement to refrain from trying the chance of an appeal. It may, therefore, be expected that when that right comes to be fully understood and generally known, an appeal will be preferred against every sentence, and the great mass of the criminal business of the country will have to be done twice over."

70. "Under the former Regulations the Courts of Circuit, whose powers have since been transferred to the Sessions Judges, were authorised, upon petitions presented to them within a limited period, to call upon the Magistrate for his proceedings in any case, and to pass such orders thereupon as they might deem proper and consistent with the Regulations. Similar authority was also vested in the Court of Nizamut Adawlut over all inferior tribunals, and it is renewed in the Act now under consideration. This we apprehend to be the correct principle by which liability to error on the part of the subordinate tribunals should be guarded against, such an interposition of authority did not imply any right of appeal by a convicted prisoner, and was not open to the objections with which that right would be attended. The petition on which superior authority was interposed, could only in a loose sense be regarded as at all partaking of the nature of an appeal."

71. *Sections* XXIII. *and* XXIV., *Regulation* IX. *of* 1807.—And in a later Despatch, dated 3rd April, 1854, remarking on the reply of the Nizamut Adawlut to the foregoing observations, the Hon'ble Court's opinion is thus repeated. "We are aware that it was competent to the superior tribunals, upon petitions presented to them, to call for proceedings in criminal trials, and to pass such orders upon them as might seem just and proper. This exercise of authority, as we observed in the Despatch above referred to, constitutes the correct principle by which liability to error on the part of the

* Despatch from Hon'ble Court, No. 1 of 1843, dated 1st February.

subordinate tribunals should be guarded against, but the *petition*, on which it may be interposed, can only in a loose sense, as we also observed, be regarded as at all partaking of the nature of an appeal. In such a sense only we conceive the term *appeal* to have been used in the Section pointed out by the Nizamut Adawlut. Otherwise it would imply that the right of appeal belongs to the prosecutor as well as to the prisoner, and it would require that the execution of every sentence should be deferred until the period after which the right ceases had expired, and that every case appealed should undergo complete investigation by the appellate jurisdiction, although, *primâ facie*, there might be no ground whatever to doubt the justice and propriety of the original decision."

72. "The statement furnished by the Nizamut Adawlut shows that the number of cases disposed of in 1843, in the Lower Provinces, amounted to 31,751, and the number of cases appealed to, 5,212, or a sixth part of the whole. This is a large proportion of the criminal business of our system of judicature which has had to be done twice over, and it can hardly be doubted that the proportion would greatly increase, if it came to be fully understood and generally known that every appeal must be received as a matter of right, and must be completely investigated before the original sentence could be carried into execution."

73. "We therefore continue to think that in passing Act XXXI. of 1841, the analogy of civil has been erroneously applied to criminal judicature, and that the provisions of that Act require to be reconsidered and revised."

74. It is much to be wished that the sound advice of the Honourable Court should now be followed; for, unless this be done, such is the fondness for appeal in this country, that every addition to courts of first instance must be accompanied inevitably by a proportionate addition to courts of Appeal.

75. *Nomination of Jurors.*—Under the plan of the law commissioners, the High Court is to make rules for the qualification, appointment, and other matters relating to jurors.* I am clear that the High Court had better be kept from this and all other executive business. A better system was, I think, proposed in the Draft Jury Bill prepared by the late Mr. Bethune in 1849, and published in the Gazette of 31st October, 1849. By this, the executive officers of government, the collector—controlled by the commissioner and by the government itself—was to frame the Jury Lists. However this may be done, I should desire to see as much honour and dignity as possible attached to the rank of a juryman. Perhaps it may not be possible here, any more than in England, to make the duty attractive; but something may be done to surround it with honour, and to make, as it were, some amends for the trouble and responsibility it must occasion.

76. *Nomenclature.*—Perhaps names are not much worth debating about, but, referring to the nomenclature of the law commissioners, I confess to a prejudice in favour of "*Deputy Magistrate*" and Assistant Magistrate, as compared with the long and, in the mouths of the natives, unmeaning and unintelligible appellations of "*Judge of a subordinate Criminal Court of the first class*," and "*Judge of a subordinate Criminal Court of the second class*."

77. It is impossible to imagine that anybody will ever use all these words in the hurry of business, and the process of abbreviation may possibly be somewhat arbitrary and uncertain. Besides, I have an old-fashioned objection to calling a "*Magistrate*" a "*Judge*," and this, I fancy, will be shared by the natives, who have long been accustomed to associate distinct meanings with the terms "*Judge*" and "*Magistrate*." If possible, then, I would put in a plea for the old terminology.

78. I make no remark in this place on the proposed constitution of the "High Court" of the Law Commissioners, nor on any other part of their

* Chap. XIX., Section 267.

plan that does not immediately bear on the administration of Criminal Justice, and thus on the improvement of the Police.

79. *Roads.*—I have now recapitulated the five chief improvements which seem to me to be required to place the Police of Bengal on a footing of reasonable promise, from which it may gradually advance to a better and still better condition. There is, however, yet another measure which can hardly be omitted in this place, and which may seem of itself almost as important as any of the foregoing. I allude to a measure for the establishment of sufficient means of communication with the interior of Districts. It cannot, indeed, be necessary to dwell on the importance of roads and communications to the well-doing of any Police system. No system can work well while our Police Stations and our large Towns and Marts in the interior are cut off from the chief Zillah Stations and from one another by the almost entire absence of roads, or even (during a large part of the year) of the smallest bridle-roads or foot-paths. It may be impossible, in the present state of our resources, to make all over our Zillahs such roads as are fit at all times for wheeled carriages; but where better and broader roads cannot be made, it ought to be an indispensable part of our system to have from the chief Zillah Station to all Police Stations in the interior, and from each Police Station to the neighbouring Stations, at least a raised and bridged foot or bridle-path, so that a man, a horse, a bullock, an elephant, or a palankeen should at all times of the year be able uninterruptedly to pass and repass. There are but few of our Zillahs where this might not be done at a comparatively small expense, if the land were available; and of so much public import is it to have land available for such a purpose, that I should not think it unjust to propose a law, making it binding on all Zemindars, and other proprietors of land, to give up sufficient lands for the purpose, free of all cost to the State, except of any standing crops or agricultural produce. In most parts of Bengal the Zemindars would do this willingly without any law, and the benefit to the surrounding lands would be of itself sufficient to over-pay the value of the land given.

80. By so digging the earth for the road as to form a small canal, a means of water communication in the rains might be secured, which would be of the highest value to agriculture and commerce, and which would easily bear a light Toll, sufficient to pay for the repair (at least) of the road and the canal.

81. I think that the construction and repair of such roads ought to be an essential duty of each Magistrate and Division Magistrate; that the expense should be estimated and passed once a year, separate from all other public works, and should be considered and calculated on as one of the charges of the Police. Such a system, fairly established, and energetically kept up, would, by facilitating the movements of Magistrates, of Police Officers, of despatches, of complainants, and of witnesses, do as much for the improvement of the Police as any measure that could be devised, and without it I doubt if any measures could be fully successful.

82. *Omlah.*—It is a matter not absolutely essential, yet surely of much importance, in this and other branches of the public service, that means should be adopted for encouraging and rewarding good service among the native ministerial Officers of our Courts, popularly called "*the Omlah.*"

83. It is usual to run down this class of men with undistinguishing severity, and to attribute to their pernicious influence the greater part of the mischiefs which beset our Courts and impede the administration of justice. To a large and unhappy extent these imputations are, it must be owned, but too well deserved. Yet even here reprobation has been too indiscriminate, and too little regard has been had to the trials and temptations by which this class of Officers is assailed and surrounded, to the real services which they render, to the extraordinary knowledge of business, industry, and ability by which so many of them are distinguished, and to the general neglect with which they are treated by the Government they serve.

84. They are for the most part paid at a rate that almost necessitates corruption; they have at the best little to look forward to as the honourable reward of a life of incessant toil; and they are liable to be turned off, and not seldom are turned off, without warning, and with the most trifling compensation, on any sudden change or remodelling that may occur in the offices to which they are attached.

85. Yet in the tours which I make through these Provinces, I have found much oftener than I anticipated, and in various parts of the country, old, faithful, and useful servants of this class, to whose long, zealous, and often strikingly honest and uncorrupt labours, the most convincing testimony is borne by all persons, European and Native, with whom they have come into contact.

86. On such men as these I am occasionally solicited to bestow some official promotion as a reward for their past service and as an incentive to the diligence and honesty of others. To these solicitations I have never been unattentive, and I have done all that I could to encourage meritorious Native functionaries of this class, by promoting them as far as I was able. But our system seldom permits of this kind of reward being bestowed. The most honest and capable Serishtadar cannot rise as a Judge without passing through the grade of a Moonsiff; and for this he must undergo an examination, which is always insuperably distasteful to a mature man of business, and which is intended to prove, in younger candidates for office, that aptitude and that knowledge of which the old Serishtadar has notoriously been long possessed, and which he has proved by a quarter of a century of constant and approved transaction of affairs. For a Deputy Magistrate he may be fitted by knowledge and experience, but seldom by personal activity or past habits; and indeed, as Natives of a certain age are remarkable for the absence of that pliability and versatility which enable a man to change himself with his circumstances, it is seldom that any of the most able and experienced ministerial *omlah*, who have long distinguished themselves in subordinate positions, are found to succeed if transferred to situations of a different and more independent character.

87. *Civil Order of Merit.*—I am satisfied, however, that it would be greatly to the interest and advantage of Government if some means were devised of systematically rewarding all marked and distinguished service on the part of these and other Native Civil Servants of the State, and I have longed wished to see a civil Order of Merit established for this purpose, with various grades or classes, and moderate pecuniary advantages varying with each class.

88. It would not be difficult to frame a scheme for this purpose, which should cost in money nothing worth consideration, but which might, and probably would, produce the most beneficial effect on the character and conduct of the whole body of Native Civil Servants. I desire to submit this suggestion for the consideration of higher authority.

89. *Station Guards.*—It may not be indispensable to the improvement of the Police, but it is a thing very much to be desired for the security of the public peace, that there should be available at the headquarters of each station a small but well drilled and trustworthy guard, to be used in case of riot or of opposition to the ordinary Police. The same guard might be available for Treasury guards and Escorts, and for guarding the Jails, and other duties of a like kind; and it would often save much harassing duty to the regular troops. I have already proposed the raising of civil Police Corps for this purpose, of which the expense would be met in part by a reduction of the present very inefficient Jail and Treasury guards. The Supreme Government has sanctioned the raising of one such Corps to be employed chiefly in the Sonthal Pergunnahs; and as regards the main proposition a reference has been made to the Hon'ble Court.

90. *Honorary Magistrates.*—It has been recommended, and the recom-

mendation has recently been much canvassed, that commissions as Honorary Magistrates should be issued to certain carefully-selected Indigo Planters and Zemindars, so as to enlist the wealth and influence of the Mofussil in the administration of its affairs. In favour of this proposition it has been urged that the Zemindars and Planters do now, avowedly, and with the entire consent and satisfaction of the rural population, administer in all small matters just that simple, ready, and paternal justice among their Ryots, which the Ryots best understand and appreciate; and that the jurisdiction which is thus assumed and exercised without law, being in itself useful and acceptable to the people, ought rather to be exercised with the full countenance and support of the law: that whether the law give it or withhold this jurisdiction, nothing can prevent the natural effect of wealth, position, influence, and authority among a docile and subservient population; and that it would be wise to enlist in the service of law and order that power which is now sometimes used against the public peace, and is at best, as between authority and crime, too often neutral, if not, indeed, sometimes ranged on the side of criminals and against the law: that many irregularities now caused by the exercise of unlawful power would cease, if this power were clothed with legal dignity and responsibility; and that by raising the position we should raise and confirm the character and improve the conduct of the entire class in question. On the other hand, it is replied that, as regards the Zemindars, they are, with rare and hardly ascertained exceptions, hard, selfish, corrupt, and grasping, or indolent, facile, and indifferent to the public good, while they are almost always ignorant and prejudiced. And that, as regards Planters, they have but too often, under a system which undoubtedly involves a certain extent of forced cultivation, interests so opposed to those of their neighbours and dependants, as to make it in the highest degree unjust and dangerous to intrust them with legal powers, which the very best might sometimes be tempted, and the worst would always be ready, to use for the prosecution of their own lawful objects. That although Indigo Planters are as a class greatly improved during the past twenty or thirty years, and often the willing and energetic instruments of much public and private benefit to the neighbourhoods in which they carry on their important avocations, yet they have not yet altogether got the better of a tendency to right themselves in cases of dispute without waiting for tardy processes of law; and there is still too much jealousy between them and their Native neighbours, and too many constantly recurring causes of quarrel between them to render it possible to intrust to any of them powers which, however honestly they might, and probably in many instances would, be used, would nevertheless always be contemplated with doubt and suspicion by those around them, and could never be otherwise than unpopular in the hands of even the most esteemed and worthy.

91. Although I somewhat lean towards the opinion that a careful and judicious enlisting into the service of the public of the rich and powerful Zemindars and Planters of the interior has in it much that seems to promise well, and that it should at all events be kept in view as a measure to be at some, perhaps distantly future, time gradually accomplished, I am not yet in a position to recommend it for present adoption. I have, however, called on a number of experienced Officers for their views on the subject, and I may hereafter be able to offer a more decided opinion regarding it.

92. *Vernacular Education.*—Lastly, I would express my decided conviction that, although the measures I have now proposed, improved and amended as they cannot fail to be during the further discussion to which they will be subjected, will in due time produce an improvement in the state of the Bengal Police which cannot otherwise be effected, they are all of secondary importance, compared with the enlightenment of the people among whom they are to operate, and by whose co-operation alone they can be made fully effectual for the general good. While the mass of the people remain in their present state of ignorance and debasement, all laws and all systems must be comparatively

useless and vain. Above all things that can be done by us for this people is their gradual intellectual and moral advancement, through the slow but certain means of a widely-spreading popular system of Vernacular Education, and money laid out on this great engine of improvement will, in the end, prove better spent and more enduringly profitable than on the working of the most excellent system of administration by the most efficient and costly establishments.

93. This greatest of our plans for the benefit of our Indian fellow-subjects has now under happy auspices been commenced. I earnestly trust that it may be prosecuted with persevering determination; that no reasonable expense will be spared to give it activity and extension, and that a large proportion of the rising generation may be embraced within its powerful and beneficent operation.

30*th April*, 1856. (Signed) F. J. HALLIDAY.

NOTE BY MR. SECRETARY GREY.

It has for some years been matter of complaint by the public in the Mofussil, and more especially the English public, that the office of Magistrate in Bengal is held by Officers whose junior standing in the service and consequent inexperience do not qualify them for the exercise of the very responsible duties which devolve upon them.

For several years the propriety of re-uniting the offices of Magistrate and Collector, has been thought of and discussed, one of the main objects of such re-union being to place the Chief Magisterial power in every District in the hands of men of mature age and long experience in India.

It has been thought by most people that such a measure could not fail to produce good, because, while on the one hand the same average amount of natural inferiority and natural superiority was likely to be found in an equal number of men selected from two different ranks in the service, it was on the other hand inevitable that the men of the one rank—that is, those of the longer standing—would possess a far greater amount of official experience and of acquaintance with the country and its people.

It has not been supposed, having regard to the manner in which the Land Revenue in Bengal is raised, that any theoretical objection founded upon European ideas would be urged against the junction of Revenue and Magisterial authority in the same hands, and this seemed the less likely, from the circumstance that in eleven of the Bengal Regulation Districts and in all the Non-Regulation Districts such union of authority actually obtained; this being the case, too, it may be remarked in all the Districts where the permanent settlement does *not* prevail.

After being talked about for some years, the proposition to re-unite the offices of Magistrate and Collector was at length formally made by Lord Dalhousie in April, 1854. The proposition was submitted to the Government of India, and no notice of it being taken for some months, the Lieutenant Governor, in October of the same year, called the attention of the Supreme Government to the subject, and solicited permission to take advantage of then expected vacancies to re-unite the office of Magistrate and Collector in some four or five Districts which were named.

This request was, however, refused in January, 1855, and a Minute of the Honourable Mr. Grant's was sent for the Lieutenant Governor's perusal, in which Lord Dalhousie's proposition was strongly objected to. The Lieutenant Governor communicated his views upon the question to the Supreme Government in February, 1855, and since that date, nothing more has been heard on the matter from the Supreme Government.

The subject has, however, intermediately been twice brought incidentally to the notice of the Supreme Government. In September last the Lieutenant Governor, in applying for an increase to the Uncovenanted Executive Service, took occasion to observe that such assistance though greatly needed, would not cure one great evil of the present condition of the service, namely, the evil of advancing very young Officers to appointments of responsibility and importance.

This evil, it was remarked, could only be cured by one of three measures, one of which was the re-uniting of the offices of Magistrate and Collector.

No reply to this communication has been received.

The second occasion on which the subject of placing the Chief Magisterial and Chief Revenue Control in a District in the same hands was brought under the notice of the Supreme Government, was in the instance of the Districts of Bhaugulpore and Beerbhoom, when a portion of the Magisterial Jurisdiction of each of those Districts was taken, after the Sontal insurrection, to form a Non-Regulation Province. It was then recommended by the Lieutenant Governor *as a measure of economy*, that the separate Magistracies of Bhaugulpore and Beerbhoom should be abolished, and that the Collectors of those Districts should be made also Magistrates; to this proposition the Supreme Government at once assented.

With the above exception, the Magistrate-Collector question has not apparently advanced since Lord Dalhousie made his proposition two years ago.

My object in bringing the subject now briefly to the notice of the Lieutenant Governor, is to beg his attention to a Comparative Statement which I have prepared, showing the standing of the Magistrates in Bengal, that is to say of the Officers actually officiating as such at three different periods, namely in April, 1850, April, 1854 (the date of Lord Dalhousie's proposition), and April, 1856.

This statement will be found, I think, to show an urgent need of *some* means being adopted to procure greater experience in the Magistrate's Office than is now obtained.

The average standing of the Magistrates of the 25* Districts which have separate Magistrates, was in 1850, nine years and eight months. The average standing of the officers now serving as Magistrates in the same Districts is only six years and ten months.

In 1850, there were only two Magistrates below seven years' standing, now there are 15 such.

The youngest Officer officiating as a Magistrate in 1850, was of five years' standing, the youngest Officer now officiating as Magistrate is of less than three years' standing.

In the case of 1850, I believe it was a temporary appointment merely, as the Directory shows several Officers of one and two years' senior standing not acting as Magistrates. In the present year when Mr. Wigram was appointed to act as Magistrate of Beerbhoom, there was at the time no Officer between him and Lord Ulick Browne, the next junior Acting Magistrate, who was qualified and available for a Magistrate's appointment.

Unless the number of the service available for duty in Bengal is increased at least to the strength at which it stood in 1850, or some other remedy be adopted, it is clear that the present state of things will continue.

(Signed) W. Grey,

Secy. to the Govt. of Bengal.

20th April, 1856.

* That is excluding the 24-Pergunnahs

	Magistrate's length of service in 1850.	Magistrates' length of service in 1854.	Magistrates' length of service in 1856.
Behar	17— 1	11— 4	5— 6
Beerbhoom	17— 1	6—11	2— 9
Shahabad	15—10	5—11	11— 0
Tirhoot	13— 8	8— 3	7—11
Mymensing	12— 7	9— 0	7— 5
Jessore	12— 4	8—10	6— 3
Dacca	9— 7	8— 4	5— 3
Sarun	9— 4	9— 4	6— 3
Patna	9— 3	8— 5	5— 6
Dinagepore	8— 6	11— 3	6—10
Monghyr	8— 6	8— 5	4— 7
Hooghly	8— 2	9— 0	6— 0
Midnapore	7— 6	6— 6	8— 6
Rajshahye	7— 6	8— 5	6— 4
Howrah	7—11	5— 4	6— 7
Purneah	7— 3	7— 7	9— 7
Tipperah	7— 4	11— 4	9— 6
Burdwan	7— 3	7— 6	5— 6
Chittagong	7— 3	10— 4	6—10
Nuddeah	7— 1	13— 4	8— 6
Backergunge	6— 4	5— 5	7— 5
Moorshedabad	5— 0	9— 2	5— 1
Sylhet	9— 6	5— 7	7— 7
Bhaugulpore	10— 3	8— 9	10— 3
Rungpore	10— 8	6—11	5— 0
25÷	242— 9	211— 2	171—11
	9— 8	8— 5	6—10

BENGAL:

ITS LANDED TENURE AND POLICE SYSTEM.

SPEECH

ON

A MOTION FOR INQUIRY IN THE HOUSE OF COMMONS, JUNE 11, 1857.

BY

THE HON. A. KINNAIRD.

WITH AN APPENDIX.

1857.

BENGAL SYSTEM OF GOVERNMENT.

Government of Bengal.

Mr. Speaker,

Sir,—As one well convinced that in very many espects our government in India has been productive f much good to that country taken as a whole, I laim the attention of this House while I endeavour o set before them, as briefly and as faithfully as I can, he present condition of the Lower Provinces of Bengal, as an exception to that fact, if we are to elieve the testimony of residents in that country.* I lo this, Sir, because undoubtedly on us lies the re-ponsibility of securing for the people of India the est government that is attainable. I am not actuated y the slightest feeling of hostility, either to the Government or to the East India Company, both of which I have generally supported with reference to ndia; but I am now painfully convinced that hitherto ve have failed to secure to the natives of the Lower Provinces of Bengal those blessings for which Govern-nents exist; and let me impress upon this House the remendous magnitude of the claims of our Indian

Responsibility of the House of Commons.

---

* I have given the evidence in support of my resolutions at greater length in this pamphlet than I was able to do in the House luring the debate, as it would have occupied too much time.

empire. The age in which we live is an age of wonders; but certainly not one of the least is the almost utter indifference that has hitherto been manifested here to these claims, and to the interests of one of the mightiest empires of the world, committed to us, as was well said by my Right Honourable friend, the late President of the Board of Control, not for the selfish purpose of our own aggrandisement, but that we should raise it to the participation of the same privileges which we ourselves nationally enjoy.

Magnitude of claims.

Neglect.

Yes, Sir, we have neglected our duty to India; let us repair that neglect, and at least give some earnest and constant attention to its claims for the future. When the interests of 30,000 of our gallant soldiers in the Crimea were thought to be neglected, how wide spread the sympathy. When the 7,000,000 of Ireland were afflicted by a sore famine, how generous the response to the cries of distress. But these numbers sink into absolute insignificance in comparison with the numbers on whose behalf I feel it my duty to plead to-night.

Population of India 150 or 160 millions.

In India, 150 or 160 millions of human beings (a sixth of the population of the world,) are under the sway of the British Crown. A population greater in number than the combined populations of European Russia, of Austria, of France, and of Great Britain, and six times greater than the population of all the other British Colonies taken together.

Comparison with other Colonies.

Lower Provinces of Bengal.

But, as I have intimated, I intend to confine my observations to the state of the Lower Provinces of Bengal, which of themselves form an area of about

290,000 square miles, and contain a population of from 40 to 45 millions. These have been for nearly a century, more or less, under the dominion of England, and being our first possession, *there* have been committed, I apprehend, our greatest mistakes in government, and mistakes of such a nature that it is exceedingly difficult to rectify them. It is only since 1854, after the renewal of the East India Company's Charter in 1853, that Bengal has even had a separate governor. Again, the system of landed tenure, established by Lord Cornwallis in 1792, has been a source of boundless misery. Good in theory, and if honestly carried out, all those provisions in it calculated to protect the poor have been practically lost sight of. It is known by the name of the Perpetual Settlement, and the Zemindary System. Founded with the most benevolent intentions, praised by Pitt and Dundas at home, and by Lord Wellesley (Lord Cornwallis's successor) in India, while the Court of Directors congratulated themselves on having at length done their duty by the establishment of institutions so admirably adapted to promote the welfare of the people of Bengal, I impute blame to no one with regard to its adoption. All I say is, that, as it has been carried out, its results have been most disastrous to the people of Bengal. Compare the state of the Lower Provinces with the North-West Provinces, which have more recently come under our sway, and you will see in the latter the beneficial results of good government, and in the former the evils of grinding oppression. While in eight years, Lord Dalhousie, in the Punjaub, which

Oldest possession and worst governed.

Separate Governor, 1854.

Perpetual Settlement, 1792.

North-West Provinces.

Punjaub, 1848. came into our possession in 1848, created a system of government said to be free from all the defects developed in the older provinces, and with due allowance for the weakness of the native character, a perfect model of excellence. But in Bengal our institutions *Contrast of Bengal.* are pronounced a failure; and some who know the country, feel that we are on the eve of a crisis, for not only are things bad, but in many respects they are growing worse. Let this House just consider that the Europeans, who are the governing class, are but a handful compared with the natives, less than 100,000 against 150 millions, and you will at once perceive that our power rests on prestige. Destroy this by any violent shock, and our power is gone. The Hindoos are no doubt a patient people, but there is a limit to human endurance, and if we overpass that limit, who can predict the consequence?

Petition of the Missionaries. The petition of the missionaries which I had the honour to present to this House at the close of the last Session, had its origin in their knowledge of the miseries of the people. They first addressed themselves to the Lieutenant-Governor of Bengal, Mr. Halliday, *Refusal of its prayer.* and the Governor-General in Council; but the petition which they presented for inquiry into the social condition of the people of Bengal, was dismissed with the usual official assurances that inquiry was useless; that the evils, though great, were exaggerated; and that remedies would be applied which inquiry would only delay; though Mr. Halliday and even Mr. Grant himself, in their answers, practically admitted the truth of nearly all their representations. I feel persuaded, judging from his former policy, that had Lord Dalhousie been Governor-General, he would have granted the enquiry. As it is, they had no resource but to address themselves to the Parliament of England, with the hope that we would listen to the cry of oppression; which, whether we hear it or not, is rising up from the millions of Bengal. That they are justified, nay much more than justified in the course they have taken, I unhesitatingly maintain; and that their testimony is of the greatest value, and deserving the highest credit, I conscientiously believe. Of no one party, but connected with various Christian denominations, conversant with the every day lives of the people, unconnected with the Government and the Civil service, gentlemen of British birth and liberal education, with English ideas of justice, what one body in India is so calculated as they to take a just view of the social condition of the people? *They are, in fact, the only body in India who have no class interests to serve.* These are not days when men can discredit the testimony of missionaries—they are too well known and appreciated. The name of Livingstone alone forbids it. Two of their number, Dr. Duff and Mr. Mullens, are on the Council of the New University, and three are native ministers.

Petition to Parliament.

Claims to be listened to.

Duff, and Mullens.

I am the more induced to bring this question under the notice of the House, that in 1843 the Parliamentary Inquiry was terminated, before this question of the social condition of the people was mooted.

No inquiry when Charter was renewed, 1843.

This House will agree with me, that a Government

that does its duty, should, at least, secure to the subjects of that government these four things :—

1. The administration of justice.
2. Security to life and property.
3. Protection to all classes, poor as well as rich.
4. Exemption from excessive taxation.

It becomes, therefore, my duty in submitting the resolutions which I am about to move to this House, to give them such information as is within my power, on these several points; and if I succeed in shewing that on all these points our administration is radically and grievously defective, I must believe that they will take some effectual steps to secure for these our fellow-subjects those rights to which they are as much entitled as ourselves.

Our administration defective.

I must claim the indulgence of the House, if I enter at some length into the accounts given of the present social condition of Bengal, as the strength of my appeal lies in the facts of the case; and therefore a summary glance at these would fail to communicate the impression which I am anxious to convey to the House; and let me say at the outset, that it is my aim to understate rather than to overstate the case, which in truth needs no colouring of mine to make the picture more gloomy—it is gloomy enough of itself.

Facts.

I shall take up the subjects of inquiry in the following order :—1st. The Perpetual Settlement and Zemindary system, which will include the taxation of the people; and 2ndly, the Police system, and the administration of justice.

I. The Zemindary System.

"To understand the system of landed tenure in Bengal, we must bear in mind that the Hindoo cultivators are the tenants of the Government. The Government is not only the ruler, but the landlord. The land tax, therefore, which constitutes the bulk of the revenue, is virtually rent. From 1772 to 1792 it was the custom to farm out the collection of the revenue to the highest bidders for terms of ten years. Since 1792, when Lord Cornwallis established what is called the Permanent Settlement, the land has been permanently invested in the hand of the Zemindars, who have an hereditary right to the district allotted to them, on condition that they pay to Government the prescribed amount of tax. It seems to have been his wish to raise up an aristocracy in Bengal like that in England. By the same act, the peasant who holds from the zemindar has an equal right to his small holding as the zemindar has to his district, so long as he pays his assessed rent; *but his legal rights are worthless, as he has no power to enforce them.* As an example of the oppression he endures—if a zemindar, on account of the failure of crops, obtains a remission of the tax to Government, having gained it for himself, he still exacts the tax from the ràyat, carries the account over to the next year, and charges him interest; the ràyat is from that hour practically a slave."

Zemindaree System.

Ràyat.

"The simple fact is, that Lord Cornwallis provided, with the settlement, a series of measures to protect the cultivator; and while that settlement has been upheld with sacred care, these measures have been *utterly disregarded.* The cultivator experiences no benefit from one of them. He can get no lease, no receipts; he has no protection against arbitrary and extortionate cesses in addition to his rent. But more than this, the Government had one object—*to get its land tax under the settlement.* What then? It gave the zemindars enormous powers, and reduced the cultivators to slavery."

Regulation, No 7. "In 1799, a regulation (*No.* 7) was passed, giving the zemindars powers to summon, and, if necessary, *compel*, the personal attendance of their tenants to settle rents, adjust accounts, measure boundaries, or '*any other* just purpose.' Under this, nearly every zemindar has his own bludgeon men, his own court, his own prison; aye more, as it is universally believed, his own modes of torture. This law and the Regu-
No. 5. lation *Five of* 1812 together constitute almost the most severe laws in the world, in the form of laws of distraint; and inconceivable misery is occasioned by them. Nothing whatever in the shape of an attempt to relieve the people has been heard of since *a proposed* measure in 1824, *which was not carried.* Bengal has been neglected in a most extraordinary manner; the condition of the people has not been a matter of Parliamentary inquiry; the real state of the case is known only to a few civil servants, who all these years *have done nothing*, and are utterly unable to explain their neglect; in fact, there is in Bengal an amount of suffering and debasement which probably you could not find exceeded, or even equalled, in the slave states of America."

This last is the testimony of a long resident in India, and a judicial person.

In answer to the question whether the lower provinces have deteriorated, I am told :—

"It can scarcely be said with strict accuracy that Bengal and Behar are *deteriorating*, when the agricultural produce of these provinces has been doubled, perhaps trebled, in the last 60 years. The increase of the exports of the Gangetic valley creates, year by year, greater surprise; but with all these elements of prosperity daily developed, the ràyat alone lan-
Causes of deterioration. guishes, and his condition has deteriorated and is deteriorating. This may be attributed to two causes. 1. The over population of Bengal, which is emphatically a *pauper warren.* Nine-tenths of the people live only by tilling the soil, and they must

have land to cultivate, or starve. The zemindar is therefore able to make his own terms, and to impose whatever exactions he pleases. If one man refuses to take the land, there are others ready to bid for it. For this evil of over population there is one remedy alone, a system of emigration to Assam, to Aracan, and to Pegu, where labour is scanty, and exorbitantly paid. The 2nd cause of this wretchedness is the absence of any institutions of our creation, which effectually protect the poor from oppression. In this respect Bengal is worse off than Behar, where the more manly population restrains oppression and extortion by resistance."

Again, I am told:—

"The power of the zemindar arises partly from his position as a great landlord among a submissive tenantry and a feeble executive government; and partly from the laws of distraint commonly called the Panjum (5th) and Huftum (7th), the very sound of which freezes the blood of the poor ràyat. These laws are oppressively severe, and enable a zemindar at any time to sell up a refractory or obnoxious tenant. The tenant has his remedy in a law suit, which is no remedy at all; for the zemindar is careful to keep up his influence and interest in the courts by bribery, by intrigue, and by systematic and organised collusion with the native ministerial officers, who form a rampart round the solitary English judge, which he is seldom able to break through." *Zemindaree System.*

The authority which I first quoted, says on this point—

"A few shillings will buy any number of false witnesses; and the police take the strongest side."

The *Friend of India*, Sept. 1852, said:—

"A whole century will scarcely be sufficient to remedy the evils of that perpetual settlement, and we have not yet begun

Its baneful influence. the task. Under its baneful influence a population of more than twenty millions have been reduced to a state of such utter wretchedness of condition, and such abjectness of feeling, as it would be difficult to parallel in any other country."

Another writer says:—

Revenue System. "The revenue system has also contributed a very large share towards the production of this state of things. It has ever been regarded as the first of duties on the part of every government official in Bengal to secure at all costs the revenue. Every right, hereditary or acquired, has been sacrificed to revenue, until, of all insecurities, the tenure of land has been the most precarious and uncertain. The absolute power wielded by the collector for the purposes of revenue has been delegated to the zemaindar for the acquisition of rent. For how could the zemaindar pay revenue if he could not secure the payment of his rents? Hence the promise of the Government, to secure to the hereditary tenures of Bengal the rights possessed at the time of the perpetual settlement, has been faithlessly broken, and so far as legal protection goes, the ràyat is at the mercy of the zemindar. He *has* rights, and rights too recognised by law, but the law gives him no means of securing them, nor any protection against invasion on the part of the stronger. Even where the law is open to the ràyat, the costliness, the chicanery, the corruption of the courts are such as to operate as a complete barrier to success."

Again:

"The Government are again in fear of a Santhal outbreak, or rather an insurrection of the Coles, the neighbours of the Santhals, in the hills of Central India. The same causes are at work to produce it. A high revenue charge, the extortions of usurers, and the police, are likely to bring about the same result."*

---

* As an illustration of the working of the zemindaree system among the Coles, I subjoin this account sent to me by a judge in India, of what took place only last year, till the English magistrate found that the native deputy magistrate could not be trusted in cases where Christianity was involved. The writer says, "The persecutions of the Christians are this year more fearful and unheard of than ever before. The native assistant to the Magistrate is of one mind with the zemindars. . . . . . Dismissing and fining the Christians, and robbing, plundering, beating them, is the order of the day in all the Christian villages. Sometimes it happens that in one day Christians of three or four villages are coming to us, lamenting that their houses, threshing noors, or fields, were plundered. Meanwhile these shameless plunderers put law-suits in the Court, stating that the Christians have plundered their fields, and against as many Christians as they possibly can at once, that no witnesses may remain to give evidence against their statements. . . . Tuesday last, the threshing floor of a Christian was plundered, and he so much beaten, that he fell down for dead. . . . . . He had a severe stroke over the forehead, two teeth broken, and was so much beaten and trampled upon, that he was not able to stand. . . . . We hear that the zemindars, who have caused this cruelty, and have plundered our brethren, came into the Cutcherry (Court house) yesterday, saying, 'There may come a Christian of our village complaining that we have beaten him, this is a lie. He was drunk, fell, or injured himself, and therefore we beg that his complaint against us may not be accepted.'" Again, "They, as well as all the villagers, conceal themselves every night outside the village, because the zemindars have sworn to plunder and to burn the village. . . . . . The zemindars have laid a strange plan. They intend to bind all those who will come in the beginning of the new year to engage for fields, by signature upon stamp paper, not to become Christians, and to submit to all whatever the zemindars will ask from them, and to all labour they may put upon them." Again, in a letter dated 12th December, 1856, it is said, "The night before last the house of our brethren at ———, was burnt down to the ground. A short time ago he had been plundered. . . . . On the same day, in the same village, another brother was bound, and continually cold water poured upon him; meanwhile, others stood by fanning him, to torture him with cold. In another village, ———, the zemindar caught four Christians, imprisoned them, and threatened to beat them with shoes. But as soon as the rumour spread in the village, all the people gathered before the zemindar's house, and asked him to relieve the brethren, which was done. But now the zemindar put a law-suit into the Cutcherry against the whole village, stating that they have attacked his house, intending to plunder it." This account, which has only recently reached me, is valuable as an illustration of what is done by zemindars and native assistant magistrates, when not sufficiently controlled by English magistrates, willing to do their duty. It is well

In the appendix to the Missionaries' petition, there are these statements :—

"The purchaser of an estate must be prepared to contest numerous lawsuits with his neighbours, to keep in his pay a

---

to observe that as the zemindars are not the proprietors of the land, they can have no legal right to make conditions with their rayats, that they shall in fact be their slaves; or, at any rate the Government has a right to say, we forbid such conditions, as the Government is the proprietor of the land.

I shall cite one more case, which is in some respects more melancholy, inasmuch as the decree of the English magistrate in favour of some persecuted Christians in the village of Baropakhya, in the district of Backergunge, in Bengal, was reversed by an experienced Sessions Judge. This case is also important, because the decision of the Sessions Judge was reviewed in the Sudder court, at Calcutta, which is the supreme court of appeal in civil cases, at the instance of Mr. Halliday, the Lieutenant-Governor. The Sudder unanimously decided that the judgment of the Sessions Judge was wrong, and that he ought to have sustained the conviction of the magistrate. But notwithstanding this, the criminals could not be re-tried, having been acquitted by the Judge, and set at liberty; and the poor native Christians remain to this day deprived of their lands and property. The Sessions Judge is, however, to be removed. The facts are briefly these. Fourteen native Christians were on the night of the 1st of July, 1855, forcibly seized, bound, beaten, and carried away from their homes; one was tortured, and all were carried about the country for six weeks, while their lands were given to others. The Magistrate, on the 28th of November, sentenced their invaders to imprisonment and labour. This judgment was appealed against, and the defendants were admitted to bail. On the 6th of January, 1856, the prisoners were all acquitted by the Sessions Judge, and released; while the police were commended; and he endeavoured to fasten an accusation on the Christians themselves of having fraudulently got up the case. The *Dacca News* thus refers to this melancholy subject :—

"There is nothing so convincing to our minds of the absolute necessity of a Parliamentary Commission, to inquire into the state of this country, as the fact that the minds of men living in India become accustomed to a certain way of looking on the things that exist around them, and see nothing at all uncommon in events that would strike an Englishman, fresh from England, with horror and disgust. We were conscious of this indifference in ourselves when we read the pamphlet by Mr. Underhill, detailing the sufferings of the Baropakhya Christians. What—said we to ourselves—is the man making such a fuss about? The Christians were only carried off, and *chullaumed* about the country for a month and a half; only one man seems to have been a little tortured. The Magistrate commits to the Judge their persecutors, and the Judge does—what most Company's judges do—decides against the Christian, European, or body of club-men sufficiently powerful to overawe theirs, and to make two or three quarterly payments to the collector, before the estate has yielded him any income. It is owing to these difficulties that so few English capitalists have laid out their money in the purchase of land in Bengal."

"An able Government officer once remarked in a conversation with the writer, that 'the reason why the lower provinces are called *settled*, must be, because everything in them (concerning boundaries) is *unsettled*, just as *lucus* is so called *a non lucendo*.'"

---

native. It is quite a common case—has happened to ourselves a hundred times; we are quite accustomed to be decided against. Messrs. Page and Underhill cannot expect to fare better than other European 'interlopers.' Throughout Mr. Kemp's decision run two ideas that are stereotyped in Anglo-Indian minds, which are, that the 'interloper,' whether missionary or planter, who comes before the courts, is either a fool—(this idea is not so absurd)—or a knave; that he must always be the oppressor, and can never be oppressed, or he would have righted himself; and that native Christians—'apostates' from heathenism, as Mr. Kemp politely calls them—must be rascals. These ideas are universal in India; so universal, that even the traduced classes themselves concur in them.

"It is with regret that we have read Mr. Kemp's decision. The conclusion we are irresistibly led to form, from this perusal, is, that Mr. Kemp had decided the case, on the abovementioned Anglo-Indian principles, before he had ever seen a paper in the case, and then tried to defend his conclusion from papers afterwards furnished to him. Mr. Kemp is one of the Company's crack judges. What must the others be?

"But the case of the Baropakhya Christians is but a drop in the bucket to what is daily suffered in Burisâl. For several years, before Planters dared to speak out, we tried, in the correspondence columns of the *Englishman*, to excite public attention to the state of that unhappy district. We have heard of a Darogah getting Rs. 3,000 in a single case. We have heard of a Thannah Mohurrir, whose salary is Rs. 7 a month, returning home after six months with savings amounting to Rs. 600. We have heard that the salt peons receive a salary of Rs. 4 a month, out of which they are expected to provide a boat, which alone costs Rs. 7 monthly. Were things worse in Oude? Did we annex Oude because 500 villages were depopulated? We can show as many in Tipperah. We were blamed because we said the name of Englishman had begun to stink in the nostrils of the people. Have not the planters of Serajgunge, in their petition, proved that our assertion was no exaggeration? We *must* have a Parliamentary Commission."

"A 'statute of frauds' should be enacted, declaring the prevalent practice of *benami* (anonymous or pseudonymous) possession to be illegal. The ostensible owner should be treated by the law as the real owner to all intents and purposes. The system of secret trusts, now prevalent, is a gigantic fabric of iniquity and fraud, to which the world probably cannot furnish a parallel."

Zemindaree System.

"The position assigned to zemindars by the law, is very peculiar. They are neither bonâ fide landowners, nor bonâ fide fiscal officers, appointed to collect the land-tax. They are almost all, however, in the habit of treating their ràyats not merely as their tenants, but as their serfs. They call themselves rajahs or kings, and the ràyats their subjects. They almost universally either claim more than their due, or else they claim it in an improper manner, for it is not easy to determine what really is their due. They exact contributions from their ràyats when a marriage or a birth or a death takes place in the family. They exact contributions for the avowed purpose of observing funeral rites in commemoration of their dead ancestors, and of celebrating the annual heathen festivals. These practises are almost universal. In numerous localities they exact from the ràyats gratuitous labour in the field or at the oar; and compel the poor people to allow them, without payment, the use of their cattle or of their boats, if they possess any. It is not unusual, especially at a considerable distance from the civil stations, for zemindars to go still further in the abuse of their power, by inflicting imprisonment and torture upon any ràyat who may have incurred their displeasure."

Can we wonder that witnesses of such a state of things should, before the last charter was granted, have addressed Parliament thus:—

"That your petitioners believe, that a strict and searching inquiry into the state of the rural population of Bengal, would lead your Honourable House to the conclusion, that they commonly live in a state of poverty and wretchedness, produced chiefly by the present system of landed tenures and the extortion of zemindars, aggravated by the inefficiency and the cruelties of the peace-officers, who are paid by the Chowkedarry tax or by the Government."

Or that later still, they should thus have addressed Lord Dalhousie, when his government was drawing to a close, with the hope that should the subject ever be discussed in Parliament, he would bring to bear upon it his ability and influence.

"The conviction that even after returning to England, and commencing afresh to take an active part in the labours of the imperial legislature, your lordship will always endeavour to promote the welfare of India, encourages us to give expression to the wish that your lordship's special attention might be directed to the lamentable condition of the peasantry of Bengal, to the causes of that condition, and to the best means of ameliorating it. We take the liberty of alluding to this subject not merely because we know both from our own experience, and from the testimony of other missionaries, that the present working of the zemindaree system is one of the most powerful obstacles to the spread of Christianity in this country; but also because we are convinced that it is a great and growing evil, particularly when considered in connection with the general character, both of zemindars and ràyats. It encourages the concealment, and consequently the commission of crime. It impedes the administration of justice; and whilst it emboldens the rich to set the law at defiance, it leads the poor to despair of obtaining redress, even against the greatest wrongs that may be inflicted upon them. We have reason to believe that a spirit of sullen discontent prevails even now among the rural population, from an impression that Government is indifferent to their sufferings. The zemindaree system may be convenient as a fiscal measure; but, on the other hand, the experience of sixty years proves that it tends to demoralize and pauperize the peasantry, and to reduce this fair and fertile land to a condition similar to that under which Ireland suffered so grievously and so long."

Or can we wonder that they should have adressed the Lieutenant-General of Bengal, and through him the Governor-General in Council, in these words?—

"That your Petitioners recognise in the perpetual settlement an important boon to the whole presidency, in its limitation of the land tax, and they regard that settlement as the probable foundation of great national prosperity. But in the practical operation of the system, your Petitioners observe two distinct classes of evils.

"*First*, the under tenures are insecure; the rents of the cultivating classes are capriciously varied; and the interests of those classes are virtually unprotected.

"*Secondly*, the zemindars are armed with extraordinary and excessive powers.

"That your Petitioners believe it to be notorious, that the intentions of the laws for securing leases to the tenants; for securing them receipts on their payments of rent; for limiting within just bounds the rents reserved in leases; and for checking the custom of exacting abwabs and other arbitrary additional charges and cesses, are commonly frustrated and defeated. On the other hand, the power of the zemindars, (as recognised in Reg. VII. of 1792, Sec. 15, cl. 8,) to compel the personal attendance of their tenants, for the adjustment of rent and other purposes, is, particularly in many parts of the country, a substitute for the regular and ordinary processes of the law, and is virtually the subjection of the tenants to a state of slavery. And, further, this evil is in many instances greatly aggravated, by the estates being held in co-tenancy, so that several shareholders, who are often in a state of conflict, equally exercise an arbitrary and unrestrained authority.

"That while this law thus presses severely on the tenants, your Petitioners observe, that from the increased cultivation of the soil, and the greatly increased value of its produce, the zemindars, who were primarily regarded simply as collectors of the land tax or farmers of the revenue, entitled to a fair profit on the returns, derive a revenue greatly in excess of the revenue which they pay to Government. And thus, contemporaneously, while the zemindar has been rising in wealth and power, the tenant has been sinking into penury and dependence, subject to illegal and exhausting exactions, harassed by contending proprietors, and oppressed by the exercise of extra-judicial powers.

"That your Petitioners are compelled to add, that other evils increase the wretchedness of the condition to which a tenant is thus reduced. The village chowkedars are the servants of his landlord; the government police are corrupt, and he cannot vie with his landlord in purchasing their favour; the courts of justice are dilatory and expensive, and are often far distant from his abode, so that he has no hope of redress for the most cruel wrongs; and he is frequently implicated in affrays, respecting disputed boundaries, in which he has not the slightest personal interest. Ignorant of his rights, uneducated, subdued by oppression, accustomed to penury, and sometimes reduced to destitution, the cultivator of the soil in many parts of this Presidency, derives little benefit from the British rule, beyond protection from Mahratta invasions.

"If fixity or permanence of tenure were established, then, immediately, as your Petitioners believe, the tendency would be to establish just relations between the landlord and the tenant from the highest to the lowest; and that principle, your Petitioners therefore earnestly desire to see adopted and carried out. At present it is infringed, in the first instance, by the right of the Goverment to sell the land for arrears of revenue, and thereby avoid the under-tenures with some few exceptions; and then, still more, by the entire absence of protection to the tenants, and the undefined relations of landlord and tenant through the Presidency.

"That your Petitioners believe that they have truly and accurately represented the condition of the cultivating classes. Your Petitioners believe it to be true, that superadded to the evils they endure from a corrupt and inefficient police, and an administration of civil and criminal justice which confessedly requires extensive improvement, they are liable to be constantly harassed by the conflicting and unsettled claims either of contending shareholders of joint estates, or of contending neighbouring proprietors; by the severe laws of distraint and arrest; by the power of their superior landholders, whether zemindars or middlemen, to compel personal attendance at their pleasure; by illegal exactions; by the unfixed nature of their tenures; and by the prevalent custom of refusing both leases and receipts."

II. Police and Justice.

I must now turn to the police system, and the administration of justice, and inquire how far this is calculated to remedy such a state of things. I will cite a few authorities on these points.

Petition, 1853, *by* 1800 *Persons.* "A separate petition, signed by 1,800 Christian inhabitants of Bengal, was presented to Parliament in 1853, in which they stated that the 'police of the Lower Provinces totally fails as respects the prevention of crimes, apprehension of offenders, and protection of life and property; but it is become an engine of oppression and a great cause of the corruption of the people;' 'that torture is believed to be extensively practised on persons under accusation;' and that 'all the evil passions are brought into play, and ingenuities of all kinds, both by people and police, are resorted to;' and this petition also bore strong and emphatic testimony to the wretched condition of the people, and the unsatisfactory state of the judicial system."

Again, the missionaries, in their petition to the Governor-General in Council, make this statement; and one of the points they here notice is almost *the only one not admitted by Mr. Halliday* in his Minute on their petition, namely the feeling *of discontent and hatred* arising in the people. If they are not discontented and angry they must indeed be a marvellous people; and I for one should think the evidence of the missionaries more worthy of credit than even Mr. Halliday's *on this point*, considering that he has not permanently resided among the people since 1843, when he became Secretary to the Government of Bengal.

Missionaries' Petition to Legislative Council.

"That your Memorialists would now look to his Lordship, the present Governor-General in Council, and the Legislative Council of India, at this season of peace and financial prosperity, to deal with these important matters with adequate earnestness, and with a view to comprehensive and complete reforms. *Your Memorialists feel themselves bound to declare, that they view with alarm, as well as sorrow, the continuance of the evils which they have so long deplored, and the effects of which are seen in the demoralization and the sufferings of the people; and that they believe that measures of relief can with safety be delayed no longer; as from the information they have acquired, they fear that the discontent of the rural population is daily increasing, and that a bitter feeling of hatred towards their rulers is being engendered in their minds.*

"That a Bill, called an Affray Bill, was read a first time in

Council about three years ago, the object of which was to render liable for affrays, not merely the ignorant clubmen who are hired, or the dependent tenants who are compelled to take part in them, but those also for whose benefit they are undertaken, and without whose connivance they would not occur; and that your Memorialists believe, that the official information by which the necessity for that measure was proved to the Government in 1853, would satisfy the present Government, that practices are common, in the Mofussil, of reckless lawlessness and violence, and that there is such an indifference to human life and suffering, as indicates a fearful state of demoralization and anarchy."

A long resident in India says on this point—

"The police is not the worst in the world, only because, in the proper acceptation of the term, there is no police at all, but a system of organised chicanery and oppression."

The *Friend of India* says—

Friend of India.

"Disgust is lost in astonishment at the mysterious principle of cohesion by which it is still held together."

Another writer says—

Torture by the Police.

"In my last I intimated that torture by the police was not confined to the presidency of Madras. I will now substantiate my assertion. And in order to avoid all doubt, the instances I shall give shall be taken from the records of the Sudder Nizamut Adawleet, the highest court of appeal in all criminal cases, and other unquestionable authorities. The district of Dinagepore, in which Malduh is situated, lies some 200 miles to the north of Calcutta. On the 14th November, 1853, seven police officers proceeded to arrest Bhador Nussoo, on the charge or dacoity, that is burglarious robbery. One officer was a darogah, the chief of the police of that division; the second was the next in command; the rest were common policemen. The prisoner was first bound hand and foot, and beaten. The darogah himself then beat him with a whip on the back. As the stolen property was not forthcoming, the man was again beaten. The poor wretch now pointed at some property as stolen, which in fact belonged to the man with whom he lived. It did not satisfy his tormentors, and he was beaten senseless. At the order of the chief officer, a bamboo was now brought, on which he was slung, tied hand and foot. On reaching the cowshed, where the police had other prey, he was found to be dead. The beating was skilfully performed by sharp raps on the joints, also by punching and poking him with sticks so as to leave no external marks. By the medical officer it was considered that the further torture had been used of rolling two sticks fastened together down the thigh and leg. This was done to extort from the man the plundered property and the names of his accomplices. After all, it would appear that he was innocent.*

"Only in January last three police officers were convicted at Saharunpore of torturing, beating, and starving ten men, in order to obtain information of some robbery. The torture was suspension from a tree by the arms, like that mentioned above. This was continued for several days. One man died. At Ahmenabad, a police officer was dismissed for suspending a man to a beam by the hair of his head, and having had the man beaten while thus suspended. It is a very common mode of torture by the police to put red pepper, or the dust of chillies, into the eyes of prisoners or suspected thieves, to make them confess."—(*Cheevers*, p. 216.)

---

* I do not advert to the system of torture with the view of implicating the Government, who, I believe, have done what they can to abolish it, but because it is hardly possible to take a just view of the miseries inflicted by the police without adverting to it. It will take years to eradicate it, as the system prevails throughout society in India: even parents will torture their children, and it has come down to the people from their ancestors as a venerable institution.

"A few years ago the house of the missionary of Dinagepore was assaulted by dacoits. He escaped, but his native preacher was killed. Several men were convicted, chiefly on their own confession, and punished for the crime. During the trials the attention of the judge was called to the state of the prisoners' feet. They bore evident marks of torture. No notice, however, was taken of the fact. Not long after, a gang of robbers was arrested, which it was proved had committed the crime. The punished men were innocent, and the confessions which led to their conviction had been extorted by the cruelest and most atrocious means.

"But these instances are enough. Ask any judge or magistrate in Bengal, and he will tell you that torture is practised by his police; that the object is not to discover the criminal, but some one who will confess the crime. Often the police are bribed by the guilty party. If the crime cannot be hidden, an innocent man is seized, and by tortures of the most atrocious kind, he is induced to confess that he has committed the offence. It is so notorious, that criminal prosecutions are often dismissed by the magistrates, because the confessions are obviously constrained. Nor will the practice cease until the confessions of prisoners are deemed of less importance than they are by the administrators of justice.

"It would occupy too much room to detail to your readers how these gentry oppress the peasantry of Bengal. How the appearance of the police in a village is a signal to bury food and treasure, or for the inhabitants to flee. How any offender, if rich enough, may usually bribe the thief-taker, and even purchase his good offices to fasten the crime upon an unoffending neighbour. How torture is not unfrequently employed to extort money, or confessions of guilt, or accusations against innocent men. All this, and much more, is so common in Bengal, that the sufferings of the rāyat now pass unheeded, the commonness of such things has produced indifference.

Inexperience of Magistrates.

"But this is not all. The evil is increased by the inexperience of the persons appointed to the magisterial office. On arriving in this country the juvenile civil servant is placed under a superior to gain a knowledge of business, and to prepare for future service. But so low in estimation, or rather in the scale of emolument, has the Honourable Company placed the magistrate's office, that it is for the most part filled by young and 'therefore unqualified' men. The introduction of these inexperienced men has largely increased of late years. In 1850 the average standing of magistrates was nine years and eight months; it is now so low as six years and ten months. No wonder that Mr. Halliday should affirm that 'our magistracy is losing credit and character, and our administration is growing perceptibly weaker.' The evil is greatly increased by the confined nature of the civil service itself. It is not large enough to supply the demands for efficient officials which are increasingly made upon it, with the increasing area of our Eastern dominions. Besides which, the magnitude of the population committed to the jurisdiction of one man far exceeds the powers of the most able and experienced official. It is a mockery of government to expect that one man can efficiently discharge the duties arising out of the police and judicial administration of half a million of people.

Frequent changes of Officials.

"There is, however, another evil, and one of great magnitude, to which Mr. Halliday does not refer, but which ought not to have been passed over—I mean, that of the frequent removals from place to place, and from office to office, of the servants of the Company. Scarcely is a man seated in his chair, than he is whisked off to another spot. He is appointed to another district, and often very different kind of labour, of course in all cases obtaining a higher remuneration. Thus in the district of Dacca, the average time of continuance in the magistrate's office has been for the last twenty years not ten months, scarcely a sufficient period to learn the names of the chief towns of the district which the individual is appointed to govern.

"I will take a name or two at random from the Register of Civil Servants and their appointments, just to elucidate the extent of this evil. Here is a well-known name among Indian officials, Lushington—Henry Lushington. He arrived in India the 14th of October, 1821. Up to May 9, 1842, he had filled no less than twenty-one offices—a change every year. But during this time he returned to Europe twice, and was absent from India four years and a quarter. His occupancy of each office therefore averages scarcely *nine* months.

"Thousands of square miles of country, inhabited by millions of people, would have neither justice nor protection, were it not for the illegally assumed power of the planter and zemindar. There are districts in which the magistrate's court is sixty miles away, and in one case I know of a judge having to go 140 miles to try a case of murder, so wide does his jurisdiction extend. This very district contains upwards of two millions of people; yet to govern it there are just two Europeans, and one of these spends a considerable portion of his time in sporting, shooting wild animals, and hunting deer."

There are but 70 European magistrates—1 to 460,000. An old resident in India says, there are three or four cases of a single magistrate to more than a million souls. This is in a country where roads are *very* scarce.

A writer before quoted, says—

"No man in his senses will resort to a court of law in Bengal. The result is only sure to that side which can lie with most assurance, and bribe with the longest purse. What with delay, the inefficiency of the magistrates and judges, the unblushing corruption which prevails from the highest to the lowest official, the civil servant only excepted, justice is the scarcest of all commodities in Bengal. There is no doubt of it. In every part of Bengal which I have visited, I never met with but one opinion about it. From Burdwan in the north-west, to Chittagong in the far south-east, the testimony of all classes of people is uniform; all agree that the courts of the Company are nests of corruption, perjury, and injustice. I have already spoken of the faultiness of the judicial and police administration. I may be pardoned this continual reference to it. It is truly the spring of by far the larger part of the evils under which the people of Bengal suffer. An unexpected proof of this has just occurred, and the source of it is the highest authority in the country. No man has a more wide and perfect knowledge of Bengal than Mr. Halliday, its *Mr. Halliday's Minute.* able Lieutenant-Governor. In a Minute he has lately recorded he has laid bare the existing system to its core. Well may the editor of *The Friend of India* remark, 'The execution of justice in Bengal depends, therefore, upon men whose first hope is to escape starvation, and their second is to avoid the just expiation of their deeds upon the gallows.' I hope that not a day will be lost by some member of the House of Commons in moving for the production of this remarkable Minute or Report on the judicial administration of Bengal."

This most remarkable Minute I am happy to inform the House that I have seen, and I hold in my hand a reprint of it. I must be permitted to read some extracts to the House.

MINUTE BY THE HON'BLE THE LIEUTENANT-GOVERNOR OF BENGAL.

POLICE AND CRIMINAL JUSTICE IN BENGAL.

Police.—For a long series of years complaints have been handed down from administration to administration regarding the badness of the Mofussil police under the Government of Bengal, and as yet very little has been done to improve it. Such efforts as have occasionally been made for this purpose, have been usually insufficient to meet the greatness of the evil; partial remedies have failed to produce any extensive benefit; and, during long intervals, the Government has appeared to fold its hands in despair, and to attempt nothing new, because the last tried inadequate measure had ended in inevitable disappointment.

3. *Former Measures.*—For what, after all, has been done to improve the police during the last thirty years? We have ceased, it is true, to expect integrity from darogahs with inadequate salaries and large powers, surrounded by temptations, and placed beyond the reach of practical control; and we have somewhat curtailed the excessive and unmanageable extent of our magistrate's jurisdictions by the gradual establishment of thirty-three* sub-division magistrates. But beyond this, and not speaking at present of the special and peculiar machinery lately set up in a few districts for the suppression of dacoity, I know not what else has been attempted; and, even with regard to these two instalments of improvement, the halting, hesitating way in which they have been effected has prevented the full benefit which might otherwise have been expected from them. Before the first of these improvements, our stipendiary police in the Regulation Provinces consisted of some four hundred and eighty-four darogahs or thannadar, scattered at distant intervals over a territory of 150,000 square miles, and a population of 35,000,000 souls—being, say, one darogah or superior police officer to 309 square miles and 72,314 souls. Each of these potent functionaries was paid rupees 25 a month—avowedly less than he could live and move about upon—and each had under him, generally, a mohurir or clerk, and a jemadar or head constable, on salaries

* This is now the number of sub-divisions in the Regulation Provinces.

ranging from rupees 4 to 8 a month each, but with powers equal on most occasions to the darogah himself. Subordinate to these at each thannah was an establishment of from ten to twenty burkundauzes or constables, often deputed with large powers into the interior, and paid, each man, from rupees 3-8 to 4 a month—a salary notoriously inadequate. It was a step in the right direction, doubtless, when the government of Lord Auckland determined thenceforth to pay no darogah less than rupees 50 per mensem, and to allow to one hundred of the number rupees 75, and to fifty of them rupees 100 per mensem. But the good of all this was tarnished by the omission to do anything for the lower grades of police officers. For it was impossible to become a good darogah without an apprenticeship; and when the apprenticeship was to be served in the midst of great power, great temptation, and the traditions of unavoidable corruption in the station of a thannah mohurir on rupees 7 a month, what was to be expected from such a training?—or how, train the darogah as you might, could you expect purity and integrity until you had cleansed away from about him the foul atmosphere of corruption necessarily engendered by the aggregation of ill-paid and unscrupulous underlings with whom bribery and extortion were almost a necessity, and had long been the habit of their lives?

4. *Recent Recommendation.*—I last year submitted to the Government of India an earnest recommendation, founded on Mr. Dampier's propositions, for an increase to the salaries of mohurirs, jemadars, and burkundauzes, by a system of gradation.* And, unless financial difficulties interpose, I cannot

* Full details of the proposed measure, and cogent arguments for its adoption, will be found in Mr. Grey's letter to the Government of India, No. 774, of 30th April, 1855. It was proposed to divide mohurirs into three grades, on rupees 30, 35, and 40 per mensem; jemadars into three grades, on rupees 10, 15, and 20; and of the burkundauzes, one-fourth at rupees 6 per mensem, one-fourth at rupees 5, and the rest on rupees 4. The whole increased cost to be incurred would be rupees 338,609 per annum.

doubt that this measure must ultimately be honoured by the approval of the Governor-General in Council. But if this be not granted, all thought for the improvement of the police will, I fear, be but thought thrown away.

5. *Sub-division Magistracies.*—Beyond all doubt, we shall ever fail to establish a good and trustworthy system of police, unless—together with other improvements—we establish a close, constant, and vigorous control over our police agents, and a ready access to justice for all persons, so that the appeal of the weak against the strong may be at all times possible and effectual.

6. Throughout the length and breadth of this country, the strong prey almost universally upon the weak, and power is but too commonly valued only as it can be turned into money. The native police, therefore, unless it be closely and vigorously superintended by trustworthy officers, is sure to be a scourge to the country in exact proportion to its strength and power. For this indispensable superintendence, no adequate provision has ever yet been made; nor can any provision be considered adequate which does not supply, at least, one capable and trustworthy magistrate for every two, or, at most, every three thannahs. At present, however, our establishments do not comprise more than seventy executive magistrates, covenanted and uncovenanted, over four hundred and eighty-four * thannahs, being at the average rate of about seven-and a-quarter thannahs to each magistrate — a proportion much below what is requisite; and the distribution of even this number of magistrates is extremely irregular.

7. *Village Chowkeydars.*—Of the vast importance of the rural police, the village chowkeydars, and the strong necessity for fortifying and improving their character and position, there

* I find this the number of thannahs in the Regulation Provinces in the Appendix to the Circular Orders of the superintendent of police printed in 1854.

has never been but one opinion. Yet, though more than one expedient for this purpose has been devised and discussed, nothing has ever been carried into execution, and it is a lamentable, but unquestionable fact, that the rural police, its position, character, and stability as a public institution, have, in the Lower Provinces, deteriorated during the last twenty years. It is now diminished in number and impaired in efficiency, while its rights have been seriously and successfully attacked and undermined; so that, unless some speedy measures be taken to save it, it is in danger of perishing altogether from the face of the land, and passing out of use, if not out of remembrance.

10. The great difficulty indeed regarding the village police, which has been commented upon by all who have directed their attention to the subject since the beginning of the century, is that they are inadequately and uncertainly paid. They are kept in a permanent state of starvation, and though in former days magistrates battled for them with unwilling zemindars and villagers, and were encouraged by Government to do so, it has been discovered in later times that this is all against the law. Village watchmen are now declared to have no legal right to remuneration for service, and (the help of the magistrate being withdrawn) they have no power to enforce their rights, even if they had any rights to enforce. Hence they are all thieves or robbers, or leagued with thieves and robbers, insomuch that when any one is robbed in a village, it is most probable that the first person suspected will be the village watchman.

12. Yet, miserably impaired as the institution of the village police has become, it is still true that no police can be effective without their help, and that, as stated in the Minute of Lord Hastings, dated 2nd October, 1815, "It is from the chowkeydars that all information of the character of individuals, of the haunts and intentions of robbers, and of everything necessary to forward the objects of police, must ordinarily be obtained; they are the watch and patrol to which the community looks

for its immediate protection, and on the occurrence of a crime, the darogah's only mode of proceeding is to collect the watchmen of all neighbouring villages, and to question them as to all the circumstances, with a view to get from them that information which they only can afford."

13. The village chowkeydars are in short the foundation of all possible police in this country, and upon their renovation, improvement, and stability depends the ultimate success of all our measures for the benefit of the country in the prevention, detection, and punishment of crime. To what a state of corruption, however, this important branch of the police system had fallen, was strongly illustrated by the late Mr. Bethune, in his Minute of the 27th May, 1851, of which the following is an extract:—

"The evidence I have seen of this is now thirteen years old, but the complaints recently made of outrageous dacoities and acts of violence point rather to a deterioration than to an improvement of the practical working of the system since that time. I took the following striking comparison from Speede's Criminal Statistics of Bengal, in which some of the results obtained by the Police Commissioners in 1837, have been digested and arranged in a tabular form. The returns made to Government for the years 1833-4-5-6, show the average number of persons annually convicted for crimes and offences* *of all kinds* in those years to be 31,843, and taking the population of the districts to which these returns apply to have been 38,717,874, as estimated in the magistrates' returns, the proportion is about 1 convict to 1,219 persons.

"The Commissioners of 1837 obtained also a return of chowkeydars dismissed from the police force during the years 1835-6-7, with the causes of dismissal.† *Were they no worse than the rest of the population*, the number of persons among

---

* Speede's Criminal Statistics, page 149; and page 174.

† Speede's Appendix, page 7.

them guilty of *every kind of offence known to the calendar*, at the rate of 1 in 1,219, would be under 107 annually, or 321 in the three years included in the return. What were the facts? The whole number of chowkeydars dismissed for misbehaviour in those three years, instead of 321, is 1,130.

Of whom for murder and Thuggee . .	19
Burglary	39
Robbery and theft	357
	415

that is to say:—

"Nearly one-fourth more, in proportion to their number, *for these heinous crimes*, than were convicted in all the Lower Provinces of Bengal *for all offences of every kind.*"

The whole is summed up by the Commissioners in the following terms:—

"The most urgent necessity exists for a thorough revision throughout the country. The establishment (of village watchmen) is described not only as utterly useless for police purposes, but as a curse instead of a blessing to the community. *It is even a question whether an order issued throughout the country to apprehend and confine them would not do more to put a stop to theft and robbery than any other measure that could be adopted.*"

14. Various plans have been proposed for amending this state of things, and a good deal of paper has been covered with written discussions regarding them, but nothing has ever been done; so that many persons have come to think it a thing impossible to do any good in that direction, and have ceased from all effort accordingly.

18. *Administration of Criminal Justice.*—I am satisfied, however, that it will be vain to improve the agency for the detection and apprehension of criminals, unless we improve also the agency for trying them.

Police reform, in India at least, is a word of large signification, and extends to our criminal judicatories as well as to the magistracy and constabulary organisation. At present our criminal judicatories stand in need of much amendment, and unfortunately the method of amending them is a question which admits of much diversity of opinion.

19. They certainly do not command the confidence of the people.

20. That this is the case may, I think, be inferred from many parts of Mr. Dampier's elaborate reports. I have myself made much personal inquiry into this matter during my tours. Whether right or wrong, the general native opinion is certainly that the administration of criminal justice is little better than a lottery, in which, however, the best chances are with the criminals; and I think this also is very much the opinion of the European Mofussil community.

21. No complaint is more common among magistrates and police officers of every grade than that of the disinclination of the people to assist in the apprehension and conviction of criminals. From one end of Bengal to the other the earnest desire and aim of those who have suffered from thieves or dacoits, is to keep the matter secret from the police, or, failing that, so to manage as to make the trial a nullity before the courts. Something of this is due perhaps to the natural apathy of the people, though it cannot fail to be observed on the other hand that where they have any object to gain, the same people show no apathy or unreadiness, but remarkable energy and perseverance, in civil and criminal prosecutions. More no doubt is due to the corruption and extortion of the police, which causes it to be popularly said that dacoity is bad enough, but the subsequent police inquiry very much worse. But after allowing for both these causes, no one, conversant with the people, can have failed to remark how much of their strong unwillingness to prosecute is owing to the deep sense which pervades the public mind of the utter uncertainty of the proceedings of our courts, and the exceeding chances of

escape which our system allows to criminals. Often have I heard natives express, on this point, their inability to understand the principles on which the courts are so constituted or so conducted, as to make it appear in their eyes as if the object were rather to favour the acquittal then to insure the conviction and punishment of offenders; and often have I been assured by them that their anxious desire to avoid appearing as prosecutors arose in a great measure from their belief that prosecution was very likely to end in acquittal, even, as they imagined, in the teeth of the best evidence, while the acquittal of a revengeful and unscrupulous ruffian was known by experience to have repeatedly ended in the most unhappy consequences to his ill-advised and imprudent prosecutor.

22. That this very general opinion is not ill-founded may, I think, be proved from our own records.

23. Appended to this Minute, is a note and certain statistical returns prepared by Mr. Secretary Buckland, from which it may be gathered that for fourteen burglaries committed, only one burglar is punished; and that even in thefts, which are matters of easier detection and punishment, the average proportion of convictions is only of three persons to eight offences.

26. From any sentence passed by a magistrate beyond a fine of rupees 50, or one month's imprisonment, there may be an appeal to the sessions judge, and from every sentence passed by a sessions judge there may be an appeal to the Sudder Court. Of the total 4,000 persons annually committed to the sessions for heinous crimes, it appears that the conviction of 1,735 takes place in the sessions effectually, and of 332 in the referred trials to the Sudder; so that of the whole number committed, very nearly one-half is eventually acquitted.

27. That a very small proportion of heinous offenders are ever brought to trial, is matter of notoriety. It now appears that half of those brought to trial are sure to be acquitted.

Is it to be expected, then, that the people should have confidence in our system, or that they should show any desire to assist the police, knowing as they do from experience the miserable results to be obtained?

28. I must say that this appears to me the weakest point of our whole system, and that which most loudly calls for an effectual remedy. No doubt the badness of the police and the inefficiency of the tribunals act and re-act on each other, and both are concerned in bringing about the deplorable existing consequences. But until the tribunals are reformed, I can see no use in reforming the police, and I think it will be money thrown away to attempt the latter unless we are determined vigorously to insist on the former. We have been hitherto debating about both for many years without much practical effect, and in the meantime, to take only one crime, and only the seven districts round about Government House, we have seen dacoities increase from 82 in 1841, to 524 in 1851! It is true that under a special agency this has since been reduced to 111 in 1855. But the operations of this agency have shown more than anything else the utter inability of our ordinary institutions to cope with the enormous social evil that is ever rising up in defiance before it.

29. *Inexperience of Magistrates.*—Even if our tribunals were all we could wish, and if our police were fully reformed, what would it avail us so long as our superintending magistracy was for the most part in the hands of inexperienced and therefore unqualified young men? Yet this has not only been long the notorious fact, but peculiar and accidental circumstances, partly temporary and partly arising out of the constitution of the civil service, have at this moment made the inexperienced condition of the magistracy more observable than it has ever been before, while it seems certain that the evil during several succeeding years is likely very seriously to increase I have appended to this paper a note by Mr. Grey on this very

subject.* Those who are conversant with the working of our system are aware that this is (under present rules) an evil that cannot be resisted; while it exists, although certain of our young magistrates often display efficiency and ability beyond their years, yet on the whole our magistracy is losing credit and character, and our administration is growing perceptibly weaker, and yet I grieve to be obliged to affirm that the evil will infallibly increase within the next three years unless an early remedy be applied. Does anybody imagine that while this lasts our Bengal police can be reformed?

30. *Five Measures Proposed.*—It appears to me then that in order to an effectual improvement of the police in the Lower Provinces, the following principal measures are indispensably necessary:—

(1.) The improvement of the character and position of the village chowkeydars or watchmen.

(2.) Adequate salaries, and, I may add, fair prospects of advancement to the stipendiary police.

(3.) The appointment of more experienced officers as covenanted zillah magistrates.

(4.) A considerable increase in the number of the uncovenanted or deputy magistrates.

(5.) An improvement in our criminal courts of justice.

40. We must do our utmost to carry the people with us in our police reforms; at present they will readily admit old

---

* The average standing of the magistrates of the 25 districts which have separate magistrates, was in 1850, nine years and eight months. The average standing of the officers now serving as magistrates in the same districts is only six years and ten months.

In 1850, there were only two magistrates below seven years' standing, now there are 15 such.

The youngest officer officiating as a magistrate in 1850, was of five years' standing, the youngest officer now officiating as magistrate is of less than three years' standing.

(Signed) W. Grey,
Secy. to the Govt. of Bengal.

20th April, 1856.

established obligations to maintain village watchmen in a certain customary proportion to the size of each village, and to pay them after a certain usage, which differs somewhat in different villages, but has long been accommodated to old habits and customs in all. They will not, however, regard with favour a distinct and precise taxation for a new police, the application of which they will doubt, and the object of which they will be very likely to misunderstand; and, unfortunately, our knowledge of the people and our intercourse with them, through distantly placed, often inexperienced, and but too frequently changed, Mofussil magistrates, is not sufficiently intimate and cordial to allow as yet of our acquiring their confidence, and thereby their co-operation, in plans for the improvement of their old institution. Hereafter, when we shall have placed trustworthy magistrates in adequate numbers, and in the centre of manageable jurisdictions, I do not doubt that we shall be able gradually to influence the people more effectually than we can now pretend to do, and so to carry them with us as to obtain their intelligent assent, and with it their hearty assistance to all our measures. We must, in short, obtain their confidence in our magistracy and police system before we can hope for their co-operation, and this cannot be expected under our present imperfect organisation.

43. *More experienced Magistrates.*—The third measure on my list relates to the youth and inexperience of the covenanted magistrates. This is a very serious evil, and it is absolutely necessary to remedy it. It arises out of the numerical inadequacy of the covenanted service to supply the number of offices required by the existing system. It has been a matter of reproach to the service for many years, but it has very much increased of late, owing to the growing disproportion of men to offices. It has, in a manner painfully perceptible to me in my visits to the different districts, impaired the force, dignity, and efficiency of our administration in the interior; and in all

cases in which the youth and inexperience of the officer is not, as it sometimes is, counterbalanced by unusual ability and force of character, it has brought the all-important authority of the zillah magistracy into marked slight and disregard, and sometimes into actual contempt. It is certain still more to increase under the present system, and no addition to the number of the service can remedy it for many years to come.

The nature of the duties and responsibilities of collectors' offices requires that they should be held by officers of a certain standing and experience; but the actual work of those offices has become, with a few exceptions, so notoriously light, that full leisure is left for the efficient performance of a magistrate's business; and there is undoubtedly nothing in the nature of the two duties in these provinces, where the collection of the Government revenue is almost mechanical, and the interference of the collector in the realisation of the zemindar's rent from his tenants is purely judicial, to make them in the smallest degree incompatible. To re-unite them, therefore, is now the mere dictate of prudence. It will at once place the superintending magistracy of each district in experienced hands, will economise labour, will remove a standing reproach against the Government, and will restore to the Mofussil administration that strength and weight which the present youth and inexperience of our "boy magistrates" have very sensibly and seriously impaired. This measure was proposed by Lord Dalhousie in 1854, and the reasons in its favour which then existed have been greatly enhanced by the occurrences of the past two years. I earnestly trust that the advantages which it offers, and which are enjoyed by all other parts of India, including all our recent acquisitions, will no longer be denied to Bengal, where, in fact, they are most urgently needed, and where the theoretical objections to the system, weak as I believe them to be everywhere else, have literally no kind of practical application.

By those who object to this, in my judgment, most useful

and necessary measure, two methods have been proposed of remedying the great present evil, which nobody denies, of the youth and inexperience of the magistrates. One is to make the magistrates and collectors, as it were, change places; to let the young and inexperienced officers become, after their present brief training, collectors on the present salaries of magistrates, and to let them thence rise to the office of magistrate, receiving in that office the salary now given to collectors.

This would merely transfer a disease from one part of the administration to another part, and cure the defect in the magistracy at the expense of the efficiency of the revenue department. The revenue department, not less than the magistracy, requires maturity of standing and experience, and the Government, as well as the people, would suffer if the office of collector were placed generally in young, inexpert, and unpractised hands.

45. If this were done, the step to which the junior now rises from his first and insufficient training, instead of being as now that of a magistrate in full charge of a district as large as three counties, would be, with perhaps the same or nearly the same pecuniary advantages, the more suitable position of a deputy or subordinate to the experienced collector magistrate, and the Zillah magistracies, instead of being in the hands of youngsters of three, and perhaps even less than three, years' standing, would not be attained to under a standing of at least ten years, and probably much more.*

46. *Increase of Deputy Magistrates.*—The next necessary measure is an increase to the magistracy, and this can only be by an increase to the number of uncovenanted deputy magistrates.

47. It is vain to talk of police reform so long as the police are under no closer superintendence than that of a magistrate from 30 to 60 miles off (or even more), in a country where, owing

---

* Our present junior collector is of eleven years' standing, and this is at a time of unusually rapid promotion.

to the nature of the climate and the want of means of communication, a distance of 10 miles is often more than equivalent to 50 miles in England. I will not here parade any statistical facts. Every one acquainted with the country knows how few and far between are our magistrates in the interior, as compared with even the worst organised country in Europe, and every one admits that one of the first steps towards improvement must be to have magistrates at such tolerably convenient distances, that each functionary shall not be at all events more than a few hours' journey from the most distant village in his jurisdiction.

The additional establishments, allowing for some reduction in the present Zillah magistrates' establishment, would certainly bring the expense up to five lacs and a half per annum, or say, with some additional Thannahs, six lacs. For this amount, however, I think this very desirable, not to say necessary reform, might be made. And even then, and after adding the amount of rupees 3,38,609, required to render adequate the pay of Mohurirs, Jemadars, and Burkundauzes,* which would raise the total additional annual expense to rupees 8,88,609, or say, after allowing for all defects of the estimate, ten lacs of rupees, the police charges of Bengal would still be only a little more than the police charges of the North-Western Provinces.† And it must be by no means left out of sight, that the diminution of expenditure at present, in consequence of the diminished numbers of junior civil servants, as compared with the year 1850, is more than a lac and a half of rupees ;‡ and as it is in a great measure owing to this diminution, that an addition is required to the uncovenanted magis-

---

* See para. 4 of this Minute.

† Provincial Police charges, 1851–52, Bengal, rupees 10,31,386. N.W. P., rupees 16,97,607. See para. 15 of Mr. Secretary Grey's letter to the Government of India, No. 2137, of 30th September, 1855.

‡ The actual difference is rupees 1,54,440.

trates, it is reasonable to set off a large part of this lac and a half, say at least a lac, against the additional charge now asked for, thus reducing the total to a maximum of nine lacs per annum.

79. *Roads.*—I have now recapitulated the five chief improvements which seem to me to be required to place the police of Bengal on a footing of reasonable promise, from which it may gradually advance to a better and still better condition. There is, however, yet another measure which can hardly be omitted in this place, and which may seem of itself almost as important as any of the foregoing. I allude to a measure for the establishment of sufficient means of communication with the interior of districts. It cannot, indeed, be necessary to dwell on the importance of roads and communications to the well-doing of any police system. No system can work well while our police stations and our large towns and marts in the interior are cut off from the chief Zillah stations and from one another by the almost entire absence of roads, or even (during a large part of the year) of the smallest bridle-roads or foot-paths. It may be impossible, in the present state of our resources, to make all over our Zillahs such roads as are fit at all times for wheeled carriages; but where better and broader roads cannot be made, it ought to be an indispensable part of our system to have from the chief Zillah station to all police stations in the interior, and from each police station to the neighbouring stations, at least a raised and bridged foot or bridle-path, so that a man, a horse, a bullock, an elephant, or a palankeen should at all times of the year be able uninterruptedly to pass and repass. There are but few of our Zillahs where this might not be done at a comparatively small expense, if the land were available; and of so much public import is it to have land available for such a purpose, that I should not think it unjust to propose a law, making it binding on all zemindars, and other proprietors of land, to give up sufficient lands for the purpose, free of all cost to the State, except of

any standing crops or agricultural produce. In most parts of Bengal the zemindars would do this willingly without any law, and the benefit to the surrounding lands would be of itself sufficient to over-pay the value of the land given.

80. By so digging the earth for the road as to form a small canal, a means of water communication in the rains might be secured, which would be of the highest value to agriculture and commerce, and which would easily bear a light toll, sufficient to pay for the repair (at least) of the road and the canal.

81. I think that the construction and repair of such roads ought to be an essential duty of each magistrate and division magistrate; that the expense should be estimated and passed once a year, separate from all other public works, and should be considered and calculated on as one of the charges of the police. Such a system, fairly established, and energetically kept up, would, by facilitating the movements of magistrates, of police officers, of despatches, of complainants, and of witnesses, do as much for the improvement of the police as any measure that could be devised, and without it I doubt if any measures could be fully successful.

But, Sir, clear and decided as is Mr. Halliday's testimony, we have no evidence that even his testimony is not considered exaggerated by the Supreme Council of India, which consists of only five members besides the Governor-General himself; for the Minute of Mr. Halliday, sent in to the Council, is dated 30th April, 1856, and yet in October of the same year we find Mr. Dorin writing to the Court of Directors in answer to the Memorialists, in language in direct opposition to Mr. Halliday's Minute; and in the same paper which has been laid on the table of this House,

I am still more surprised to find some of the statements of Mr. Grant, because he does in *very important* points declare his *agreement* with the missionaries.*

Now, Sir, Mr. Dorin and Mr. Grant are *the two civil* members of the Supreme Council, appointed by the Government; while Mr. Halliday is neither in the Supreme nor in the Legislative Council.

Whole subject demands investigation.

I think this House must be convinced, from the statements I have just brought before them, that the whole subject demands a thorough investigation; not an investigation that is to stop any measure now in progress for the amelioration of these evils; not an investigation which is to array class against class, and promote discord; but a calm, patient, investigation, such as English gentlemen are capable of making, and the result of which ought to be submitted to this House. If I am asked what object would be attained by inquiring into facts which are admitted to a great extent (to say the least) by the authorities in Bengal, I would say there are three objects to be attained by a public inquiry

Object of inquiry.

1st object.

1st. That it would put all men (who care to know) into possession of the facts which some men only now know. Does the Governor-General know them? Does this House know them? I am tempted to add, Do the Court of Directors know them?

2nd object.

2ndly. That it would put the stamp of the Government of India, the stamp of authority, on the authenticity of the facts, so that it would be impossible to

---

* See Appendix.

have official denials of those facts from interested parties, either in India or at home.

And 3rdly, and lastly, that the knowledge of the publicity given to the existence of the evils, must in the nature of things quicken the activity both of the Supreme and the Legislative Councils of India, to devise and to push forward measures of fundamental reform, so that we should have no more such answers as Mr. Dorin's to the petitions of missionaries; and, on the other hand, that we should cease to have obstructions put in the way of such measures as the one lately introduced into the Legislative Council, by Mr. Grant, on the sale of land for arrears, as I understand from a letter I received from Calcutta, only last week, is now the case. And (to refer to another most important subject), we should perhaps cease to hear of such a fact as this, that when the Indian authorities were themselves desirous of putting down the cruel swinging festivals in Bengal, as *has been done* in Madras and Bombay, they were prevented doing so by a despatch from the Court of Directors at home. Nothing, I think, can give a better illustration of the importance of such a public and special inquiry, than what has just occurred with reference to the pauper lunatics in Scotland.

3rd object.

Mr. Grant's Bill.

Swinging Festivals.

Sir,—I say that this House is responsible in this matter, and we have a right to know whose statement is correct, the missionaries, who say that there is wide-spread disaffection as the consequence of misrule; or the Government authorities, who deny the statement. There is a higher power than all the authorities in India, and than the Court of Directors at home, and that is the Ministers of the Crown, and those Ministers are responsible Ministers. And if we would hold up our heads among the nations as the defenders of right and justice, we must see that our own rule in India is just and pure. What avails our representations to Turkey, our indignation at the corrupt officials there, for not carrying out the more enlightened views of the Sultan, if we allow the native officials in India to take bribes, to oppress, to defraud, and for the sake of a miserable economy, give such a small staff of efficient magistrates that they cannot, if they would, control their subordinates. Let us wipe our own hands of guilt. I said, Sir, miserable economy. And why did I say so? Why, but because I believe that one great cause of misgovernment in India is, that for a long time it was governed not so much for the good of the people, as to enrich ourselves. And even now, Mr. Grant and Mr. Halliday agree that the reform of the police is a mere question of money.

Ministers of Crown responsible.

I feel confident that my Right Honourable friend, the President of the Board of Control, desires to do justice to the people of India, and I cannot doubt that the noble lord at the head of the Government, would be more than willing to promote the welfare of all the subjects of the British Crown, whether black or white; and what can I wish better for him, than that he who has been the tried friend of the African black, the supporter all over the world of liberty and humanity, against oppression and misrule; who stopped diplomatic intercourse with a European ruler, because he used his authority to oppress his subjects; that he should be known also as the maintainer of the rights of the millions of Hindustan. If my Right Honourable friend answers in reply to what I have said, that measures of reform are in progress, then I claim his support for my second Resolution, which requests that a statement of those measures may be sent home, and laid on the table of the House.

And if any one demurs to the truth of my statements, I can only see in this a fresh reason for inquiry, as we cannot both be right. If I am right, then I have asked the very least that can be asked. I have purposely abstained from asking for a Royal Commission to be sent out from England, lest it should weaken the hands of the Indian authorities in the eyes of the natives, who do not understand constitutional Government; but I cannot believe, that any evils that could result from an inquiry instituted by the Indian Goverment, for the sake of giving us the information we want, would at all counterbalance the advantages that would result from it. During the siege of Sebastopol, who were right in their statements of wants and necessaries, the private or the public authorities?

Sir, I consider that the present Government of India is on its trial. Four years have passed away since it assumed its present form, and nothing to alleviate these evils has been done for Bengal, whatever has been talked about.

The north-west provinces may be enjoying a good system of government. The Punjab, thanks to that distinguished nobleman who so ably presided for many years over the Government of India, may be under a still more perfect system, but what is this to the 35 millions of Bengal? Sir, it is for them I plead. I fully recognise the importance of many things that have been done, such as abolishing the Government connection with idolatry, destroying sutteeism, infanticide, thuggism, human sacrifices; introducing a system of education for the people; and more recently the legal recognition of the marriage of widows; but again I say, this does not alter the fact of the miserable social condition of the inhabitants of Bengal.

I have not consciously overstated one fact, and I surely shall not appeal in vain to those who acknowledge the supreme authority of Him who says "Thou shalt not wrest judgment; thou shalt not respect persons, neither take a gift. That which is altogether just shall thou follow."

I beg to move—

1*st Resolution.*—"That, from representations made to this House, there is reason to believe that the present administration of the Lower Provinces of Bengal does not secure to the population the advantages of good government, but that the mass of the people suffer grievous oppression from the police, and the want of proper administration of justice."

2*nd Resolution.*—"That, in the opinion of this House, it is desirable that Her Majesty's Government should take immediate steps with a view to the institution of special inquiries into the social condition of the people; and to ascertain what measures have been adopted in consequence of the oppression under which a large proportion of the inhabitants of the Lower Provinces are now said to be suffering, more especially with reference to the system of landed tenures, the state of the police, and the administration of justice; and also that such report be laid upon the table of the House."

[*Note.*—Since this Pamphlet was in the press, I regret that the sad tidings from India too truly confirm the Missionaries' statement of the existence of disaffection. And, in a private letter just received from Calcutta, these observations occur:—"In the Minutes published on Sir E. Perry's motion, on the Missionaries' Memorial for Inquiry, you will have noticed the confidence with which the warnings about disaffection were disregarded as altogether needless and groundless. This present event may show who is most likely to be right. All was said to be peace in Affghanistan till the rising in Cabul."]

APPENDIX.

It is supposed by some that the existence of Mr. Halliday's Minute of April 1856 is a proof that the Government authorities are sufficiently alive to the miserable condition of Bengal. And it was even said, as a reply to my speech, that I relied on public testimony for my facts; whereas I only relied upon it as a confirmation of private testimony; and even with respect to the Minute of Mr. Halliday, the House of Commons is indebted to me for their knowledge of it; as, though extracts from it were moved for by Sir Erskine Perry, they were not given, on the ground that it had not reached the India House or the Board of Control. A comparison, however, of that Minute with a later Minute in answer to the Memorial of the Missionaries, which has been laid on the table of the House, and which was dated September 1856, seems to give some clue both to the neglect of Mr. Halliday's suppressed Minute, and to the unaccountable slowness of the authorities in India in providing remedies for known evils. Such delay appears to me the more inexcusable, as Mr. Halliday has himself, in the Minute of April 1856, not only pointed out the evils of the police and judicial systems, but suggested the remedies.

Mr. Halliday.

Let it be borne in mind that Mr. Halliday is not the Government, but the servant of the Government; and till he can persuade the Government to move, his hands are tied. But as his Minute was publicly recognised in the late debate as an authority, its existence when it shall be laid before us, substantially obtains what I sought in my late motion for inquiry, as far as the police and judicial systems are concerned. For, 1st. It brings the facts before the eye of the public. 2ndly. It stamps those facts as authentic, with the seal of Government authority. And, 3dly, In conjunction with the late debate, which has given it publicity, it is calculated to urge on the Government to measures of reform. In this point of view I have gained the object of my motion, though the House declined to give a decided opinion upon the subject. All that is needed now is an equally lucid report on the Zemindaree system, and I have little doubt that the Lieutenant-Governor would have most valuable suggestions to make upon it if he had any hope of getting them carried out or seriously entertained, and that it could be vastly ameliorated; and that some measures such as the redemption of the Land Tax could be devised to improve the country without breaking faith as to the Permanent Settlement. But I much fear that the real difficulties will be found in the Supreme Council of India. Mr. Halliday was appointed Lieutenant-Governor of Bengal in 1854, and, we find in the note of his secretary, Mr. Grey, dated April 1856, appended to his first Minute, that he called the attention of the Supreme Government, as early as October 1854, to a proposed measure of police reform, suggested by Lord Dalhousie; but his proposal was objected to and refused: and when again he mooted the question in February 1855, apparently no answer was even returned to him. In September 1855, he again brought forward the subject, and again received no reply! A fourth proposal on the same subject was accepted, probably because it was recommended *as a measure of economy*.* To say the least, this neglect on the

---

* *Extract from Note by* MR. SECRETARY GREY.

"After being talked about for some years, the proposition to re-unite the offices of Magistrate and Collector was at length formerly made by Lord Dal-

part of the Supreme Council of the Lieutenant-Governor's suggestions, even when backed by Lord Dalhousie's opinion, does not seem very propitious for reforms, particularly those

---

housie in April 1854. The proposition was submitted to the Government of India, and no notice of it being taken for some months, the Lieutenant-Governor, in October of the same year, called the attention of the Supreme Government to the subject, and solicited permission to take advantage of then expected vacancies to re-unite the office of Magistrate and Collector in some four or five Districts which were named.

"This request was, however, refused in January 1855, and a Minute of the Honourable Mr. Grant's was sent for the Lieutenant-Governor's perusal, in which Lord Dalhousie's proposition was strongly objected to. The Lieutenant-Governor communicated his views upon the question to the Supreme Government in February 1855, and since that date nothing more has been heard on the matter from the Supreme Government.

"The subject has, however, intermediately been twice brought incidentally to the notice of the Supreme Government. In September last the Lieutenant-Governor, in applying for an increase to the Uncovenanted Executive Service, took occasion to observe that such assistance, though greatly needed, would not cure one great evil of the present condition of the service, namely, the evil of advancing very young officers to appointments of responsibility and importance.

"This evil, it was remarked, could only be cured by one of three measures, one of which was the re-uniting of the offices of Magistrate and Collector.

"No reply to this communication has been received.

"The second occasion on which the subject of placing the Chief Magisterial and Chief Revenue control in a District in the same hands, was brought under the notice of the Supreme Government, was in the instance of the districts of Bhaugulpore and Beerbhoom, when a portion of the Magisterial jurisdiction of each of those districts was taken, after the Sontal insurrection, to form a Non-Regulation Province. It was then recommended by the Lieutenant-Governor, *as a measure of economy*, that the separate magistracies of Bhaugulpore and Beerbhoom should be abolished, and that the Collectors of those districts should be made also Magistrates; to this proposition the Supreme Government at once assented.

"With the above exception, the Magistrate-Collector question has not apparently advanced since Lord Dalhousie made his proposition two years ago.

"My object in bringing the subject now briefly to the notice of the Lieutenant-Governor, is to beg his attention to a Comparative Statement which I have prepared, showing the standing of the Magistrates in Bengal, that is to say of the Officers actually officiating as such at three different periods, namely in April 1850, April 1854, (the date of Lord Dalhousie's proposition,) and April 1856.

"This statement will be found, I think, to show an urgent need of *some* means being adopted to procure greater experience in the Magistrate's office than is now obtained."

20th April, 1856. (Signed) W. GREY,
Secy. to the Govt. of Bengal.

involving increased expenditure. We now come to April 1856, when that most extraordinary Minute of Mr. Halliday's, describing in fact the condition of Bengal when he assumed the Government, was sent in to the Supreme Council. One should at least have supposed that such a document, coming from such an authority, and on such a subject, would have commanded immediate attention. But what do we find? That up to the time of the debate in the House of Commons, the Supreme Council had not even thought it worth while to send it home to the Court of Directors. The present Governor-General, Lord Canning, having only reached India a few weeks before this Minute was sent in to the Council, was perhaps scarcely aware how important a document had been placed on the shelf of the council chamber. I say emphatically placed on the shelf, for how otherwise is it possible to account for the letter of Mr. Dorin, sent home to the Court of Directors? and even for some of Mr. Grant's opinions on the subject of the Missionaries' Memorial?

Missionaries' Memorial.

I now come to the consideration of the circumstances of this Memorial. It was presented to Mr. Halliday, in September 1856, and it asked for inquiry into the whole social condition of Bengal. Had the Memorialists taken Mr. Halliday's own Minute, they would have found in it alone, I think, a justification of the strongest assertions in their Memorial. Why Mr. Halliday so strongly objected to it, and thought the evils exaggerated, I cannot say, unless he felt aggrieved at the slowness of the Council in commencing reforms, and wished to insinuate that he had inquired enough. One passage in his second Minute gives countenance to this idea, where he says—

"The time present is, as regards those things, not the time for investigation but for action, and anything that is likely to delay action on those points will impede the very consummation which the Memorialists so greatly desire. Nothing would so surely, or so long, delay the completion of the necessary improvemements in the police and in the judicial system, as a commission for a new inquiry into those subjects, and, *on that ground alone, further inquiry is to be deprecated.*"

The Governor-General not having had experience, as he said, could only generally declare his agreement with Mr. Halliday, and his respect for the missionaries themselves. Of course he must have relied very much on the opinions of the civil members of his Council, Mr. Dorin and Mr. Grant, in refusing the missionaries' petition for inquiry. It seems, therefore, of the highest importance to ascertain what hope we may entertain for Bengal from their recorded opinions.

Mr. Dorin thus writes on the 10th of October—

"I agree entirely in the view taken of this Memorial by the Honourable the Lieutenant-Governor of Bengal. *Mr. Dorin.*

"There can be little question of the unsatisfactory condition of the rural population of the districts of Bengal Proper; *but whether this state of things arises from defects which the Government can remedy*, or is engendered by physical causes over which the Government can exercise no control, *may be open to very grave doubt.*

"In respect to such sources of social disorder as would admit of action being taken on them, I believe the Government are in possession of sufficient information to enable them to proceed with *reasonable promptitude and decision*: upon other heads of inquiry suggested by the reverend missionaries, no information, however extensive, would justify the Government in taking any action whatever.

"The jarring of class interests will assuredly not assist the progress of social organization, nor am I altogether sanguine that the amendment of the law, or the improvement of the police, or the still more potent engine of the spread of education, will very materially eradicate the evils of which the Memoralists complained.

"I believe those evils to arise in a great degree from *the physical structure of* the people, and *that nature and climate* have at least as much to do with them as any defect in the civil administration of the country.

"The civil and criminal law is essentially the same *in the North-western provinces as in Bengal, and the state of the police is little better in the Upper Provinces than in the Lower;* so that, if the faultiness of the law, or of the police, were the cause of the social evils experienced by one portion of the population, they might be regarded as producing similar results on the other. No one avers that this is the case, or that the condition of the peasantry of the north-western provinces is so debased as that of Bengal.

"And, for one reason, why? because they are men. They are a fine manly race, replete with physical courage, who will not submit to be pillaged by every privileged, or unprivileged, plunderer; men who will stand up for their own rights, and defend their property as soon as they have acquired it. But will a Bengallee do this? Will he lift a finger in defence of either life or property, or is there a particle of physical or moral courage in his composition? I cannot say that I have ever heard of it.

"I believe there is not a more timid human being than a Bengallee on the face of the earth, and we have had only too palpable proof of it on recent occasions."

I suppose Mr. Dorin would admit that the Dacoits, themselves Bengallees, will occasionally lift up a finger. But I have a more serious objection to make to this extract: to say the least, it argues the most extraordinary ignorance in a member of the Supreme Council. Mr. Halliday had in April asserted two things with respect to the police; first, that the expenditure of £100,000 a year more on the magistracy and police of Bengal, was a necessary measure of reform; and secondly, that nearly that amount is spent annually in the North-west provinces more than is spent in the Lower.* In other words, the police of the North-west provinces are well paid, while the police of the Lower provinces are ill paid, or not paid at all; and yet Mr. Dorin argues that the social evils of Bengal cannot

---

* *See* page 41.

be attributed to the faultiness of the police, otherwise the same evils would exist in the North-west provinces.

Mr. Dorin further says—

"What can be done for such people as these, who will do nothing for themselves? What Government interference can supply that foundation of moral improvement, that self-reliance which nature itself seems to have denied? It is almost a law of nature that cowards should be either slaves or tyrants, and I fear this describes but too truly the general condition of the population of this fertile province. It may be that the zemindaree system has failed in practice; yet it was not necessarily a bad system, nor was it founded on unstatesmanlike principles. Its object was to create a substantial intermediate interest in the community, a landed aristocracy, from which the genial flow of social influences might reasonably have been expected; and, if it has failed in producing this effect, the fault is more with the unsuitable materials on which it operated, than in the principle of the measure itself. English and Bengallee nature are not alike, and it has not followed that the theory of a system which might be abundantly adapted to the constitution of England was equally applicable to the atmosphere of Bengal. The Memorialists should not blame the system so much as the people; and, in like manner, where they descant, as they do most justly, on the iniquities of the police, they should remember that the police of England is not perfect, and that if the police are expected to protect the people, it is at least equally required that the people shall help the police; and, what is more to the purpose, that the people shall, to a very great extent, have reasonable reliance on themselves. *Mr. Dorin.*

"The crime of dacoity is frightfully prevalent, yet is it possible to suppose it could be so extensive if the people could be persuaded to do anything in their own defence? Dacoits are as little disposed to face danger needlessly as any other class of the community, and vigorous resistance would soon extirpate the system; but where is this found? The very timidity of the people is an inducement to the crime, and yet it cannot be expected that there should be a policeman in every man's house. The extortion of the police is notorious; yet, if men will submit to extortion in silence, how is the remedy to be provided? The omlah of the courts of law are accused of being corrupt; yet, if suitors will favour the corruption, how is justice to be pure? No doubt the police is capable of vast improvement, and a Sikh police has recently been organised for the Sonthal pergunnahs, in despair of finding a Bengallee policeman who was fit to be trusted; yet, unless the people are prepared to make some exertion for themselves, I do not see how a well-ordered police, or an amended code and administration of the law, can effect very much in diminution of social evils."

Mr. Halliday. Yet Mr. Halliday had told the Supreme Council in his Minute, that the village police are all thieves and robbers, or all leagued with them; that it was popularly said that dacoity is bad enough, but the subsequent police inquiry very much worse;* and that "*the omlah are for the most part paid at a rate that almost necessitates corruption.*"—Minute, Sect. 84. And who are the suitors that favour the corruption? Why, the zemindars who oppress the ryots.

Mr. Dorin's opinion seems to be, that the more a people need the protection of Government, the less they ought to expect to find it; and it never seems to have crossed his mind that the institutions under which the Bengallees live, may have helped to form their nature. On one point, I do most sincerely agree with Mr. Dorin, namely, that English and Bengallee natures are not alike. Were we subjected to such a state of administration as Mr. Halliday describes for six months, I think there would be a rising from the Cheviot Hills to the Land's End. As it is, I believe that there is an insurrection in one part of Bengal or another, annually; but it is treated as a savage demonstration, and put down by force. Mr. Dorin adds—

"I do not say all this in order to argue that any amelioration of

---

* *See* pp. 31—35.

the social evils which beset the population of Bengal is impossible, but to show that, in my opinion, there are natural and physical difficulties in the way of improvement, the remedy also of which is beyond the reach of any Government, or of any inquiry that could be pushed to the fullest extent desired by the most enthusiastic philanthropist."

I certainly cannot be surprised at the regret expressed by Lord John Russell in the course of the debate, that Mr. Dorin should be in the Supreme Council at all.

If we turn to Mr. Grant's Minute, we have the satisfaction of finding this important admission—

" The Memorial of the Missionaries, transcribing and adopting a previous petition to Parliament, mentions the following as evils existing in Bengal, ' which it falls properly within the scope of Government to meet and control,' and which they say ' appear to be on the increase:'— *Mr. Grant.*

"(1) Insecurity of life and property in many districts.

"(2) Numerous gang robberies perpetrated annually with impunity.

"(3) Constant scenes of violence, in contentions respecting disputed boundaries between the owners of landed estates.

" The Memorialists maintain that the radical cause of these evils is the inefficiency of the police and of the judicial system; that a well-organised police, with a more extensive and more effective judicial system (besides giving the required security to life and property), would do much to check the outrages that arise out of disputes about land; and, moreover, that in order to a cure of this last evil, the cause which leads to disputes about land, namely, the insecurity of title and possession, must be removed by, first, the complete survey of the land; secondly, a system of registration; and thirdly, ' laws to obviate the infinite mischief of the universal system of secret trusts.'

" Upon this important head, I beg to record my complete concurrence with the Memorialists, both as to the existence and extent of the evils, and the nature of the remedies.

"For many years past I have never lost an opportunity of pressing upon the highest authorities the injustice with which Bengal is treated in regard to the expenditure allowed to her for police. This is no question of system; it is purely a money question. Without a very large additional expenditure, nothing can be done; with twelve or fifteen lacs a year to give, the money could hardly be misspent. We have reason to believe that the days of this crying evil are numbered."

We may notice here how entirely Mr. Grant agrees with Mr. Halliday in thinking that the Bengal police are inadequately paid, differing therefore from Mr. Dorin. But while this whole statement is encouraging, we have, on the opposite side, to place the following remarks, nearly at the commencement of his Minute, in explanation of his opposing the Memorial for inquiry.

Mr. Grant. "All that remains in the Memorial of substantially disputable matter, are the assertion that bitter hatred of their rulers is now in course of being engendered in the minds of the Bengal ryots; and the severe and unqualified charges made by the Memorialists, as a class, against the class of zemindars universally.

"I do not suppose that many besides the Memorialists share in their belief upon the first point; and if the fact were as they believe, such a commission to prove it, as they propose, would be too dangerous an experiment to try.

"I do not mean to make light of this belief: I could make light of no belief entertained in a quarter entitled to so much respect on a question of such importance. I am sure that this assertion would not have been thus formally made on what were not thought strong grounds. But there is a great inconsistency, to my understanding, between this assertion and other assertions made with equal confidence in the same Memorial. The alleged feeling is imputed to the extreme and peculiar social evils to which the ryot of Bengal is said to be subject; and all the evils of which the ryot can be conscious are traced by the Memorialists, if I understand them, to extortions, and tyranny, and general misconduct of the zemindars, and to the immediate consequences of the zemindaree system, inadequately checked as it is by the police and judicial system provided by the rulers. Now our police is, I dare say, not very much better than it was, but there is no reason to imagine that it is worse. The increase in the pay of police darogahs has done undeniable good, to a certain extent. In other respects our judicial system is vastly better than it was; and the improvement has been all in the direction of the ryot, by bringing justice (though still much too far from him) much nearer to him than it was. Of late years magisterial officers have been largely increased in number, and more dispersed over the country than formerly. Moonsiff's courts, the courts of the ryot, as effective courts of civil justice, may be said to be the creation of the last 30 years; and their improvement in quality, year by year, is unquestioned. Of late, then, the checks provided by the rulers have been vastly improved upon the whole, and, so far as the rulers are concerned, in appearance, as well as in reality, there has been in this generation much to soothe, nothing to irritate, and most certainly nothing to engender the bitter hatred attributed to the ryot. The zemindars, therefore, and the zemindaree system, according to the Memorialists, are the cause of all. To them, the Memorialists allege, are due the alleged social evils, which evils are alleged to be now engendering bitter hatred of their rulers in the breasts of the Bengal ryots of the present day. Now this string of allegations would all be consistent enough, if the zemindaree system were a novelty. But how stands the fact? Be that system good or bad, it is no novelty; it is not even a creation of the British Government. We found the system, and the zemindars themselves, in full force. We have left the zemindars but the shadow of the power they then had; in many respects we have left them not even the shadow of it. For such power as is left them, I can think of no personal interest they can have had then in using it well, that they have not in an equal or greater degree now; and certainly they have more to fear in using it ill now than they had then. How is it, then, that if social evils really exist to such an extreme degree as to embitter the ryot's spirit, and if zemindars and the zemindaree system are the immediate causes of those evils, this bitterness is only now beginning to be engendered, a generation or two after the assumed enemy has been, to say the least, partially bound down? Why did it not begin to arise in the ryot's breast whilst the zemindar, with no better disposition and many fewer responsibilities, had 20 times his present power for evil?

"As, in my judgment, all these suppositions, namely, the extreme degree of the evils, their cause and their effect, cannot be true, and one is no more credible than the other, I can see no reason for adopting any. To me they have all much more the appearance of having been entertained as consequences of different theories, than as the results of wary and unprejudiced observation."

It is remarkable that Mr. Halliday, in his Minute, distinctly states that for 20 years past the police *have* deteriorated, and that the magistracy is losing credit and character, and the administration growing perceptibly weaker;* and in one passage, in the 43rd section of his Minute, he uses these words—

Mr. Halliday.

"The youth and inexperience of the covenanted magistrates has been a matter of reproach to the service for many years, but it has very much increased of late, owing to the growing disproportion of men to offices. It has, in a manner painfully perceptible to me in my visits to the different districts, impaired the force, dignity, and efficiency of our administration in the interior; and in all cases in which the youth and inexperience of the officer is not, as it sometimes is, counterbalanced by unusual ability and force of character, it has brought the all-important authority of the Zillah magistracy into marked slight and regard, and sometimes into actual contempt. It is certain still more to increase under the present system . . . from 1793 to 1830 . . . . the magistrate was the officer most experienced and highest in rank in the district; and he was therefore looked up to with a degree of respect, the recollection of which to those who, like myself, have known 'the Mofussil'

---

* *See* pp. 31, 36, 37.

(country) in those old days, suggests a painful contrast with the uninfluential and comparatively insignificant position of the juvenile functionaries, many of whom I have found ineffectually presiding over the Zillah magistracies in my recent tours."

We find then that Mr. Grant and Mr. Halliday are at variance in their opinions; and as the former has, I understand, been very little in the Mofussil at all, I must believe that Mr. Halliday's opinion is the correct one, and regret that Mr. Grant so differs with him: and herein may be seen perhaps one of the causes in operation to retard reforms. Then again, we did not find the *present* zemindaree system in operation. Those two regulations also, the 7th and the 5th, which are the terror of the ryots, were passed in 1799 and 1812, under our administration.

With regard to Mr. Peacock, the legislative member of the Council, we can get no light from him on the question at all.

I now turn therefore to the answer from the Court of Directors, in approval of the refusal of a commission of inquiry; and in that answer I see that the Court agree with Mr. Dorin and Mr. Grant in some of the statements I have adverted to. The Directors thus write—

Court of Directors.

"It needs no commission of inquiry to inform us that the peasantry of Bengal are subjected, by their landlords, to arbitrary and illegal demands, on religious and other occasions, beyond, and independent of, the sums which they pay as rent. The demand and payment are made in a way which does not admit of the interference of the police; but the courts of justice would deal with all such levies of money as extortionate exactions. To the courts, however, the people do not appeal for protection in such cases. They submit to the demands, either because they consider them as having the sanction of prescription, or because, *as shown by Mr. Dorin, they are too timid to resist payment. The Memorialists seem not to be aware of the difficulty of forcing protection upon a people beyond the point at which they are prepared to accept it*, and to lend their own aid in securing it

"We observe with great satisfaction that the Lieutenant-Governor expresses his 'absolute dissent from the statement made, doubtless in perfect good faith, that the people exhibit a spirit of sullen discontent, on account of the miseries ascribed to them: and that there exists among them that bitter hatred to the Government which has filled the Memorialists, as they declare, with alarm as well as sorrow.' Much, as already shewn, has been done to remedy the evils to which the Memorialists advert, and to inspire confidence in the Government. 'Much,' as observed by Mr. Grant, 'to soothe, nothing to irritate, and most certainly nothing to engender the bitter hatred attributed to the ryot.'"

In other words, the Court of Directors are astonished that defenceless sheep will not accept the protection of the savage wolf.

It seems perfectly clear that the Directors had not seen Mr. Halliday's Minute, or that if they had seen it, they had not attended to it, and that I was not very far wrong when I asked, Do the Court of Directors know the evils?

Only one other point I need advert to in the answer from the Court, where they say—

Court of Directors.

"Measures for the reform of the police are now under the consideration of the Government; codes of procedure, to simplify and facilitate the administration of justice, both civil and criminal, are before the Legislative Council; measures specially directed to the suppression of gang robbery have, for some time, been in active operation in those districts of Bengal in which that crime has most extensively prevailed. Of the endeavours of the Government, and its officers, in this direction, the Memorialists can scarcely be altogether ignorant. Immediately in connexion with the statement, that the evils to which they advert appear to be on the increase, they allege, 'that gang robberies of the most daring character are perpetrated annually, in great numbers, with impunity.' The contrary of this is the fact; for, instead of increasing, the number of gang robberies had decreased, in the districts referred to, from 439 in 1851, to 168 in 1854 (the reports for which year are the last we have received in detail), and the decrease was still progressing: the most formidable gang of dacoits had been broken up, and upwards of 200 of their members had been convicted, of whom 180 had been transported for life."

That this is no answer whatever to the Memorialists is clear from Mr. Halliday's own statement on this very point. Mr. Halliday says, quoting from the Minute of Mr. Bethune, of the 27th May, 1851, that the complaints recently made of outrageous dacoities, and acts of violence, point rather to *a deterioration* than to an improvement of the practical working of the system of police thirteen years previously, when one-fourth more in proportion to their number were convicted in the lower provinces for murder, thuggee, burglary, robbery, and theft, than the rest of the population, for all offences of every kind. Mr. Halliday says further in his first Minute, that in the seven districts, *about Government House*, dacoities had increased from 82 in 1841, to 524 in 1851! And then he adds, "It is true that under *a special agency*, this has since been reduced to 111 in 1855. *But the operations of this agency have shown more than any thing else the utter inability of our ordinary institutions to cope with the enormous social evil that is ever rising up in defiance before it.*"* So that the answer to the Memorialists is entirely beside the mark, and if Mr. Halliday is to be believed, the Memorialists on this point are right, and the Court of Directors wrong. Mr. Grant also, as we have seen, agrees with the Memorialists here. *Mr Halliday*

The conclusion I draw from the whole is, that unless the action of Parliament, as the exponent of public opinion in England, is brought to bear on the Government of India, these social wrongs will be denied or softened down, and remedies

---

* *See* page 36.

delayed as they have hitherto been. For all the evidence I have brought, is evidence drawn from a period later than the last Charter in 1853.

I sincerely rejoice that the President of the Board of Control is responsible to the Parliament of England for the good government of India. In the late debate, he expressed surprise that I had done an injustice to the Directors, in not referring to their despatch of 24th September, 1856, recognising the evils of which I complained. Now, in the first place, though the paper containing that despatch is headed "Police System, Bengal," it appears to me only to refer to Bengal in common with the rest of India, and not as requiring any special attention; and secondly, it is certainly extraordinary that in resisting my motion for *inquiry*, and falling back upon Mr. Halliday's opinion expressed one week before this very despatch was written, namely, September 18, that the time for action was come, the despatch should conclude thus, "We have thrown out the foregoing remarks, *merely as suggestions*, upon a subject to which we attach very great importance; and we desire that you will take the subject into your early consideration, and *after communication with the other* Presidencies, *report fully to us your sentiments* as to the expediency of the general reorganisation of the police throughout India, upon some such system as that which obtains with respect to the police in the Punjaub, and as to the mode and cost of the proposed reform." So that from this despatch, to which Mr. Vernon Smith referred me, and for which I had moved myself, I gather that in September the Court of Directors did not agree with Mr. Halliday that the time for action was come. The only difference between the Court in September and myself in June is, that I asked that the result of the Bengal inquiry should be laid on the table of the House of Commons; and this is a most important difference, I admit.

Indeed this is *the* point of my motion, as I fully believe that reams of paper have been covered with suggestions. Indeed, the Lieutenant-Governor seems weary of fruitless schemes, and Mr. Grant the same. But why have they been fruitless? Because all has been private. And because it is very difficult to fasten responsibility where there are three governing powers. My object has been to bring all into the light of day as the means of producing action, and public inquiry seemed the only mode likely to be successful in attaining this object.

I wish to add a few words with respect to the Missionaries themselves. Had the evils they deplored not been exactly those which they would discover in the course of their labours, there might be ground for the assertion that they have been stepping out of their province. But even with respect to the question of the landed tenure, which is the most political question they have touched, I have shewn in this pamphlet, that it most seriously affects the state of Christian ràyats under heathen zemindars, and also the success of Christian missions; as in the case where the zemindars proposed to make a condition of their lease that the ràyats should not turn Christians, and this in a country where not to get land is to starve.

I have always considered as one of the first rights of Englishmen, the right to petition Parliament; and yet in the late debate, the exercise of that birthright of Englishmen was ridiculed by a so-called Liberal Member of the House of Commons, the honourable Member for the Tower Hamlets. I say much more than that the Missionaries had a right to petition,—I maintain that they would have been chargeable with a neglect of duty, had they, knowing such terrible evils to exist, held their peace. It has been said that the early Apostles did not do so. But were the Apostles responsible for the crimes committed by the Roman government? The Missionaries share in the responsibility attaching to every Englishman of bringing his influence to bear on the Government in correcting abuses. The Missionaries belong to the governing class in India, which are the English. Some of them would adorn our House of Commons, and might perchance have sat in it had they not given themselves to their noble work. Dr. Duff probably knows more of India than any Member of that House. What would such an objector say, if in the remoter districts of England the police were to commit murder and to shelter murderers, to rob, to be worse than the rest of the population, and some of the more powerful inhabitants were to seize the houses and the property of their defenceless neighbours, as was done in Baropakhya, and to be protected by a Magistrate in so doing? What would he say if the Clergy of the district, were to hold their tongue because the Apostles contented themselves with preaching the Gospel, without abusing the Roman Government? Whatever might be said by this objector, I believe the country would execrate such Ministers.

But what is more extraordinary still, it seemed almost to be believed that I had stepped out of my line of duty; and that because I had presented the Missionaries' petition, it would have been an improper interference with the Government of India had I carried a motion founded on that petition. May not any Member make any motion he pleases? Is it not the duty of the House of Commons to interfere with Governments?

And is it not a new doctrine that a commission of inquiry supersedes the authorities? Did it do so in Ceylon? or in Ireland? or in Canada? or in the late war? Such an argument indicates the weakness of the cause to be defended.

I was also called the mouthpiece of the Missionaries; I have no objection to that appellation, only I was not their mouthpiece. My motion was a thoroughly independent one. I did not even rely on the Missionaries' assertions (however true) for my evidence. My Right Honourable friend, the President of the Board of Control, noted this in the debate, as if I ought to have done so. Why it would have been suicidal to do so. The question I wished the House to decide upon, was, whether the Missionaries were right in their assertions; and I think I have proved that they were in all essential points right. If I succeed in fixing the attention of thoughtful men in England and Scotland on the social condition of India, and in arousing the House of Commons in any degree from their past indifference to that country, I believe that the Government will take up the subject in earnest; and though it may be very difficult to make the various governing bodies in India and at home agree as to the measures they shall adopt, yet I believe that they will be forced into agreement, and that Bengal itself, after a century of misrule, will have cause, abundant cause, to rejoice at having been brought under the sway of the British Crown.

FINIS.

THE

REVELATIONS OF AN ORDERLY,

BEING

AN ATTEMPT TO EXPOSE THE ABUSES OF ADMINISTRATION BY THE RELATION OF EVERY-DAY OCCURRENCES IN THE MOFUSSIL COURTS.

BY

PANCHKOUREE KHAN

1857

PREFACE.

The following pages were originally written for and published in the "*Benares Recorder*." The object of the writer was to state in simple language, facts that had come under his own observation; and to expose abuses in the subordinate administration of the Courts, that are universally acknowledged to exist. A varied experience of twenty-one years in different departments of the government service, had given him some insight into the native character; and he was desirous of shewing the public in general and young officials in particular, the several modes that the natives have of "*throwing dust*" in the eyes of their European superiors.

The writer was also desirous of pointing out to the authorities a few of the weak points of the system of Policy and Revenue. He could not presume to do this in his own person; and he made use of the fictitious agency of "an Orderly," to relate his own varied experience.

The writer of these pages once for all, begs leave to state, that nothing tending to the personal disparagement of any individual, was intended. He earnestly hopes that no offence has been taken at any of his remarks; and he throws himself upon the indulgence of the public, in once more intruding on their notice.

Missing Page

Page No. 1

To this I replied, that I was only the more puzzled to find out the secret of his system. That he could do nothing for any suitor for justice; nor could he bar access to the Huzoor.* How then could one make money?

My sapient friend, said Suntokhea, I was not aware that you were so green. We have scores of ways of making money, even when our masters are vigilant and cautious, and vainly imagine that because, forsooth, they take the trouble to do the work themselves, no person will give fees. I will describe some few of the processes by which we receive money.

A great man's Mooktyar or Karindah† is sent by his master to wait on the Huzoor. He is admitted into the entrance hall, where he remains unnoticed for a couple of hours. To all his prayers, to give intimation to the Huzoor of his presence, a deaf ear is turned. Until fairly exhausted, the Karindah offers me a rupee. This is spurned, and I ask him whether he thinks I *could* possibly take *one* rupee? The poor man, driven to desperation, offers me five rupees. On this I pocket the affront, put on my sweetest smile; declare that he is a perfect *ushraf*;‡ and intimate to my master, that such a one craves an interview. Five rupees you will say is but a small morsel. I allow it; but then these delicate bits come frequently.

Again, every rich native gentleman, who is in the habit of visiting the "*Saheban Aleeshan*,"§ fees us orderlies on every festival. Suppose my gentleman becomes a non-conformist to our rules, or is in any way inclined to be bumptious, he finds that in the next visit he pays the Huzoor, his suwaree‖ remains unnoticed in the compound; or if he enters the entrance room, no one will so much as give him a chair to sit upon. If he becomes impatient, we recommend his going away as the Huzoor is busy, and has positively prohibited intrusion My gentleman finds himself at a non-plus; and is glad to compromise by paying us *all* double fees, and giving a solemn promise of good behaviour for the future

But, said I, *Suntokhea Singh*, suppose one of these gents were to inform the Huzoor of your tricks, how would you get out of the scrape?

Why, replied he, nothing is easier -No man will dare to inform against his having given fees to the servants of the Huzoor, because he would criminate himself. He can merely complain of useless detention. On this the Huzoor wigs us and desires us, under pain of his displeasure, not to keep people waiting at his door, without at once apprising him. Well, the next people that call, are at once ushered into the presence, whether the Huzoor be busy or not. His patience becomes exhausted, and he scolds again for indiscriminate admission. To this we reply most submissively, that we had the Huzoor's own orders. He despairs of managing us, and we have our own way.

* Literally, the presence † Attorney or representative, or agent.
‡ Gentleman. § Gentlemen of exalted dignity applied, par excellence, to the dignitaries of the British Government. ‖ Carriage.

Again, suppose a thanadar does not purchase our favor, nothing is easier than getting him turned out. Of course we dare not meddle directly; but we watch our opportunity, and when we find the Saheb idle, we talk in stage-whispers, and invent some scandal or lie against the thanadar, which one tells to another by way of news. A second states, that he also has heard such a story of the thanadar, and mentions it. A third says, that the thanadar is a *nimukharam*,* for he abuses the Magistrate Saheb Bahadoor; and says, he does not care for him, so long as he does his duty. These whispers are overheard and operate like slow poison, and on the occasion of the first irregularity occurring, our stories are (perhaps unconsciously) remembered against the unfortunate thanadar and he is suspended, *sine die*—which is in fact a dismissal.

I took leave of friend Suntokhea in admiration of his inventive talents, fully resolved to fee him for his interest in getting a berth as a Burra Saheb's orderly myself, when, should I succeed, I may be able to withdraw the curtain which hides other mysteries.

CHAP. II.

HOW THE MOONSHEE JEE SCHOOLS PANCHKOUREE AS TO THE MODE OF PROCEEDING.

I promised to pay my quondam friend and present patron two months' pay, on obtaining a chupprass† and before long I was recommended to the "Dipty Saheb," whose orderly I, in due course, became. I consoled myself with the reflection that ere long I should get some small pickings, which would amount in the aggregate to something comfortable. But several weeks passed, and I found I could pocket nothing; for none but petty matters were tried by my master. In despair I consulted Suntokhea once more.

What a simpleton you are, friend Panchkouree, to be in a fix about such a trifle. The Deputy Saheb has the "Surasurreee"‡ department. Where two parties contest a case, one must lose. The gainer, as an established *dustoor*,§ pays for the decision in his favor. It is an undoubted prerogative of the Huzoor's orderly to receive a fee, as also that of the Mohurir ‖. Thus a double object is gained. You will get a daily fee of at least 4 or 8 annas; and by and bye become the agent between the *decreedar*¶ and the Mohurir; you will have the latter under your thumb, and can compel him to improve your prospects. But, said I, the Saheb is said to be sharp; should he discover my inter-

* Unfaithful to salt, an ingrate. † A badge.
‡ Summary Department for decision of cases between landlord and tenant.
§ Custom. ‖ Writer or Clerk. ¶ Decree holder.

ference, he will punish me ; on what pretext then shall I demand a fee from the *decreedar*.

Friend Panchkouree, replied Suntokhea, believe me that your Saheb is as blind a mole as the rest of them. How is he to discover anything? The *decreedars*, for their own sake, will not tell tales ; and one leaves the presence on so many occasions, that so long as somebody is within hail, the absence for a few minutes, of an orderly, is unnoticed. Ask boldly ; I am confident of the result ; and do you not fail to give me part of your earnings.

Well, next day, as soon as a case was decided, I quietly sneaked out of the room ; and following the *decreedar*, significantly held out my palm To my joy and surprise he slipped a rupee into it, and whispered me to give the Moonshee his share. I thought that bad luck would come of a division of such spoils, so I uttered an *alhumduloollah* ! !* and stroking my beard entered the presence with increased gravity. The same experiment was repeatedly tried with varied success as to the amount · in no case was I utterly disappointed.

After a few days the Moonshee called me to his house. and asked me whether I had made any money? I called the Prophet to witness that nobody thought of offering me a cowree. Friend, he said, have I not seen thee follow out the *decreedars ;* surely it was not without a purpose, and without some result? So help me Allah, Moonshee Saheb, I answered, that I received nothing but scurrilous abuse. Who am I that a zumeendar should pay me aught? The Moonshee, at length, told me that it was established as an ancient rule, that whosoever gained a cause should give a *douceur* to the Umlah That in future I should demand fees in the Moonshee Jee's name ; and that I should retain one-fourth for myself and fellow chupprasees, and give him three-fourths, for himself and his friends This I readily agreed to, and then the Moonshee Jee schooled me how I was to behave on certain occasions which I proceed to describe.

Suppose an order is passed, calling for a *kyfeut*† from the Sheristah ;‡ nobody ever thinks of executing the order before the lapse of a week at least. If the plaintiff be importunate, and the saheb desire you to ascertain why the *kyfeut* has not been written, you take the complainant out with you, and ask him what he will give if you get the *kyfeut* written at once? The poor wretch, tired of waiting for days, gladly offers a rupee. You pocket it ; go to the Muhafiz-duftur,§ and say that the Saheb has sent word, that if the order is not at once executed he will be fined roundly. The matter is ended at once, and we divide the spoil. If the party will not pay, you go and enquire why the *kyfeut* is not written? The answer is, that some important papers are called for by a superior authority ; and the Muhafiz-duftur begs that the Huzoor will give him a few days' grace. The harrassed litigant finds it cheaper to pay a rupee than to be

* Thanksgiving, praise to God.
† Memorandum of report.
‡ The native Record-keeper.
§ Record-keeper.

kept cooling his heels at the court for weeks, and gives in at last, paying his fees with interest.

Again, it is the established practice for a zumeendar to pay a fee of one rupee for every jummabundee* that is filed in the office. This is taken by the Muhafiz-duftur and Qanoongoes.† But, friend Panchkouree, it is cruelly hard that you and I should not partake of the spoil. So look sharp; and whenever you hear a zumeendar complain to the Huzoor that his jummabundee, although given in, has not been filed, try and make a bargain: go and bully the Qanoongo and Muhafiz-duftur, as if with the Saheb's *hookoom*.‡ The zumeendar will fee you, and we will divide like good friends.

Various hints did I receive and act upon; and I need not say that I not only made lots of money, but generally contrived to keep the lion's share of the prey to myself. I was not satisfied, however, with such small game; and was resolved on the first opportunity to change my service, for one of greater emolument and higher station.

Chap. III.

HOW PANCHKOUREE MAKES MONEY, WHILE A SHERIFF'S OFFICER, OR PROCESS SERVER.

Having solved the golden problem, and being fixed in my purpose to build a pukka house and to possess some landed property, I took the earliest opportunity of taking my congé, of the Dipty Saheb, and being transferred to the staff of the Nazir.§ Now this official is the chief executive, and his chuprasees share in the prestige of his name, as well as in the emoluments of his office. Being a stranger, I of course, had the fag, without any of the profits. But I was becoming quite a man of the world and a practical philosopher, so I consoled myself with the reflection, that when my *kismut*‖ ordained it I should be as great a man as my friend Suntokhea Singh. Most diligently did I do the Nazir Saheb's bidding. Most assiduous was I in filling his chillum; bringing him water; running after his palkee or garee, until I fairly won his confidence, and was looked upon by all persons as his especial favorite.

I found that a deal of money was to be made and by the simplest process in the world. The Dipty Saheb issued a summons for the appearance of a petty defaulter of revenue. The "*tullubana*¶" is paid by the plaintiff but if he does not make a "*moamlah*"** with us, the process is never served. Several of these writs are entrusted to one man; but the majority of

* Rent-roll. † Fiscal officers. ‡ Order § Sheriff. ‖ Fate
¶ Money for serving a process. ** Compromise.

them are never out of the *kummurbund** of the chuprasee. When the period allowed for serving them has elapsed, a *kyfeut* is given in to the effect, that "the plaintiff would not indicate the party named, and that, therefore, the serving of the process was impossible." Perhaps the plaintiff protests that no chuprasee ever went to the village. The Nazir is summoned. On being spoken to, he sends for me, and sharply asks whether the summons was served or not? I call the prophet to witness that the plaintiff's allegation is a lie; that I did go for three several days, but that the plaintiff would not indicate the defendant. Upon this, the Saheb issues a warrant of apprehension, which is entrusted to me to execute, and the plaintiff not only pays the *tullubana* a second time, but pays the piper, by feeing me roundly to apprehend the defaulter. But I shall relate another process of making money and deceiving the Collector or Deputy. Bulbhuddur Singh is purchaser of the rights and interests of Duldhupput Misr in the village of Undhadhoond; but what these rights *may* be, I do not pretend to know. He gets a deed of possession from the Civil Court and proceeds to the village to collect his rents. He finds that Duldhupput is one of the small fry of proprietary brotherhood that has no direct concern in the management of the village. He examines the Putwaree's papers, and is puzzled to know what he has purchased. Most men would content themselves with chewing the cud of resignation; but Baboo Bulbhuddur Singh is a man of another stamp; and he resolves on playing the artful dodger; and picks out a couple of needy asamees† who are not scrupulous as to truth. He offers to pay them five rupees each, if they will but appear before the Collector Saheb, and acknowledge that they are cultivators of Mouza Undhadhoond, and that Baboo Bulbhuddur is *the* zemindar, and entitled to receive the revenue. What is the man driving at? you enquire. Have patience and you will see.

Baboo Bulbhuddur presents a petition in the '*Surasurree*' department, praying that Ramdeenooa Chumar and Durshunooa Ahir be coerced to pay him two rupees each for five biswas of land cultivated by each in the village of Undhadhoond. A *kyfeut* is called for from the office, as to whether Baboo Bulbhuddur be zemindar? The return is that 'he is auction purchaser, and that his name is recorded in lieu of Duldhupput Misr.' A process is served against the defaulters Ramdeenooa and Durshunooa; who having been paid, and schooled beforehand, appear before the Huzoor and acknowledge the justness of the claim, and agree to pay, if a little grace be vouchsafed. This is called '*ekbaldawee*'‡ and decree for the paintiff is ordered.

Some weeks afterwards, Baboo Bulbhuddur Singh proceeds to the village of Undhadhoond to collect his rents. The zemindars turn out and oppose him, and, perhaps, a serious affray is the result. The Baboo now complains in the Fouzdaree Adalut for forcible dispossession, under the provisions of Act 4 of 1840, or

* Waist-band. † Villagers. ‡ Admission

as it is commonly known '*Akut Chakaroom.*' He refers to the case decided by the 'Dipty Saheb,' in which he obtained decree for rent: he shews the order of the Civil Court for putting him in possession. He cites Ramdeenooa and Durshunooa as witnesses to his possession. He summons me to prove that when I served the process against the asamees, I observed that he was in possession of Mouza Undhadhoond. And as he pays well, and we have all sworn through thick and thin, the odds are that Bulbhuddur Singh is 'ordered to be put in possession of the property disputed.' Upon the strength of which he manages, gradually, to get the entire estate.

One day the Nazir was directed to oust a cultivator, who had a large *jote** in the village of *Undhadhoond*; and previous to deputing me, he took me aside and schooled me how I should act. I made fifty rupees by this one job, and shall describe the whole of the proceedings. If a landlord obtain a decree for rent against an asamee, he may pray for a process of ouster, any time within twelve years. The asamee is summoned. I am feed for *not* serving process, and return the order with a *kyfeut* that the defendant will not come out of his house—is in short '*rooposh.*'† The unfortunate cultivator is ordered to be dispossessed of his fields for his contumacy. I go out with a force of peons and uproot everything already grown by the cultivator; and aid the landlord in re-ploughing the fields.

Should the landlord imagine that he can carry out the Collector Saheb's order without giving us fees; it gives us no concern. We make a bargain with the other party, and if the worst comes to the worst on going out to put the landlord in possession, we, instead of doing so, pretend scruples of conscience as to uprooting crops about to ripen—and report to the Saheb, in a well-got-up *kyfeut*, that the *decreedar* is a '*zalim*'‡ and a '*moofsidh*'§—that Bulbhuddur Singh's reputation is so well-known to the Huzoor, that it does not need for the slave to represent, &c &c, and the asamee keeps possession of his field.

CHAP. IV.

HOW PAUNCHKOUREE GETS ON TO THE PAY LIST OF A WEALTHY NATIVE.

I was directed by the Nazir, one day, to apprehend a revenue defaulter, or to bring his principal Karindah before the Huzoor. The defaulter was a Nawabzadeh, and the apprehension of even his steward would be looked upon as a disgrace. However the Collector Saheb Bahadoor passed the order to the Nazir, and it was my province to obey orders. I proceeded at once to the Nawab Saheb's house, with two other chuprasees, and present-

* Tillage. † In hiding. ‡ Tyrant. § Rascal.

ing the warrant, desired them to accompany us to the Nazir. We had a broad hint to quit, for the warrant was thrown back to us, and a cry of "*mar*, *mar*"* raised, that induced us to bolt in double-quick time. Next day a formidable *kyfeut* was given in to the Huzoor. I had heard that the Karindah was wont to come daily to the Kacherree to consult the Sheristadar. I was on the look out, and the moment he appeared I ran and informed the Huzoor, who at once ordered his apprehension. He was in quod for three days; and his master soon paid the amount due by him for his man's release. This was a grand moral lesson for the Nawab Saheb; and the next time he took care not to insult people in power. But when I went to make my salam I was gratified with a fee and promises for the future.

A fruitful field is the abkaree system, and the license granted to opium and drug farmers to oppress the people, and screw money out of them. I say license given, because they make use of their farming license to be guilty of all kinds of villany. I was directed one day to execute a search warrant for contraband opium. The *theekadar*† sent for me, made much of me, and put five rupees into my hand. I asked no questions, but knew very well that I was expected to do something for my fee. Several of the farmer's people accompanied me to the house to be searched. I authoritatively called out to the owner of the house to admit me to search for contraband opium. The man was a wealthy Bunneah; and appearing to be conscious of his innocence, at once opened the door and admitted us. I saw one of the farmer's men quietly deposit a bundle of something under some rubbish, and after rummaging about he ferreted out his own bundle, which he held up in triumph to us as *the* contraband opium we had been desired to search for. The poor Bunneah was horror-stricken, and appealed to me; but having received a retainer I dared not to defend the poor man. I swore he was a liar; called out to the witnesses, before whom the opium was taken out of the Bunneah's house, to remember what they had seen and to depone to that effect before the Huzoor. The Bunneah in desperation offered me fifty rupees to release him. But as I could not do so, after having proceeded so far, I abused him and calling all persons to witness that he had offered a bribe; bundled him off to the Saheb Bahadoor. He was fined 100 rupees, of which one-fourth was carried to the account of Government, one half was given to the farmer's people, and the remaining fourth was bestowed on me.

I thought this plan of making money was an admirable one; but was resolved to try whether more money could be made by siding against the theekadar instead of with him. I had not long to wait, when an order was passed by the Dipty Saheb to search the house of a well-known courtezan. The theekadar sent for me; but I would not go; and during the night I paid a visit to *Madame Dilfureb*,‡ she received me haughtily; but I

* Beat. † Farmer. ‡ Proper name—Enticer of the heart.

soon convinced her of my power to molest or protect her; and I was not only treated to "every delicacy of the season," but to her blandest smiles. I ascertained that she had a quantity of opium in the house, which her servants made up into *mudduck*, or little pellets for smoking. This we carefully hid; and next morning I accompanied the theekadar's men to the house of *Madame Dilfureb*. I insisted upon the people being searched in the presence of a police burkundaz previous to entering the lady's house. One fellow had a large bundle of *kuffa*,* which was boned by the police and the search proceeded; of course nothing was found. I duly reported the delinquency of the theekadar's people, who were roundly fined, and I not only received a handsome fee from *Dilfureb*, but additional marks of respect and esteem.

The farmers of the abkaree make large profits, not by the sale of drugs, but by holding a threat of searching honest people's houses in *terrorem* over them; they seize contraband articles, extort money from the contrabandists, who are too glad to compromise with them, rather than be sent up to the Collector Saheb, and the farmer is glad to let them off for what he can screw out of them, because he gets the *whole*, and has neither the onus nor trouble of furnishing proof of the guilt of the parties. It is *only* in cases of public seizure when the farmer dares not suppress the case, that rich contrabandists are sent up for punishment, or where the parties are too poor to be squeezed; and the farmer's interest requires him to cram the maw of the penal law with a few victims.

Chap. V.

ZUBBURDUST MISR AND LALLA RAMBALUK; AND HOW THEY ROSE BY ACCUSING THE INNOCENT, WHEN THEY COULD NOT FIND THE GUILTY PERSONS.

I had become acquainted with every "*Jack in office*," and as we had many little "*soirées*" of our own, and in a friendly manner compared notes with one another, I was at once able to perceive that amongst us flunkies I was a very little creature indeed. That my friend Suntokhea was but a gudgeon, while others might not inaptly be called the sharks and alligators of our legal sea My eyes glistened at the objects in prospect, and my whole frame quivered with emotion, as I listened to my friends, when they related the ways and means *they* had of making money. Every man of them had one pukka house or more. Ranges of shops in the bazars they had contrived to convert into their own property, and in their mohullas,† they were "cocks of the walk," and who dared compete with them when they chose to cock-a-doodle-doo? I shall proceed to give some of their histories.

* Rags steeped in poppy milk, and twisted tightly together. † Wards.

Zubburdust Misr was a strong, black, middle aged man, with an "oily-gammonish" kind of look about him that deceived every body. He was a burkundaz on the receipt of 4 Rs. per mensem, and had been on the staff of the well-known thief catcher, Lalla Rambaluk, thanadar of Zalimgunje, district of Beinsafpoor. A set of miscreants, whom nobody could trace, were going about the country poisoning and robbing the lieges. Parties used to be found lying dead, or dying near wells, or in the suraces, stripped of everything, and without any marks of violence. The Civil Surgeon, on making a post-mortem examination, could only affirm that they had been poisoned, he presumed with *dhutoora*. The men "died, and their corpses presented no outward signs of violence." The greatest consternation prevailed. The Magistrate reported the circumstance to Government, and got a wigging for his pains; and he in consequence issued an order to "stop the pay of all the thanadars" until the delinquents were discovered. Upon this Rambaluk was sent for, and directed to produce the poisoners, under penalty of the Huzoor's severe displeasure. Everything that man could do was done, but we could make no thing of the case; so like Lord Burleigh we solemnly shook our heads and pronounced the affair a mystery!

Again, it was reported that four travellers had been poisoned and robbed. Two died, but two recovered after a deal of trouble. The survivors deposed that they had made a long march, and about noon-day having come to a shady peepul tree on the road-side, close by which there was a well of sweet water, they sat down to refresh themselves. They had nothing to eat but a little "*chubenah*,"* which humble fare appearing to excite the compassion of a party of travellers, who were also seated under the peepul, they offered them some "*suttoo*,"† which having eaten, they suddenly became insensible. They stated that sundry articles of silver, such as bangles, armlets, &c., were in their bundles; the whole of which had been taken by the poisoners.

Again the most thundering orders were fulminated to the police. The Kotwal and all the thanadars were sent out to hunt for the poisoners; but nobody could give any information as to their whereabouts. At last Rambaluk sent for me. Brother Zubburdust Misr, said he, you know that Bhowanee Pershad Sahoo is a notorious *thangeedar*, (receiver of stolen property) and that of late he has not given us any but the smallest fees. Go at once to his house, search it, and produce the silver articles, according to the Huzoor's orders. I at once twigged his meaning; but wishing to gammon him, I insinuated—'but Lallah Shaheb, the Sahoo must have in his *dokan*‡ scores of bangles and armlets, how am I to know which are the ones that the poisoned travellers owned?' To this Rambaluk replied—you and I should understand one another by this time Zubburdust Misr. Ask no silly questions, but go and produce the articles from Bhowanee Pershad's house, and there will be no difficulty in iden-

* Parched peas. † Parched peas and barley ground into meal. ‡ Shop.

tifying them. I went as directed; and producing my warrant, proceeded to business. The Sahoo asked me if I were mad to be searching the house of an old friend? He denied having any of the stolen property; and talked very much about his "*izzut*."* Friend Sahoo, I enquired, how will you account for having such a variety of silver and golden ornaments as yonder chest contains. (Here I pointed towards an old acquaintance, which was carefully concealed). He understood me and offered me a hundred rupees, which I at once pocketed. I was afraid, however, to return to Lallah Rambaluk without *any* silver ornaments; so I took from the Sahoo sundry bits of silver that *had* been bangles and armlets—and after *sumjhaoing*† him, asked him in the presence of witnesses, whence he had procured them? He replied that a woman called Lutchminea, by caste a Brahminee, had sold them to him two days previously; I took Bhowanee Pershad and the bits of silver to Lallah Rambaluk, who, after cogitating for a few moments, uttered a devout "*Sree—Sree—Sree*," and looking at me triumphantly, exclaimed that the whole plot was unravelled, and in two days our faces should be made white before the Huzoor. The Sahoo paid the thanadar another 50 rupees, and was released on bail.

We then apprehended Lutchminea, and asked her to confess. But she persisted in denying all knowledge of the bits of silver or of the gang of poisoners. Give her a remembrancer, Zubburdust Misr, said Rambaluk. I took a large loose bag, containing decayed and dried chillies, and put it over her head, with a few shakes. In a few moments she was nearly suffocated, and when she recovered her senses she said she would confess to whatever we bid her. Her confession was taken in the thanna before three witnesses, and according to her statement we proceeded to seize Debee Misr, and Singha Ram. Both these worthies denied the charge; but they were old offenders and required a little *sumjhaoing*.‡ They were kept out exposed to the fierce rays of a vertical sun for a couple of hours, and when fainting from heat and thrist, they were treated to the chilly bag. They readily confessed before witnesses. Now here was a beautiful case for the Magistrate. The surviving travellers had sworn to having received *suttoo* from a party consisting of a woman and two men, who called themselves Bramins. Two men and a woman had confessed to the crimes of poisoning and robbing. The bits of silver they alleged to be part of the property robbed from the travellers. What booted it, that the travellers could not identify the robbers or the bits of silver? They had barely seen the robbers for a moment, and the bangles, &c., had been broken up. But the robbers freely confessed, and all was right.

The Huzoor was delighted at our success. Promised great things to Rambaluk Lallah, and made me a Jumedar of police

* Respectability. † Tutoring. ‡ Here used for punishing.

at once. The defendants confessed before the Magistrate. They had been imprisoned previously for mal-practices; and they were sent for trial by the Sessions Judge. The Sahoo got off on the pretext that he was ignorant of the silver having been stolen property; and stated that he had voluntarily given it up to me; and named Lutchminea as the party from whom he had purchased it. Here Zubburdust Misr paused to enjoy my astonishment.

Friend, I said, what you have just related gives me the highest respect for your abilities. But surely the Sahebs are not gulled so readily! I also have played a few tricks, but had no notion of such wholesale consummate art as you mention. How were the alleged poisoners punished by the Judge Saheb?

Zubburdust Misr sighed deeply, or affected to do so, and continued thus:—I had disbelieved that "Ram Jee"* interfered directly in the matters of this world; but the issue of the case I have related gave me serious matter for reflection. You shall judge for yourself. Two days remained for the trial of the poisoners before the Junab Saheb Judge,† when a *roobakaree*‡ was received by the Magistrate from the officiating Joint Magistrate of a neighbouring district (a young, headstrong, opiniative boy, one that *would* do everything himself, and not trust to his *Omlah*. One can never depend upon *what* they do) purporting that a gang of poisoners, consisting of two men and a woman had been taken by the police just as they were rifling some travellers to whom they had administered *dhutoora*. That they had a very miscellaneous collection of all kinds of silver and golden ornaments; and that finding denial of no avail, as they had been caught in the act of robbing, they had confessed to having poisoned and robbed sundry people at different times, and that they had heard some innocent persons had been apprehended, and were committed for trial by the Sessions Judge, in the zillah of Beinsafpoor. They pointed out the property taken from the travellers, which, together with copy of their confession, was sent to the Magistrate of Beinsafpoor.

Here was a go! The Saheb Magistrate raved and swore at the whole of the police. The men and woman who had confessed, were asked why they had confessed? and out came the whole story. This would have gone for nothing, but the travellers swore to the identity of the property sent by the boy Joint, and there could be no doubt as to the innocence of the parties we had apprehended. The upshot was, that the Kotwal, Lalla Rambaluk, and two other thanadars, were turned out, and I was reduced to a burkundaz, in which place I have continued ever since.

I was determined to ascertain some more interesting matters, but the "soiree" broke up, and I proceeded to my home.

* God. † My Lord, the Judge. ‡ Proceeding.

CHAP. VI.

A THANADAR PUNISHED FOR AN HONEST REPORT.

I happened to be in the room, one day, when a fine-looking young fellow, in the undress of a sepoy, came up to the desk of the Joint Magistrate, and salamed to him. The Saheb Joint asked him what he wanted? He stated that his name was *Lootcha Singh*, that he was alleged to have been murdered three years back; and that as he understood his uncle had been transported to another district, on account of the alleged murder as a felon for life, he had come to exculpate him. The Saheb was not a little astonished; but he is one of those energetic men who never hesitates over a resolution, but at once carries it out. He sent for the *misl** of the case, and I heard read as follows:—

"*Gudha Purshad*, thanadar of *Bewuqoofpoor*, reported to the Magistrate, that *Lootcha Singh*, a resident of *Fussadgunj*, was missing. That nobody could give any account of him. That he had a criminal intrigue with his own brother's wife. That this brother was absent, but the intrigue having come to the knowledge of *Lootcha Singh's* uncle, *Zalim Singh*, it was suspected that *Lootcha Singh* had fled, nobody knew whither. Upon this, the Magistrate suspended *Gudha Purshad*, thanadar, recorded his conviction that *Lootcha Singh* had been murdered by his own relations, in revenge for the intrigue with his brother's wife. That the thanadar of *Bewuqoofpoor* had been bribed to send up a false statement of the case. That the Kotwal of the city be directed to go at once to the village of *Fussadgunj*; and within a fortnight to produce the murderers of *Lootcha Singh* with the necessary proofs, under penalty of dismissal.

"Within the fortnight the Kotwal reported to the Magistrate that, "*baikbul Huzoor*,"† he had apprehended the murderer of *Lootcha Singh*, who proved to be his uncle, *Zalim Singh*; and that the murderer not only confessed his crime, but that strong circumstantial evidence went to criminate him, &c., &c. The defendant, *Zalim*, made a free confession before the Magistrate. He deponed that a criminal connection had existed between *Lootcha Singh* and *Phooljhurea*, wife of his own brother, who was absent. That fear of loss of caste resulting, should the intercourse be fruitful, he had first remonstrated with *Lootcha Singh*; but finding him deaf to reproof, he murdered him one night, and threw his body the same night into the Ganges. No question was asked the prisoner, and the confession having been written in a corner of the room, out of ear-shot of the Saheb, was attested by him and three witnesses, as a free and unextorted confession of murder.

* File of papers of a case. † By the good fortune of the presence

"Sundry witnesses deponed to having heard of the existence of a criminal intimacy between the deceased and his brother's wife *Phooljhurea*. That they heard defendant reprove the deceased; and that certain witnesses heard defendant threaten to kill him. But nobody saw the deed done. Nobody was found. There was no bloody weapon—no marks of a struggle, or other indication of violence. The Magistrate committed *Zalim Singh* to take his trial before the Sessions Judge for the wilful murder of his nephew *Lootcha Singh*.

"The prisoner confessed before the Judge. The witnesses corroborated what they had previously deponed to. The law officer gave a *futwa* of "*kissas*"* and the Judge referred the *misl* of the case to the Suddur Nizamut Adalut, and recommended that *Zalim Singh* should be hanged.

"In due course of time the file of papers was laid before their worships, the Judges of the Court of Nizamut Adalut. One Judge concurred in opinion with the Sessions Judge and was for hanging *Zalim Singh*. But, for the credit of the "*Saheban Aleeshan*,"† the second Judge, Mr. ———, differed entirely from all the other sahebs. He observed, that *Zalim* had himself gone to the thanah of *Bewuqoofpoor*, and reported that *Lootcha Singh* was missing. That the Magistrate had merely attested his deposition, without putting a single question to him. That the wording of the confessions, as recorded before the Kotwal, the Magistrate and Sessions Judge, were almost similar, verbatim; that although the evidence went to prove that a family dispute had occurred, and that the prisoner *Zalim* had been heard to threaten *Lootcha Singh;* yet that there was no proof of the murder having been committed at all, as the '*corpus delicti*,' the only positive proof was wanting. He, therefore, voted against capital punishment, and recommended that the prisoner be confined for life; or until *Lootcha Singh* turned up.

"The whole of the Judges concurred with Mr. ——, and *Zalim Singh*, branded on the forehead as a felon, was transported to Goruckpore. *Gudha Purshad* was turned out and declared to be incapable of again serving Government, and the Kotwal received a very oily purwanah of good-conduct, and a reward of 500 rupees.

"The Saheb Joint recorded the deposition of *Lootcha Singh*. He stated that he had had a criminal connection with *Phooljhurea*. That he was afraid of his uncle *Zalim;* and hearing on the evening of his alleged murder, that a regiment of sepoys was encamped only a few miles off, and was proceeding to Bengal, he went and enlisted, and accompanied the regiment to Bengal. That having heard, incidentally, that his uncle *Zalim Singh* had been transported as a felon, he had taken leave, returned to his village; and come to the Huzoor to declare the whole truth.

"The Saheb did not lose a day in sending for *Zalim Singh* from Goruckpore; and when he was questioned, I made it a point to

* Retaliation—as blood for blood. † Gentlemen of exalted rank.

be present. The Saheb told him that he was free, as his nephew was proved to be alive. The poor victim of the law burst into tears, threw himself at the Saheb's feet, and pointing to his branded brow, asked the Joint Magistrate of what use would freedom be to him, when he bore the mark of Cain for life? He was asked why he had confessed three several times? He submitted, that the Saheb himself would have done so under similar circumstances. That he was kept in a privy, with putrid ordure up to his knees all night, and exposed to the influence of a burning sun all day. Until, maddened by the treatment, and wishing for death, at any rate, a release from his intolerable torture, he confessed just as he had been tutored to do by the Kotwal. He stated that not a question had been put to him by the Magistrate or Judge; and that on attempting to speak, he was rebuked. He said that his release was a matter of indifference, as he was broken-hearted, and could not shew his face again in the company of honest men, owing to his branded brow.

"The Saheb Joint sent up a strong representation to the Nizamut Adawlut. He recommended that the Kotwal should be dismissed, made to refund the reward he had received, and tried criminally for having trumped up a false case of murder. That *Gudha Purshad* should be employed again and receive a reward from Government; and that poor *Zalim Singh* be supported at the expense of the state for life. This was asking only what was due from the Government. But what was the result.

"Poor *Zalim* was, of course, released, but no provision was made for him, nor any recompence awarded for his branded forehead. *Gudha Purshad* remained unnoticed. And as for the Kotwal, not only did he *not* disgorge the reward of 500 rupees given him for his iniquity, but he was retained in possession of his appointment; and for ought I know, is still a 'Jack in office.'

"I saw that the *Saheb* was very greatly disgusted at all this; but he was helpless, and was obliged to swallow his indignation. I could not help reflecting, however, on the cruelty of the punishment of branding or '*Godena,*' and Government has always objected to mutilation of a limb, because the culprit is thereby rendered helpless for life. But a branded felon, if ever released, is punished even more severely than by mutilation. He is morally degraded and rendered an outcast from the society of men. The mark has mutilated his moral character, and disqualified him from resuming a reputation, of which he was innocently deprived, and he ought no longer to be made liable for raising his hands against those who point to that mark as a disgrace and a reproach. It were well if our legislators gave the subject the reflection it merits, and repealed the damning law.* But I forget that I am a poor, ignorant orderly, and must not presume to give a hint even to my betters."

* Act of 1849 has been promulgated, prohibiting the branding of convicts.

Chap. VII.

A PORTRAIT OF A PROSPEROUS POLICEMAN.

I was connected with *Jubbur Khan* by marriage; and we saw each other frequently. *Jubbur Khan* was confidential orderly to *Nimaz Khan*, one of the officials of police; and he had played his cards so cleverly that he had a considerable sum of money in cash, besides jewels with which his wife and children were bedecked. Some five years ago my friend was a poor devil of a *burkundaz*,* his own clothes were ragged, and his appearance was meagre. His wife and children were in rags and half-starved. Whereas now he is as unctuous-looking a man as ever lived upon a *pouh* of *ghee*† per diem. Of course we frequently compared notes; and this is the marrow of his story.

When a suitor goes to the thannah, it is the duty of *Jubbur Khan* to take him aside and enquire how much he will give for settling the case in his favor. A bargain is driven, and the utmost squeezed out of the party that can possibly be obtained. Even a pair of shoes, a *topee*,‡ or a *kummurbund*§ are accepted, in the absence of anything more valuable. Of course *Jubbur Khan* swears to his patron that he takes nothing for himself, and is content, like a well-behaved jackall, to feast on the lion's leavings; but not a day passes without his pocketing something handsome; and many is the time that the lion's share has fallen to his lot. He told me that his cue was to get up a *moamlah*‖ against some rich *Muhajun*,¶ or other wealthy person. For then, if the rich man would not fork out handsomely, nothing was easier than to word the *kyfeut* of the police report, so as to induce the *Hakim*** to issue an order for a *tuhkeekat*,†† and then a golden harvest was reaped. For instance—a man well dressed (as every swindling blackguard may be) appears in the thannah and gives a formal complaint against a *nouputtee Muhajun*‡‡ for the abduction of his sister, or daughter, or wife. Now such a charge is not cognizable; but, like an artful dodger, *Jubbur Khan* tells the complainant to state that the woman had 500 rupees' worth of jewels on her person, which the defendant has also robbed him of. The complainant takes the hint and depones accordingly; and as he expects to get a handsome sum of money from the *Muhajun* for giving in a *razeenama*§§ he gives a fee of 25 rupees to *Nimaz Khan*, and *Jubbur* is sent to the *Muhajun's* house with warrant.

Jubbur Khan blusters and bullies the unfortunate *Muhajun*, and producing his warrant, declares that, although much against his wish, he must take *Dumree Lall* to the thannah. The *Muhajun* gives 100 rupees for a day's respite, and *Jubbur Khan* returns to the thannah. Next day he goes again to the *Muhajun*,

* Police constables are so called. † Half a pound of clarified butter.
‡ Cap. § Waistband. ‖ Case. ¶ Banker. ** Official governor.
†† Enquiry. ‡‡ Highest caste of banker. §§ Compromise.

who sends his confidential man with another 100 rupees to *Nimaz Khan*. At first the *Karindah* is well bullied, his master abused, and a threat held out that every mother's son shall be *chalaned*.* At length *Jubbur Khan* folds his hands before *Nimaz Khan*, and after lauding him to the skies, as the soul of honour and peerless amongst the undaunted, entreats that the thanadar would reflect for a moment, whether it be possible for a man of such respectability as *Dumree Lall Sahoo* to have committed such an act as the prosecutor charges him with. That *Dumree Lall* is a *nouputtee Muhajun*, and a man of reputed munificence; whereas he had heard from several people that the prosecutor is a *Dullal*† and a *budmash*,‡ etc. Here the *Mohurir* and *Jumadar* edge in a word in praise of *Dumree Lall* and in abuse of the prosecutor. *Nimaz Khan* relaxes the austerity of his countenance, and acknowledges that he *had* heard of *the hounsilah*§ of *Dumree Sahoo*, etc. He takes the *Karindah* into a private apartment, and after a short while dismisses him. The prosecutor is sent for, abused most heartily, and threatened with all the most unheard-of severities, if he again presumes to make such a false complaint against people of respectability. The *Dullal* respectfully enquires whether the small sum of 25 rupees had been received by the thanadar or not. He appeals to *Jubbur Khan*; but one and all turn upon him, call him a liar and scoundrel, and he is summarily kicked out. A report goes up to the Saheb Magistrate, simply intimating that a charge of abduction had been brought by a *Dullal* against *Dumree Lall Sahoo*; that the *Huzoor* knows well the character of *Dullals*, and that as the charge was not cognisable by the police, the prosecutor was referred to the "*Adalut-ool-alea*,"‖ And thus ends the farce.

Jubbur Khan gave me a very amusing account of the clever way in which a part of stolen property, chiefly jewels and gems, is appropriated by the police, after recovery. A party complains that he has been robbed of a large amount of jewels and precious stones. Part is found; and almost always one or more choice specimens are reserved for the thanadar. It is scarcely probable that *every* thing stolen will be recovered; consequently the occasional loss of any part of the property is put down to the account of the thief. But no one ever thinks of suspecting the police. And if suspicion be excited "*cheh faedah* ?"¶ Where is the proof?

Jubbur Khan was desired one day to apprehend a suspected coiner, who had been circulating a quantity of base coin. Such is the cleverness of these fellows, that it is asserted as a fact, that the very day the new Company's rupee was circulated, a supply of the base coin was simultaneously sent into the bazaar. The coiners never utter their own coin; but have

* Sent to the magistrate. † Broker. ‡ A bad character. § Liberality.
‖ The exalted seat of justice. ¶ Cui bono?

agents of every grade, who pass a few base rupees along with a number of good ones. Well, friend *Jubbur* proceeded boldly to the house of *Jalea Pershad*, and calling out to him, declared he had come to intimate the Huzoor's orders. He was desired to remain outside, until the women were put out of the way; and after a quarter of an hour's delay, he was ushered in, with extreme civility, into the presence of *Jalea Pershad*. *Jubbur* produced his warrant, and told him that he must accompany him at once to *Nimaz Khan*, and bullied him roundly for keeping him so long a time at the door. *Jalea Pershad* begged of him to be pacified; declared his readiness to accompany him at once; and, before leaving his house, put a gold-mohur into *Jubbur Khan's* hand, and begged of him to mention nothing of the detention outside *Jalea's* house. The *Sahoo* took a bag of a hundred *inducements* with him in case of need, and departed with *Jubbur Khan*.

On reaching the thannah, the first order given is to put *Jalea Pershad* in the stocks. He is taken away for the purpose; but whispers to *Jubbur Khan* to tell *Nimaz Khan* that he has brought a *nuzzur** for his worship The thanadar receives the inducements, and finds them sufficiently weighty to remove the prisoner's feet from the stocks. He is introduced into a decent room apart from the others, and his people are permitted to bring in his *bistoor*,† and to make him as comfortable as circumstances will permit.

Of course *Jalea Pershad* gets off, minus the *inducements*, for there is no proof against him. And *Jubbur Khan* swears, that not only did he not see anything suspicious in *Jalea's* house, but that he was at once admitted therein.

In short, by *Jubbur Khan's* statement, the execution of a search warrant, or a warrant of apprehension, may be always evaded if the delinquent is able to *oil palms*. For, as he candidly confessed, the *Sirkar Bahadoor*‡ gives me four rupees a month, and the offer of a sum equivalent to six months' pay, often, or occasionally, ought not to be resisted by an orderly.

CHAP. VIII.

THE MOOKTYAR TRIBE ILLUSTRATED BY EXAMPLES.

There are a set of miscreants that infest the courts, than whom a greater nuisance does not exist; I mean the *Mooktyars*, or Attorneys. Without any pretence to education, without any legal knowledge, they derive a maintenance by fomenting quarrels, by mystifying their clients by misquotations, of the "*Qanoon-i-Sircar*,"§ and the "*circoolar chittees*,"‖ and the "*cant-*

* Good-will offering. † Carpet bedding. ‡ The State.

§ Regulations of Government. ‖ Circular orders.

ractions"[*] of the Nizamut Adalut. Noisy declamation and lying are their talent, and extreme impudence is their privilege. Rebuked, fined, turned out as they have been, they contrive to creep in again, as soon as there is a change of administration. Many an amusing scene have I witnessed, and many a *rise* do they take out of the *hakims*.

Lutees Pershad is a well-known character. Like the immortal practitioners, Dodson and Fogg, he undertakes cases on *spec.* If his client cannot pay, it does not signify; he contents himself with the client's signature to a bit of stamp-paper, an I O U in short. Months afterwards, the client is astonished to find that his little property is attached in execution of a decree, passed in favour of the decree-holder, *Lutees Pershad.* Houses, shares of villages, orchards, have thus dropped in "*by accident*" into the maw of this worthy.

I was in the room, when he presented a petition on the part of *Chenala Begum*,[†] *purdah nusheen*, praying that the magistrate would punish one *Syud Moofukhur-ood-Doulah*, a *budmash*, who had fraudulently robbed her of jewels to the amount of 10,000 rupees. The *Huzoor* ordered the *Mooktyar-namah* to be attested, when out stepped *Syud Moofukhur-ood-Dowlah*, presented a petition, and verbally declared to the *Huzoor* that the plaintiff had been a courtezan in the city, and had been taken into the keeping of his master, Nuwab . . , and that having been indiscriminate in her amours, his master had turned her out. He affirmed that she was not a *purdah nusheen*, and that *Lutees Pershad* had got up a Dodson and Fogg case. The Saheb rejected the *Mooktyar-namah*, and directed that the woman should appear in person and give her deposition upon oath, if she really had any charge to make against *Mofoukhur-ood-Dowlah*.

Next day *Lutees Pershad* intimated to the magistrate, that his client had come to the *Kucheree*[‡] in a *doolee*,[§] and begged that the *doolee* might be bodily introduced into the room. This was agreed to, and a *Mohurir*[||] proceeded to take her deposition. The *Mooktyar* was asked whether *Chenala Begum* was really inside the *doolee?* He replied in the affirmative; but *Moofukhur-ood-Dowlah* submitted that it might be somebody else. That, perhaps, the lady was right in keeping behind a *purdah*, for she was old, wrinkled, and ugly, etc. Upon this, the screen of the *doolee* was hastily thrown aside; and with a torrent of abuse, that amused and surprised everybody, out walked the lady, and going boldly to the defendant, asked how *he*, who was only nominally a man, could dare to call *her* old and ugly? She was in fact *passé*, but bore the traces of beauty, and affected extreme haughtiness. The magistrate was

* Constructions of regulations.

† A female of reputed respectability—one sitting behind a screen.

‡ Office. § Covered conveyance, carried by men. || Writer—scribe.

not a little amused at the scene ; but he proceeded to business, and took the woman's deposition on oath. A few cross questions made her confess that the charge of robbery was false—that she had been a common prostitute—had been in keeping of Nuwab .. .. .., and that *Moofukhur-ood-Dowlah* was a lover of hers—that he had discarded her—and that by the advice of *Lutees Pershad*, she had personated a *purdah nusheen*, and trumped up a charge of robbery against her old flame. Of course, *Chenala Begum* was fined for a false and malicious complaint; and *Lutees Pershad* was fined roundly for having caused the false complaint to be instituted.

A clever *Mooktyar*, one *Lallah Door-undesh* once played off a fine trick on a *rayther* soft Joint Saheb. There had been a serious affray in the country and two men died of *lathee* wounds. A consideration was given to the thanadar, who ordered the corpses to be burned and thrown into the river ; and a report was sent up to the *Huzoor*, to the effect that a slight *mar peet** had taken place ; but that the *fidwee*† had proceeded to the spot, and satisfied himself that the affray had been so trifling, as to be unworthy of notice. That *Joot Bhur*, Goraet,‡ had indeed informed him that two men had died who were concerned in the affray, but having made due inquiry, he, the *fidwee*, had ascertained that the deceased had been laid up with fever for three months, and that they must have died of natural disease. That in the "*ukkil-nakhis*"§ of the thanadar no further investigation was needed, and he recommended that *Joot Bhur* be dismissed. While the Joint Saheb was in deep meditation, puzzled what to do, up walks *Lallah Door-undesh*, and salaming profoundly, offers a petition, purporting that his client was son and heir to one of the deceased, and declared that the deceased did really die of disease, and that the heir prayed that the "*razeenama*"‖ be accepted. The *Huzoor's* countenance gleamed with satisfaction at this untying of the Gordian knot ; and turning approvingly to *Lallah Door-undesh*, he enquired whether the petitioner were present ? An answer was given in the affirmative, and a lad of twelve years produced. The Saheb then asked the *Mooktyar*, whether the boy was really and in truth the heir to the deceased ? To which *Door-undesh* replied, with a becoming smirking humility, "Can the *Huzoor* imagine that any one would presume to think that the *Huzoor could* be deceived ? "*Jenab-i-allei*"¶ knows that such a thing is impossible, and that he, the "*Doulut-i-Khawah*"** is incapable of deception." The Saheb, entirely satisfied, cocks his hat and tells the Moonshee—"*bukot khoob, razeenama munzoor, misl dakhil duftur.*"†† The poor Moonshee endeavours to remind the Saheb that there are strong presumptions of homicide having been committed—that there is no proof that the boy, who gave the *razee-*

* Beating. † Slave. ‡ Village watchman.
§ Defective judgment. ‖ Compromise ¶ Great lord. ** Desirer of riches.
†† "Very well. The compromise is accepted. Put the case on the shelf."

nama, is not a fictitious personage, &c. When *Lallah Door-undesh* breaks in with—"Thus it is, sir, that the *Omlah* try to warp your impartial judgment, for their own base purposes; even after your honour has passed a final order, which is equal in discrimination to the judgment of Solomon." The Moonshee gets wigged for presuming to dictate to the *Huzoor*, and the parties leave the *Kucheree* in triumph.

Lallah Door-undesh not only benefits by fees from the thanadar, and the parties concerned in the affray, but his character rises to the culminating point in the regions of public opinion. People at once perceive how he can tickle the Saheb, and client after client comes with his retaining fee to entreat the services of *Lalla Door-undesh*. He walks consequentially towards his "*ekka*;" (*anglicè*, hack-cab) and meeting the Moonshee Jee, in the way, jostles him and passes on, inflated with vanity and consequence.

CHAP. IX.

THE NUISANCE OF THE DULLALS.

It is not, perhaps, generally known that in the ancient and holy city of *Kashee* (Benares) there have existed from time immemorial, and do exist at the present moment, several classes of men who live by extorting from the citizens and devout pilgrims more than is sufficient to maintain them in the most recklessly profligate career. They levy a regular and systematic "*black mail*" upon high and low, rich and poor. No rank or station is above their reach; and no person is so poor as to be unable to afford these gentry profit, either by payments in coin, or by some kind of service. The wealthy *Baboo*, the *nouputtee Muhajun*, the *Vakeels*; the *Omlah*, the very *Moonsiffs* and *Sudder Ameens* are subjected to their influence. For either by direct violence, or by a veneration for "*dustur*," these worthies are coerced. I allude to the *Pundahs*, the *Gunga Pooters*, the *Ghateas*, the *Burureahs*, the *Dullals*, a tribe of carrion-crows with which the city is infested, and under whose domination it groans. In attempting to expose the villany and oppression of a class, I shall not stoop to delineate individuals; for the law can reach them when known. But my object is to shew the public a body of miscreants, who, by their combination and the force of circumstances, defy all law; which as "*an Orderly*" I am able to do from personal experience.

Go into the *chouk** and attempt to purchase the most trivial article. Take up a pair of shoes or a shawl, and you will find a *Dullal*† at your elbow. The man praises one thing, abuses another; beats down the price of the vendor authoritatively; and you are surprised that such disinterested officiousness should be shown to a stranger in a crowded *chouk*. The man

* Market-square. † Broker

civilly offers to take you whithersoever you please; and to assist you in purchasing whatever you may require. You return home wondering what was the man's inducement to waste his own time in chaffering for you?—I lift the curtain to shew you that the vendors and your "*chaperone*" are in league; that your complaisant friend is a *dullal*, who takes very good care to lower the vendor's price only so much as to admit of his coming in for a handsome *dusturee*.* The difference between the bazar price, and the amount price of the article sold, is the "*huq*"† of the *Dullal*! You will ask whether the vendor may not himself pocket the whole of the money? I answer, that he dare not. The whole of the *Dullals* would cabal against him; would cry down his wares; would thrash him within an inch of his life; would by force prevent purchasers from attending his shop. "Can such things be?" you ask. Can the authorities submit tamely to such outrages. Why do not the parties who are cheated or bullied, complain to the Magistrate? They *have* tried the experiment, and although in a few instances successful, they have generally failed in obtaining redress from want of judicial proof. Moral conviction is one thing, and judicial proof another. And were a Magistrate to punish on moral conviction alone, his judgment would, in all probability, be reversed by the Judge in appeal; who, having to form *his* judgment by the *written evidence*, must be guided by *judicial proof alone*. Let me illustrate the practices of the *Dullals* by an example.

The largest, if not the only, wholesale grain market in Benares is the *Trilochun bazar*, between the city and the *Burna Sungum ghat*. Here as elsewhere, the *Dullals* have established their sway. One of the principal of these was *Bisheshur Singh*, who contrived by some means or other to eke out a comfortable subsistence by his iniquitous practices. If a boat put to at the ghat, and any transaction with the grain market was negotiated, *Bisheshur* claimed his *huq*. If the grain were attempted to be sold direct to the owner of the *Gunje*, *Bisheshur Singh* gathered his band of *Dullals* together, got up a scrimmage, and himself lodged the first complaint in the thannah; but the proprietor of the *Gunje*, *Sheikh Chalah*, was a cautious and canny cove, and managed always to escape being saddled with the onus of these rows. *Bisheshur Singh* waited patiently until there was a change in the administration; and no sooner was a new Magistrate appointed, than he presented a thundering petition to the *Huzoor*, purporting that the *Gunje*‡ was public property—that the former *Hakims* had removed all taxes and cesses, and had declared every person at liberty to land and sell his grain at will—that *Beoparees*§ brought large fleets of boats, laden with grain for the use of the city, but that owing to the great oppression of *Sheikh Chalah* they would not land the grain. That a tax of so much per boat was

*Customary douceur. † Right. ‡ Market. § Grain Merchants.

taken by the *Sheikh* from every *Beoparee*, that the grain was forcibly stacked in the granaries of the *Trilochun*, and that the *Sheikh* took a fixed sum per maund for selling the grain, &c. Scores of similar petitions were filed by parties calling themselves *Beoparees*.

To these charges, *Sheikh Chalah* merely replied, that he was owner of the grain market at *Trilochun*—that he made large advances to *Beoparees* in distant provinces, who brought or sent the grain to his market; that he provided *chokedars** for the protection of the boats—that he afforded accommodation to the *Beoparees* for their grain in his ample store-houses, where it remained until sold—that he supplied money to the *Beoparees* on the hypothecation of their grain—that in short, he was merely a *broker* on a large scale; and received from the *Beoparees* only that brokerage, which mutual convenience and long usage, had established. The Saheb Magistrate desired his Assistant to go the next morning and make enquiries on the spot; and I accompanied him as his orderly. When the Assistant reached the bazar, there was a great crowd, crying out "*Coompanee ka dohaee !*† *Saheb Shistant ka dohaee !*" The *Chota Saheb*‡ seemed quite perplexed, and asked the people what they had to say? "*dohaee ! dohaee ! Sheikh Chalah* has ruined us and cheated us," was all he heard. Upon this, turning round to me, he sagaciously asked "Panchkouree, are these poor people very ill that they want *dowaee ?*§ Why do they not go to the Doctor?" I humbly submitted that they were not ill, but cried for justice, or *dohaee*. But, said the Saheb, *dowaee* or *dohaee*, it is all one; for the poor men appear to be grievously oppressed. Here, Moonshee, *sowal purho*.|| Some fifty petitions were read; the petitioners answered to their names, and the puzzled *Saheb Shistant*¶ looked at one, and then at another, and yawned from the sheer fatigue of thinking so profoundly. I whispered in his ear, "May it please the *Jenab-i-alee* to enquire whether the petitioners in the crowd present are real *Beoparees* or not? Your slave recognises them as *Budmashus Dullals*." The hint was taken, and the Saheb himself put the question to every petitioner: "*Toom kone?*" *Dullal hyee Khodawund*,"** was the invariable answer. "Very strange," said the *Saheb Shistant*, "where are the oppressed and aggrieved *Beoparees?* Turn out the rascals, *Darogah*, and bring me the *Beoparees* from the bazar and the boats." Several *Beoparees* presented themselves; who denied that they had any cause of complaint against *Sheikh Chalah*—that they paid him brokerage by the custom of the country—but that they *had* to complain against *Bisheshur Singh* and his rascally *Dullals*, who by the abuse and cajolery, cheated them out of small sums of money daily. The *Saheb Shistant* represented matters truly to the Magistrate, who "*dakhill duftured*" the case.

* Watchmen. † Cry for Justice. ‡ Young Gentleman. § Medicine.
|| Read the Petition. ¶ The Assistant. ** Who are you? A broker, Sir.

"Why was not the principal, *Bisheshur Singh*, punished?" you ask. For a plain reason. He would have appealed to the *Saheb Allee Jah*,* the Judge. He would have proved by the evidence of fifty witnesses that he had received, as his father had done before him from time out of mind, a fixed rate for every boat that arrived at the ghat—that the owner of the bazar was the oppressor, etc., etc., and the Magistrate's order would have been reversed. It is true, justice is a grand thing: but who can expect it without *judicial proof?*

As a commentary on the courts of the *Coompanee Bahadoor*, I shall relate a fact. Some five-and-twenty years ago, an *Afghan* appeared with his servant, a Hindoostanee, in the Magistrate's Court at Moradabad. He, upon oath, declared that he had caught his servant in the act of stealing a fistfull of rupees. The servant denied. "Where are your witnesses, my friend?" said the Magistrate to the *Afghan*. The *Mogul*, after a moment's reflection, collared his servant, and beating him soundly, called out, "Why did you not, you scoundrel, bring witnesses, when you came to rob me?" Whether the Magistrate took the hint or not, I know not.

CHAP. X.

THE PUNDAHS, THE PRELATICAL ORDER OF BRAHMINISM.

The "*Pundahs*," in the holy city of *Kashee*, are the *prelates* of their priesthood, and, like every other calling in India, the sacred offices are even hereditary. They are not bound to celibacy. Their wealth is enormous. Their lives are a tissue of profligacy, arrogance, fraud, and deceit; and as for morals, "*they never had any*." Like the Papal pretensions of universal supremacy, they arrogate to themselves privileges, and superiority over the laity; and assert them with a haughtiness exceeding that of *Thomas-à-Becket*. The daily offerings at the celebrated temples and the shrines they contain, are collected by officiating priests who account to the *Pundahs*. The annual income of the temples is enormous; for, like the Papal church, the Hindoo system of religion allows of the compounding of every sin—from a peccadillo to homicide—for a consideration; and the greater the amount of guilt, the larger, of course, is the propitiatory offering, and the greater the profit of the priests. The ordinary ceremonials and sacrificial rites are performed by the "*Poojerees*." The *Pundah* officiates only on grand occasions, when some wealthy *Rajah* or *Baboo* makes his advent in *Kashee*, and offers to propitiate the gods by an offering, in proportion to the enormity of his sins. Then, indeed, the satellites of the "*Sree Pundah Jee*" are on the alert; and desperate becomes the conflict of wits, between cupidity on one side, and superstition mixed with avarice on the other.

* Gentleman of exalted rank.

When his Highness the ex-Peishwa came to *Kashee*, after the death of his father, and solicited the *Pundah* of the great temple of *Visheswar* to assist him in the fulfilment of his vows, he refused to do so, until the Maharajah should fill with coined silver the *houz*, or font of the temple. This was acceded to; and it was found that one lakh and twenty-five thousand rupees were required for that purpose. A goodly breakfast, I ween, and sufficient for a time to stay the cravings of a morbid sacerdotal appetite. On other occasions he is induced to attend the temple, when some zealous votary lures him thither with the promise of an after-recreation, in which "the choicest specimens of the sweet songstresses of Ind" enrapture the senses by their voluptuous song and dance. The *Pundahs* like the elders of old, are connoisseurs of beauty; and those who cannot afford the lure of wealth, make use of the lure of beauty to ensure the honour of the *Pundah's* presence.

The office of *Pundah* is hereditary; and where the family has increased, a division of the profits of the temple proceeds is always made. Fierce contentions take place among the brotherhood for their shares, and then the easily-gotten wealth of the *Pundahs* finds a channel for itself into the pockets of the Vakeels of the Civil Courts. Tact and ability, however, render one of the parties superior to the others; and he becomes, in fact, the *Pundah Jee*.

The *Pundahs* do not confine themselves to the affairs of their temples, but are landed proprietors and money-lenders. They mix themselves up in the affairs of everybody, and make for themselves enemies by the unfairness of their dealings, or by pushing their creditors to extremity, by bribing the myrmidons of the law to ruin the creditors by the law. "*Ayarub Koomar Swamee*" was one of these Hindoo prelates, and was recipient of the superfluous wealth of the *Dukhan*. Lakhs of rupees flowed into his coffers to lay out in "*poojha-pat*" for the benefit of the donors. The *Swamee* offered up vicarious sacrifices in the names, and for the benefit of the senders; and he himself, by his sanctimonious office, so throve by pretending to dispense the charity of others, that his reputed wealth was enormous, besides being proprietor of houses and lands and villages. One evening, at dusk, as *Ayarub Koomar Swamee* proceeded to the temple of "*Keedarnath*" to perform certain rites; and, as he perambulated the temple, previously to entering therein, he was shot dead with a pistol, which burst in the assassin's hand. But although hundreds of persons witnessed the deed, nobody recognised the homicide, and he made off. Some days afterwards, a man from the *Telingah* country was found in the haunts of some noted *budmashes*, with his right hand injured by the explosion of gunpowder. The Magistrate succeeded in adducing sufficient proof to hang him; but it was never known for certain, who had instigated the homicide. As usual, in such cases, the most contradictory and absurd reports were spread; but the most probable conjecture is, that some rich party, with whom he was at law, and whom he had pushed hard, had instigated the murder.

Many a dark deed has been done, and is done, in the extensive houses of these *Pundahs* and *Poojarees*. While the gong is loudly sounding, and scores of athletic priests are blowing *sunkhs** in the numerous temples that are dotted about and around the houses, the last expiring shriek of some victim is, perhaps, suppressed by the noise. Disobedient "*chelas*,"† victims of jealousy, and unnatural crimes, die by slow torture, or poison, or famine. No intimation is, or can be, given to the police; for none but the initiated and privileged may enter these houses, sanctified by the numerous temples. And who, but the most devoted and trust-worthy, are ever permitted to see the dark places where crime is committed. It is believed generally, but I speak not from experience (for being of the faith of *Islam*, I am not permitted to approach such places), that in the innermost recesses of several temples, is a shrine dedicated to "*Devee*" or "*Bhowanee*;" those infernal Deities whose delight is in blood, where children of tender age are enticed, and offered up on certain occasions. Frequent are the reports made to the police that children are missing—the informants suspect nobody; and no trace of the innocents is ever found. Can it be that they are the victims of the horrible suspicion I have alluded to?

A *Pundah* consulted some learned Brahmins about the horoscope of his infant son, his first-born. It was foretold that the shadow of the child would press heavily upon the fortunes or life of the father. The *Pundah* took the infant in his arms, fondled it with apparent delight. On returning it to the mother's arms it was a breathless corpse. He had squeezed the nape of the neck, to prevent the fulfilment of the horoscope!!! Some person inimical to him lodged a formal complaint before the Magistrate. The Magistrate, after taking the deposition of the informant, summoned the *Pundah* to appear in person and answer to the charge of infanticide. He evaded process for a long while; but, at last, was forced to appear before the *Huzoor*. But what can simple honesty of purpose in a Magistrate do against the combinations of wealth and venality? The *Pundah* was acquitted "from want of judicial proof."

As for the *Poojarees*, "whose name is legion," their mal-practices are the theme of every discourse. They are the usual heirs of all persons dying intestate, when the deceased have any property to leave. Their quarrels form the bulk of the cases in the Civil Courts. Instead of the monastic rigidity of morals, which they obtain credit for, they are more than suspected of all the vices imputed to the monks. How rapidly-soever the Hindoos of the present day may be casting off the shackles of an enslaving creed, and they begin to think for themselves, and to believe that all mankind has emanated from one Supreme Divinity; yet they are influenced by their *Poojarees* and *Pundahs* more than I can describe. One besetting practice has long existed; for men,

* Large shells. † Disciples—Scholars.

whose marriages have proved unfruitful, to take their wives to the shrines appropriated for the purpose, and to leave them there, for a period of weeks or of months; and such is generally the efficacy of the practice that fertility is the result, to the joy and belief of the happy husband.

CHAP. XI.

THE GHATEAS, GUNGAPOOTRAS, AND AGHORPUNTS.

I said that the "*Pundahs*" of the temples in "*Kashee*" are a curse to the city. How then shall I describe the "*Gungapootras*" and the "*Ghateas*" who, like a foul ulcer, are daily increasing, and eroding the vitals of their deluded victims? From the *Burna Sungam ghat* to the *Assee,* a distance of some five miles, the bank of the Ganges is besprinkled with temples, *cutcha chubootras*, or wooden platforms, called *tukht poshes* that overlook the brink of the holy stream; and scarcely a cubit's length is left for a landing-place for boats and travellers. Every one of these *chubootras* or *tukhtposhes,* is occupied by its proprietor, who sits cross-legged, in the simple dignity of nudity with his "*chundun*"* and flowers, mumbling out in a measured and monotonous voice the names of their favored divinities. Every orthodox Hindoo, as he comes out of the broad bosom of *Gunga-maee*, makes an offering to the *Ghatea;* who, in return, marks his forehead with *chundun,* and pronounces a blessing on him. But when the bathers are foreigners, they are not permitted even to approach the stream, in places occupied by the *Ghateas,* until they pay down the sum demanded from them. Numerous are the petitions given in to the Sabeb Magistrate Bahadoor against these *Ghateas,* and frequently an order is passed to the police to see that the complainants are not prevented from taking a dip. In such cases the *Ghateas* commence a volley of curses, the most foul and blasphemous that can be imagined. And what Hindoo can stand out against the curses of a *Brahmin* and a *Ghatea?* The bathers appeal to the police burkundazes, but they coolly say, "We have no orders to prevent the *Ghateas* from speaking." If a small *douceur* be offered, it is indignantly rejected, and the bathers reflect that if a considerable gratuity is to be given, they had better conform to the "*dustur,*" and give it to the *Ghateas* as "*poon.*"†

Some of these *Ghateas* go to the most distant provinces, and join a troop of pilgrims coming to Benares. Or they follow in the wake of some Rajah or Baboo, who has vowed to perform a tour of pilgrimages. The whole of the party are then dubbed "his *jijmans*"‡ by the *Ghatea*. He considers them under his special protection. No one else may take a fraction from them; and the *Ghatea* and *his* partners alone reap the harvest. If other *Ghateas* interfere, serious affrays ensue; and the Magistrate is bewildered with their mutual complaints and recrimina-

* Sandal wood. † Good work. ‡ A person who employs priests.

tions. Suppose that the rich pilgrims choose to assert independence of will, and to make presents to other *Ghateas*, then the parties, who think themselves aggrieved, threaten to stab themselves in the presence of the pilgrims; and rather than be responsible for shedding the blood of a *Ghatea*, they are fain to give in on any conditions.

The "*Gungapootras*" are "sons of the Ganges," and exercise despotic sway in their domain of the "*Munkurnika*." Their numbers are considerable; and in the division of spoil, desperate conflicts occur. But they know that "union is strength; and consequently always combine to hunt the common prey—the Hindoo public. The "*Munkurnika*" is a reservoir lined with flags of hewn stone on the bank of the Ganges. During the rise of the river, it is filled with the sacred stream. Besides which, a puny springlet dribbles into this basin from the land-side; and during the hottest season of the year, suffices to keep up a filthy puddle, rendered more and more impure by the daily immersion of hundreds; but nevertheless, this filthy semifluid matter is looked upon by the Hindoo as the purest of the pure—the cleanser from sin and moral impurity. The "*Koondh*" is thronged every morning by votaries, each with his silver in hand, to bestow upon his *Gungapootra*, and eager to plunge into the basin of holy water. And who dares venture to take a dip in it without first obtaining the permission of the *Gungapootras?* He would run the risk of being beaten to death; or of being found "*suffocated by accident*," as he dipped into the *Koondh*. Mr. Prinsep gives the following account:—

"*Gungapootras* (sons of the Ganges), who enjoy hereditary possession of most of the ground between high and low water mark: the third sort consists of *muths* or *murhees* (small temples), erected at the expense of pilgrims and others; they generally have a flat roof to serve still as a *chubootra* for the proprietor or *Ghatea* to sit upon, who not unfrequently allows the temple to fall into premature decay, and sells the space again to another pious dupe. As a criterion of the value of such property, it may be mentioned, that when Maharaja Sindea, in 1829, wished to repair the dilapidated ghat of Beereswur, next adjoining to *Munkurnika ghat*, he could not obtain the good will of the *Gungapootras* under 15,000 rupees, although they were promised the reconstruction of their *chubootras*, and their right of occupancy was to remain unfringed."

These *Gungapootras* and *Ghateas* are generally the greatest "*budmashes*" in the place. There is not a crime or enormity of which they are not suspected, but of which they are supposed to be incapable. Violent assaults on women and boys, with criminal intent, are common; but very few such cases are ever reported by the police, or if reported, they are slurred over and represented as "*tukrar-i-khufeef*."* The assailants are protected by their wealth and their position; and unless the complainants can afford to pay more largely than the *Ghateas*, they are not

* A petty dispute.

likely to obtain redress. A common practice among the disreputable of these *Ghateas* is to jostle a well-dressed woman, and to snatch from her nose or ears the golden jewels she wears. In dense crowds of thousands, cooped up in narrow thoroughfares, it is not easy to catch these miscreants; and if caught, they easily evade proof by giving the robbed jewel to their companions, who pass it from one to another with the rapidity of thought.

The most loathsome sight at the *ghats* are the "*Aghorpunt fuqueers*," (*Anglicè* Ogres), practical philosophers, who affect to disbelieve that there is any difference between things, and who avow that any difference depends upon the imagination. A cuff or a kick is as immaterial to them as a blessing. They go about *in puris naturalibus* with a fresh human skull in their hands, (off which they had previously eaten the putrid flesh, and from which afterwards with their fingers scooped out the brain and eyes) into which is poured whatsoever is given them to drink. They pretend to be indifferent whether it be ardent spirits or milk, or foul water. Their food is the first thing that offers, whether it be a putrid corpse, cooked food, or ordure. With matted hair, blood-red eyes, and body covered with filth and vermin, the *Aghorpunt* is an object of terror and disgust to everybody. He looks rather a wolf, ready to destroy and then devour his prey, than a human being. I once saw a wretch of this fraternity eating the head of a putrid corpse, and as I passed by he howled and pointed to me; and then scooped out the eyes and eat them before me. I had my matchlock in my hand, and was within an ace of putting a ball into his head, for I deemed him a wolf; and, in fact, he was a brute.

A Magistrate took up a monster of this sort drinking liquor out of a bloody human skull. He was in a fearful state of intoxication, and had a kind of Malay crease, a spiral dagger about a cubit long, a blow from which would have been death. The Magistrate had him taken up at once. On referring to the records of the office, it was ascertained that the wretch had been thrice imprisoned in jail for rape, for assault amounting almost to homicide, and for being a vagrant. The Magistrate ordered him to furnish heavy security for his good behaviour; or in default, to be imprisoned for three years. In all such cases the Magistrate is bound to make a report to the Judge, who sent for the *misl* of the case, and released the *Aghorpunt*.

Should not such monsters in human shape rather be incarcerated for life as a disgrace to humanity? Or would the precepts of Islam not sanction the wholesale slaughter of such brutes? But the Hindoos themselves look upon the *Aghorpunts* with veneration; and none of them would dare to drive him away from their doors. Strange infatuation in a people to worship incarnations of the divinity in every bestial shape, and to respect men even lower than the brutes.

Chap. XII.

General Venality and Perjury of Officials.

A practice has long prevailed, although it is less frequent now than it used to be, for people who were at feud, or when the object was to extort money from wealthy individuals, to wound themselves, and to charge others with the crime. In the good old days when Magistrates were content to look through the spectacles of their Omlah, the practice was rife; and many an innocent man has been punished by imprisonment for years through the perjury of witnesses and the venality of officials. *Jubbur Khan* assured me that he saw a *budmash* of the Mohulla *Hurha*, who had cut his throat from ear to ear with a *tulwar*, merely to criminate a neighbour, whom he suspected of an intrigue with his wife; that the man's wound took six months to heal; and that he was not imprisoned for having made a false and malicious charge, solely owing to the desperate manner in which he had wounded himself. *Jubbur Khan* was a party in investigating a case of this nature; and I shall relate the particulars as I heard them from him.

'*Sheo Suhaee Singh*, alias *Singha*, had been repeatedly imprisoned for gambling, aggravated assaults, and *budmashee*. He managed to insinuate himself into the good graces of some of the officials of the *Kotwalee*, and he used to be constantly seen at the Kotwalee, on pretence of attending on the bazaar that is daily held in the *chouk* to the eastward of the Kotwalee. Extensive ranges of stone and brick shops have lately been built by the exertions of the Magistrate Bahadoor, and wealthy Muhajuns and brokers have settled therein, for the protection afforded them by the vicinity of the police station of the city. The old Kotwalee is to the south of the new one, with only a road between; and any row taking place on the road should at once be suppressed by the police who are on the spot. But the focus of a policeman's vision is dependent entirely on circumstances, and should not be judged of by an ordinary standard.

'One dark night, between the hours of nine and ten, not fifty, years ago, two cloth Muhajuns, *Balkishan Dass* and *Bootchnoo*, alias *Ram Kishun*, were returning to their houses for the night, accompanied by *Bisheshur Singh*, a retainer, and some other followers. As they approached the *phatuk** of the old Kotwalee they were rushed upon by three men, calling out '*mar—mar*.' The Muhajuns and their party gathered close together for mutual defence, when, in the twinkling of an eye, one of the assailants was seen weltering in his blood lying on the ground. His companions shouted '*dakah—dakah*,'† and a Jemadar of police and a *phatukbundee* ‡ came to the rescue as if by magic. The Muha-

* Gateway. † Dacoity—Robbery. ‡ Watchman of the gateway.

juns and their party were thunderstruck, and could neither advance nor retreat from fear and surprise. The wounded man proved to be one *Bhyro Ahir*, alias *Gujjoo*, who declared to the witnesses that *Bisheshur Singh* had wantonly cut him down with a sword, as he and *Singha* and another were peaceably passing the Muhajun's party on the high-road. *Singha* sang to the same tune, and the Jemadar Saheb apprehended the Muhajuns and *Bisheshur Singh*, and took them all to the Kotwalee. I need not describe how the feet of the Muhajuns were put into the stocks, nor how they were freed therefrom; suffice it, that after the usual *tuhkeetkat* (which means ascertaining nothing, and fleecing and bullying the Mohulla people) the case was sent up to the Saheb Bahadoor, the report purporting that the charge of assault and wounding with a sword was fully proved against the Muhajuns.

'The Magistrate, instead of having the depositions of parties taken in the '*sheristah*,' or in a corner of his own room, was one of those *hakims* that would do every thing himself. So he boxed the prosecutor and defendants together before himself, and kept the witnesses at a distance, and apart from one another. The prosecutor, on oath, recognised *Bisheshur Singh* as the party who had cut him down with a sword without enmity or provocation; deponed that his companion *Singha* snatched away the naked sword from *Bisheshur's* hand and seized him, and delivered him to the police, who came up just then. *Singha* swore in the same strain, with this difference, that *Bisheshur Singh* threw his own sword down after wounding *Gujjoo*. On being asked what he had been doing at that time of night with *Gujjoo*, he alleged that they had met by accident near the Kotwalee. The police Jemadar and *phatukbundee* gave the same story. The defendants denied the charge. They alleged that they were proceeding homewards; and that as they were passing the Kotwalee, *Gujjoo* and *Singha* rushed at them, *Singha* having a drawn sword in his hand; that they stopped suddenly, and *Singha* cut down his companion *Gujjoo*, threw down the sword, and crying out '*dakah—dakah*,' seized *Bisheshur Singh* and made him over, with his whole party, to the Jemadar of police and *phatukbundee*, who appeared so suddenly as to lead to the conclusion that they expected to hear of the attack, and that, in fact, they were accomplices. The *Muhajuns* gave in a similar defence, and asked whether people of their caste and profession were in the habit of using swords, and assaulting such well-known *budmashes* and desperadoes as *Gujjoo* and *Singha*?

'The magistrate himself instituted inquiries, and ascertained from the Jemadar and *phatukbundees* stationed at '*Rajah-ka-durwazah*,' that *Gujjoo* and *Singha* had attempted to pass their post about an hour before they met the party of *Muhajuns*; but seeing *Singha* with a sheathed *tulwar* in his hand, they prevented their passing, and turned them back. Certain *budmashees* who were in jail, and old friends of *Singha*, recognised the *tulwar* as a favourite weapon of his. In short, from the whole of the bearings of the case it was plain that the charge against the *Muhajuns* was false and malicious, therefore they were released. And as *Singha* had contradicted himself in two distinct depositions given upon oath, in such a manner as to amount to *perjury*, he was committed to the Sessions, and was sentenced to imprisonment with labour in irons for seven years.'

Another common trick of the *budmashes* is to entice people of decent condition into their private houses, with seductive solicitations, and after amusing them to keep them there until they put their names to papers, just by way of showing specimens of their autographs. They have documents ready cut and dry on stamp papers of different value, duly witnessed by people who are in their pay, or who participate in their frauds, to be converted into penal bonds for value received. Months afterwards the unfortunate visitor is accosted in any public place, in the presence of numerous witnesses, and asked for the amount of his (extorted) bond. Of course the debt is denied, and the demander is cursed only for his pains. But the *budmash* calls people to witness that he *did* ask his debtor to pay the amount of his bond, which he refused to discharge. An action for debt is instituted. The *budmash* produces the bond before the Moonsiff. The witnesses are summoned, and are merely asked, 'Did you witness this *tumassook*?' 'I did, your worship,' is the reply, 'this is my signature.' The witnesses, before whom the *budmash* demanded the amount of the bond, also confirm the plaintiff's allegation. The defendant can only deny the claim, and submit that the bond was extorted. 'Where is the proof?' says the Moonsiff. 'I have none,' is the reply. And a decree is given in favour of plaintiff with costs. It is only when '*Greek meets Greek*' that the result is different. Then the defendant acknowledges the deed; but alleges that he has paid the amount with interest; and files a receipt for the amount of the bond, with interest at twelve per cent, duly attested by three '*credible*' witnesses, who appear before the Huzoor, and swear to their signatures, as well as to having seen the money repaid to the plaintiff. Here then *is* a go! and to decide according to justice is not an easy matter.

A celebrated Judge and Legislator, a just and honest man, who knew the native character well, candidly confessed, that whenever he had such a posing case before him, he desired the *Sheristadar* to read away—he shut his eyes, as if in deep cogitation—while all the beholders conceived that he was weighing the merits of the case mentally; he was, in truth, making up his mind to decide, according to the doctrines of chance, whether it should be as the number of flies on the *punkah* were odd or even!—'Odd for plaintiff,' the Judge mentally resolves—he opens his eyes, looks at the *punkah*, and counts *two flies* against the plaintiff. '*Hookoom hooah ke, udum-suboot men, moqudummah dismiss ho.*'* Verily, this man was 'a Daniel.'

* It is ordered, that, owing to want of proof, the case be dismissed.

Chap. XIII.

BULBHUDDER SING PERSONATES A RAJAH; TAKES A GREAT HOUSE; AND DECAMPS AT NIGHT WITH HIS PLUNDER.

In my last I hinted at the practice of the *budmashes* of forcing people to give them bonds for sums never lent to them; and then of ruining them by sueing for the amount in the subordinate Civil Courts. I now proceed to notice another abuse of daily occurrence. This is the constant and grinding oppression of the '*phereedars*,'* who are servants of the *budmashes* and usurers, and who go about forcing poor people to give them a portion of that pittance which they earn, literally, by the toil of their hands and the sweat of their brows.

A poor widow supports herself and children by slaving at the *chukkee* (grinding mill) day and night—if that can be called *support*, where the poor creatures contrive, with all their toil, to earn a few ounces of meal, or perhaps, *four pice* a day; out of which a *phereedar*, who had lent her a rupee five years' back, and who had received back double the sum, continues to demand *two pice* a day! In vain she pleads that she has repaid him—in vain urges that she must give her children food, even if she herself starve. He throws her on the ground, kicks her, and drags her about, until human nature can stand it no longer, and she faints! The neighbours hear a noise and run to the poor woman's house, just as the *phereedar* is leaving it. They see her lying insensible and give her aid. But the *phereedar* gives them a hint, that if they dare to give evidence in the matter he will serve them in the same way. The poor widow begs of her neighbours the sum of eight annas to purchase a stamped paper on which alone a petition may be written; and she begs of some compassionate *Mooktyar* (*a rara avis*) to engross the petition for her, she presents this to the Saheb Magistrate, and with tears and loud cries implores his protection. He orders her deposition to be taken on oath; and in consideration of her extreme indigence directs that enquiry be made through the police. The *thanadar* goes to the spot, asks every witness what he knows in the matter? The invariable reply is, that the witness knows nothing. I will suppose the *thanadar* to be an honest man as far as ordinary circumstances are concerned, and that he really intends to do justice in this case. What *can* he do? The witnesses named by the poor widow turn against her, and the *thanadar* is obliged to report that '*charge is not proven by the witnesses of the prosecutrix*.' Now, how can the Magistrate punish? Where is the *legal proof?* The witnesses dare not give honest evidence! 'Of what use then are laws and legal and police establishments?' you ask, I

* Vagabonds.

answer, that they are only fit to awe the weak. There is no law that has yet been passed, that a clever scoundrel cannot break through. And thanks to the policy of an enlightened age, *the spread of education* is only enabling the natives to become keener rogues. Every common '*gunwar*'* quotes his '*kantractions*'† and '*surkoolar hookoom*;'‡ and nine out of ten of the hangers-on of the courts know only so much of English as to render them dangerous eaves-droppers.

A common mode of swindling in the city of *Kashee* as practised by the clever *budmashes* is, for one of the party to personate a Rajah on a visit of ceremony to the holy city; while his companions pretend to precede him and hire a stately *huvelee* in '*Dal-ka-Munduvee*,' which they furnish for the nonce. *Bulbhuddur Singh* sits in state as *Rajah Guchpuch Rae*, bedecked in false gems, and dressed in shawls and *kimkhabs* (*anglicè* kingcobs). His retainers go about the city, and entice shawl-merchants and jewellers to the Rajah's house. They arrive with costly wares, and eagerly proceed to expose them; but the Rajah turns an indifferent eye upon them, and declares they are not sufficiently choice for *him*. The *Soudagurs*§ promise to return next day. In the mean time the song and dance proceed with fierce revelry. Six sets of the best dancing women exert their lungs and limbs, and go through every fascinating movement to delight and amuse *Rajah Guchpuch Rae*. Where is my treasurer, exclaims the Rajah. Bid him bestow a largess of 100 *Ushurfees*‖ on these soul-enslaving terrestrial houries. A retainer, after going through the farce of a search, respectfully approaches his Highness, and intimates that the treasurer has not yet arrived. The *nimukharam! behaeyah!*¶ exclaims the Rajah. Here fellows, see that a proper treasurer be in attendance on the morrow, to whom we shall deliver our treasure and *toshehkhanah.*** The Rajah enjoys himself until no longer able to sustain excitement; and then the *gundrupins*†† retire, and the torches are extinguished.

Next day, there are several candidates for the honor of the treasurer's office, who eagerly offer to serve. The salary is 200 rupees a month, says the Rajah, and I hate accounts; constant attendance and implicit obedience are all I require. After rejecting some, His Highness fixes upon *Lalla Umbeka Sahaee*, who receives a well-worn shawl as a *khillut*‡‡ and an immense key. He ventures to ask where the treasury is? And is told to wait until the *huzrut* has leisure to show it to him. In the mean time the Rajah suddenly recollects that he has immediate occasion for 1,000 rupees, and he shouts out: 'Here Bahadoor, take 1,000 rupees from *Lalla Umbeka Sahaee* and give it to *Bisheshur Singh*, and be sure to take a receipt for the money. Tell him it is the price of a ring I bought of him for my favourite *Goolbe-*

* Villager. † Constructions of regulations. ‡ Circular Orders.
§ Tradespeople. ‖ Gold Mohurs. ¶ Unfaithful to salt. Shameless.
** Place for keeping valuables. †† A caste of Hindoo Nautch-girls.
‡‡ Dress of honour.

har.' *Bahadoor* asks the treasurer the money. The poor man looks aghast, and shews huge key as all he has received of the Rajah's treasure. But *Bahadoor* tells him that *Rajah Guchpuch Rae* never fails to cut off the ears of a disobedient servant. So the hint is taken, and the *Lalla* gives an order on his *Shroff* in the city for the amount. And *Bahadoor* at once proceeds to realise the money. As evening approaches shawl-merchants and jewellers again appear and press their wares on the Rajah. They see *Lalla Umbeka Sahaee* figuring as treasurer. They are old acquaintances; and they ask him the amount of *Guchpuch Rae's* treasure. In reply to which, he simply shews *the* key, about a foot in length. The merchants open out their wares to entice the Rajah; but he says he will wait until all his things arrive. They offer to leave their bundles for the Rajah and his ladies to choose, which is agreed to with apparent indifference. The song and dance proceed as usual until midnight, when, as usual, the torches are extinguished.

Next morning, what a change has taken place. One old man is seated at the doorway, dosing over a *chillum* of *ganjah.* No other sign of life is visible in *Rajah Guchpuch Rae's* palace. The treasurer arrives first, opens and rubs his eyes, and asks the old man where the Rajah and his people have gone? He replies, that they decamped before dawn. In due course, the *Muhajans,* the jewellers, and birds of song arrive, but nothing of the Rajah is to be found; and smoke-stained walls, and filth, and litter about the rooms, alone betray that revelry *had been* there! The jewellers and *Muhajuns* turn in wrath upon *Lalla Umbeka Sahaee*, and tax him with having aided to cheat them. They proceed first to abuse, and then to beat him. In vain the poor man shews the huge key, and laments his thousand rupees lost for ever. They drag him to the Kotwal, and charge him with having cheated them; and the defrauded treasurer remains in durance vile for a week at least; and gets off at last, on proving himself to be one of the victims of this system of swindling, and after feeing the police myrmidons pretty roundly.

Who is ever to find out what worthy personated *Rajah Guchpuch Rae*, when hundreds and thousands of travellers are daily passing to and from the holy city?

I happened to be present at a curious decision by a Saheb who had magisterial powers. A *Muhajun* desired his nephew to purchase a piece of *kimkhab.* He did so, but cut off a yard for his own use. The *Muhajun* charged the lad with theft. After hearing all parties, the *Hakim* most sapiently ordered, that the *Muhajun* should pay a fine of ten rupees, and his nephew receive ten stripes. "For God's sake, sir," begged the *Muhajun*, "do not inflict stripes on my nephew, for the whole family will be disgraced. And what offence have I committed worthy of fine." The Saheb sharply remarked, "That the *Muhajun* deserved to be fined for having a rogue as an accomplice; and the nephew deserved stripes, because he had stolen a yard of *kimkhab*"*!!!* The order was carried out.

CHAP. XIV

THE GHATS AT BENARES DURING AN ECLIPSE.

Have any of my readers had the curiosity to visit the ghats during the occurrence of an eclipse of the sun or moon? If not, I would urge them to go once on such an occasion. The living tide that keeps pouring in from all the principal roads into the city some time before the event, is of itself an imposing and interesting spectacle. The human wave, as it rolls along the streets, gains accession from every lane and bye-way, and is at once amassed upon the banks of the holy stream, the *Ultima Thule* of the grand struggle—the eternal hum—the shout—the struggles, as the strong push away the weak to open a passage for themselves, afford a vast field for study to the contemplative. Then, again, the variety of costume, the drapery of every possible hue, captivate the attention of those who delight in the philosophy of dress; but, above all, the enormous crowd brought to a stand still—the living mass squeezed together in a small space, at once conveys to the mind the enormous fecundity of the human species. Contemplate them closely, and if you have been accustomed to read human nature, you will see in every face expressions of the feelings that are ruling within. Philosophers of every shade might, at such gatherings, find subjects for study and instruction. But let me now leave generalities, and enter into particulars.

Look at the crowd, the struggle yonder shows that an official, or a rich native gentleman, is pushing forward. The one is mounted in a tonjon, the other is on horse-back. The troop of people running with switches in their hands are their followers; they are striking the feet of the rabble shouting "*furuk, furuk*;"* but still they cannot penetrate the crowd; the horseman is obliged to stop, and the tonjon is forced up from the shoulders of the bearers above upon the heads of the crowd, with the occupant in a perilous position.

Suppose you have managed to reach the *Munkurnika ghat* in safety. By all means have a boat ready there for your reception; hasten on board, and take an elevated position, that you may compass as much of the spectacle on shore as possible, and drop down the river leisurely. What do you see? A vast concourse of living heads upon the surface of the water, bobbing up and down in alternate succession; and, O! horrors among them, several loathsome corpses gyrating in the eddies made by the bather; nor are they shunned, although the effluvia from them is sufficiently powerful to kill a horse. There a young girl rises from her immersion, and finds a dead body in her arms. She transfers it, without any sign of disgust, to an octogenarian female neighbour, whose charms have long been veiled over by a

* Aside, be off.

net-work of wrinkles, and who now sees an emblem of what she is soon likely to be, but she loathes it not—she passes it on with becoming civility. Now, you see a stout, upright man, the very figure-head of a sepoy, with a manikin, perhaps two years old, seated on his shoulder, holding on like grim death by the hair of his father's head, while the elderly gentleman gives him a dip to his great delight, although not free from the chances of suffocation. Nor are the scenes along the ghats solemn and purely ceremonial. Love has its dominion here also, but in its grotesque and primitive shape. Behold yonder are a group of beautiful nymphs, gracing the chocolate coloured stream like rich lotuses in full bloom. Mark that young man with a smooth brow and athletic frame; he has been viewing the nymphs for some time, he can no longer resist their charms, he dives, now he rises among them; he looks amorously upon them all, and then gravely utters his apology, with mock solemnity—*ushanan kea pushnan nea, to nam lea permeshur ka—bom, bom, bom.* One girl ventures to look at him, and seeing that he is a love of a man, returns a glance of fire, and inadvertently drops a flower; he picks it up, and keeps it as a token. Now, for some fun:—the *chevaliers d'Industrie* are busy yonder. Do you see that group of females bedecked with costly jewels, bathing as if it were by themselves, see that girl taking a dip, a nimble-fingered gentleman dives simultaneously, the nymph rises suddenly *muyah-re-muyah mere nuthnee gye.** This attracts attention, and the spoiler escapes. You hear another scream soon after, *duyah-re-duyah mere balee gye,*† sure enough her pendants are gone: there stands one with a nose rent clean to the nostril, and the other with bleeding ears. But this is nothing—often has the female entire been carried off for the sake of what she had on her person, and the *mugger*‡ gets credit for the abduction. The riflers are expert divers, and are sure to emerge in a crowd of bathers unperceived, roaring *bom, bom, Mahadeo,* a sort of thanksgiving for the furtive success.

Dropping down, you have a splendid panoramic view of the stone ghats and buildings, the minarets, observatory, musjids, and everything that renders Benares remarkable. You then proceed to *Burna Sungum,* where the crowd is, perhaps, most dense. Here the same farce of ceremonials is going on as elsewhere, and the same plunder is as active as ever under all manner of ingenious contrivances; but this ghat is remarkable for the scene which occurred there some years ago. The river had been insidiously undermining it for several years, and on that occasion the weight of the crowd was more than it could bear, and it suddenly gave way, carrying hundreds and hundreds of helpless beings into the jaws of death. Nor was this all, the alarmed multitude made a retrograde movement, and thousands were crushed under the tread of the panic-stricken crowd. The police

* Mother! O mother! my nose-ring is gone!
† Nurse! O nurse! my ear-ring is gone!
‡ The alligator.

reported that one thousand individuals had perished! But the officials like to deal with even and low numbers; it is a convenient way of stripping horror of its disgusting features.

Such events furnish rare opportunities to the gentlemen who live by their wits to practise their dexterity and earn their utmost. Bangles, ear-rings, armlets and nose-rings, disappear as well from the persons of the living as from the bodies of the dead; females generally are the victims. How the things are carried off, and by whom, is a profound mystery.

One brawny fellow is carrying the body of a young woman, carefully wrapped from head to foot, bewailing the unfortunate and untimely death of his sister. The crowd respectfully make way. He carries her to the nearest unfrequented spot, and lays her down. She is stone dead, and her nose, ears, arms and feet are all stripped of their ornaments. No longer useful to the dead, he leaves the corpse on that spot, and goes to seek for the living;—a wife, or perhaps, some other female relative; but where is she? Alas! gone. He becomes conscious of another bereavement, and is plunged in the depths of misery; and perhaps becomes the immediate victim of lacerated feelings. Alas, poor Hindoo! had you no well of clear water in your vicinity to purify yourself and family with?

A curious story is yet told of a *dome* who flourished and was *finished* in the days of "*Junab William Welburfurs Burrud Saheb Bahadoor.*" He was a most expert diver. One day while loitering for prey at the *Munkurnika ghat*, where the family of a rich *Muhajun* were bathing, he espied among them a woman richly decorated with jewels; in a moment he contrived to get into the river, and after playing about according to his wont, he dived and disappeared; the jewelled lady also disappeared; neither the one nor the other was seen to rise again, and her friends were under the impression that some fierce alligator had taken a fancy to her, and perpetrated the elopement. Several days afterwards a devout person who had cleansed himself of his sins in the river, and was just stepping out on shore, accidentally put his foot under a stone step, and there felt something soft. He was immediately filled with suspicions, and communicated his alarm to others. Some *domes* were sent for and the body extricated from its cell; it was the remains of the *Muhajun's* lady, denuded of all its costly ornaments. Suspicion rested on no one: but the *dome*, who had committed the horrid outrage, was, some months afterwards, detected offering the jewels for sale; they were recognised as the property of the deceased. The *dome* confessed, and expiated his crime on the gallows.

CHAP. XV.

THE FERRIES, HOW THEY ANSWER A GOVERNMENT MONOPOLY.

The *Ghat Manjhees*, *ghat and ferry thikadars*, and the *Chowdhurees* of *hackeries*, or, in other words, the heads of guilds and corporations are, perhaps, as great curses to the community, as any other of the thousand evils under which it groans. Frequently and anxiously the Magistrates have tried to devise plans for the prevention of oppression; but the best concerted schemes have failed, from the extraordinary reverence of "*the dustoor*"* to which the Natives of this country bow with as much deference as they do to their priests. Where proof of oppression can be produced by a complainant, punishment will necessarily follow. But I confess that no *preventive* measure occurs to me.

No boat of any kind puts to at any ghat, or leaves the ghats of Benares, without the consent of the *Ghat Manjhee* and without feeing him. No one can hire a boat, but a per-centage is put on for the *Ghat Manjhee: Soudagurs* employ this worthy to procure boats for them; and he puts down his own allowance in the bill, as coolly as if he held a Queen's patent to make the charge. A European traveller applies to the Magistrate for boats, to proceed up or down the country. The Kotwal is ordered to procure them. Even *he* can do nothing without the *Ghat Manjhee*, who furnishes the boats, as well as directs the *rates*, with reference to his own commission. They are in league with the *Churundars*† of boats, and with the servants of *Muhajuns*, to defraud the Insurance Companies. A very common trick is, to unload good boats and let them to *Soudagurs*, and to put the packages or other goods on unsound boats, *after* the boats have been reported to the Agents and passed on. But the grand gains are on extraordinary occasions, when boats are pressed for the use of the army. *Then* the *Ghat Manjhee* is attended by the *chupprasees* of the Magistrate and the Commissariat officer; and they go about the Ghats, forcibly detaining private boats until fee'd; and even throwing out sacks of grain, to rot or to be stolen, on the banks of the river. If the owner of the boat or of the grain, protests or makes any opposition, he is summarily dealt with, by receiving a sound thrashing; and then of being bundled away to the thanah, as a contemner of authority. If a representation be made to the Magistrate, and he attempt to put down such practices, the *Ghat Manjhee* and police take good care that the proper number of boats are not furnished; and rather than run the risk of detaining troops, a Magistrate is forced to wink at such practices.

The ferries of every large river are annually farmed to the highest bidder, on condition that he keep a sufficient number of

* Custom—A facetious and learned man, proposed that all the gods of the Hindoo Pantheon should be shelved, and the god *Dustoor* set up in their stead.

† Supercargo.

good boats, properly manned, at every ferry. A stone slab is affixed at the principal landing-places, stating the rates authorised by the Saheb Magistrate, written in Persian and Nagree; and on proof of any departure from these rates, the farmer is punishable. But it is a universal complaint, that the farmers at the ferries are the greatest extortioners: and who, for the sake of one or two pice, would leave his occupation, or postpone his journey for several days, to prosecute the *ijaradar* for extortion and infringement of the rules? And if a complainant does come forward manfully, to expose a public abuse, he must induce some fellow-travellers to remain also as witnesses. In all cases, judicial proof is difficult to obtain; and the prosecutor is worried and exhausted for his pains—besides being out of pocket.

Some European recruits were crossing the river at Rajghat; and my master, the *Nazir Saheb*, was directed to be in attendance, and to see that no useless delays occurred. I accompanied him, of course. We saw large boats, with about fifty Europeans on board; each worked across the river, merely by the swinging motion of the rudder. On landing the men, the boatman was pushing off, but the *Nazir* called out to me to seize him. I did so. "Where are the three boatmen, you scoundrel, as directed in your pottah?" said the enraged *Nazir*. The "*Gorah log** so hurried us, that my two oar-men did not come up in time." Upon this, I was desired to give him some gentle admonitions, which I did, in the shape of sundry hard boxes on the face, and some kicks on his "*Western parts.*" We watched other boats as they came to the ghat, but in almost all, there was a great deficiency of *danrees*.† "Go, Panchkouree," said the *Nazir* to me, "and drag that fellow, *Gunput Singh*, to me. I will take him before the *Huzoor* and get his *ijarah* cancelled, for thus endangering the safety of the *Cumpanee ka Gora*. I joined in the virtuous indignation of the *Nazir*, and proceeded to *Gunput's* house. "Come in, Bhaee Panchkouree Khan," said the wily farmer, "and take a *chilum* of delicious *ganjah*." But I was not to be caught so easily, and I began to bluster and to threaten to collar the farmer. "Oh! my friend," he said, "have a moment's patience. I had forgot to repay you the five rupees I owe you for a tulwar I bought from you. Here is the money." I felt the full force of his persuasive rhetoric, and pocketing the money, began smoking the *chilum* pleasantly. After a time *Gunput* asked me why he had been sent for? I explained. "Is that all?" he said, "I will settle it at once." He accompanied me to the *Nazir*, and most obsequiously salamed to him. The *Nazir* commenced a volley of abuse, in which kind mention of the farmer's sister and daughter was made. But the farmer of the ferries, without moving a muscle of his countenance, put a little *chit* into the *Nazir's* hand; and it was wonderful to observe the sedative influence of that slip of paper. The *Nazir* and the *Ijaradar* went away from the ghat, I following in

* Europeans. † Boatmen.

astonishment; and a report was made to the *Huzoor* that the *Gorah log* had crossed over without accident!!

It was during the height of the floods in the month of August, in the year——, that a ferry-boat was observed rushing down the river with frightful rapidity. There were about seventy-five human beings on board; and the water was scarcely six inches from the edge of the boat. There were but two boatmen; one at the helm, and the other at an oar. The boat got into an eddy, and the strength of the boatmen was unequal to extricate her. She went round once, and canted over, head-foremost, and not a vestige of boat or of the passengers was there! The farmer of the ferries was fined for his neglect, in not seeing to the efficiency of his boats. But was that punishment at all sufficient for the loss of so many lives? Surely a case of this kind may be construed into *homicide from neglect,* and should be punishable by several years' imprisonment.

The *Choudhurees of hackeries* are great men in their way, and are the occasion of much annoyance to the lieges. At every "uddah" (or stand), and in every market square, an emissary of the *Choudhuree* attends to look after his master's interests. When hackeries are required by *Soudagurs* and *Muhajuns,* these *Choudhurees* are the parties who provide them. They are rather moderate in their requisitions from the proprietors of carts, and limit their *dustooree* to only two annas in the rupee—being *one-eighth!* When hackeries are required for the public service, and an order for impressing them is passed by the Magistrate and Commissariat, *then* is the *Choudhuree* in his glory. Travellers, with their wives and children, are summarily dismounted, and with their property, lodged under the first convenient tree—strings of carts laden with grain, are taken possession of, and the contents lodged on the road-side. No complaints are listened to, and unless *oil of palms* is freely used to slip out of the clutches of the press-gang, escape is impossible. For every ten carts ordered for the public service, a hundred at least are pressed. "Why?" you ask, in your innocence, O happy ignorance! Suppose you have ten good carts with three bullocks to each—the feed of thirty bullocks cannot be less than four rupees a day. Or we will suppose that servants and all come to five rupees a day. Now suppose the owner to be a bumptious fellow who will not fork out. He is trotted backwards and forwards, first to the Kotwalee; then to the Sudder bazar; then to the *Saheb Kumsuriut.* He is not paid a fraction until the troops march; and he may be a fortnight or three weeks, feeding his cattle and his servants "*bakhyr-khwah-i-Koompanee.*"* Now the moment he was pressed, had he had the sense to have slipped twenty rupees into the *Choudhuree's* hand, or half that sum into the hand of the *burkundazes,* he would, I conceive, have been a considerable gainer. Do you twig?

* For the good of the Company.

CHAP. XVI.

TARDINESS OF THE COURTS.

Many people have complained, and hundreds do still daily complain, of the tardiness of the Courts. Of the slowness with which the sword of justice falls upon the offending victims, and the uncertainty attending it, whether it shall remain suspended in mid-air, or whether it shall fall on an offending, or an innocent head? I shall endeavour to give my readers a peep behind the curtain, and to show them how and why it is that such business prevail.

It has been my lot, as an *Orderly*, to serve under several *Hakims*, and being of an inquisitive turn, I have watched their modes of procedure with interest; and have, I hope, made profitable use of my observations. One *Hakim* has a *shoukh** of turning every thing *oolta-poolta*.† Nothing that has been proposed or done by his predecessor *can* be right. Nobody *can* take a correct view of any thing but himself. He objects to a time-honoured usage, and asks the spectacled *Serishtadar*,‡ "*Keon kon ayeen ba moojib*?"§ The old man, almost old enough to be his grandfather, stands before the *Huzoor* with folded hands, and replies, "*Zabitah yeh hye, Khodabund, koodamut seh.*"‖ "*Zabitah be d—d. Ayeen dekhao.*"¶ Upon this, the case pending before the *Huzoor* is deferred, and Indexes and Guides, to which the Native cannot have access, because they have never been translated, are consulted; the construction of the regulations, on which the *dustoor-ool-umul* (rules of practice) has been based, is rejected as a false interpretation of the law; and the whole system of local usage is upset, after it had gone on for thirty years. I will allow that the construction of the law *may* have been wrong, yet the mere change of any mode of procedure, after a period of thirty or forty years, is in itself to be deprecated in a people so tenacious of "*dustoor*" as the people of *Hindoostan*. The fault of the administration is, that officials have it in their power to alter the rules of practice as they please. And instead of every zillah being governed on uniform principles, the modes of procedure of no two zillahs are similar.

Again, there are *Hakims* who are content to look *only* through the spectacles, and to hear *only* through the ears of their *Omlah*. To every remonstrance he replies, "*Never make any enquiries yourself, or you will ruin the case.*" With such an official an unanswerable argument is, "*Zabitah yeh hye*" Every thing goes to rack and ruin from the *Hakim's* easy and yielding temper. He shews too much deference to the opinions of his officers; seldom exercises his own judgment; in some instances he has not leisure to do so—in others *he will not*.

* A fancy. † Topsy-turvy. ‡ Head Native Official.
§ Well! By what regulation is it? ‖ This is the practice, Sir, from time out of mind. ¶ Practice be d—d. Look at the regulation.

Where so much depends upon the *mizzaj** of a functionary, and he has it in his power to do evil or to do good, with but little control over his own actions; of course, the necessary supervision over subordinates must be considered a contingency depending on chance. In some districts it is so *overdone* that the services of the subordinate officials are lost to the State. In others, it is so imperfectly and weakly exercised, that the subordinate officials, in every department, are the *de facto* rulers.

Another cause of the existing abuses is the *uncertain tenure of office* of all Native officials, from a *Serishtadar*, *Kotwal*, or *Thanadar* down to an *Orderly*. Where people have almost unlimited power to do good or to do evil; and they may be turned out at a moment's notice, either for any presumed offence, or from dislike on the part of the *Huzoor*, and when such dismissals are, in reality, final, without the benefit of an unprejudiced hearing on appeal, of course an incumbent must be a fool to allow any moral considerations to check his venality. "Let us eat and drink to-day, for to-morrow we die," is their motto. Accordingly, in forty-nine out of fifty officials, the practice is to *do nothing without a fee*. The greatest vigilance on the part of the *Hakims* will not put a stop to this evil, *while the tenure of office is uncertain;* and I shall mention some of the ways and means whereby money is daily made in the *Fouzdaree*, Revenue, and Civil Adaluts, leaving it to the learned Councillors and the *Hakiman Aleeshan* to devise some remedy for the abuses, which, as an *Orderly*, I have been a witness to hundreds of times.

I think I once heard my master, the *Nazir Saheb*, say that in all cases of dismissal of any subordinate, receiving more than 10 *rupees* per month in the revenue department, a report was to be made to the "*Junab-Aleejah-Saheb Commissioner Bahadoor.*" And that there is a positive order from the Court of Directors, that no *Thanadar of police* should be discharged on light and insufficient grounds. The *Nazir* further mentioned, that all dismissals of *Thanadars* were to be reported to the Commissioner of police. "How is it then, *Nazir Saheb*," I enquired, "that *Meer Jubburdust Khan*, your worship's cousin, and *Lulloputto Khan* were turned out of their *Thanadarees*, merely from some dislike taken to them by the Magistrate *Bahadoor?*" "I do not know," replied the *Nazir*, "but they appealed to the *Junab Commissioner* of police, and got no redress." "And how comes it," asked *Jubber Khan*, "that *Meer Boorbuck Khan* has been appointed a *Thanadar*, when he is so confirmed an opium-eater as to be never sober? Is there ever such a thing as an *imtihan*† undergone?" The *Nazir* sighed, stroked his beard, and said, "*Ullah Kureem tooee janteh ho!*"‡

In almost all instances, connected with the *Mofussil Thannas*, the *Darogahs* and all the *Burkundazes* are in a plot against

* Disposition.—Temper.

† Trial—examination.

‡ Merciful God! Thou only knowest!

the Magistrate to defer execution of his orders, until they cannot help themselves. In petty cases, after the deposition of a plaintiff has been taken, his witnesses are summoned by *Subpœna*. The defendant can afford to bribe the witnesses, or he may bully them to hide themselves. The *Nazir* returns a *kyefut* that the witnesses are "*rooposh*," and the *Thannadar* is directed to apprehend them and send them to the *Kutcheree*. The first thing he does, is to send word to the parties that an order for their apprehension has been received. If the witnesses or the defendant readily fork out, the warrant, after being delayed for a week or two, is returned to the Magistrate with an intimation that the witnesses are "*rooposh*." But suppose the parties do not stump up? Why then, they are forced out of their houses and sent in to the *Huzoor* in the most ignominious manner. Thus, it will be seen, if a defendant can intimidate, or bribe witnesses not to attend, and if he pay the *Thannadar* for their *non-apprehension*, a common case of abuse or slight assault, which should have been decided at once, is spun out for a month, or more. For suppose the Magistrate order that the personal property of witnesses be distrained, even then the same farce is gone through. Perhaps none may be forthcoming; and if distrained, they may not be sold before the expiration of six months. And in all my experience I have never yet heard of the sale of such distrained property.

Again, suppose there is an affray, and the parties are *caught in the very act*. They name exculpatory witnesses, who *must* be summoned. "Why? in the name of common sense, if witnesses can prove upon oath that they were taken while engaged in an affray?" you ask. Because a finding in such cases is deemed by the appellate authorities to be faulty, the case is uselessly prolonged, while the witnesses *drop* in by ones and twos, and they allege that they "saw defendants twenty days ago ploughing their fields all day, and that defendants were, therefore, not engaged in the affray." On being asked what day they refer to? They reply that they cannot tell. What were they doing at the time of the row? They were not there, and never so much as heard of it!!! It is for such trash that the case is deferred, week after week, and if a Magistrate be ever so anxious to do ready justice, he cannot do so, because his order would be reversed on appeal.

CHAP. XVII.

PROCEEDINGS OF THE POLICE.

On occasions of suspicious death, burglaries and robberies, the police are in their glory. A dead *fœtus* is found lying in the middle of a cross road. The *Goraet* (called *go-right*, because he always *goes wrong*) proceeds to the *thanna*, and informs the *Than-*

nadar that a "*laash*"* is found! that the umbilical cord has not been cut, and that the child must have been purposely and wantonly exposed to meet a fatal end. The *Darogahjee* cross-questions the *Goraet*, and ascertains that a suspicion of an intrigue between *Kulloo Kulwar*, only son of the rich *Sahoo Bhowanee Kulwar*, and *Mosummat Lutchminea*, a young widow, had for some time been current in the village of ——. The *Goraet* declared that he was positive the child was their's "How far is the house of the *Sahoo* from the place where the *fœtus* was found?" "Only *five coss Darogahjee!*" "Is *Bhowanee Sahoo* rich?" "*Lakhorupea ka doulut hye khodabund.*"† "The very man," says the *Darogah Saheb*. "Here, *Jubber Khan*, go and bring me *Kulloo Kulwar* and *Lutchminea*, while I send a report to the Magistrate Bahadoor." While *Jubber Khan* is going on his errand, the *Thannadar* sends the putrid *fœtus* to the Magistrate, and intimates, "that the practice of infanticide is daily increasing—that the *Huzoor* is aware that "*the turukkee khuah*"‡ has not the power to investigate such charges without an order from the *Huzoor*—that the *Goraet* had given such information as to induce the *fidwee* to believe that he could trace the parties, &c., &c." To this the Magistrate replies—"Make the investigations *husb-i-zabitah*."§

Jubber Khan brings over *Kulloo Kulwar* and his reputed *Dulcinea*: and they are at once put into the stocks as proved malefactors. But they have not come to the *thanna* alone. A *Chumarin*, an old, withered hag, who deals in drugs and philters, is also brought as a witness against the parties. She swears, that, some nine months back, she was sent for to the house of *Lutchminea*, who asked her whether she could administer any potion to hide the effects of love! That she, the witness, did give her a powder, for which she received one rupee. But the prisoner, *Lutchminea*, flatly denied that she ever had a child, and alleged her readiness to undergo an examination by midwives. The *Thannadar* has his wits about him, however, and does not think proper to permit an examination. Next morning the old *Sahoo Bhowanee Kulwar* comes over to the thanna to bespeak the *Darogahjee's* good offices; and he ventures to hint that his son is innocent. "What have I to do with that, *Sahoo jee?* The *Goraet* swears to your son's guilt, and the *Daee* swears that *Lutchminea* bought a powder from her. I have the Magistrate *Bahadoor's hookoom* to apprehend and *chalan* the parties, and go they shall. The *Kutcheree* is only twenty miles off, and if your son and *Lutchminea* are innocent, of course the *Saheb Bahadoor*, whose justice is as famed as that of the renowned *Nousherwan*, will release them." The *Sahoo* finds that he must bleed, and pour out the contents of some of his beloved money-bags He accordingly makes a bargain with the *Darogah*, to release his son at once, for one hundred rupees cash. "Very good," says his worship,

* Corpse. † He is worth lakhs of rupees, your honour.
‡ Hoper for exaltation. § According to practice.

"release *Kulloo*." But Mr. *Kulloo* refuses to budge a foot, unless his beloved *Lutchminea* is permitted to accompany him, and old *Bhowanee* is forced by his son to pay fifty rupees in addition for her release. They are released, and go their way rejoicingly; while the *Thannadar* orders a *kullean*, and whiffs away in delight, uttering an occasional *Ulhum-dool-illah!** Of course a report is made to the *Saheb* Magistrate *Bahadoor*, that there is no proof against the accused parties—that the *Goraet* is a liar and a *moofsid*† for having implicated *Kulloo* and *Lutchminea*; and that, in the *fidwee's ukhul nakis*,‡ the *Goraet* is deserving of punishment. The unfortunate wretch is suspended by orders of the Magistrate, and is eventually dismissed from service and imprisoned.

A gentleman once ran off with the daughter of a respectable *Moosulman Zumeendar*, one *Loll Cawn*§ (*anglicè*, red ears). The father was indignant, and complained to the Magistrate, and begged that the *Kotwal* be at once sent with a warrant to search the *Saheb's* house for his beloved *Shukkur Lub*.|| A most stringent order is passed by the Magistrate *Bahadoor*. The *Kotwal* proceeds in state, and demands admittance to the house of the *Saheb*. The *Saheb* comes out himself, receives the *Kotwal* very graciously, and begs of him to walk in. A purse of fifty gold-mohurs is slipped into the *Kotwal's* hand, and the *Saheb* tells him, "My friend, you are an honest man, and a man of intelligence, and you have a warrant to search my house for a woman known as *Shukkur Lub*, a daughter of that worthy man, *Loll Cawn*. Search, in Gods' name; but you need not break open my boxes and almirahs, in which my valuables are kept." The *Kotwal* searches every room; every hole and corner is examined in the presence of the *posse commitatus*, and half-a-dozen witnesses from the neighbourhood; but no woman is forthcoming. "Search the beds and the pillows - rip open the *newar*¶ of the beds, shouts the *Kotwal*; "perhaps the woman may be hid there. But nothing suspicious even is found. The *Kotwal* goes away, and reports everything duly to the Magistrate; forgetting, of course, to mention that a purse of fifty gold-mohurs had been put into his hand, and that it was, in fact, at the time of making the report, in a secret pocket in his vest. "Did the Saheb actually abduce the girl?" you enquire; "and was she really in his house when a search was made by the *Kotwal*?" To be sure she was. Being a beautiful creature, a pearl of price, the *Saheb*, who was a wealthy *Soudagur*, would have gone to any expense to retain his beautiful *Shukkur Lub*, and she was snugly ensconced in a large clothes' almirah, which was not looked into by the *Kotwal*!

The indigo planters in every district are great sufferers by the trespass of cattle. Indeed, the *Ahirs* commonly take their herds

* Thanksgiving to God.
† Blackguard.
‡ The slave's defective judgment.
§ This is, of course, a gross corruption.
|| Proper name—Sugar-lipped
¶ Broad tape, with which beds, in India, are commonly bottomed.

into indigo fields for cheap pasturage with malicious intent; and a body of them, armed with *lathees*, accompany the cattle, to protect them in case of ejection or seizure for trespass; desperate affrays with the planters' servants occur. It is true that a special enactment for the protection of the indigo crops was passed in 1832; but still the planters cannot always obtain redress. The *Thannadars* are either in their pay, and oppress the people for the planters, or they are against them, because they are unwilling to purchase protection from the officials. A curious and laughable story was told me some time ago, which I shall relate for the edification of my readers. A planter was greatly annoyed by the trespass of cattle in his indigo fields. He seized them repeatedly, and sent them to the *thanna;* but the *Thannadar* was not his friend, and the cattle were invariably released. One day the planter was dining with the Magistrate, and, in the course of conversation, asked whether he could shoot any cattle he found in his fields, without subjecting himself to punishment? "By no means," said the Magistrate. "Can I maim them, by wounding a limb?" No, you would in that case be punished." "O hang it, I could dock them, surely?" "Why, yes, there is no great harm in docking them, I imagine," said the Magistrate. Some few days afterwards the *Thannadar* reported that the *Saheb Godam** had sent in twenty head of cattle, minus their tails. The *thannadar* begged to send them in to the Magistrate for inspection and orders. They were ordered to be sent in with their owners. On the same day the planter wrote to the magistrate and some other friends to favour him with their company at dinner They went; the covers were laid, and the soup produced. It was pronounced delicious by all the company, and by the Magistrate in particular; and all parties went away satisfied with their host's hospitality.

A few days afterwards a summons was received by the planter to attend at the Fouzdaree Court, and to answer a charge brought against him for mutilating cattle. He appeared in person, and after hearing the charge and the proofs, readily acknowledged that he had cut off the tails of twenty head of cattle from the very roots, because he had found them grazing in and destroying his indigo plants. "But good God, sir, what could you do with so many tails?" "Do, sir? Why, I asked a number of friends to dinner, and they and I acknowledged that it was not only humanity to remove the caudal appendages which daily subjected them to the severest tortures under the hands of the unfeeling *Ahirs*, but a just retribution for the damage done by them with their other extremity; and as to the utility of the tails —we had never eaten finer oxtail soup in our lives." The Magistrate laughed heartily, and dismissed the case.

* Owners of factories are so designated.

Chap. XVIII.

CONSPIRACY TO OVERTURN THE BRITISH GOVERNMENT WHICH ENDED IN A STATE TRIAL, AND AN ACQUITTAL OF THE SUSPECTED GUILTY PARTY.

The *moghalitah-deehee** of the subordinate officials, of every grade and denomination, is a constant source of vexation to the superior officers of every department, and a general subject of complaint I have already mentioned a few instances in which dust has been thrown in the eyes of the *Hakims*, and I shall proceed to notice a few more.

The *Nazir Saheb* directed me to proceed to Patna, to make enquiries connected with a revenue defaulter, and by a singular coincidence I witnessed some strange proceedings, which I shall endeavour to describe for the edification of your readers.

In the ancient and well-known city of Patna, there lived once upon a time one *Syud Bakur*, who rejoiced in the honorable distinction of being one of the *Khas Sowars* to the *Huzoor Saheb Magistrate Bahadoor*. He was so highly favoured by his *Nuseeb*† and the *mehurbanee*‡ of the *Saheban Aleeshan* that he rose to the *chief Darogah of Shubgushtee*§ in the aforesaid city. A curious system exists of having two Superintendents of police, whose duty it is to go about and to keep the Magistrate informed of the doings of the *Darogahs* of police, and to find out and let the *Huzoor* know the *Nufs-ool-hal*‖ of any important *mokudumma*¶ that may be pending. I need hardly remark how very important such an office is, and how greatly a *Darogah of Shubgushtee* has it in his power to influence the decision of any case. Nor how much he has the means of ruining or forwarding the views of any *Darogah* of police. My conviction is, that a Magistrate, who is not readily accessible at all hours to the people under his charge, is unfit for his trust. He should hear every thing that anybody may have to say, but he shoud never take aught for granted that he hears without proof or strong presumption.

It was discovered by the authorities that a conspiracy for the subversion of the British government was in embryo. For years the flame had smouldered, but the *iqbal*** of the *Koompanee Bahadoor*, and the bayonets of their army, prevented any outbreak in the provinces. The immediate cause of disaffection was the resumption of the *muafee*†† lands. Hundreds of proud Mahommedan Chieftains, who lived in affluence, and who depended solely upon their *muafees* for the support of themselves and their numerous retainers, were reduced to poverty. But matters were not matured—" the pear was not ripe." Yet it was evident that a cloud had come over the prosperity of the *Koompanee Bahadoor*. Their

* Deceit—humbug. † Lucre. ‡ Favour. § Night-watch.
‖ Actual facts—The pith of the matter. ¶ Case.
** Fortune. †† Rent-free lands.

arms had met with a reverse in Kabool. The Sikhs were in force on the Sutledge, and threatened the overthrow of the British Government. The Nepalese, secure in their hill fastnesses, and protected by the formidable belt of *Turaee*, which intervened between their country and the provinces of the plain, were eager to measure swords with the *Koompanee.* It was more than suspected that an intrigue was carried on between the Courts of Lahore and Katmandoo; and that they mutually communicated their intentions in regard to the invasion of Hindoostan. The mistaken system of education of the Natives in European literature had prepared hundreds of youths for employment by the Rajahs and Nawabs, whose duty it was to translate the English newspapers to their Highnesses. The tone of the letters of the local newspapers was generally improper, inasmuch as it shewed the Native Princess that the writers freely canvassed the measures of Government and pointed out the weak points of its policy. The military force at every station and in every large cantonment was accurately known through the medium of the local Press. The way in which the Nepalese could act against the British authority most effectively was pointed out by the writers of inflammable articles. Who then can wonder that the Nepalese were intriguing with the Native army, to turn upon their employers? And who can wonder that disaffected parties arrayed themselves to second the wishes of the Court of Katmandoo? Even the Rajahs, who lived under the British protection in the vicinity of Nepal, were suspected of covertly aiding and abetting the enemies of the Government which fostered them.

The principal Agents in the matter were *Khwajeh Saheb,* a wealthy and influential Zemindar—*Shah Gubbur-ood-deen,* a holy Syud, whose influence over the Moosulmans was great, as a *Peerzadah,* or son of a prophet—*Rahut Allee,* a noted forger and *budzat,** but exceedingly clever, and very much feared for his unscrupulous villany—*Syud Bakur,* the *Darogah* of *Shubqushtee*—and *Moofsidh,* a common regimental Moonshee, then with the —— Regiment of Native Infantry. The ostensible grievances were, the general resumptions of *muafee,* and the *messing system of the jails*—the former of which, it was pretended, had deprived thousands of their means of maintenance, and the latter was complained of as a measure to make all persons incarcerated in the jails, "*Christans.*" The Sepoys were egged on to mischief by the Regimental *Moonshee,* by being reminded of the daily-increasing bad faith of their *Feringhee* masters; of their inability to retain their stupendous Empire in India without their aid; and the certainty of any new power making such conditions with them for their general secession as would insure to the sepoys great privileges and high dignity. The Moosulmans were reminded that they were a conquered race—conquered by the "dogs" they still abhorred and despised. The Hindoos were told that the messing system of the jails and the practice of transportation beyond

* Bad character.

seas, as in force among the *Ungrez Bahadoor*, were slow, but sure modes of undermining the time-honored usages of Brahminism. The day fixed for the *denouement* of the plot was the festival of the *Mohurrum*, when the constant noise attendant on the processions would tend to mislead the authorities as to any riot that might actually occur.

But one of the Mahommedan Native officers of the —— regiment, who had only been partially admitted behind the curtain of intrigue, becoming alarmed at the result of the projected insurrection, and fearing also the loss of his snug berth, informed the Major of the regiment of what had been concocting so industriously for months. The Major, like a wary soldier, at once proceeded to the residence of the regimental *Moonshee* and apprehended him and seized all his papers. When these were read, the whole plot was unravelled, and all that remained for the authorities to do, was to order the apprehension of the principal conspirators, and to adopt measures for the suppression of any disturbance that might occur during the *Mohurrum* processions.

But how shall I describe the panic that prevailed among the generality of the English community, who, instead of joining together and acting in concert, were too much frightened to think or act concertedly in adopting remedial measures for the emergency. It was given out, and believed in the station, that the Surveyors and Planters, in the district and in the neighbouring zillahs, had been murdered, and that the troops at Dinapore and its neighbourhood would shortly become subject to the same fate. Extra troops were stationed at the "*Golghur*" (that stupendous monument of the folly and ignorance of a by-gone generation) and the Treasury. The ladies were requested to seek the protection of the troops; and the Subaltern on duty being asked by a lady whether the sepoys' muskets were ready for action; replied, "Yes, *ma'am, they are loaded with large charges to try 'em.*" Reports were rife that the Planters, the settlement Officer, and the Surveyors, in the Chumparun district, had been massacred; indeed the majority of the European residents at Patna were in, what is vulgarly called, a horrible funk. It required but an outbreak, headed by a resolute leader, and the raising of the green standard of the Prophet, to excite a general insurrection, that, in the state of affairs above described, would have ended in a second Kabul tragedy.

The Magistrate issued the most stringent orders for the apprehension of the parties implicated in the papers of the regimental Moonshee; but for a while his efforts were fruitless. The usual return of *rooposhee** was made to all the Magistrate's warrants for apprehension. At length *Reket Allee* was taken. As for the *Khwajeh Saheb* his capture appeared to be so doubtful, that the Magistrate went to his house, personally, in the night, and forced his way into his bed-room; but although the bed was warm,

* In hiding.

and it was evident that it had been occupied only just before, yet the *Khwajeh* could not be apprehended. Reader, perhaps you require to be told, that the confidential *Syud Bakur* upon whom the Saheb Magistrate depended in his greatest emergencies, was in the pay of the *Khwajeh* and *Reket Allee?* The holy *Syud* was hereditary Chief of the *Bhurrooas;** (please refer to Shakespeare's dictionary for the exact meaning of the term) and received a portion of the earnings of all the "*birds of song*" in the city of Patna and its suburbs. The *Khwajeh Saheb* had a sister of the *Syud* as a favourite mistress; and whenever the Magistrate ordered the seizure of the *Khwajeh, Syud Bakur* managed to give him timely notice to escape. At length, however, all the alleged conspirators were apprehended, and confined separately, and great were the expectations of the whole country as to the steps that would be adopted for their punishment.

While matters were in this unsatisfactory state the *Mohurrum* approached. The "*Katulka-rat*" (night of massacre) is at hand, and detachments of troops are ordered hither and thither to protect the several parts of the town. When, suddenly, a hue and cry are heard "*Dakoo! Dakoo!—telingah ayah; Bhago, Bhago!*"† The detachments rushed as they best could through the crowd, that was flying in every direction, frightening them the more; but where the *Dakoos* were nobody could tell. Troops were ordered from cantonments, and the greatest fears for the fate of the opium factory, and the European residents in that part of the station, prevailed. The night passed off wearily and sleeplessly, and parties congratulated one another in the morning on their escape from death or ravishment. The houses of the European residents at the station, I am noticing, are situated in small groups along the bank of the Ganges river, and extend over a length of eight or ten miles, and consequently the inhabitants are unable to assist each other in time of need.

But patience, reader, and see what the morrow shall bring forth.

CHAP. XIX.

PROCEEDINGS AGAINST THE CONSPIRATORS.

Next morning there was a gathering together of all the notables, and one eagerly questioned the other as to what he knew, or had heard, of the occurrences of the night? But nobody seemed to know what had originated the panic of the previous evening. Parties went up all the one hundred and forty-three steps leading to the pinnacle of the *Golghur*,‡ and from thence

* Pimps. † Dacoits!—Dacoits! The sepoys are come. Run! Run!

‡ Round-house.—It was intended for a granary, and a preservative from famine; but it cannot contain one week's supply for the city of Patna, and remains a remarkable monument of ignorance and folly.

anxiously surveyed the whole country round with telescopes, to ascertain, if possible, what was the cause of the secret dread that weighed like an incubus on them. But nothing could be discovered—all appeared in a state of repose. At length, as the morning advanced, *Syud Bakur* reported to the authorities, that *a camel* had been frightened by the *tom-toming* and firing of the procession, and had rushed into the crowd upsetting right and left all that came in his way. The mob shouted '*Dakoo!*' and a panic spread like wildfire!!!

The fate of the residents of the opium factory still remained to be ascertained, and also of the detachment that had been sent for their protection and that of the Government stores. A Subaltern was despatched on horseback, and on his reaching the godowns, he was agreeably surprised to hear shouts of merriment. 'Hallo! Captain Snooks, how are you all?' asked the Sub.—'Jolly,' said Snooks, 'I never passed a pleasanter night, and trust I may have several more such nights yet. Nothing but broiled bones and beer and billiards all night, my boy. What d'ye-call-'em and I were right jolly.'

But the trial of the conspirators was to come on, and people anxiously waited the decision of the authorities. It was expected that severe punishment would be resorted to, as an example to the whole of Hindoostan. The proofs, as far as I could ascertain from the officials of the Adalut, were, *first*, that letters from *Moonshee Reket Allee*, *Syud Gubur-ood-deen* and *Khwajeh Saheb* were found in the house of *Moonshee Moofsidh*, urging him to the performance of 'the good work'—promises of large reward were held out for the future—intimation that several lakhs of rupees were at his disposal for the work in hand. *Second*, the confessions of some of the native officers, that they had been tampered with by the *Moonshee*, and that an insurrection was in agitation. *Third*, the confession of *Moonshee Moofsidh* himself, that he was a tool of *Reket Alee* and *Gubur-ood-deen Shah*, with whom he had frequent conferences, and who alleged that they were Agents for the Rajah of Nepal, and the influential Zemindars of the neighbourhood.

The *Khwajeh Sabeb*, *Reket Alee* and *Guburood-deen Shah*, flatly denied the charges brought against them, and alleged that they had never seen *Moonshee Moofsidh*. They denied the genuineness of the letters found in the possession of *Moonshee Moofsidh*, and alleged that they, as well as the seals, were fabrications. They called the Court's attention to the fact, that in a number of cases which had been tried, and parties implicated on the strength of documentary evidence, the letters adduced in proof had turned out to be forgeries, trumped up by the enemies of the accused, to ruin their fair fame. They loudly and bitterly protested that they had been forced from their homes and kept in durance as felons on, at best, but weak presumption. That the Magistrate had acted with the zeal and ardour of youth, for which he himself was culpable.

All this was openly discussed in the bazar, and, of course, people differed in their opinions. But the general impression was, that the parties were really guilty of a conspiracy; and the knowing ones said, that if they were recognised by *Moonshee Moofsidh*, there could be no doubt but that they would be blown off from a cannon's mouth, as a grand '*moral lesson*' to the world of India, of which Shah Soojah had set an example in Affghanistan. At the same time it was hinted that a sum of twenty-five thousand rupees had been offered to *Moonshee Moofsidh* to fail in the identification, and that a very *hoshyar* and *chalak Saheb** was expected from Calcutta to assist in the defence of the conspirators. And that *other modes* of propitiating the clemency and biassing the judgment of the *Saheban Aleeshan* would also be adopted. I could not help wondering how communication could be effected with a prisoner, guarded by sepoys, by other prisoners, who were themselves confined in a mass of brick-work like the *Golghur*. So being of an inquisitive turn of mind, I determined to find out the secret. I made myself very agreeable, and mixed freely with the *Jacks in office*, and in a convivial moment learned the trick. Suppose a prisoner is confined under the bayonets of sepoys, he must be permitted to eat bread. The preparer of food is bribed, and a short note is *put into a chupatee*,† or a sentence is written on a plate, and when the bread is taken up, the prisoner reads what is written, and expunges the characters. A short moral sentence is always a hint to the prisoner. For instance, '*May the blessed Prophet bring you comfort in this bread.*' Or, '*Cheer up, friend! that which is written is written.*'

Well, the trial came on before the extraordinary commission appointed for the purpose. The defendants were all brought up before their worships, and confronted with *Moonshee Moofsidh*. He persisted in his story, that he had had several interviews with *Reket Alee* and *Gubur-ood-deen Shah*, but that the *prisoners were not the parties !!!* What was to be done? The old woman called by us the *Koompanee Bahadoor*, had been frightened. The *Burra Sahebs* had made a great report to the *Council*. The safety of the empire was supposed to have been jeopardised. Some of the most influential people of the country had been apprehended—even that paragon of Darogahs, *Syud Bakur* the *nimuk-purwardah*‡ of the *Saheb log*, who was so highly honoured, that the *Lord Saheb ka Miss*§ had taken his likeness; even he was proved to have been in league with the conspirators.

But a very influential *Saheb*, a *burra admee*, had come to make *shifarush*‖ for the conspirators. *Syud Bakur* also exerted all his powers as chief '*Bhurooa*,' and mollified the *mizzaj* of some of the *Saheban Aleeshan* by discreetly sending forth his

* Clever and sharp gentleman.

† A flap of unleavened bread, something like a Scotch bannock.

‡ Cherished with salt. § Miss Eden is alleged to have taken the likeness of the worthy Syud Bakur. ‖ Friendly or powerful intercession.

sweetest birds of song to warble their dulcet notes in the ears of the *Sahebs.* The result was, that all the prisoners were released *from want of legal proof.*

However, the knowing ones were of opinion that the acquittal of the prisoners was a political dodge ; and, under the circumstances, the wisest course that could have been pursued. To have brought conviction home to the prisoners would have been to shew the people of Hindoostan, that the Sirdars and Zemindars, who were fostered by the *Koompanee,* were eager for a change of Rulers – the police officials and the Sepoys of the *jungee pultuns* were unfaithful to their *salt*—that *Moulvee Reket Alee,* and others like him, who had been honoured with important revenue and judicial trusts, were ready to turn upon the *Koompanee's* government, that the conspiracy had been suppressed in the bud, and that the parties implicated were known. And it was good policy to let the world know, that the *Koompanee Bahadoor* did not doubt the fidelity of her army.

REVELATIONS OF THE REVENUE DEPARTMENT.

Chap. XX.

THE REVENUE SETTLEMENT, AND THE ORDINARY AND EXTRAORDINARY WAYS AND MEANS WHEREBY THE OFFICIALS MAKE MONEY.

I have 'said my say' as to matters in *Fouzdaree :* and shall now give my readers a few revelations in the *revenue* department of the State. This as well as the police, comes home to every man's door. The *Putwarree** system ; the *Muhukma Commissioner-koorkee ;*† the *Qanoongoes ;*‡ the *Suzawuls ;*§ the *Tuhseeldars ;*|| and *Peshcars* ; the *Sheristadar*¶ and his satellites, are all deserving of notice : the *revenue settlements,* and the ordinary and extraordinary ways and means whereby the officials make money, and the zemindars and *putteedars* lose their estates ; all these are worthy of prominent mention. I have been myself a humble ryot, and have felt the insolence and oppression of the 'Jacks in office.' I have had the produce of my little field, which, with the labour of my wife and little ones, I had matured and expected to reap, attached and sold, despite my complaints to the *Hakims.* But my office of '*Nazir's Orderly*' has shewn me strange scenes, which it shall be my business to describe faithfully to my fellow-ryots, as a beacon to prevent them from suffering from the oppressions carried on under the sanction of the law, and as a duty to my present employers, the

* Village Accountant. † Office of Commissioner of Distraint.
‡ Revenue Officers. § Trustee for sequestrated estates.
|| Native Revenue Collectors. ¶ Head Native Official.

Saheb Koompanee Bahadoor, whose *nimuk-purwurdah** I am, from sanctioning them under false colouring. The *Saheban Aleeshan* little dream of the hundreds of ways in which grinding oppression is practised under their very noses. Be they ever so vigilant, they are deceived by the native officials, and it is only by some lucky chance that they stumble upon the practices which pervert the intentions of justice. If they be ever so clear-sighted, they are made to see through the eyes of others. How is this possible? you indignantly ask—Are not the Civil Servants of the Government the élite of England? Are they not some of them acknowledged to be the most talented men of the country? Has not this class furnished some of the ablest Statesmen in the world? All this I acknowledge. But what can they do? I have stood behind the chair of the *Collector Saheb*, and I have seen him absolutely unable to go through the official drudgery of the day. I have seen him defer a case day after day, in the vain hope that he would find time for investigating it thoroughly. But, alas! such leisure could not be found. I have seen his subordinate European officials similarly puzzled with work. How then can you be surprised, that these gentlemen are obliged frequently to let their decisions pass under the force of circumstances they cannot overcome, in order to shew a good *nuksha*† to the Board. Hence, I say, they require promptings from people who are behind the scenes.

I had held possession of my *jote* of five beegahs of land in the village of Moobarukpoor, for upwards of fifteen years, and my progenitors had possession for upwards of half a century. We had never paid more than two rupees a beegah, or ten rupees per annum, to our old zemindar. We were protected by the *kawaneen-i-sircar*;‡ which declares that '*no khoodkasht*,§ *chupperbund asamee shall be liable to enhancement of revenue, except in due course of law*,' and I reposed in confidence on the *insaf*‖ of the *sircar*. But *Bulbhudder Singh* had purchased the village by private sale; and he had served all the *asamees* with a notice to quit, or to pay four rupees a beegah I went to the '*Dipty Saheb*,' and gave in an *oozerdaree*;¶ and after hearing both sides, the *Dipty Saheb* ruled that *Bulbhudder Singh* was merely '*kibaladar*;' that as such he was merely a *kaemmukam* (locum tenens) of the zemindar, and could not legally demand enhancement of rent from a *koodkasht ryot*. That even were *Bulbhudder nilamdar, ba illut baqee*,** he was debarred by Reg. V. of 1812, and Act 1, of 1845, which expressly declared 'that no auction-purchaser shall have the power to enhance the rate of *khoodkasht chupperbund asamees*.' 'Hear him,' said I, 'hear him! here is wisdom! Here is a true *ryot*†† *purwur*!'

* Salt-cherished, *i. e.*, supported.
† Report. ‡ Regulations of Government.
§ Cultivators having hereditary right of occupation.
‖ Justice. ¶ Objection.
** Auction-purchaser of an estate sold for balance of Government revenue.
†† Cherisher of ryots.

But, lo! no sooner was my field ripe for the sickle, than a fellow put into my hands a dirty bit of paper, with unintelligible Nagree characters written thereon, which he verbally told me was the *Putwaree's wasil-baqee*, shewing that I owed *Bulbhudder Singh* the sum of ten rupees! I could not read; so I took the paper, in great dismay, to a *Lallah* in the next village, and he read as follows:—

Account of receipts and balance for the year 1253 Fusilee, Panchkouree Asamee Mouroosee.

Five beegahs jote, at the rate of 4 rupees a beegah, in all 20 rupees for the entire year.

For the first half year, due 15 rupees—received 5 rupees.

Balance claimed	10	rupees	
Add interest for 15 days . . .	0	2	0
Mursoom (dues) Putwaree ..	0	0	6
Total due to Bulbhudder Singh	10	2	6

(Signed) GUJJUB LALL, *Putwaree*.

Seeing how prompt justice was rendered me by the *Dipty Saheb* on a former occasion, I again waited on him, loudly demanding justice. '*Dohaee! Dipty Saheb! Dohaee Koompanee Bahadoor!*' 'Fool!' said the *Dipty*, what are you bawling yourself hoarse for? I can listen to nothing unless you present a petition on stamped paper.' 'But, sir,' I urged, 'my crops are distrained; my wife and children will starve, unless speedy justice be rendered. And from whence shall I get funds to purchase a stamp, and to pay for engrossing the petition?' All that I could get for my pains was, to be turned out of the room for my importunity.

But finding no help for it, I sold my *pugree*, and purchased a stamp, and getting a petition written, which I fondly conceived would have melted a heart of stone, presented it next day. The *Dipty Saheb* at once passed an order to this effect—'the petitioner is at liberty to give security to the *kibaladar* for the amount of distress, or to deposit the money in the treasury; and then to institute a '*bejah koorkee*'* suit—ordered that the petition be —'*dakhil duftur*.'†

'But, *Junab-i-alee!*'‡ I entreated. 'I sold my very pugree to enable me to present a petition on stamped paper to your honor; and do you call this redress? I ask the prophet to witness that the demand is unjust and illegal, and you desire me to deposit 15 *rupees*. Where, in the name of the prophet, shall I get that sum?' But the *Dipty Saheb* plainly told me that he was helpless, and that unless I did as he directed, he could give me no redress. Finding myself *lachar*,§ I borrowed fifteen rupees from the village Muhajun, at the rate of four pice per mensem,

* A suit for replevin.

† Struck off the file.

‡ Great lord.

§ Helpless.

interest, upon each rupee, or 75 *per cent. per annum! ! !* (read this, ye ghosts of usurers and learn a lesson from the unsophisticated mild Hindoo) and deposited the money, and had my crops released for the nonce from the *distress*.

CHAP. XXI.

THE CASE OF THE POOR RYOT.

I had a very moving petition drawn out by *Lallah Seetul Pershad*, commencing with '*zoolm hae layek insaf, wuh jour hae kabil iltifat*.* I set forth, that I was a hereditary *asamee*, and by the *Qawaneen-i-Sirkar* was not obnoxious to enhancement of rent;—that I had a jote of five beegahs of land in *mouza Moobarukpoor*, and had never paid the old zemindars more than two rupees a beegah, or ten rupees per annum, for *malgoozaree*;—that I had paid five rupees, and when the balance became due was ready to pay it;—that *Bulbhudder Singh, the kibaladar*, had wantonly served me with a notice to pay him four rupees a beegah, but that owing to the *insaf-i-nousherwanee*† of the *Huzoor*, the notice was declared to be illegal;—that notwithstanding, *Bulbhudder Singh*, whose *budmashee* and *zoolm* were well known to the *Junab*, had levied distress on my fields to force me to pay an unjust demand; and I prayed for justice.

Bulbhudder Singh's Mooktyar, Lalla Debee Purshad, presented a defence, in which he stated that his client was purchaser of the village, and had served a notice to all the *asamees*, under the provisions of Regulation V. of 1812. He quoted several *Nuzirs* (precedents) by which his client was borne out in enhancing the rents, &c. &c. *Gunga Dass, Putwaree*, deponed that he had written the *jumma wasil baqee*,‡ on the score of which distraint of Panchkouree's property had been made—that the account was correct at the rate of four rupees a beegah, and that the sum demanded, viz., 10 rupees, 2 annas, 6 pice, was justly due. I could stand this no longer, and shouted out, '*Ay! Junab-i-Alee!* that man is a liar. He is a *Putwaree*, and every *Putwaree* is a liar. Zemindars have silver rings in the noses of the *Putwarees*, and therewith lead them as they please.' The *Saheb* asked the *Putwaree* whether more than ten rupees per annum had ever been realized from Panchkouree. To which a negative was returned. 'How then do you say that the excess of demand is just?' The *Putwaree* submitted that he acted according to the orders of *Lallah Debee Purshad*. The *Dipty Saheb* decreed for me with costs, and ruling that the distress was vexatious and illegal, released me from the remainder of *Bulbhudder's* claim. But *Lallah Debee Purshad* was not satis-

* Tyranny is a fit (subject) for justice, and oppression is a fit (subject) for attention.

† Justice worthy of Nousherwan.

‡ Account of receipts and balance.

fied. He asked whether the *Hakims*, whose orders he had quoted, were ignorant of the laws, that their judgments were to be overruled summarily? And the *Lallah* began quoting so many *kantractions* and *surkoolar chittees*, that my liver became as water. But the *Saheb* ordered him to be turned out, and bade me be of good cheer, and to go and reap my harvest. And I did so with a joyous heart, well pleased that I had got the better of both the *Putwaree* and *Bulbhudder*.

But, lo! a month afterwards I was served with a notice from the *Moonsiff's* Court, intimating that *Bulbhudder Singh* had complained against me for the amount of annual *malgoozaree*, praying the Court to authorise his charging me four rupees a beegah; or 20 rupees for my jote per annum. I went to *Seetul Purshad* and asked him to write a petition for me; but he told me that this was a *lumburee moquddumma*,* and that I must consent to undergo considerable expense, and to employ a regular *Vakeel*. I was in despair. I had not a rupee in the world, so was obliged to pledge my pair of oxen to the village *Muhajun* to raise funds for the defence of this suit. But I rested my hopes on the blessed prophet and *insaf* of the *Hakiman-i-Adawlut*.

My Vakeel recapitulated the arguments used by the *Dipty Saheb*, and quoted a host of regulations and *kantractions*. But the *Moonsiff* merely asked the *Putwaree* whether the *itilanamah* had been served upon Panchkouree agreeably to Regulation V of 1812? To this the *Putwaree* replied in the affirmative. I myself did not deny it, but produced copy of the *Dipty's roobukaree*, in which the notice itself was pronounced illegal. But the Moonsiff threw away the *roobukaree* with contempt—'*Kuon Dipty Kullectur our kuon Hakim-i-Adawlut Dewanee.*' (Oh ye Gods; Does he pretend to compare the *Dipty's* contemptible intellects with mine!) The Moonsiff then asked the *Putwaree* whether the lands of my jote were capable of paying four rupees a beegah, and what were the general rates of the district? The *Putwaree* submitted that my jote was worth five rupees a beegah; that was the average rate of the village. The Moonsiff decreed for *Bulbhudder*, casting me, and declaring me liable to pay four rupees a beegah in future. My Vakeel advised me to appeal, but I stared stupidly in his face. 'Do not you understand me, friend,' he said; 'appeal to the *Saheb Judge Bahadoor*, and you will be righted. The Moonsiff has warped the law from fear of *Bulbhudder*, and the Judge Saheb will reverse his decree.' 'Oh! Vakeel,' I answered, 'where, in the name of the prophet, am I to get more money to fight with *Bulbhudder*? I have sold my oxen; I have lost my cause; I shall be ousted out of house and home, and you tell me to appeal!' Could appeals be heard without putting us poor *ryots* to ruinous expense, they would be salutary; but as matters are, the *long purse will always carry the day against a poor man.*

* Regular Civil Suit.

I had observed *Bulbhudder* in the Moonsiff's Court, standing alongside his Vakeel. He seemed to be troubled with a curious nervous movement of the right hand across his throat. And whenever the eyes of the Moonsiff and *Bulbhudder* met, the latter invariably put his open hand, edgewise, to his throat. This always made the Moonsiff turn pale and look another way. What the exact interpretation of this sign may be, I know not. But I had lost my cause, and was not particular to ascertain the meaning of signs and telegraphs.

Bulbhudder took the earliest opportunity to sue me before the *Dipty Saheb* for the next *kist*, according to the Civil Court's decree. I appeared in person, and confessed that the Moonsiff had decreed against me, and that *Bulbhudder's* cause was a good one this time. 'Do you intend appealing?' quoth the *Saheb*. 'No, Sir,' I replied, 'I give in, and only pray that my jote may be given to any one else. If *Bulbhudder* will release me of all claims, I will resign my jote.' God and the Prophet know that the *Saheban Aleeshan* have a peculiar mode of administering their own laws. One *Hakim* passes an order to a certain effect, and another passes one diametrically opposite to it. Both fancy themselves to be right; either the laws are *enigmas*, or the administrators are overinstructed in them God help us poor *ryots*!*

Chap. XXII

THE ZEMINDARS AND COLLECTORS.

I showed in my last how I had been forced from my *jote;* and it was in consequence of my distress that I applied to my friend *Suntokee*, the result of which may be seen, by referring to the two first chapters of these revelations.

I observed that I alone was not the sufferer. During my incumbency as an '*Orderly*,' I have witnessed scenes, that if described with ordinary rhetoric, would induce my readers to think that I am not dealing with facts, but endeavouring to harrow their feelings with imaginary tales of distress. I will leave such matters for the ingenuity of romance-mongers, and give you the naked truth, which requires no high colouring to render it interesting. There lived, in the village of *Tundah*, an opulent cultivator, by name of *Bhawanee Singh*. His ancestors had been the *Zemindars* of the village; but during the first revenue settlements by *Joonateen Dunkeen Bahadoor*, his father had refused to enter into the necessary engagements, alleging that the assessments were too heavy, so that at the time of my

* The glorious uncertainty of the law is, perhaps, in no instance, so well exemplified as in the different constructions of officials on this subject of exemption from enhancement of rent Order upon order has been promulgated, only to render "confusion worse confounded."

story, *Bhawanee Singh* was cultivator of fifty *beegahs* of as fine land as you would desire to see for miles around. The *malgoozaree* on these lands was one rupee eight annas a *beegah*, or seventy-five rupees per annum. The *Zemindars* of *Tandah* were also opulent men, and were never a day behind the fixed time for payment of the "kists"* due to the *Sircar*. But the *talooq*† was known to be profitable, and was coveted by the Vakeel and *Umlah*; and a plot was entered into between them to force it to be sold, when they would pounce upon it as legal prey, and appropriate it as their own.

It is well known that no native, how rich soever, will pay money the moment it falls due, unless he has the dread of punishment or disgrace before him It is a practice in the revenue courts of the *Sircar Bahadoor*, to issue dustucks for the *malgoozaree* the very day the kist (instalment) becomes due. This was not done in the village of *Tandah* for three several kists; and the *Zemindar* became careless, and did not pay his next instalment. The *Huzoor* was duly informed of the default. He inquired how the *Zemindar* could be a defaulter when he was known to be opulent; and whether a *dustuck*‡ had been served on him? "Yes, your honour," was the reply. "Here it is, duly signed and sealed." "Serve him with a second dustuck; and direct the *Nazir* also to send a smart *Molazim*,§ to ascertain the cause of *Dowlut Singh's* default." The order was obeyed, and the *Nazir Saheb* despatched me on this service. "Go *Bhaee Panchkouree Khan*," said he, "and bring that *Moofsidh Dowlut Singh* to his senses." At the same time he gave me a knowing look that intimated he had something more to say. I made a great bustle, pretended to start at once, but took myself straight to the *Nazir's* house. Here I found *Moulvee Vaqeel* and *Lalla Moonshee* waiting for me. They detained me until the arrival of the *Nazir*; and I then received instructions to go to *Dowlut's* village; but instead of bullying him for the rent of the *Sircar Koompanee*, to give him all the best compliments of the *Nazir* and the *Moonshee jee*. "Tell him," said they, "that we are his best friends – that he need not trouble himself about the *malgoozaree*, for that the *Saheb* collector will never find out that he is in balance, while we choose to befriend him."

Well, I proceeded to *Dowlut Singh's house* in *Tandah*, and most affectedly sported my *chuprass*, so that anybody could not fail to observe it, and announced myself as having come from the *Nazir*. *Dowlut Singh* came out in a fright, gave me a *charpaee* to sit upon, and anxiously asked "What I had come about?" I was bent upon lining my own purse, so I answered, by telling him "that his *malgoozaree* was not paid, and that the *Saheb* collector had sent me to apprehend him."

* Instalments.

† Estate. The peculiarity of tenure is too prolix for a marginal note.

‡ Warrant.

§ Servant on the regular establishment.

"Where is the *dustuck*?" he inquired. I showed him the notice, with the *Huzoor's* signature, and the broad seal of office. Upon this he appeared to reflect; and after awhile, he said, "You must be tired. *Khan Saheb*, walk in, and I will see whether I cannot make you comfortable." I did so, performed my ablutions, filled my hookah, and puffed away insolently, and expatiated on my influence with the Nazir, and of *Nazir's* and *Moonshee's* influence with the *Huzoor*. "But, *Dowlut Singh*," I said, "you know that *ushraf log** do not exert their influence for nothing. However, thank God, that *you* do not require our *shifarish*,† for you owe the *Sircar* but a paltry two thousand rupees, and that is as nothing to such as you are, *Dowlut Singh*." But I saw poor *Dowlut* wince; and after coaxing me a good deal, he began to tell me how he, and the *Nazir*, and *Moonshee*, had been on the best possible terms —how he had been advised by them to be in no hurry to pay the kists due to the *Sircar*—how he had expended all the money on his son's marriage—how the *Muhajun*, with whom he had money dealings, refused to advance money without his mortgaging his *talooq*. "And now, *Khan Saheb*, my hope rests with you, and your influence with the *Nazirjee*. Here is a small sum for *pan-tumbakhoo*."‡ I looked at the money, and to my disgust it was only five rupees. So I indignantly threw it down, and rising as if to go, I said, "*Salam Thakoorjee*, I shall inform the *Huzoor* that you refused to come with me." *Dowlut Singh* hastily ran and laid hold of my hand, and bade me sit down. His little son ran into the *suhun*,§ where we were seated, and I saw a *kuldar ushurfee*‖ which was hung round the boy's neck, and remarked how well it looked. The old *Rajpoot* took it from his boy's neck, and put it into my hand, with a knowing look, as if deprecating any refusal. I took it, stroked my beard, and enlarged upon my official influence.

Having thus cleverly secured about four months' pay, I turned on another tack, and told *Dowlut Singh* that the *Nazir* and *Moonshee* had confidentially desired me to communicate their sentiments to him. I then gave him all the "*soft sawder*" I could think of, and left him, quite assured that he need not trouble himself about his *talooq*, and the *malgoozaree* due to the *Sircar*. I informed the *Nazir* and *Moonshee* of the success of my mission; but, of course, said not a word about the goldmohur.

The Collector was informed of *Dowlut Singh's* back-sliding; and after wading through the *nathee*¶ of papers, and satisfying himself that the notices had (*apparently*) been served, he made a report to the *Sudder*, and obtained leave to sell the *talooq* for the balance due to Government. In the days I mention, sales were not so scrupulously conducted as they now are; and poor *Dowlut* was not aware of the impending calamity

* Respectable people. † Good word. ‡ Betel-nut and tobacco.
§ Entrance, verandah. ‖ Old gold Mohur. ¶ File.

until one day before the sale. He rushed into the *Kacherree* and protested to the Collector that he had never been served with a single notice; and plainly charged the *Moonshee* and *Nazir* with corruption and *fussadh*.* "Bring the *misl*," coolly said the Saheb. It was brought, and the Collector *Bahadoor* himself turned over the pages. "Here are the *dustucks*, *Dowlut Singh*, and your signature duly affixed. Call the *mushkooree peadahs*."† They came and swore to having served the *dustucks*. "Sir," said the *Nazir*, "I sent Panchkouree Khan, a *molozim*, to bring the defaulter, and here is his *kyfeut*." I was sent for, and no sooner did I appear, than *Dowlut* roared out, "*Ay! dhurmoaotar*!‡ that is the blackguard who brought me a message from the *Nazir* and *Moonshee*, not to pay the revenue, and he fleeced me of a gold-mohur." I looked sternly at *Dowlut*, and quietly submitted to the *Huzoor* that the man was mad! I call the blessed prophet to witness, *Junab-i-alee*, that I did not so much as get a drink of water in the village of *Tandah*, and that I took some pieces of bread with me which I ate! If the *Huzoor will* listen to such calumny, how can the servants of the *Sircar* be safe? Here the whole of the officials present hummed forth a similar complaint. The Collector was in despair, and ordered the sale to take place next day, if the entire balance were not paid.

Suffice it to say, that the money was not paid—that the *taloog* of *Tandah* was sold, and purchased by *Lalla Moonshee* and *Moulvee* Vakeel. That *Dowlut Singh* appealed to the *Alee Jah Commissioner Bahadoor*, but could get no redress, as the papers were right, and that the auction-purchasers got possession. The next chapter will show what they did, and how *Bhawanee Singh* was dealt with.

Chap. XXIII.

Oppression of the Ryots.

No sooner was the sale of *Tandah* concluded, than *Moulvee* Vakeel obtained a *kibalah*§ and *umuldustuk*‖ and took formal possession. Notice for enhancement of rent was served on every *ryot*, and among others, *Bhawanee Singh*, and his fifty *beegahs* of *mouroosee jote*,¶ were not forgotten. He had always paid one rupee eight annas, per *beegah*, and was now directed to pay five rupees. But he was a tough old *Rajpoot* and merely laughed the notice to scorn. However, *Moulvee* Vakeel was not a man to give in while a quirk or quibble was at hand, or a sheer face of brass could frown forth withering terrors; so as soon as the first *kist* became due, he instituted summary process

* Malice – conspiracy.
† Men hired for an occasion.
‡ Oh! merciful Avater (of God).
§ Deed of sale
‖ Warrant for putting in possession.
¶ Hereditary culture.

against him. The case was prepared by the *Umlah*, and heard before the *Saheb Shistant*, who had recently joined.

There were, first, the *Putwaree's wasil baqee*; second, copy of the notice served on defendant, declaring him liable to pay five rupees her *beegah*; third, the Collector's *kibalah* to the auction-purchaser. To all these, old *Bhawanee Singh* simply referred to the fact, that he was a resident hereditary cultivator, from the cession of the province to the *Sircar Koompanee Bahadoor*—that he held a *pottah* signed by the *Saheb Kullan Joonateen Dunkeen*—that by the regulations of the *Sircar*, he was exempt from enhancement of rent—and that, please *Ramjee*! he would not pay a fraction more than he had done. While the *Saheb Shistant*, sate with a becoming gravity, with his beaver hat knowingly cocked on his head, Moulvee Vakeel eagerly said, '*Junab-i-alee*! did your honour ever hear such insolence as has been uttered by that fellow? He says he will not pay a pice more than the *Malgoozaree* he has paid, even if your worship order it!!! He presumes to defy the *Hakim*!' 'Well, well,' pettishly said the *Saheb*; "*choop ruho*.* What are the sale-regulations, *Moonshee*?' Now the reader will remember that the *Moonshee* was a joint proprietor with the Vakeel; and his cue, therefore, was to mislead; so he turned up Regulation V. of 1812, Sec. 9. "Here, sir, is the kanoon. Moulvee Vakeel did serve the notice for enhancement of *Malgoozaree*, and is clearly entitled to decree in the present suit." Decree for plaintiff was given accordingly. This is grand, thought old *Bhawanee Singh* "*diggruee to pah, lekin roopyea to mor pase bah*."† After a month the decree was executed, and the usual process for apprehension of the person was issued. The *Mushkore* that served the writ, was thrashed soundly by *Bhawanee's* three sons, who were taken up for the assault by the *Thanadar*; and *chalaned* and sentenced to six months' imprisonment each, and old *Bhawanee* himself, heart-broken and disconsolate, delivered himself up to the *Nazir*. The case was called, the decree read, and *Bhawanee* asked whether he would pay the amount? "No, I will not," was his reply. "For fifty years my father and I have never paid more than one rupee eight annas a *beegah*, and not a pice more shall I pay." He was sent to jail. Moulvee Vakeel next gave a petition to the *Saheb Shistant* for the sale of *Bhawanee's* property. This was ordered of course; but it was strange that six fine cows, two stone sugar mills, and a stack of grain, were sold for only eighteen rupees. The sale was sanctioned; but as the whole amount of decree was not paid, old *Bhawanee* was, therefore, allowed to rot in jail.

When the next instalment became due to the auction-purchaser, a summary suit was again filed to the usual processes, the return of the *Nazir* was "*rooposh*." But the defendant and his sons were in jail; how then could the suit be defended?

* Be quiet. † He has obtained decree, but the rupees are in my hands.

The result was, an *exparte* decree for Moulvee Vakeel. This decree was also executed; and the *Nazir's kyfeut* was, that the defendant was in jail in a suit of the decree-holder, Moulvee Vakeel. He was sent for from the jail; but pleaded insolvency, and was released.

Bhawanee was at large—his sons also were released; and they commenced ploughing their fields like men. They vowed that Moulvee Vakeel should rue the day he ever thought of oppressing them. Old *Dowlut Singh* and his stalwart progeny were also paupers; and in the whole village a feeling of hatred and revenge was engendered against the *Nilamdar*.* But the *Moulvee* was not one that would rashly venture his person within a village, the inhabitants of which were inimical to him; and he laughed at the deadly threats of the tribe of *Rajpoots*.

He sent his *Karindah*, however, to *tuhseel*,† and on the first night of his arrival at the *chownee*‡ it was fired; and he and his party were knocked down with *lattees*, as they ran out to escape the devouring flame.

This was what the Vakeel had longed for and had anticipated, and he smoothed down his beard with the hand of satisfaction, and prepared to act. Meantime, *Dowlut Singh* and his stalwart sons, and old *Bhawanee* and his sons, were so alarmed at their own violence, and frightened for the consequences, that they left their homes and fled. A very exaggerated report was made to the Magistrate, of a case which required no colouring to heighten its enormity. The wounded men were sent into hospital, and weeks passed before they were declared to be convalescent; the defendants were not forthcoming until they were proclaimed as outlaws, when they made necessity a virtue, and gave themselves up. They were tried, fully convicted, and sentenced to imprisonment for seven years. Thus Moulvee Vakeel got possession of the entire *talooq*, at the expense of a few broken bones to his retainers.

This result made a serious impression on me. I reflected that my own case was not parallel in hardship. For here were zemindars and old *istimraree puttadars*§ turned out of their fields, and irretrievably ruined in purse and reputation, by the machinations of a man who had risen from the dregs of the people to be a Vakeel; by the sheer force of villany, aided by, it must be confessed, great talent. Here were the well-meaning regulations of a Government that would be paternal, misconceived and distorted, to suit the views of interested parties. And the *Hakims*—what were they doing? Alas! I saw, by my own practice, that they were as children in our hands; their various duties so interfere one with another, that a portion only could possibly be performed.

But there is such a thing as retributive justice even in this life. Moulvee Vakeel managed to keep possession of the en-

* Auction-purchaser.

† Realise rents. ‡ Village office. § Holder of leases in perpetuity.

tire *talooq*, to the exclusion of *Lalla Moonshee*. The latter worthy did not dare to contest the matter with the former, for fear of exposing his own share in the nefarious practices that have been related. The two foul animals hunted in couple, while there was prey in view; but as soon as it was captured and consumed, the strongest fell on the weak one and devoured him.

Chap. XXIV.

THE MOCKERY OF AN ADJUDICATION.

Most of my readers are aware that "*summary suits*" for rent or replevin (known as *moquddummat sursurree*, or *bejah tulbee*) are heard and decided by a Covenanted Assistant to the Collector, or by the "*Dipty Saheb*." But, perhaps, all are not aware that the proof in such cases is based entirely upon the *Putwarees'* * accounts. For any claim that is doubtful, the parties are referred to the civil courts. But as no witnesses may be examined, the *Putwaree* has it entirely in his power to depone for *zemindar* or for *ryot*, exactly as his own interest may bias him. He produces a *Jummabundee*† and the village accounts, which are confessedly dictated by the *zemindar* himself. He asserts that the *ryot* owes the *zemindar* so much money, and has not paid it, *because it is not mentioned in his accounts*! while the poor *ryot* calls his *deotas*‡ to witness for him, and names the *Muhajun* to whom he pledged his bullocks for that money to pay his rent; and he names witnesses in whose presence the money was paid. But the inexorable *Dipty* merely asks him "*Putwaree yah zemindar ka ruseed rukhteh ho?*"§ "*Nuhee, ryot purwur!*"|| Decree for plaintiff is the certain result. But who shall blame the Assistant or Deputy, when they are so desired to do, and are forbidden to make aught approaching to judicial investigation? The *jummabundee* itself—the principal, if not only documentary evidence in suits for rent or replevin—is a tissue of falsehoods and errors Pick out any one, or a dozen at random, and try and reconcile the discrepancies. You will find the same number of the field, the same *jumma* and area, put down against two or three distinct *asamees*, in the same number of distinct entries. "Why?" you ask. "Merely to enable the *Zemindar* and *Putwaree* to charge one or the other party with the *malgoozaree*, according to the necessity of the occasion." "But is there not an establishment of Deputy Collectors, *Tuhseeldars*, *Qanoongoes* and Mohurrirs, to examine records and to rectify errors, wilful or unintentional?" "True; but how can one man set through the work of four? The comparison is slurred over, and the people suffer."

* Village accountant. † Register of holdings. ‡ Deities.
§ Do you hold the receipts of Zemindar or Putwaree?
|| No, cherisher of the ryot.

But to illustrate my allegations with a tale—"There lived in the village of *Bhurturra* one *Ramkishoon Koonbee*, who had a *jote* of seven *beegahs* of land, which had devolved on him as his inheritance. He was industrious an prosperous, and always paid his rent of twenty-one rupees per annum to *Bulbhuddur Singh*, the *Nilamdar*, *Ramkishoon's* sons had grown up, however, and leaving two of them to manage the fields, he, with one son, took service with the Rajah of Bettiah. They had been absent two years at the period of my tale. A *beegah* of land that had been left fallow, was about to be ploughed by *Ramkishoon's* sons for sugar-cane, when *Debee Lalla*, with five strapping *lattheals*,* forcibly stopped them, and ploughed the field themselves. On the lad's remonstrance, *Debee Lalla* told them *that their father had been dispossessed two years ago!* They were too weak to fight, so went to another of their fields, and commenced tilling it vigorously. A year-passed away, and *Ramkishoon Koonbee* returned to *Bhurturra;* and his sons told him the story of their dispossession from part of the *jote*. The old fellow's blood was up, and he filed a petition in the *sursurree* for *bedakhilee*.† The *Putwaree* was summoned, and deponed upon oath to the dispossession of *Ramkishoon* from his entire *jote three years ago!* that *Ramkishoon* had fled from his village, and that the *Nilamdar* had made a *bundobust* of the seven *beegahs* of land with *Ramdechul Singh*, who had paid the *malgoozaree* regularly. Great was the horror of the poor *Koonbee*. He produced receipts given to his sons for the money they had paid the *Karindah*, *Debee Lalla*. He swore that he was in possession of six *beegahs* of his old *jote*, and begged of the *Saheb* to look at the accounts. This was done; but lo! the past two *jummabundees* bore the name of *Ramdechul Singh*, as cultivator of the fields formerly held by *Ramkishoon Koonbee*. What could the *Saheb* do? *Ramkishoon's* case was dismissed, and he was referred to the civil courts for redress."

Here was a poor cultivator, resident and hereditary, dispossessed first of one field by force, and then of all the rest, by an unscrupulous *Nilamdar* and a rascally *Putwaree*. Had the *Qanoongo* first reported to the *Huzoor*, that an entry in the *Jummabundee* had been made, contrary to the preceding year's papers, an enquiry would have been ordered, and the false entry corrected. But the more inaccuracies there are in a *Jummabundee*, the greater is the fee demanded for filing it; and if the *Douceur* be sweet enough, there is never any difficulty in getting the *Huzoor's* signature affixed to it. Even enquiries made in person by the *Hakims*, and on the spot where a dispute exists, do not always tend to elicit the truth. An officer of experience, and one who could see through a mill-stone as well as most of his neighbours once had a case pending before him, in which, the question at issue was the hereditary right to a grove

* Men armed with clubs.

§ In the summary department, for dispossession.

of mangoe trees. The *Saheb* ordered his tents to be pitched in the disputed grove, and proceeded thither. He observed some villagers with loads of wood on their heads, and others carrying grass, passing close by his tents. "Here, fellows!" he exclaimed, "come hither." But they threw down their loads and ran, as if for their lives. The *chupprasees* of the *Huzoor* pursued and brought them back. "What made you run away?" angrily asked the *Saheb*. "From fear of your worship," they replied. They were then asked "if they knew to whom the grove of trees belonged?" They replied, "that the trees were planted by *Jeet Singh*, grandfather of *Ishwur Singh*, one of the parties; and that all the world knew that *Ishwur* was in possession."

Now the truth was, that the witnesses were purposely sent through the grove by *Ishwur Singh*, who in reality had no right to the grove of trees, nor was he in possession thereof. But the *ruse* told, and the *Saheb* decided for the clever rogues. He recorded, that he had learned from "*hur ek rahgeer, jo ittifaqun oos raste jata tha!*"* that the grove was the property of *Ishwur Singh*; and decree was given accordingly.

The filing of the *Putwaree's* papers is a tax to the entire district; and when the *Saheban Borud* issue stringent orders to the Collectors to expedite the delivery of the papers, then comes a glorious harvest to us orderlies. The *Dipty* sends first one dustuck upon the Zemindar and *Putwaree*, then a second, and a third. They are at length brought before the man "in a little brief authority," and the culprits tremble for the result. "Has the *tullabana* been paid?" "No, your honour." "Then put the *Putwaree* in the *Nazir's* guard; and place an extra *peadah* on the zemindar until the *tullabana* has been paid." The zemindar alleges that the *peadah* only served him with the notice four days ago; but he is turned out summarily. He offers to pay whatever is demanded; but the *peadah* coolly asks *ten rupees* This is refused indignantly; but every day the bullying increases, and the extra day's *tullabana* is added to the first demand, until the *Zemindar lachar*, gives the *peadah* all he demands, to get away to his quiet home, far from the harpies of the *Kacherrees*. But what is the law? There is no penal law by which the zemindar may be coerced to file the *jummabundee*. The only punishment the law contemplates, is to debar any *Zemindar* the privilege to sue for his rent in *any* court, if the *jummabundee* is not filed; and yet each village is mulcted from five to ten rupees per annum; and a parcel of vagabonds, called "*mushkooree peadahs*," fatten illegally on the villagers. *In every district where the Putwaree's papers are filed regularly, and before the beginning of the year, a legion of these mushkoories is let loose upon the Zemindars, to force them to do as the Saheban Aleeshan desire.*

* From every passer-by, who, accidentally, was going that road.

Chap. XXV.

EUROPEAN AGENCY EMPLOYED BY GOVERNMENT IS INCOMPETENT FOR THE PUBLIC SERVICE REQUIRED FROM IT.

A *Mahajun* had purchased the village of *Bahadoorpoor*, and his *Karindahs* suggested that by doubling the rents of every cultivator, he would get a clear profit of a hundred rupees per mensem. How was this miracle to be effected? You shall see. A *jummabundee* was given to the *Qanoongo* to be filed in the Collector's office, but the increase shewn was so alarming, that he did not dare to attest it. He gave a *kyfeut* to the *Huzoor* to the effect, that "there was an increase in the *jumma* certainly, but that the *nilamdar* alleged that the *asamees* had agreed to the enhancement of rent on his consenting to dig wells, etc., for them." The *Saheb* ordered the *Qanoongo* to go out himself to assemble the *asamees*, and to report faithfully whether they had really consented to the increase? And if so, to get the signatures of the majority affixed to the *jummabundee*. This was pretended to be carried out, and a month had not elapsed when the *Qanoongo* again presented the *jummabundee* with his *kyfeut* to the *Huzoor*, asserting that the names of all the cultivators had been affixed to the document in the presence of himself and the *Putwaree*. What could the *Saheb* do? The *jummabundee* was signed and sealed, and ordered to be filed among the records.

In such cases, the *dodge* is to realise what sums may be recovered from the *ryots*, without instituting *summary suits* or distraining the property of any defaulting tenant; the object being to establish a confidence among the *asamees* in the *jummabundee*, while the fictitious *jumma* is being worked into substitution. Well, two years roll away, and just as the standing crops are fit for the sickle, the cultivators are astonished at receiving notices of distress, and to their disgust, every man finds his *malgoozaree* doubled. Half the inhabitants rush into the Collector's presence, crying out that their crops are ripe, but that the *nilamdar* will not allow them to be cut. The *Saheb*, to get them away, orders the *Peshcar* to compromise the matter in dispute. The *Peshcar* is too great a man, however, to go out that day—but a week afterwards he proceeds to the "*chhaonee*" of the village, and gets well feasted by the *nilamdar*. The *ryots* are brow-beaten and abused, and the *Peshcar* even lends his myrmidons to assist the *nilamdar* in annoying the people. They leave the village in despair; and again the Saheb Collector is assailed with cries of "*Dohaee! Collector Saheb, Dohaee Koompanee Bahadoor!*" But on enquiry, it appears that the *Peshcar* has not returned from his investigation; and all that *can* be done is to issue a stringent order to the *Peshcar* to expedite his enquiries. At length, the *kyfeut* of the *Peshcar* is given in to the effect, that he had carefully examined the village account of the *past two years*, and had found that the *nilamdar* merely wanted his just dues from the *ryots*; to realise which he had distrained their crops. The *Saheb Bahadoor* was very busy, and the cultivators were directed to give *malzaminee* to the *Commissioner Koorkee*, and then to institute "*Bejah Koorkee*" suits. Now, in all these orders, strict attention, in conformity with the regulations, was paid, but the villagers, tired and disgusted at the dilatoriness of *summary* proceedings, left the *Kacherree* in despair, and made a compromise with the *nilamdar*!!

A *ryot*, even well to do in the world, can with difficulty find money-security for twenty-five or fifty rupees when his crops (upon which he depends for support) are under distraint; a poor man, under such a calamity, *must* give in to his landlord, or be ruined, in spite of the vigilance and extreme desire of the *Hakims* to render justice.

I have attempted to shew that it is quite in the power of the *Qanoongoes* and *Putwarees* to falsify the village papers according to their own wishes, or the instigation of the parties by whom the doing so is made profitable to them. Let the *Saheban Aleeshan* call for *kyfeut* from the first, or examine the latter on oath, they will find that the *whole truth* cannot be extracted from them. It is only when such officers as Mr. O—— and Mr. M—— have leisure to make the investigations themselves, that I have seen the truth dragged out as if with cart-ropes. I shall mention a case in point.

Lalla Lukhmee Lall had been a Government *Vakeel*, and had contrived to acquire considerable landed property, besides a large sum of ready money. At a sale, ordered by the Civil Court, he had purchased the rights and interests of *Goorbuksh Singh* in the village of *Guhora* for a very inconsiderable amount. By applying golden spectacles to the eyes of the *Qanoongo* and *Putwaree*, he managed to get his name entered as "*auction purchaser of the rights of Goorbuksh Singh Lumbardar of Guhora.*"* Now, it so happened, that the *Lumbardar's* name only had been entered in previous *jummabundees*, and the *Lalla* as purchaser of his rights, naturally took his place. The other sharers of the village alarmed, petitioned the Collector to cause their names also to be entered in the *jummabundee*, but the *Putwaree* and *Qanoongo* declared that their names were not in any previous years' *jummabundee*, nor in the *Putteedaree's statement* or "*Wagiboolurz*" of the *Mohtimin Bundobust*.† The papers were duly examined; and as the name only of *Goorbuksh Singh* was found therein, the *Saheb* disallowed the objections raised, and ordered *Lukhmee Lall's* name to remain as sole proprietor. It was only by undergoing a ruinously expensive law-suit, that the poor *Putteedars* gained their rights. You ask, naturally, how it happened that the several sharers failed to have their names recorded in the Collector's books? I will tell you in a few words.

* The party who pays the Government revenue into the treasury
† Settlement officer.

There are two brothers, joint-proprietors of an estate. They live in perfect harmony, and the name of the elder only is recorded as proprietor. The younger dies, leaving six sons, who of course, are entitled to one-sixth share each of their father's share. But they have always seen the estate managed by their uncle, and they will not interfere with the old man. Calamities of season occur, and the lads require money for their marriages, and a *Muhajun* is thought of. The emissaries of the *Lalla* recommend their Master as a considerate man and an *ushraf*, and he lends the old man money. The *Lalla* prosecutes in a court of law, in which he is an influential member himself—gains a decree—executes it—sells the rights of the old man, who was the sole *recorded* proprietor—buys them himself, and gets his name recorded in the government register. Now, the *Putwaree* and *Qanoongo* knew very well the exact state in which matters stood; and had they been honest men, and done their duty to the people and to the State, so serious an error as has been noticed, could never have happened. The dispossessed *Pulteedars* did get redress, it is true; but after an expenditure ruinous to their purse, through a tedious litigation and endless appeals, sufficient of themselves to cool the courage and energies of most men.

And after obtaining decrees from the Civil Courts, what use are they in nine cases out of ten? The *diggureedar* petitions the court to distrain cattle belonging to A. Immediately B. comes forward, and proves his possession; and although they are full-brothers, and collusion between them is manifest, yet the cattle are released. Another party sues for sale of a *Nuwab's* property consisting of houses and lands. His wife at once objects on the score of their being part of her marriage-dower! Her Vakeel produces the deed of settlement, and the property is released. In short, if the Legislative Council and the Suddur Courts had endeavoured to devise a means to harrass decree-holders, and to give them only "*the shells of the oyster*" for their speculations in matters of law, they could not have hit upon a more ingenious mode than confirming to them the present rules of practice, as regards the sale of property in execution of decrees.

CHAP. XXVI.

THE KOMMISHNUR KURKI.

The *Qanoongo* fattens most when it is the misfortune of any village to be made "*Kham Tuhseel*,"—*i. e.* where the *zemindar* becomes a defaulter, and no person offers to take a farming lease for a term of years and pay the balance; the Collector appoints a manager on his own part, called a *Suzawul*, to collect the rents, and in most cases the *Qanoongo* is chosen to fill this office. The first thing done, is to go to the village, assemble inhabitants, and ask for the *nuzurana* (good-will offering) for the *Sircar*. Nothing but silver is ever taken from the majority, but the *Suzawul* is content to commute the cash payment to the offering of a fat sheep. As soon as the sheep has been digested, the *asamees* are again summoned to adjust the new *jummabundee ba-moojibi hookoom Saheban Borud.** The *Brahmuns* are let off, lest they should curse the *Lalla*; but from every other caste, from 4 annas to 8 annas a beegah is rigorously exacted. As these sums are intended for the *Suzawul's* private purse, they are from a mere infirmity in the memory, omitted in the village accounts. The *zemindar's* dues are always enforced by the *Sircar's* representative. The shepherds present the younglings of their flocks; the barbers shave him, and sooth him to rest, or gently arouse him by the delicious pressure of the limbs known as *shampooing*; sometimes the young *Nayins* (barberesses) take the place of their husbands to lull the *Suzawul* to rest—the *Telees* furnish sufficient oil for a lamp to burn throughout the night—and thus a *Suzawul*, in charge of a large estate, is *the* picture of a happy man in the enjoyment of rural felicity and rural affluence. Many a feast do his friends receive at the expense of the villagers, and who would not feast, "eat, drink, and be merry," when all the material cost nothing? A case comes on before the Saheb Collector; the *Qanoongo* is ordered to attend. He cannot be found. Where is he? Nobody can tell. The *Nazir* roars out to me, "Go, Panchkouree, and bring that *Suhalunkar*,† that *Nimukharam*,‡ to the *Huzoor*. Go to his house; and if not there, go to the village of *Sundaha*, where he may be playing the *Suzawul*."

There is a trite saying, that "experience maketh fools wise." I should, when I first took service, have girded up my loins, and gone in search of the *Suzawul* at once; but I reflected on the inutility of hurried measures; so I went to my own house, ate a good dinner, rested comfortably, and departed next morning to search for the *Suzawul*. I went to his house, but the inmates had not heard of him for several days. I then proceeded to *Sundaha*, and while yet a good way from the *Chhaonee*, heard the music of a *Seringee* § and the screeching of a "*Ramzanee*."‖ I boldly made up to the assembled company, and inquired for the *Suzawul*. There was the fat *debauchee*, with a *hookah* in hand, indolently puffing and gazing on the "charming nautching damsel," and now and then varying the monotonous gravity of his deportment, by a nod or a yawn. He appeared intoxicated with *bhung*, and the flashes of light from the *Ramzanee's* eyes; utterance had forsaken him, although the time was barely past noon. "*Wah! Wah!*¶ *Qanoongojee*," I said; "the *Huzoor* remembered you yesterday; and since no person could tell whither you had

* Register of holdings, according to the orders of the Board of Revenue.
† Shirker of duty. ‡ Unfaithful to salt. § Native fiddle. ‖ Dancing woman.
¶ Well done!

gone, I have been desired by my master the *Nazir Saheb*, to bring you to the presence, and to report faithfully how I saw you engaged. *Inshallah*;* I shall make such a report as will be remembered by you." The *Suzawul*, although pretty well steeped in inebriety, was sobered at once by my salutation. He got up, begged of me to be seated next to himself, a *chillum* was handed to me, a kid was sent for, for a *pulao* for me. I reflected that I should act like a fool if I did not enter into the spirit of the moment: so I ungirdled my *kummerbund*, took off my *pugree*, puffed at the *chillum*, and ogled the dancing wench. I will draw a veil over the rest of the evening. Suffice it to say that I was convinced *Suzawulship* was an office of no small importance in the revenue departments of the State.

Next morning the *Qanoongo* and myself proceeded to the *Kacherree*, and I duly reported to the *Nazir* that the *Suzawul* was busy all day in collecting the rents for the *Sircar*, and that he could not possibly have come away sooner than he did.

But *the* great man, "*who plays fantastic tricks before high heaven*," is the *Kommishnur Koorkee*; and I have watched his doings with much edification. He has his *Sudder Kacherree*, and writes his *roobakarees* like a *Hakim*. As far as I could learn from the *Mooktyars* and *Mohurrirs* of the Collector's office, the duties of this officer are simply those of an Ameen of distraint and sale, for which he is entitled to a commission of ten per cent. *on the proceeds of sale*. And in the event of a compromise, or non-completion of sale, from any cause whatsoever, he is entitled to *five per cent. on the valuation of the property distrained*; the resources from this commission *only* would amount to about 35 or 40 rupees per mensem. The *Kommishnur Saheb* has to pay the rent of a suitable *kacherree*. He has a *Mohurrir* on seven rupees a month, *and six Chuppraseees*, at least, to whom he must give three rupees each. Thus, little enough, it would appear, is left for the provision of the great man, himself. He has, generally, a wife and several children at home. He sports a horse or palkee, keeps one or two servants, and a comely woman-servant, who acts as his *khidmutgar*. Money must be found for these expenses, and, by the blessing of the *Deotas*, who watch over the prosperity of the mysteries of chicanery, it is never wanting. Without tiring my readers with all the minutiæ of trickery, I shall just give a few examples of extortion.

A. sues B. for one hundred rupees, due to him as *malgoozaree*. He attaches property worth 50, but appraised at 25 rupees. The usual processes are gone through, and the property sold for 25 rupees. Out of this sum, the *Kommishnur* coolly deducts ten per cent. on the *zur-dawee* (amount of claim), which, in this case, is *ten rupees*, and the party who levied the distress receives but 15 rupees; whereas the *Kommishnur* was legally entitled to a tenth of 25 rupees, or 2 *rupees*, 8 *annas only*, instead of *ten rupees*. This iniquitious practice of misappropriation has been so far checked,

* Please God!

that is is not openly exhibited in the accounts, as it used to be in the "good old days."

Again, A. distrains the property of B. for an alleged claim of 100 rupees, but the property is appraised at only *ten rupees*. But a sale is not effected, owing to a compromise. Now, had a sale taken place, the *Kommishnur* would legally have received one-tenth of ten, or one *rupee*. But since no sale took place, he is entitled only to eight annas; however, he takes half the usual commission, or five per cent. *on the amount of claim*, from the unfortunate ryot, whose property had been distrained; *or five rupees*! It will thus be made manifest that he modestly takes only *ten times* the commission for doing nothing, instead of that which he would have received for effecting a sale ! ! !

An *asamee* has been allowed to cut his *khurreef** crop without his rent being demanded. He is in debt, and has paid away the greater part of his produce to the village *Muhajun;* when he finds *two beegahs* of half-grown *sugar-cane* distrained, and notice of sale advertised. If allowed to come to maturity, and the juice to be worked into *goor*, the two *beegahs* of cane would yield from 150 to 200 rupees; but the *zemindar* is resolved to ruin him. The poor *ryot* runs to the *Collector Saheb*, or the *Saheb Dipty*, and petitions against his grinding oppression. He is told to give *malzaminee*,† and to institute *Bejah Koorkee*.‡ He hypothecates the standing crops to his *Muhajun*, who becomes his surety, and the case is instituted. After the usual forms, the case is heard. The *ryot* does not deny that the claim is just, but pleads that if he had time granted him, he would pay the demand, and still save himself from ruin. The *Saheb* says, "*Wajib haee*."§ But the *Mooktyars* ask whether the zemindar is not entitled to receive the malgoozaree from the produce of the soil? They allege that the *khurreef* was cut and sold by the *ryot*, without paying the zemindar his dues; and that if the *Saheb Buhadoor* will now interfere, how is the zemindar to pay the revenue due to the *Sircar?* The *Moonshee-jee* quietly folds his hands to say his *iltimas*;|| and he urges that the sale of standing crops is authorised by usage. The case is dismissed and the sale ordered. And the poor ryot has the option of either permitting his half-grown crops to be purchased by the zemindar (*ism furzee*) in a fictitious name at a twentieth of the value, or of borrowing money from the *Muhajun* on the hypothecation of the crops, *at seventy-five per cent. per annum interest*.

Well, thought I, the *Koompanee ka Raj* is a paternal and fostering *Raj* for the poor ryots!

"Ill fares the land, to hastening ills a prey,
Where wealth accumulates and *men* decay;
Princes and Lords may flourish, or may fade,
A breath can make them, as a breath has made;
But a bold peasantry, their country's pride,
When once destroyed can never be supplied"

* Crop sown in the rains, and cut in October. † Money security.
‡ Suit for replevin. § It is correct. || Humble representation.

Chap. XXVII.

Local Juntee.—the Collector and Civil Surgeon.

There is an anomalous kind of court called the "*local juntee*" or *muhakimah aoukaf*—in English, local agency, which is as mysterious and uncontrollable as the *Supreme Court*, of which people say and hear so much. It is a simple enough court in itself, and *might* be made very useful; for it was established simply to look after the interests of government in *escheats*, from what cause soever, and to guard against the misappropriation of endowments for religious purposes of all creeds. The Collector and Civil Surgeon are the *ex-officio* local agents in every district; but they are at liberty, with the sanction of Government, to associate any other official with them, whose services may be found expedient. What could have induced our legislators to drag in the *Doctor Saheb* into the junta I know not; for there are no emoluments of office; and the work is "vexatious to a degree." Any blackguard in the city, of what caste or persuasion soever, that wishes to annoy, or to screw money out of a wealthy neighbour, gives in a *sowal*, signed *Khyr-khwah-i-sircar*,* alleging that his houses and lands are the *Nuzool* (property) of the State. If people are wise, they buy off the *Khyr-khwah*, otherwise they involve themselves with a mysterious power, that may, whenever it pleases, claim half the city, and contest the ownership of the property in the civil courts. This court is also notable for the *deliberation* of its decisions. Nobody can find out when the court sits; and the holy prophet only knows how long a case may be pending—it may be for days, or weeks, or months, or years! It bangs the equity side of the Supreme Court, by chalks, in its lentissimo progress. There is a characteristic story current in this city, of the late Mr Augustus Brooke, who was for so many years the Governor's Agent, and at one time chief judge of the provincial court of appeal. When he found a case so voluminous as to alarm his nerves, or (knowing the parties) he was convinced that the case was vexatious, he sent for the *Vakeels* of the litigants and said, "*Bhulla Babajan! ub myn mokuddumma ko ghourkhana men bhejta hoon*" (Well, my dear sons, I shall now send the case to my office of deliberation). The parties in such cases generally made a slow salam, and returned to their homes, satisfied that the deliberations of the *Huzoor* were postponed *sine die*; in other words, the case was burked. The result was understood, therefore the parties in despair never attended; a year afterwards, the cases were struck off the files in default. The sittings and judgments of the *local agency* are pretty similar.

* Well-wisher of Government.

Sometimes, however, when the local agents do bestir themselves for the public interests, they find their good intentions thwarted by parties who produce decrees of civil courts in their favor, for tenements and property that are undoubtedly public, and therefore inalienable. A wealthy individual builds a fine *suraee** for the accommodation of travellers, and to perpetuate his name, makes the establishment one of benevolence. His grandson after his death, gets in debt; and his creditor, after getting a decree in his favor from the civil court, indicates the *suraee* as the property of the defendant. He surrenders to them his rights and interests, the *suraee* is sold and the purchaser, as *malik*, levies his dues from the "*Bhutearahs*," who keep the stalls—in plain words, he levies a fixed hire from every occupant of the *suraee*; and this goes on for years. An energetic Collector happens to be appointed, who in character is a *ghureeb purwour*;† and knowing his duty, endeavours to recover for the agency the control over the *suraees*, mosques, *dewals*, wells, &c., which have slipped into individual hands, as the property of the public, which of course he maintains is inalienable: he asserts the right of the Government, through their local agents, to interfere and prevent this misappropriation of public property. But the *fact of possession for thirty years* ruins the cause, and the Civil Court decides against the agents.

A wealthy individual dies, leaving large property in houses, lands, villages, and ready money, by will, to be devoted to the performance of the rites of the Hindoo religion. An executor by will is also appointed. Some fifty years elapse, and a *Khyrkhwah* petitions the local agents to take possession of, and manage the property, on the score of misappropriation of funds, alienation of property, etc. Lengthened investigation takes place, law-suits are instituted, and won by the agents of the *Sircar*, and they take possession of the remainder of the property. Heirs of the original testator and the heirs of the legatee repeatedly come forward to take the management into their own hands; but the lion's grip is not more easily relaxed than the possession of the *local juntee*. The parties are referred to the Civil Courts, and the fact of malversation having been once proved against the legatee, the courts always decide for the *Sircar*. "But how are the funds appropriated?" you enquire. You will scarcely believe it, but on the faith of *Islam*, I swear that the money goes to feed the *Pundahs*, *Ghateahs*, *Poojarees*, and the host of the Brahminical tribe. I have witnessed with horror and astonishment, the daily rations of rice, *dall*, *atta*, *ghee*, doled out by order of the local agents, and the produce of several gardens, the flowers of the season, taken to the *dewals*, for offerings to the idols therein enshrined. Here, thought I, are the *Saheban Aleeshan*, who abuse the pure faith of *Islam*, and ridicule the *bootpurustee*‡ of the Hindoos; here are the direct organs and representatives of Government fostering idol-wor-

* Inn. † Cherisher of the poor. ‡ Idol-worship.

ship! I wished devoutly, that I had the power to appropriate the whole of the funds towards the building and endowment of a *musjid*;* for then I should have constituted myself the *moctuwullee*,† and have enjoyed in this life the blessings promised by the prophet to the faithful hereafter. But I consoled myself with the reflection, that idol-worshippers and their aiders and abettors would alike burn in the fires of Jehunnum.

I remarked, as a most singular fact, that in the large and rich city of *Kashee*, it *never* happened that any person, possessed of large property died without heirs and intestate. *Well-wishers* give in *sowals* purporting that *Baboo Fullanah* died intestate and without heirs; praying that the property should be confiscated to the use of government, and that the well-wisher be duly provided for. But a fellow at once comes forward, with a *Bukhshisnamah* (deed of gift) duly registered and witnessed, to prove himself the legal owner. The witnesses are summoned and examined on oath; and they swear to every particular of the deed of gift. Government is *flummuxed* (as the *Persians* say); and a clever scoundrel, who is no more entitled to the property than I am, enjoys the fruits of his nefarious ingenuity. Thus it happens also, that *Gosaeens* and *Mohunts* never die heirless. A favorite *Chelah*, or a well-favoured youth retained for the "*Dhundah*"‡ of the *Muhunt* or *Gosaeen*, generally manages to come in as heir.

But to cheat the government is a common practice of every day, and is considered a glorious achievement. It is when two, or three, or more heirs contest a property, and *every claimant produces a deed in his favour duly authenticated and registered*, that the skill of the parties is to be admired. Greek meets Greek. The party or parties in possession let the other claimants "do their worst." *They* sue in *forma pauperis* (emphatically known as "*papuree*") and are put to no expence in stamps and *Vakeel's* fees. But the unfortunate wight in possession has to pay every authorised and every possible kind of fee; and after spending some thousands, gets a decree in his favour, with costs chargeable to plaintiffs. They make their *salams* and leave the court, while the decree-holder finds it impossible to recover a *dumree*.§ As for the costs of stamped paper due by the pauper to Government, it is hopeless in most cases to expect to recover. The fact is, our legislators, from a too tender regard to justice, have encouraged the institution of suits in *forma pauperis*, to the great detriment of their own stamp revenue; and to the infinite annoyance of the legislators. Thus a beggar composedly claims *ten lakhs of rupees* as his inheritance, and gets a hearing without paying a cowree, while the defendant has to defend the case wantonly brought against him at an expence of several thousands.

* Mahomedan mosque. † Officiating priest.

‡ Personal Attendance. § A fractional part of a pice.

CHAP. XXVIII.

THE SURVEY AND OTHER OPERATIONS IN THE N. W. PROVINCES.

Most of my readers have heard of *Jan Burd Saheb Bahadoor's* famous *bundobust* of the North Western Provinces But few know the details of that settlement, and of the causes which rendered it a failure. My readers, therefore, will pardon a dry chapter, when it is written not so much for their amusement as for their instruction.

The whole of the ceded and conquered provinces laboured under the disadvantage of short leases for the revenue for a term of five or ten years. This unsettled people's minds; and there was a perpetual struggle between Government and the *zemindars*—on the part of the first to augment the revenue to its full proportion, which it was firmly believed stood clipt and reduced by low official jugglery, and on the other, to reduce the jumma by every mode of lying, fraud and bribery. The periodical revision of settlements, naturally forced upon the Government the retention of a large establishment for the express purpose of making the required settlements, and burdened it besides with the expense of highly-paid Revenue Boards, as well as their deputations over various parts of the country. The great desiderata were the precise limits of each estate, and, therefore, the exact area. This led to the appointment of young gentlemen of the Civil Service, as *Settlement Officers*, under Regulation VII. of 1822, and the employment of *Revenue Surveyors* to carry out the revenue measurements in the most efficient manner. The object was to settle at once, and for ever, the endless disputes of contested boundaries; to fix an equitable assessment on the lands with reference to the existing means and future capabilities of the villages from the Surveyor's returns and the Settlement Officer's personal observations; and to make long leases of twenty or thirty years with the *zemindars*, and thus induce them to lay out their capital in the improvement of the soil. In short to save, by one grand effort, the expense perpetuated by keeping up large establishments as had hitherto been the practice.

But the root of the evil was the ignorance of the officers to whom the work was intrusted, as to the exact nature of what they were required to perform The young Settlement Officers had to learn the rudiments of the revenue system, and the Surveyors were not instructed to prepare their papers, so as to tally in all points with the *records of the Collector's Office*. In the essential point of lists of estates in each *purgunnah* the returns of the survey and settlement officers differed materially. A confusion was made between *muhals and mouzahs* * In many

* A *muhal* is any portion of land which has a distinct entry in the revenue rent-roll. A *mouzah* means the lands of a village. Thus, a village may contain many *muhals;* and a *muhal* may be composed of several portions of separate and distinct mouzahs.

instances, the Collector, the Settlement Officer and Surveyor, were at open feud, or were privately bent on playing at cross-purposes, and thwarting each other. The Surveyors conceived that their duty was confined to measuring the lands in each *hulka, chukker*, or separate estate, as defined by the Settlement Officer. The Settlement Officer had a very difficult duty to perform. He had to show a great increase in the aggregate jumma of each *purgunnah*, and yet was to satisfy the people. At first these paper settlements and the undigested reports that accompanied them appeared to satisfy the superior authorities; but the *working* of the system proved bad. *Zemindars* could not afford to pay yearly losses. They tried a desperate game, and neglected the cultivation to induce a remission of revenue. Their estates were sold to recover the balances due to the *Sircar*. The new purchasers rack-rented the tenants, who fled, and affairs became worse than ever. Then came the Revenue Surveys, and a desperate struggle arose of bribery on the one hand, on a large scale, to prevent the real areas and resources of villages from being brought to light; and on the other hand, a vigorous endeavour to arrive at the actual truth by searching investigations. My readers will decide for themselves which party was likely to get the upper hand in the strife. It is notorious that every Native official, of whatever grade, not only was promoted by gigantic strides, but they all contrived to improve the opportunity for their own benefit—"*ba doulut Sircar!*"

The *principle* of the Revenue Settlements was excellent, and evinced the wisdom and practical skill of the legislature, and of the many able men who composed the Boards of Revenue. But the great mistake was to saddle the important undertaking with an order to go through a fixed quantity of work within a definite time, and to make the assessments as high as the country could possibly bear with reference to its means. It is true that several orders were issued to the Settlement Officers to make the *bundobusts* light, in order that the people might not be overburdened, at the same time keeping in view that government should receive its just dues. But to this order there could be but one construction, and it was like telling a cook to slaughter a calf, and then out of superfluous humanity to shed tears over the untimely fate of the unfortunate animal. Wherever remission was suggested, or an increase recommended, disproportionate to the *apparently* existing means, so many explanations were called for that officials grew wary and wise, and tried to square the statements so as to *appear* faultless. And yet it is hard to blame the higher officials for their suspicions. While some Settlement Officers, like the late lamented "*James Muir*," zealously and honestly pursued their arduous course amidst the blessings of thousands; others again contented themselves with hunting and shooting through the length and breadth of the district entrusted to them, and formed their opinion of the nature and value of the soil they had ridden over, intent only on their "*shikar.*" But I have gone far enough with my *prolegomena*, and shall return to the beginning of my subject, and show how the work proceeded.

A set of hungry *Ameens* were let loose upon the district, whose duty it was to set up earthen *termini* at every angle of the boundary of each estate. Of course they were paid by the job, but they were open to persuasion, when offered in the shape of coin; and when offers were not voluntary and satisfactory, they, by fair means or by foul, extorted large sums from the zemindars. On the least attempt at backing out, they were reported as men inclined to palm frauds to the *Peshkar*, who in turn sent up the reports to the Settlement Officers, and the Zemindars were roundly fined. Suppose the demarcation of a *purgunnah* completed, then the survey operations commenced.

First and foremost, a fat *Tindal* went to *every* large village, and gathering the notables together, he announced to them that the "*Paemash-ka-luskur* would encamp therein; and, mind friends he would say, "get ready ten thousand *maiks* (tent pins), large supplies of straw, and *chuppurs* for the stables and cook-rooms of the *Sahebs* of the establishment. This hint was always sufficient to induce the Zemindars to shell out handsomely, and to beg of the *Tindal* to represent to the "*Saheb-i-Mussah*"* that the village was not adapted for an encampment. The *Tindal* knew very well that the village was too much out of the way to be chosen by the Surveyor, so he pocketed the rupees, went on his way to the next large village, and repeated his experiment of selecting an encampment with similar success. Well, the encampment has been at length selected, and parties of *khulasees* sent out to prepare the villages for survey.

This process consisted in fixing the theodolite stations, and removing any obstructions in a direct line between every two stations, so as to admit of as correct chain-measurements as possible. But the line-cutters had a fine harvest. A rich crop of sugar-cane, or a fine old mangoe tree, or a peepul, held in veneration by the villagers, *would* come into the direct line. If the zemindars paid freely, the station was removed to one side to avoid the trees or the crops. If they asserted independence, a report of opposition to the survey was made, and in most cases the villagers were heavily mulcted by the Settlement Officer.

* Surveyor.

Chap. XXIX

PROCEEDINGS OF THE SURVEYORS.

The lines being prepared for survey, parties of Surveyors were sent out to measure the boundaries. This used to be carefully and satisfactorily done at first by European Assistants; but it was discovered in the course of time that it was *cheaper* to use Native Agency and to pay 25 rupees a month to a boundary Surveyor, instead of 150 or 200 to an Assistant. This notable discovery, however, did not answer its end. The Governor-General of the day, Lord William Bentinck, convened a meeting of *Revenue Surveyors* (officers in the military service) at Allahabad; and then and there resolved to carry through the great work *at once* by the employment of Native Agency under European supervision. It took some time, of course, to train Natives to their work; but it *was* at length accomplished, and the work then got on as rapidly as the projectors had anticipated. But the new *material* had odd notions of honesty, and, of course, adopted it, as it seemed to be most beneficial to individual interests. The Tindals nearly lost their monopoly, and the gathering of the harvest devolved on more influential hands. The *Lalla Saheb*, or, as he used sometimes to be styled, the *Kumpass-wala*, claimed and took the lion's share of the perquisites. But you ask, "How were the perquisites obtained?" Why, a common trick was for the *Kumpass-wala* to adjust his theodolite, and to pretend surprise that the magnetic needle would not play. The Tindal would anxiously inquire what was wrong. The *khulasees* would do the same. The zemindars present would thus have their curiosity excited, and would crowd round the theodolite with gaping mouths. At last the Tindal would venture to ask the *Lalla Saheb* whether the usual morning *pooja* to the instrument had been performed? This acted as a flapper to the *Lalla*; and he asked his next neighbour, a zemindar, to put a rupee on the glass of the needle. It was done; but deuce a bit would it move. The attraction is not sufficiently strong, he would say, try another. This was done until the patience of the villagers was exhausted, and they had put down as many as ten rupees. The *Lalla* gingerly touched the catch, and the needle swung round to the astonishment and edification of the villagers. The rupees were pocketed, and divided afterwards among the whole of the party. But the ordinary mode was to induce the zemindars to believe that the *Kumpass-wala* had it in his power to increase or decrease the area of the village by a single squint at the *Kumpass*.

Many an amusing story did I hear of this wonderful *Kumpass*. It possessed the power of reversing everything observed. Hence, if you looked through the *doorbeen** at a fort, everything *inside* was revealed! Thus the *Feeringhees* so readily took forts: not by skill or by valour, but by means of the wonderful power of the *doorbeen*. A young *Rajpoot*, who was a gay deceiver among the

* Telescope.

softer sex, asked whether the *doorbeen* would shew a woman with her head downwards. "To be sure it would," was the reply. "But what is your object?" "Why," said he, "if the feet be uppermost, the clothes must fall down over the head, and what fun that would be!" The story got wind; and if ever a village woman approached a *Kumpass-wala's* party, she squatted down, and covered herself well; so that no exposè should take place, if the *doorbeen* were directed at her.

The boundary survey over, a party of detail measurers went out to measure the cultivation. If the zemindar feed highly, a good portion of cultivated land was put in as fallow or waste; and specifications of soil noted so favourably as to induce a belief that the cultivation was not highly productive. The item of irrigation was exaggerated in the same manner. There were *no* wells, *no* ponds, *no* streamlets to furnish an adequate supply of water. If the zemindar did not pay, then a picture diametrically opposite was drawn and submitted. The cultivation was increased; every deserted field on which the furrow of a plough was faintly visible, was included under the head of cultivation. The barren waste was entered as "arable," and even tracts of pure sand were represented as fertile. Every field was highly irrigated, and the sources of irrigation multiplied

It was soon found that a detail-survey, such as I have attempted to describe, was of little service to the Settlement Officer. There was, in the first place, no data for an *asameewar* settlement; and, secondly, the extent of cultivation was more than doubtful. Then was introduced the admirable mode of *khusrah surveys*; a most excellent mode of procedure if you can look sufficiently sharp after the *Ameen*, to force him to be honest and correct. The mode of procedure was as follows Well-trained *Ameens* were sent to sketch and measure *each separate field* with an iron chain, which was occasionally tested at head-quarters. This map, when completed, was called a "*shujrah*;" and exhibited every detail on a large scale. A register-book, called a "*khusrah*," shewed the number of every field, the name of the cultivator, the length and breadth, the area in local *beegahs*, the denomination of soil, and whether the field was irrigated or otherwise, and from what source. But the evil was, that the Surveyor was bound to perform a certain quantity of work within a fixed time; and it was physically impossible for him to look after a hundred or more *Ameens*, spread over a wide tract of country. A natural jealousy between the establishments of the Surveyor and Settlement Officer induced the latter to scrutinize too carefully the work of the Surveyor's *Ameens*, and at last a compromise was effected. The Settlement Officer placed at the Surveyor's disposal an establishment of examiners and testers, who reported to the Surveyor; and this officer *re-tested* the work of the Settlement Officer's men. This was done by drawing, at random, red lines over the surface of the field map; on which lines the examiners proceeded, and so did the Surveyor himself. But it will be palpable to the understanding of everybody, that only a small portion of the *khusrah* work *could* be thus tested. This arrangement, however, was a grand thing for the Surveyor; for the papers having once been filed in the Surveyor's office, with the verification of the Settlement Officer's testing *Ameens*, the responsibility was removed from the former department, and saddled upon the latter. But I shall proceed to give the reader some notion of the "*modus operandi*" of the *khusrah Ameens*.

At the commencement of the *khusrah* surveys the simple and unsophisticated mode of measurement with *ropes* of Indian hemp, or thongs of leather, was adopted. But let any one that chooses try the experiment; and he will be astonished at the difference of measurement with the same rope, when in a dry, and when in a wet state. Testing was out of the question; for the most startling discrepancies were put down to the score of contraction and expansion of the ropes! To prevent such excuses, iron chains, formed of a stated number of links, and of the size of half a square of a local *beegah* were introduced. I may as well say that every *beegah*, whatever may be its size, is a square of twenty "*lutthas*" or poles. Each chain was therefore divided into *ten lutthas;* and each *luttha* into ten links. If a zemindar paid handsomely, each *luttha* was lengthened by the addition of one link; and if he would not pay, it was shortened in the same proportion. Thus the area of every field, and consequently of the entire cultivation, was increased or decreased to a considerable degree. Where bribery took root to any extent, it went throughout the establishment of the *testers* and the *Mohurrirs* and *Moonshees* of the Survey and Settlement office; and every return was *fudged,* as school-boys term it.

It once so occurred, that in a whole *purgunnah* of a certain district, the survey papers shewed *no irrigation* throughout its entire length and breadth. The Surveyor and Settlement Officers resolved to see with their own eyes, and sent their tents into the *purgunnah.* Next morning they proceeded to inspect several villages It was in the month of November, when, if the rains closed early, irrigation is resorted to for producing the young *rubbee* crops. Marks of old water-courses were to be seen in abundance, but not a well was visible. Very odd! they thought; "Let us follow these water-courses from the fields, and see where they will lead to." It was done; but it ended in a large stack of bajra-stalks (*kurbee*). They tried another, and a third, but the result was similar. At last, grown desperate, they commenced removing a stack, when several of the villagers begged of them to desist, lest some accident should occur. They *did persist,* however, and discovered that a well was hidden by the stack of kurbee!!! They tried several more experiments, with the same satisfactory result. The *Ameens* were fined heavily, and the *testers* turned off! and so disgusted was the Settlement Officer at the trick played upon him, that he taxed every field at the highest rate of a field properly irrigated, whether it had such advantage or not.

CHAP. XXX.

THE SETTLEMENT OFFICERS' DUTIES.

In the matter of irrigation, soil, average of produce, name of the holder of the field, and even his *caste*, the *Ameens* reaped a rich harvest. I have already shewn how statements regarding the first were falsified. As the criterion of the produce of the soil generally is formed from its quality, the returns were ordinarily made to suit the ultimate views and ends of the *Ameens.* The name of the holder was a most important point, and which the Surveyors themselves did not understand rightly; and the changes under this head occasioned serious mischief. The distinction of *Seer lands** and *Sikhmee Asamees*† and hereditary cultivators was not understood, or not regarded. When an opulent *Asamee* of the Rajpoot or Brahmin castes asserted independence, and would not pay, he was recorded as a "*Chumar!*" When the register of holdings was publicly tested, and *fullanah Chumar* called, no answer was returned from sheer pride of caste; and the unfortunate wight was obliged to petition the Settlement Officer, and to fee the *Qanoongo* and *Mohurrirs* handsomely to get his name correctly entered. But what I have said was merely the light skirmishing of irregular troops—the real seat of war was the *Kacherree-i-paemash;* and the chief plunderers were the *Moonshees* and their satellites in that department.

When a *Khusrah* was tested and signed by the Surveyor, it was sent into the *Moonsheekhanah.* Now, the signature was confined to the leaf shewing the *total area.* Nightly durbars were held by the *Moonshee-jee*, and large sums were paid him to *falsify the papers entirely.* The page shewing the total area, and bearing the Surveyor's signature, was the same, but the details were entirely changed. This was proved to have occurred in the *district of Futtehpoor;* and what guarantee is there that similar tricks and deception were not, more or less, universal?

The survey-papers are at length prepared, and such as they are, sent to the Settlement Office. What did the *mohtimim bundobust* do to correct them? He could not cry down the *khusrahs*, because his own establishment had pronounced them to be correct. The most that was attempted was a revision of the names of the cultivators, *ferisht ba dulmewesee*; but the same causes that disfigured the accuracy of the survey papers, were here also in full operation, and the result was "confusion worse confounded."

* Lands entered in the names of proprietors, and cultivated either by themselves or their under-tenants.

† Under-tenants, whose names are not registered.

Now came the actual responsibilities of the Settlement Officers' duties. He had to fix a rental upon each *muhal.* He had to apportion the *malgoozaree* of each *ryot* to the extent of his holding. He had to adduce reasons for the reduction or increase of the revenue The proper mode would have been for the *Saheb mohtimm* to proceed into *every village* and judge for himself, and *then* to decide this important point. But, alas! few had the inclination to take so much trouble; and even if they had, they were hampered by the orders of the superior authorities. They were expected to go through a certain quantity of work; and to save their credit they did so, but to the frustration of the object for which government had appointed them. A common mode was to divide each *purgunnah* into a number of imaginary portions—assuming that each portion consisted of similar soil and facilities for irrigation Suppose, in passing his order, the *Mohtimm bundobust* were to declare that such a *purgunnah* had the finest soil and was extremely well watered: a Zemindar present insinuated, with folded hands, "*Gureeb purwar mera sub dhurtee bullooa hace! panee nahee!*"* The *Saheb* would say, "Did I not ride through the *purgunnah* on my way to shoot tigers?" "But, sir, my village is five coss off the road!" "What of that, fellow! am I blind, or shall I see through *your* eyes?" The *Saheb* chuckled at his own wit, and the *Sherishtadar* and *Peshcars,* as in duty bound, laughed sardonically, and exclaimed—"*Ayee! kumbukht! Huzoor undha hae!!!*"†

Thus it will be seen, that, by assuming an arbitrary standard, a false valuation of the estates was, as a consequence, made. Scores of really profitable *muhals,* that were assessed on the *average,* were very greatly under-rated; while other estates that were poor, and whose productiveness fell *under* the average by being lumped with their more profitable neighbours, were irretrievably ruined. The reports of settlement were plausible enough and read well; but the results of experience prove the falsity of the data upon which the settlement operations were based. In calculating the means of a village, the ordinary mode was to take the average of the rates of *malgoozaree,* and thereby multiply the number of *beegahs* under cultivation, to deduct therefrom the ordinary village expenses, and ten per cent. for the Zemindar's *malikana* (or dues for right of management), and the balance was the government *jumma.* Suppose an estate with 1,000 *beegahs* of cultivation, and the average *malgoozaree* rate to be three rupees a *beegah,* the gross assets would be assumed at 3,000 rupees. There are two *chowkedars* and one Goraiat at two rupees a month each, and a *Putwaree* at four rupees. The annual expense would be 120 rupees. The *mali-*

* Cherisher of the poor! the whole of my lands are sand—there is no water!

† Oh! evil fortune! is "the presence" blind?

kana at ten per cent. would be 300 rupees. The accounts would stand thus:—

Hal hasil (present assets) .... Rs.	3,000
Deduct *malikana* at 10 per cent...	300
Rupees.	2,700
Deduct wages of village servants, ...	120
Balance, or Government revenue	2,580

By the above calculation it will be seen that the Government revenue bore the extraordinary proportion of 86 *per cent on the gross returns.*

But the duties of a Zemindar do not consist only in receiving the rents from the *ryots*. He is obliged, or he *should* be obliged, to make advances to the needy villagers for seed, for the purchase of cattle, and for alleviating calamities of season. He is obliged to renew old wells, to dig new ones, and to incur a pretty considerable figure in *nuzzurs* to the *Qanoongo*, the *Tahseeldar*, and the *Darogah* of police. None of these items are ever taken into account; and however much the notion of allowing or conniving at such fees may be repudiated, yet *they are extorted;* and, therefore, some allowances should be made for this *secret service* expense. Let any one that is doubtful, purchase a pair of oxen and a plough, and cultivate one or five, or ten *beegahs* of land. Let him set down carefully every item of expenditure, including the expense of irrigation. Let him add to all this the ground rent to the Zemindar and the interest on the money expended. Then take the current or average price of grain and bhoosa, and set both calculations of expenditure and profit in juxta-position, he will then have some notion of the large profits of an agriculturist.

But the roguery of the Zemindars themselves was amusing; and the way in which they cheated the Settlement Officers astonished me. One fellow had 150 beegahs of very inferior land on one side of his estate, and during the demarcation he himself cut it off from his village. The neighbouring Zemindar was only too glad to get 150 beegahs for nothing that did not belong to him; so he held his tongue. On the opposite side of the village there were some exceedingly rich fields, which the Zemindar claimed as a portion of his estate that he had been fraudulently deprived of. About two years after, when the *bundobust* was being made, he petitioned that his estate was estimated at 1,000 beegahs, whereas the survey made the area 750 beegahs. He alleged that a neighbouring village had a larger area than he was assessed for, and prayed that the papers of the last *bundobust* should be examined. He gained his point, and at a trifling expense gained 150 beegahs of the richest land for the same quantity of the worst description abandoned in another direction.

In the *Turaee*, vegetation is so rank, that lands, deserted for a couple of years, are so thickly covered with long grass jungle as to induce a belief that the plough had never furrowed it. The unconscious Surveyor and Settlement Officer shot *floriken* and *black partridges* in these plots of land; and, of course, readily believed that they were part of the uncultivated jungle. The *bundobust* over a hundred ploughs rooted up the grass, and smiling fields of plenty rewarded the Zemindar and cultivator for their ingenuity in deception.

CHAP. XXXI.

THE DEPUTIES' DUTIES.

I have hitherto spoken of the Settlement Officers only, and shall now notice the *Deputies* who played a very important part in the settlement operations. In most instances, they adjudicated all disputes connected with the revenue; and an appeal lay from their decisions to the Settlement Officer, in the same way as appeals lay from the orders of the latter, to the Commissioner of Revenue. In most instances the Deputies employed on settlement were Natives of the country, Hindoos of the *Kayesth* tribe and *Moosulmans*. There were queer stories told of some of these worthies; and complaints of a serious nature were, on more than one occasion, made to the highest authorities against them; but the petitions were disregarded. "We cannot afford to listen to complaints against men who get through their work so well" —or, "Whenever a public officer does his duty the people are sure to abuse him, and to charge him falsely," &c., was the usual way of disposing of these matters. Of course, this leaning in their favor inspired them with fresh confidence, and they went to work under the hope of impunity. If these gents would not work well, it was not imputed to their inefficiency or unwillingness; but their salaries were increased to induce them to exert themselves! Thus conduct which would have sufficed to damage the reputation and prospects of an European officer, most extraordinarily went to elevate the character and fortunes of the Natives, an anomaly that at this distant time we are surprised to find was gravely sanctioned.

I was much amused at the way in which zemindars were hunted out and discovered, and rights forced upon people who had ceased to *hope* for them. But, it may be said, that it is never too late to do justice. True, I reply; if the justice (so called) to one does not involve a greater injustice to another. In the North-Western Provinces entire *purgunnahs* were held by single individuals, who called themselves Rajahs—for instance, *purgunnahs Koothar* and *Powaeen*, in zillah *Shajehanpore*—who had usurped property by the sharp argument of the sword, previous to the acquisition of the province by the British

Government, and were afterwards, for years, recognised as proprietors without question. These large proprietors mismanaged their property, and rack-rented the *ryots*, and the local government ordered *Mofussil* settlements to be made with the *Purdhans* and *Moquddums*. The entire management was taken out of the hands of the *Talooqdars*, and they were allowed a per centage, or *malikana*, on the Government assessment. But there was a peculiarity in the tenures of the *province of Benares*; and it is to this province that my allusion applies as to the hunt for zemindars.

The peculiarity in the tenure was this. When *Junab Jonatheen Dunkeen Bahadoor* made his famous ten years' settlement of *Sircar* Benares, previous to completing an *istimraree*, or perpetual *bundobust* for the Government revenue, engagements were entered into with the zemindar, or with any parties that would accept of the offered conditions. In A. D. 1795, when the perpetual settlement was completed, *farming arrangements* were made in all those *muhals*, the zemindars of which would not engage with Government, or where the zemindars' rights were not clearly proven. The *revenue* was fixed in perpetuity; but it was ruled by *Dunkeen Bahadoor* that on proof of the rights of zemindars before the Civil Courts, they were to be put in possession of the zemindaree in dispute. Some parties *did* prove their rights, and *did* get possession through the Civil Courts. But in a great number of instances, the farmers, or their heirs, had kept undisputed possession since 1795, up to 1840-41, when the revision of settlement took place. The common feeling and the public opinion were in favour of the old farmers. They had held possession for *forty-five years*, during which time no person claimed the zemindaree. They had fulfilled every condition of their agreement, and naturally looked upon themselves as the *de facto* zemindars. But it was ruled that farmers had no rights; and to pretend to regard them as zemindars was absurd. The settlement Officers were directed to find out the heirs, lineal or collateral, of the old zemindars, and to make zemindaree settlements with them.

A period of nearly half a century had elapsed and the generation contemporary with *Dunkeen Bahadoor's bundobust* had passed away. But to hunt out their heirs was the object to be effected, and the Settlement Deputy Collectors were ordered on this duty. No sooner was it known to the people at large that such was the desire of the *Sircar*, than scores of claimants for dormant zemindarees started into existence. One proved that he was in possession of a mangoe tree which had once formed part of a grove that had been planted by his ancestor, who was zemindar. Another alleged that the mounds of an old *gurhee*, or fort, in the village, had been in possession of his grandfather. A third asserted that a *pukka* well, in ruins, on the roadside, had been built by his progenitor (*ajah* or *mooris alah*—means like the Scotch expression *forbears*, indiscriminately applied to any progenitor beyond a grandfather.) Some of the grey-beards of the village deponed accordingly as their memories were prompted by the influence of *silver*. The Qanoongo managed to get hold of a dirty bit of paper called a "*polindah*," in which it was mentioned that a certain individual was zemindar prior to the British Government, and the Qanoongo *had heard* that the said person was an ancestor of one of the claimants. Well, to cut short the story, a settlement was made with one of these parties to the entire exclusion of the farmer resident for nearly half a century.

People were amazed at such proceedings. They shrugged their shoulders and said "*Kea kurreh; hookoom Hakim ka haee!** It would surely have been an act of grace becoming our rulers to have boldly asserted that as no parties had proved their rights to the zemindaree when formerly invited to do so, the rights had escheated to Government; and that in consideration of the long possession of the *Moostajirs*,† Government had made over those rights of zemindaree to them. But this was not done, and there appeared to be a confusion of ideas on the subject; for it not unfrequently occurred that a Deputy's order was reversed by the Settlement Officers, and the Settlement Officer's order reversed by the Commissioner, whose order was again upset by the Board, in one continual round of cross-purposes.

A common occurrence was to lengthen out the proceedings of the Deputies as unmercifully as it was possible; so that no *European* patience could stand the verbiage and the round-about allusions of the *roobukarees*. Every one knows how easy it is for a Native writer to spin out to endless length what could have been expressed in a few lines; and my readers will not be greatly surprised to learn that when the appeals from the Deputies' proceedings were numerous, the patience of the appellate authority was exhausted, and was glad to leave matters alone, except in cases of glaring partiality.

The preparation of the *putteedaree* papers, and the declaring the shares of the several proprietors, was a source of great gain; and as this part of the work was also hurried, it was badly done, and gave dissatisfaction to the people. Some parties that had no right whatever to any portion of an estate, managed to get themselves re-recorded proprietors, and one clever rogue, *Pudarut Singh*, contrived to acquire large possessions. *Pudarut* first of all used A. in the Civil Court for a twelve anna share, or three-fourths of the village of *Danealpoor*. A notice was duly served on A., and he replied, that he was not in possession, and knew nothing of *Pudarut's* claim, but still he had to defend a vexatious suit. Upon this, *Pudarut sumjhaoed* him and offered to pay costs of suit, and to give him a hundred rupees into the bargain if he would file an *ekbal dawee*. "You can lose nothing my friend, for I wish to fight it out with

* What can be done? It is the order of the rulers. † Farmers.

Ameer Alee; and if I get *Danealpoor*, you will obtain possession of a quarter as my *Putteedar* for nothing." The bait was swallowed, and an *ekbal dawee* filed. *Pudarut Singh* bided his time with consummate patience; he was not fool enough to contest the ownership of *Danealpoor* with *Ameer Alee*, for he was aware he would not succeed. But after the conclusion of the revision of settlement, *Pudarut Singh* very coolly put his claim for three-fourths, or 12 annas in every estate that had been settled with A. The *ekbal dawee* filed in the Civil Court, in the case of *Danealpoor*, was adduced by *Pudarut* as a proof of his right, his claim was acknowledged, and he was put in possession.

Chap. XXXII.

THE DUTY OF THE REVENUE AUTHORITIES.

The settlements over, and the *putteedaree* papers prepared, there still remained the very important matter of preparing the *jummabundees* (registers of holdings). If that which concerns the greatest number be of the greatest importance, then the *jummabundees* were the most important part of the settlement work. It was "the book" of the poor cultivator, and by it, mainly, would be decided every case of dispute for rent or replevin between landlord and tenant. The enlightened, humane and distinguished gentleman who governs at this moment the destines of the N. W. Provinces, was fully aware of the importance to be attached to these papers. *Junab Jan Burd Saheb* reiterated his injunctions on this head; but they made a grand mistake, in taking for granted that their orders would be carried out. And hither again the *incubus* that weighed painfully on the settlement operations transferred its morbid weight. *The work was to be done within a given time.* The Deputies issued *dustucks* upon the zemindars, and forced them to pay *tullubana* until the jummabundees were filed. The *Putwarees* were seized, brought into camp, and coerced to prepare the papers on a model they did not understand, and which could only have been properly prepared in the villages themselves, the *ryots* had few opportunities to object to the entries respecting themselves, and the register of holdings was an imaginary register, prepared by the *Putwaree* at random, to escape duress, or instigated by parties who had a design to effect. The superior authorities directed that a copy of the *Jummabundee* of every village should be proclaimed by beat of drum in the village; and then be kept in the most public place for fifteen days, to enable people to satisfy themselves of its correctness. But few of the cultivators, comparatively, can read; and those that could, and were curious, tried the experiment; but found that the pages "were a sealed book to their understanding." A villager found that numbers were fixed on his fields. Nobody could tell him how they were to be recognised in the field. He was dissatisfied and gave a petition on stamp paper to the Deputy, objecting to the *Jummabundee*. The *Putwaree* was asked to explain what was equally unintelligible to himself. He asked the villager— "*Tor Jote men lumber dus bah?*"* "*Gosyneah janeh!*"† was the reply. "*Urreh! lumber dus pokhur oopur bah yanuhee?*"‡ "*How?*" granted the *ryot*. "Again, is not No. 5 in your *jote?*" "The Lord knows!" "What, is not the field to the west of No. 100 in your jote?" "No." The *Putwaree*, however, swore it was; and the entry remained as it stood at first.

I cannot call the attention of the revenue authorities too strongly to this important point—the correction of the *jummabundees*. It should have been a work of time and of patient, laborious, and *honest* investigation. The Deputies should have been forced to pitch such a number of camps in every *purgunnah*, as would have enabled them to redress the real or imaginary wrongs of every *asamee* by personal and pains-taking local inquiry. What is palpable to the understanding at a glance, can never, except by some lucky chance, be elucidated by the examination of witnesses. I have shewn that the *jummabundee* papers were filed according to a form that was not understood, and which, by a ridiculous misinterpretation, was known as the "*nuksha-i-paragraff*" (Because a Settlement Officer directed the preparation of the papers according to a certain paragraph of the Board's Circular orders.) In this, all that was attempted was to fix, as they best might, the numbers of every field on the holdings of the several *asamees*, so as to make the *jummabundee* tally, *apparently*, with the Survey and Settlement papers. No thought was given to exhibit the actual state of things, or to correct inaccuracies that crept in during a course of years.

I will relate what actually occurred within the limits of Sircar Benares, not ten years ago, to shew the necessity of personal inspection. There was a village, in which the zemindar alleged, that the river Ganges had swallowed up *three hundred beegahs* of the best land, subsequent to the survey of the district; and he therefore prayed that a corresponding reduction in the *jumma* should be made. Inquiries were made through the *Qanoongo* and *Putwaree*, who deponed on oath to the fact of the alleged encroachment of the river. The *Huzoor* allowed the remission, "*Ta hookoom sanee.*"§ In another case, the same officer received a petition from certain zemindars and *ryots*, praying that the revenue on *one hundred and fifty beegahs* of land be remitted, on the score of "*Bullooa-boord.*"|| This was also allowed, "*Ta molahaza Huzoor.*"¶ As most of my readers will be puzzled to know what "*Bullooa boord*" means, I will explain by telling

* Is No. 10 in your Jote (holding)?
† God knows.
‡ What? Is not No. 10 on the tank?
§ Until further orders.
|| Smothered in sand.
¶ Until inspection.

them that the literal translation is, *buried under sand*. The claim in this instance was founded on the allegation, that one hundred and fifty *beegahs* of rich land had been so covered over by the sand of the Ganges river, as to be no longer culturable. It so happened for the punishment of the iniquities of the aforesaid petitioners, that the investigation of these two cases was made over to an officer who could understand the survey papers, and who was not in the habit of trusting implicitly to *kyfeuts*, however well attested; and he mounted his horse and rode to the spot. On comparing the *shujrah* (or field map) with the spot alleged to have been destroyed by the encroachment of the river, he found, to his astonishment, that the entire fields were intact, and that, owing to the high bank of the river and its escarpment, it was physically impossible for the river to be guilty of any usurpation of seignioral rights. And on proceeding to the spot alleged to have been buried under sand, he found, to his surprise, that the fields indicated in the petition for remission were the *richest and best cultivated in the vicinity!!!* The proper orders were passed, and the *Putwarees* punished by dismissal from office. Now, I would ask, how was it possible for any officer to satisfy himself as to the merits of the case before him, such as I have described, without personal inspection?

And since the jummabundees prepared by the Settlement Deputies were not attempted to be vested by personal inspection, another error was allowed to creep in, which shewed the ingenuity of the zemindars, but was no proof of their foresight. In some resumed *maufee** villages, where the settlement officers were ordered to assess the *muhal* at half the calculated assets, the exmaufeedars exhibited a false rental, in which every *asamee* was put down at one-half of his actual rate of *malgoozaree*. The consequence was that the Government jumma was fixed at *one-fourth* of the actual assets, instead of *one-half*. The jummabundee "*paragraff*" being duly filed, a year or two was allowed to elapse, and then the zemindar petitioned the Collector to be permitted to increase the rates, alleging that he had *just found out* that the *Putwaree* had falsified the *mohtimim's paragraff*. But this prayer was denied, on the ground that he had been guilty of deception, and had wilfully caused his *Putwaree* to mis-state facts, and that he must abide by the consequences. In a similar manner several zemindars filed jummabundees, barely equalling the Government revenue in amount, in the hope that a reduction in the revenue would be made. But a settlement in perpetuity is not so easily set aside, and the invariable result of such roguery was to the loss of the zemindar, and the gain of the *ryot*.

Ever since the jummabundee of the Settlement Office, what has ever been attempted to correct it? *Nothing*. The rule seems to be to warp every succeeding year's *paragraffs*, so as to

* Exempt from revenue.

correspond with the papers filed at the Settlement. The names of defunct parties are entered, as the cultivating *asamees*, and, despite the natural fluctuations in village rentals, the papers are made to correspond, year after year, with almost literal exactness. But how is this to be remedied ? Let one Deputy be set apart for these jummabundees and summary suits *alone*, in every district ; and if there be still complaints of error, why, turn him out. The present strength of the establishment is insufficient for more than the current duties.

Chap. XXXIII.

Moonsiffs, Sudder Ameens, Principal Sudder Ameens, Zillah Judges and the Sudder Dewanee Adalut.

I have endeavoured to expose a few of the blemishes in the administration of the Revenue and Criminal departments ; and I shall now notice the *Dewanee Adalut*. My readers will not expect much legal knowledge from "*An Orderly*, so I shall confine myself to noticing facts that have occurred, and which do occur every day in these Courts, and the truth of which may be verified by any one that chooses to make inquiry of the *people*. With all the present extra machinery of Government in this department, the several grades of *Moonsiffs, Sudder Ameens, Principal Sudder Ameens,* and learned Judges, the system does not work to the satisfaction of the people. As in a piece of machinery having a multiplicity of wheels, the stoppage of a minor wheel will prevent the revolution of the larger ones, so in the machinery of the *Dewanee* Courts the wheels are sometimes checked now at the small end, presently at a medium one, and again at the main wheel, which appears to move all the rest ; and the whole will not go on smoothly until they are sufficiently greased by the "*oil of palms*" in the minor division. And here I would have it distinctly understood that my remarks will apply not to any individual, or to any zillah, but to the whole system, as a machine, in which there are some screws loose.

As in duty bound, let me begin at the lowest end, and show how justice is done by a Moonsiff. The son of a *Lalla* earning *ten rupees* a month, who from childhood is, of necessity, conversant with all the petty chicanery and fraud practised around him, becomes a Mohurrir, or writer to a *Vakeel*. He is brought up at the feet of *Gamaliel* like *Paul*, to become a persecutor ; and as in Paul's case, a miracle must be worked for his conversion. After a few years, the lad finds that he can aptly quote the regulation or construction, or precedent which gained such and such a case. He has a tenacious memory, and is naturally sharp-witted, and aspires to become a Moonsiff. He fees the *Serishtadar*, who certifies to his respectability to the judge, who allows his name to be entered as a candidate, and he is permitted to stand an examination. In the statement presented to the judge, the lad styles himself zemindar; because, forsooth, his father has a *on e pie* share in a small village, which may yield him, perhaps, 24 rupees per annum. In the questions put to the candidates, little else is required to answer them than a retentive memory and a knowledge of the usages of the Courts. No questions are put to test their having been well-grounded in jurisprudence; no attempt to ascertain the nature of their education, and the depth or shallowness of their understanding. The lad passes his examination, receives his diploma, and, when a vacancy occurs and fortune favours him, he is elevated to the rank and office of a Moonsiff.

Behold the *Lalla* is dropped, and changed for the title of a *Rae Bahadoor* by virtue of his office. He dons an *ummama* or turban, and envelopes himself in an ample *kubba*. He seats himself crossed-legged in a chair (to be on a par with his superior, the *Saheb* Judge) and moves about his head like a porcelain "*Chinese Mandarin,*" and occasionally shakes his caput like a "Burleigh" to show his extraordinary wisdom. For, be it known, that the heavier a *Kayesth's* head is stuffed with the jargon of the law, the more violently must it play at "*See-saw*" during his pretended or real cogitations. A case comes on. *Baboo Dabee Dyal Singh* versus *Mosummat Dilchusp*, claiming 100 rupees, with interest thereon at 12 per cent: The *Vakeel* of plaintiff produces the bond duly signed and witnessed. The writer of the bond and the witnesses are summoned. They depone upon oath to the fact of having witnessed the defendant come to the house of the plaintiff, and of her having received the coin, and of her having asked them to witness the transaction. The defendant is served with a notice according to established form. She sends for a *Vakeel* and asks advice. It is a cursed lie, she tells him; the bond is a fabrication, and the plaintiff and witnesses unknown to her. She asks the *Vakeel* whether he believed *she* would condescend to borrow a paltry hundred rupees, when, from the *Baboo* to the *Rajah*, all are the slaves of her youthful charms? The *Vakeel* shakes his head in incredulity, and assures her of his best services, but hints that it will be necessary for her to *prove* that she did *not* receive the money, and did *not* write the bond. She throws her fingers out in the face of the *Vakeel* with a "*tobah*!" and desires him to get a decree in her favour and to leave her in peace. The *Vakeel* thinks over the matter, but can find no loop-hole for his client to creep through, except the Moonsiff *Saheb* himself favour her, or that fraud and lying on one side be encountered with a similar array on the other side. He wisely adopts the latter course. He suborns witnesses, who prove that Mosummat *Dilchusp* did send by them the sum of one hundred rupees to *Baboo Debee Dyal Singh*, the plaintiff, with ten rupees for interest thereon. A receipt is produced, which the witnesses recognise upon oath as being the receipt of the plaintiff, and the case is dismissed with costs.

Answer me, ye sapient! who is to blame for using such questionable means to escape the fangs of the law? And yet, without opposing fraud by fraud, how is villany to be encountered. Moral obligations must cease to have influence when the law, which is supposed to protect, is not sufficient to check the atrocious practices which subvert its best ends. Hence ignorant men like myself and my brethren, infer that if the law cannot protect us, we must do so ourselves; and since the law cannot penetrate through the mysterious veil of villany and punish it signally, we must adopt cunning to overthrow conspiracy.

A very false argument is commonly made use of to defend the selection of Moonsiffs from the lower orders of the people—viz, that they are intimately acquainted with the prejudices, the feelings, and the customs of the country; and that they will, therefore, more readily afford satisfactory justice to the *people*, than officials who have no common interest with them. But this is the cant of theory. Ask the *people* themselves, and they will tell you what is acknowledged in all parts of the world, that the *people* naturally look up to the well-born and the well-educated as their protectors; and that they commonly distrust those who have risen from their own level to a higher sphere. The ties of private life *must* operate with more or less force, and bias the judgment; and very few have the moral resolution to withstand the importunity of near connections. This is not sufficiently attended to, and Moonsiffs are appointed to districts where they have been born and bred and where natural associations must bias their judgments. Besides, Hindoo society is so constituted, that deference and respect are paid by the inferior castes to the higher. Were a *Brahmin* to threaten to stab himself if a suit went against him, would any *Koyesth Moonsiff* or *Sudder Ameen* take upon himself to decree against him? These considerations have influence every day, and to a greater degree and extent than most readers can imagine.

Between the Moonsiff and the superior grades to which he may rise, the only difference consists in their different salaries and their degrees of power. The nature of the man continues the same, but his appetite is increased; and why should this surprise people? A *nuzzur* varies in proportion to the status of the party to whom it is offered, and an offering to a small deity, which will be held meet for his dignity, will be an insult to a bigger one, who has been used to hecatombs In all these grades of office, as in most others, a great evil exists: I allude to the mode adopted of judging of an official's ability and efficiency by certain statements which are called for, monthly, by the superior Courts. These forms are dry statistics of work done; they cannot show *how* that work was done. Some of the most efficient and honest of our judicial officers—those who are most popular with the *people*—are they that are in bad repute with the *Suddur*. Let me mention one name, and to my humble praise the whole city of *Kashee* will respond—Mr. *James*.

Campier; although respected and revered by the people, he is all but ridiculed in the annual reports of the *Suddur*. As his best eulogium, I will simply say, that he is *a poor man*; and with one exception (the late Moluvee Gholam Yahea) I know no other of whom this can be truly said. In such cases, why is not an occasional *toy* given as a reward? A watch, a ring, a standish may be given as a proud distinction; and the favour will not be wanting in effect, if it be properly bestowed.*

CHAP. XXXIV.

OFFICERS OF JUSTICE

"*In the good old days*," when Judges received the munificent salary of 300 *rupees* per mensem, the practice of the Courts was to extort in fees from the plaintiff and defendant so much as to enable the Judges to live in splendour, and to retire with princely fortunes. The late Mr. Brooke used frequently to relate how he was enabled to live up to ten thousand rupees a month when his Honourable Masters paid him *three hundred*! Never a petition that was presented was filed, until the party had given a fee to the *Huzoor*, in proportion to the amount or value of the property contested. This was done, as a matter of course, until the final proceeding, when the party who gained the cause presented the Judge with a *Shookranah* (or thanksgiving-offering). Since those days a very different system of payment has been adopted, and the fees are pocketed by Government in the shape of proceeds of stamps. The restrictions on every class of public officers has produced a salutary effect; but every order may be evaded. Even the order lately passed, directing every Judge to write the summing-up (*wujoohat*) in his own hand-writing, is practised in letter, but not in spirit. In many instances, the *Serishtadar* writes the *roobukaree* as usual; the English writer translates the summing-up; and the Judge corrects it and re-writes it!!! Others again, who are men of talent, and quite capable of doing their duty, *have not leisure for the purpose*!—they are so busy in playing at billiards, shooting, or horse-racing; so the work, for which they are paid, is left to be done by their Native officials. But, generally speaking, these are solitary exceptions, and not the rule. An official of this stamp, some years ago, was desirous of proceeding at once to Calcutta to attend some races. He sent for his *Serishtadar*, and desired him to make three parcels of all the cases pending. "Mind, my friend," said the learned Judge, "I shall be absent for one month. Meantime, write the usual orders in every case, and write the decrees for plaintiff in the cases contained in this

* What could be more impressive than a public acknowledgment of good service by a governor; and a public presentation of a token of the respect and consideration of Government?

parcel; non-suit all the second, and dismiss all the third" !!! Here was an equitable distribution of justice! The same officer was inclined to favour a party in a suit before him, and he desired the *Serishtadar* to decree for plaintiff. While the *roobukaree* was in course of preparation, the party alluded to waited on the Judge, and entreated of him to befriend him. The *Serishtadar* was sent for, and asked whether the "*hookoom monasib*"* had not been passed? "Yes junab-i-alee!" Upon this, further enquiry was made; and the Judge found out that he had intended *to dismiss the case*! The *Serishtadar* was desired to do so accordingly; but he had pocketed a handsome fee from the plaintiff, and was what is called "in a fix." He was forced to obey the *Huzoor's* order, but inserted a sentence that rendered the dismissal of the suit nugatory: he quoted Regulation X of 1813, which is applicable only to the *abkaree*. The plaintiff appealed; and as the order was grounded on false premises, it was of course reversed.

There used to be a very common practice in former years of gentlemen that were found unqualified for the important duties of Collector of Revenue, to be promoted to Judgeships. My readers will doubtless call to mind several such. There was one very well known in this neighbourhood, who was notoriously the puppet of his *Serishtadar*. This latter worthy used to wait in person on the *Huzoor* every morning, with a list of the cases that would be called on that day, and the *Saheb Judge* wrote against each case "*decree*" or "*dismiss*,' as he was prompted. In full *Kacherree*, after going through the farce of hearing all the pleadings and depositions, he would decide as had been previously concerted. The *Serishtadar*, although very corrupt, was a very able officer, and the *Saheb* not only seldom had his orders reversed, but was accounted a *wise personage* by the *Suddur*. This gentleman could not tolerate the idea of a European being in Court as a party. One day, a respectable English planter, who had a case in Court, and who could not account for the delay, went in person into the Court. The sapient Judge in a blustering voice demanded his business? He submitted that he had business, and respectfully enquired whether the Court was not an open one? "No, sir," was the rejoinder; "it is not. Go out, sir, and send your constituted *Vakeel*" !!!

The same Judge had a case before him, in which the thing contested was a village, the localities of which were unknown to everybody. However, the learned Judge had discovered that the village contained an area of seventy-five *beeguhs*. He decreed accordingly, and a precept was issued to the Collector to put the decree-holder in possession. The Collector respectfully intimated to his *worship*, that if he would depute some person to point out the land decreed, he would duly put the decree-holder in possession. The Judge wrote back, "that it was his

* Proper order.

province to *order*, not to point out how his order was to be executed." The result was, as might have been anticipated, that the order is in abeyance at this very moment. Verily, this man was a *Solomon !*

An Indigo Planter in a neighbouring district took some lands for sowing indigo. His name may have been Smith, or Brown, or Thomas ; so we shall call him *Mr. Thomas*, as the name is a good old name, and sounds well. Mr. Thomas was allowed to sow the indigo seed without opposition ; but when the plant had sprung up, one *Ram Deehul Singh* claimed the land as his and demanded the rent. "Very hard," thinks Mr. Thomas, "to be obliged to pay twice ;" and he told the man to go to law. For he had taken the lands on the good faith of *Fureb Singh*, with whom he had interchanged agreements, and to whom he had made an advance of capital. *Ram Deehul Singh* accordingly instituted a suit against Mr. Thomas for possession of the indigo lands. There was no doubt that he was the rightful owner, so he obtained a decree in his favour, and to be put into possession of his lands immediately. Now, Mr. Thomas's head Mohurrir, or *Goomashta*, was brother to the *Decree Nuvees* of the Court ; and the loss and inconvenience to Mr. Thomas, if the indigo were uprooted, were duly explained to the *Sherishtadar* ; and he took upon himself to add to the decree, "*after the indigo is cut*"—thereby keeping the decree-holder out of his own for eighteen months ! ! !

It is a good old custom for a writer, who may have ventured to appear before the public, to take leave of his indulgent readers in a formal address, and to mention the inducements that led him to "take up his pen." I accordingly thank my readers for their favourable notice of my endeavours to amuse, as well as to instruct them. I was induced to make "*An Orderly*" endeavour to expose the trickery and vice of the Courts, as the only means in my power to bring so important a matter before the public, and prominently before the authorities ; in the hope that steps would be taken to remedy the evils brought to notice. I had no personal enmity to revenge ; no personal friendship to serve ; no ambitious object to attain. If the truths I have written have the effect of remedying *one single evil* that may press heavily upon the *ryot*, in that shall be my reward. Reader, farewell ! with a low *salaam*, I say to one and all, *Khoda Hafiz* *

PANCHKOUREE KHAN.

* God preserve you.

THE END.